MAX-PLANCK-INSTITUT
FÜR AUSLÄNDISCHES ÖFFENTLICHES RECHT
UND VÖLKERRECHT

Beiträge zum ausländischen öffentlichen Recht und Völkerrecht

Begründet von Viktor Bruns

Herausgegeben von
Armin von Bogdandy · Anne Peters

Band 268

Last but not least, I wish to express my deepest gratitude to my family for having always been there when I needed them, to my friends for never letting me cease laughing and singing during the tougher parts of my academic journey, and to Professor Steffen Hindelang for his selfless academic advice and his unfaltering friendship and support.

Preface

This work is based on my doctoral thesis, which was accepted at Humboldt-University Berlin in 2014. It is closely linked to a large-scale research project on 'Treaties and Subsequent Practice'. This project was funded by the German Research Foundation (DFG) and contributed to a project of the United Nations' International Law Commission (ILC) on 'Subsequent Agreements and Subsequent Practice in Relation to Interpretation of Treaties' led by Special Rapporteur Georg Nolte.

The interrelationship between these projects generated valuable synergies. On the one hand, the thesis informed part of the Special Rapporteur's final report on the topic. On the other hand, it profited from deep insights into the ILC's work. Being part of the Special Rapporteur's research staff, I was fortunate to have had the chance to substantially contribute to various stages of the ILC's project and to coordinate reports for the earlier 'Study Group on Treaties over Time'.

An academic work may label one single author. However, it will always be the product of many people: First of all, I wish to thank Professor Georg Nolte for entrusting me with an ambitious and demanding position within the research project on 'Treaties and Subsequent Practice' and for having supervised my doctoral thesis. Professor Nolte continuously encouraged me to develop my own thoughts and ideas and to always remain critical towards simplistic truths.

In addition to Professor Gerd Seidel, who gave the second review on my doctoral thesis, I am very grateful to Professor Janbernd Oebbecke and his staff at the University of Muenster. During my undergraduate studies, they set an unparalleled example of cordial, sincere, and sympathetic collegiality, which will inspire me throughout my professional career.

I also gratefully acknowledge the support of the German Academic Scholarship Foundation (Studienstiftung des deutschen Volkes). Its merit doctoral scholarship did not only entail personal space and freedom for finishing my thesis but also offered a stimulating academic environment.

ISSN 0172-4770 ISSN 2197-7135 (electronic)
Beiträge zum ausländischen öffentlichen Recht und Völkerrecht

ISBN 978-3-662-54936-0 ISBN 978-3-662-54937-7 (eBook)
https://doi.org/10.1007/978-3-662-54937-7

Library of Congress Control Number: 2017953943

Springer

Printed on acid-free paper

This Springer imprint is published by Springer Nature
The registered company is Springer-Verlag GmbH Germany
The registered company address is: Heidelberger Platz 3, 14197 Berlin, Germany

Katharina Berner

Subsequent Agreements and Subsequent Practice in Domestic Courts

Springer

Contents

List of Abbreviations

AC	Appeal Cases
AFDI	Annuaire Français de Droit International
AIDI	Annuaire de l'Institut de Droit International
AIR	All India Reporter
AJIL	American Journal of International Law
ALI	American Law Institute
All ER	All England Law Reports
ALR	Australian Law Reports
AÖFV	Amtsblatt der Österreichischen Finanzverwaltung (Official Gazette of the Austrian Fiscal Administration)
ARSIWA	Articles on the Responsibility of States for Internationally Wrongful Acts
ASA	Archiv für Schweizerisches Abgaberecht
ASDI	Annuaire Suisse de Droit International
ASIL PROC	American Society of International Law Proceedings
ATF	Australian Tax Forum
AVR	Archiv des Völkerrechts
AWACS	Airborne Early Warning and Control System
AYBIL	Australian Yearbook of International Law
BBl	Bundesblatt (Swiss Federal Law Gazette)
BC Int'l & Comp L Rev	Boston College International and Comparative Law Review
Berkeley J Int'l L	Berkeley Journal of International Law
BFH	Bundesfinanzhof (German Federal Fiscal Court)
BFHE	Entscheidungen des Bundesfinanzhofs (Official Collection of the German Federal Fiscal Court)
BGBl (Austria)	Bundesgesetzblatt (Austrian Federal Law Gazette)
BGBl (Germany)	Bundesgesetzblatt (German Federal Law Gazette)
BGE	Entscheidungen des Schweizerischen Bundesgerichtes (Official Collection of the Swiss Federal Court)
BGer	Schweizerisches Bundesgericht (Swiss Federal Court)

BGH	Bundesgerichtshof (German Federal Court of Justice)
BGHSt	Entscheidungen des Bundesgerichtshofes in Strafsachen (Official Collection of the German Federal Court of Justice for Decisions in Criminal Matters)
BGHZ	Entscheidungen des Bundesgerichtshofes in Zivilsachen (Official Collection of the German Federal Court of Justice for Decisions in Civil Matters)
BMF (Austria)	Bundesfinanzministerium (Austrian Federal Ministry of Finance)
BMF (Germany)	Bundesfinanzministerium (German Federal Ministry of Finance)
BS	Bereinigte Sammlung der Bundesgesetze und Verordnungen (Revised Compilation of Swiss Federal Acts and Ordinances)
BStBl	Bundesteuerblatt (German Federal Tax Gazette)
Bus L Int'l	Business Law International
BVerfG	Bundesverfassungsgericht (German Federal Constitutional Court)
BVerfGE	Entscheidungen des Bundesverfassungsgerichts (Official Collection of the German Federal Constitutional Court)
BVerwG	Bundesverwaltungsgericht (German Federal Administrative Court)
BVerwGE	Entscheidungen des Bundesverwaltungsgerichts (Official Collection of the German Federal Administrative Court)
B-VG	Bundes-Verfassungsgesetz Österreich (Austrian Federal Constitutional Law)
BVGE	Sammlung der Entscheidungen des Schweizerischen Bundesverwaltungsgerichts (Official Collection of the Swiss Federal Administrative Court)
BVGer	Schweizerisches Bundesverwaltungsgericht (Swiss Federal Administrative Court)
BYIL	British Yearbook of International Law
CAT Committee	Committee against Torture
CCNR	Central Commission for the Navigation of the Rhine
CEDAW Committee	Committee on the Elimination of Discrimination against Women
CFA	Committee on Fiscal Affairs
Chi-Kent L Rev	Chicago-Kent Law Review
CHRYB	Canadian Human Rights Yearbook
CJEU	Court of Justice of the European Union
CJLJ	Canadian Journal of Law and Jurisprudence
CLR	Commonwealth Law Reports
Col J Transnat'l L	Columbia Journal of Transnational Law

Col LR	Columbia Law Review
Commw L Bull	Commonwealth Law Bulletin
COP	Conference of States Parties
Cornell Int'l LJ	Cornell International Law Journal
CRC Committee	Committee against Torture
CTS	Consolidated Treaty Series
DALT	Draft Articles on the Law of Treaties
DLR	Dominion Law Reports
DSB	WTO Dispute Settlement Body
DTA	Double taxation agreement
DVBl	Deutsches Verwaltungsblatt
DVjs	Deutsche Vierteljahrsschrift für Literaturwissenschaft und Geistesgeschichte
ECOSOC	United Nations Economic and Social Council
ECtHR	European Court of Human Rights
EJIL	European Journal of International Law
EJLS	European Journal of Legal Studies
EPL	European Public Law
ETS	European Treaty Series
EU	European Union
EUROCONTROL	European Organisation for the Safety of Air Control
ExCom	Executive Committee of the High Commissioner's Programme
FCA	Federal Court of Australia
FCAFC	Federal Court of Australia: Full Court
FCR	Federal Court Reports (Australia)
Fletcher F World Aff	Fletcher Forum of World Affairs
FYBIL	Finnish Yearbook of International Law
Geo Wash Int'l L Rev	George Washington International Law Review
GG	Grundgesetz (German Basic Law)
GJIL	German Yearbook of International Law
GOJIL	Göttingen Journal of International Law
Hague YB Int'l L	Hague Yearbook of International Law
Harv Int'l LJ	Harvard International Law Journal
Hastings Int'l & Comp L Rev	Hastings International and Comparative Law Review
HCA	High Court of Australia
HKLJ	Hong Kong Law Journal
HKLRD	Hong Kong Law Reports & Digest
HL	House of Lords
HLR	Harvard Law Review
HRC	Human Rights Committee
Hum Rts L Rev	Human Rights Law Review
IACtHR	Inter-American Court of Human Rights

ICESCR Committee	Committee on Economic, Social and Cultural Rights
ICJ	International Court of Justice
ICLQ	International and Comparative Law Quarterly
ICON	International Journal of Constitutional Law
ICSID	International Centre for Settlement of Investment Disputes
IDI	Institut de Droit International
IJIL	Indian Journal of International Law
IJRL	International Journal of Refugee Law
ILA	International Law Association
ILC	International Law Commission
ILO	International Labour Organization
ILR	International Law Reports
Int CL Rev	International Community Law Review
Int'l L Ass'n Rep Conf	International Law Association Conference Reports
Int'l L	International Lawyer
Int'l LF D Int'l	International Law FORUM du droit international
Int'l Tax & Bus Law	International Tax & Business Lawyer
Intertax	Intertax (International Tax Review)
IO	international governmental organisation
ISAF	International Security Assistance Force
ITLOS	International Tribunal for the Law of the Sea
IWC	International Whaling Commission
J Transnat'l L & Pol'y	Journal of Transnational Law and Policy
JA	Juristische Arbeitsblätter
JIEL	Journal of International Economic Law
JILP	NYU Journal of International Law and Politics
JR	Judicial Review
JRLS	Jerusalem Review of Legal Studies
JWT	Journal of World Trade
Law & Pol'y Int'l Bus	Law & Policy in International Business
Law & Prac Int'l Cts & Tribunals	Law & Practice of International Courts and Tribunals
LNTS	League of Nations Treaty Series
LQR	Law Quarterly Review
MBB	Maandblad Belasting Beschouwingen
Mich J Int'l L	Michigan Journal of International Law
Minn L Rev	Minnesota Law Review
NATO	North Atlantic Treaty Organization
NGO	international non-governmental organisation
NILR	Netherlands International Law Review

NJIL	Nordic Journal of International Law
NJW	Neue Juristische Wochenschrift
NVwZ	Neue Zeitschrift für Verwaltungsrecht
NZCA	New Zealand Court of Appeal
NZLR	New Zealand Law Reports
OECD	Organisation for Economic Co-operation and Development
OEEC	Organisation for European Economic Co-operation
OJ	Official Journal of the European Communities
PC	Privy Council
PCA	Permanent Court of Arbitration
PCIJ	Permanent Court of International Justice
PD	Law Reports, Probate, Divorce & Admiralty Division
QB	Law Reports, Queen's Bench (3rd Series)
RBDI	Revue Belge de Droit International
RCADI	Recueil des Cours de l'Academie de Droit International de la Haye
RFH	Reichsfinanzhof (German Imperial Fiscal Court)
RG	Reichsgericht (German Imperial Court of Justice)
RGBl	Reichsgesetzblatt (German Imperial Law Gazette)
RGDIP	Revue Générale de Droit International Public
RIAA	Reports of International Arbitral Awards
RQDI	Revue Québécoise de Droit International
S Ct	Supreme Court Reporter (USA)
SCC	Supreme Court of Canada
SCD	Special Commissioners' Decisions
SCR	Supreme Court Reports (Canada)
SR	Systematische Sammlung des Bundesrechts (Compendium of Swiss Laws)
Stan L Rev	Stanford Law Review
Stat	United States Statutes at Large
STC	Simon's Tax Cases
Stud Transnat'l Legal Pol'y	Studies in Transnational Legal Policy
Student Advoc	The Student Advocate
Tax L Rev	Tax Law Review
Tex Int'l LJ	Texas International Law Journal
Tulsa J Comp & Int'l L	Tulsa Journal of Comparative & International Law
U Colo L Rev	University of Colorado Law Review
UCLA L Rev	UCLA Law Review
UKHL	United Kingdom House of Lords
UKPC	United Kingdom Privy Council
UKSC	United Kingdom Supreme Court
UNCITRAL	United Nations Commission on International Trade Law
UNGA	United Nations General Assembly

UNHCR	Office of the United Nations High Commissioner for Refugees
UNSG	Secretary General of the United Nations
UNTS	United Nations Treaty Series
US Const	Constitution of the United States of America
US	United States Supreme Court Reports
Va J Int'l L	Virginia Journal of International Law
Val UL Rev	Valparaiso University Law Review
Vand J Transnat'l L	Vanderbilt Journal of Transnational Law
VfGH	Verfassungsgerichtshof Österreich (Constitutional Court of Austria)
VfSlg	Sammlung der Erkenntnisse und Beschlüsse des Verfassungsgerichtshofes (Official Collection of the Constitutional Court of Austria)
Victoria U Wellington L Rev	Victoria University Wellington Law Review
VwGH	Verwaltungsgerichtshof Österreich (Administrative Court of Austria)
WEU	Western European Union
WLR	Weekly Law Reports
WTAM	World Trade and Arbitration Materials
WTO	World Trade Organisation
Yale LJ	Yale Law Journal
YBILC	Yearbook of the International Law Commission
ZaöRV	Zeitschrift für ausländisches öffentliches Recht und Völkerrecht

Table of Cases

Australia

A v Minister for Immigration & Ethnic Affairs [1997] HCA 4, (1997) 190 CLR 225

Commonwealth Minister for Justice v Adamas [2013] HCA 59, (2013) 304 ALR 305

De L v Director-General Department of Community Services (NSW) [1996] HCA 5, (1996) 187 CLR 640

Great China Metal Industries Co Ltd v Malaysian International Shipping Corporation Berhad [1998] HCA 65, (1998) 72 ALJR 1592

Macoun v Commissioner of Taxation [2015] HCA 44, (2015) 326 ALR 452

Maloney v The Queen [2013] HCA 28, (2013) 298 ALR 308

Minister for Home Affairs of the Commonwealth v Zentai [2012] HCA 28, (2012) 289 ALR 644

Minister for Immigration and Multicultural and Indigenous Affairs v QAAH of 2004 [2006] HCA 53, (2006) 231 ALR 340

Minister for Immigration v Ibrahim [2000] HCA 55, (2000) 204 CLR 1

SZATV v Minister for Immigration [2007] HCA 40, (2007) 233 CLR 18

Thiel v Federal Commissioner of Taxation [1990] HCA 37, (1990) 171 CLR 338

Victrawl Pty Ltd v Telstra Corporation Ltd [1995] HCA 51, (1995) 183 CLR 595

Commissioner of Taxation v SNF (Australia) Pty Ltd [2011] FCAFC 74, (2011) 193 FCR 149

Commissioner of the Australian Federal Police and the Commonwealth of Australia v Magno and Almeida [1992] FCA 566, (1992) 37 FCR 298

Diatlov v Minister for Immigration and Multicultural Affairs [1999] FCA 468, (1999) 167 ALR 313

McDermott Industries (Aust) Pty Ltd v Commissioner of Taxation [2005] FCAFC 67, (2005) 142 FCR 134

Minister for Immigration & Multicultural & Indigenous Affairs v Al Masri [2003] FCAFC 70, (2003) 197 ALR 241

Minister for Immigration and Citizenship v Anochie [2012] FCA 1440, (2012) 209 FCR 497

Minister for Immigration and Citizenship v MZYYL [2012] FCAFC 147, (2012) 207 FCR 211

NBGM v Minister for Immigration & Multicultural & Indigenous Affairs [2006] FCAFC 60

Rezaei v Minister for Immigration and Multicultural Affairs [2001] FCA 1294

Rishmawi v Minister for Immigration & Multicultural Affairs [1997] FCA 829, (1997) 77 FCR 421

Semunigus v Minister for Immigration & Multicultural Affairs [1999] FCA 422

SRYYY v Minister for Immigration & Multicultural & Indigenous Affairs [2005] FCAFC 42, (2005) 147 FCR 1

Austria

VfGH, Judgment of 14 October 1986, VfSlg 11073

VfGH, Judgment of 1 March 1990, VfSlg 12281

VfGH, Judgment of 15 March 1990, VfSlg 12326

VfGH, Judgment of 29 September 1994, VfSlg 13881

VfGH, Judgment of 15 October 1998, VfSlg 15309

VfGH, Judgment of 29 June 2011, VfSlg 19434

VfGH, Judgment of 12 September 2013, U 1053/2012-14

VfGH, Judgment of 25 September 2015, V 41/2015-11

VwGH, Judgment of 8 November 1995, 95/01/0070

VwGH, Judgment of 20 December 1995, 95/01/0104

VwGH, Judgment of 21 March 1996, 94/15/0128

VwGH, Judgment of 31 July 1996, 92/13/0172

VwGH, Judgment of 17 December 1996, 95/01/0127

VwGH, Judgment of 18 December 1996, 96/20/0793

VwGH, Judgment of 10 December 1997, 94/20/0002

VwGH, Judgment of 21 May 1997, 96/14/0084

VwGH, Judgment of 21 March 2003, 2000/20/0189

VwGH, Judgment of 30 March 2006, 2002/15/0098

VwGH, Judgment of 20 February 2009, 2007/19/0535

VwGH, Judgment of 23 February 2010, 2008/15/0148

Belgium

Cour de cassation de Belgique, Judgment of 28 May 2004, case no F.02.0078.F <http://jure.juridat.just.fgov.be>

Cour de cassation de Belgique, Judgment of 9 May 2008, case no F.06.0124.F <http://jure.juridat.just.fgov.be>

Canada

Pushpanathan v Canada (Minister of Citizenship and Immigration) [1996] 2 FC 49, 191 NR 247

Chan v Canada [1995] 3 SCR 593, 128 DLR (4th) 213

Ezokola v Canada (Citizenship and Immigration) [2013] SCC 40, 361 DLR (4th) 1

Németh v Canada (Justice) [2010] 3 SCR 281, 2010 SCC 56

Pushpanathan v Canada (Minister of Citizenship and Immigration) [1998] 1 SCR 982, (1998) 160 DLR (4th) 193

Ward v Canada (Minister of Employment & Immigration) [1993] 2 SCR 689, 103 DLR (4th) 1

Yugraneft Corp v Rexx Management Corp [2010] 1 SCR 649, 2010 SCC 19

Court of Justice of the European Union

Case C–386/08 *Brita GmbH v Hauptzollamt Hamburg-Hafen* [2010] ECR I–1289

Case C–126/97 *Eco Swiss China Time Ltd v Benetton International NV* [1999] ECR I–3055

European Court of Human Rights

Al-Adsani v UK [GC] ECtHR 2001–XI

Al-Saadoon and Mufdhi v UK App no 61498/08 (ECtHR, 2 March 2010)

Demir and Baykara v Turkey [GC] App no 34503/97 (ECtHR, 12 November 2008)

Dudgeon v UK (1981) Series A No 45

Golder v UK (1975) Series A No 18

Goodwin v UK [GC] ECtHR 2002–VI

Hassan v UK [GC] App no 29750/09 (ECtHR, 16 September 2014)

Inze v Austria (1987) Series A No 126

Lithgow v UK (1986) Series A No 102

Loizidou v Turkey (1995) Series A No 310

Marckx v Belgium (1979) Series A No 31

Mazurek v France ECtHR 2000–II

Öcalan v Turkey [GC] ECtHR 2005–IV

Saadi v UK [GC] App no 37201/06 (ECtHR, 28 February 2008)

Germany

BFH, Judgment of 6 August 1985, VII R 41/83, BFHE 144, 483–87

BFH, Judgment of 9 October 1985, I R 128/80, BFHE 145, 341–48

BFH, Judgment of 14 December 1988, I R 148/87, BFHE 155, 374–80

BFH, Judgment of 1 February 1989, I R 74/86, BFHE 157, 39–44

BFH, Judgment of 10 July 1996, I R 4/96, BFHE 181, 158–61

BFH, Judgment of 25 October 2006, I R 81/04, BFHE 215, 237–42

BFH, Judgment of 17 October 2007, I R 5/06, BFHE 219, 518–29

BFH, Judgment of 27 August 2008, I R 64/07, BFHE 222, 553–59

BFH, Judgment of 2 September 2009, I R 90/08, BFHE 226, 267–75

BFH, Judgment of 2 September 2009, I R 111/08, BFHE 226, 276–83

BFH, Judgment of 11 November 2009, I R 15/09, BFHE 227, 419–31

BFH, Decision of 19 May 2010, I B 191/09, BFHE 229, 322–36

BFH, Judgment of 9 February 2011, I R 54/10, BFHE 232, 476–85

BFH, Judgment of 25 May 2011, I R 95/10, BFHE 234, 63–71

BFH, Judgment of 12 October 2011, I R 15/11, BFHE 235, 401–6

BFH, Judgment of 10 January 2012, I R 36/11 <http://www.juris.de>

BFH, Judgment of 13 June 2012, I R 41/11, BFHE 237, 360–67

BFH, Decision of 11 December 2013, I R 4/13 <http://www.juris.de>

BFH, Judgment of 16 January 2014, I R 30/12 <http://www.juris.de>

BFH, Judgment of 10 June 2015, I R 79/13 <http://www.juris.de>

BFH, Judgment of 25 November 2015, I R 50/14 <http://www.juris.de>

BGH, Decision of 11 April 1957, 4 ARs 9/57, BGHSt 10, 221–27

BGH, Judgment of 23 March 1976, VI ZR 150/74, [1976] NJW 1587–88

BGH, Decision of 20 October 1981, X ZB 3/81, BGHZ 82, 88–100

BGH, Judgment of 16 June 1982, I ZR 100/80, BGHZ 84, 339–45

BGH, Judgment of 3 November 1992, 5 StR 370/92, BGHSt 39, 1–36

BGH, Decision of 16 August 2000, XII ZB 210/99, BGHZ 145, 97–104

BGH, Decision of 29 May 2013, XII ZB 530/11, [2013] NJW 3095–98

BGH, Judgment of 21 April 2016, I ZR 43/14 <http://www.juris.de>

BGH, Decision of 6 October 2016, I ZB 13/15 <http://www.juris.de>

BVerfG, Judgment of 29 July 1952, 2 BvE 2/51, BVerfGE 1, 372–96

BVerfG, Decision of 10 March 1971, 2 BvL 3/68, BVerfGE 30, 272–88

Hong Kong

Ng Ka Ling v Director of Immigration [1999] 1 HKLRD 315

Ubamaka v Secretary for Security [2011] 1 HKLRD 359

India

Godhra Electricity Co Ltd v The State of Gujarat [1975] 2 SCR 42

HHM Shantidevi P Gaikwad v Savjibhai Haribhai Patel [2001] AIR 1462 (SC)

International Arbitral Awards

Arbitration regarding the Iron Rhine ('Ijzeren Rijn') Railway (Belgium v the Netherlands) (2005) 27 RIAA 35–125

Case concerning a Dispute between Argentina and Chile concerning the Beagle Channel (Argentina v Chile) (1977) 21 RIAA 53–264

Case concerning the Interpretation of the Air Transport Services Agreement between the United States of America and France, Signed at Paris on 27 March 1946 (France v USA) (1964) 16 RIAA 5–74

Chamizal Case (Mexico v USA) (1911) 11 RIAA 309–47

CMS Gas Transmission Company v Argentine Republic (Decision on Preliminary Objections) (17 July 2003) ICSID Case No ARB/01/8

Continental Shelf Arbitration (UK v France) (1977) 18 RIAA 3–413

European Molecular Biology Laboratory Arbitration (EMBL v Germany) (Arbitration Tribunal) (1990) 105 ILR 1–74

Island of Palmas Case (USA v the Netherlands) (1928) 2 RIAA 829–71

PCA, *Bay of Bengal Maritime Boundary Arbitration (Bangladesh v India)* (7 July 2014) <http://www.pca-cpa.org/showpage.asp?pag_id=1376>

Sempra Energy International v Argentine Republic (Award) (28 September 2007) ICSID Case No ARB/02/16

Tariffs Applied by Canada to Certain US-Origin Agricultural Products NAFTA Arbitral Panel (Secretariat File No CDA-95-2008-01) Final Report of the Panel (2 December 1996) <registry.nafta-sec-alena.org/cmdocuments/0c7973b9-1088-4221-99a5-e279075380b0.pdf>

Tax Regime Governing Pensions Paid to Retired UNESCO Officials Residing in France (France v UNESCO) (2003) 25 RIAA 231–65

WTO, *EC—Bananas III—Second Recourse to Article 21.5 Report of the Appellate Body* (26 November 2008) WT/DS27/AB/RW2/ECU, WT/DS27/AB/RW/USA <http://docsonline.wto.org>

WTO, *EC—Chicken Cuts—Report of the Appellate Body* (12 September 2005) WT/DS269/AB/R, WT/DS286/AB/R <http://docsonline.wto.org>

WTO, *EC—Computer Equipment—Report of the Appellate Body* (5 June 1998) WT/DS62/AB/R, WT/DS67/AB/R, WT/DS68/AB/R <http://docsonline.wto.org>

WTO, *Japan—Alcoholic Beverages II—Report of the Appellate Body* (4 October 1996) WT/DS8/AB/R–11/AB/R <http://docsonline.wto.org>

WTO, *US—Gambling—Report of the Appellate Body* (7 April 2005) WT/DS285/AB/R <http://docsonline.wto.org>

WTO, *US—Hot-Rolled Steel—Report of the Appellate Body* (24 July 2001) WT/DS184/AB/R <http://docsonline.wto.org>

WTO, *US—Stainless Steel (Mexico)—Report of the Appellate Body* (30 April 2008) WT/DS344/AB/R <http://docsonline.wto.org>

Young Loan Arbitration on German External Debts (Belgium, France, Switzerland, UK, and USA v Germany) (1980) 19 RIAA 67–145

International Court of Justice

Anglo-Iranian Oil Co Case (UK v Iran) (Jurisdiction) [1952] ICJ Rep 93–115

Applicability of the Obligation to Arbitrate under Section 21 of the United Nations Headquarters Agreement of 26 June 1947 (Advisory Opinion) [1988] ICJ Rep 12–35

Avena and Other Mexican Nationals (Mexico v USA) [2004] ICJ Rep 12–73

Case concerning Kasikili/Sedudu Island (Botswana v Namibia) [1999] ICJ Rep 1045–109

Case concerning Maritime Delimitation and Territorial Questions between Qatar and Bahrain (Qatar v Bahrain) (Jurisdiction and Admissibility) [1994] ICJ Rep 112–28

Case concerning Sovereignty over Pulau Ligitan and Pulau Sipadan (Indonesia v Malaysia) [2002] ICJ Rep 625–86

Case concerning the Arbitral Award Made by the King of Spain on 23 December 1906 (Honduras v Nicaragua) [1960] ICJ Rep 192–218

Case concerning the Arbitral Award of 31 July 1989 [1991] ICJ Rep 53–76

Case concerning the Dispute regarding Navigational and Related Rights (Costa Rica v Nicaragua) [2009] ICJ Rep 213–72

Case concerning the Right of Passage over Indian Territory (Portugal v India) (Merits) [1960] ICJ Rep 6–46

Case concerning the Rights of Nationals of the United States of America and Morocco (France v USA) [1952] ICJ Rep 176–214

Case concerning the Temple of Preah Vihear (Cambodia v Thailand) (Merits) [1962] ICJ Rep 6–38

Certain Expenses of the United Nations (Article 17, Paragraph 2, of the Charter) (Advisory Opinion) [1962] ICJ Rep 151–81

Constitution of the Maritime Safety Committee of the Inter-Governmental Maritime Consultative Organization (Advisory Opinion) [1960] ICJ Rep 150–72

Corfu Channel Case (UK v Albania) (Merits) [1949] ICJ Rep 4–38

Fisheries Case (UK v Norway) [1951] ICJ Rep 116–44

LaGrand (Germany v USA) [2001] ICJ Rep 466–517

Military and Paramilitary Activities in and against Nicaragua (Nicaragua v USA) (Merits) [1986] ICJ Rep 14–150

North Sea Continental Shelf (Germany v Denmark) [1969] ICJ Rep 3–56

Pulp Mills on the River Uruguay (Argentina v Uruguay) [2010] ICJ Rep 14–107

Reservations to the Convention on Genocide (Advisory Opinion) [1951] ICJ Rep 15–69

Sovereignty over Pedra Branca/Pulau Batu Puteh, Middle Rocks and South Ledge (Malaysia v Singapore) [2008] ICJ Rep 12–102

Territorial Dispute (Libyan Arab Jamahiriya v Chad) [1994] ICJ Rep 6–42

Whaling in the Antarctic (Australia v Japan) Judgment of 31 March 2014 <http://www.icj-cij.org/docket/files/148/18136.pdf>

New Zealand

Attorney-General v X [2007] NZCA 388

Attorney-General v Zaoui (No 2) [2005] 1 NZLR 690

C v H [2009] NZCA 100

Lena-Jane Punter v Secretary for Justice, ex p Adam Punter [2004] 2 NZLR 28

Ye v Minister of Immigration [2009] 2 NZLR 596

Permanent Court of International Justice

Case concerning the Payment in Gold of Brazilian Federal Loans Contracted in France (France v Brazil) PCIJ Rep Series A No 21

Case of the SS 'Lotus' (France v Turkey) PCIJ Rep Series A No 10

Competence of the ILO in regard to International Regulation of the Conditions of Labour of Persons Employed in Agriculture (Advisory Opinion) PCIJ Rep Series B No 2

Competence of the ILO to Regulate, Incidentally, the Personal Work of the Employer (Advisory Opinion) PCIJ Rep Series B No 13

Jurisdiction of the Courts of Danzig (Advisory Opinion) PCIJ Rep Series B No 15

Jurisdiction of the European Commission of the Danube (Advisory Opinion) PCIJ Rep Series B No 14

Question of Jaworzina (Polish-Czechoslovakian Frontier) (Advisory Opinion) PCIJ Rep Series B No 8

Switzerland

BGer, Judgment of 14 June 1912, BGE 38 I 165

BGer, Judgment of 13 October 1967, BGE 93 II 354

BGer, Decision of 22 May 1968, BGE 94 III 35

BGer, Judgment of 17 February 1971, BGE 97 I 359

BGer, Judgment of 27 June 1996, BGE 122 II 234

BGer, Judgment of 8 April 2004, BGE 130 III 430

BGer, Decision of 8 March 2006, BGE 132 III 389

BGer, Judgment of 21 November 2011, BGE 137 I 305

BGer, Judgment of 19 September 2012, BGE 138 II 524

BGer, Judgment of 25 September 2012, BGE 138 III 708

BGer, Judgment of 17 April 2015, 2C_1176/2013, BGE 141 II 233

BVGer, Judgment of 18 December 2007, C-2019/2007

BVGer, Judgment of 11 September 2008, E-4207/2006, BVGE 2008/34

BVGer, Judgment of 16 January 2009, BVGE A-2677/2007

BVGer, Judgment of 21 January 2010, BVGE 2010/7

BVGer, Judgment of 18 June 2010, D-1308/2010

BVGer, Judgment of 25 August 2010, E-2190/2010

BVGer, Judgment of 11 March 2011, A-6641/2010

BVGer, Judgment of 12 May 2011, A-4683/2010

BVGer, Judgment of 20 September 2011, E-5012/2006

BVGer, Judgment of 20 September 2011, E-7449/2009, BVGE 2011/29

BVGer, Judgment of 23 July 2012, A-1246/2011

BVGer, Judgment of 3 January 2014, D-6370/2013

United Kingdom of Great Britain and Northern Ireland

Attorney General for Canada v Attorney General for Ontario [1937] AC 326 (PC)

Hoani Te Heuheu Tukino v Aotea District Maori Land Board [1941] UKPC 6, [1941] AC 308

Thomas v Baptiste [1999] UKPC 13, [2000] 2 AC 1

Malone v Metropolitan Police Commissioner [1979] ch 344

Salomon v Customs and Excise Commissioners [1967] 2 QB 116

The Parlament Belge (1879) 4 PD 129

UBS AG v Revenue and Customs Commissioners [2005] STC (SCD) 589

A v Secretary of State for the Home Department [2004] UKHL 56, [2005] 2 AC 68

Al-Sirri v Secretary of State for the Home Department [2012] UKSC 54, [2013] 1 AC 745

Al-Waheed v Ministry of Defence [2017] UKSC 2, [2017] WLR(D) 50

Assange v The Swedish Prosecution Authority [2012] UKSC 22, [2012] 2 AC 471

Barras v Aberdeen Steam Trawling & Fishing Co [1933] UKHL 3, [1933] AC 402

British Airways Board v Laker Airways Ltd [1984] UKHL 7, [1985] AC 58

Bucnys v Ministry of Justice, Lithuania [2013] UKSC 71, [2013] 3 WLR 1485

Deep Vein Thrombosis and Air Travel Group Litigation [2005] UKHL 72, [2006] 1 All ER 786

Fothergill v Monarch Airlines Ltd [1980] UKHL 6, [1981] AC 251

HH v Deputy Prosecutor of the Italian Republic, Genoa [2012] UKSC 25, [2013] 1 AC 338

HJ (Iran) v Secretary of State for the Home Department [2010] UKSC 31, [2011] 1 AC 596

Horvath v Secretary of State for the Home Department [2000] UKHL 37, [2001] 1 AC 489

Hoxha v Secretary of State for the Home Department [2005] UKHL 19, [2005] 1 WLR 1063

James Buchanan & Co Ltd v Babco Forwarding and Shipping (UK) Ltd [1978] AC 141 (HL)

Januzi v Secretary of State for the Home Department [2006] UKHL 5, [2006] 2 AC 426

JH Rayner (Minsinc Lane) Ltd v Department of Trade and Industry [1990] 2 AC 418 (HL)

Jones v Ministry of Interior for the Kingdom of Saudi Arabia [2006] UKHL 26, [2007] 1 AC 270

King v Bristow Helicopters Ltd (Scotland) [2002] UKHL 7, [2002] 2 AC 628

Kramer v Attorney General [1923] AC 528 (HL)

Owners of Cargo Lately Laden on Board the MV Erkowit v Owners of the Eschersheim (The Eschersheim, the Jade and the Erkowit) [1976] 1 WLR 430 (HL)

Philippson v Imperial Airways Ltd [1939] AC 332 (HL)

Quazi v Quazi [1980] AC 744 (HL)

R (Adams) v Secretary of State for Justice [2011] UKSC 18, [2012] 1 AC 48

R (Adan) v Secretary of State for the Home Department [2000] UKHL 67, [2001] 2 AC 477

R (Al-Jedda) v Secretary of State for Defence [2007] UKHL 58, [2008] 1 AC 332

R (European Roma Rights Centre) v Immigration Officer at Prague Airport [2004] UKHL 55, [2005] 2 AC 1

R (Mullen) v Secretary of State for the Home Department [2004] UKHL 18, [2005] 1 AC 1

R (Pinochet) v Commissioner of Police for the Metropolis [2000] 1 AC 147, [1999] UKHL 17

R (Sivakumuran) v Secretary of State for the Home Department [1987] UKHL 1, [1988] AC 958

R (ST Eritrea) v Secretary of State for the Home Department [2012] UKSC 12, [2012] 2 AC 135

R v Asfaw [2008] UKHL 31, [2008] 1 AC 1061

R v Ireland [1997] UKHL 34, [1998] AC 147

Rio Tinto Zinc Corp v Westinghouse Electric Corp (Nos 1 and 2) [1978] AC 547 (HL)

RT (Zimbabwe) v Secretary of State for the Home Department [2012] UKSC 38, [2013] 1 AC 152

Secretary of State for the Home Department v K [2006] UKHL 46, [2007] 1 AC 412

Sepet v Secretary of State for the Home Department [2003] UKHL 15, [2003] 3 All ER 304

Sidhu v British Airways [1997] AC 430 (HL)

Smith v The Ministry of Defence [2013] UKSC 41, [2014] 1 AC 52

T v Secretary of State for the Home Department [1996] UKHL 8, [1996] AC 742

ZH (Tanzania) v Secretary of State for the Home Department [2011] UKSC 4, [2011] 2 AC 166

United States of America

Abbott v Abbott 560 US 1, 130 S Ct 1983 (2010)

Air France v Saks 470 US 392, 105 S Ct 1338 (1985)

Atkins v Virginia 536 US 304, 122 S Ct 2242 (2002)

Charlton v Kelly 229 US 447, 11 S Ct 897 (1913)

Eastern Airlines, Inc v Floyd 499 US 530, 111 S Ct 1489 (1991)

El Al Israel Airlines, Ltd v Tsui Yuan Tseng 525 US 155, 119 S Ct 662 (1999)

Factor v Laubenheimer 290 US 276, 54 S Ct 191 (1933)

Itel Containers Intern Corp v Huddleston 507 US 60, 113 S Ct 1095 (1993)

Kolovrat v Oregon 366 US 187, 81 S Ct 922 (1961)

Lawrence v Texas 539 US 558, 123 S Ct 2472 (2003)

Lozano v Montoya Alvarez 134 S Ct 1224 (2014)

Maximov v US 373 US 49, 83 S Ct 1054 (1963)

Medellin v Texas 552 US 491, 128 S Ct 1346 (2008)

Nielsen v Johnson 279 US 47, 49 S Ct 223 (1929)

O'Connor v US 479 US 27, 107 S Ct 347 (1986)

Olympic Airways v Husain 540 US 644, 124 S Ct 1221 (2004)

Pigeon River Imp, Slide & Boom Co v Charles W Cox, Ltd 291 US 138, 45 S Ct 361 (1934)

Roper v Simmons 543 US 551, 125 S Ct 1183 (2005)

Ross v McIntyre 140 US 453, 11 S Ct 897 (1891)

Sale v Haitian Centers Council, Inc 509 US 155, 113 S Ct 2549 (1993)

Sullivan v Kidd 254 US 433, 41 S Ct 158 (1921)

Sumitomo Shoji America, Inc v Avagliano 457 US 176, 102 S Ct 2375 (1982)

Thompson v Oklahoma 487 US 815, 108 S Ct 2687 (1988)

Trans World Airlines, Inc v Franklin Mint Corp 466 US 243, 104 S Ct 2691 (1984)

US v Stuart 489 US 353, 109 S Ct 1183 (1989)

Weinberger v Rossi 456 US 25, 102 S Ct 1510 (1982)

Zicherman v Korean Air Lines Co, Ltd 516 US 217, 116 S Ct 629 (1996)

Table of Treaties

Multilateral

Agreement on the Taxation and Customs Regime for Gasoil Consumed as Board Supply in the Navigation on the Rhine (signed 16 May 1952, entered into force 28 January 1954) BGBl (Germany) 1953 II 532 (Gasoil Agreement)

American Convention on Human Rights (signed 22 November 1969, entered into force 18 July 1978) 1144 UNTS 123 (Pact of San José; IACHR)

Charter of the United Nations (adopted 26 June 1945, entered into force 24 October 1945) 1 UNTS XVI (UNC)

Constitution of the World Health Organization (signed 22 July 1946, entered into force 7 April 1948) 14 UNTS 185 (WHO Constitution)

Convention against Torture and Other Cruel, Inhuman or Degrading Treatment (adopted 10 December 1984, entered into force 26 June 1987) 1465 UNTS 85 (CAT)

Convention for European Economic Co-operation (signed 16 April 1948, entered into force 28 July 1948) 888 UNTS 141

Protocol on the Revision of the Convention for European Economic Co-operation of 16 April 1948 (signed 14 December 1960, entered into force 30 September 1961) 888 UNTS 179

Convention for the Protection of Human Rights and Fundamental Freedoms (signed 4 November 1950, entered into force 3 September 1953) 213 UNTS 222 (European Convention on Human Rights; ECHR)

Protocol 7 to the European Convention for the Protection of Human Rights and Fundamental Freedoms (signed 22 November 1984, entered into force 1 November 1988) ETS No 117 (Protocol 7 ECHR)

Convention for the Unification of Certain Rules relating to International Carriage by Air (signed 12 October 1929, entered into force 13 February 1933) 478 UNTS 371 (Warsaw Convention)

Protocol to Amend the Convention for the Unification of Certain Rules relating to International Carriage by Air Signed at Warsaw on 12 October 1929 (signed 28 September 1955, entered into force 1 August 1963) 478 UNTS 371 (Hague Protocol)

Convention Instituting the Definitive Statute of the Danube (adopted 23 July 1921, entered into force 1 October 1922) 26 LNTS 187

Convention of the World Meteorological Organization (signed 11 October 1947, entered into force 23 March 1950) 77 UNTS 143 (WMO Convention)

Convention on International Civil Aviation (signed 7 December 1944, entered into force 4 April 1947) 15 UNTS 295 (ICAO Convention)

Convention on International Trade in Endangered Species of Wild Fauna and Flora (signed 3 March 1973, entered into force 1 July 1975) 993 UNTS 243 (CITES)

Convention on the Civil Aspects of International Child Abduction (signed 25 October 1980, entered into force 1 December 1983) 1343 UNTS 89 (Hague Abduction Convention)

Convention on the Conservation of Migratory Species of Wild Animals (signed 23 June 1979, entered into force 1 November 1983) 1651 UNTS 333 (CMS)

Convention on the Contract for the International Carriage of Goods by Road (signed 19 May 1956, entered into force 2 July 1961) 399 UNTS 189 (CMR)

Convention on the Elimination of All Forms of Discrimination against Women (adopted 18 December 1979, entered into force 3 September 1981) 1249 UNTS 13 (CEDAW)

Optional Protocol to the Convention on the Elimination of All Forms of Discrimination against Women (adopted 6 October 1999, entered into force 22 December 2000) 2131 UNTS 83 (CEDAW-OP)

Convention on the Grant of European Patents (signed 5 October 1973, entered into force 7 October 1977) 1065 UNTS 199 (European Patent Convention)

Convention on the Inter-Governmental Maritime Consultative Organization (signed 6 March 1948, entered into force 17 March 1958) 289 UNTS 48

Convention on the Law Applicable to Contractual Obligations (signed 19 June 1980, entered into force 1 April 1991) 1605 UNTS 59 (Rome Convention)

Convention on the Limitation Period in the International Sale of Goods (signed 14 June 1974, entered into force 1 August 1988) 1511 UNTS 3 (Limitation Convention)

Convention on the Presence of Foreign Forces in the Federal Republic of Germany (signed 23 October 1954, entered into force 6 May 1955) 334 UNTS 3

Convention on the Prevention and Punishment of the Crime of Genocide (signed 9 December 1948, entered into force 12 January 1951) 78 UNTS 277

Convention on the Prevention of Marine Pollution by Dumping of Wastes and Other Matter (signed 29 December 1972, entered into force 30 August 1975) 1046 UNTS 120 (London Convention)

Convention on the Prohibition of the Development, Production and Stockpiling of Bacteriological (Biological) and Toxin Weapons and on their Destruction (signed 10 April 1972, entered into force 26 March 1975) 1015 UNTS 163 (Biological Weapons Convention; BWC)

Convention on the Reduction of Statelessness (adopted 30 August 1961, entered into force 13 December 1975) 989 UNTS 175 (Statelessness Convention)

Convention on the Rights of the Child (adopted 20 November 1989, entered into force 2 September 1990) 1577 UNTS 3 (CRC)

Optional Protocol to the Convention on the Rights of the Child on a Communications Procedure (adopted 19 December 2011, entered into force 14 April 2014) UN Doc A/RES/66/138 (CRC-OP 3)

Convention on the Recognition and Enforcement of Foreign Arbitral Awards (signed 10 June 1958, entered into force 7 June 1959) (New York Convention)

Convention on the Settlement of Investment Disputes between States and Nationals of Other States (signed 18 March 1965, entered into force 14 October 1966) 575 UNTS 159 (ICSID Convention)

Convention on the Settlement of Matters Arising out of the War and the Occupation (signed 26 May 1952, entered into force 5 May 1955) 322 UNTS 219

Convention on Treaties (signed 20 February 1928, entered into force 29 August 1929) (1935) 29 AJIL Supp 128 (Havana Convention)

Convention relating to Civil Procedure (adopted 17 July 1905, entered into force 27 April 1909) 199 CTS 1

Convention relating to Civil Procedure (adopted 1 March 1954, entered into force 12 April 1957) 286 UNTS 265

Convention relating to the Status of Refugees (adopted 28 July 1951, entered into force 22 April 1954) 189 UNTS 137 (Refugee Convention)

Protocol relating to the Status of Refugees (adopted 31 January 1967, entered into force 4 October 1967) 606 UNTS 267 (Refugee Protocol)

Convention relating to the Status of Stateless Persons (signed 28 September 1964, entered into force 6 June 1960) 360 UNTS 117 (Stateless Persons Convention)

Convention Respecting the Laws and Customs of Warfare on Land (signed 18 October 1907, entered into force 26 January 2010) 36 Stat 2277 (Hague Land Warfare Convention)

Covenant of the League of Nations (adopted 29 April 1919, entered into force 10 January 1920) 225 CTS 195

Customs Convention on Containers (signed 18 May 1956, entered into force 4 August 1959) 338 UNTS 103 (1956 Containers Convention)

Customs Convention on Containers (signed 2 December 1972, entered into force 6 December 1975) (1972 Containers Convention)

EUROCONTROL International Convention relating to Cooperation for the Safety of Air Navigation (signed 13 December 1960, entered into force 1 March 1963) 523 UNTS 117 (EUROCONTROL Convention)

General Act of the International Conference at Algeciras relating to the Affairs of Morocco (signed 7 April 1906, entered into force 31 December 1906) 201 CTS 39 (Act of Algeciras)

International Convention for the Regulation of Whaling (signed 2 December 1946, entered into force 10 November 1948) 161 UNTS 72 (Whaling Convention; ICRW)

International Convention for the Suppression of the Financing of Terrorism (signed 9 December 1999, entered into force 10 April 2002) 2178 UNTS 197 (ICFST)

International Covenant on Civil and Political Rights (adopted 16 December 1966, entered into force 23 March 1976) 999 UNTS 171 (ICCPR)

Optional Protocol to the International Covenant on Civil and Political Rights (adopted 16 December 1966, entered into force 23 March 1976) 999 UNTS 171 (ICCPR-OP 1)

International Covenant on Economic, Social and Cultural Rights (adopted 16 December 1966, entered into force 3 January 1976) 993 UNTS 3 (ICESCR)

Optional Protocol to the International Covenant on Economic, Social and Cultural Rights (adopted 10 December 2008, entered into force 5 May 2013) UN Doc A/63/435 (ICESCR-OP)

Maritime Labour Convention (signed 23 February 2006, entered into force 20 August 2013) (2006) 45 ILM 792 (MLC)

North American Free Trade Agreement between the United States of America, Canada and Mexico (signed 17 December 1992, entered into force 1 January 1993) 32 ILM 289 (NAFTA)

North Atlantic Treaty (signed 4 April 1949, entered into force 24 August 1949) 34 UNTS 243 (NATO Treaty)

Statute of the International Court of Justice, annexed to the Charter of the United Nations (adopted 26 June 1945, entered into force 24 October 1946) 1 UNTS XVI (ICJ Statute)

Statute of the Permanent Court of International Justice (adopted 16 December 1920, entered into force 20 August 1921) 6 LNTS 379 (PCIJ Statute)

Treaty of Peace between the Allied and Associated Powers and Germany (signed 28 June 1919, entered into force 10 January 1920) 255 CTS 188 (Treaty of Versailles)

Treaty on European Union (signed 7 February 1992, entered into force 1 November 1993) 1759 UNTS 3 (TEU)

Treaty of Nice Amending the Treaty on European Union, the Treaties Establishing the European Communities and Certain Related Acts (signed 26 February 2001, entered into force 1 February 2003) 2701 UNTS No 47937 (Treaty of Nice)

Treaty of Lisbon Amending the Treaty on European Union and the Treaty Establishing the European Community (signed 13 December 2007, entered into force 1 December 2009) 2702 UNTS No 47938 (Lisbon Treaty)

UNIDROIT Convention on International Factoring (signed 28 May 1988, entered into force 1 May 1995) 2323 UNTS 373

UNIDROIT Convention on International Financial Leasing (signed 28 May 1988, entered into force 1 May 1995) 2321 UNTS 195

United Nations Convention against Corruption (signed 31 October 2003, entered into force 9 December 2003) 2349 UNTS 41 (UNCAC)

United Nations Convention on Contracts for the International Sale of Goods (signed 11 April 1980, entered into force 1 January 1988) 1489 UNTS 3 (CISG)

United Nations Convention on the Carriage of Goods by Sea (signed 31 March 1978, entered into force 1 November 1992) 1695 UNTS 3 (Hamburg Rules)

United Nations Convention on the Law of the Sea (signed 10 December 1982, entered into force 16 November 1994) 1833 UNTS 3 (UNCLOS)

Vienna Convention for the Protection of the Ozone Layer (signed 22 March 1985, entered into force 22 September 1988) 1513 UNTS 293 (Ozone Convention)

Vienna Convention on Diplomatic Relations (adopted 18 April 1961, entered into force 24 April 1964) 500 UNTS 95 (VCDR)

Vienna Convention on Succession of States in respect of Treaties (adopted 22 August 1978, entered into force 6 November 1996) 1946 UNTS 3

Vienna Convention on the Law of Treaties (adopted 23 May 1969, entered into force 27 January 1980) 1155 UNTS 331 (VCLT)

Bilateral

Agreement between Belgium and Luxembourg for the Avoidance of Double Taxation and the Regulation of Certain Other Matters with respect to Taxes on Income and Fortune (signed 17 September 1970, entered into force 30 December 1972) 870 UNTS 167 (1970 Belgian–Luxembourg DTA)

Agreement between the Federal Republic of Germany and the Kingdom of Belgium for the Avoidance of Double Taxation and the Regulation of Certain Other Matters with respect to Taxes on Income and Fortune, Including the Business Tax and Land Taxes (signed 11 April 1967, entered into force 30 July 1969) 704 UNTS 361 (1967 German–Belgian DTA)

Agreement between the Federal Republic of Germany and the Swiss Confederation for the Avoidance of Double Taxation with respect to Taxes on Income and on Capital (signed 11 August 1971, entered into force 29 December 1972) 2545 UNTS 207 (1971 German–Swiss DTA)

Protocol to the Agreement of 11 August 1971 between the Federal Republic of Germany and the Swiss Confederation for the Avoidance of Double Taxation with respect to Taxes on Income and on Capital (signed 17 October 1989, entered into force 30 November 1990) 2546 UNTS 343 (1971 German–Swiss DTA, as amended in 1989)

Protocol to the Agreement of 11 August 1971 between the Federal Republic of Germany and the Swiss Confederation for the Avoidance of Double Taxation with respect to Taxes on Income and on Capital (signed 21 December 1992, entered into force 29 November 1993) 2546 UNTS 357 (1971 German–Swiss DTA, as amended in 1992)

Agreement between the Government of Australia and the Government of the French Republic for the Avoidance of Double Taxation and the Prevention of Fiscal Evasion with respect to Taxes on Income (signed 13 April 1976, entered into force 21 September 1977) 1072 UNTS 379 (1976 Australian–French DTA)

Protocol Amending the Agreement of 13 April 1976 (Australia–France) (signed 19 June 1989, entered into force 19 July 1990) 1583 UNTS 491

Agreement between the Government of Australia and the Government of the People's Republic of China for the Avoidance of Double Taxation and the Prevention of Fiscal Evasion with respect to Taxes on Income (signed 17 November 1988, entered into force 28 November 1990) 1642 UNTS 3 (1988 Australian–Chinese DTA)

Agreement between the Government of the Commonwealth of Australia and the Government of the Republic of Singapore for the Avoidance of Double Taxation and the Prevention of Fiscal Evasion with respect to Taxes on Income (signed 11 February 1969, entered into force 4 June 1969) 708 UNTS 228 (1969 Australian–Singaporean DTA)

Protocol Amending the Agreement of 11 February 1969 (Australia–Singapore) (signed 16 October 1989, entered into force 5 January 1990) 1571 UNTS 500

Agreement between the Kingdom of the Netherlands and the Federal Republic of Germany for the Avoidance of Double Taxation with respect to Taxes on Income and Fortune and Various Other Taxes, and for the Regulation of Other Questions relating to Taxation (signed 16 June 1959, entered into force 18 September 1960) 593 UNTS 43 (1959 Dutch–German DTA)

Additional Protocol to the Agreement between the Kingdom of the Netherlands and the Federal Republic of Germany for the Avoidance of Double Taxation with respect to Taxes on Income and Fortune and Various Other Taxes, and for the Regulation of Other Questions relating to Taxation (signed 13 March 1980, entered into force 1 January 1981) 1225 UNTS 340

Agreement between the Principality of Liechtenstein and the Republic of Austria for the Avoidance of Double Taxation with respect to Taxes on Income and Fortune (signed 5 November 1969, entered into force 7 December 1970) 771 UNTS 149 (1969 Liechtenstein–Austrian DTA)

Agreement between the Republic of Austria and the Federal Republic of Germany for the Avoidance of Double Taxation with respect to Taxes on Income and Capital and to Trade and Property Taxes (signed 4 October 1954, entered into force 7 September 1955) 1972 UNTS 277 (1954 Austrian–German DTA)

Agreement between the Republic of Austria and the Swiss Confederation for the Avoidance of Double Taxation in the Field of Taxes on Income and on Capital (signed 30 January 1974, entered into force 4 December 1974) 2176 UNTS 297 (1974 Austrian–Swiss DTA)

Agreement in Implementation of Article III of the Panama Canal Treaty (Panama–USA) (signed 7 September 1977, entered into force 1 October 1979) 1280 UNTS 201 (1977 Article III Implementation Agreement)

Convention between Belgium and France for the Avoidance of Double Taxation and the Establishment of Rules of Reciprocal Administrative and Legal Assistance with respect to Taxes on Income (signed 10 March 1964, entered into force 17 June 1965) 557 UNTS 13 (1964 Belgian–French DTA)

Convention between Germany and the Persian Empire regarding Conditions of Residence (signed 17 February 1929, entered into force 11 January 1931) 111 LNTS 241 (1929 German–Persian Establishment Agreement)

Convention between Italy and Switzerland concerning Frontier Traffic and Grazing (signed 2 July 1953, entered into force 17 February 1956) 257 UNTS 99

Convention between the French Republic and the Federal Republic of Germany for the Avoidance of Double Taxation and the Establishment of Principles for Reciprocal Administrative and Legal Assistance with respect to Taxes on Income and Fortune, Business Taxes and Land Taxes (signed 21 July 1959, entered into force 4 November 1961) 770 UNTS 325 (1959 French–German DTA)

Additional Protocol to the Convention between the French Republic and the Federal Republic of Germany for the Avoidance of Double Taxation and the Establishment of Principles for Reciprocal Administrative and Legal Assistance with respect to Taxes on Income and Fortune, Business Taxes and Land Taxes of 21 July 1959 (signed 20 December 2001, entered into force 1 June 2003) BGBl (Germany) 2002 II 2370

Convention between the German Reich and the Swiss Confederation for the Prevention of Double Taxation in the Matter of Direct Taxes and Succession Duties (signed 15 July 1931, entered into force 29 January 1934) 144 LNTS 389 (1931 German–Swiss DTA)

Additional Agreement to the Convention of 15 July 1931 between the Swiss Confederation and the German Reich for the Prevention of Double Taxation in the Matter of Direct Taxes and Succession Duties (signed 11 January 1934, entered into force 29 January 1934) 144 LNTS 449

Additional Protocol to the Agreement between the German Reich and the Swiss Confederation for the Avoidance of Double Taxation in the Area of Direct Tax and Inheritance Tax of 15 June 1931 (signed 9 September 1957, entered into force 20 April 1959) BGBl (Germany) 1959 II 408

Convention between the Government of Australia and the Government of the United States of America for the Avoidance of Double Taxation and the Prevention of Fiscal Evasion with respect to Taxes on Income (signed 6 August 1982, entered into force 31 October 1983) 1424 UNTS 37 (1982 Australian–US DTA)

Protocol Amending the Convention between the Government of Australia and the Government of the United States of America for the Avoidance of Double Taxation and the Prevention of Fiscal Evasion with respect to Taxes on Income (signed 27 September 2001, entered into force 12 May 2003) 2260 UNTS 117

Convention between the Government of the Republic of Singapore and the Swiss Confederation for the Avoidance of Double Taxation with respect to Taxes on Income and on Capital (signed 25 November 1975, entered into force 17 December 1976) SR 0.672.968.91 (1975 Singaporean–Swiss DTA)

Convention between the Republic of Austria and the Portuguese Republic for the Avoidance of Double Taxation with respect to Taxes on Income and Fortune (signed 29 December 1970, entered into force 27 February 1972) 823 UNTS 277 (1970 Austrian–Portuguese DTA)

Convention between the United States of America and Canada relating to the Avoidance of Double Taxation and Fiscal Evasion in the Case of Income Taxes (signed 4 March 1942, entered into force 15 June 1942) 124 UNTS 271 (1942 US–Canadian DTA)

Convention between the United States of America and His Majesty the King of Italy (signed 11 June 1884, entered into force 24 April 1885) 24 Stat 1001

Convention between the United States of America and the Federal Republic of Germany for the Avoidance of Double Taxation with respect to Taxes on Income (signed 22 July 1954, entered into force 20 December 1954) 239 UNTS 135 (1954 US–German DTA)

Convention between the United States of America and the Federal Republic of Germany for the Avoidance of Double Taxation and the Prevention of Fiscal Evasion with respect to Taxes on Income and Capital and to Certain Other Taxes (signed 29 August 1989, entered into force 21 August 1991) 1708 UNTS 52 (1989 US–German DTA)

Convention between the United States of America and the Swiss Confederation for the Avoidance of Double Taxation with respect to Taxes on Income (signed 2 October 1996, entered into force 1 January 1998) BBl 1997 II 1104 (1996 US–Swiss DTA)

Convention for the Avoidance of Double Taxation and the Settlement of Other Questions connected with Direct Taxes (Germany–Italy) (signed 31 October 1925, entered into force 1 January 1926) 53 LNTS 245 (1925 German–Italian DTA)

Convention on the Surrender of Criminals (Italy–USA) (signed 23 March 1868, entered into force 17 September 1868) 15 Stat 629 (1868 Italian–US Extradition Treaty)

Establishment and Consular Agreement (Italy–Switzerland) (signed 22 July 1868, entered into force 1 May 1869) BBl 1868 III 416

Extradition Convention between the United States of America and Her Britannic Majesty (signed 12 July 1889, entered into force 4 April 1890) 26 Stat 1508 (Blaine-Pauncefote Convention)

Gámez-Bonilla Treaty (Honduras–Nicaragua) (signed 7 October 1894, entered into force 24 December 1896) reproduced in *Case concerning the Arbitral Award Made by the King of Spain on 23 December 1906 (Honduras v Nicaragua)* [1960] ICJ Rep 192, 199

Joint Declaration of the Government of the United Kingdom of Great Britain and Northern Ireland and the Government of the People's Republic of China on the Question of Hong Kong (signed 19 December 1984, entered into force 27 May 1985) <http://www.cmab.gov.hk/en/issues/joint3.htm> (Sino–British Joint Declaration)

Panama Canal Treaty (Panama–USA) (signed 7 September 1977, entered into force 1 October 1979) 1280 UNTS 3

Treaty between the German Empire and Switzerland on Extradition and Mutual Assistance in Criminal Matters (signed 24 January 1874, entered into force 20 July 1874) RGBl 1874, 113 (1874 German–Swiss Extradition Treaty)

Treaty between the Grand Duchy of Baden and the Swiss Confederation Acting in Particular on Behalf of the Canton of Schaffhausen in Respect of the Continuation of the State Railways of the Grand Duchy of Baden through the Territory of the Canton of Schaffhausen (signed 30 December 1858, entered into force 28 February 1859) SR 0.742.140.313.62 (1858 Baden–Swiss Railway Treaty)

Treaty of Amity and Commerce (Japan–USA) (signed 29 July 1858, entered into force 4 July 1859) 12 Stat 1056

Treaty of Commerce and Navigation between Austria and the Netherlands (signed 28 March 1929, entered into force 13 August 1930) 109 LNTS 39 (Austrian–Dutch Commerce and Navigation Treaty)

Treaty of Friendship, Commerce and Navigation (Japan–USA) (signed 2 April 1952, entered into force 30 October 1953) 206 UNTS 143

Treaty on Commerce and Consuls (Japan–USA) (signed 17 June 1857, entered into force 17 June 1857) 11 Stat 723

Treaty to Define and Settle the Boundaries between the Territories of the United States and the Possessions of Her Britannic Majesty in North America, for the Final Suppression of the African Slave Trade, and for the Giving up of Criminals, Fugitive from Justice in Certain Cases (USA–UK) (signed 9 August 1842, entered into force 13 October 1842) 8 Stat 572 (Webster-Ashburton Treaty)

Table of Documents

Alston, Philip, 'Final Report on Enhancing the Long-term Effectiveness of the United Nations Human Rights Treaty System' (27 March 1997) UN Doc E/CN.4/1997/74

Assembly of States Parties to the Rome Statute of the International Criminal Court, 'Elements of Crimes' (9 September 2002) ICC-ASP/1/3, Part II-B

BBl 1912 I 527f No 19

BMF (Austria), 'Erlaß Z 1246/1/3-IV/4/86 betreffend die Besteuerung wesentlich beteiligter Gesellschafter-Geschäftsführer nach dem österreichisch-deutschen Doppelbesteuerungsabkommen' (22 December 1986) AÖFV No 32/1987

BMF (Germany), 'Deutsch-belgisches Doppelbesteuerungsabkommen; Verständigungsvereinbarung mit dem belgischen Finanzministerium vom 15. Dezember 2006 über die Zuordnung des Besteuerungsrechts bei Abfindungen an Arbeitnehmer' (10 January 2007) BStBl I 2007, 261

BS 12 p 278 No 2

BS 12 p 314 No 2

CAT Committee, 'General Comment No 2' (24 January 2008) UN Doc CAT/C/GC/2

——, 'Rules of Procedure of the Committee against Torture' (13 August 2013) UN Doc CAT/C/3/Rev.6 (CAT Committee Rules of Procedure)

CEDAW Committee, 'General Recommendation No 6' (1988) UN Doc A/43/38

——, 'Concluding Observations on Switzerland's First and Second Periodic Report on Implementation of the CEDAW' (18 August 2003) UN Doc A/58/38(SUPP)

——, 'Rules of Procedure of the Committee on the Elimination of Discrimination against Women' (28 May 2008) UN Doc HRI/GEN/3/Rev.3 (CEDAW Committee Rules of Procedure)

——, 'Concluding Observations on Switzerland's Third Periodic Report on Implementation of the CEDAW' (14 August 2009) UN Doc CEDAW/C/CHE/CO/3

——, 'General Recommendation No 28' (16 December 2010) UN Doc CEDAW/C/GC/28

CESCR, 'Rules of Procedure of the Committee on Economic, Social and Cultural Rights' (1 September 1993) UN Doc E/C.12/1990/4/Rev.1 (CESCR Rules of Procedures)

——, 'Concluding Observations on the Netherlands' Second Periodic Report on Implementation of the ICESCR' (16 June 1998) UN Doc E/C.12/1/Add.25

——, 'Concluding Observations on Germany's Third Periodic Report on Implementation of the ICESCR' (4 December 1998) UN Doc E/C.12/1/Add.29

——, 'Concluding Observations on Canada's Third Periodic Report on Implementation of the ICESCR' (10 December 1998) UN Doc E/C.12/1/Add.31

——, 'General Comment No 11' (11 May 1999) UN Doc E/C.12/1999/5

——, 'General Comment No 13' (8 December 1999) UN Doc E/C.12/1999/10

——, 'Concluding Observations on Germany's Fourth Periodic Report on Implementation of the ICESCR' (24 September 2001) UN Doc E/C.12/1/Add.68

——, 'Concluding Observations on the United Kingdom's Fourth Periodic Report on Implementation of the ICESCR' (5 June 2002) UN Doc E/C.12/1/Add.79

——, 'General Comment No 17' (12 January 2006) UN Doc E/C.12/GC/17

——, 'Concluding Observations on Austria's Third Periodic Report on Implementation of the ICESCR' (25 January 2006) UN Doc E/C.12/AUT/CO/3

——, 'Concluding Observations on Canada's Fourth and Fifth Periodic Report on Implementation of the ICESCR' (22 May 2006) UN Docs E/C.12/CAN/CO/4 and E/C.12/CAN/CO/5

Charter of Fundamental Rights of the European Union [2007] OJ C303/1

Committee on Human Rights Law and Practice, 'Interim Report on the Impact of the Work of the United Nations Human Rights Treaty Bodies on National Courts and Tribunals' (2002) 70 Int'l L Ass'n Rep Conf 508–55

——, 'Final Report on the Impact of Findings of the United Nations Human Rights Treaty Bodies' (2004) 71 Int'l L Ass'n Rep Conf 621–702

Council Framework Decision 2002/584/JHA of 13 June 2002 on the European Arrest Warrant and the Surrender Procedures between Member States [2002] OJ L190/1 (Framework Decision)

CRC Committee, 'General Comment No 5' (27 November 2003) UN Doc CRC/GC/2003/5

——, 'General Comment No 6' (1 September 2005) UN Doc CRC/GC/2005/6

——, 'General Comment No 7' (20 September 2006) UN Doc CRC/C/GC/7/Rev.1

——, 'General Comment No 10' (25 April 2007) UN Doc CRC/C/GC/10

——, 'General Comment No 12' (20 July 2009) UN Doc CRC/C/GC/12

——, 'Rules of Procedure of the Committee on the Rights of the Child' (16 April 2013) UN Doc CRC/C/4/Rev.3 (CRC Committee Rules of Procedure)

ECOSOC Res 1655 (LII) (1 June 1972) UN Doc E/RES/1655(LII)

ECOSOC Res 1705 (LIII) (27 July 1972) UN Doc E/RES/1705(LIII)

ECOSOC Res 1985/17 (28 May 1985) UN Doc E/RES/1985/17

EUROCONTROL, 'General Conditions of Employment Governing Servants at the EUROCONTROL Maastricht Centre' (1 August 2013) <http://www.eurocontrol.int/sites/default/files/publication/files/general-conditions-employment-maastricht.pdf>

Fitzmaurice, Sir Gerald, 'First Report on the Law of Treaties' [1956-II] YBILC 104–28

Harvard Draft Convention on the Law of Treaties (1935) 29 AJIL Supp 657–65

HRC, 'General Comment No 22' (27 September 1993) UN Doc CCPR/C/21/Rev.1/Add.4

——, 'General Comment No 24' (11 November 1994) UN Doc CCPR/C/21/Rev.1/Add.6

——, 'General Comment No 27' (1 November 1999) UN Doc CCPR/C/21/Rev.1/Add.9

——, 'General Comment No 31' (26 May 2004) UN Doc CCPR/C/21/Rev.1/Add.13

——, 'General Comment No 6' (27 May 2008) UN Doc HRI/GEN/1/Rev.9 (Vol I)

——, 'General Comment No 34' (12 September 2011) UN Doc CCPR/C/GC/34

——, 'Rules of Procedure of the Human Rights Committee' (11 January 2012) UN Doc CCPR/C/3/Rev.10 (HRC Rules of Procedure)

ILC, 'Report of the International Law Commission on the Work of its 11th Session' (20 April–26 June 1959) [1959-II] YBILC 87–123

——, 'Report of the International Law Commission on the Work of its 16th Session' (11 May–24 July 1964) [1964-II] YBILC 173–227

——, 'Summary Records of the 16th Session of the International Law Commission' (11 May–24 July 1964) [1964-I] YBILC 1–343

——, 'Summary Records of the 18th Session of the International Law Commission' (4 May–19 July 1966) [1966-I/2] YBILC 1–351

——, 'Draft Articles on the Law of Treaties with Commentaries' [1966-II] YBILC 187–274

——, 'Documents of the 31st Session of the International Law Commission' (14 May–3 August 1979) [1979-II/1] YBILC 1–246

——, 'Report of the International Law Commission on the Work of its 48th Session' (6 May–26 July 1996) [1996-II/2] YBILC 1–145

——, 'Report of the International Law Commission on the Work of its 58th Session' (1 May–9 June and 3 July–11 August 2006) UN Doc A/61/10

——, 'Fragmentation of International Law: Difficulties Arising from the Diversification and Expansion of International Law—Report of the Study Group of the International Law Commission' (13 April 2006) UN Doc A/CN.4/L.682

——, 'Report of the International Law Commission on the Work of its 60th Session' (5 May–6 June and 7 July–8 August 2008) UN Doc A/63/10

——, 'Report of the International Law Commission on the Work of its 61st Session' (4 May–5 June and 6 July–7 August 2009) UN Doc A/64/10

——, 'Report of the International Law Commission on the Work of its 64th Session' (7 May–1 June and 2 July–3 August 2012) UN Doc A/67/10

——, 'Report of the International Law Commission on the Work of its 65th Session' (6 May–7 June and 8 July 2013) UN Doc A/68/10

——, 'Provisional Summary Record of the 3160th Meeting' (7 May 2013) UN Doc A/CN.4/SR.3160

——, 'Report of the International Law Commission on the Work of its 66th Session' (5 May–6 June and 7 July–8 August 2014) UN Doc A/69/10

——, 'Report of the International Law Commission on the Work of its 67th Session' (4 May–5 June and 6 July–7 August 2015) UN Doc A/70/10

——, 'Provisional Summary Record of the 3303rd Meeting' (28 June 2016) UN Doc A/CN.4/SR.3303

——, 'Provisional Summary Record of the 3307th Meeting' (8 July 2016) UN Doc A/CN.4/SR.3307

Institut de Droit International, 'De l'interprétation des traités—Rapport et projet de résolutions présentés à l'Institut de Droit International' (1950) 43 AIDI 366–640

——, De l'interprétation des traités' (1956) 46 AIDI 317–49

——, 'Résolution sur l'interprétation des traités' (1956) 46 AIDI 358–9

——, 'Resolution—The Activities of National Judges and the International Relations of Their State' (1993) 65-II AIDI 318–23

International Human Rights Instruments, 'Report on the Working Methods of the Human Rights Treaty Bodies relating to the State Party Reporting Process' (25 May 2005) UN Doc HRI/MC/2005/4

——, 'Guidelines on the Independence and Impartiality of Members of the Human Rights Treaty Bodies (Addis Ababa Guidelines)' (2012) UN Doc HRI/MC/2012

Joint Position 96/196/JHA of 4 March 1996 Defined by the Council on the Basis of Article K.3 of the Treaty on European Union on the Harmonised Application of the Definition of the Term 'Refugee' in Article 1 of the Geneva Convention of 28 July 1951 relating to the Status of Refugees

Koskenniemi, Martii, 'Report of the Study Group on Fragmentation of International Law: Difficulties Arising from the Diversification and Expansion of International Law' (13 April 2006) UN Doc A/CN.4/L.682

Lauterpacht, Sir Hersch, 'De l'interprétation des traités—Observations complémentaires et projet définitif de résolutions, présentés à l'Institut de Droit International' (1952) 44 AIDI 197–223

NAFTA Free Trade Commission, 'Notes of Interpretation of Certain Chapter 11 Provisions' (31 July 2001) <http://www.sice.oas.org>

Nolte, Georg, 'Annex A—Treaties over Time—In Particular: Subsequent Agreement and Practice' in ILC, 'Report of the International Law Commission on the Work of its 60th Session' (5 May–6 June and 7 July–8 August 2008) UN Doc A/63/10

——, 'First Report on Subsequent Agreements and Subsequent Practice in relation to Treaty Interpretation' (19 March 2013) UN Doc A/CN.4/660

——, 'Second Report on Subsequent Agreements and Subsequent Practice in relation to Treaty Interpretation' (26 March 2014) UN Doc A/CN.4/671

——, 'Third Report on Subsequent Agreements and Subsequent Practice in Relation to the Interpretation of Treaties' (7 April 2015) UN Doc A/CN.4/683

——, 'Fourth Report on Subsequent Agreements and Subsequent Practice in Relation to the Interpretation of Treaties' (7 March 2016) UN Doc A/CN.4/694

OECD, 'Recommendation of the OECD Council concerning the Model Tax Convention on Income and Capital' (23 October 1997) Doc C(97)195/FINAL

——, 'Resolution of the Council concerning the Participation of Non-Members in the Work of Subsidiary Bodies of the Organisation' (8 July 2004) Doc C(2004)132/FINAL

——, 'Resolution of the OECD Concil Revising the Mandate of the Committee on Fiscal Affairs' (13 November 2008) Docs C(2008)147 and C/M(2008)20

OEEC, 'Resolution of the Council Creating a Fiscal Committee' (19 March 1956) Doc C(56)49/Final

UN Conference on the Law of Treaties, 'Summary Records of the Plenary Meetings and of the Meetings of the Committee of the Whole' (First session, Vienna 26 March 1968) UN Doc A/CONF.39/11

——, 'Summary Records of the Plenary Meetings and of the Meetings of the Committee of the Whole' (Second session, Vienna 9 April–22 May 1969) UN Doc A/CONF.39/11/Add.l

——, 'Reports of the Committee of the Whole' (Vienna, 26 March–24 May 1968 and 9 April–22 May 1969) Official Records: Documents of the Conference, UN Doc A/CONF.39/11/Add2

UN, 'Model Double Taxation Convention between Developed and Developing Countries' (2011) UN Doc ST/ESA/PAD/SER.E/21

UNGA Res 174 (II) (21 November 1947) UN Doc A/519

UNGA Res 319 (IV) (3 December 1949) UN Doc A/RES/319(IV)

UNGA, 'Survey of International Law in relation to the Work of Codification of the International Law Commission: Preparatory Work within the Purview of Article 18, Paragraph 1, of the International Law Commission—Memorandum Submitted by the Secretary-General' (1949) UN Doc A/CN.4/1/Rev.1

UNGA, 'Statute of the Office of the United Nations High Commissioner for Refugees' Annex to UNGA Res 428 (V) (14 December 1950) UN Doc A/RES/428(V) (UNHCR Statute)

UNGA Res 1166 (XII) (26 November 1957) UN Doc A/RES/1166(XII)

UNGA Res 2166 (XXI) (5 December 1966) UN Doc A/6516

UNGA Res 2958 (XXVII) (12 December 1972) UN Doc A/RES/2958(XXVII)

UNGA Res 3274 (XXIX) (10 December 1974) UN Doc A/RES/3274(XXIX)

UNGA Res 31/36 (30 November 1976) UN Doc A/RES/31/36

UNGA Res 48/116 (18 February 1994) UN Doc A/RES/48/116

UNGA Res 48/118 (24 March 1994) UN Doc A/RES/48/118

UNGA Res 50/152 (9 February 1996) UN Doc A/RES/50/152

UNGA Res 52/103 (9 February 1998) UN Doc A/RES/52/103

UNGA Res 56/83 (12 December 2001) UN Doc A/RES/56/83

UNGA Res 63/123 (11 December 2008) UN Doc A/RES/63/123

UNHCR ExCom Conclusion No 8 (XXVIII), 'Determination of Refugee Status' (12 October 1977)

UNHCR ExCom Conclusion No 25 (XXXIII), 'General Conclusion on International Protection' (20 October 1982)

UNHCR ExCom Conclusion No 77 (XLVI), 'General Conclusion on International Protection' (20 October 1995)

UNHCR ExCom Conclusion No 81 (XLVIII), 'General Conclusion on International Protection' (17 October 1997)

UNHCR, 'Guidelines on International Protection No 3: Cessation of Refugee Status under Article 1C(5) and (6) of the 1951 Convention relating to the Status of Refugees (the "Ceased Circumstances" Clauses)' (10 February 2003) UN Doc HCR/GIP/03/03

——, 'Guidelines on International Protection No 6: Religion-Based Refugee Claims under Article 1A(2) of the 1951 Convention and/or the 1967 Protocol relating to the Status of Refugees' (28 April 2004) UN Doc HCR/GIP/04/06

——, 'Ergänzende Stellungnahme des UNHCR zu den Voraussetzungen der Beendigung der Flüchtlingseigenschaft nach Art 1 C (5) 1 des Abkommens von 1951 über die Rechtsstellung der Flüchtlinge (Genfer Flüchtlingskonvention)' (October 2005) <http://www.refworld.org/docid/48abd5570.html>

——, 'Guidance Note on Extradition and International Refugee Protection' (April 2008) <http://www.refworld.org/docid/481ec7d92.html>

——, 'Handbook on Procedures and Criteria for Determining Refugee Status under the 1951 Convention and the 1967 Protocol relating to the Status of Refugees' (December 2011) UN Doc HCR/1P/4/ENG/REV.3 (UNHCR Handbook)

USA, 'Model Income Tax Convention' (15 November 2006) <http://www.irs.gov/pub/irs-trty/model006.pdf

Vereinbarung gemäß Art. 15a B-VG über Vorhaben in der Bundeshauptstadt Wien, an welchen der Bund und das Land Wien interessiert sind (Austria–Vienna) (signed 9 May 1979, entered into force 20 December 1979) BGBl (Austria) 18/1980

Waldock, Sir Humphrey, 'First Report on the Law of Treaties' [1962-II] YBILC 27–80

——, 'Third Report on the Law of Treaties' [1964-II] YBILC 5–65

——, 'Sixth Report on the Law of Treaties' [1966-II] YBILC 51–103

Wood, Sir Michael, 'Second Report on Identification of Customary International Law' (22 May 2014) UN Doc A/CN.4/672

Chapter 1
Introduction

*Auctoritas, non veritas facit legem.**

1.1 Preliminary Reflections upon Interpretative Power

In some ways, concluding a treaty is like dropping a message in a bottle into the sea. Its contracting parties carefully contemplated what they might agree on; they sought to reach genuine compromises or attempted to conceal irreconcilable disagreement. Eventually, they succeeded in agreeing on one particular treaty. In doing so, they granted rights or undertook obligations vis-à-vis each other, or otherwise shaped the international legal order within which they exist.

But irrespective of how much care was laid into the treaty's drafting process, its parties will not have succeeded in creating a perfect agreement. The treaty may, for example, witness developments of a political, social, or scientific nature that were unforeseeable. When establishing the North Atlantic Treaty Organisation (NATO) in 1949,[1] its founding members hardly envisaged the dimension of new threats such as international terrorism, mass influx of refugees, or illicit drug trafficking that emerged after the Cold War. Similarly, in 1929 the parties to the Warsaw Convention[2] only

[*] Thomas Hobbes, *Leviathan, sive De materia, forma, & potestate civitatis ecclesiasticæ et civilis* (2nd edn, Typis Joannis Thomsonii 1678) 133.

[1] North Atlantic Treaty (signed 4 April 1949, entered into force 24 August 1949) 34 UNTS 243 (NATO Treaty).

[2] Convention for the Unification of Certain Rules relating to the International Carriage by Air (signed 12 October 1929, entered into force 13 February 1933) 137 LNTS 11 (Warsaw Convention).

K. Berner, *Subsequent Agreements and Subsequent Practice in Domestic Courts*, Beiträge zum ausländischen öffentlichen Recht und Völkerrecht, https://doi.org/10.1007/978-3-662-54937-7_1

vaguely expected that airplanes would become a means of mass transport one day;[3] or that medical knowledge would allow detecting physical causes for particular psychic injuries. Such cases raise the question whether a treaty is capable of operating in an evolving environment. If its parties cannot agree on amending the treaty and if it is too inflexible for informal adaptation, it may ultimately 'fall into obsolescence'.[4]

In addition to this general challenge, which becomes increasingly acute once a treaty reaches a certain age, every treaty inevitably suffers from the inherent imperfections of human language. The words and phrases that make up a treaty hardly ever carry only one single meaning. Almost every treaty is ambiguous.[5] To resolve this ambiguity and to determine their correct meaning at a given moment in time and in a given context, treaties are subject to a process called 'interpretation'.[6] During their lives, treaties are interpreted by different actors such as international courts and tribunals, international governmental and non-governmental organisations (IOs and NGOs), executives and legislatures of the contracting parties, and, last but not least, domestic courts. Applying a treaty without having (consciously or unconsciously) determined its meaning is almost impossible.[7]

Interpreters therefore wield an enormous but often underestimated power. Like someone who receives a message in a bottle, they are called on to decipher the meaning of a document without positively knowing what it has been created for. The outcome of their attempt to do so can be assessed in multiple ways. It can be assessed in terms of convincing or unconvincing, morally right or wrong, or politically suitable or unsuitable. But from a legal perspective, the interpretative outcome should, in the first place, be assessed in terms of correct or incorrect. Treaties are not concluded by accident. They are the result of a concordant will of sovereign States or other actors, whose overriding importance is reflected in the basic principle *pacta sunt servanda.* As James Crawford succinctly remarked, 'it is too often forgotten that the parties to a treaty, that is, the states which are bound by it at the relevant time, own the treaty. It is their treaty. It is not anyone else's treaty.'[8] A 'correct' interpretation is not the one which the interpreter personally considers suitable. Instead,

---

[3] While the first scheduled airline flight took off in 1914, the commercial aviation industry did not grow significantly until after World War II, see Tom Heppenheimer, *Turbulent Skies—The History of Commercial Aviation* (Wiley & Sons 1995) 1; Isabella Diederiks-Verschoor and Pablo Mendes de Leon, *An Introduction to Air Law* (9th edn, Kluwer 2012) 3.

[4] Georg Nolte, 'Annex A—Treaties over Time—In Particular: Subsequent Agreement and Practice' in ILC, 'Report of the International Law Commission on the Work of its 60th Session' (5 May–6 June and 7 July–8 August 2008) UN Doc A/63/10, 365.

[5] See in particular Herbert Hart, *The Concept of Law* (3rd edn, OUP 2012) 124 f; see further Sir Hersch Lauterpacht, 'Some Observations on Preparatory Work in the Interpretation of Treaties' (1935) 48 HLR 549, 571.

[6] See 1.3.1.2.

[7] Wolfram Karl, *Vertrag und spätere Praxis im Völkerrecht—Zum Einfluss der Praxis auf Inhalt und Bestand völkerrechtlicher Verträge* (repr, Springer 2012) 1, 22.

[8] James Crawford, 'A Consensualist Interpretation of Article 31(3) of the Vienna Convention on the Law of Treaties' in Georg Nolte (ed), *Treaties and Subsequent Practice* (OUP 2013) 31.

a correct interpretation is the one that comes closest to implementing this concordant will. Otherwise, concluding treaties would be utterly pointless.

In contrast to many domestic legal systems, public international law offers legally binding rules that regulate the interpretative process. These rules, which are commonly considered as reflecting customary international law,[9] are laid down in articles 31–33 of the Vienna Convention on the Law of Treaties (VCLT).[10] Article 31 VCLT contains the so-called 'general rule' of interpretation.[11] This 'general rule' consists of the various elements that are, in a single combined operation,[12] to be taken into account as primary means of interpretation. In particular, article 31(1) VCLT requires that treaties are to be interpreted in good faith in accordance with the ordinary meaning to be given to the terms of the treaty in their context and in the light of its object and purpose. Article 32 VCLT stipulates supplementary means of interpretation and article 33 VCLT offers rules for the interpretation of treaties that are authenticated in two or more languages.[13]

As part of the general rule, article 31(3) VCLT provides that there shall be taken into account, together with the context, any subsequent agreement between the parties regarding the interpretation of the treaty or the application of its provisions (a), and any subsequent practice in the application of the treaty which establishes the agreement of the parties regarding its interpretation (b). In addition, article 32 VCLT implicitly authorises that recourse may be had to subsequent agreements and subsequent practice that do not meet all criteria of the general rule ('other' subsequent agreements and subsequent practice).[14] Formally enjoying the same status as any other primary or supplementary means of interpretation, subsequent agreements and subsequent practice (hereinafter in short referred to as 'subsequent conduct')[15] are a peculiarity that has received surprisingly little attention so far. In

---

[9] Whereas the customary status of arts 31 and 32 VCLT is widely acknowledged, the customary status of art 33 VCLT is more doubtful. For more details, see 3.2.

[10] Vienna Convention on the Law of Treaties (signed 23 May 1969, entered into force 27 January 1980) 1155 UNTS 331 (Vienna Convention; VCLT).

[11] See 3.3.1.

[12] See 3.3.3.

[13] See 3.3.2.

[14] Draft conclusion 1(4) in ILC, 'Report of the International Law Commission on the Work of its 65th Session' (6 May–7 June and 8 July–9 August 2013) UN Doc A/68/10, 13.

[15] See Georg Nolte, 'Report 1—Jurisprudence of the International Court of Justice and Arbitral Tribunals of Ad Hoc Jurisdiction relating to Subsequent Agreements and Subsequent Practice' in id (ed), *Treaties and Subsequent Practice* (OUP 2013) 174. cf also *Case concerning Maritime Delimitation and Territorial Questions between Qatar and Bahrain (Qatar v Bahrain)* (Jurisdiction and Admissibility) [1994] ICJ Rep 112, 122 [28]. The ILC did not expressly endorse this terminology. Nevertheless, it also occasionally used the term 'subsequent conduct' as a general category, see eg draft conclusion 4 with commentary in ILC, 'Report of the International Law Commission on the Work of its 65th Session' (6 May–7 June and 8 July–9 August 2013) UN Doc A/68/10, 34 [11]. Other authors have rejected the generic term 'subsequent conduct' as being inappropriate, albeit for different reasons. According to

the academic discourse, they have mostly been perceived as tools to informally adapt treaties to changing conditions. While some commentators focused on the benefits of informal adaptation over formal amendment mechanisms, others highlighted its dangers by evoking the image of 'treaties set on wheels.'[16] This important but nonetheless one-sided focus has neglected another peculiarity.

Subsequent agreements and subsequent practice open the interpretative process for more actors than only the individual interpreter himself. Via subsequent agreements and subsequent practice, the contracting parties retain considerable influence on their treaty. This actually distinguishes the contracting parties from individual interpreters. The interpreter is merely called on to identify the correct meaning of the terms of the treaty. As this study is going to show, the parties, in contrast, can, through their subsequent conduct, actively influence the treaty's meaning. Hence it is in fact misleading to compare treaties to messages in a bottle. Sender and recipient of this message regularly do not communicate with each other directly and in real time. Nevertheless, the sender may furnish the latter with hints as to how his message ought to be understood. From this perspective, articles 31 and 32 VCLT do not merely establish another technical rule of interpretation. Instead, they also contain a more principled decision as to how interpretative power shall be distributed and exercised.

The exact scope of this power not only depends on how articles 31 and 32 VCLT are understood in the abstract. It also depends on how interpreters approach them in interpretative reality. This reality most probably deviates from the 'ideal' conception of subsequent conduct under the Vienna rules. Are interpreters willing to accept that the contracting parties are the 'true masters' of the treaty and retain some interpretative power over its meaning? Do interpreters recognise that the general rule of interpretation evenly vests this power in the parties as a whole? Or do interpreters instead concede to some parties a stronger influence on the treaty's meaning than to others? Which types of subsequent agreements and subsequent practice are

---

Richard Gardiner, *Treaty Interpretation* (2nd edn, OUP 2015) 259, the term 'conduct' merely denoted *any* behaviour of States. For this reason, 'subsequent conduct' could not be used to refer to subsequent practice because the latter implied a certain degree of repetition. As this study does not follow the narrow understanding of 'practice' advocated by Gardiner, his reasoning does not mitigate against using the term 'subsequent conduct' as suggested. For a broader understanding of 'practice', see 4.3.1.1 and draft conclusion 4 with commentary in ILC, 'Report of the International Law Commission on the Work of its 65th Session' (6 May–7 June and 8 July–9 August 2013) UN Doc A/68/10, 31 f, esp 35 [16]. Karl, *Vertrag und spätere Praxis* (n 7) 112, in contrast, argues that the term 'subsequent conduct' implied that it was limited to conduct (or behaviour) of State parties only. Since Karl does not restrict practice under art 31(3)(b) VCLT to State practice, he rejects 'subsequent conduct' as a generic term for both subsequent agreements and subsequent practice, too. Agreeing that the term 'practice' encompasses the practice of parties and non-party entities alike (see 4.3.1.2), this study, however, submits that the ordinary meaning of the term 'conduct' is open to a similarly broad construction.

[16] Georg Ress, 'Verfassungsrechtliche Auswirkungen der Fortentwicklung völkerrechtlicher Verträge—Überlegungen zum Verhältnis des Grundgesetzes zur Europäischen Wirtschaftsgemeinschaft und zur Europäischen Menschenrechtskonvention' in Walther Fürst, Roman Herzog, and Dieter Umbach (eds), *Festschrift für Wolfgang Zeidler* (de Gruyter 1987) 1779.

regarded as an admissible exercise of interpretative power under articles 31 and 32 VCLT? And how does this exercise of interpretative power impact on the treaty's meaning?

Interpretative practice that may shed light on questions like these occurs on various occasions. Unlike in the past, a large part of it is now generated at the national level and through the jurisprudence of domestic courts.[17] With its increasing importance, treaty law now also regulates matters that used to be largely governed by domestic law.[18] When domestic courts render a decision, they can no longer exclusively rely on domestic legal rules but increasingly have to apply treaty law and international law rules of treaty interpretation as well.[19] Today, domestic courts generate much interpretative practice. Their jurisprudence promises to vividly reflect the difficulties in applying subsequent agreements and subsequent practice. In an ideal world, interpreters such as domestic courts may be conceived as trustees that faithfully attempt to implement the contracting parties' concordant will. But in reality, they may pursue their very own agenda and—consciously or unconsciously—divert from this will.

As interpreters, domestic courts act in a way that can be described as a 'dédoublement fonctionnel' ('role splitting').[20] Although they are primarily State organs, they also effectively act as international agents. Thus, domestic courts fall between two stools. On the one hand, they are supposed to apply international law rules of treaty interpretation and to maintain neutrality instead of unduly discriminating in favour of or against particular contracting parties. On the other hand, domestic courts are actors created by a particular national legal system. They are probably more familiarised with domestic interpretative rules than with the requirements under articles 31–33 VCLT; their own legal system may impose constitutional impediments for relying on subsequent agreements or subsequent practice; they may simply lack the necessary language skills to be able to identify subsequent agreements or subsequent practice; and they may be influenced by particular cultural or political values and feelings of loyalty towards their own State, which prevent them from giving equal weight to each party's conduct.[21]

---

[17] See generally Eyal Benvenisti, 'Reclaiming Democracy: The Strategic Uses of Foreign and International Law by National Courts' (2008) 102 AJIL 241.

[18] Francesco Francioni, 'International Law as a Common Language for National Courts' (2001) 36 Tex Int'l LJ 587, 587.

[19] cf Michael Wood's Foreword in Gardiner, *Treaty Interpretation* (n 15) xv.

[20] For his theory of 'dédoublement fonctionnel', see Georges Scelle, 'Le phénomène du dédoublement fonctionnel' in Walter Schätzel (ed), *Rechtsfragen der internationalen Organisation—Festschrift für Hans Wehberg zu seinem 70. Geburtstag* (Klostermann 1956) 324 f. Instead of exclusively focusing on domestic courts, Scelle adopts a broader perspective by examining both adjudicative, legislative, and law enforcing functions at the national and international level.

[21] cf Reem Bahdi, 'Truth and Method in the Domestic Application of International Law' (2002) 15 CJLJ 255, 261, who describes the pitfalls of cultural relativism when interpreting international legal instruments; Eyal Benvenisti, 'Judicial Misgivings regarding the Application of International Law: An Analysis of Attitudes of National Courts' (1993) 4 EJIL 159, 161 f, who criticises that domestic courts tended to protect 'short-term governmental interests.' See further id, 'Comments on the Systemic Vision of National Courts as Part of an International Rule of Law' (2012) 4 JRLS 42, 45.

In the end, the research question that guides this study is about interpretation and power: *based on the jurisprudence of domestic courts, this study aims at finding out how subsequent agreements and subsequent practice within the meaning of articles 31 and 32 VCLT have been applied in interpretative practice.* In other words, it is not asked whether domestic courts faithfully apply articles 31 and 32 VCLT. The latter question is one that lends itself to being answered in the affirmative or in the negative. Still, this question also presupposes a reasonably clear understanding of subsequent agreements and subsequent practice under the Vienna rules. Such understanding, however, still appears to be lacking. By deliberately chosing an open-ended question instead, this study leaves room for the interpretative practice of domestic courts to challenge and shape the perception of these means of interpretation.

1.2 Current State of Research

Until recently, subsequent conduct has attracted comparatively little attention. This has changed since the International Law Commission (ILC) decided to include the topic 'Treaties over Time' in its long-term programme of work in 2008.[22]

Initially, the ILC approached the topic in the form of a Study Group chaired by Georg Nolte.[23] Based on successive reports prepared by its Chairman, the Study Group considered the jurisprudence of the International Court of Justice (ICJ) and arbitral tribunals of *ad hoc* jurisdiction,[24] jurisprudence under special regimes,[25] and subsequent agreements and subsequent practice of States outside of judicial or quasi-judicial proceedings.[26] In 2012, the ILC changed its working format and appointed Nolte as Special Rapporteur for the topic 'Subsequent Agreements and Subsequent Practice in relation to the Interpretation of Treaties'.[27]

---

[22] ILC, 'Report of the International Law Commission on the Work of its 60th Session' (5 May–6 June and 7 July–8 August 2008) UN Doc A/63/10, 355 [353]. See also UNGA Res 63/123 (11 December 2008) UN Doc A/RES/63/123. The decision to include the topic in its long-term programme of work originates in a proposal by Georg Nolte, which was contained in an informal working paper and which was later published as Annex A to the Commission's Report of 2008, see Nolte, 'Annex A' (n 4).

[23] ILC, 'Report of the International Law Commission on the Work of its 61st Session' (4 May–5 June and 6 July–7 August 2009) UN Doc A/64/10, 360 [218]–[19].

[24] Nolte, 'Report 1—ICJ and Arbitral Tribunals' (n 15) 169–209.

[25] id, 'Report 2—Jurisprudence under Special Regimes relating to Subsequent Agreements and Subsequent Practice' in id (ed), *Treaties and Subsequent Practice* (OUP 2013) 210–306.

[26] id, 'Report 3—Subsequent Agreements and Subsequent Practice of States outside of Judicial or Quasi-Judicial Proceedings' in id (ed), *Treaties and Subsequent Practice* (OUP 2013) 307–86.

[27] ILC, 'Report of the International Law Commission on the Work of its 64th Session' (7 May–1 June and 2 July–3 August 2012) UN Doc A/67/10, 6 [22].

In 2013, the Commission considered Special Rapporteur Nolte's first report[28] and provisionally adopted five draft conclusions with commentaries.[29] These annotated conclusions address the general rule and means of treaty interpretation (draft conclusion 1), subsequent agreements and subsequent practice as authentic means of interpretation (draft conclusion 2), the interpretation of treaty terms as capable of evolving over time (draft conclusion 3), the definition of subsequent agreement and subsequent practice (draft conclusion 4), and the attribution of a treaty related practice to a State (draft conclusion 5).

In 2014, the ILC considered Special Rapporteur Nolte's second report[30] and provisionally adopted five further draft conclusions with commentaries.[31] These annotated conclusions elaborate on the identification of subsequent agreements and subsequent practice (draft conclusion 6), possible effects of subsequent agreements and subsequent practice in interpretation (draft conclusion 7), the weight of subsequent agreements and subsequent practice as a means of interpretation (draft conclusion 8), the agreement of the parties regarding the interpretation of a treaty (draft conclusion 9), and decisions adopted within the framework of a Conference of States Parties (COP) (draft conclusion 10).

In 2015, the ILC considered Special Rapporteur Nolte's third report[32] and provisionally adopted an annotated draft conclusion on subsequent agreements and subsequent practice regarding the interpretation of constituent instruments of international organizations (draft conclusion 11).[33] Having analysed subsequent conduct in great depth, the ILC and its Special Rapporteur have not addressed the interpretative practice of domestic courts until this study was finalised and made available to the Special Rapporteur.

Drawing on this study's findings,[34] the Special Rapporteur published his fourth report in 2016. This report proposed draft conclusions on the pronouncements of expert bodies (draft conclusion 12) and on domestic court decisions (draft conclusion 13). Reaffirming this study's findings, draft conclusion 13 contains recommendations and guidelines for domestic courts.[35] When the ILC considered the report,

[28] Georg Nolte, 'First Report on Subsequent Agreements and Subsequent Practice in relation to Treaty Interpretation' (19 March 2013) UN Doc A/CN.4/660.

[29] ILC, 'Report of the International Law Commission on the Work of its 65th Session' (6 May–7 June and 8 July–9 August 2013) UN Doc A/68/10, 12–48.

[30] Georg Nolte, 'Second Report on Subsequent Agreements and Subsequent Practice in relation to Treaty Interpretation' (26 March 2014) UN Doc A/CN.4/671.

[31] ILC, 'Report of the International Law Commission on the Work of its 66th Session' (5 May–6 June and 7 July–8 August 2014) UN Doc A/69/10, 170–217.

[32] Georg Nolte, 'Third Report on Subsequent Agreements and Subsequent Practice in Relation to the Interpretation of Treaties' (7 April 2015) UN Doc A/CN.4/683.

[33] ILC, 'Report of the International Law Commission on the Work of its 67th Session' (4 May–5 June and 6 July–7 August 2015) UN Doc A/70/10, 84–103.

[34] Georg Nolte, 'Fourth Report on Subsequent Agreements and Subsequent Practice in Relation to the Interpretation of Treaties' (7 March 2016) UN Doc A/CN.4/694, 37.

[35] ibid 43.

it regarded draft conclusion 13 as 'somewhat unusual' because it did not simply 'clarify … the pertinent rules of interpretation as such' but made recommendations addressing specific actors.[36] It therefore hesitated to adopt draft conclusion 13 and the Special Rapporteur withdrew his proposal in that regard.[37] At the same time, he urged the Commission to include findings from the report in the commentaries to the draft conclusions to further nuance and improve them.[38]

In scholarly literature, subsequent conduct has only recently begun to increasingly attract attention, too. An instructive early work is a monograph by Wolfram Karl, which was originally published in 1983.[39] This monograph is not primarily concerned with subsequent practice pursuant to articles 31 and 32 VCLT. Instead, it addresses a more general notion of subsequent practice, whose effects are not limited to the interpretation of treaties but also encompass their modification and termination. Although Karl occasionally mentions domestic court cases to illustrate his reasoning, he does not systematically discuss domestic jurisprudence.

Other commentators have focused on important specific aspects of the topic such as subsequent conduct and evolutive interpretation[40] or subsequent conduct and international investment or trade law.[41] Moreover, subsequent conduct is also covered by more general contributions on interpretation such as the treatises by Richard Gardiner[42] and Ulf Linderfalk,[43] or the commentaries on the VCLT that have been published by Oliver Dörr and Kerstin Schmalenbach,[44] Mark Villiger,[45] or

[36] ILC, 'Provisional Summary Record of the 3303rd Meeting' (28 June 2016) UN Doc A/CN.4/SR.3303, 13.

[37] cf id, 'Provisional Summary Record of the 3307th Meeting' UN Doc A/CN.4/SR.3307, 6.

[38] cf ibid, 6.

[39] Karl, *Vertrag und spätere Praxis* (n 7). See also generally Rahim Moloo, 'When Actions Speak Louder Than Words: The Relevance of Subsequent Party Conduct to Treaty Interpretation' (2013) 31 Berkeley J Int'l L 39.

[40] Eg Julian Arato, 'Subsequent Practice and Evolutive Interpretation: Techniques of Treaty Interpretation over Time and Their Diverse Consequences' (2010) 9 Law & Prac Int'l Cts & Tribunals 443; Rahim Moloo, 'Changing Times, Changing Obligations? The Interpretation of Treaties over Time' (2012) 106 ASIL PROC 261; id, 'The Relevance of Subsequent Party Conduct' (n 39) 51 f.

[41] Eg Anthea Roberts, 'Power and Persuasion in Investment Treaty Interpretation: The Dual Role of States' (2010) 104 AJIL 179; Alexander Feldman, 'Evolving Treaty Obligations: A Proposal for Analyzing Subsequent Practice Derived from WTO Dispute Settlement' (2009) 41 JILP 655.

[42] Gardiner, *Treaty Interpretation* (n 15).

[43] Ulf Linderfalk, *On the Interpretation of Treaties—The Modern International Law as Expressed in the* 1969 *Vienna Convention on the Law of Treaties* (Springer 2007).

[44] Oliver Dörr and Kirsten Schmalenbach (eds), *Vienna Convention on the Law of Treaties—A Commentary* (Springer 2012).

[45] Mark Villiger, *Commentary on the* 1969 *Vienna Convention on the Law of Treaties* (Martinus Nijhoff 2009).

Olivier Corten and Pierre Klein.[46] Yet, none of these works focuses in greater detail on the interpretative practice of domestic courts.

Instructive initial overviews of subsequent conduct in domestic jurisprudence have been offered by authors such as David Bederman and Evan Criddle,[47] who addressed subsequent agreements and subsequent practice alongside other means of interpretation and based on a defined part of US jurisprudence. Similar works have been published in Germany, Austria, and the UK.[48] But while these surveys examine the interpretative practice of domestic courts, they only touch upon subsequent conduct in passing.

On the whole, a more comprehensive analysis of how subsequent agreements and subsequent practice have been applied in the interpretative practice of domestic courts is therefore still missing. In particular, there has been no attempt to develop a deeper understanding of subsequent agreements and subsequent practice in the light of their historical origins and the Vienna rules of interpretation as a whole and to critically re-examine this understanding against the background of domestic jurisprudence. By filling this gap, this study aims at drawing empirically-informed conclusions not only about a sensible approach to article 31(3)(a) and (b) and article 32 VCLT but also, on a more general level, about the distribution of interpretative power upon which these provisions are founded.

1.3 Scope of this Study

Based on the jurisprudence of domestic courts, this study examines how subsequent agreements and subsequent practice within the meaning of articles 31 and 32 VCLT have been applied in interpretative practice. Its scope is therefore limited in several respects.

[46] Olivier Corten and Pierre Klein (eds), *The Vienna Conventions on the Law of Treaties—A Commentary* (OUP 2011).

[47] David Bederman, 'Revivalist Canons and Treaty Interpretation' (1993) 41 UCLA L Rev 953; Evan Criddle, 'The Vienna Convention on the Law of Treaties in US Treaty Interpretation' (2003) 44 Va J Int'l L 431.

[48] See in particular Ondolf Rojahn, 'Die Auslegung völkerrechtlicher Verträge in der Entscheidungspraxis des Bundesverwaltungsgerichts' in Rudolf Geiger and Wilfried Fiedler (eds), *Völkerrechtlicher Vertrag und staatliches Recht vor dem Hintergrund zunehmender Verdichtung der internationalen Beziehungen—Symposion vom 28. bis 30. Januar 1999 in Leipzig* (Nomos 2000); Bernd Meyring, *Die Entwicklung zustimmungsbedürftiger völkerrechtlicher Verträge nach ihrem Abschluss und ihre Auswirkungen in der deutschen Rechtsordnung* (Berliner Wissenschafts-Verlag 2001); Christoph Schreuer, 'The Interpretation of Treaties by Domestic Courts' (1971) 45 BYIL 255; Francis Mann, 'The Enforcement of Treaties by English Courts' (1958) 44 Transactions of the Grotius Society 29; Ian Sinclair, 'The Principles of Treaty Interpretation and their Application by the English Courts' (1963) 12 ICLQ 508; Francis Jacobs and Shelley Roberts (eds), *The Effect of Treaties in Domestic Law* (Sweet & Maxwell 1987).

1.3.1 Treaty Interpretation

Subsequent agreements and subsequent practice are two of those means of treaty interpretation that are laid down in articles 31–33 VCLT. As such, they are generally considered to reflect customary international law rules of treaty interpretation.[49] In consequence, this study is concerned with the interpretation of a particular source of public international law, namely treaties. Other sources of public or private international law, national law, or private or public law contracts are not considered by this work.

1.3.1.1 Treaties

'Treaties' for the purpose of this study are those agreements that satisfy the requirements of article 2(1)(a) VCLT. This provision defines 'treaties' as international agreements concluded between States in written form and governed by international law. The term 'agreement' refers to any form of a 'meeting of minds' between the parties.[50] This 'meeting of minds' describes the core idea behind treaties. But article 2(1)(a) VCLT stipulates further requirements. Firstly, the agreement must have been concluded between States.[51] Agreements between IOs or between States and IOs are not covered by the Convention. Secondly, they must have been concluded in writing. This is because written agreements possess a stronger probative value than unwritten ones.[52] Hence, there must be some 'written record' of the terms of the agreement.[53] And thirdly, the agreement must be 'governed by international law'.

---

[49] See 3.2.

[50] Villiger, *Commentary on the VCLT* (n 45) 77; see also Georg Schwarzenberger, *International Law as Applied by International Courts and Tribunals* (3rd edn, Stevens 1957) vol 1, 491.

[51] Jan Klabbers, *The Concept of Treaty in International Law* (Kluwer 1996) 47 f. As regards the international law conditions for statehood, see generally James Crawford, 'State' in Rüdiger Wolfrum (ed), *The Max Planck Encyclopedia of Public International Law* (OUP 2012).

[52] Philippe Gautier, 'Article 2—1969 Vienna Convention' in Olivier Corten and Pierre Klein (eds), *The Vienna Conventions on the Law of Treaties—A Commentary* (OUP 2011) 38. To explain why the Convention only covers written agreements, Gautier further contends that treaties were commonly concluded in writing anyway. This, however, may be doubted. As the ILC points out, 'in modern practice international agreements are' indeed 'frequently concluded… by less formal instruments.' See ILC, 'Draft Articles on the Law of Treaties with Commentaries' [1966-II] YBILC 187, 189 [7].

[53] Gautier, 'Article 2' (n 52) 38. As regards the difficult question when an agreement is governed by international law, which eventually hinges on the intentions of the parties, see Jan Klabbers, 'Informal Agreements in International Law: Towards a Theoretical Framework' (1994) 5 FYBIL 267, 278 f.

This requirement excludes agreements whose execution is principally governed by the domestic law of one of its parties.[54]

The concept of 'treaty' within the meaning of customary international law is similar but not identical to the definition contained in article 2(1)(a) VCLT.[55] Treaties that satisfy the Convention's requirements also constitute treaties for the purpose of customary international law.[56] The latter, however, neither requires treaties to be concluded in writing nor between States.[57] For academic purposes, this broader understanding entails advantages in that it covers more and more diverse phenomena. Nevertheless, this study embraces the narrower definition under article 2(1)(a) VCLT. The reasons for this are twofold. Firstly, treaties concluded between IOs or between States and IOs raise special problems that cannot adequately be addressed in a study that primarily focuses on treaties between States.[58] And secondly, the Vienna rules are specifically designed to interpret *written* language. Interpretation, as regulated by articles 31–33 VCLT, presupposes some kind of text as a logical starting point for the interpretative process.[59]

1.3.1.2 Interpretation

Subsequent agreements and subsequent practice are means of treaty interpretation. This study analyses how these means are applied in the interpretative practice of domestic courts. It does not, at least not primarily, assess how domestic courts contribute to the formation of subsequent agreements and subsequent practice. Their jurisprudence rather serves as an empirical basis for understanding how these means of interpretation operate.

This endeavour—like any other work that focuses on aspects of treaty interpretation—presupposes that one comprehends what 'interpretation' means. Yet, the meaning of 'interpretation' is difficult to define. This difficulty is exacerbated by the fact that the Convention itself refrains from providing a working definition. This study neither claims nor purports to be of a linguistic nature. Nevertheless, it appears reasonable to form an idea about what interpretation means if one writes (or reads) about it.

---

[54] id, *The Concept of Treaty in International Law* (n 51) 55 f; Gautier, 'Article 2' (n 52) 40 f.

[55] cf art 3 VCLT, which preserves the legal force of agreements that do not satisfy the Convention's requirements.

[56] Gautier, 'Article 2' (n 52) 34.

[57] ibid 35 f, 39 f; Villiger, *Commentary on the VCLT* (n 45) 80 f [15] f.

[58] cf, *mutatis mutandis*, ILC, 'DALT' (n 52) 187 [2]. As regards subsequent agreements and subsequent practice and IOs, see in particular Nolte, 'Third Report' (n 32). See also Christopher Peters, 'Subsequent Practice and Established Practice of International Organizations—Two Sides of the Same Coin?' (2011) 3 GOJIL 617 and id, *Praxis Internationaler Organisationen—Vertragswandel und völkerrechtlicher Ordnungsrahmen* (Springer 2016).

[59] See 1.3.1.2 and 3.3.1.1.

In conventional language, 'interpretation' means as much as 'expounding the meaning of something'.[60] From a non-legal perspective, one may give a meaning to phenomena like music, paintings, or even facial expressions. In a legal context, one may equally interpret various different phenomena such as unilateral statements, oral, or written agreements. Treaty interpretation, however, is, as its name suggests, solely concerned with determining the 'meaning' of a treaty, ie a written agreement concluded between States. But what is the 'meaning' of a treaty?

The Convention's drafting history suggests that the interpretative process ultimately aims at 'ascertaining the intention of the parties'.[61] Initially, Sir Humphrey Waldock's draft articles on treaty interpretation were criticised by several ILC members for not sufficiently emphasising the parties' intention.[62] Despite this criticism, the final Draft Articles on the Law of Treaties (DALT) do not expressly mention the parties' intention. The accompanying commentary, however, clarifies that the rules on treaty interpretation were designed to appreciate 'the meaning which the parties may have intended to attach to the expressions that they employed in a document.'[63]

The cardinal role of the parties' intention has been widely recognised.[64] In particular, the ILC recently acknowledged that treaties constituted 'embodiments of

---

[60] See 'interpret, v' *Oxford English Dictionary Online* (September 2014, OUP) <http://www.oed.com/view/Entry/98205?rskey=FSg5IV&result=2>.

[61] ILC, 'DALT' (n 52) 219 [5].

[62] Eg Eduardo Jiménez de Aréchaga in id, 'Summary Records of the 16th Session of the International Law Commission' (11 May–24 July 1964) [1964-I] YBILC 1, 34 [10]; Shabtai Rosenne in ibid 36 [13]; Abdul Tabibi in ibid 276 [25]; Obed Pessou in ibid 278 [46]; Milan Bartoš in ibid 279 [64]; Radhabinod Pal in ibid 286 [51]; Alfred Verdross in ibid 287 [61].

[63] ILC, 'DALT' (n 52) 218 [4]. See also Eirik Bjorge, *The Evolutionary Interpretation of Treaties* (OUP 2014) 89.

[64] In particular *Case concerning the Dispute regarding Navigational and Related Rights (Costa Rica v Nicaragua)* [2009] ICJ Rep 213, 241 [58]. See already Hugo Grotius, *De jure belli ac pacis libri tres* (Francis Kelsey tr, reprod, Hein 1995) 409: 'The measure of correct interpretation is the inference of intent from the most probable indications'; Emer de Vattel, *The Law of Nations or the Principles of Natural Law* (Charles Fenwick tr, repr, Hein 1995) 201: '… the sole object of a lawful interpretation is to discover the intention of the maker or makers of the treaty.' See also Sir Hersch Lauterpacht, *Private Law Sources and Analogies of International Law: With Special Reference to International Arbitration* (Longman 1927) 187; Sir Gerald Fitzmaurice, 'The Law and Procedure of the International Court of Justice: Treaty Interpretation and Certain Other Treaty Points' (1951) 28 BYIL 1, 3; James Brierly, *The Law of Nations—An Introduction to the International Law of Peace* (5th edn, OUP 1955) 251; Mustafa Yasseen, 'L'interprétation des traités d'après la Convention de Vienne sur le Droit des Traités' (1976) 151 RCADI 1, 16; Heribert Köck, *Vertragsinterpretation und Vertragsrechtskonvention—Zur Bedeutung der Artikel 31 und 32 der Wiener Vertragsrechtskonvention* 1969 (Duncker & Humblot 1976) 26 f; Ian Sinclair, *The Vienna Convention on the Law of Treaties* (2nd edn, MUP 1984) 115; Campbell McLachlan, 'The Principle of Systemic Integration and Article 31(3)(c) of the Vienna Convention' (2005) 54 ICLQ 279, 287; James Crawford, *Brownlie's Principles of Public International Law* (8th edn, OUP 2012) 379.

the common will of their parties'.[65] Based on this observation, it confirmed that 'interpretation must seek to identify the intention of the parties.'[66] This emphasis on the parties' intention is qualified by the fact that, under the Vienna rules, 'the text must be presumed to be the authentic expression of the intentions of the parties.'[67] In other words, interpretation under the Vienna rules aims at 'giving effect to the expressed intention of the parties, that is, their intentions as expressed in the words used by them in the light of the surrounding circumstances.'[68]

In consequence, the parties' intention is an 'objectivised' intention of the parties as a whole; properly understood, the parties' intention is a 'construct'.[69] As Oliver Dörr notes, '[t]o be ascertained by interpretation is … the intention in the sense of the true meaning of the text of the treaty rather than the intention of the parties distinct from it.'[70] Similarly, the ILC pointed out that the parties' intention was their intention 'as determined through the application of the various means of interpretation'[71] and not 'a separately identifiable original will'.[72]

For the purpose of this study and in the light of the foregoing considerations, treaty interpretation under articles 31–33 VCLT therefore refers to the process of determining a treaty's meaning by ascertaining the objectivised intention of the parties.

---

[65] Commentary on draft conclusion 2 in ILC, 'Report of the International Law Commission on the Work of its 65th Session' (6 May–7 June and 8 July–9 August 2013) UN Doc A/68/10, 23 [8].

[66] Commentary on draft conclusion 3 in ibid 27 [9].

[67] id, 'DALT' (n 52) 220 [11]. See also Yasseen, 'L'interprétation des traités' (n 64) 25; Paul Reuter, *Droit international public* (6th edn, Presses universitaires de France 1983) 145; Crawford, *Brownlie's Principles* (n 64) 379.

[68] Arnold McNair, *The Law of Treaties* (repr, Clarendon Press 2003) 365. See also Oliver Dörr, 'Article 31—General Rule of Interpretation' in id and Kirsten Schmalenbach (eds), *Vienna Convention on the Law of Treaties—A Commentary* (Springer 2012) 552 [3].

[69] Bjorge, *The Evolutionary Interpretation of Treaties* (n 63) 2 f. See also Rudolf Bernhardt, *Die Auslegung völkerrechtlicher Verträge insbesondere in der neueren Rechtsprechung internationaler Gerichte* (Heymann 1963) 34; Yasseen, 'L'interprétation des traités' (n 64) 16; Linderfalk, *On the Interpretation of Treaties* (n 43) 32 f; Crawford, *Brownlie's Principles* (n 64) 379. The parties as a whole are those parties for whom the treaty is in force at the moment when it is being interpreted, see art 2(1)(g) VCLT for the Convention's definition of the term 'party' and Linderfalk, *On the Interpretation of Treaties* (n 43) 31.

[70] Dörr, 'Article 31' (n 68) 552 [3].

[71] Commentary on draft conclusion 3 in ILC, 'Report of the International Law Commission on the Work of its 65th Session' (6 May–7 June and 8 July–9 August 2013) UN Doc A/68/10, 27 [9].

[72] ibid.

1.3.2 Inter-State Level

At the inter-State level, there are numerous actors that may interpret treaties by taking account of subsequent agreements and subsequent practice. First of all, one commonly thinks of international courts and tribunals such as the ICJ,[73] the European Court of Human Rights (ECtHR),[74] or the World Trade Organisation's (WTO) Appellate Body.[75] International courts and tribunals like these are the main, or at least the most prominent interpreters of treaty provisions. Yet, treaties primarily postulate rights and duties for their parties. For this reason, a large part of treaty interpretation occurs at the national level, as a daily routine, and, in particular, as part of domestic judicial decision-making.

1.3.2.1 Domestic Judiciaries

From a functional perspective, domestic courts can be considered as part of a 'global community of courts'.[76] This community divides judicial competences between different bodies.[77] Aside from domestic courts, it mainly consists of international courts, tribunals, and other quasi-judicial bodies.

Several treaty regimes establish a permanent judicial or quasi-judicial body that is competent to interpret a particular international agreement. Examples include, at the global level, the International Tribunal for the Law of the Sea (ITLOS),[78] the WTO Dispute Settlement Body (DSB) with panels and an Appellate Body,[79] and the Human Rights Committee (HRC).[80] At the regional level, judicial and quasi-judicial

[73] See generally Shabtai Rosenne, 'International Court of Justice (ICJ)' in Rüdiger Wolfrum (ed), *The Max Planck Encyclopedia of Public International Law* (OUP 2012); Robert Kolb, *The International Court of Justice* (Hart 2013).

[74] Jochen Frowein and Wolfgang Peukert, *Europäische Menschenrechtskonvention—EMRK-Kommentar* (3rd edn, Engel 2009) 437–616; Mario Oetheimer and Guillem Palomares, 'European Court of Human Rights (ECtHR)' in Rüdiger Wolfrum (ed), *The Max Planck Encyclopedia of Public International Law* (OUP 2012).

[75] See generally Peter-Tobias Stoll, 'World Trade Organization, Dispute Settlement' in Rüdiger Wolfrum (ed), *The Max Planck Encyclopedia of Public International Law* (OUP 2012); Peter Van den Bossche and Werner Zdouc, *The Law and Policy of the World Trade Organization—Text, Cases and Materials* (3rd edn, CUP 2013) 244–314.

[76] Anne-Marie Slaughter, 'A Global Community of Courts' (2003) 44 Harv Int'l LJ 191, 192.

[77] Matthias Herdegen, 'Interpretation in International Law' in Rüdiger Wolfrum (ed), *The Max Planck Encyclopedia of Public International Law* (OUP 2012) [3] f.

[78] ITLOS settles disputes arising under the United Nations Convention on the Law of the Sea (signed 10 December 1982, entered into force 16 November 1994) 1833 UNTS 3 (UNCLOS) and related instruments.

[79] The DSB settles disputes arising under WTO-related agreements.

[80] The HRC settles disputes arising under the International Covenant on Civil and Political Rights (signed 16 December 1966, entered into force 23 March 1976) 999 UNTS 171 (ICCPR) and its protocols.

bodies under special regimes include the Court of Justice of the European Union (CJEU),[81] the ECtHR,[82] and the Inter-American Court of Human Rights (IACtHR).[83] Other treaties merely provide for an institutional infrastructure in which judicial dispute settlement takes place on an *ad hoc*-basis. Prime examples of such *ad hoc* adjudication are the arbitral tribunals under bilateral and regional investment agreements that refer to the Convention on the Settlement of Investment Disputes between States and Nationals of Other States.[84] In addition, there are non-specialised courts and tribunals like the ICJ to which contracting parties can refer disputes although their treaty does not establish its own dispute settlement body.[85]

Thus, international courts, tribunals, and other quasi-judicial bodies undeniably play an important role as regards treaty interpretation.[86] Although they also apply other sources of international law,[87] treaty interpretation is one of their core functions. Since they are established by and solely operate within the international legal order, these bodies should be naturally inclined to apply international rules of treaty interpretation—be it the Vienna rules, customary principles of interpretation, or rules that take account of the special features of the treaty that is being interpreted.[88]

---

[81] The CJEU settles disputes arising under European Union law.

[82] The ECtHR settles disputes arising under the Convention for the Protection of Human Rights and Fundamental Freedoms (signed 4 November 1950, entered into force 3 September 1953) 213 UNTS 222 (European Convention on Human Rights; ECHR).

[83] The IACtHR settles disputes arising under the American Convention on Human Rights (signed 22 November 1969, entered into force 18 July 1978) 1144 UNTS 123 (Pact of San José; IACHR).

[84] Convention on the Settlement of Investment Disputes between States and Nationals of Other States (signed 18 March 1965, entered into force 14 October 1966) 575 UNTS 159 (ICSID Convention).

[85] Treaties conferring jurisdiction on the ICJ include the United Nations Convention against Corruption (signed 31 October 2003, entered into force 9 December 2003) 2349 UNTS 41 (UNCAC) (see art 66(2)), the International Convention for the Suppression of the Financing of Terrorism (signed 9 December 1999, entered into force 10 April 2002) 2178 UNTS 197 (ICFST) (see art 24 (1)), and the Vienna Convention for the Protection of the Ozone Layer (signed 22 March 1985, entered into force 22 September 1988) 1513 UNTS 293 (Ozone Convention) (see art 11).

[86] McNair, *The Law of Treaties* (n 68) 355.

[87] cf art 38 of the Statute of the International Court of Justice, annexed to the Charter of the United Nations (signed 26 June 1945, entered into force 24 October 1946) 1 UNTS XVI (ICJ Statute).

[88] One example is art 1131(2) of the North American Free Trade Agreement between the United States of America, Canada and Mexico (signed 17 December 1992, entered into force 1 January 1993) 32 ILM 289 (NAFTA). Under this provision, interpretative notes issued by the Free Trade Commission are binding on Chapter 11 arbitral tribunals. Thus, art 1131(2) NAFTA deviates from subsequent agreements under art 31(3)(a) VCLT because the latter are not vested with binding force. Another example is the so-called living instrument approach that has been developed by the ECtHR to interpret the ECHR in an evolutive manner. See generally Alastair Mowbray, 'The Creativity of the European Court of Human Rights' (2005) 5 Hum Rts L Rev 57.

As regards domestic courts, the picture is very different. This is because domestic courts more often apply and interpret national legal instruments than international law in general and treaty law in particular.

When interpreting treaties, domestic courts are in an uncomfortable situation. On the one hand, domestic judges are primarily trained in national legal methodology and it is this methodology which they mostly apply. While some elements of the Vienna rules may have an analogue in the national legal order, others—like subsequent agreements and subsequent practice—may have no such counterpart. On the other hand, domestic courts that are unfamiliar with international law rules of treaty interpretation risk violating treaty obligations undertaken by their *forum* State. Thus, they may even incur their *forum* State's international responsibility.[89]

1.3.2.2 Accessibility and Reliability of Jurisprudence

An essential part of defining the scope of this study was to select those States whose jurisprudence would be analysed. This selection had to find an important balance. A too narrow scope would have made it impossible to draw general conclusions from the ensuing analysis. An overly broad scope, in contrast, might have led to less substantiated and reliable conclusions.

The final selection reflects a compromise between these two options in that it only limits the empirical basis where it was necessary to do so for practical constraints. Due to its author's language skills, only those States were selected whose official language includes English, French, or German. Exceptions were only made if a State accurately translated its jurisprudence into one of these languages. Moreover, only those States were selected whose jurisprudence has regularly and reliably been published for a considerable period of time.

Based on the foregoing considerations, several States inevitably had to be excluded from the scope of this study.[90] In consequence, this study can hardly claim to be representative of *all* legal traditions, geographical regions, or cultures but inevitably leaves room for further research on subsequent agreements and subsequent practice in domestic courts. Arranged in alphabetical order, this study initially included the following States: Australia, Austria, Belgium, Canada, France, Germany, Hong Kong (as part of the People's Republic of China), India, Israel, Kenya, New Zealand, South Africa, Switzerland, the Philippines, the UK, and the USA.

When identifying potentially relevant case law, it became apparent that the jurisprudence of some States yielded only very few or no results. These scattered and

[89] cf McNair, *The Law of Treaties* (n 68) 346.

[90] These States include, eg, Nigeria, whose law reporting is interrupted for considerable periods of time, and Egypt, whose electronic law reporting in English is regularly out of service.

isolated references to subsequent agreements and subsequent practice (so they existed in the first place) did not allow drawing general and reliable conclusions. Hence the scope of this study had to be limited further. The final scope of this study includes the following States: Australia, Austria, Belgium, Canada, Germany, Hong Kong (as part of the People's Republic of China), India, New Zealand, Switzerland, the UK, and the USA.

1.3.2.3 Sample Period

The Vienna Convention on the Law of Treaties marks the normative point of reference upon which this study is based. This study's sample period therefore runs from 1969 when the Vienna Convention was adopted to the spring of 2017 when this study was finalised for publication. The later date at which the Convention entered into force, in contrast, was considered irrelevant. This is because, as is explained in Chap. 4, States and other actors have not only regarded the Vienna rules as part of treaty law. Instead, articles 31 and 32 VCLT have quickly been regarded as a reflection of customary international law, too. In consequence, domestic courts and other interpreters may have relied on subsequent conduct within the meaning of the Convention irrespective of whether their *forum* State had already become bound by the Convention.

1.3.3 Intra-State Level

At the intra-State level, there are numerous actors at different levels of State hierarchy that interpret treaties and may therefore rely on subsequent conduct. In spite of that, this study focuses on the interpretative practice of only one group, namely domestic courts. In addition to domestic courts, executive and legislature also frequently confront questions of treaty interpretation. A State's executive, for example, may need to interpret a treaty when attempting to lawfully execute treaty provisions or national legislation that implements treaty provisions. Both legislature and executive may interpret a treaty when discussing drafts for national legislation that is meant to implement a treaty. Furthermore, they may interpret a treaty when the former wishes to conclude a treaty whose provisions might conflict with already existing treaty obligations or domestic legislation.

In contrast to executive and legislature, domestic courts have only comparatively recently begun to consciously, proactively, and purposefully engage in treaty interpretation.[91] This is mainly due to two reasons. Firstly, the number of treaties as such, and in particular of those that impact on formerly domestic affairs, has dramatically

---

[91] See in particular Eyal Benvenisti and George Downs, 'National Courts, Domestic Democracy, and the Evolution of International Law' (2009) 20 EJIL 59, 60.

increased over the last decades.[92] And secondly, some impediments and 'avoidance techniques'[93] to treaty interpretation by domestic courts have begun to erode.[94] Dualist approaches to international law, for instance, no longer prevent courts from interpreting treaties.[95] Moreover, 'political questions'[96] or 'acts of State'[97] are no longer totally kept away from judiciaries.[98] Against this background, international legal scholarship has increasingly analysed how domestic courts deal with public international law issues in general and treaty law issues in particular.[99] Yet, some aspects have attracted little attention so far. By examining how subsequent agreements and subsequent practice have been applied in the interpretative practice of domestic courts, this study attempts to close one of the remaining gaps.

In doing so, it focuses on the jurisprudence of the highest domestic courts. This is because cases that raise difficult interpretative questions are often brought before high courts anyway. Moreover, reliance on subsequent conduct (ideally) requires some comparative legal research. Such research, in turn, regularly requires resources which high courts are more often equipped with than lower courts. In addition, the former constitute the upper end of a State's judicial hierarchy so that their approach to subsequent conduct is more authoritative and representative than that of inferior courts.

---

[92] See the preamble in Institut de Droit International, 'Resolution—The Activities of National Judges and the International Relations of Their State' (1993) 65-II AIDI 318, 319; Jenny Martinez, 'Towards an International Judicial System' (2003) 56 Stan L Rev 429, 441 f; cf also Francioni, 'National Courts' (n 18) 588; José Alvarez, 'The New Treaty-Makers' (2002) 25 BC Int'l & Comp L Rev 213, 216; Benvenisti, 'Reclaiming Democracy' (n 17) 245 f; Benvenisti and Downs, 'National Courts' (n 91) 61 f; Antonios Tzanakopoulos, 'Domestic Courts as the "Natural Judge" of International Law: A Change in Physiognomy' (2012) 3 Select Proceedings of the European Society of International Law 155, 159.

[93] See generally Benvenisti, 'Judicial Misgivings' (n 21). cf also August Reinisch, *International Organizations before National Courts* (CUP 2000) 35 f.

[94] See arts 1 and 2 in Institut de Droit International, 'Resolution' (n 92) 321.

[95] Eg Schreuer, 'The Interpretation of Treaties by Domestic Courts' (n 48) 257 f; David Sloss, 'Treaty Enforcement in Domestic Courts—A Comparative Analysis' in id (ed), *The Role of Domestic Courts in Treaty Enforcement—A Comparative Study* (CUP 2009) 8; Gibran van Ert, 'Dubious Dualism: The Reception of International Law in Canada' (2010) 44 Val UL Rev 927, 931 f; Tzanakopoulos, 'The "Natural Judge"' (n 92) 161 f.

[96] See generally Louis Henkin, 'Is There a "Political Question" Doctrine?' (1976) 85 Yale LJ 597.

[97] See generally McNair, *The Law of Treaties* (n 68) 358–63; Fausto de Quadros and John Dingfelder Stone, 'Act of State Doctrine' in Rüdiger Wolfrum (ed), *The Max Planck Encyclopedia of Public International Law* (OUP 2012).

[98] McNair, *The Law of Treaties* (n 68) 362; David Bederman, 'Deference or Deception: Treaty Rights as Political Questions' (1999) 70 U Colo L Rev 1439, 1441.

[99] Published work includes eg Benvenisti, 'Judicial Misgivings' (n 21); Thomas Franck and Gregory Fox (eds), *International Law Decisions in National Courts* (Transnational Pub 1996); Karen Knop, 'Here and There: International Law in Domestic Courts' (2000) 32 JILP 501; Benvenisti, 'Reclaiming Democracy' (n 17).

1.4 Outline and Methodology

This study is divided into nine chapters. Framed by an introductory and a concluding chapter, they are grouped into two main parts. Part I, which comprises Chaps. 2–4, seeks to set the stage for the ensuing analysis of domestic jurisprudence by providing its historical and doctrinal underpinning. In doing so, it proceeds chronologically and from the general to the specific. Chapter 2 traces the origins of subsequent agreements and subsequent practice within the meaning of articles 31 and 32 VCLT. These origins may not only have inspired the ILC when preparing its Draft Articles on the Law of Treaties but their legacy may continue to influence present-day interpreters. Chapter 3 places subsequent agreements and subsequent practice in their broader legal context by shortly delineating the genesis of the Vienna rules, the interrelationship between articles 31 and 32 VCLT and customary international law rules of treaty interpretation, and the interplay of their various components. Chapter 4 concludes by elaborating on the meaning of subsequent agreements and subsequent practice pursuant to article 31(3)(a) and (b) and article 32 VCLT.

Part II is dedicated to subsequent agreements and subsequent practice in the jurisprudence of domestic courts. Although articles 31 and 32 VCLT provide for a general framework in which they shall or can to be taken into account, several questions about subsequent agreements and subsequent practice remain unclear, leave room for discretion or even misunderstandings. Against this background, the jurisprudence of domestic courts may help to gain a better understanding of these means of interpretation by demonstrating how they operate in interpretative practice. This interpretative practice is analysed in Chaps. 5–8. At this point, it is useful to make a few additional remarks on how potentially relevant case law has been selected. When they discuss or even rely on subsequent conduct, domestic courts sometimes do[100] and sometimes do not[101] cite the Vienna rules. Therefore, it would

[100] See eg VfGH, Judgment of 1 March 1990, B195/89, VfSlg 12281, 4; VfGH, Judgment of 29 September 1994, V97/93, VfSlg 13881, 14; VfGH, Judgment of 29 June 2011, F1/11, G7/11, VfSlg 19434, 36; *Yugraneft Corp v Rexx Management Corp* [2010] 1 SCR 649, 2010 SCC 19 [21] (Rothstein J); BVerfGE 90, 286, 364; 104, 151, 207; BVerwGE 80, 249, 253; 104, 254, 256; 109, 1, 7; *Lena-Jane Punter v Secretary for Justice, ex p Adam Punter* [2004] 2 NZLR 28 [61] (Glazebrook J); *Ye v Minister of Immigration* [2009] 2 NZLR 596 [61] f (Lord Glazebrook); *R (Mullen) v Secretary of State for the Home Department* [2004] UKHL 18, [2005] 1 AC 1 [47] (Lord Steyn); *R (Al-Jedda) v Secretary of State for Defence* [2007] UKHL 58, [2008] 1 AC 332 [38] (Lord Bingham); *Assange v The Swedish Prosecution Authority* [2012] UKSC 22, [2012] 2 AC 471 [67] (Lord Phillips).

[101] See eg *Victrawl Pty Ltd v Telstra Corporation Ltd* [1995] HCA 51, (1995) 183 CLR 595 [16] (Brennan J); *Attorney-General v X* [2007] NZCA 388 [38] f (Young P); *SZATV v Minister for Immigration* [2007] HCA 40, (2007) 233 CLR 18 [68]–[74] (Kirby J); *Maloney v The Queen* [2013] HCA 28, (2013) 298 ALR 308 [14] (French J); BVerfGE 112, 1, 33; 59, 63, 94 f; BGHZ 82, 88, 94; 145, 97, 99 f; BFHE 222, 553, 558; *James Buchanan & Co Ltd v Babco Forwarding and Shipping (UK) Ltd* [1978] AC 141 (HL), 153 (Lord Wilberforce); *Trans World Airlines, Inc v Franklin Mint Corp* 466 US 243, 260 f, 104 S Ct 2691 (1984); *Air France v Saks* 470 US 392, 404, 105 S Ct 1338 (1985); *O'Connor v US* 479 US 27, 34, 107 S Ct 347 (1986); *US v Stuart* 489 US 353, 370, 109 S Ct 1183 (1989).

not have been conducive to exclusively focus on those cases in which domestic courts expressly cited articles 31 and 32 VCLT.

It is impossible to accurately predict the cases in which domestic courts will cite articles 31 and 32 VCLT. Nonetheless, one can roughly distinguish three situations in which they are more likely to do so.[102] Firstly, domestic courts will be more likely to cite these provisions when the interpretative issue has serious—eg social, political, or financial—implications beyond the case at hand.[103] Here, reliance on subsequent conduct and express invocation of the Vienna rules seems to increase a court's power of persuasion when being critically scrutinised by the general public or during some form of judicial review. Secondly, domestic courts (or better: individual judges) will be more likely to cite articles 31 and 32 VCLT when they deliver a separate opinion.[104] Once again, reliance on subsequent conduct and express invocation of the Vienna rules apparently serve to increase persuasiveness of the judge's legal reasoning when facing enhanced legal scrutiny. And thirdly, domestic courts will be more likely to cite articles 31 and 32 VCLT when other actors or secondary sources that have come to their attention have expressly invoked these provisions.[105]

But in fact, express citation of articles 31 and 32 VCLT does not guarantee that a court faithfully aligns its approach to subsequent agreements and subsequent practice to the requirements laid down by the Vienna rules. Vice versa, courts that do not cite articles 31 and 32 VCLT may nevertheless discuss and rely on subsequent agreements or subsequent practice and thus help to understand how these means of interpretation operate in practice.[106] For these reasons, the analysis in Part II is

---

[102] The following aspects, in contrast, neither seemed to influence whether a court cited arts 31 and 32 VCLT nor whether arguments based on subsequent conduct were discussed at all: The *forum* State's legal tradition; whether the *forum* State and/or the other parties to the treaty were (already) a party to the Vienna Convention; and whether the treaty had been concluded before the Vienna Convention had entered into force (see art 4 VCLT on the Convention's non-retroactivity).

[103] See eg BVerwG, Decision of 7 February 2008, 10 C 33/07 <http://www.juris.de> [31]; *Mullen* (n 100) [47] (Lord Steyn).

[104] See eg *Commissioner of the Australian Federal Police and the Commonwealth of Australia v Magno and Almeida* [1992] FCA 566, (1992) 37 FCR 298 [26] (Einfeld J); *R v Asfaw* [2008] UKHL 31, [2008] 1 AC 1061 [125] f (Lord Mance).

[105] See eg *Minister for Immigration v Ibrahim* [2000] HCA 55, (2000) 204 CLR 1 [140] (Gummow J); VfGH, Judgment of 14 October 1986, B79/86, VfSlg 11073, 8; *Ubamaka v Secretary for Security* [2011] 1 HKLRD 359, 394 (Fok J); *Attorney-General v Zaoui (No 2)* [2005] 1 NZLR 690 [130] (Glazebrook J); BGer, Judgment of 8 April 2004, 4C.140/2003, BGE 130 III 430, 439; BVGer, Judgment of 21 January 2010, BVGE 2010/7, 103 f; *Hoxha v Secretary of State for the Home Department* [2005] UKHL 19, [2005] 1 WLR 1063 [70] f (Lord Brown).

[106] See eg *Németh v Canada (Justice)* [2010] 3 SCR 281, 2010 SCC 56 [52] f (Cromwell J); BVerfGE 30, 272, 276, 278; 59, 63, 95; 68, 1, 81 f; *Buchanan* (n 101) 153 f (Lord Wilberforce), 161 (Lord Salmon); *Sidhu v British Airways* [1997] AC 430 (HL) 443 (Lord Hope); *Trans World Airlines* (n 101) 256 f; *O'Connor* (n 101) 34; *Stuart* (n 101) 370; *Eastern Airlines, Inc v Floyd* 499 US 530, 547 f, 111 S Ct 1489 (1991); *Zicherman v Korean Air Lines Co, Ltd* 516 US 217, 226, 116 S Ct 629 (1996); *El Al Israel Airlines, Ltd v Tsui Yuan Tseng* 525 US 155, 167, 119 S Ct 662 (1999).

not based on a formalistic selection of cases in which domestic courts expressly cited articles 31 and 32 VCLT. Instead, it takes a broader perspective by taking into account those cases in which domestic courts discussed, relied on, and sometimes even surprisingly failed to discuss arguments based on subsequent agreements or subsequent practice.

This study's empirical basis was compiled by consulting primary and secondary sources alike. Online databases supplemented traditional and printed sources since they can more easily be scanned for decisions on a particular issue or even particular keywords. As already indicated, the keywords that were used to scan these databases not only included obvious ones such as 'article 31(3)(a) VCLT', 'subsequent practice',[107] 'subsequent agreement',[108] or 'Vienna Convention'.[109] Instead, they also included broader notions such as 'conduct',[110] 'treaty',[111] 'interpret',[112] 'dynamic',[113] 'evolutive',[114] 'consent',[115] 'acquiescence',[116] 'modify',[117] or 'over time'.[118] These keywords were then supplemented by Boolean operators to generate more results.

Domestic court cases that are mentioned in this study are cited as they are cited in their own jurisdiction. References to unreported decisions use neutral citations so that they can be found in one of the following online databases:[119]

- Australia: <http://www.austlii.edu.au> and <http://www.westlawinternational.com>
- Austria: <http://www.alex.onb.ac.at> and <http://www.ris.bka.gv.at>
- Belgium: <http://www.juridat.be>
- Canada: <http://www.canlii.org> and <http://www.westlawinternational.com>
- Germany: <http://www.juris.de>
- Hong Kong: <http://www.hklii.hk> and <http://www.westlawinternational.com>
- India: <http://www.judis.nic.in>
- New Zealand: <http://www.nzlii.org> and <http://www.westlawinternational.com>
- Switzerland: <http://www.bger.ch> and <http://www.bvger.ch>

---

[107] In French: 'pratique ultérieur' or 'pratique suivie'; in German: 'spätere Praxis'.

[108] In French: 'accord ultérieur'; in German: 'spätere Übereinkunft'.

[109] In French: 'Convention de Vienne'; in German: 'Wiener Übereinkommen'.

[110] In French: 'comportement'; in German: 'Verhalten' or 'Übung'.

[111] In French: 'traité'; in German: 'Vertrag'.

[112] In French: 'interpréter'; in German: 'auslegen' or 'interpretieren'.

[113] In French: 'dynamique'; in German: 'dynamisch'.

[114] In French: 'évolutif'; in German: 'evolutiv'.

[115] In French: 'consentement'; in German: 'Zustimmung'.

[116] In French: 'consentement tacite'; in German: 'stillschweigende Zustimmung'.

[117] In French: 'modifier'; in German: 'modifizieren'.

[118] In French: 'avec le temps'; in German: 'im Laufe der Zeit'.

[119] All internet sources were last accessed on 1 March 2017.

- UK: <http://www.bailii.org> and <http://www.westlawinternational.com>
- USA: <http://www.heinonline.org> and <http://www.westlawinternational.com>

Based on the case law that was identified in the various research steps, Chaps. 5–8 more closely analyse how subsequent agreements and subsequent practice have been applied in the interpretative practice of domestic courts. To start with, Chap. 5 explores the legal status and effects of subsequent agreements and subsequent practice. As regards their status, it is examined whether domestic courts treat subsequent agreements and subsequent practice like any other primary or supplementary means of interpretation or assign to them an 'enhanced'[120] or even lower status than the Vienna rules require. As regards the effects of subsequent agreements and subsequent practice, Chap. 5 then asks whether domestic court rely on these means of interpretation to support particular types of results such as extensive, restrictive, dynamic, or static interpretations.

Chapter 6 addresses an astonishing discrepancy. Notwithstanding their legal relevance at the international level, subsequent agreements are only seldom mentioned by domestic courts. Without claiming to exhaustively explain this discrepancy, it focuses on three conceivable causes. Firstly, Chap. 6 examines to which extent the number of contracting parties to a treaty may influence the relevance of subsequent agreements. Secondly, it draws attention to the fact that domestic courts generally requested solid evidence to establish the existence of subsequent agreements. And thirdly, it explains why domestic courts may be prevented from relying on subsequent agreements due to real or perceived constitutional impediments.

Next, Chap. 7 takes up a particularly contentious issue, namely the relevance of non-party practice under article 31(3)(b) VCLT. On its face, this provision does not require practice that is attributable to a contracting party.[121] Based on this observation, Chap. 7 investigates whether domestic courts have attached any interpretative value to non-party practice when relying on article 31(3)(b) VCLT. By way of example, it focuses on three distinct kinds of non-party practice, namely the output of treaty bodies, documents published by the Office of the UN High Commissioner for Refugees (UNHCR), and the Model Convention on Income and Capital and related documents that have been published by the Organisation for Economic Co-operation and Development (OECD) as a guide for existing and future double taxation agreements (DTAs).

To close the analysis of domestic jurisprudence, Chap. 8 asks how domestic courts have approached the normative heart of subsequent practice under the general rule, namely the notion of 'agreement'. Under article 31(3)(b) VCLT, practice merely serves as evidence to reveal an understanding of the terms of the treaty that is shared by its parties. This provision does not attach any interpretative value to single pieces or even an accumulated body of practice but only to the parties' agreement.[122] As

[120] cf Nolte, 'Report 1—ICJ and Arbitral Tribunals' (n 15) 171 f.

[121] See 4.3.1.2.

[122] See 4.1.

argued in Chap. 4, article 31(3)(b) VCLT ought to be interpreted restrictively so as to require the agreement of *all* parties. This raises two central questions. Firstly, how should interpreters deal with one or more parties' inaction when trying to establish the parties' agreement? And secondly, how may interpreters establish the parties' agreement when they do not consider practice of all parties but rather select the practice upon which they rely?

In conclusion, Chap. 9 sums up the findings of the previous chapters. This summary contains final observations not only on how domestic courts have responded to the distribution of interpretative power enshrined in article 31(3)(a) and (b) and article 32 VCLT. In addition, it also asks how the consequences of their response may influence the international legal order on the long run.

Part I
Subsequent Agreements and Subsequent Practice

Chapter 2
The Origins of Subsequent Agreements and Subsequent Practice

Subsequent agreements and subsequent practice are nowadays commonly associated with and discussed as part of the VCLT. Yet, the understanding of subsequent agreements and subsequent practice as laid down in the Convention is not the only conceivable one. When the ILC for the first time formulated rules of treaty interpretation, it did so by 'trying to isolate and codify the comparatively few general principles which appear to constitute general rules for the interpretation of treaties.'[1] This quotation from Special Rapporteur Sir Humphrey Waldock suggests that he must have had some sources of inspiration to rely on when preparing his first draft articles on treaty interpretation. Chap. 2 therefore purports to identify these sources of inspiration by searching for and analysing the origins of subsequent agreements and subsequent practice.

In order to identify and analyse the origins of subsequent agreements and subsequent practice, this Chapter takes a three-pronged approach. In a first step, it focuses on international legal doctrine during the period of classical international law, in the nineteenth and early twentieth centuries, and in the form of State-sponsored and private efforts to codify the law of treaties or rules of treaty interpretation during the twentieth century (2.1). In a second step, it offers an overview of the jurisprudence of the Permanent Court of International Justice (PCIJ) and the ICJ as the main and traditionally authoritative reference points for understanding the relevance of subsequent agreements and subsequent practice at the beginning of the twentieth century (2.2). In a third step, it then concentrates on domestic jurisprudence to see whether domestic courts had been familiar with subsequent agreements and subsequent practice before these means were codified with the Vienna Convention (2.3).

[1] ILC, 'Draft Articles on the Law of Treaties with Commentaries' [1966-II] YBILC 187, 218 [5].

K. Berner, *Subsequent Agreements and Subsequent Practice in Domestic Courts*, Beiträge zum ausländischen öffentlichen Recht und Völkerrecht, https://doi.org/10.1007/978-3-662-54937-7_2

2.1 International Legal Doctrine

2.1.1 'Classical' Writers

The foundations of public international law as it is known today were mainly laid in the so-called period of classical international law. This period is commonly considered to run from the beginning of the seventeenth century or the Peace of Westphalia in 1648 to the Congress of Vienna in 1815.[2] Writers of that period, such as Hugo Grotius (1583–1645), Samuel Pufendorf (1632–1694), Christian von Wolff (1679–1754), and Emer de Vattel (1714–1767), influenced the understanding of international law at that time and are still often quoted today. To the extent that issues of treaty interpretation were addressed at all, it would therefore be interesting to know whether these representatives of classical international law already recognised some forms of subsequent agreements and subsequent practice as means of interpretation or whether these means of interpretation were still unknown in those days.

Strictly speaking, the Dutchman Hugo Grotius predates the period of classical international law. Nonetheless, he is traditionally regarded as one of the intellectual founding fathers of the way of legal thinking that emerged during this era.[3] In 1625, he published an extensive treatise on the law of nations that was influenced by the work of Alberico Gentili (1552–1608) and entitled *De iure belli ac pacis*

[2] Randall Lesaffer, 'The Classical Law of Nations (1500–1800)' in Alexander Orakhelashvili (ed), *Research Handbook on the Theory and History of International Law* (Edward Elgar 2011) 408 f. There exists some disagreement as to the when the period of classical international law exactly began. Some authors broadly refer to the beginning of the 17th century or the first publication of Grotius' *De jure belli* (1625), see eg Stephen Neff, 'A Short History of International Law' in Malcolm Evans (ed), *International Law* (OUP 2003) 31 f and Lesaffer, 'The Classical Law of Nations (1500–1800)' (n 2) 408 f. Others instead regard the Peace of Westphalia (1648) as the central turning point that marked the transition to classical international law. See eg Wilhelm Grewe, *The Epochs of International Law* (de Gruyter 2000) 279 f and Heinz Durchhardt, 'From the Peace of Westphalia to the Congress of Vienna' in Bardo Fassbender and others (eds), *The Oxford Handbook of the History of International Law* (OUP 2012) 628 f. As regards the problems associated with such 'periodisation' and the inconsistencies of the various attempts to divide the history of international law into different periods, see generally William Butler, 'Periodization and International Law' in Alexander Orakhelashvili (ed), *Research Handbook on the Theory and History of International Law* (Edward Elgar 2011) 379 f.

[3] Neff, 'History of International Law' (n 2) 9; Peter Haggenmacher, 'Hugo Grotius (1583–1645)' in Bardo Fassbender and others (eds), *The Oxford Handbook of the History of International Law* (OUP 2012) 1099. In recent literature, Grotius' contribution to legal thinking during this period has been increasingly challenged. According to some authors, Grotius was in fact more a Medieval thinker than 'great pioneer of "modern" thinking', see Grewe, *The Epochs of International Law* (n 2) 191 f. See generally Ernst Lewalter, 'Die geistesgeschichtliche Stellung des Hugo Grotius' [1933] DVjs 262.

libri tres.[4] Chapter XVI of this treatise deals with the interpretation of treaties by combining abstract maxims,[5] natural law concepts,[6] and concrete legal principles.[7] But although he extensively elaborated on treaty interpretation, Grotius seems not to have recognised any forms of subsequent agreements or subsequent practice as admissible means of treaty interpretation.

Looking at the works of Pufendorf, Wolff, and Vattel, one finds no traces of subsequent agreements and subsequent practice either. In his book *De jure naturae et gentium libri octo,*[8] the German jurist Samuel Pufendorf equally dedicated a full chapter to aspects of treaty interpretation. Repeating several examples already mentioned by Grotius, the interpretative rules which Pufendorf proposes largely deal with cases of contradictions[9] or ambiguities intentionally interpreted to the other party's detriment.[10] More abstract rules of treaty interpretation can be found in the sixth volume of Christian von Wolff's *Jus naturae: Methodo scientifica pertractatum.*[11] Nonetheless, the German polymath von Wolff did not fully abandon the interpretative approach of his predecessors, who combined abstract maxims, natural

[4] For Gentili's influence on Grotius, see Peter Haggenmacher, 'Grotius and Gentili: A Reassessment of Thomas E. Holland's Inaugural Lecture 1' in Hedley Bull, Benedict Kingsbury, and Adam Roberts (eds), *Hugo Grotius and International Relations* (Clarendon Press 1990) 133 f. In his principal work on public international law, Gentili addresses some aspects related to treaty interpretation, see eg Alberico Gentili, *De iure belli libri tres* (John Rolfe tr, Clarendon Press 1933) vol 2 (translation of the edition of 1912) 145 f, 369, 425. Yet, it contains no references to subsequent agreements or subsequent practice as means of treaty interpretation.

[5] Grotius postulates, eg, that words are generally to be understood in their natural sense or that technical terms are to be explained according to their technical usage. See Hugo Grotius, *De jure belli ac pacis libri tres* (Francis Kelsey tr, reprod, Hein 1995) 409, 410 f. On such abstract maxims, see generally David Bederman, *Classical Canons—Rhetoric, Classicism and Treaty Interpretation* (Ashgate 2001).

[6] Eg Grotius, *De jure belli ac pacis libri tres* (n 5) 409, where Grotius introduces the concept of 'good faith'.

[7] These concrete principles provide specific answers to specific problems, which are often taken from historic examples. For instance, Grotius explains how to properly interpret the words 'Carthage shall be free' or how to proceed with a treaty that had been entered into with a king when the king had been expelled from his kingdom. See ibid 417 f, 420.

[8] Samuel Pufendorf, *De jure naturae et gentium libri octo* (William Oldfather tr, repr, Hein 1995) 793–824 (Ch XII).

[9] See ibid 798, where Pufendorf describes the following dilemma: There are two laws, one of which stipulating that a statue of a tyrannicide be placed in the gymnasium and the other stipulating that no statue of a woman be erected in the gymnasium. As Pufendorf illustrates, it becomes necessary to reconcile these apparently contradictory laws by way of interpretation if it is a woman who kills a tyrant.

[10] See eg ibid 801: Two parties made a truce for thirty days. Arguing that such truce did not include the nights, one party attacks the other at night.

[11] Christian von Wolff, *Jus naturae—Methodo scientifica pertractatum* (Rengersche Buchhandlung 1746).

law concepts, and concrete legal principles; and like them, he did not consider subsequent agreements and subsequent practice worth mentioning.

Perhaps it was Emer de Vattel who came closest to developing truly abstract rules of treaty interpretation. His work *Le droit des gens, ou principes de la loi naturelle* even contained rules of interpretation that are still familiar today, such as rules on systematic interpretation to ensure coherence of the treaty as a whole[12] or on interpretation based upon the treaty's object and purpose.[13] But despite this level of abstraction and although he aimed at discovering the intentions of the contracting parties,[14] Vattel did not seem to attach any interpretative weight to subsequent agreements or subsequent practice either.

2.1.2 'Post-Classical' Writers

The period between the nineteenth and early twentieth century witnessed and shaped the works of the 'post-classical' writers of international law. These writers were not only well versed in the works of classical international law. They also witnessed that relations and interaction between States intensified steadily[15] so that the relevance of treaties and treaty interpretation increased, too.[16] Representative of that period are scholars such as Robert Phillimore (1810–1885), Lassa Oppenheim (1858–1919), Charles Hyde (1873–1952), and Ludwig Ehrlich (1889–1968), who were among the first to acknowledge and elaborate on subsequent agreements and subsequent practice as means of interpretation.

Perhaps more a judge and politician than an academic was Robert Phillimore.[17] Nevertheless, his *Commentaries on International Law,* which were first published in 1854/1855, were widely received during the nineteenth century.[18] Chapter VIII

---

[12] Emer de Vattel, *The Law of Nations or the Principles of Natural Law* (Charles Fenwick tr, repr, Hein 1995) 206 f.

[13] ibid 207 f.

[14] ibid 200 f.

[15] As regards the establishment of international governmental organisations (IOs) as one manifestation of the growing need for international co-operation and the settlement of conflicting interests by treaties, see Hans-Ulrich Scupin, 'History of International Law, 1815 to World War I' in Rüdiger Wolfrum (ed), *The Max Planck Encyclopedia of Public International Law* (OUP 2012) [57] f, [69], [75] f. More generally on the growth of 'international legislation', Neff, 'History of International Law' (n 2) 20 f.

[16] As regards the increased relevance of treaty law, see Alexander Orakhelashvili, 'The 19th-Century Life of International Law' in id (ed), *Research Handbook on the Theory and History of International Law* (Edward Elgar 2011) 441–44.

[17] John Noyes, 'Christianity and Theories of International Law in Nineteenth-Century Britain' in Mark Janis and Carolyn Evans (eds), *Religion and International Law* (Martinus Nijhoff 1999) 247.

[18] ibid 247 f.

of the second volume dealt with the interpretation of treaties. Although Phillimore prevalently cited the works of Grotius, Pufendorf, and Vattel and thus followed up on their exposition of rules of treaty interpretation, he also addressed what he called 'authentic interpretation.'[19] Defined as 'the exposition supplied by the Lawgiver himself',[20] his concept of authentic interpretation is vaguely reminiscent of subsequent agreements and subsequent practice. Notably, one of his footnotes suggests that it was Roman law from which he derived the underlying idea for his concept of authentic interpretation. In this footnote, he quoted the *Codex Iustinianus,* which provided: *Tam conditor quam interpres legum solus imperator iuste existimabitur*—by law, the emperor is regarded to be the only one who gives as well as interprets the law.[21]

This reference to authentic interpretation may be regarded as an early predecessor to subsequent agreements and subsequent practice. Yet, Phillimore's understanding of authentic interpretation considerably differed from subsequent agreements and subsequent practice as laid down in the Vienna rules. Firstly, Phillimore did not consider authentic interpretation as interpretation stricto sensu (which in his view only encompassed dogmatic interpretation).[22] And secondly, the only form of authentic interpretation which he conceived of was interpretation by way of concluding a new treaty.[23] But despite these differences, Phillimore's work is instructive because it suggests that it was a Roman law formula, revived by authors like him, from which subsequent agreements and subsequent practice as means of interpretation originate.

Phillimore's exposition of rules of treaty interpretation was followed up by Lassa Oppenheim. Oppenheim, a legal positivist who was born in Germany and who had started his career in the field of criminal law, did not focus on international law before he moved to the UK in 1895.[24] All the same, he became one of the leading scholars of modern international law. In 1905, he published the first edition of his magnum opus *International Law: A Treatise*. The second edition of this work, revised by Oppenheim himself, was published in 1912. According to him, there existed no customary or conventional law rules of treaty interpretation at that time.[25] For this reason, Oppenheim limited his account to those 'rules on interpretation which recommend themselves.'[26] Just as Phillimore's work, this account contained

[19] Robert Phillimore, *Commentaries upon International Law* (T & J W Johnson, Law Booksellers 1855) vol 2, 72.

[20] ibid.

[21] ibid vol 2, 72 at fn 1, quoting the *Codex Iustinianus* 14, 12.

[22] ibid vol 2, 72.

[23] ibid.

[24] Mathias Schmoeckel, 'Lassa Oppenheim (1858–1919)' in Bardo Fassbender and others (eds), *The Oxford Handbook of the History of International Law* (OUP 2012) 1152 f.

[25] Lassa Oppenheim, *International Law—A Treatise* (2nd edn, Longman 1912) vol 1, 583.

[26] ibid vol 1, 586.

ideas that were reminiscent of subsequent agreements and subsequent practice as means of interpretation.

In Oppenheim's view, treaty law rested on the contracting parties' consent.[27] This observation led him to conclude that no alternative interpretation was admissible if the parties themselves preferred a particular construction.[28] Distinguishing two forms of interpretation made by the parties themselves, he noted that '[t]hey may either agree informally upon the interpretation and execute the treaty accordingly; or they may make an additional new treaty and stipulate therein such interpretation of the previous treaty as they choose.'[29] Moreover, he argued that

> [i]f the meaning of a stipulation is ambiguous and one of the contracting parties, at a time before a case arises for the application of the stipulation, makes known what meaning it attributes to the stipulation, the other party or parties cannot, when a case for the application of the stipulation occurs, insist upon a different meaning. They ought to have previously protested and taken the necessary steps to secure an authentic interpretation of the ambiguous stipulation.[30]

Thus, Oppenheim acknowledged that the parties' subsequent conduct should be relevant to the interpretation of treaties. What he first described, ie informal agreement on a certain interpretation and the application of the treaty accordingly, seems to combine subsequent agreements and subsequent practice. In addition, he accepted that one party needs to react in order to prevent a certain interpretation deduced from another party's active conduct. To the extent that Oppenheim's approach to subsequent agreements and subsequent practice was inspired by Phillimore, he went even further. Notably, he detached subsequent agreements and subsequent practice as means of interpretation from their Roman law origins and instead linked them to the principle of consent.

In the early twentieth century, the idea that the parties' conduct should influence treaty interpretation also emerged in American international legal thinking. At that time, Charles Hyde, an American professor of international law and member of the Permanent Court of Arbitration (PCA), was a central figure among international legal scholars. He became especially known for his work *International Law, Chiefly as Interpreted and Applied by the United States*, which was first published in 1922.[31] Its passage on treaty interpretation goes back to an earlier contribution published in 1909. In his 1909 article 'Concerning the Interpretation of Treaties', Hyde noted:

> Where various inferences may be reasonably deduced from the conduct of the signatory parties under given circumstances, it is obviously unjust to assert as a rule that any one of them should be controlling. It is only the single reasonable inference which must be deduced from the conduct of the contracting parties which can be safely trusted.[32]

[27] ibid vol 1, 583.

[28] ibid.

[29] ibid. Notably, Oppenheim only considered the latter alternative, ie interpretation by way of a new treaty, as amounting to authentic interpretation.

[30] ibid vol 1, 586.

[31] Charles Hyde, *International Law—Chiefly as Interpreted and Applied by the United States* (Little, Brown & Co 1922).

[32] id, 'Concerning the Interpretation of Treaties' (1909) 3 AJIL 46, 55.

In his 1922 work, he observed that '[c]ontracting States have at times, during the years following the conclusion of an agreement, placed a definite construction on the terms thereof; and this circumstance has been controlling in the minds of arbitrators in construing the compact.'[33] To support this observation, Hyde quoted the *Chamizal Case,* in which arbitrators had indeed identified and relied on 'subsequent treaties [between the parties] and their consistent course of conduct in connection with all cases arising.'[34]

Another scholar of the twentieth century, who unreservedly acknowledged the relevance of subsequent practice, was Ludwik Ehrlich. Ehrlich was a Polish judge and academic who had, among others, served as an *ad hoc* judge at the PCIJ. In his lecture on 'L'interprétation des traités', held at the Hague Academy of International Law in 1928, Ehrlich discussed 'practical interpretation'

> qui résulte … du fait que le traité dont il s'agit a été exécuté d'une certaine manière par les parties elles-mêmes immédiatement après sa confection. Ce serait là un cas particulier de l'interprétation historique et notamment de l'interprétation usuelle. Pour la distinguer de ces autres méthodes, on pourrait l'appeler interprétation pratique, ou bien interprétation quasi-authentique.[35]

To give an example of such practical interpretation, Ehrlich pointed at the jurisprudence of the PCIJ, which had equally endorsed this means of interpretation by that time.[36] As he explained,

> [l]'interprétation pratique ou quasi-authentique, qui est une manière de procéder pour dégager la volonté des parties, se distingue de l'interprétation authentique, qui est la constatation expresse par les parties contractantes de la manière dont elles entendent une clause de leur accord.[37]

Summing up his observations on practical interpretation, Ehrlich remarked:

> On a vu que l'interprétation que nous avons proposé de désigner sous le nom d''interprétation pratique,' ou sous le celui d''interprétation quasi-authentique' est admise dans la pratique comme une des méthodes d'établissement de la volonté des parties. Elle se base sur la présomption, qui est la manière dont les parties ont d'abord appliqué, ou permis

---

[33] id, *International Law* (n 31) 72.

[34] ibid, quoting *The Chamizal Case (Mexico v USA)* (1911) 11 RIAA 309, 23.

[35] Ludwik Ehrlich, 'L'interprétation des traités' (1928) 24 RCADI 5, 48 [fn omitted]. In English [translated by the author]: '… which lies … in the fact that the parties themselves have executed the treaty in a particular manner immediately after its conclusion. Such practical construction constitutes a special case of historical and, in particular, functional interpretation. To distinguish this one from other methods, one may call it practical or quasi-authentic interpretation.'

[36] ibid 48 f. For the jurisprudence of the PCIJ, see below at 2.2.1.

[37] ibid 50. In English [translated by the author]: '… practical or quasi-authentic interpretation, which is one way to elucidate the intention of the parties, needs to be distinguished from authentic interpretation, which is the parties' express explanation of how they understand a particular provision of their agreement.'

> d'appliquer, le traité, qui correspondait à leur volonté, plutôt que l'interprétation différente que l'une des parties prétendrait soutenir plus tard. Car il s'agit toujours de la volonté des parties telle qu'elle existait au moment de la conclusion du traité, et le principe de la bonne foi dicte cette présomption qu'en exécutant ou permettant d'exécuter le traité d'abord d'une certaine manière, on s'en tenait à la volonté primitive dont, dans le temps, on était plus près.[38]

These quotations reveal that Ehrlich distinguished between authentic interpretation stricto sensu on the one hand and practical interpretation or quasi-authentic interpretation on the other. In contrast to the former, practical interpretation did not have to take the form of express stipulations by the parties. Helping to discover the intention of the parties, practical interpretation instead authorised the interpreter to consider the application of the treaty (not necessarily by the parties themselves) as an implied evidence of this intention. As Ehrlich clarified, such evidence of the parties' common intention was not to be confused with an interpretation advocated by one party alone.

2.1.3 State-Sponsored and Private Codification Efforts

With the beginning of the twentieth century, rules of treaty interpretation were not only discussed by individual academics. They also formed part of the first attempts to codify the law of treaties. These attempts were carried out, among others, under the auspices of the International Conferences of American States, the Harvard Research on International Law, the Institut de Droit International (IDI), and the American Law Institute.

The International Conferences of American States—their alternative designation as Pan-American Conferences elucidates that these Conferences were in fact meetings of the Union of American Republics—produced essentially two documents on the law of treaties; yet, only the second mentioned subsequent practice. The Havana Convention on Treaties,[39] which was adopted at the Sixth International Conference of American States in 1928, contained no provisions on treaty interpretation. A

[38] ibid 130 [fn omitted]. In English [translated by the author]: 'We have seen that the interpretation that we proposed to refer to under the notions 'practical interpretation' or 'quasi-authentic interpretation' is recognised in interpretative practice as one method to establish the parties' intention. It rests on the presumption that the way in which the parties once applied or authorised to apply the treaty corresponds to their common intention, more than any other interpretation which one of them may later wish to adopt. Because we are always concerned with the parties' intention as it existed when they concluded the treaty, the principle of good faith equally supports the presumption that, because the parties once applied or authorised to apply the treaty in a particular manner, we should respect that original intention which is, from a temporal perspective, closer to the treaty's conclusion.'

[39] Convention on Treaties (signed 20 February 1928, entered into force 29 August 1929) (1935) 29 AJIL Supp 128 (Havana Convention).

less formal document that was adopted at the Seventh International Conference of American States in 1933, in contrast, exclusively dealt with treaty interpretation.[40] Article 8 of this document provided that, in order to establish the scope of an article, the acts of the contracting parties subsequent to the convention should be taken into account, in so far as they may be pertinent.

In addition, article 2 called on interpreters to prefer that interpretation which the parties had made together. The authors of the 1933 document thus believed that subsequent conduct was relevant for treaty interpretation. Read alone, article 8 did not specify under which conditions subsequent acts of the contracting parties could be taken into account. In particular, it remained unclear how many contracting parties had to participate in such acts. But read together with article 2, one may argue that interpretations based on acts attributable to all parties and indicating their common agreement were regarded more persuasive than those resting on the acts (or the assent thereto) of only some parties. In sum, the 1933 document thus both acknowledged the relevance of subsequent practice and emphasised the idea of consensus or common agreement of all parties.

Only two years later, the 1935 Harvard Draft Convention on the Law of Treaties was published.[41] Unlike the Havana Convention, this draft covered treaty interpretation in general and addressed subsequent practice. Moreover, this draft should prove far more influential than the document on treaty interpretation adopted by the Pan-American Conference in 1933. The Draft Convention was part of the Harvard Research in International Law, a project organised by the Harvard Law School in the late 1920s and 1930s. Initially, this project served to support the League of Nations' Committee of Experts in its codification efforts. Under the directorship of Manley Hudson (1886–1960), then professor of public international law at Harvard Law School and later the first Chairman of the ILC, the Harvard group prepared draft conventions and commentaries on 13 key topics of public international law. Among these topics was the law of treaties, for which James Garner (1871–1938), then professor of political science at the University of Illinois, was responsible.[42]

Article 19 of the Harvard Draft Convention, which consists of 36 articles in total, dealt with the interpretation of treaties. Its lit (a), whose language sounds vaguely familiar, read:

> A treaty is to be interpreted in the light of the general purpose which it is intended to serve. The historical background of the treaty, *travaux préparatoires*, the circumstances of the parties at the time the treaty was entered into, the change in these circumstances sought to be effected, the subsequent conduct of the parties in applying the provisions of the treaty, and the conditions prevailing at the time interpretation is being made, are to be considered in connection with the general purpose which the treaty is intended to serve.

---

[40] The text is reproduced as an appendix to the Harvard Draft Convention on the Law of Treaties (1935) 29 AJIL Supp 1225–26.

[41] Harvard Draft Convention on the Law of Treaties (1935) 29 AJIL Supp 657–65 (Harvard Draft).

[42] James Kenny, 'Manley O Hudson and the Harvard Research in International Law 1927–1940' (1977) 11 Int'l L 319, 326.

None of the means of treaty interpretation enlisted in article 19 was to take precedence over the others; instead, all of these 'factors' equally served to elucidate the treaty's true meaning, ie its underlying purpose.[43] To this end, the draft quite naturally mentioned subsequent practice, here referred to as 'subsequent conduct', as one of these factors. The commentary on article 19 attached even greater importance to subsequent practice by admitting that 'in interpreting the treaty, the conduct or action of the parties thereto cannot be ignored'.[44] Supporting this assertion, it further emphasised that courts—not only the PCIJ and international arbitral tribunals but also domestic courts—frequently relied on subsequent practice when determining the meaning of the terms of a treaty.[45] Although article 19 did not mention subsequent agreements, the commentary clarified that such agreements could equally be taken into account. According to the Harvard Research project, it was 'too obvious to need to comment that the same parties which created an instrument by agreement may also, by agreement, place upon it such interpretation as they wish.'[46]

In addition to elucidating the significance of subsequent agreements and subsequent practice as means of interpretation, the commentary also specified which practice constituted 'subsequent practice' (or 'subsequent conduct') within the meaning of draft article 19: 'If all the parties to a treaty execute it, or permit its execution, in a particular manner, that fact may reasonably be taken into account as indicative of the real intentions of the parties or of the purpose which the instrument was designed to serve.'[47] According to the commentary, only practice of all the parties carried sufficient power of persuasion to be relevant to the process of interpretation. Of course, this qualification only related to subsequent agreements and subsequent practice within the meaning of the Harvard Draft. Nevertheless, it is worth remembering when trying to gain a better understanding of subsequent conduct within the meaning of the Vienna Convention. This is because much of the work of the Harvard Research project was known to and taken into account by the ILC when it undertook to codify certain areas of international law.

Another early attempt to codify the law of treaties was the one undertaken by the Institut de Droit International from 1950–1956. Being a private association of legal experts of various nationalities, the IDI's aims are to 'develop the law and act so that it might be implemented.'[48] Once the Institute's plenary assembly has taken a certain topic on its agenda, a scientific commission meets for regular discussions that normally culminate in the adoption of a resolution on this topic.[49] On 19 April 1956

---

[43] cf Harvard Law School, 'Harvard Draft Convention—Comment on Article 19' (1935) 29 AJIL 937, 938.

[44] ibid 966.

[45] ibid 966 f.

[46] ibid 968.

[47] ibid 966.

[48] See the Institute's website at <http://www.idi-iil.org>.

[49] Peter Macalister-Smith, 'Institut de Droit International' in Rüdiger Wolfrum (ed), *The Max Planck Encyclopedia of Public International Law* (OUP 2012) [18].

and based on the work of its Rapporteur Sir Hersch Lauterpacht (1897–1960), the IDI adopted a resolution that laid down the following rules of treaty interpretation:[50]

> Estime que lorsqu'il y a lieu d'interpréter un traité, les Etats, les organisations et les juridictions internationales pourraient s'inspirer des principes suivants:
>
> *Article premier*
>
> 1. L'accord des parties s'étant réalisé sur le texte du traité, il y a lieu de prendre le sens naturel et ordinaire des termes de ce texte comme base d'interprétation. Les termes des dispositions du traité doivent être interprétés dans le contexte entier, selon la bonne foi et à la lumière des principes du droit international.
> 2. Toutefois, s'il est établi que les termes employés doivent se comprendre dans un autre sens, le sens naturel et ordinaire de ces termes est écarté.
>
> *Article 2*
>
> 1. Dans le cas d'un différend porté devant une juridiction internationale il incombera au tribunal, en tenant compte des dispositions de l'article premier, d'apprécier si, et dans quelle mesure, il y a lieu d'utiliser d'autres moyens d'interprétation.
> 2. Parmi ces moyens légitimes d'interpréter se trouvent:
>   a) Le recours aux travaux préparatoires;
>   b) La pratique suivie dans l'application effective du traité;
>   c) La prise en considération des buts du traité.

The reference to subsequent practice ('pratique suivie') was included at a very late stage of the Institute's work on the topic. It goes back to a proposal of the German member Wilhelm Wengler (1907–1995) to mention subsequent practice in article 1 of the IDI's Resolution. To explain his proposal, Wengler had emphasised:

> En effet, il s'instaure très souvent une certaine uniformité dans la manière dont les parties au traité entendent telle ou telle phrase du traité en exécutant celui-ci. Il importe peu si l'on

[50] Institut de Droit International, 'Résolution sur l'interprétation des traités' (1956) 46 AIDI 358, 358–59. In English [translated by the author]:

> It is believed that, when interpreting a treaty, States, international organisations, and international dispute settlement bodies may be guided by the following principles:

First article

1. The parties having expressed their agreement on the text of the treaty, it is necessary to take the natural and ordinary meaning of the terms of this text as the starting point for any interpretation. The terms of the treaty ought to be interpreted in their full context, in good faith, and in the light of the principles of international law.
2. If, however, it is clear that the terms of treaty are employed in a different sense, the natural or ordinary meaning of these terms ought to be rejected.

Article 2

1. Where a dispute is brought before an international court or tribunal, account should be taken of the provisions of article 1, to determine whether, and to which extent, it is necessary to use additional means of interpretation.
2. These additionally admissible means of interpretation include:
   a) Recourse to the *travaux préparatoires*;
   b) Subsequent practice in the application of the treaty;
   c) Considering the purposes of the treaty.

> parle d'un accord tacite d'interprétation ou d'une coutume particulière entre les parties concernant l'interprétation des traités. En tout cas, de telles pratiques uniformes dans l'application effective des traités par les parties … sont extrêmement importantes pour l'interprétation du traité par le juge international ou même le juge national, qui doivent tenir compte de cette pratique même si l'intention originale des parties au temps de la conclusion du traité a peut-être été différente.[51]

The British member Wilfred Jenks (1909–1973) objected that it 'ne semple pas oportun de faire mention d'une question aussi complexe et spéciale dans les dispositions très générales de l'article premier.'[52] Due to this objection, Wengler's proposal was eventually moved to article 2 of the resolution. Moreover, Rapporteur Lauterpacht pointed out that subsequent practice had to be 'constante'—a qualification not rejected by the other members but still missing in the final resolution.[53] Apart from these incidents, the Institute hardly discussed the proposal to include subsequent practice. This shows that its members largely agreed with the final conception of subsequent practice and that they endorsed Wengler's explanation for including subsequent practice. This explanation suggested that there was often uniform practice in the application of a treaty that was inherently valuable for interpreting the treaty, irrespective of considering such practice as a tacit agreement or as something less formalised, and irrespective of whether it deviated from the parties' original intention. Thus, the proposal dissolved subsequent practice from the original intention of the parties and introduced a dynamic element into the process of treaty interpretation.[54]

---

[51] id, 'De l'interprétation des traités' (1956) 46 AIDI 317, 334. In English [translated by the author]: 'In fact, the meanings which the contratcting parties confer on the treaty by applying it often display a considerable degree of uniformity. It it immaterial whether we speak of a tacit interpretative agreement or of a particular rule of customary law between the parties regarding the treaty's interpretation. In any case, such uniform practice of the parties in the application of the treaty … is highly important for the interpretation of the treaty by an international or national judge, who must take such practice into account even if it deviates from the parties' original intention when the treaty was concluded.'

[52] ibid. In English [translated by the author]: 'It does not appear opportune and appropriate to mention such a complex and special issue among the very general provisions of the first article.'

[53] ibid 339.

[54] For subsequent practice as evidence of the parties' original intention, see eg *Article 3, Paragraph 2, of the Treaty of Lausanne* (Advisory Opinion) PCIJ Rep Series B No 12, 24 and Georg Nolte, 'Report 1—Jurisprudence of the International Court of Justice and Arbitral Tribunals of Ad Hoc Jurisdiction relating to Subsequent Agreements and Subsequent Practice' in id (ed), *Treaties and Subsequent Practice* (OUP 2013) 175 f; *Corfu Channel Case (UK v Albania)* (Merits) [1949] ICJ Rep 4, 24 f; *Anglo-Iranian Oil Co Case (UK v Iran)* (Jurisdiction) [1952] ICJ Rep 93, 107. See further Francis Jacobs, 'Varieties of Approach to Treaty Interpretation: With Special Reference to the Draft Convention on the Law of Treaties before the Vienna Diplomatic Conference' (1969) 18 ICLQ 318, 328; Giovanni Distefano, 'La pratique subséquente des états parties à un traité' (1994) 40 AFDI 41, 46.

The Second Restatement of the Foreign Relations Law of the United States, published in 1965 and prepared by the American Law Institute (ALI), contains the last serious and concise summary of rules of treaty interpretation before the Vienna Convention was adopted.[55] Section 146 of the Restatement proclaims the following basic function of treaty interpretation:

> The extent to which an international agreement creates changes, or defines relationships under international law is determined in case of doubt by the interpretation of the agreement. The primary object of interpretation is to ascertain the meaning intended by the parties for the terms in which the agreement is expressed, having regard to the context in which they occur and the circumstances under which the agreement was made. This meaning is determined in the light of all relevant factors.

It then lists various criteria or factors for interpretation in order to ascertain and give effect to the purpose of the treaty which it was, so it appeared from the terms used by the parties, intended to serve. Apart from the ordinary meaning, which always has to be considered as a relevant factor, all criteria are ranked equally. As one of these criteria, s 147(1)(f) mentions 'the subsequent practice of the parties in the performance of the agreement, or the subsequent practice of one party, if the other party knew or had reason to know of it.'

Two aspects about the Restatement are noteworthy in that they distinguish this approach to treaty interpretation from others of that time. Firstly, the Restatement expressly commits itself to ascertaining the meaning intended by the parties as the ultimate goal of treaty interpretation. And secondly, it seems to uncouple subsequent practice from the agreement of all parties. Section 147(1)(f) does not expressly require practice that establishes the parties' agreement. Moreover, inactive parties merely need to have 'had reason to know' of relevant active conduct by other parties. Such constructive knowledge does not necessarily preclude acquiescence and hence a finding of agreement.[56] Taken together, these factors nonetheless suggest that the Restatement neither positively requires nor implicitly attaches great importance to the parties' agreement.

In sum, the Restatement proposes a very inclusive concept of subsequent practice. Not the parties' agreement but rather practice as such serves as an argument. A possible explanation for this open concept may be the Restatement's overall

---

[55] The relevant ss of the Second Restatement are reproduced in Jacobs, 'Varieties of Approach to Treaty Interpretation' (n 54) 344 f. In 1987, the ALI published a comprehensive revision of the Second Restatement, see American Law Institute, *Third Restatement of the Law—The Foreign Relations Law of the United States* (American Law Inst Pub 1987). Section 325 of the Third Restatement (Interpretation of International Agreement) follows art 31(1)(3) VCLT in that it provides:

> 1. An international agreement is to be interpreted in good faith in accordance with the ordinary meaning to be given to its terms in their context and in the light of its object and purpose.
> 2. Any subsequent agreement between the parties regarding the interpretation of the agreement, and subsequent practice between the parties in the application of the agreement, are to be taken into account in its interpretation.

[56] See 8.1.1.

approach to treaty interpretation. Unlike alternative approaches, it does not distinguish between relevant and irrelevant means of interpretation but admits any means (or factor) as long as it helps to achieve the ultimate goal of ascertaining the intention of the parties. As shown below, this extreme intentionalist approach was rejected by the drafters of the Vienna Convention.[57] At the same time, they also rejected the inclusive concept of subsequent practice (and subsequent agreement) by codifying an alternative approach that does not admit any practice (or agreement) as a primary means of interpretation but rather makes reliance on subsequent practice (and agreements) subject to certain conditions.[58]

2.1.4 Conclusion

Reconsidering the overview of international legal doctrine, it has been instructive to learn that subsequent agreements and subsequent practice cannot be traced back to the era of classical international law; in others words, the writings of that time cannot have influenced contemporary concepts of subsequent agreements and subsequent practice.

Instead, it was the work of 'post-classical' writers of the nineteenth and early twentieth century that began acknowledging subsequent agreements and subsequent practice as means of interpretation, albeit still in a rudimentary form and often under the more general notion of authentic interpretation. The work of Phillimore suggests that subsequent practice ultimately originates from Roman law, under which a single person, namely the emperor himself, inherently possessed the power not only to make but also to interpret the law. Other 'post-classical' writers separated the notion of authentic interpretation from its Roman law origins and instead linked it to consensus-based principles of party autonomy. In the end, the reasons for relying on subsequent practice remained the same. Whenever writers of the nineteenth and early twentieth century tried to justify reliance on subsequent practice, they emphasised that he (or those) who made the law should also have the power to interpret it. While accepting that relevant practice could be of an informal nature, nineteenth and early twentieth century writers already began to indicate that only interpretations attributable to all contracting parties carried special weight in the interpretative process.

State-sponsored and private efforts to codify the law of treaties during the early twentieth century not only endorsed subsequent practice as a means of interpretation but also gave more concrete contours to it. While some documents like the 1935 Harvard Draft Convention specifically required *practice of the parties* to the treaty, the 1956 IDI Resolution merely required *a practice* in the application of the treaty. A recurring theme was the importance of consensus or the idea of the parties as the masters of the treaty. Isolated practice and practice not resting on the parties' agreement were not dismissed completely. Nevertheless, these forms of practice

[57] See 3.1.

[58] See 3.1, 4.2, and 4.3.

were regularly not ascribed special weight but subordinated to conduct establishing the agreement of all parties.

Subsequent agreements, in contrast, have hardly been mentioned in international legal doctrine before the Vienna Convention was adopted. Only the commentary on the 1935 Harvard Draft Convention clarified that interpretative agreements could also be taken into account when interpreting a treaty. Other scholarly work did not separately address subsequent agreements alongside subsequent practice. Still, this does not necessarily mean that interpretative agreements were considered irrelevant. In the light of the broad and unrefined understanding of subsequent practice, it is equally possible that international legal doctrine did not yet distinguish between subsequent practice and informal interpretative agreements but rather included the latter into the notion of subsequent practice.

2.2 Judicial Settlement of International Disputes

Section 2.2 delineates the origins of subsequent agreements and subsequent practice in international dispute settlement.[59] The ILC demonstrated that subsequent agreements and subsequent practice have been applied by courts of general jurisdiction, by arbitral tribunals of *ad hoc* jurisdiction, and by judicial and quasi-judicial bodies under special regimes before and after the adoption of the Vienna Convention in 1969.[60]

[59] In accordance with art 33 of the Charter of the United Nations (signed 26 June 1945, entered into force 24 October 1945) 1 UNTS XVI (UNC), one can distinguish two forms of international dispute settlement mechanisms, namely arbitral and judicial dispute settlement. Judicial dispute settlement bodies are of a permanent nature and 'made up of independent judges which are entrusted with adjudicating international disputes on the basis of international law according to a pre-determined set of rules of procedure', see Christian Tomuschat, 'International Courts and Tribunals' in Rüdiger Wolfrum (ed), *The Max Planck Encyclopedia of Public International Law* (OUP 2012) [1]. Arbitral dispute settlement bodies, in contrast, are established *ad hoc* and their composition is determined by the parties themselves, see generally Charles Brower, 'Arbitration' in Rüdiger Wolfrum (ed), *The Max Planck Encyclopedia of Public International Law* (OUP 2012).

[60] See the various references to relevant case law in the commentaries on the Commission's draft conclusions 1–10 in ILC, 'Report of the International Law Commission on the Work of its 65th Session' (6 May–7 June and 8 July–9 August 2013) UN Doc A/68/10, 9–48 and id, 'Report of the International Law Commission on the Work of its 66th Session' (5 May–6 June and 7 July–8 August 2014) UN Doc A/69/10, 166–217. See also Georg Nolte, 'First Report on Subsequent Agreements and Subsequent Practice in relation to Treaty Interpretation' (19 March 2013) UN Doc A/CN.4/660, 14 [31]–19 [41]; id, 'Report 1—Jurisprudence of the International Court of Justice and Arbitral Tribunals of Ad Hoc Jurisdiction relating to Subsequent Agreements and Subsequent Practice' in id (ed), *Treaties and Subsequent Practice* (OUP 2013) and id, 'Report 2—Jurisprudence under Special Regimes relating to Subsequent Agreements and Subsequent Practice' in id (ed), *Treaties and Subsequent Practice* (OUP 2013).

For this reason, it is unnecessary to comprehensively re-examine the pre-Convention approach to subsequent conduct in international dispute settlement. The following discussion instead purports to offer a general orientation by highlighting the main tendencies in international dispute settlement before 1969. In doing so, it concentrates on the jurisprudence of the PCIJ (2.2.1) and the ICJ (2.2.2) as the main and traditionally authoritative reference points for understanding the relevance of subsequent conduct.

2.2.1 *Permanent Court of International Justice*

The PCIJ was established pursuant to article 14 of the Covenant of the League of Nations[61] and effectively carried out its judicial work from 1922 to 1940.[62] During this period, the Court delivered 65 decisions in total, comprising both advisory opinions and decisions in contentious proceedings.[63] Decisions of the Court were only binding *inter partes* and in respect of the particular case.[64] Nevertheless, the Court frequently cited its earlier decisions and tried to contribute to the development of consistency and stability in decision-making.[65]

Many of the Court's decisions concerned aspects of treaty interpretation.[66] For this reason, one would expect that it regularly relied on subsequent agreements and subsequent practice once these means of interpretation had entered into its case law. But contrary to this expectation, the Court's jurisprudence presents an ambivalent picture. On the one hand, it recognised the 'familiar principle that where a contract is ambiguous, resort may be had to the manner of performance in order to ascertain the intention of the Parties.'[67] On the other hand, the overall number of cases in which the Court relied on subsequent conduct is rather small. And while the Court did take account of subsequent practice as a means of interpretation in a few cases, subsequent agreements have hardly played any role in its jurisprudence.

The earliest decision in which the Court mentioned subsequent practice is its second advisory opinion on the *Competence of the ILO in regard to International*

---

[61] Covenant of the League of Nations (signed 29 April 1919, entered into force 10 January 1920) 225 CTS 195.

[62] Although the Court formally existed until 18 April 1946, it already stopped working in 1940 because of the beginning of World War II. See Shabtai Rosenne, 'Permanent Court of International Justice (PCIJ)' in Rüdiger Wolfrum (ed), *The Max Planck Encyclopedia of Public International Law* (OUP 2012) [13].

[63] See arts 39 and 65 of the Statute of the Permanent Court of International Justice (signed 16 December 1920, entered into force 20 August 1921) 6 LNTS 379 (PCIJ Statute).

[64] See art 59 PCIJ Statute.

[65] Rosenne, 'Permanent Court of International Justice (PCIJ)' (n 62) [31].

[66] id, 'Permanent Court of International Justice (PCIJ)' in Rüdiger Wolfrum (ed), *The Max Planck Encyclopedia of Public International Law* (OUP 2012) [39].

[67] *Case concerning the Payment in Gold of Brazilian Federal Loans Contracted in France (France v Brazil)* PCIJ Rep Series A No 21 at 119.

Regulation of the Conditions of the Labour of Persons Employed in Agriculture.[68] This case dealt with the question of whether competences of the International Labour Organisation (ILO) under its constituent document, Part XIII of the Treaty of Versailles,[69] also extended to agricultural labour. Adopting a predominantly textual approach to interpretation, the Court eventually concluded that they unambiguously did.[70] Nonetheless, the Court added that 'if there were any ambiguity … [it] might, for the purpose of arriving at the true meaning, consider the action which has been taken under the treaty.'[71] But despite having just rejected any ambiguity, the Court then examined the contracting parties' conduct concerning the ILO's competences.[72] This examination showed that more than two years had passed since the Treaty of Versailles had been ratified until the parties had begun to question its competences regarding agricultural labour; in the meantime, the contentious issue had 'repeatedly been discussed and had been dealt with in one form or another'.[73] Hence, the parties' practice, which essentially consisted in not addressing the contentious issue, confirmed the Court's preliminary interpretation. Although the Court quite naturally took account of subsequent practice, it assumed just as naturally that it could only do so after having consulted other means of interpretation and concluded that the terms of the treaty were ambiguous.[74]

The advisory opinion on the *Question of Jaworzina (Polish-Czechoslovakian Frontier)* helps to shed further light on the Court's attitude towards subsequent conduct although it did not raise issues of treaty interpretation.[75] As its name indicates, this opinion discussed if and to which extent the delimitation of the Polish-Czechoslovakian frontier in the region of Spisz (Jaworzina) was still open. Instructed by the Principal Allied Powers, the Conference of Ambassadors had divided Spisz between Poland and Czechoslovakia and determined the frontier line on 28 July 1920. Both Poland and Czechoslovakia had agreed to be bound by such determination. Nevertheless, Poland later contested the frontier line and argued that its determination was neither complete nor final. A note of the Drafting Committee formed by the Conference of Ambassadors, dated 21 October 1922, as well as letters by the President of the Conference to the Polish and Czechoslovak Ministers, dated 13 November 1922, seemed to confirm this view.[76] The Court therefore

[68] *Competence of the ILO in regard to International Regulation of the Conditions of Labour of Persons Employed in Agriculture* (Advisory Opinion) PCIJ Rep Series B No 2.

[69] Treaty of Peace between the Allied and Associated Powers and Germany (signed 28 June 1919, entered into force 10 January 1920) 255 CTS 188 (Treaty of Versailles).

[70] *Competence of the ILO (Agricultural Labour)* (n 68) 39.

[71] ibid.

[72] ibid.

[73] ibid 39 f.

[74] Nolte, 'Report 1—ICJ and Arbitral Tribunals' (n 54) 176.

[75] *Question of Jaworzina (Polish-Czechoslovakian Frontier)* (Advisory Opinion) PCIJ Rep Series B No 8.

[76] ibid 34 f.

had to decide whether these documents could be taken into account to interpret the decision of 28 July 1920 or whether the decision was not open to subsequent interpretation because of its final nature. Notably, it first emphasised the 'established principle that the right of giving an authoritative interpretation of a legal rule belongs solely to the person or body who has power to modify or suppress it' and even quoted 'the traditional principle: *ejus est interpretare legem cujus condere*.'[77] But due to the clear language of the decision of 28 July 1920,[78] it then concluded that the Conference had accomplished its task and therefore no longer retained the power to subsequently interpret its decision.[79]

Another example of the Court's approach to subsequent practice is its advisory opinion on the *Competence of the ILO to Regulate, Incidentally, the Personal Work of the Employer*.[80] Background to this opinion was that the ILO had drawn up and proposed labour legislation to protect certain classes of workers that incidentally regulated the same work when performed by these workers' employers. The case thus centred on the interpretation of Part XIII of the Treaty of Versailles, which defined the ILO's competences. Article 387 of said Treaty only generally provided that the ILO was established for the promotion of the objects set forth in the Preamble. The Preamble envisaged in broad terms the promotion of humane working conditions of labour and the protection of workers. Yet, no provision explicitly permitted or prohibited the ILO from taking measures that incidentally regulated work performed by employers. However, Part XIII of the Treaty provided for a first meeting of the ILO's General Conference and the parties had taken the issue of 'the extension and application' of the Convention prohibiting 'the use of white phosphorus in the manufacture of matches' onto the Agenda of this first Conference.[81]

The prohibition primarily protected those employees who manufactured matches and thus directly came into contact with white phosphorus (a highly toxic substance); but in addition, it could not be excluded that the prohibition also protected, incidentally, some employers from being exposed to white phosphorus. In the Court's view, addressing the white phosphorus issue qualified as a 'contemporaneous practical interpretation made by the High Contracting Parties of the scope of the competence which they had conferred upon the International Labour Organization'.[82] Based on this observation, it finally held that the ILO possessed the contentious competence to incidentally regulate the personal work of the employer.[83] Compared to other decisions, the Court attached considerable importance to the parties' subsequent conduct. Nevertheless, it did not seem to abandon its tendency

[77] ibid 37.

[78] ibid 36 f.

[79] ibid 37.

[80] *Competence of the ILO to Regulate, Incidentally, the Personal Work of the Employer* (Advisory Opinion) PCIJ Rep Series B No 13.

[81] ibid 19.

[82] ibid.

[83] ibid 14.

to subordinate subsequent conduct to other means of interpretation. Instead, the Court merely relied on it because other means of interpretation had failed to resolve the remaining ambiguity of the contentious provisions. Thus, this opinion reconfirms the impression that the PCIJ considered subsequent conduct as a supplementary means of interpretation in the sense of what later became article 32 VCLT.[84]

The advisory opinion on the *Jurisdiction of the Courts of Danzig* constitutes a 'backslide' since it more openly treated subsequent practice as an auxiliary means of interpretation.[85] By virtue of the 1921 Definitive Agreement in regard to officials between the Polish Government and the Free City of Danzig, Danzig railway officials had passed into the service of the Polish administration. The Court had to decide whether the Agreement conferred jurisdiction upon the Danzig courts to hear pecuniary claims by these railway officials against the Polish administration. The answer to this question depended on whether the Agreement itself (and not national law passed to implement it) governed the relationship between administration and officials. After a thorough analysis of the text of the Agreement, the Court concluded that it did.[86] Nevertheless, it sought to reinforce its conclusion by additionally referring to 'the manner in which the Agreement ha[d] been applied' by the parties.[87] This reference was a rather cursory one, the Court being content to observe that the parties had apparently considered the Agreement to have been duly brought into effect; this implied, in its view, that neither party had considered it necessary to incorporate the Agreement into domestic law.[88]

A final example of the Court's approach to subsequent practice is its advisory opinion on the *Jurisdiction of the European Commission of the Danube* in the river sector between the cities of Galatz and Braïla.[89] The various questions relating to the Commission's jurisdiction were primarily governed by the 1921 Convention Instituting the Definitive Statute of the Danube.[90] One of these questions related to the correct method for determining the dividing line between the competences of the European Commission and the Romanian authorities. While Romania had argued that the limits between the respective competences were of a territorial nature,[91] the Court firmly rejected that view.[92] Admitting that the Statute's wording itself was not particularly instructive, the Court relied on extrinsic material to justify its

---

[84] cf Nolte, 'Report 1—ICJ and Arbitral Tribunals' (n 54) 176.

[85] *Jurisdiction of the Courts of Danzig* (Advisory Opinion) PCIJ Rep Series B No 15. See also Nolte, 'Report 1—ICJ and Arbitral Tribunals' (n 54) 176.

[86] *Jurisdiction of the Courts of Danzig* (n 85) 18 f.

[87] ibid 15, 20.

[88] ibid 20 f.

[89] *Jurisdiction of the European Commission of the Danube* (Advisory Opinion) PCIJ Rep Series B No 14.

[90] Convention Instituting the Definitive Statute of the Danube (signed 23 July 1921, entered into force 1 October 1922) 26 LNTS 187.

[91] *European Commission of the Danube* (n 89) 61.

[92] ibid 62 f.

conclusion.[93] In particular, it referred to the subsequent conduct of the Special Commission—the Special Commission for the Question of the Jurisdiction of the European Commission of the Danube—and the governments concerned, albeit without going into further details.[94]

2.2.2 International Court of Justice

In 1946, the International Court of Justice succeeded the PCIJ as the principal judicial organ of the United Nations.[95] Until the adoption of the Vienna Convention in 1969, the ICJ had disposed of about 50 cases in the form of advisory opinions and judgments and decisions in contentious proceedings.[96] Although ICJ decisions are only binding *inter partes,* the Court has, like its predecessor, regularly emphasised the need for continuity and stability in its case law.[97] The following examples of cases are taken from the period before the Convention was adopted. They may therefore indicate whether the ICJ has followed up on its predecessor's approach to subsequent agreements and subsequent practice or not. In this regard, it will be interesting to see whether the ICJ has started to take account of subsequent agreements and whether it has developed more precise contours of subsequent practice.

In its advisory opinion on the *Constitution of the Maritime Safety Committee,* the ICJ indeed followed up on the PCIJ's approach to subsequent practice.[98] According to article 28(a) of the Convention on the Inter-Governmental Maritime Consultative Organization,[99] the Maritime Safety Committee should consist of 14 members elected by the Assembly from the members, governments of those nations having an important interest in maritime safety, of which no less than eight shall be the largest ship-owning nations. Having rejected the view, asserted by some States, that the Assembly had discretion in determining the 'largest ship-owning nations', the Court assumed that the correct standard for this determination was one based on the States' strength of tonnage. But since article 28(a) did not even mention the term 'tonnage', it was unclear how a State's tonnage should be defined. Only two alternatives were conceivable: Either tonnage meant the tonnage beneficially owned by

[93] ibid 60 f.

[94] ibid 63.

[95] See art 92 UNC.

[96] For an overview of the cases that have been referred to the Court since 1946, see the Court's website at <http://www.icj-cij.org>.

[97] Shabtai Rosenne, 'International Court of Justice (ICJ)' in Rüdiger Wolfrum (ed), *The Max Planck Encyclopedia of Public International Law* (OUP 2012) [112].

[98] *Constitution of the Maritime Safety Committee of the Inter-Governmental Maritime Consultative Organization* (Advisory Opinion) [1960] ICJ Rep 150.

[99] Convention on the Inter-Governmental Maritime Consultative Organization (signed 6 March 1948, entered into force 17 March 1958) 289 UNTS 48.

the nationals of a State,[100] thus taking account of private and State ownership; or it meant a State's registered tonnage, which was independent of any such ownership.

In the Court's view, only '[a]n examination of certain Articles of the Convention and the actual practice which was followed in giving effect to them throws some light on the Court's consideration of the question.'[101] Therefore, it closely analysed the practice of the organisation itself[102] and of the organisation's member States.[103] This analysis eventually led it to conclude that the only criterion that the parties could have thought of when drafting article 28(a) was the States' registered tonnages.[104] On the one hand, the parties' practice was central to the ICJ's reasoning and readily taken into account. But on the other hand, other means of interpretation would not have cast any light on the interpretative question. Hence, this decision does not evidence that the ICJ had deviated from its predecessor's approach to subsequent practice. In other words, it does not refute the impression that the Court originally regarded subsequent conduct as an auxiliary and subsidiary means of interpretation to which 'more or less "clear" terms [were] largely immune.'[105]

The same impression arises from the ICJ's reliance on subsequent practice in the *Case concerning the Arbitral Award Made by the King of Spain on 23 December 1906*.[106] This case was brought by Honduras against Nicaragua. Honduras argued that the latter had failed to comply with the arbitral award of the King of Spain, which attempted to settle a boundary dispute between the two States.[107] Nicaragua, however, denied Honduras' claim. In its view, the award was invalid because the treaty on which it was based[108] had already expired when the King had accepted his office as arbitrator and rendered his award.[109] This line of argument relied on article XI of the Treaty, which stipulated that it should expire after a period of ten years.[110] However, the Treaty failed to specify the date at which it would enter into force. Nicaragua had argued that it had entered into force at the date of signature, ie on

[100] *Maritime Safety Committee* (n 98) 167.

[101] ibid.

[102] ibid 168 f.

[103] ibid 168.

[104] ibid 169.

[105] cf Nolte, 'Report 1—ICJ and Arbitral Tribunals' (n 54) 180. See, however, id, 'Report 1—Jurisprudence of the International Court of Justice and Arbitral Tribunals of Ad Hoc Jurisdiction relating to Subsequent Agreements and Subsequent Practice' in id (ed), *Treaties and Subsequent Practice* (OUP 2013) 180, where he demonstrates that the Courts jurisprudence after 1969 no longer supports this conclusion.

[106] *Case concerning the Arbitral Award Made by the King of Spain on 23 December 1906 (Honduras v Nicaragua)* [1960] ICJ Rep 192.

[107] ibid 195 f.

[108] Gámez-Bonilla Treaty (Honduras–Nicaragua) (signed 7 October 1894, entered into force 24 December 1896) reproduced in *Arbitral Award Case* (n 106) 199.

[109] ibid 197 f.

[110] ibid 207 f.

7 October 1894.[111] To support its interpretation, it had referred to article IX of the Treaty, which provided that the requirements of ratification and exchanges thereof should not hinder the organisation of a Mixed Commission under the Treaty.[112] That the Commission was to be organised before the date of ratification necessarily implied that the Treaty must have entered into force before ratification, too.[113] Honduras, in contrast, contended that the Treaty had entered into force at the date of the exchange of ratifications, ie on 24 December 1896.[114]

Rejecting Nicaragua's contextual argument, the Court adopted the latter view and emphasised the parties' subsequent conduct.[115] As the Court observed, both Honduras and Nicaragua had agreed on the King of Spain as arbitrator on 2 October 1904; had they believed that the Treaty would expire five days later, their agreement would have been completely senseless.[116] Moreover, on the very date of the alleged expiry, Nicaragua's President had sent a telegram to the Spanish Minister to Central America to praise the King as prospective arbitrator.[117] Although said Minister had suggested extending the period of the treaty,[118] neither of the two governments took action to do so but proceeded with the arbitration.[119] Against this background, the Court was convinced that neither party had considered the treaty to expire that soon.[120] Hence it concluded that the Treaty had not entered into force until the date of ratification, that the arbitral award was given during the duration of the Treaty, and that the award was therefore valid and binding on Nicaragua.[121]

This case again shows that—at least when reliance on other means of interpretation would not have been helpful—the ICJ was prepared to treat practice-based arguments as being decisive for the outcome of a case. Furthermore, it illustrates how accurately the Court examined subsequent practice when planning to base its interpretation on this practice. In the *Arbitral Award Case*, the ICJ mentioned not only practice of the claimant alone or of both parties but also unilateral conduct of the defendant to support its line of argument. One may certainly speculate why the Court attached so much importance to the parties' conduct in this case; perhaps it was because the Treaty itself or other means of interpretation did not resolve the contentious issue. Besides, this case shows how the Court dealt with a special problem concerning subsequent practice, namely the interpretative value of silence. Here it was the parties' silence, or non-reaction to the Spanish Minister's suggestion

[111] ibid 208.

[112] ibid.

[113] ibid.

[114] ibid.

[115] ibid.

[116] ibid.

[117] ibid.

[118] ibid 209.

[119] ibid.

[120] ibid.

[121] ibid.

to extend the Treaty's period. In this regard, the Court clarified that the parties' silence in itself did not carry any weight; whether such silence acquired interpretative value depended on external circumstances in the light of which it was appropriate (or not) to assume that the parties would have reacted to prevent their silence from being interpreted as consent.[122]

In the *Case concerning the Temple of Preah Vihear,*[123] the ICJ subsequently confirmed that silence or omission may establish agreement if 'the circumstances were such as called for some reaction' by the inactive party 'within a reasonable period.'[124] Subject of the dispute was territorial sovereignty over the region of the Temple. To support its claim to sovereignty,[125] Cambodia principally relied on a map that had been drawn up by French officials at the request of the Siamese government.[126] Thailand, in contrast, contended that the map was erroneous and not legally binding.[127] Having adopted a 'merely passive attitude', it therefore argued that it had never consented to the frontier line as expressed on the map.[128] Nevertheless, the Court eventually held that Thailand had acquiesced in the map.[129] This was because the map, which purported to represent the outcome of the work of delimitation, had been disseminated widely.[130] While still requiring an agreement regarding the contentious issue, the Court thus simultaneously clarified that the necessary agreement did not presuppose active conduct. Instead, it could also be established through an omission to act that qualified as acquiescence. For the purpose of distinguishing acquiescence from simple silence, the Court's *Temple* judgment does not offer a clear-cut standard. Still, it identifies a major and still existing challenge in connection with applying subsequent practice as a means of treaty interpretation.[131]

In its advisory opinion on *Reservations to the Convention on Genocide,*[132] the ICJ addressed another question that has remained crucial for present-day interpreters, namely how they may identify sufficiently consistent practice that is capable of supporting a particular interpretation. In this case, the Court had to decide whether or not the effectiveness of a reservation to the Genocide Convention[133] required the assent of

[122] For the ICJ's approach to silence and omission after the adoption of the Convention in 1969, see in particular Nolte, 'Report 1—ICJ and Arbitral Tribunals' (n 54) 32–39.

[123] *Case concerning the Temple of Preah Vihear (Cambodia v Thailand)* (Merits) [1962] ICJ Rep 6.

[124] ibid 23.

[125] ibid 20 f.

[126] Cambodia was part of French Indo-China until its independence in 1953. Until 1939 and between 1946–49, Thailand was named Siam.

[127] *Temple of Preah Vihear* (n 123) 21.

[128] ibid.

[129] ibid 21 f.

[130] ibid.

[131] On the issue of silence and agreement, see 8.1.

[132] *Reservations to the Convention on Genocide* (Advisory Opinion) [1951] ICJ Rep 15.

[133] Convention on the Prevention and Punishment of the Crime of Genocide (signed 9 December 1948, entered into force 12 January 1951) 78 UNTS 277.

all the parties to the Convention. The Convention itself did not address this issue. For this reason, the Court first had recourse to the preparatory work of the Convention and emphasised its special object and purpose.[134] Next, it took account of the 'subsequent attitude' of the contracting parties,[135] ie the practice of States that had made reservations and the practice of the other contracting parties in relation to these reservations. Yet, these various forms of practice did not suffice to support one or the other interpretation.[136] On the contrary, the Court more generally indicated that it was not acceptable to randomly pick out any practice to support the desired interpretation but that interpreters must take account of the whole array of practice to a treaty and then assess whether this practice was sufficiently consistent to support a certain interpretation.[137]

In the *Case concerning Rights of Nationals of the United States of America in Morocco,*[138] the Court again refused to adopt a particular interpretation because the parties' practice that had been relied on was not sufficiently consistent. In a counter-claim, the USA had asserted that its nationals enjoyed immunity from a Moroccan consumption tax provided by a Dahir ('decree') of 28 February 1948.[139] This claim raised the question of how the value of merchandise was to be determined for customs purposes under articles 95–97 of the 1906 Act of Algeciras.[140] In this regard, both France[141] and the USA had apparently attempted to rely on the practice of the competent customs authorities to support their respective views.[142] But when the Court examined how the value of merchandise had been determined in practice, it observed that the competent authorities had failed to apply one or the other method in a consistent manner.[143] Their practice being inconsistent, it failed to support both the French and the US view.[144] Instead, the Court decided to interpret article 95 of the Act in a flexible manner so that various factors had to be taken into account when determining the value of imported goods.[145]

---

[134] *Genocide Convention* (n 132) 22, 24 f.

[135] ibid 25.

[136] ibid 25 f. As Nolte, 'Report 1—ICJ and Arbitral Tribunals' (n 54) 178 f explains, such inconsistency regularly prevented the Court from narrowing down the meaning of more general terms.

[137] *Genocide Convention* (n 132) 25 f.

[138] *Case concerning the Rights of Nationals of the United States of America and Morocco (France v USA)* [1952] ICJ Rep 176.

[139] ibid 203 f.

[140] General Act of the International Conference at Algeciras relating to the Affairs of Morocco (signed 7 April 1906, entered into force 31 December 1906) 201 CTS 39 (Act of Algeciras). As to the dispute concerning the correct method of calculation, see *Rights of Nationals* (n 138) 207 f.

[141] Morocco was a French colony until 1956.

[142] *Rights of Nationals* (n 138) 210.

[143] ibid 208 f.

[144] ibid 211.

[145] ibid. See also Nolte, 'Report 1—ICJ and Arbitral Tribunals' (n 54) 198.

As can be seen from this case, an inconsistent practice did not necessarily prevent the Court from drawing conclusions from such practice. Although the Court was unwilling to rely on such practice to adopt a particular interpretation of the contentious provisions, it nevertheless relied on it to hold that the contentious provisions must not be interpreted restrictively but accommodated more than one interpretation.[146] Moreover, this case reveals the range of actors whose conduct the Court was prepared to take into account. It considered not only practice of high organs of State as in the *Case concerning the Arbitral Award Made by the King of Spain on 23 December 1906*; the conduct of lower authorities such as customs authorities was considered relevant, too, if they were tasked with implementing the contentious provisions.

The cases mentioned above must not obscure the fact that subsequent practice was not completely uncontroversial with the judges of the Court. Shortly before the Vienna Convention was adopted, the ICJ delivered an advisory opinion on *Certain Expenses of the United Nations (Article 17, Paragraph 2, of the Charter).*[147] At first sight, the opinion is more relevant for studies on organisational practice since it is this special type of practice which the majority took into account.[148] This reliance on organisational practice was severely criticised by Judge Spender, who contended that it was misconceived to equate organisational practice with subsequent (State) practice.[149] For the purpose of this study, it is his general comments that are worth mentioning:

> The legal rationale behind what is called the principle of 'subsequent conduct' is I think evident enough. In essence it is a question of evidence, its admissibility and value. Its roots are deeply embedded in the experience of mankind.
>
> A man enters into a compact usually between himself and another. The meaning of that compact when entered into whether oral, or in writing, may well be affected, even determined, by the manner in which both parties in practice have carried it out.
>
> That is evident enough. Their joint conduct expresses their common understanding of what the terms of their compact, at the time they entered into it, were intended to mean, and thus provides direct evidence of what they did mean. That conduct on the part of both parties to a treaty should be considered on the same footing is incontestable. It provides a criterion of interpretation. It is however evident enough—despite a flimsy and questionable argument based upon what appears in *Iranian Oil Company* (*ICJ Reports* 1952, pp 106–107)—that the subsequent conduct of one party alone cannot be evidence in its favour of a common understanding of the meaning intended to be given to the text of a treaty....
>
> In the case of multilateral treaties the admissibility and value as evidence of subsequent conduct of one or more parties thereto encounter particular difficulties. If all the parties to a multilateral treaty where the parties are fixed and constant, pursue a course of subsequent

[146] See in particular ibid 178, where he explains that subsequent conduct not necessarily concretises particular terms of a treaty but may also have the effect of interpreting terms more broadly.

[147] *Certain Expenses of the United Nations (Article 17, Paragraph 2, of the Charter)* (Advisory Opinion) [1962] ICJ Rep 151.

[148] ibid 160, 165.

[149] ibid 185 f (diss op Judge Spender). As this study does not focus on the special case of organisational practice, it does not go further into this criticism.

> conduct in their attitude to the text of the treaty, and that course of conduct leads to an inference, and one inference only, as to their common intention and understanding at the time they entered into the treaty as to the meaning of its text, the probative value of their conduct again is manifest. If however only one or some but not all of them by subsequent conduct interpret the text in a certain manner, that conduct stands upon the same footing as the unilateral conduct of one party to a bilateral treaty. The conduct of such one or more could not of itself have any probative value or provide a criterion for judicial interpretation.[150]

This quotation reveals that Judge Spender deemed it necessary to remind his fellow judges that subsequent practice must be taken for what it is, namely a piece of evidence to elucidate the 'common understanding' of the parties to the treaty regarding its true meaning. It was therefore obvious to him that subsequent practice enjoyed full and unreserved probative value only if a given practice could somehow be attributed to *all* contracting parties. Not denying that unilateral conduct may play a role in the interpretation of treaties, Judge Spender consequently emphasised the reduced probative value of unilateral practice as opposed to practice (be it active conduct or true acquiescence) of all the parties.

Thus, Judge Spender endorsed the idea of two different types of subsequent practice. According to his reasoning, subsequent practice may, on the one hand, qualify as a primary means of interpretation standing 'on the same footing' as the original treaty. On the other hand, 'other' subsequent practice, ie practice that cannot somehow be attributed to all parties, may qualify as a supplementary means of interpretation, whose reduced probative value not only justifies but even mandates conceding to it a lower interpretative weight.

2.2.3 Conclusion

Both the PCIJ and the ICJ acknowledged that subsequent practice can help to elucidate the correct meaning of the terms of a treaty. Still, neither of them frequently had recourse to it until the Vienna Convention was adopted. Moreover, neither of them seems to have often relied on subsequent agreements. Since the number of cases in which the PCIJ and the ICJ relied on subsequent practice is rather limited, too, inferences about their general approach to subsequent practice before the adoption of the Vienna Convention ultimately remain matters of conjecture. Nonetheless, it is possible to carefully draw some provisional conclusions.

The PCIJ's recourse to subsequent practice can be linked to the same idea that prevailed in international legal doctrine, namely that the one who created a legal rule naturally and as a matter of course possesses the right to determine its meaning. Nevertheless, the Court mostly treated subsequent practice as a subsidiary, auxiliary means of interpretation.[151] This may explain why the Court's references to subsequent practice tended to be rather cursory. Since the interpretations which the Court intended to adopt had regularly already been established and substantiated by

[150] ibid 190 f (diss op Judge Spender).

[151] Nolte, 'Report 1—ICJ and Arbitral Tribunals' (n 54) 176, 180.

relying on other means of interpretation, it was not necessary to go into details and to examine the pertinent practice more closely. Furthermore, the Court regularly referred to the practice of all instead of just few parties. This suggests that it either required such practice to be at least based on the agreement of all parties or that, in the extreme, all parties must have participated in it.

The ICJ's jurisprudence differs from that of its predecessor in terms of quality but not of quantity. Although it had not unequivocally abandoned the idea of subsequent practice being subordinate to other means of interpretation, the ICJ adopted a more sophisticated approach to subsequent practice than the PCIJ. In particular, it seemed to be more sensitive towards the difficulties concerning practice as a means of interpretation. In *Reservations to the Convention on Genocide,* for instance, the Court implicitly criticised reliance on few examples of practice without having conducted a thorough and comprehensive analysis of all potentially relevant instances of practice.[152] While it took account of practice originating from different levels of State hierarchy, it emphasised that all instances of practice, taken together, must be sufficiently consistent to support one particular interpretation. A special issue that emerged in the *Case concerning the Arbitral Award Made by the King of Spain on 23 December 1906*[153] and in the *Case concerning the Temple of Preah Vihear*[154] is the interpretative value of silence. In this regard, the Court stressed that silence in itself could not be considered as relevant but that its interpretative value depended on and must be assessed in the light of the circumstances of the individual case.

2.3 Domestic Jurisprudence

A preliminary survey indicated that German, Swiss, and US jurisprudence would offer the largest body of relevant case law. Domestic courts in other jurisdiction, in contrast, hardly ever relied on subsequent conduct before the Vienna Convention was adopted. For this reason, this Chapter examines, by way of example, decisions of German (2.3.1), Swiss (2.3.2), and US courts (2.3.3) prior to the adoption of the Convention in 1969. Since this study concentrates on decisions of the highest domestic courts, the following examples are equally taken from high courts only.

2.3.1 Germany

To start with, this Chapter identifies and analyses precursors to subsequent agreements and subsequent practice in the jurisprudence of German supreme courts. The courts whose jurisprudence has been taken into account are the same as those

[152] For the analysis of this case, see 49 f.

[153] For the analysis of this case, see 47 f.

[154] For the analysis of this case, see 49 f.

examined in Part II, namely the Federal Constitutional Court (*Bundesverfassungsgericht;* BVerfG), the Imperial Court of Justice (*Reichsgericht;* RG) and the Federal Court of Justice (*Bundesgerichtshof;* BGH), the Federal Administrative Court (*Bundesverwaltungsgericht;* BVerwG), the Imperial Fiscal Court (*Reichsfinanzhof;* RFH) and the Federal Fiscal Court (*Bundesfinanzhof;* BFH). Although these courts produced a large body of case law on issues of treaty interpretation, arguments based on subsequent practice emerged in two BGH cases only. References to subsequent agreements, in contrast, have even been non-existent.

The first case that mentioned some form of subsequent practice is a decision of the German Federal Court of Justice on the interpretation of the 1874 German–Swiss Extradition Treaty.[155] Article 1(1) of said Treaty stipulated that the contracting parties 'undertook' to extradite certain persons who had committed specific crimes. Para 2, in contrast, provided that the parties 'could' also extradite persons who had only attempted to commit a crime. The different wording of these paragraphs—'undertake' and 'could'—raised the question of whether extradition for attempted crimes was at the discretion of the contracting parties or whether para 2 equally contained an obligation to extradite. To resolve this question, the Court decided to consider the parties' 'practical construction' of the contentious provision.[156]

First of all, it noted that the German *Reichstag* had interpreted para 2 so as to contain an obligation,[157] whereas a higher regional court had favoured the opposite view.[158] Thus, Germany's internal practice had been split on this question. And while the Swiss Federal Council (*Bundesrat*) had refused to recognise any obligation to extradite,[159] German and Swiss administrative practice in executing the Treaty supported the *Reichstag's* view. Although there had been several extradition proceedings which could have caused the same dispute as in the present case, the parties had apparently never addressed this issue. In the end, the Court concluded that both parties must have believed that they were obliged to extradite even in the case of attempted crimes.[160] Dismissing both purely internal German and Swiss practice, the Court attached decisive weight to the parties' common ('external') application and interpretation of the contentious provision.[161] This case is instructive in three respects. Firstly, it shows that the German Federal Court of Justice was prepared to consider different forms of State practice originating from different actors. Secondly, it distinguished between internal and external practice. And thirdly, it

[155] Treaty between the German Empire and Switzerland on Extradition and Mutual Assistance in Criminal Matters (signed 24 January 1874, entered into force 20 July 1874) RGBl 1874, 113 (1874 German–Swiss Extradition Treaty).

[156] BGHSt 10, 221, 224 f.

[157] ibid 223.

[158] ibid.

[159] ibid 225.

[160] ibid.

[161] ibid.

stressed the importance of uniform practice by refusing to consider internal practice that failed to be sufficiently uniform.

The second German decision that mentioned subsequent practice concerned the 1955 Convention on the Settlement of Matters Arising out of the War and the Occupation.[162] Under article 7 of the Convention, Germany undertook to legally recognise judgments and decisions in criminal matters rendered by authorities or courts of the three Allied Powers in- and outside of Germany. Because article 6(11) of the Convention provided that article 7 did not apply to crimes against humanity and war crimes, it was questionable whether this recognition also applied to judgments and decisions concerning these crimes. Mainly relying on the drafting history of the Convention, the Court was convinced that it did not.[163] To support its conclusion, it shortly added that this interpretation was in conformity with German and British practice. To exemplify this practice, the Court mentioned a decree issued by the German Federal Minister of Justice[164] and a letter from the British Embassy in Bonn to the German prosecuter's office in Hamburg.[165] But while the Court acknowledged that these statements were relevant for the interpretation of the Convention,[166] it apparently considered it neither necessary nor even useful to examine whether there was any practice by the other parties to the Convention.

Departing from its earlier approach to subsequent practice, this selectiveness may indicate that the Court considered it superfluous to establish the agreement of *all parties*. In the alternative, it may, however, also illustrate that the Court regarded subsequent practice as carrying interpretative weight in itself. This would mean that the Court did not deem it necessary to even try to link subsequent practice to the parties' agreement.

2.3.2 *Switzerland*

The Swiss Federal Supreme Court is the only Swiss supreme court that apparently took account of subsequent conduct before the Vienna Convention was adopted. In sum, the total number of relevant cases does not approach that of the US Supreme Court.[167] But in contrast to its US and German counterparts, the Swiss Federal Supreme Court not only took account of subsequent practice but even considered a subsequent agreement in one case.

---

[162] Convention on the Settlement of Matters Arising out of the War and the Occupation (signed 26 May 1952, entered into force 5 May 1955) 322 UNTS 219.

[163] BGHSt 12, 36, 39 f.

[164] ibid 41.

[165] ibid.

[166] ibid.

[167] See below at 2.3.3.

An early example of subsequent practice in Swiss jurisprudence is a judgment on the 1874 German–Swiss Extradition Treaty. Under this Treaty, the parties could request extradition of persons who had either committed one of the offences listed in the Treaty or who had participated in one of these offences. The person whose extradition Germany had requested had, however, only aided and abetted someone who had committed an extraditable offence. Because such aiding and abetting was not listed among the extraditable offences, the question arose whether the term 'participation' could be interpreted so as to include both participation stricto sensu and aiding and abetting.[168] Preferring an extensive interpretation, the Court principally relied on the parties' practice under the Treaty as it was reflected in earlier extradition proceedings that had raised the same issue.[169] In these proceedings, Germany had complied with a Swiss request and thus indicated—as had Switzerland through its request in the present case—that it interpreted the term 'participation' in an extensive way.[170] Besides, Switzerland had even reconfirmed this interpretation by unconditionally accepting the extradition and by reporting the case in the Federal Council's annual report to the Federal Assembly (*Bundesversammlung*).[171]

In a judgment on the interpretation of article 1(A)(2) Refugee Convention,[172] the Court examined subsequent practice in a similarly detailed fashion. Article 1(A)(2) Refugee Convention stipulates that the term 'refugee' shall apply to any person who, as a result of events occurring before 1 January 1951 and owing to well-founded fear of being persecuted for reasons of race, religion, nationality, membership of a particular social group or political opinion, is outside the country of his nationality and is unable or, owing to such fear, is unwilling to avail himself of the protection of that country. At issue was whether an alleged Hungarian refugee, who had fled Hungary due to the events occurring in Hungary in autumn 1956 and who had later married a German national, could be considered a refugee or not.[173] Despite the clear wording of the contentious provision, the Court held that the Hungarian did satisfy the requirements for refugee status because the temporal limit included events which had occurred after 1 January 1951 if they were at least caused by events having occurred before this date.[174]

[168] BGer, Judgment of 14 June 1912, BGE 38 I 165, 170 f.

[169] ibid 171.

[170] ibid 173.

[171] ibid.

[172] Convention relating to the Status of Refugees (signed 28 July 1951, entered into force 22 April 1954) 189 UNTS 137 (Refugee Convention).

[173] The question of the Hungarian's refugee status was relevant since the Court's jurisdiction for divorcing the marriage between him and his German wife depended on this status. The Protocol relating to the Status of Refugees (signed 31 January 1967, entered into force 4 October 1967) 606 UNTS 267 (Refugee Protocol), which later removed this temporal limitation, had not yet entered into force for Switzerland when the judgment was delivered.

[174] BGer, Judgment of 13 October 1967, BGE 93 II 354, 362.

In order to justify this extensive interpretation, the Court referred to various examples of subsequent practice to the Convention.[175] As it observed, the Swiss Federal Council had approved a 1957 report by the Swiss Federal Department of Justice and Police that endorsed this extensive interpretation.[176] Besides, the UNHCR and most European member States in the UNHCR Executive Committee (ExCom) had equally confirmed this interpretation.[177] Next, the Court concentrated on German practice because the defendant, the Hungarian's wife, was a German national and Germany therefore had, in the Court's view, a special interest in the case.[178] To illustrate German practice, the Court analysed judicial practice, internal administrative practice, and an official circular by the German Home Office.[179] Although it acknowledged that practice by political and administrative agencies was not legally binding as such,[180] the Court nevertheless concluded that it could hardly reject an interpretation supported by the practice of those contracting parties that had an interest in the case.[181]

At first sight, this case suggests that the Court approached subsequent practice in a reflected manner. Nevertheless, its line of reasoning reveals some weaknesses. On the one hand, the Court critically weighed the practice before it by arguing that German practice was particularly important and by focusing on the European member States in the UNHCR ExCom.[182] This implies that the Court sought to present its practice-based arguments convincingly. As the interpretation adopted by the Court appears to go beyond the ordinary meaning of the contentious provision, the burden to justify its interpretation must have been comparatively high. It is therefore not surprising that the Court attempted to demonstrate that its interpretation was in accordance with the parties' subsequent practice. On the other hand, the Court seems to have failed to notice that its interpretation might also affect other contracting parties whose practice it had disregarded; besides, it had not addressed the fact that the UNHCR ExCom is a subsidiary organ of the UNGA[183] so that it may be more convincing to consider statements in the Committee as contributing to organisational practice instead of practice of individual contracting parties to the Refugee Convention.[184] As these considerations relate to the basic question of how

175 ibid 360 f.

176 ibid 360.

177 ibid.

178 ibid 361.

179 ibid.

180 ibid 362.

181 ibid.

182 European member States in the UNHCR ExCom had a special interest in the case because they were particularly affected by Hungarian refugees due to their geographical location.

183 UNGA Res 1166 (XII) (26 November 1957) UN Doc A/RES/1166(XII).

184 As regards organisational practice, see also the case of the OECD at 7.3 f.

many parties must agree on a particular interpretation, the Court's reasoning implies that it had not (yet) developed a more elaborate approach to practice as a means of interpretation.

A year before the Vienna Convention was adopted, the Swiss Supreme Court delivered a judgment in which it not only relied on subsequent practice but also on a subsequent agreement. This case concerned the formalities for sending debt collection instruments between Switzerland and Italy. At issue was whether such instruments could be sent by simple postal delivery or whether their delivery had to satisfy higher standards. The delivery of debt collection instruments was governed by the 1905[185] and 1954 Conventions on Civil Procedure[186] (which both Italy and Switzerland had ratified) and by an establishment and consular agreement concluded between Italy and Switzerland in 1868.[187] Articles 6 of the 1905 and 1954 Conventions stipulated that debt collection instruments could be delivered by standard post if two conditions were met: first, if there was no agreement between the parties prohibiting postal delivery; and second, if the party on whose territory delivery was to take place had not objected. Discussing whether there was any agreement prohibiting postal delivery between Switzerland and Italy,[188] the Court referred to an Italian–Swiss Protocol implementing the 1868 agreement on consular matters. Article III of this Protocol stipulated that Italian and Swiss courts should communicate directly with each other in all matters concerning delivery of requests in civil and criminal matters.

Read on its own, this provision did not necessarily suggest that it also applied to service of process. An exchange of notes between the Italian Embassy in Bern and the Swiss Federal Department on Police and Justice, however, endorsed said interpretation.[189] The agreement reflected in this exchange of notes had even been subsequently confirmed by circulars sent to the cantonal governments, by the Federal Council's annual report, and in a footnote contained in the Revised Compilation of Federal Acts and Ordinances for the Years 1848–1947.[190] Eventually adopting this interpretation, the Court attached great weight to this evidence. Notably, the Court did not solely rely on the exchange of notes, although it was drafted in clear terms. Instead, it recounted additional examples of practice to reconfirm both the existence and the correct content of the parties' agreement.

---

[185] Convention relating to Civil Procedure (signed 17 July 1905, entered into force 27 April 1909) 199 CTS 1.

[186] Convention relating to Civil Procedure (signed 1 March 1954, entered into force 12 April 1957) 286 UNTS 265.

[187] Establishment and Consular Agreement (Italy–Switzerland) (signed 22 July 1868, entered into force 1 May 1869) BBl 1868 III 416.

[188] BGer, Decision of 22 May 1968, BGE 94 III 35, 38 f.

[189] ibid 40.

[190] BBl 1912 I 527 f No 19; BS 12 p 278 No 2; BS 12 p 314 No 2.

2.3.3 United States of America

The analysis of US Supreme Court cases closes the overview of precursors to subsequent agreements and subsequent practice in domestic jurisprudence. Its case law on matters of treaty interpretation reveals that the Court took account of subsequent practice but not of subsequent agreements. On closer examination, these references to subsequent practice display three distinct features that are addressed in greater detail below. Firstly, the Court often referred to subsequent practice interchangeably with the more general notion of 'practical construction'. Under this notion, the Court considered how a treaty had been applied in practice in order to draw conclusions about how the respective provision must be interpreted.[191] Second, the Court did not confine itself to cursory references to subsequent practice but tended to closely analyse various forms of potentially relevant conduct. And lastly, the Court often favoured the interpretation that was supported by US practice.

A case which illustrates the high degree of overlap, if not identity, between 'practical construction' and subsequent practice is *Pigeon River Imp, Slide & Boom Co v Charles W Cox, Ltd.* This case concerned the interpretation of article 2 of the Webster-Ashburton Treaty.[192] Article 2 stipulates that all water communications and all usual portages along the line from Lake Superior to the Lake of the Woods, and also Grand portage, from the shore of Lake Superior to the Pigeon river, as now and actually used, should be free and open to the use of citizens and subjects of both countries. Nevertheless, Pigeon River Company (a US corporation) had demanded tolls from Charles W Cox, Ltd (a Canadian corporation) for the use of improvements which Pigeon River Company had made in the Pigeon River, a boundary stream between Minnesota (USA) and the Province of Ontario (Canada). Pointing out that article 2 of the Treaty guaranteed that water communications be free and open,[193] the Canadian corporation had refused to pay the tolls. Pigeon River Company, however, had contended that the Pigeon River had been incapable of use prior to the Company's improvements and that the guarantee of free and open use under article 2 of the Treaty was qualified by the words 'as now and actually used'. The River having been innavigable when the Treaty was concluded, article 2 did not apply and its charge of tolls was not prohibited by the Treaty.[194]

The contentious expression 'as now and actually used' was in itself rather ambiguous. For this reason, the Court 'look[ed] to the practical construction that has been

[191] See in particular *Pigeon River Imp, Slide & Boom Co v Charles W Cox, Ltd* 291 US 138, 45 S Ct 361 (1934).

[192] Treaty to Define and Settle the Boundaries between the Territories of the United States and the Possessions of Her Britannic Majesty in North America, for the Final Suppression of the African Slave Trade, and for the Giving up of Criminals, Fugitive from Justice in Certain Cases (USA–UK) (signed 9 August 1842, entered into force 13 October 1842) 8 Stat 572 (Webster-Ashburton Treaty).

[193] *Pigeon River* (n 191) 152.

[194] ibid.

placed upon it'.[195] Next, it closely examined how the contracting parties themselves had dealt with the question of improvement works and tolls. On the part of the USA, it observed that the legislature of Minnesota had in fact authorised the charge of toll,[196] that the US Congress had acquiesced in Pigeon River Company's improvements,[197] and that the Secretary of the Interior had imposed no regulations or conditions on the improvement project.[198] In the Court's view, these acts could not be taken as reflecting the intention of the USA to modify or even violate the Treaty but rather constituted forms of perfectly permissible practical construction.[199] On the part of Canada, the Court noted that the Province of Ontario had equally authorised complementary works and tolls for their use on the Canadian side of the river and that even the Canadian Supreme Court had subsequently confirmed this practice.[200] In addition, it pointed out that neither Canada nor the USA had ever claimed that the other party was in breach of the Treaty due to authorising the charge of tolls.[201] Based on these observations, the Court eventually held that article 2 of the Treaty could indeed not be interpreted so as to prohibit the tolls charged by Pigeon River Company.[202]

In this case, the Court employed the notion of 'practical construction' to accurately take account of both parties' subsequent practice. In many cases involving an analysis of 'practical construction', the Court even announced that it would take account of the conduct of all parties to the respective treaty.[203] Nevertheless, cases discussing 'practical construction' must be treated with care. Despite prior announcements to the contrary, the Court often only elaborated on the conduct of one or few parties or uncompromisingly gave priority to US practice.[204] This can be seen in the case of *Factor v Laubenheimer*.[205] Here the Court was asked to determine whether the UK could request extradition of the petitioner for a behaviour that was criminalised in the UK but not in Illinois (USA) where the petitioner had been captured and from where extradition was sought. In the petitioner's view, extradition was unlawful by virtue of the double-criminality rule under the Webster-Ashburton Treaty as supplemented by the Blaine-Pauncefote Convention.[206]

---

[195] ibid 158.

[196] ibid.

[197] ibid 159.

[198] ibid.

[199] ibid 160 f.

[200] ibid 161.

[201] ibid.

[202] ibid 163.

[203] See eg *Ross v McIntyre* 140 US 453, 467, 11 S Ct 897 (1891); *Kolovrat v Oregon* 366 US 187, 194, 81 S Ct 922 (1961); *Sullivan v Kidd* 254 US 433, 442 f, 41 S Ct 158 (1921); *Nielsen v Johnson* 279 US 47, 52 f, 49 S Ct 223 (1929).

[204] See eg *Ross* (n 203) 467.

[205] *Factor v Laubenheimer* 290 US 276, 54 S Ct 191 (1933).

[206] Extradition Convention between the United States of America and Her Britannic Majesty (signed 12 July 1889, entered into force 4 April 1890) 26 Stat 1508 (Blaine-Pauncefote Convention).

The pertinent provisions of these treaties being rather ambiguous, the Court decided to look at the diplomatic correspondence of the contracting parties as well as their practical construction.[207] Notably, the Court mainly focused on US practice and largely ignored that of the UK. Admitting that this construction was not 'conclusive',[208] it nevertheless relied on an interpretation by the US State Department that was contained in diplomatic correspondence.[209] That this interpretation conflicted with a previous court order, ie that US practice, taken as a whole, was far from being uniform, did not matter to the Court. As regards UK practice, the Court matter-of-factly remarked that the UK government had never 'expressly yielded' to the US Department's interpretation.[210]

Thus, the Court displayed a very deferential attitude towards the interpretation adopted by the US executive. This deference was promptly criticised by three Justices in a dissenting opinion. Calling attention to UK practice, they demonstrated that the UK had consistently advocated the very opposite interpretation.[211] Moreover, the dissenters questioned the legitimacy of the practice relied on by the majority by stressing that the author of the pertinent correspondence had been personally prejudiced and that his interpretation had in fact never been followed in practice.[212] In sum, the dissenters revealed two major weaknesses of the majority's line of argument. Firstly, they pointed out that the majority had disregarded relevant UK practice by unduly concentrating on the US executive. And secondly, they showed that the majority, by deferring to the interpretation adopted by the US executive at any price, had concealed or overlooked the fact that this interpretation did not even reflect the view of the US executive as a whole.

In *Ross v McIntyre*, the Court took a similarly deferential approach. This case raised the question of whether certain provisions of the Japanese–US Treaty on Commerce and Consuls[213] were applicable alongside a treaty concluded one year later.[214] The answer depended on article 12 of the later Treaty, which revoked the earlier Treaty because all of its provisions were incorporated into the later one. This provision allowed for two different interpretations: the first to the effect that the prior Treaty was completely revoked, the second to the effect that the revocation was limited to those provisions that were incorporated into the later. Emphasising the 'practical construction given to the alleged revocation by the authorities of both countries', the Court eventually took the second view.[215] But in substantiating its

207 *Factor* (n 205) 294 f.

208 ibid 295.

209 ibid 295 f.

210 ibid 298.

211 ibid 317–21 (diss op Butler, Brandeis, and Roberts JJ).

212 ibid 319 f (diss op Butler, Brandeis, and Roberts JJ).

213 Treaty on Commerce and Consuls (Japan–USA) (signed 17 June 1857, entered into force 17 June 1857) 11 Stat 723.

214 Treaty of Amity and Commerce (Japan–USA) (signed 29 July 1858, entered into force 4 July 1859) 12 Stat 1056.

215 *Ross* (n 203) 467.

motives for doing so, it only elaborated on the US side. In this regard, it referred to consular regulations of 1888, correspondence between the US Minister to Japan and the US Secretary of State, and legislation adopted by Congress to implement the later Treaty.[216] Having analysed this material, the Court apparently considered it futile to enquire how Japanese authorities had construed the contentious provision in practice because it did not mention Japanese practice at all. Consequently, the Court once again did not, as it had originally announced, examine the practice of the authorities of both countries but exclusively discussed how the USA had unilaterally interpreted the Treaties.

A final example of the Court's deferential attitude is the case of *Charlton v Kelly*,[217] which differs from the cases just described in that the Court at least mentioned the other party's practice. Nonetheless, it eventually held that the interpretation reflected in US practice should prevail. This case concerned the interpretation of the 1868 US–Italian Extradition Treaty.[218] As the Treaty only referred to 'persons' without explicitly excluding citizens, Italy had asked the USA to extradite an American citizen. The petitioner, however, had argued that the Treaty had to be interpreted so as not to allow a State to extradite its own citizens. The petitioner's view was supported by the subsequent practice of Italy, which was reflected in correspondence between the Italian Foreign Minister and the US Secretary of State. This correspondence revealed that Italy had refused to extradite its own citizens under the Treaty in the past.[219]

Nevertheless, the Court did not to attach weight to this practice and instead favoured the opposite interpretation. Its preferred construction was supported by the consistent practice of the USA—both under the 1868 Treaty and under extradition treaties with other States—only to refuse extradition of its citizens if the respective treaty explicitly provided for such an exception. Moreover, the Court pointed out that the USA had protested against the Italian position.[220] Although it acknowledged that the construction of a treaty by the political department of the government was not conclusive, it nonetheless attached 'much weight' to the practice of the USA.[221] Italy, in contrast, was considered to have possibly breached the Treaty with the interpretation it had so far adhered to.[222] But since the 1868 Treaty did not expressly stipulate whether or not its parties were obliged to surrender their own citizens, the interpretation eventually favoured by the Court was not the only conceivable

---

[216] ibid 467–69.

[217] *Charlton v Kelly* 229 US 447, 11 S Ct 897 (1913).

[218] Convention on the Surrender of Criminals (Italy–USA) (signed 23 March 1868, entered into force 17 September 1868) 15 Stat 629 (1868 Italian–US Extradition Treaty), as amended by the Convention between the United States of America and His Majesty the King of Italy (signed 11 June 1884, entered into force 24 April 1885) 24 Stat 1001.

[219] *Charlton* (n 217) 465 f.

[220] ibid 466 f.

[221] ibid 468.

[222] ibid 475.

one. Notwithstanding the Court's general tendency to pay deference to US practice, neither US nor Italian practice appeared more convincing. The parties' practice being inconclusive, the Court had therefore better not based its interpretation on any of them but solely relied on other means of interpretation instead.

2.3.4 Conclusion

Before the Vienna Convention was adopted, domestic courts relied less frequently on subsequent agreements and subsequent practice than international judicial dispute settlement bodies. Apart from jurisprudence in Germany, Switzerland, and the USA, references to subsequent agreements and subsequent practice were very rare or even non-existent. Although the reasons eventually remain a matter of speculation, one may wonder whether this was because domestic courts were largely unfamiliar with subsequent agreements and subsequent practice as potentially useful means of treaty interpretation. In the alternative, one can also imagine that some courts saw no need to consider subsequent agreements and subsequent practice when interpreting a treaty. In other words, the adoption of the Vienna Convention and the growing acceptance that its rules of interpretation reflect customary international law may have had two effects: they either raised awareness among domestic courts for the usefulness of these means of interpretation or created a feeling of obligation to employ them—irrespective of whether or not the individual State has already ratified the Convention.

In Germany, the Federal Court of Justice seemed to be the only court to mention subsequent practice at all. Yet, the Court did not consider it necessary to justify relying on subsequent practice but did so quite naturally. The way in which the Court took account of subsequent practice was far from being uniform. In one case, the Court discussed various instances of practice of both contracting parties and carefully distinguished between internal or intra-State practice and external or inter-State practice. Since the parties' internal practice was inconsistent and in part conflicted with their external practice, the Court favoured the interpretation supported by the latter. In the other case, its examination of subsequent practice was more superficial and selective. Although the pertinent treaty was a multilateral one, the Court only considered the practice of two parties and did not even ask whether the other parties had also generated relevant practice. Looking for agreement between all parties in the one but not in the other case, one can therefore note that the Court had not yet developed a coherent approach to subsequent practice but rather relied on it in an intuitive way.

The pre-VCLT approach to subsequent agreements and subsequent practice displayed by Swiss supreme courts hardly differs from that of their German counterparts. The Swiss Federal Supreme Court was the only Swiss supreme court that relied on subsequent practice at all. But in contrast to the German Federal Court of Justice, it also had recourse to a subsequent agreement in one case. Like its German counterpart, the Swiss Federal Supreme Court refrained from explaining why subsequent conduct should influence the interpretation of treaties. The comparatively detailed way in which the Court discussed subsequent agreements and subsequent practice implies that it had indeed reflected on the interpretative weight of subsequent agreements and subsequent practice in different situations. Its jurisprudence suggests that the Court considered it important to unequivocally demonstrate that the practice of all parties (in the case of bilateral treaties) or all parties that had a special interest in the case (in the case of multilateral treaties) supported the contentious interpretation.

The largest body of case law on subsequent practice—before the Vienna Convention was adopted—can be found in the jurisprudence of the US Supreme Court. Its jurisprudence illustrates that the Court was prepared to take account of various forms of practice and especially of executive practice. These forms of practice mostly included unilateral practice such as governmental instructions, official interpretations by members of governmental departments, diplomatic notes by governmental agencies, unilateral statements by *chargés d'affaires*, or official reports of commissions. Bilateral practice, in contrast, mostly took the form of diplomatic correspondence between the respective contracting parties. Looking for precursors to subsequent practice in the jurisprudence of the US Supreme Court, it is almost impossible not to mention 'practical construction'. Announcing to consider the parties' practical construction, the Court examined how one party, some parties, or all parties had applied the treaty. Its understanding of 'practical construction' therefore also covered the conduct of all parties to the treaty and thus overlapped with subsequent practice as a means of treaty interpretation.

Such overlap, however, has not been the rule. In many cases, the Court in fact invoked the parties' 'practical construction' to pay deference to the US executive. Hence it would be mistaken to generally equate 'practical construction' with subsequent practice. Even if the Court had initially announced to analyse the practice of all parties to a treaty, it sometimes exclusively concentrated on US practice or considered this practice decisive. Especially when the Court had identified an interpretation adopted by the US executive, it almost certainly disregarded any other practice, be it that of other branches of the State or that of other parties to the treaty.

Chapter 3
Subsequent Agreements and Subsequent Practice in Context: The 1969 VCLT

Subsequent agreements and subsequent practice are now explicitly listed in article 31(3)(a) and (b) VCLT. In addition, recourse may be had to 'other' subsequent conduct, ie agreements and practice that do not meet all criteria of the general rule, under article 32 VCLT.[1] To fully understand the significance of subsequent agreements and subsequent practice under the Convention, it is necessary to consider them as part of a broader context. Subsequent agreements and subsequent practice within the meaning of the Convention do not operate in a legal vacuum but, ideally, in accordance with the Convention's scope of application and alongside other means of interpretation that jointly influence the result of the interpretative process. In any event, it is the Convention itself which, in its article 31(1), stresses the importance of the context. For these reasons, Chap. 3 provides an overview of the Convention as such and the Vienna rules of interpretation in particular.

To that end, it briefly recounts the genesis of the Convention and the Vienna rules of interpretation (3.1) before elucidating the interrelationship between articles 31 and 32 VCLT and customary international law rules of treaty interpretation. (3.2). Highlighting the ILC's role in drafting the Convention, it is asked whether the oft-repeated dictum that these provisions are a reflection of customary international law might actually be oversimplistic. To conclude this contextual overview, Chap. 3 sets out the Vienna rules of interpretation as a whole (3.3) by examining the 'general rule' under article 31 VCLT (3.3.1), the 'supplementary means of interpretation' under article 32 VCLT (3.3.2), and finally the relationship of these various means of interpretation (3.3.3).

[1] Draft conclusion 1(4) in ILC, 'Report of the International Law Commission on the Work of its 65th Session' (6 May–7 June and 8 July–9 August 2013) UN Doc A/68/10, 13.

K. Berner, *Subsequent Agreements and Subsequent Practice in Domestic Courts*, Beiträge zum ausländischen öffentlichen Recht und Völkerrecht, https://doi.org/10.1007/978-3-662-54937-7_3

3.1 Genesis of the Vienna Convention and its Rules of Interpretation

Nowadays, international practitioners and academics alike quite naturally refer to the Vienna Convention. But when the ILC placed this topic on its agenda in 1949, it appeared very unlikely that the international community would ever succeed in codifying the law of treaties. And indeed, more than 30 years passed since that date until the Convention entered into force on 27 January 1980. Even Trygve Lie, UN Secretary General (UNSG) in 1949, who had recommended the Commission to take up this topic,[2] had noted with some foresight that

> there is hardly a branch of the law of treaties which is free from doubt and, in some cases, from confusion .... The field of interpretation of treaties continues to be overgrown with the weed of technical rules of construction which can be used—and are frequently used—in support of opposing contentions.[3]

Undeniably the most time-consuming part of these 30 years was taken up by the work in the ILC. During the 17 years until the ILC submitted its final draft on the law of treaties to the UN General Assembly (UNGA), four Special Rapporteurs had been seized with this topic: James Brierly (1949–1952), Sir Hersch Lauterpacht (1952–1954), Sir Gerald Fitzmaurice (1954–1961), and Sir Humphrey Waldock (1961–1966).[4] Although all of them made important contributions during their terms of office, it was not until Waldock's appointment that the ILC changed priorities and finally decided to set the law of treaties high on its agenda.[5] While the reports prepared by Waldock's predecessors received scant attention,[6] the ILC

---

[2] UNGA, 'Survey of International Law in relation to the Work of Codification of the International Law Commission: Preparatory Work within the Purview of Article 18, Paragraph 1, of the International Law Commission—Memorandum Submitted by the Secretary-General' (1949) UN Doc A/CN.4/1/Rev.1, 51 f.

[3] ibid 52.

[4] Notably, all Special Rapporteurs on the law of treaties were British international lawyers, see Ian Sinclair, 'The Vienna Conference on the Law of Treaties' (1970) 19 ICLQ 47, 50. This peculiarity may raise the question of whether their nationality and the related familiarity with the common law legal system influenced the final outcome of the ILC's work on the law of treaties.

[5] Until Waldock was appointed as Special Rapporteur, topics other than the law of treaties took up most of the ILC's time. The Commission itself admitted that 'it ha[d] hitherto been prevented from seriously taking up the subject of the law of treaties'. See ILC, 'Report of the International Law Commission on the Work of its 11th Session' (20 April–26 June 1959) [1959-II] YBILC 87, 88 [8]. See also Oliver Lissitzyn, 'Efforts to Codify or Restate the Law of Treaties' (1962) 62 Col LR 1166, 1167. See further Mark Villiger, *Commentary on the* 1969 *Vienna Convention on the Law of Treaties* (Martinus Nijhoff 2009) 34 [13], who remarks that '[w]hile the Convention may bear only few signs of earlier drafts and reports, there can be no doubt that it was moulded mainly by Sir Humphrey.'

[6] cf Sir Humphrey Waldock, 'First Report on the Law of Treaties' [1962-II] YBILC 27, 28 f.

discussed the six reports submitted by him at great length. At the same time, the ILC fundamentally revised its approach to the law of treaties. With Waldock's appointment, it was settled that the Commission's work should ultimately result in a draft convention instead of a code—a point on which there had previously been many debates.[7] Apart from settling these debates, Waldock's work warrants special attention for another reason. Even at that time, some voices in legal literature and even in the Commission had doubted that treaty interpretation was a suitable subject to be dealt with in any convention on the law of treaties.[8] Waldock, however, also solved this point of controversy.[9]

Having devoted his first two reports to other topics,[10] Waldock submitted his first draft provisions on treaty interpretation with his 'Third Report' in 1964. Naturally, he could not build on his predecessors' reports since they had refrained from covering interpretation. Nevertheless, Waldock did have some sources of inspiration. As he himself explained,[11] he was inspired by the work of the IDI[12] and studies on the jurisprudence of the ICJ by Sir Gerald Fitzmaurice (in his private capacity).[13] Altogether, Waldock's first draft provisions consisted of six articles.[14] In respect of

[7] Sir Gerald Fitzmaurice, 'First Report on the Law of Treaties' [1956-II] YBILC 104, 106 f. Fitzmaurice believed that 'any codification of the law of treaties, such as the Commission is called upon to carry out, should take the form of a *code* and not of a draft convention.' In his view, it was simply inappropriate to conclude a treaty dealing with the law of treaties because such treaty would be governed by the very rules it stipulated; besides, he considered that a treaty was the right instrument for stipulating rights and duties, not, however, for setting out principles and abstract rules as dominated the existing (customary) law of treaties. In the light of his scepticism towards elaborating a draft convention, the Sixth Committee decided to leave this question open for the time being. The reasons for ultimately opting for a draft convention were twofold: First, a convention promised to be more effective in 'consolidating the law', and second, the procedure to concluding a convention should give new States a chance influence the formation of the law of treaties. See Waldock, 'First Report' (n 6) 160 [17].

[8] See eg Taslim Elias and Gilberto Amado in ILC, 'Summary Records of the 16th Session of the International Law Commission' (11 May–24 July 1964) [1964-I] YBILC 1, 22 [24], 23 [39]. cf, by way of contrast, Chairman Roberto Ago in ibid 23 [34], who objected that the 'interpretation of treaties… was of capital importance for the Commission's work and for the law of treaties in general' and added that 'certainty of the law of treaties depended mainly on certainty of the rules of interpretation.'

[9] cf Sir Humphrey Waldock in ibid 275 [2].

[10] His first report of 1962 covered conclusion, entry into force, and registration of treaties whereas his second report of 1963 dealt with validity, duration, and termination of treaties.

[11] Sir Humphrey Waldock, 'Third Report on the Law of Treaties' [1964-II] YBILC 5, 55 [10].

[12] See 2.1.3.

[13] Sir Gerald Fitzmaurice, 'The Law and Procedure of the International Court of Justice 1951–4: Treaty Interpretation and Certain Other Treaty Points' (1957) 33 BYIL 203.

[14] Waldock, 'Third Report' (n 11) 52 f. The texts of those provisions that are relevant to this study are reproduced below:

subsequent agreements and subsequent practice, two main points of interest emerge from this tentative draft. First, Waldock distinguished between (subsequent) interpretative agreements on the one hand and subsequent practice on the other. While classifying the former as part of the context under draft article 71(1)(a), he referred to subsequent interpretative practice as part of the 'other means of interpretation'. These 'other means of interpretation' correspond to what finally became the supplementary means of interpretation under article 32 VCLT.

Article 70
General rules

1. The terms of a treaty shall be interpreted in good faith in accordance with the natural and ordinary meaning to be given to each term—
    (a) in its context in the treaty and in the context of the treaty as a whole; and
    (b) in the context of the rules of international law in force at the time of the conclusion of the treaty.
2. If the natural and ordinary meaning of a term leads to an interpretation which is manifestly absurd or unreasonable in the context of the treaty as a whole, or if the meaning of a term is not clear owing to its ambiguity or obscurity, the term shall be interpreted by reference to—
    (a) its context and the objects and purposes of the treaty; and
    (b) the other means of interpretation mentioned in article 71, paragraph 2.
3. Notwithstanding paragraph 1, a meaning other than its natural and ordinary meaning may be given to a term if it is established conclusively that the parties employed the term in the treaty with that special meaning.

Article 71
Application of the general rules

1. In the application of article 70 the context of the treaty as a whole shall be understood as comprising in addition to the treaty (including its preamble)—
    (a) any agreement arrived at between the parties as a condition of the conclusion of the treaty or as a basis for its interpretation;
    (b) any instrument or document annexed to the treaty;
    (c) any other instrument related to, and drawn up in connexion with the conclusion of, the treaty.
2. Reference may be made to other evidence or indications of the intentions of the parties and, in particular, to the preparatory work of the treaty, the circumstances surrounding its conclusion and the subsequent practice of parties in relation to the treaty, for the purpose of—
    (a) confirming the meaning of a term resulting from the application of paragraph 1 of article 70;
    (b) determining the meaning of a term in the application of paragraph 2 of that article;
    (c) establishing the special meaning of a term in the application of paragraph 3 of that article.

Article 73
Effect of a later customary rule or of a later agreement on interpretation of a treaty

The interpretation at any time of the terms of a treaty under articles 70 and 71 shall take account of—
    (a) the emergence of any later rule of customary international law affecting the subject-matter of the treaty and binding upon all the parties;
    (b) any later agreement between all the parties to the treaty and relating to its subject-matter;
    (c) any subsequent practice in relation to the treaty evidencing the consent of all the parties to an extension or modification of the treaty

In other words, at this early stage Waldock still appeared to consider subsequent practice less important for determining the meaning of the terms of the treaty than (subsequent) interpretative agreements. Second, it is noteworthy that Waldock assigned an additional function to subsequent practice alongside that of being a means of interpretation. Draft article 73(c) expressly acknowledged that subsequent practice may not only indicate the parties' common intention to interpret but also their intention to modify the treaty. Accepting that the line between interpretation and modification may be blurred in practice,[15] Waldock thus stressed that it was both possible and necessary to differentiate between interpretation and modification.[16]

When the ILC discussed Waldock's 'Third Report', his fellow Commission members largely welcomed the pertinent paragraphs on treaty interpretation in general and (subsequent) interpretative agreements and subsequent practice in particular. Elaborating on the proposed distinction between subsequent practice as a supplementary means of interpretation and subsequent practice that extended or modified a treaty, Waldock emphasised that

> it was only when that practice was concordant that it could be regarded as having the value of an authentic interpretation. In the case of multilateral treaties, the subsequent practice of only some of the parties was not automatically excluded as a means of interpretation; if it did not cover a broad group of parties it would, of course, only serve as an indication, and more evidence would be required in support of the alleged interpretation. It was for that reason that he had dealt with the matter of subsequent practice in two different provisions.[17]

Nevertheless, some Commission members doubted that Waldock's first draft adequately reflected the weight to be given to subsequent practice. Antonio de Luna, for example, contended that subsequent practice should not be regarded as a supplementary means of interpretation only as it 'had a more objective character and also a greater measure of certainty than *travaux préparatoire*.'[18] In the same vein, Gilberto Amado admitted that he was

> disturbed to note that some members wished to give so much weight to the *travaux préparatories*. He did not dispute their value in the interpretation of a treaty, but, after all, words were often used to hide thoughts, and in negotiating a treaty States were concerned mainly to advance their interests. The *travaux préparatoires* should not therefore be placed on the same footing as such a traditional practice as authentic interpretation by States.[19]

[15] The term 'amendment' describes formal treaty changes whereas the term 'modification' refers to informal changes, see Wolfram Karl, *Vertrag und spätere Praxis im Völkerrecht—Zum Einfluss der Praxis auf Inhalt und Bestand völkerrechtlicher Verträge* (repr, Springer 2012) 20.

[16] Waldock, 'Third Report' (n 11) 60 [25]. As regards the difficulty of distinguishing between interpretation and amendment, see also Oliver Dörr, 'Article 31—General Rule of Interpretation' in Oliver Dörr and Kirsten Schmalenbach (eds), *Vienna Convention on the Law of Treaties—A Commentary* (Springer 2012) 555 [76].

[17] Sir Humphrey Waldock in ILC, 'Summary Records of the 16th Session of the International Law Commission' (11 May–24 July 1964) [1964-I] YBILC 1, 282 [3].

[18] Antonio de Luna in ibid 285 [36].

[19] Gilberto Amado in ibid 286 [55].

Trying to sum up the objections against Waldock's approach to subsequent practice, Chairman Roberto Ago therefore suggested that

> the practice of parties might be classified into three categories: first, a practice which was not very definite but which was an auxiliary element in interpretation; second, a wholly concordant and definite practice, which was tantamount to a kind of interpretative agreement; and, third, practice which was equivalent to the amendment of the treaty.[20]

In the end, the Commission decided to slightly amend Waldock's first draft.[21] As a result of this amendment, (subsequent) interpretative agreements and subsequent practice were placed on an equal footing. This was achieved by slightly degrading the former and upgrading the latter: While (subsequent) interpretative agreements

---

[20] Chairman Roberto Ago in ibid 298 [58].

[21] ibid 315 f. The texts of those provisions that are relevant to this study are reproduced below:

Article 70
General rule (concerning the interpretation of treaties)
1. A treaty shall be interpreted in good faith in accordance with the ordinary meaning to be given to each term—
 (a) in the context of the treaty and in the light of its objects and purposes, and
 (b) in the light of the rules of international law in force at the time of its conclusion.
2. The context of the treaty, for the purposes of its interpretation, shall be understood as comprising in addition to the treaty, including its preamble and annexes, any agreement or instrument related to the treaty and reached or drawn up in connexion with its conclusion.
3. There shall also be taken into account, together with the context,
 (a) any agreement between the parties regarding the interpretation of the treaty;
 (b) any subsequent practice in the application of the treaty which clearly establishes the understanding of all the parties regarding its interpretation.

Article 71
Cases where the meaning of a provision is in doubt
Recourse may be had to further means of interpretation, including the preparatory work of the treaty and the circumstances of its conclusion, in order to verify or confirm the meaning resulting from the application of article 70, or to determine the meaning when its interpretation according to article 70—
 (a) leaves the meaning ambiguous or obscure; or
 (b) leads to a result which is manifestly absurd or unreasonable in the light of the objects and purposes of the treaty.

Article 69A
Modification of a treaty by a subsequent treaty, by subsequent practice or by customary law
The operation of a treaty may also be modified—
 (a) by a subsequent treaty between the parties relating to the same subject matter to the extent that their provisions are incompatible;
 (b) by a subsequent practice of the parties in the application of the treaty establishing their agreement to an alteration or extension of its provisions; or
 (c) by the subsequent emergence of a new rule of customary law relating to matters dealt with in the treaty and binding upon all the parties.

had been part of the context under Waldock's first draft, they were now only to be taken into account together with the context. This was because it was held that agreements adopted years after the original treaty could hardly be regarded as part of the treaty's context.[22] Subsequent practice, in contrast, which had been previously listed among the 'other means of interpretation', was now also to be taken into account with the context and hence classified as part of the general rule under draft article 70.

At the same time, any reference to practice by individual parties was deleted since some Commission members had insisted that only common practice should be taken into account.[23] Nonetheless, Special Rapporteur Waldock reiterated that subsequent practice by only some parties 'could be very important, especially in the case of multilateral treaties.'[24] For this reason, he proposed that such 'practice of individual parties might be mentioned in the commentary as one of the other forms of evidence, without its being given special importance.'[25]

Moreover, the Commission moved the provision on treaty modification by subsequent practice from behind the provisions dealing with treaty interpretation in front of them, thus linking it more closely to those on the amendment and modification of treaties. In doing so, the Commission meant to clarify that modification by subsequent practice 'had nothing to do with interpretation'[26] but concerned cases 'where subsequent practice could not be reconciled with the ordinary meaning of a treaty though purporting to be an application of it.'[27]

At the end of its 16th session in 1964, the Commission formally voted on the draft articles of treaty interpretation and provisionally adopted them with only few abstentions.[28] In accordance with the Commission's procedure, the draft was then submitted to the UNGA, its Sixth Committee,[29] and to governments for consideration. Having completed the first reading of all of Waldock's draft articles at its 16th session in 1964, the Commission spent its 17th and 18th sessions in 1965 and 1966 reconsidering the draft in second reading. For that purpose, the Special Rapporteur had revised the provisional draft articles in the light of observations and comments

[22] Eg Chairman Roberto Ago in ibid 311 [19].

[23] Eg Milan Bartoš and Grigory Tunkin in ibid 314 [72], [75].

[24] Special Rapporteur Sir Humphrey Waldock in ibid 314 [74].

[25] ibid 314 [76].

[26] Antonio de Luna in ibid 296 [37].

[27] Special Rapporteur Sir Humphrey Waldock in ibid 296 [39].

[28] Draft art 70 as a whole was adopted unanimously, draft art 71 was adopted by 13 votes to none with two abstentions, and draft art 69A was adopted unanimously, see ILC, 'Summary Records of the 16th Session of the International Law Commission' (11 May–24 July 1964) [1964-I] YBILC 1, 317 f.

[29] The Sixth Committee is the UNGA's legal committee. See generally Huw Llewellyn, 'United Nations, Sixth Committee' in Rüdiger Wolfrum (ed), *The Max Planck Encyclopedia of Public International Law* (OUP 2012).

made by governments and debates in the UNGA and its Sixth Committee.[30] In terms of (subsequent) interpretative agreements and subsequent practice, this draft did not contain any fundamental changes.

It was discussed at the Commission's 18th session in 1966, during which it also reconsidered the order of all draft articles and added commentaries to each of them. At its 893rd meeting on 18 July 1966, the Commission unanimously adopted its final text of the draft articles, which consisted of 75 articles in total.[31] The full

---

[30] Sir Humphrey Waldock, 'Sixth Report on the Law of Treaties' [1966-II] YBILC 51, 91, 101. The texts of those provisions that are relevant to this study are reproduced below:

Article 68
Modification of a treaty by subsequent practice
The operation of a treaty may be modified by subsequent practice of the parties in the application of the treaty establishing their agreement to an alteration or extension of its provisions. In the case of a multilateral treaty, the rules set out in article 67, paragraph 1, apply to an alteration or extension of its provisions as between certain of the parties alone.

Article 69
General rule of interpretation
1. A treaty shall be interpreted in good faith in accordance with the ordinary meaning to be given to its terms in the light of:
   (a) The context of the treaty and its objects and purposes;
   (b) The rules of international law;
   (c) Any agreement between the parties regarding the interpretation of the treaty;
   (d) Any subsequent practice in the application of the treaty which establishes the common understanding of the meaning of the terms as between the parties generally.
2. Nevertheless, a meaning other than its ordinary meaning shall be given to a term if it is established that the parties intended the term to have that special meaning.
3. The context of the treaty, for the purposes of its interpretation, shall be understood as comprising in addition to the treaty any agreement or instrument related to the treaty which has either been made by the parties or has been made by some of them and assented to by the others as an instrument related to the treaty.

Article 70
Further means of interpretation
Recourse may be had to further means of interpretation, including the preparatory work of the treaty and the circumstances of its conclusion, in order to verify or confirm the meaning resulting from the application of article 69, or to determine the meaning when the interpretation according to article 69:
   (a) Leaves the meaning ambiguous or obscure; or
   (b) Leads to a result which is manifestly absurd or unreasonable in the light of the objects and purposes of the treaty.

Article 71 (deleted and contents transferred to article 69 as new paragraph 2).

[31] ILC, 'Summary Records of the 18th Session of the International Law Commission' (4 May–19 July 1966) [1966-I/2] YBILC 1, 335 [138].

draft, including commentaries, formed part of the Commission's 1966 report to the UNGA.[32] The provisions on treaty interpretation of this final draft hardly differed from articles 31–33 VCLT anymore. In contrast to previous versions, this last one distinguished most clearly between agreements made in connexion with the conclusion of the treaty, which were part of the context, and subsequent agreements, which were only to be taken into account with the context. With this final draft, the terminology used to define subsequent agreements fully corresponded to that employed for subsequent practice.

The Commission having completed its task, it was for the UNGA to decide how to further proceed with the law of treaties. The Assembly eventually decided to convene an international conference of plenipotentiaries to negotiate and conclude a convention on the law of treaties based on the Commission's draft.[33] This approach

---

[32] id, 'Draft Articles on the Law of Treaties with Commentaries' [1966-II] YBILC 187, 177 f. The texts of those provisions that are relevant to this study are reproduced below:

Article 27
General rule of interpretation
1. A treaty shall be interpreted in good faith in accordance with the ordinary meaning to be given to the terms of the treaty in their context and in the light of its object and purpose.
2. The context for the purpose of the interpretation of a treaty shall comprise, in addition to the text, including its preamble and annexes:
   (a) Any agreement relating to the treaty which was made between all the parties in connexion with the conclusion of the treaty;
   (b) Any instrument which was made by one or more parties in connexion with the conclusion of the treaty and accepted by the other parties as an instrument related to the treaty.
3. There shall be taken into account, together with the context:
   (a) Any subsequent agreement between the parties regarding the interpretation of the treaty;
   (b) Any subsequent practice in the application of the treaty which establishes the understanding of the parties regarding its interpretation;
   (c) Any relevant rules of international law applicable in the relations between the parties.
4. A special meaning shall be given to a term if it is established that the parties so intended.

Article 28
Supplementary means of interpretation
Recourse may be had to supplementary means of interpretation, including the preparatory work of the treaty and the circumstances of its conclusion, in order to confirm the meaning resulting from the application of article 27, or to determine the meaning when the interpretation according to article 27:
   (a) Leaves the meaning ambiguous or obscure; or
   (b) Leads to a result which is manifestly absurd or unreasonable.

Article 38
Modification of treaties by subsequent practice
A treaty may be modified by subsequent practice in the application of the treaty establishing the agreement of the parties to modify its provisions.

[33] UNGA Res 2166 (XXI) (5 December 1966) UN Doc A/6516.

was in line with what both the Secretariat and the Commission had recommended.[34] Said Conference was held at the Neue Hofburg in Vienna. It was split up into two sessions, the first taking place from 26 March–24 May 1968 and the second from 9 April–22 May 1969.[35] During these two sessions, delegates of 115 States as well as observers from specialised agencies and IOs attended the Conference. The States represented at the Conferences acted in three distinct formations: the Plenary, the Committee of the Whole, and the Drafting Committee.

The first session of the Conference was largely dominated by the Committee of the Whole. This Committee did most of the substantive work by debating each of the Commission's draft articles and, if necessary, proposing amendments. At its 37th and 38th meeting, the Committee discussed whether or not to retain draft article 38 (modification by subsequent practice). In the end, it decided to delete this provision.[36] Apart from that, debates mainly focused on drafting matters[37] or doctrinal questions such as whether treaty interpretation should be governed by a 'textualist', an 'intentionalist', or a 'teleological' approach.[38] Thus, the first session of the Conference ended with virtually no changes to the Commission's draft articles on treaty interpretation.

At the second session of the Conference, it was for the Plenary to read all draft articles as agreed on by the Committee of the Whole and revised by the Drafting Committee. When the Plenary dealt with treaty interpretation, it widely accepted the draft before it and introduced hardly any amendments either. At the end of the 13th plenary meeting, Roberto Ago, the President of the Conference, therefore most happily noted

> that the Conference had successfully disposed of the most controversial and difficult subject in the whole field of the law of treaties, the question of the interpretation of treaties. The section on interpretation had been condensed into a few formulas which had been adopted unanimously by the Conference. When the section had first come before the International Law Commission, many had felt that it might be unwise for the Commission to embark on a codification of so difficult a subject. He himself had taken a more optimistic view and was most grateful to the Conference for having proved him right.[39]

On 22 May 1969, the Convention was finally adopted with 79 votes. Nineteen States abstained and only France rejected the Convention. Thirty-seven out of 85 articles

[34] As regards the discussions in the ILC on which form this Conference could and should take, see ILC, 'Summary Records of the 18th Session of the International Law Commission' (4 May–19 July 1966) [1966-I/2] YBILC 1, 240 f.

[35] See generally Sinclair, 'The Vienna Conference' (n 4).

[36] UN Conference on the Law of Treaties, 'Summary Records of the Plenary Meetings and of the Meetings of the Committee of the Whole' (First session, Vienna 26 March 1968) UN Doc A/CONF.39/11, 215.

[37] ibid 185, 441 f.

[38] ibid 167 f. On the three conflicting approaches, see 3.3.3.

[39] UN Conference on the Law of Treaties 'Summary Records of the Plenary Meetings and of the Meetings of the Committee of the Whole' (Second session, Vienna 9 April–22 May 1969) UN Doc A/CONF.39/11/Add.l, 59.

were adopted unanimously. Among these articles were the Convention's rules of interpretation. Despite such broad agreement, it still took another 21 years until the Convention entered into force on 27 January 1980, 30 days after the 35th instrument of ratification had been deposited with the UN Secretary-General.[40]

3.2 The Vienna Rules as a Reflection of Customary Law

As part of the Vienna Convention and in their capacity as treaty law, the scope of application of articles 31 and 32 VCLT is limited.[41] Their true relevance is not so much related to their capacity as treaty law as to being considered a reflection of customary international law. This notion implies that the content of articles 31 and 32 VCLT is identical to customary international law rules of treaty interpretation.[42] If that were correct, these provisions would 'apply as treaty law in relation to those States which are parties to the Vienna Convention for treaties which fall within the scope of the Convention, and as customary international law between all States.'[43]

The alleged customary status of articles 31 and 32 VCLT is closely related to the ILC's role in drafting the Convention.[44] Under article 1 of its governing Statute, the Commission shall have for its object the promotion of the progressive development of international law as well as its codification.[45] The term 'progressive development' refers to the preparation of draft conventions on subjects which have not yet been

[40] Art 84 VCLT.

[41] Firstly, the Vienna rules only apply to the interpretation of treaties all of whose parties have also ratified the Vienna Convention. As of today, only 114 States have become a party to the Convention. States such as France, India, Turkey, and the USA have not ratified the Convention so far. For the current status of ratification of this and other treaties referred to in this study, see <http://treaties.un.org/>. Secondly, the Vienna rules only apply to the interpretation of written agreements concluded between States, see arts 1 and 2(1)(a) VCLT. And thirdly, they only apply to the interpretation of treaties that have been concluded by States after the date on which the Convention entered into force for these States, see art 4 VCLT.

[42] Commentary on draft conclusion 1 in ILC, 'Report of the International Law Commission on the Work of its 65th Session' (6 May–7 June and 8 July–9 August 2013) UN Doc A/68/10, 15 [4] with further references.

[43] ibid. See also Dörr, 'Article 31' (n 16) 525 [7].

[44] See 3.1.

[45] The Statute of the International Law Commission (ILC Statute) is annexed to UNGA Res 174 (II) (21 November 1947) UN Doc A/519. On the distinction between 'codification' and 'progressive development', see Arthur Watts, 'Codification and Progressive Development of International Law' in Rüdiger Wolfrum (ed), *The Max Planck Encyclopedia of Public International Law* (OUP 2012) [17]–[22]. On whether or not the ILC is still a suitable forum for codifying and developing international law, see James Crawford, 'Prospects for the Codification and Development of International Law by the United Nations: The Work of the International Law Commission' (1998) 9 FYBIL 9 and Stephen McCaffrey, 'Is Codification in Decline?' (1997) 20 Hastings Int'l & Comp L Rev 639.

regulated by international law or in regard to which the law has not yet been sufficiently developed in the practice of States.[46] 'Codification', in contrast, refers to the more precise formulation and systematisation of rules in fields where there has already been extensive State practice, precedent, and doctrine.[47] Thus, codification is concerned with identifying existing custom and recasting it into *jus scriptum*.[48]

Although the ILC Statute distinguishes between progressive development and codification of already existing customary international law, these mechanisms inevitably coincide in practice. According to the Commission, it was ultimately impossible to strictly separate development and codification of international law in the course of its work.[49] In consequence, any draft prepared by the ILC may both reflect existing customary international law, develop existing, or create new law. This also applies to the Vienna Convention on the Law of Treaties. As the Commission itself frankly admitted, its 'work on the law of treaties constitutes both codification and progressive development of international law … and … it is not practicable to determine into which category each provision falls.'[50]

For this reason, the Commission did not expressly indicate whether its draft articles on treaty interpretation reflected existing customary international law. Individual ILC members, however, doubted that they did. José Ruda, for instance, noted that 'at the present stage of development of international law, there did not as yet exist for States any obligatory rules on the subject of interpretation.'[51] Hence, the Commission's draft articles on interpretation 'would not constitute a codification of existing law; they would represent proposals for the progressive development of international law.'[52] In the same vein, some commentators contended that the

[46] Art 15 ILC Statute.

[47] ibid.

[48] Mark Villiger, *Customary International Law and Treaties—A Manual on the Theory and Practice of the Interrelation of Sources* (2nd edn, Kluwer 1997) [150]–[55]. In both alternatives, the final product will be a draft with recommendations for the UNGA on how to further proceed with the matter, see art 16(j) ILC Statute. This draft normally takes the forms of draft articles that are intended to serve as a basis for concluding an international convention. As regards codification of international law, see art 23(c) and (d) ILC Statute. Art 15 ILC Statute indicates that draft conventions are generally considered the appropriate means to progressively develop the law. In some cases, however, the ILC merely publishes a report which the UNGA then takes note of, see art 23(a) and (b) ILC Statute.

[49] ILC, 'Report of the International Law Commission on the Work of its 48th Session' (6 May–26 July 1996) [1996-II/2] YBILC 1, 84 [147], 86 [156]–[59]; see also Shabtai Rosenne, 'The Temporal Application of the Vienna Convention on the Law of Treaties' (1970) 4 Cornell Int'l LJ 1, 18; Ian Sinclair, *The Vienna Convention on the Law of Treaties* (2nd edn, MUP 1984) 11; Alain Pellet, 'Between Codification and Progressive Development of the Law—Some Reflections from the ILC' (2004) 6 International Law FORUM du droit international 15, 16 f.

[50] ILC, 'DALT' (n 32) 177 [35] [fn omitted]. See also the Convention's preamble (8th recital); Rosenne, 'The Temporal Application of the VCLT' (n 49) 2 f.

[51] José Ruda in ILC, 'Summary Records of the 16th Session of the International Law Commission' (11 May–24 July 1964) [1964-I] YBILC 1, 277 [33].

[52] ibid 277 [35].

various rules of treaty interpretation were so diverse when the Commission included the law of treaties into its agenda that there was no customary international law on treaty interpretation which the Commission could have codified.[53]

Today, it is nevertheless widely recognised that articles 31 and 32 VCLT reflect customary international law. International courts and tribunals frequently refer to articles 31 and 32 VCLT to establish customary international law rules of treaty interpretation.[54] In accordance with the prevailing view in the literature,[55] the ILC has similarly confirmed that the 'rules enshrined in articles 31 and 32 of the Vienna Convention reflect customary international law.'[56] Against

---

[53] Antoine Favre, 'L'interprétation objectiviste des traités internationaux' (1960) 17 ASDI 75, 97; Villiger, *Commentary on the VCLT* (n 5) 439 [37]; Jan Klabbers, 'Virtuous Interpretation' in Malgosia Fitzmaurice, Olufemi Elias, and Panos Merkouris (eds), *Treaty Interpretation and the Vienna Convention on the Law of Treaties—30 Years on* (Martinus Nijhoff 2010) 27; Jean-Marc Sorel and Valérie Boré Eveno, 'Article 31—1969 Vienna Convention' in Olivier Corten and Pierre Klein (eds), *The Vienna Conventions on the Law of Treaties—A Commentary* (OUP 2011) 812 [15].

[54] *Case concerning the Arbitral Award of 31 July 1989* [1991] ICJ Rep 53, 70 [48]; *Territorial Dispute (Libyan Arab Jamahiriya v Chad)* [1994] ICJ Rep 6, 19 [41]; *Case concerning Kasikili/Sedudu Island (Botswana v Namibia)* [1999] ICJ Rep 1045, 1059 [18]; *LaGrand (Germany v USA)* [2001] ICJ Rep 466, 501 [99]; *Case concerning Sovereignty over Pulau Ligitan and Pulau Sipadan (Indonesia v Malaysia)* [2002] ICJ Rep 625, 645 [37]; *Avena and Other Mexican Nationals (Mexico v USA)* [2004] ICJ Rep 12, 48 [83]; *Pulp Mills on the River Uruguay (Argentina v Uruguay)* [2010] ICJ Rep 14, 46 [65]; ECtHR, *Golder v UK* (1975) Series A No 18 [29]; *Al-Adsani v UK [GC]* ECHtR 2001–XI [55]; *Saadi v UK [GC]* App no 37201/06 (ECtHR, 28 February 2008) [61]; *Al-Saadoon and Mufdhi v UK* App no 61498/08 (ECtHR, 2 March 2010) [126]; Case C–386/08 *Brita GmbH v Hauptzollamt Hamburg-Hafen* [2010] ECR I–1289 [41]; WTO, *Japan—Alcoholic Beverages II—Report of the Appellate Body* (4 October 1996) WT/DS8/AB/R-11/AB/R <http://docsonline.wto.org> at 10–12; WTO, *US—Hot-Rolled Steel—Report of the Appellate Body* (24 July 2001) WT/DS184/AB/R <http://docsonline.wto.org> [57]; WTO, *US—Gambling—Report of the Appellate Body* (7 April 2005) WT/DS285/AB/R <http://docsonline.wto.org> [159]; WTO, *US—Stainless Steel (Mexico)—Report of the Appellate Body* (30 April 2008) WT/DS344/AB/R <http://docsonline.wto.org> [76]; *Tariffs Applied by Canada to Certain US-Origin Agricultural Products* North American Free Trade Organisation (NAFTA) Arbitral Panel (Secretariat File No CDA-95-2008-01) Final Report of the Panel (2 December 1996) <registry.nafta-sec-alena.org/cmdocuments/0c7973b9-1088-4221-99a5-e279075380b0.pdf> [118] f; *Arbitration regarding the Iron Rhine ('Ijzeren Rijn') Railway (Belgium v the Netherlands)* (2005) 27 RIAA 35, 62 [45].

[55] Patrick Daillier, Mathias Forteau, and Alain Pellet, *Droit international public—Formation du droit, sujets, relations diplomatiques et consulaires, responsabilité, règlement des différends, maintien de la paix, espaces internationaux, relations économiques, environnement* (8th edn, LGDJ 2009) 285 f; Mark Villiger, 'The 1969 Vienna Convention on the Law of Treaties—40 Years After' (2009) 344 RCADI 9, 132–33; Richard Gardiner, *Treaty Interpretation* (2nd edn, OUP 2015) 13–20; Dörr, 'Article 31' (n 16) 523 [6]. More cautious, however, Villiger, *Commentary on the VCLT* (n 5) 440 [38] f.

[56] Commentary on draft conclusion 1 in ILC, 'Report of the International Law Commission on the Work of its 65th Session' (6 May–7 June and 8 July–9 August 2013) UN Doc A/68/10, 14 [4].

this background, one may argue that—even if their initial customary status was questionable—articles 31 and 32 VCLT have gradually contributed to the emergence of identical custom as States increasingly took note of and recognised the content of these rules.[57]

This may be owed to the fact that articles 31 and 32 VCLT considerably facilitated the process of treaty interpretation. As Roberto Ago noted, these provisions

> would be useful in a number of ways: in eliminating uncertainty in the law, which was the basic purpose of codification, and in facilitating the work of arbitral bodies, but particularly between the parties and even in the case ... where a State sought to interpret a treaty to which it was not a party. Between the parties themselves, those rules could facilitate the settlement of disputes concerning the interpretation of treaties.[58]

Written law, irrespective of whether it is legally binding or not, entails advantages in terms of clarity, legal certainty, predictability, and stability if compared to the sometimes rather vague body of customary international law.[59] For this reason, States and other actors may not only refer to it because it has acquired legal force for them; in addition, references to written law may also occur out of convenience.[60] If States regularly refer to a piece of written law—such as articles 31 and 32 VCLT—their practice may gradually reflect the content of that written law. And provided that this practice becomes sufficiently widespread and accepted as law, it may eventually

[57] Sorel and Boré Eveno, 'Article 31' (n 53) 817 [28]. cf also Sinclair, *The Vienna Convention on the Law of Treaties* (n 49) 21; Kirsten Schmalenbach, 'Article 4—Non-Retroactivity of the Present Convention' in Oliver Dörr and id (eds), *Vienna Convention on the Law of Treaties—A Commentary* (Springer 2012) 83 [6].

[58] Roberto Ago in ILC, 'Summary Records of the 16th Session of the International Law Commission' (11 May–24 July 1964) [1964-I] YBILC 1, 280 [78].

[59] See esp Villiger, *Customary International Law and Treaties* (n 48) [169]–[70]. Yet, Villiger emphasises that these advantages are not absolute. The degree to which these advantages are actually realised also depends, according to him, on the willingness of the drafters to agree on the substance of the rule. Besides, they are inevitably diminished by the imperfections and inherent ambiguities of written texts. On the advantages of *jus scriptum* see also Rosenne, 'The Temporal Application of the VCLT' (n 49) 19; Nele Matz-Lück, 'The Benefits of Positivism: The ILC's Contribution to the Peaceful Sharing of Transboundary Water' in Georg Nolte (ed), *Peace through International Law—The Role of the International Law Commission: A Colloquium at the Occasion of its Sixtieth Anniversary* (Springer 2009) 137; Watts, 'Codification and Progressive Development of International Law' (n 45) [1].

[60] Villiger, *Customary International Law and Treaties* (n 48) [278]–[79], [423]–[25], who describes the persuasiveness of conventional rules due to their advantages as *jus scriptum*. See also Rosenne, 'The Temporal Application of the VCLT' (n 49) 19; Yoram Dinstein, 'The Interaction between Customary International Law and Treaties' (2007) 322 RCADI 243, 351; Ulf Linderfalk, 'Is the Hierarchical Structure of Articles 31 and 32 of the Vienna Convention Real or Not?—Interpreting the Rules of Interpretation' (2007) 54 NILR 133, 139; Villiger, *Commentary on the VCLT* (n 5) 21 [45].

harden into a rule of customary international law.[61] In other words, the written law can be regarded as a 'nucleus around which a new set of generally recognised rules may be established.'[62]

Nevertheless, little is to be gained from their widespread recognition as a reflection of customary international law. Regularly paying lip service to articles 31 and 32 VCLT does not guarantee that interpreters actually faithfully interpret treaties in accordance with these provisions. But does that mean that it is necessary to separately establish the (potentially different) content of customary international law rules of treaty interpretation? A first glance at the Vienna Convention suggests that it is. Pursuant to article 4 VCLT, articles 31 and 32 VCLT do not apply retroactively.[63] The construction of treaties whose interpretation is not regulated by the Convention—be it due to its non-retroactivity or for other reasons—is still governed by customary international law rules of treaty interpretation.[64]

In addition, non-identical customary international law rules of treaty interpretation may have superseded or even gradually modified the rules that are laid down in articles 31 and 32 VCLT. Under public international law, there is no general hierarchy between treaty law and custom.[65] For this reason, non-identical subsequent customary international law rules of treaty interpretation may have replaced articles 31 and 32 VCLT under the *lex posterior* rule.[66] Moreover, non-identical customary international law rules may prevail over articles 31 and 32 VCLT under the *lex specialis* rule if they offer more specific rules for the interpretation of, for example, human rights treaties or international investment agreements.[67]

---

[61] See in particular *North Sea Continental Shelf (Germany v Denmark)* [1969] ICJ Rep 3, 41 [71]; *Military and Paramilitary Activities in and against Nicaragua (Nicaragua v USA)* (Merits) [1986] ICJ Rep 14, 95 [177]. See also Villiger, *Customary International Law and Treaties* (n 48) [30], [130], [255] f; Riccardo Pisillo-Mazzeschi, 'Treaty and Custom: Reflections on the Codification of International Law' (1997) 23 Commw L Bull 549, 552; Villiger, *Commentary on the VCLT* (n 5) 21 [45]; Hugh Thirlway, *The Sources of International Law* (OUP 2014) 130.

[62] Dipen Sabharwal, 'Treaties are Treaties and Custom is Custom and Never the Twain Shall Meet—Examining the Interplay of Treaties and Custom in International Law' (2000) 12 Student Advoc 113, 120. cf also David Caron, 'The ILC Articles on State Responsiblity: The Paradoxical Relationship between Form and Authority' (2002) 96 AJIL 857, 866.

[63] Rosenne, 'The Temporal Application of the VCLT' (n 49) 3; Schmalenbach, 'Article 4' (n 57) 81 [1].

[64] See art 3(b) VCLT as well as recital 8 of the Convention's preamble.

[65] Villiger, *Customary International Law and Treaties* (n 48) [84]; Dinstein, 'Customary International Law and Treaties' (n 60) 404 f; James Crawford, *Brownlie's Principles of Public International Law* (8th edn, OUP 2012) 22; Rüdiger Wolfrum, 'Sources of International Law' in id (ed), *The Max Planck Encyclopedia of Public International Law* (OUP 2012) [11].

[66] cf Villiger, *Customary International Law and Treaties* (n 48) [87] f; Crawford, *Brownlie's Principles* (n 65) 23; Wolfrum, 'Sources of International Law' (n 65) [11].

[67] Villiger, *Customary International Law and Treaties* (n 48) [87] f.

The Vienna Convention does not expressly address modifications of treaty law through international custom. Draft article 68(c), in contrast, originally acknowledged that the operation of a treaty may also be modified by the subsequent emergence of a new rule of customary law relating to matters dealt within the treaty and binding upon all the parties.[68] This provision was eventually deleted because the relationship between treaty law and custom was regarded as 'too complex'.[69] Yet, the Convention's silence on that issue does not necessarily mean that such modification cannot occur.[70] In the *Continental Shelf Arbitration,* for example, the tribunal nevertheless accepted 'that a development in customary law may, under certain conditions, evidence the assent of the States concerned to the modification, or even termination, of previously existing treaty rights and obligations.'[71]

In short, articles 31 and 32 VCLT and customary rules of treaty interpretation are closely interrelated and may mutually influence each other. Yet there is no guarantee that they are identical. Against this background, the oft-repeated dictum that these provisions are a reflection of customary international law may be oversimplistic. At first sight, it appears indispensable to positively verify whether interpretative practice actually conforms to the requirements under articles 31 and 32 VCLT. Nevertheless, this necessity should not be overestimated. Albeit not impossible, it seems to be rather unlikely that deviations from articles 31 and 32 VCLT may eventually cristalise into non-identical customary law rules of treaty interpretation.

This is because deviations from articles 31 and 32 VCLT do not, in themselves, create rules of customary international law. Customary international law does not develop that easily but requires a sufficiently widespread practice that is accepted as law.[72] From a doctrinal perspective, it may be oversimplistic to regard articles 31 and 32 VCLT as a reflection of customary international law. But in the end, interpreters may assume that it is—as a general rule— appropriate to do so—provided that they remain sensitive to indications to the contrary.

3.3 The Vienna Rules of Interpretation

Section 3 of the 1969 Vienna Convention on the Law of Treaties covers the interpretation of treaties. Article 31 VCLT contains the general rule of interpretation, article 32 VCLT addresses supplementary means of interpretation, and article 33 VCLT

[68] Waldock, 'Third Report' (n 11) 198.

[69] ILC, 'DALT' (n 32) 236 [3].

[70] See eg Nancy Kontou, *The Termination and Revision of Treaties in the Light of New Customary International Law* (Clarendon Press 1994) 139; Villiger, *Customary International Law and Treaties* (n 48) [306]; Crawford, *Brownlie's Principles* (n 65) 33.

[71] *Continental Shelf Arbitration (UK v France)* (1977) 18 RIAA 3, 37 [47].

[72] Art 38(1)(b) ICJ Statute. See also draft cocnlusions 9 and 10 in Sir Michael Wood, 'Second Report on Identification of Customary International Law' (22 May 2014) UN Doc A/CN.4/672, 41, 51.

deals with the interpretation of treaties authenticated in two or more languages.[73] Before considering the Vienna rules in greater detail, it is necessary to settle a question of terminology.

During the Convention's drafting history, the ILC briefly discussed whether the term 'elements of interpretation' would be preferable over the term 'means of interpretation'.[74] Although continuing to use both terms interchangeably,[75] it was pointed out that the term ' "means" had the merit of being in fairly common use where interpretation was concerned.'[76] In 2013, this previously unresolved terminological issue re-emerged. Whereas Special Rapporteur Nolte proposed to refer to the content of the Vienna rules as 'means of interpretation',[77] other members of the Commission contended that this term misleadingly over-emphasised the distinct nature of each of these means.[78] Draft conclusion 1, which was provisionally adopted at the end of the Commission's 65th session, eventually 'opted for the term "means" rather than "elements" of interpretation.'[79] As the accompanying commentary explains, this is because the former 'evoked the notion of a tool or instrument and described their function in the interpretation process with greater precision.'[80]

In conformity with the Convention's own choice of words,[81] this study therefore also generally speaks of 'means of interpretation'. Where it uses, for linguistic

[73] In the following, this study leaves aside the special rules under art 33 VCLT because they are not relevant for the topic under consideration. The ILC did not expressly affirm the customary status of art 33 VCLT and merely recognised 'significant indications in the case law' to that effect, see the commentary on draft conclusion 1 in ILC, 'Report of the International Law Commission on the Work of its 65th Session' (6 May–7 June and 8 July–9 August 2013) UN Doc A/68/10, 16 [6].

[74] Paul Reuter in ILC, 'Summary Records of the 18th Session of the International Law Commission' (4 May–19 July 1966) [1966-I/2] YBILC 1, 201 [47].

[75] Eg ILC, 'Summary Records of the 16th Session of the International Law Commission' (11 May–24 July 1964) [1964-I] YBILC 1, 39 [48], 124 [55], 125 [68]; id, 'Report of the International Law Commission on the Work of its 16th Session' (11 May–24 July 1964) [1964-II] YBILC 173, 203 [13]; id, 'Summary Records of the 18th Session of the International Law Commission' (4 May–19 July 1966) [1966-I/2] YBILC 1, 185 [68], 188 [36], 198 [5]; Waldock, 'Sixth Report' (n 30) 94 [2], 100 [23]; ILC, 'DALT' (n 32) esp 219 [8], 220 [9], [10].

[76] Roberto Ago in id, Summary Records of the 18th Session of the International Law Commission' (4 May–19 July 1966) [1966-I/2] YBILC 1, 202 [50].

[77] Georg Nolte, 'First Report on Subsequent Agreements and Subsequent Practice in relation to Treaty Interpretation' (19 March 2013) UN Doc A/CN.4/660, 6 [8], [9].

[78] Sir Michael Wood in ILC, 'Provisional Summary Record of the 3160th Meeting' (7 May 2013) UN Doc A/CN.4/SR.3160, 3.

[79] Draft conclusion 1 in id, 'Report of the International Law Commission on the Work of its 65th Session' (6 May–7 June and 8 July–9 August 2013) UN Doc A/68/10, 11.

[80] ibid 18 [14].

[81] See art 32 VCLT.

reasons, the term 'elements', this alternation is not meant to indicate any conceptual difference.

3.3.1 *The General Rule of Interpretation*

Subsequent agreements and subsequent practice form part of the general rule of interpretation under article 31 VCLT. This 'general rule', as it is referred to in the title of article 31 VCLT, consists of four paragraphs and includes several means of interpretation. These means are the ordinary and special meaning, the context, the object and purpose, subsequent agreements and subsequent practice, and relevant rules of international law applicable in the relations between the parties.[82] After recalling the ultimate purpose of 'interpretation', the ensuing paragraphs shortly outline how these means are meant to operate. The following text of article 31 VCLT shall facilitate this overview:

> 1. A treaty shall be interpreted in good faith in accordance with the ordinary meaning to be given to the terms of the treaty in their context and in the light of its object and purpose.
> 2. The context for the purpose of the interpretation of a treaty shall comprise, in addition to the text, including its preamble and annexes:
> (a) any agreement relating to the treaty which was made between all the parties in connection with the conclusion of the treaty;
> (b) any instrument which was made by one or more parties in connection with the conclusion of the treaty and accepted by the other parties as an instrument related to the treaty.
> 3. There shall be taken into account, together with the context:
> (a) any subsequent agreement between the parties regarding the interpretation of the treaty or the application of its provisions;
> (b) any subsequent practice in the application of the treaty which establishes the agreement of the parties regarding its interpretation;
> (c) any relevant rules of international law applicable in the relations between the parties.
> 4. A special meaning shall be given to a term if it is established that the parties so intended.

As has been argued in Chap. 1, interpretation is the process of determining a treaty's meaning by ascertaining the objectivised intention of the parties. Article 31(1) VCLT emphasises that what is being 'interpreted' is the treaty itself; thus, the written agreement called 'treaty' is both the starting point and the very object

[82] 'Good faith', which is also mentioned in art 31(1) VCLT, is not a means of interpretation strictly speaking. Instead, it is rather a principle that governs the interpretative process, ie the application of the various means of interpretation referred to in arts 31 and 32 VCLT. For more details, see Villiger, *Commentary on the VCLT* (n 5) 425 [6] f; Gardiner, *Treaty Interpretation* (n 55) 168.

of interpretation.[83] Under article 31(1) VCLT, a treaty shall be interpreted in accordance with the ordinary meaning to be given to its terms in their context and in the light of the treaty's object and purpose. Here the word 'terms' means as much as that which has been written down in the sense of 'words' and 'provisions'.[84] Thus, it is the words and provisions whose meaning one determines when interpreting a treaty in accordance with article 31 VCLT.

However, words and provisions (the latter an accumulation of words) are hardly ever unambiguous. Words often carry multiple meanings. Hence the goal of the interpretative process is to determine a treaty's correct meaning by ascertaining the objectivised intention of the parties. By concentrating on the meaning of the terms of the treaty, the Convention assumes that the parties generally intend what the terms of the treaty mean. Had they not, they would and should have used a different language. They were free to choose whatever words they preferred; having done so, they—as well as those tasked with interpreting the treaty—are bound by this very choice of words. This is not to suggest that article 31 VCLT superordinated literal construction to other primary means of interpretation. Nevertheless, the Convention's concept of interpretation does not envisage constructions that are fully detached from the text of the treaty; instead, the parties' written agreement constitutes the object and demarcates the outer limits of the interpretative process.[85] In that sense, the ILC frankly declared that its DALT reflected a 'textualist approach' to interpretation 'based on the view that the text must be presumed to be the authentic expression of the intentions of the parties.'[86]

3.3.1.1 Ordinary and Special Meaning

Which meaning does the Convention consider as the correct one? Article 31(1) VCLT postulates as part of the general rule that an interpreter shall determine the 'ordinary' meaning of the terms of the treaty. This provision must be read in conjunction with article 31(4) VCLT, which requires that a special meaning shall be given to these terms if the parties so intended. Three questions arise: Firstly, what

[83] See already Mustafa Yasseen, 'L'interprétation des traités d'après la Convention de Vienne sur le Droit des Traités' (1976) 151 RCADI 1, 16.

[84] Gardiner, *Treaty Interpretation* (n 55) 164.

[85] See eg Commission member Grigory Tunkin in ILC, 'Summary Records of the 18th Session of the International Law Commission' (4 May–19 July 1966) [1966-I/2] YBILC 1, 189 [61].

[86] id, 'DALT' (n 32) 220 [11]. See also Chairman Milan Bartoš in id, 'Summary Records of the 18th Session of the International Law Commission' (4 May–19 July 1966) [1966-I/2] YBILC 1, 197 [50]: 'Although the word "text" did not appear… the rules set out gave precedence discreetly to the text of the treaty, which was right. It was better to refer to the text than to the intention or will of the parties as the source of the legal rule. For the rule was the expression of the will, and that expression was to be found in the text. Even if the will was clear, there could be no rule of written law without a text.'

does 'ordinary' mean? Secondly, what is the meaning of 'special'? And thirdly, which point in time is decisive for determining the 'ordinary' or 'special' meaning?

A systematic interpretation of paragraphs (1) and (4) of article 31 VCLT reveals that the terms 'ordinary' and 'special' meaning are mutually exclusive.[87] The latter, hinging on the intentions of the parties, addresses the case that the parties envisaged a term to carry a different meaning than that which it would normally carry.[88] An 'ordinary' meaning, in contrast, refers to the normal or regular meaning according to conventional language.[89] The text of article 31(1) and (4) VCLT suggests that terms of a treaty generally carry their ordinary meaning unless there is some evidence that the parties envisaged a special meaning.[90] Since words usually do not carry just one single meaning, the 'ordinary' or 'special' meaning regularly offers a wide range of possible meanings.[91] Hence it is the task of the interpreter to discover the most suitable of these conceivable meanings by utilising other primary and, where appropriate, supplementary means of interpretation.

Language, however, is not only ambiguous at a particular moment in time. It becomes even more ambiguous if one takes into account how meanings may change as time goes by. As one commentator noted, [l]anguage constantly varies and meanings may fluctuate from one age to the next.'[92] In the light of such changes of meaning over time, interpreters must consciously deliberate which temporal perspective they have to adopt when determining the ordinary meaning of the terms of the treaty. Is it the ordinary meaning prevailing at the time when the treaty was concluded ('historic language')?[93] Or is it the one prevailing at the time when the

---

[87] See also Sinclair, *The Vienna Convention on the Law of Treaties* (n 49) 126, who describes the special meaning of a term as a 'converse' to its ordinary meaning.

[88] Gardiner, *Treaty Interpretation* (n 55) 334.

[89] Ulf Linderfalk, 'Doing the Right Thing for the Right Reason—Why Dynamic or Static Approaches Should Be Taken in the Interpretation of Treaties' (2008) 10 Int'l Comm L Rev 109, 11; Villiger, *Commentary on the VCLT* (n 5) 426 [9].

[90] Dörr, 'Article 31' (n 16) [105]–[7]. cf also Gardiner, *Treaty Interpretation* (n 55) 339 f.

[91] ibid 183 f; Yasseen, 'L'interprétation des traités' (n 83) 26. See also Paul Reuter in ILC, 'Summary Records of the 18th Session of the International Law Commission' (4 May–19 July 1966) [1966-I/2] YBILC 1, 194 [21]. According to him, it was 'it was important to bear in mind that to speak of the "ordinary meaning " of the terms, or of words, in the context, implied that more than one ordinary meaning was possible: a meaning which did not take the context into account and another meaning which did.... When the Commission spoke of "the ordinary meaning in the context", it was choosing between several ordinary meanings in the light of the context.'

[92] Ilmar Tammelo, *Treaty Interpretation and Practical Reason—Towards a General Theory of Legal Interpretation* (Law Book Co 1967) 87.

[93] Under classical international law according to Emer de Vattel, *The Law of Nations or the Principles of Natural Law* (Charles Fenwick tr, repr, Hein 1995) 202, treaties are to be interpreted according to 'the common use of the terms at the time the treaty was drawn up.' This view was also held by Sinclair, *The Vienna Convention on the Law of Treaties* (n 49) 124: 'The ordinary meaning of a treaty provision should in principle be the meaning which is attributed to it at the time of the conclusion of the treaty.' A less categorical view was held by Yasseen, 'L'interprétation des traités' (n 83) 26.

respective interpretative question arises ('contemporary language')?[94] Shall interpreters always favour the one perspective, always the other, or either one or the other on a case-by-case basis?[95] These are the questions that underpin the debates that are led under the notions of 'static' as opposed to 'dynamic', 'evolutive', or 'evolutionary' interpretation.[96]

In approaching this inter-temporal problem, interpreters inevitably touch upon the underlying tension between legal stability and flexibility. This tension speaks for taking a case-by-case approach instead of searching for a general answer. Although sometimes invoked for that purpose,[97] the so-called doctrine of inter-temporal law does not assist in choosing between constructions based on historic and constructions based on contemporary language. According to this doctrine, which has been formulated by Judge Huber in the *Island of Palmas* case,

> a juridical fact must be appreciated in the light of the law contemporary with it, and not of the law in force at the time when a dispute in regard to it arises or falls to be settled. … As regards the question which of different legal systems prevailing at successive periods is to be applied in a particular case (the so called intertemporal law), a distinction must be made between the creation of rights and the existence of rights. The same principle which subjects the acts creative of a right to the law in force at the time the right arises, demands that the existence of the right, in other words its continued manifestation, shall follow the conditions required by the evolution of the law.[98]

Upon closer consideration, this dictum fails to solve the problem of interpreting terms whose meanings may change over time.[99] What this doctrine stipulates is that a treaty is to be interpreted according to the rules of interpretation that are presently in force, not according to those rules in force at the time when the treaty was concluded, when it entered into force or at some other point in time.[100] The inter-temporal doctrine is concerned with determining the applicable law when there are several laws that could theoretically apply;[101] it cannot, however, resolve conflicts

---

[94] Linderfalk, 'Dynamic and Static Approaches' (n 89) 111.

[95] As regards this terminology, see ibid 113.

[96] The choice between static and dynamic interpretation arising in connection with subsequent conduct are addressed in greater detail in Chapter 5. Similar questions arise when determining the 'relevant rules of international law' under art 31(3)(c) VCLT.

[97] Linderfalk, 'Dynamic and Static Approaches' (n 89) 113.

[98] *Island of Palmas Case (USA v the Netherlands)* (1928) 2 RIAA 829, 845.

[99] See in particular Linderfalk, 'Dynamic and Static Approaches' (n 89) 116; see also Sondre Helmersen, 'Evolutive Treaty Interpretation: Legality, Semantics and Distinctions' (2013) 6 EJLS 127, 145 f.

[100] Linderfalk, 'Dynamic and Static Approaches' (n 89) 116; id, 'The Application of International Legal Norms over Time: The Second Branch of Intertemporal Law' (2011) 58 NILR 147, 162 f.

[101] See Paul Reuter in ILC, 'Summary Records of the 16th Session of the International Law Commission' (11 May–24 July 1964) [1964-I] YBILC 1, 35 [9], according to whom the inter-temporal doctrine referred to the 'conflict between legal rules in time.' See also Sir

of meanings which arise if one applies a particular rule governing the interpretation of a particular treaty.[102]

Some confusion over this doctrine's scope of application may be due to the ILC's 1964 draft on the law of treaties.[103] With this draft, the doctrine of inter-temporal law found entry into that provision which later became article 31(3)(c) VCLT: 'A Treaty shall be interpreted in good faith in accordance with the ordinary meaning to be given to each term … in the light of the rules of general international law in force at the time of its conclusion (lit b).'[104] As will be recalled, the qualification 'in force at the time of its conclusion' was ultimately dropped. This was because the Commission, after some debate, recognised that its 1964 proposal was ill-suited for dealing with evolutions of the law in a comprehensive and satisfactory manner.[105]

Even under the 1964 draft, the inter-temporal element did not underpin the interpretative process as a whole. Instead, it only related to the ambit of the other rules of international law under lit (b). On the one hand, the temporal element thereby remained linked to its origins of solving conflicts of law; on the other hand, one may well argue that its original inclusion reflected a principled decision in favour of static interpretation. But even assuming that the ILC once favoured static over dynamic interpretation, this implicit preference did not last: Today, the Vienna Convention omits any reference to the doctrine of inter-temporal law.

Moreover, the Vienna Convention does not explicitly stipulate whether treaties are to be interpreted in a static or in a dynamic fashion. To be precise, the Convention does not exclude that particular terms of a treaty may be interpreted in a dynamic fashion. Yet, it does not prescribe that particular terms of a treaty are always to be interpreted dynamically and never statically either.[106] Since the choice between static and dynamic interpretation is ultimately part of the process of determining

---

Humphrey Waldock in id, 'Summary Records of the 18th Session of the International Law Commission' (4 May–19 July 1966) [1966-I/2] YBILC 1, 199 [9]: 'The question whether the terms used were intended to have a fixed content or to change in meaning with the evolution of the law could be decided only by interpreting the intention of the parties. The matter was, strictly speaking, not one of inter-temporal law; the evolution of the law affected the application of the agreement, but not its meaning. That approach was, however, probably too subtle for the purpose of drafting a convention.'

[103] cf Taslim Elias, 'The Doctrine of Intertemporal Law' (1980) 74 AJIL 285, 303 f.

[102] cf Gardiner, *Treaty Interpretation* (n 55) 291, who critically assesses whether and ultimately denies that the doctrine of inter-temporal law can be extended to resolving issues of treaty interpretation.

[104] Waldock, 'Third Report' (n 11) 199.

[105] ILC, 'DALT' (n 32) 222.

[106] Rudolf Bernhardt, 'Evolutive Treaty Interpretation, Especially of the European Convention on Human Rights' (1999) 42 GJIL 11, 16: 'Not the existence, but the extent of the evolutive or dynamic element in any treaty interpretation is the real problem.' cf also Malgosia Fitzmaurice, 'Dynamic (Evolutive) Interpretation of Treaties—Part I' (2008) 21 Hague YB Int'l L 101, 118.

the meaning of the terms of the treaty, there are good arguments for making this choice based on the Vienna rules themselves.[107] While it may thus prove useful to consider the character of the terms to be interpreted as well as the character of the treaty as a whole,[108] it is not sufficient to leave it at that without taking other means of interpretation into account.[109]

Some means of interpretation, such as subsequent agreements and subsequent practice under article 31(3)(a) and (b) VCLT as well as other rules of international law under article 31(3)(c) VCLT, may be inherently open to encompassing new developments and thus interpreting treaties in a dynamic fashion.[110] Nonetheless, it remains essential to decide on a case-by-case basis, by applying the Vienna rules as a whole, whether particular terms of a treaty must be interpreted in a dynamic or static fashion.[111]

3.3.1.2 Context

The ordinary meaning of the terms of the treaty cannot be determined in clinical isolation; instead, this determination is closely related to examining the terms in their context.[112] The context thus serves to immediately qualify the ordinary meaning. It both helps to confirm an interpretation if there appears to be only one conceivable

---

[107] cf Sir Humphrey Waldock in ILC, 'Summary Records of the 18th Session of the International Law Commission' (4 May–19 July 1966) [1966-I/2] YBILC 1, 199 [9]: 'The question whether the terms used were intended to have a fixed content or to change in meaning with the evolution of the law could be decided only by interpreting the intention of the parties.' See also Rosalyn Higgins, 'Time and the Law: International Perspectives on an Old Problem' (1997) 46 ICLQ 501, 519.

[108] For more details, see Ulf Linderfalk, *On the Interpretation of Treaties—The Modern International Law as Expressed in the* 1969 *Vienna Convention on the Law of Treaties* (Springer 2007) 73 f, who emphasises the question of whether the contentious term is not time-bound and refers to a class of phenomena that are not defined (so-called 'undefined generic referring expressions'). See also Yoshifumi Tanaka, 'Reflections on Time Elements in the International Law of the Environment' (2013) 73 ZaöRV 139, 155 f, who mentions human rights and environmental treaties as examples of those kinds of treaties that per se lent themselves to being interpreted in a dynamic fashion.

[109] cf ibid.

[110] See 5.2.2.

[111] According to the commentary on draft conclusion 3 in ILC, 'Report of the International Law Commission on the Work of its 65th Session' (6 May–7 June and 8 July–9 August 2013) UN Doc A/68/10 25 [5], this case-by-case approach finds support in the jurisprudence of international courts and tribunals, which determine 'through recourse to the various means of interpretation… whether or not a treaty term should be given a meaning capable of evolving over time.'

[112] Gardiner, *Treaty Interpretation* (n 55) 181; Matthias Herdegen, 'Interpretation in International Law' in Rüdiger Wolfrum (ed), *The Max Planck Encyclopedia of Public International Law* (OUP 2012) [12].

meaning and to choose the more suitable meaning if there happen to be two or more possible ordinary meanings.[113] To facilitate this exercise of correctly determining the treaty's meaning, the Convention itself explains what an interpreter shall take into account when looking at the context of the terms of the treaty. Article 31(2) VCLT, which defines 'context' within the meaning of the Convention, distinguishes between context in a narrow and in a broader sense. In addition, article 31(3) VCLT stipulates that certain elements are to be taken into account 'together with the context'.

The context in a narrow sense, as defined in the *chapeau* of article 31(2) VCLT, consists of the entire text of the treaty including its preamble and annexes. Examining the context in a narrow sense, interpreters may consider aspects such as grammar, syntax and punctuation, the title of the treaty or of individual provisions, the structure of the entire treaty, and so forth.[114] The context in a broader sense comprises certain documents that are extrinsic to the text and expressly mentioned in article 31(2)(a) and (b) VCLT.[115] These documents include agreements relating to the treaty that were made between all the parties in connection with the conclusion of the treaty (a), and instruments made by one or more parties in connection with the conclusion of the treaty and accepted by the other parties as an instrument related to the treaty (b).

Article 31(3) VCLT further mentions three distinct means of interpretation that shall be taken into account together with the context. These means are, on the one hand, subsequent agreements and subsequent practice (article 31(3)(a) and (b) VCLT).[116] On the other hand, these means include any relevant rules of international law applicable in the relations between the parties (article 31(3)(c) VCLT).[117] These relevant rules may comprise treaty law, customary international law, and general principles of international law.[118] Notably, article 31(3) VCLT does not regard

---

[113] Gardiner, *Treaty Interpretation* (n 55) 197.

[114] For more details, see ibid.

[115] Hence: context in a broader sense as opposed to those elements that form an integral part of the treaty. See Dörr, 'Article 31' (n 16) 549 [62], [63].

[116] Since the entire next chapter focuses on subsequent agreements and subsequent practice within the meaning of art 31(3)(a) and (b) VCLT, it is not necessary to go into details at this point.

[117] For more details, see Campbell McLachlan, 'The Principle of Systemic Integration and Article 31(3)(c) of the Vienna Convention' (2005) 54 ICLQ 279.

[118] cf art 38(1) Statute of the International Court of Justice, annexed to the Charter of the United Nations (signed 26 June 1945, entered into force 24 October 1946) 1 UNTS XVI (ICJ Statute), which lists treaty law, customary international law, and general principles of international law among the sources of international law. See also Herdegen, 'Interpretation in International Law' (n 112) [22]. As regards art 31(3)(c) VCLT, see in particular ILC, 'Fragmentation of International Law: Difficulties Arising from the Diversification and Expansion of International Law—Report of the Study Group of the International Law Commission' (13 April 2006) UN Doc A/CN.4/L.682; McLachlan, 'Systemic Integration' (n 117); Ulf Linderfalk, 'Who are "the Parties"?—Article 31, Paragraph 3(c) of the 1969 Vienna Convention and the "Principle of Systemic Integration" Revisited' (2008) 55 NILR 343.

subsequent agreements, subsequent practice, and relevant rules of international law as forming part of the context; instead, it merely stipulates that these means of interpretation shall be taken into account together with the context. Nevertheless, this difference in terminology does not entail any difference in legal consequences.[119] By stipulating that subsequent agreements, subsequent practice, and other relevant rules of international law shall be taken into account *with* the context, article 31(3) VCLT refrains from introducing any hierarchy between context in a narrow and in a broader sense under para 2 and quasi-context under para 3.[120]

3.3.1.3 Object and Purpose

Article 31(1) VCLT not only requires interpreters to determine the ordinary meaning of the terms of the treaty in their context but also in the light of the treaty's object and purpose. Compared to other means of interpretation, a treaty's object and purpose entails a higher degree of uncertainty, vagueness, and unpredictability. This is because the composite 'object and purpose' is rather vague itself and less tangible than, for example, a lexical meaning, syntax, or a given State practice.

To figure out what 'object and purpose' means, one may be tempted to split this composite into the treaty's 'object' on the one hand and its 'purpose' on the other. The Convention's *travaux préparatoires* suggest that the composite had been intentionally introduced to replace the term 'objects' that was employed in the draft article on *pacta sunt servanda.* In the ILC's view, the composite was more precise than the term 'objects'; moreover, it was considered to carry the advantage of conforming to the terminology preferred by the ICJ in its Advisory Opinion on the *Genocide Convention.*[121] Gardiner further elaborates on the difference between 'object' and 'purpose' by pointing to these terms' French origins. According to him, French public law distinguished between 'l'objet' of a legal instrument (meaning the fact that an instrument creates certain rights and obligations) and 'le but' as the

[119] Gardiner, *Treaty Interpretation* (n 55) 228.

[120] ibid; Sorel and Boré Eveno, 'Article 31' (n 53) 808 [8]. However, apparently contradicting themselves, Sorel and Boré Eveno also contend that '[s]ubsequent interpretative agreements, subsequent practice, or reference to relevant rules of public international law therefore seem more in the order of confirmation rather than assertion.' See id, 'Article 31—1969 Vienna Convention' in Olivier Corten and Pierre Klein (eds), *The Vienna Conventions on the Law of Treaties—A Commentary* (OUP 2011) 826 [42].

[121] Paul Reuter in ILC, 'Summary Records of the 16th Session of the International Law Commission' (11 May–24 July 1964) [1964-I] YBILC 1, 26 [77]; see also *Reservations to the Convention on Genocide* (Advisory Opinion) [1951] ICJ Rep 15, 23 f. For the use of the term 'quasi-context', see in particular Robert Kolb, *Interprétation et création du droit international—Esquisses d'une herméneutique juridique moderne pour le droit international public* (Bruylant 2006) 467.

more general reasons for establishing 'l'objet'.[122] But despite these terminological subtleties, practice under article 31(1) VCLT has so far largely refrained from strictly distinguishing between object and purpose; instead, it has become common to loosely invoke the composite 'object and purpose' without further explanation.[123]

This sweeping approach, however, does not facilitate the exercise of determining, or better 'deducing' a treaty's object and purpose. Sometimes, a treaty's preamble quite clearly indicates the treaty's object and purpose.[124] In other cases, it is more difficult to discover a treaty's object and purpose. In this situation, recourse to other means of interpretation—such as subsequent agreements and subsequent practice—may then assist interpreters in identifying or clarifying the treaty's object and purpose.[125]

3.3.2 Supplementary Means of Interpretation

When interpreters have exhausted the general rule of interpretation under article 31 VCLT, article 32 VCLT under certain conditions admits recourse to so-called supplementary means of interpretation. Reading the text of article 32 VCLT in full helps to understand why these means are termed 'supplementary':

> Recourse may be had to supplementary means of interpretation, including the preparatory work of the treaty and the circumstances of its conclusion, in order to confirm the meaning resulting from the application of article 31, or to determine the meaning when the interpretation according to article 31:
>
> (a) leaves the meaning ambiguous or obscure; or
> (b) leads to a result which is manifestly absurd or unreasonable.

Two aspects are worth mentioning. Firstly, the list of supplementary means that may be taken into account under article 32 VCLT is exemplary only.[126] For this reason,

[122] Gardiner, *Treaty Interpretation* (n 55) 212 f. See also Elisabeth Zoller, *La bonne foi en droit international public* (Pédone 1977) 74; Jan Klabbers, 'Some Problems regarding the Object and Purpose of Treaties' (1997) 8 FYBIL 138, 144 f; Ulf Linderfalk, 'On the Meaning of the "Object and Purpose" Criterion, in the Context of the Vienna Convention on the Law of Treaties, Article 19' (2003) 72 NJIL 429, 433 f.

[123] Klabbers, 'Object and Purpose' (n 122) 145; Gardiner, *Treaty Interpretation* (n 55) 214.

[124] See already *Genocide Convention* (n 121) 23.

[125] See draft conclusion 7(1) and the accompanying commentary in ILC, 'Report of the International Law Commission on the Work of its 66th Session' (5 May–6 June and 7 July–8 August 2014) UN Doc A/69/10, 167, 181 [8]. See also Georg Nolte, 'Report 1—Jurisprudence of the International Court of Justice and Arbitral Tribunals of Ad Hoc Jurisdiction relating to Subsequent Agreements and Subsequent Practice' in id (ed), *Treaties and Subsequent Practice* (OUP 2013) 181.

[126] Gardiner, *Treaty Interpretation* (n 55) 348.

article 32 VCLT authorises interpreters to have recourse to, among others, subsequent agreements and subsequent practice that do not meet all criteria of article 31(3)(a) and (b) VCLT.[127]

This is easily neglected because article 32 VCLT is regularly considered as reflecting a historic (and hence intentionalist) approach to interpretation by expressly mentioning the preparatory work of the treaty (*travaux préparatoires*) and the circumstances of its conclusion. This exemplary enumeration notwithstanding, some commentators have argued that article 32 VCLT covered only those means of interpretation of which 'all the treaty parties concerned … have been aware.'[128] As article 32 VCLT does not expressly envisage such restrictive interpretation, this view is not convincing. Yet, the parties' awareness may well be taken into account when establishing the interpretative weight of a particular supplementary means of interpretation.

The second notable aspect already follows from the term 'supplementary means' of interpretation as used both in the title and in the *chapeau* of article 32 VCLT. Under article 32 VCLT, supplementary means of interpretation may solely and exclusively be taken into account either to confirm a meaning resulting from the application of the general rule or to determine the meaning of the terms of the treaty if one of two alternative conditions is met. In the first alternative, supplementary means of interpretation may be taken into account if interpretation according to the general rule leaves the meaning ambiguous or obscure. In the second alternative, supplementary means of interpretation may be taken into account if interpretation according to the general rule leads to a manifestly absurd or unreasonable result.

The idea upon which the Vienna rules' distinction between primary and supplementary means of interpretation is based is the distinction between 'authentic' and 'non-authentic' means of interpretation.[129] In that sense, the notion 'authentic' emphasises the 'common will of the parties'[130] by regarding primary means of interpretation as 'objective evidence of the understanding of the parties as to the meaning of the treaty.'[131] As Grigory Tunkin, for example, explained, supplementary means of interpretation are

> not authentic means of interpretation because they did not reflect an established agreement between the parties, but they could, and often did, throw light on the origin or nature of ambiguities in the text. If the meaning of the text could not be established by the processes set out in paragraph 69, the further means of interpretation could be of use.[132]

---

[127] For more details, see 4.4.

[128] See in particular Villiger, *Commentary on the VCLT* (n 5) 446 [6].

[129] ILC, 'DALT' (n 32) 220 [10]. For the question whether their status as 'authentic' means of interpretation vests subsequent agreements and subsequent practice under art 31(3)(a) and (b) VCLT with binding force, see 5.1.1.

[130] Commentary on draft conclusion 2 in ILC, 'Report of the International Law Commission on the Work of its 65th Session' UN Doc A/68/10, 21 [3].

[131] ILC, 'DALT' (n 32) 221 [15]. See also ibid 203 [13], 204 [15]; draft conclusion 2 and the accompanying commentary in id, 'Report of the International Law Commission on the Work of its 65th Session' UN Doc A/68/10, 20 f.

[132] Grigory Tunkin in id, 'Summary Records of the 18th Session of the International Law Commission' (4 May–19 July 1966) [1966-I/2] YBILC 1, 201 [44].

Supplementary means of interpretation therefore differ from primary means of interpretation under article 31 VCLT in several respects. First, while interpreters are obliged to take account of all means of interpretation falling under article 31 VCLT ('shall be interpreted'), it is at their discretion whether they take account of supplementary means or not ('recourse may be had').[133] Second, interpreters are only allowed to take account of supplementary means of interpretation after having applied the general rule as a whole.[134] But even then, their options are restricted; in particular, they may base their interpretations on supplementary means if applying the general rule leads to an ambiguous, obscure, or manifestly absurd or unreasonable result. Otherwise, they may only consider supplementary means of interpretation to confirm interpretations already arrived at.

If one takes article 32 VCLT seriously, these remarks may appear superfluous and read like a reiteration of the wording of this provision. However, there exist continuing tendencies to ignore or level the difference between articles 31 and 32 VCLT.[135] These tendencies reflect older disputes about the correct approach to interpretation that surfaced during the debates in the ILC and in the first session of the Vienna Conference in 1968.[136] The next paragraphs therefore more closely illuminate these debates and conclude with presenting the solution offered by the Convention.

3.3.3 Interpretation as a Single Combined Operation

Understanding the interrelation between the various means of interpretation under articles 31 and 32 VCLT is as essential as understanding their content. This is because it helps to appreciate status and relevance of subsequent agreements and subsequent practice under the Convention. Besides, this understanding helps to respond to ongoing debates about the correct 'approach' to interpretation. These debates are not only of academic interest but may also influence the process of interpretation and eventually distort the results of this process. Based on these considerations, the three main conflicting approaches to interpretation are presented in a first step. In a second step, the interrelation of the various means of interpretation is then outlined and it is discussed if and how the Convention has succeeded in accommodating these conflicting approaches.

The three conflicting approaches to interpretation are commonly referred to as the textualist, the intentionalist, and the teleological approach.[137] As its designation

[133] Gardiner, *Treaty Interpretation* (n 55) 347.

[134] cf ibid 360 f.

[135] See generally Linderfalk, 'The Hierarchical Structure of Articles 31 and 32 VCLT' (n 60), who makes a strong case in favour of upholding the hierarchical structure between arts 31 and 32 VCLT.

[136] Gardiner, *Treaty Interpretation* (n 55) 348.

[137] Fitzmaurice, 'The Law and Procedure of the ICJ' (n 13) 204 f; Francis Jacobs, 'Varieties of Approach to Treaty Interpretation: With Special Reference to the Draft Convention on the Law of Treaties before the Vienna Diplomatic Conference' (1969) 18 ICLQ 318, 319 f.

indicates, the textualist approach requires interpreters to primarily focus on objectively discernible elements related to the text of the treaty.[138] Its underlying assumption is that the intentions of the parties are best reflected in the words used in the treaty.[139] Hence this approach presumes that words normally have an ordinary meaning which is either self-evident or which can be established by a textual analysis. Judge Huber, a famous proponent of the textualist approach, therefore suggested that the text of the treaty became 'sauf de rares exceptions, la seule et la plus récente expression de la volonté commune des parties.'[140] Means of interpretation that are unrelated to the text of the treaty but independently investigate into the parties' intentions, such as a treaty's *travaux préparatoires*, are consequently rejected.

Under the intentionalist approach, in contrast, the text of the treaty is only one among several equally ranked means to discover the intentions of the parties. In addition to the text of the treaty, all other means that help discovering the parties' intentions may be taken into account.[141] Proponents of this approach, such as Sir Hersch Lauterpacht, emphasise that one did not merely interpret words but treaties as a whole.[142] Public international law and treaties in particular operated on a consensual basis; in consequence, the goal of treaty interpretation was to discover the true intentions of the parties rather than an abstract construct such as 'presumed intentions'.[143] The teleological approach at first sight resembles the intentionalist approach in that it seeks to ascertain the object and purpose of the treaty.[144] However, it does not equate the object and purpose of the treaty with the intentions of the parties. The teleological approach rather assumes that a treaty's object and purpose exists independently from the parties' intentions.[145]

---

[138] David Bederman, 'Revivalist Canons and Treaty Interpretation' (1993) 41 UCLA L Rev 953, 964; Herdegen, 'Interpretation in International Law' (n 112) [7].

[139] Peter McRae, 'The Search for Meaning: Continuing Problems with the Interpretation of Treaties' (2002) 33 Victoria U Wellington L Rev 209, 212.

[140] Max Huber in Sir Hersch Lauterpacht, 'De l'interprétation des traités—Observations complémentaires et projet définitif de résolutions, présentés à l'Institut de Droit International' (1952) 44 AIDI 197, 199, quoted by Waldock, 'Third Report' (n 11) 56 [13]. In English [translated by the author]: '... apart from rare exceptions, the only and the most recent expression of the common intention of the parties.' See also Sinclair, *The Vienna Convention on the Law of Treaties* (n 49) 131 [fn omitted]: 'The text is the *expression* of the intention of the parties; and it is to that expression that one must first look.'

[141] McRae, 'The Search for Meaning' (n 139) 216; Herdegen, 'Interpretation in International Law' (n 112) [7].

[142] See Sir Hersch Lauterpacht, 'Restrictive Interpretation and the Principle of Effectiveness in the Interpretation of Treaties' (1949) 26 BYIL 48, 83 as well as his proposals in Institut de Droit International, 'De l'interprétation des traités—Rapport et projet de désolutions présentés à l'Institut de Droit International' (1950) 43 AIDI 366, 423 f.

[143] McRae, 'The Search for Meaning' (n 139) 217.

[144] Sinclair, 'The Vienna Conference' (n 4) 61. For an example of this approach, see especially art 19(a) of the 1935 Harvard Draft on the Law of Treaties.

[145] Jacobs, 'Varieties of Approach to Treaty Interpretation' (n 137) 320.

As mentioned earlier, the dispute about these conflicting approaches surfaced before and during the first session of the Vienna Conference in 1968. Before the Vienna Conference, Myres McDougal already criticised the Commission's 'destructive formalism'.[146] In his view, the 'restrictive hierarchies' advocated by the ILC rendered it uncertain that an interpreter's 'determinations bear any relation to the genuine shared expectations of the parties.'[147] As part of the US delegation to the Vienna Conference, McDougal challenged the Commission's draft by introducing an amendment that would have merged draft articles 27 and 28, upgraded the *travaux préparatoires*, and subordinated the whole interpretative process to ascertaining the common intention of the parties.[148] Defending the Commission's draft, the Uruguayan Committee Member Eduardo Jiménez de Aréchaga replied by cautioning that 'if respect for the wording of a treaty that had been signed and ratified was not something sacred, if the parties were to be allowed freely to invoke their supposed real will, an essential advantage of written and conventional law would be lost.'[149] In the end, the US proposal was rejected by a strong majority[150] and the Vienna rules of interpretation were even adopted unanimously.[151]

Although Sir Humphrey Waldock had clarified that he did not mean to 'settle any doctrinal controversy',[152] the Vienna rules embody some kind of settlement by reflecting a pragmatic and balanced approach instead of yielding to one or the other doctrinal theory.[153] At first glance, articles 31 and 32 VCLT suggest that the Convention pursues a predominantly textualist approach. First of all, the terms of the treaty form the logical starting point and remain the ultimate point of reference throughout the interpretative process. Moreover, the Convention relegates the *travaux préparatoires*—the 'Golden Calf' of the intentionalists—to a subsidiary

---

[146] Myres McDougal, 'The International Law Commission's Draft Articles upon Interpretation—Textuality Redivivus' (1967) 61 AJIL 992, 997.

[147] ibid 998.

[148] For the US proposal, see UN Conference on the Law of Treaties, 'Reports of the Committee of the Whole' (Vienna, 26 March–24 May 1968 and 9 April–22 May 1969) Official Records: Documents of the Conference, UN Doc A/CONF.39/11/Add2, 149 [269]. The statement by which Myres McDougal introduced the US proposal is reprinted in (1968) 62 AJIL 1021.

[149] Eduardo Jiménez de Aréchaga in UN Conference on the Law of Treaties, 'Reports of the Committee of the Whole' (Vienna, 26 March 1968 and 9 April 1969) Official Records: Documents of the Conference, UN Doc A/CONF.39/11/Add2, 170 [63].

[150] UN Conference on the Law of Treaties, 'Reports of the Committee of the Whole' (Vienna, 26 March 1968 and 9 April 1969) Official Records: Documents of the Conference, UN Doc A/CONF.39/11/Add2, 150 [271]: The amendment proposed by the US delegation was rejected by 66 votes to six, with 10 abstentions.

[151] See 3.1.

[152] Sir Humphrey Waldock in UN Conference on the Law of Treaties, 'Summary Records of the Plenary Meetings and of the Meetings of the Committee of the Whole' (First session, Vienna 26 March 1968) UN Doc A/CONF.39/11, 184 [66].

[153] Sorel and Boré Eveno, 'Article 31' (n 53) 808 [9].

means of interpretation.[154] Yet, this textualism is not absolute. By containing means of interpretation such as the object and purpose, subsequent conduct, and *the travaux préparatoires*, the Convention also reflects traces of intentionalist and teleological approaches to treaty interpretation.[155]

In the end, it is therefore hardly helpful to consider the Vienna rules as a choice between conflicting approaches to interpretation. What may be taken as evidencing one or the other approach may as well be explained by reasons of logic and good sense. As one commentator pointed out, '[t]he ordinary meaning of a term serves as a natural starting point, since interpretation turns on the meaning and scope of written words.'[156] Furthermore, means of interpretation that are unrelated to the text—which is 'presumed to be the authentic expression of the intentions of the parties'[157]—may indicate the parties' intention in a less reliable fashion than those intrinsic to it. This is especially true for the *travaux préparatoires* since they must not necessarily reflect the parties' true intentions but are highly susceptible to manipulation.[158] Subsequent agreements and subsequent practice, which are also extrinsic to the text of the treaty, thus constitute an exception in that they are based on objectively discernible evidence.[159] This explains why they, in contrast to the *travaux préparatoires*, are justifiably part of the general rule although they were traditionally regarded as evidence of the parties' original intentions.[160] In the light of the Vienna rules of interpretation, it is therefore appropriate to abandon the dispute about the correct approach to interpretation. Interpreters had better accept that the Convention reflects a binding and rather rational decision about how the ultimate goal of interpretation can best be achieved.[161]

---

[154] cf Jacobs, 'Varieties of Approach to Treaty Interpretation' (n 137) 326.

[155] McRae, 'The Search for Meaning' (n 139) 226, 229. See also Villiger, *Commentary on the VCLT* (n 5) 436 [31], who notes that most of the means which make up the general rule are in fact extrinsic to the text.

[156] ibid 436 [30]. cf also ILC, 'DALT' (n 32) 220 [9].

[157] ibid 220 [11].

[158] Particular caution is recommended when, eg, the material taken into account as part of the *travaux préparatoires* does not originate from the parties as a whole. When such material originates from individual parties, interpreters need to consider that individual parties may have pursued their very own agenda in consciously or unconsciously 'creating' this material. See Jacobs, 'Varieties of Approach to Treaty Interpretation' (n 137) 339. cf also Linderfalk, 'The Hierarchical Structure of Articles 31 and 32 VCLT' (n 60) 153 f. cf also, although less critical, Sir Hersch Lauterpacht, 'Some Observations on Preparatory Work in the Interpretation of Treaties' (1935) 48 HLR 549, 582.

[159] ILC, 'DALT' (n 32) 221 [15].

[160] Jacobs, 'Varieties of Approach to Treaty Interpretation' (n 137) 328; Giovanni Distefano, 'La pratique subséquente des états parties à un traité' (1994) 40 AFDI 41, 46. See also Sorel and Boré Eveno, 'Article 31' (n 53) 826 [42], who contended that subsequent practice was a matter of reintroducing the intention of the parties.

[161] McRae, 'The Search for Meaning' (n 139) 258, who stresses that the means of interpretation contained in art 31 VCLT are not an end in themselves; see also Lassa Oppenheim, Robert Jennings, and Arthur Watts, *Oppenheim's International Law* (9th edn, Longman 1992) 1271.

The Convention's rational and pragmatic approach to interpretation affects and characterises the interrelationship of the various means of interpretation under the Vienna rules. Apart from distinguishing between a general rule and supplementary means of interpretation, the Convention abstains from introducing any hierarchy between the various means of interpretation. This lack of a hierarchical structure is commonly illustrated by describing the interpretative process under the general rule as a 'single combined operation';[162] speaking of one general rule (singular) instead of several distinct rules (plural), even the title of article 31 VCLT embodies this idea of the interpretative process as a 'single combined operation'.[163] An even more illustrative description of the holistic interpretative process under the general rule originates from Special Rapporteur Sir Humphrey Waldock, who stressed that '[a]ll the various elements, so far as they were present in any given case, would be thrown into the crucible and their interaction would then give the legally relevant interpretation'.[164]

In explicit terms, this means that the elements constituting the general rule cannot be separated from each other. All means of interpretation under article 31 VCLT carry equal weight and are to be applied cumulatively.[165] Interpreters may, for example, immediately succeed in establishing a single ordinary meaning by adopting a purely textualist approach. Nevertheless, the Convention requires them to apply the other means of interpretation, too.[166] Each and every single means of interpretation will not necessarily be useful in a given case and thus ultimately influence the result of the interpretative process.[167] Besides, the interpretative weight of each means of

[162] ILC, 'DALT' (n 32) 219 [8]; Gardiner, *Treaty Interpretation* (n 55) 10.

[163] ILC, 'DALT' (n 32) 219 [8].

[164] Waldock, 'Sixth Report' (n 30) 95 [4].

[165] cf Mustafa Yasseen in ILC, 'Summary Records of the 18th Session of the International Law Commission' (4 May–19 July 1966) [1966-I/2] YBILC 1, 197 [48]: 'The means enumerated were only various aspects of the same operation; they were arranged, not in any order of precedence, but in a practical order, which was self-evident in view of the circumstances.' See also Herdegen, 'Interpretation in International Law' (n 112) [11]; Villiger, *Commentary on the VCLT* (n 5) 435 [29].

[166] ibid 435 f [29]. See further Duncan French, 'Treaty Interpretation and the Incorporation of Extraneous Legal Rules' (2006) 55 ICLQ 281, 301, who emphasises that the means of interpretation that are mentioned in art 31(2) and (3) VCLT 'are not discretionary add-ons, but prescriptive and mandatory aspects of the "general rule".'

[167] Villiger, *Commentary on the VCLT* (n 5) 436 [30]; Richard Gardiner, 'Treaty Interpretation in the English Courts Since *Fothergill v Monarch Airlines* (1980)' (1995) 44 ICLQ 920, 923. See also Santiago Bernàrdez, 'Interpretation of Treaties by the International Court of Justice Following the Adoption of the 1969 Vienna Convention on the Law of Treaties' in Gerhard Hafner (ed), *Liber Amicorum: Professor Ignaz Seidl-Hohenveldern in Honour of his 80th Birthday* (Kluwer 1998) 726 [11], who describes this feature of the Vienna rules as 'one of the most distinctive features of the Vienna Convention system, namely that interpretation of a treaty, or a provision of a treaty, is a legal operation which should combine the various permitted elements and means of interpretation as they may be present in the case, while keeping *open* the interpretation until the very conclusion of the interpretative process.'

interpretation may naturally differ in each case. By stipulating a holistic approach to interpretation, the Convention ensures, however, that all legally relevant aspects are identified and taken into account before finally adopting one interpretation.[168] This is not because the Convention cherishes one or the other approach to interpretation but because it is concerned with correctly determining a treaty's meaning by ascertaining the objectivised intention of the parties.

[168] Gardiner, *Treaty Interpretation* (n 55) 162, 185. See also ILC, 'DALT' (n 32) 218–23.

Chapter 4
Subsequent Agreements and Subsequent Practice under Articles 31 and 32 VCLT

The previous chapters traced the origins of subsequent agreements and subsequent practice under the Convention (Chap. 2) and set these means of interpretation into their broader context of the Convention and the Vienna rules as a whole (Chap. 3). Against this background, Chap. 4 now concludes the theoretical part of this study by elaborating on the meaning of subsequent agreements and subsequent practice under articles 31 and 32 VCLT.

In a first step, it examines the relationship between subsequent agreements and subsequent practice (4.1). In particular, it discusses whether the apparent difference between subsequent agreements and subsequent practice is one of quality or merely of degree. Based on this examination, it asks whether this difference—whatever its nature—entails any legal consequences. In a second and third step, Chap. 4 then concentrates on each of those requirements which a given phenomenon has to satisfy in order to qualify as a relevant subsequent agreement (4.2) or subsequent practice (4.3) under article 31(3)(a) and (b) VCLT, or as 'other' subsequent conduct under article 32 VCLT (4.4).

4.1 Relationship between Subsequent Agreements and Subsequent Practice

Subsequent agreements and subsequent practice are usually mentioned together.[1] When chairing the ILC's Study Group on 'Treaties over Time', Georg Nolte therefore tried to introduce the generic expression 'subsequent conduct' to cover both

[1] See the various contributions in Georg Nolte (ed), *Treaties and Subsequent Practice* (OUP 2013).

K. Berner, *Subsequent Agreements and Subsequent Practice in Domestic Courts*, Beiträge zum ausländischen öffentlichen Recht und Völkerrecht,
https://doi.org/10.1007/978-3-662-54937-7_4

subsequent agreements and subsequent practice.[2] One connection between subsequent agreements and subsequent practice is their common qualifier 'subsequent'. Comparing their general structure, one immediately notices that lits (a) and (b) of article 31(3) VCLT are drafted similarly, too. Both provisions mention some form of agreement of or between the parties, and both provisions expressly relate to the interpretation or application of a treaty. But despite these similarities, the Convention mentions subsequent agreements and subsequent practice under separate letters of article 31(3) VCLT. The reasons for this choice of drafting are now examined.

When interpreters invoke article 31(3)(a) or (b) VCLT, they will in both cases ultimately base their interpretations on an agreement between or of the parties regarding the interpretation (or application) of the treaty.[3] According to the ILC, the distinction between subsequent agreements and subsequent practice does 'not denote a difference concerning their authentic character.'[4] Lit (b) differs from lit (a) in that it additionally requires a certain practice that establishes the parties' agreement. Article 31(3)(a) VCLT explicitly envisages an agreement that '*ipso facto*' forms the basis of a particular interpretation.[5] This does not mean that interpreters will never need to critically examine whether an agreement in the sense of article 31(3)(a) VCLT really exists. But once they have succeeded in establishing the existence of an agreement, no further questions of proof arise.

The interpretative value of agreements under article 31(3)(a) VCLT therefore lies in the agreements themselves. The interpretative value of subsequent practice under

[2] See id, 'Report 1—Jurisprudence of the International Court of Justice and Arbitral Tribunals of Ad Hoc Jurisdiction relating to Subsequent Agreements and Subsequent Practice' in id (ed), *Treaties and Subsequent Practice* (OUP 2013) 174.

[3] Richard Gardiner, *Treaty Interpretation* (2nd edn, OUP 2015) 224. See also Giovanni Distefano, 'La pratique subséquente des états parties à un traité' (1994) 40 AFDI 41, 46 [fn omitted]: '[C]e n'est pas la pratique ultérieure en tant que telle qui fonde l'interprétation donnée par les parties du texte conventionnel, mais c'est dans l'accord (tacite) entre elles, cristallisé par leur comportement convergent et assonnant, que réside de fondement juridique de cette méthode d'interprétation.' In English [translated by the author]: '[I]t is not subsequent practice as such upon which the interpretation of the treaty's text by the parties is based but the (tacit) agreement between them, evidenced by their uniform and consistent behaviour, which constitutes the doctrinal foundation of this means of interpretation.' cf also Ulf Linderfalk, *On the Interpretation of Treaties—The Modern International Law as Expressed in the* 1969 *Vienna Convention on the Law of Treaties* (Springer 2007) 162: 'In the legal regime established by articles 31–33 VCLT, a recurring theme is that normally, a phenomenon cannot be included in the context for the interpretation of a treaty, if all parties have not accepted it.'

[4] Commentary on draft conclusion 2 in ILC, 'Report of the International Law Commission on the Work of its 65th Session' (6 May–7 June and 8 July–9 August 2013) UN Doc A/68/10, 23 [9].

[5] ibid 23 [9], 33 f [9], [10].

article 31(3)(b) VCLT equally rests on the parties' agreement.[6] In other words, the parties' agreement constitutes the normative heart of both subsequent agreements under lit (a) and of subsequent practice under lit (b) of article 31(3) VCLT. But unlike under lit (a), the agreement under lit (b) is not explicit but must be established by a given practice. In a figurative sense, practice therefore serves as a piece of evidence demonstrating the existence of an implicit agreement.[7] For this reason, interpreters need to perform an additional intellectual operation to establish the necessary link between a given practice and the parties' agreement if they wish to rely on subsequent practice under article 31(3)(b) VCLT.[8]

What does this observation suggest about the relationship between subsequent agreements and subsequent practice? Firstly, it is often difficult to precisely discern between subsequent agreements and subsequent practice. The stronger the probative value of a given body of practice, the closer this practice comes to qualifying as a genuine, explicit agreement instead of merely establishing such agreement.[9] This difficulty of discerning between subsequent practice and subsequent agreements is compounded by not imposing any formal requirements upon subsequent agreements under article 31(3)(a) VCLT.[10] Secondly, the probative value of subsequent agreements is *per definitionem* undiminished whereas the probative value and hence interpretative force of subsequent practice varies on a sliding scale. Hence the difference between subsequent agreements and subsequent practice 'lies in the manner

---

[6] See the commentary on draft conclusion 9 in ILC, 'Report of the International Law Commission on the Work of its 66th Session' (5 May–6 June and 7 July–8 August 2014) UN Doc A/69/10, 197 [2].

[7] This understanding of subsequent practice as a piece of evidence already emerged during the debates in the ILC. cf, for instance, Grigory Tunkin in ILC, 'Summary Records of the 16th Session of the International Law Commission' (11 May–24 July 1964) [1964-I] YBILC 1, 284 [23] [explanation added]: 'In connexion with the third source [subsequent practice], some doubts had arisen whether it should be considered as a secondary source or merely as a subsidiary source. He personally regarded it as having the character of a secondary source; if the subsequent practice of all the parties concurred, it could be said that there existed between the parties a tacit agreement, at least on interpretation.' See also Mustafa Yasseen, 'L'interprétation des traités d'après la Convention de Vienne sur le Droit des Traités' (1976) 151 RCADI 1, 49; Giovanni Distefano, 'L'interprétation evolutive de la norme internationale' (2011) 115 RGDIP 373, 376.

[8] cf *Case concerning Kasikili/Sedudu Island (Botswana v Namibia)* [1999] ICJ Rep 1045, 1087 [63].

[9] cf Oliver Dörr, 'Article 31—General Rule of Interpretation' in Oliver Dörr and Kirsten Schmalenbach (eds), *Vienna Convention on the Law of Treaties—A Commentary* (Springer 2012) 554 [75]. See Georg Nolte, 'Annex A—Treaties over Time—In Particular: Subsequent Agreement and Practice' in ILC, 'Report of the International Law Commission on the Work of its 60th Session' (5 May–6 June and 7 July–8 August 2008) UN Doc A/63/10 375 [24].

[10] As regards the question of whether any formal requirements apply to subsequent agreements under art 31(3)(a) VCLT, see 4.2.1 and 6.2.

of establishing the agreement of the parties' and 'the greater ease with which an agreement is established.'[11]

If an interpretation supported by a subsequent agreement conflicts with one supported by subsequent practice, the respective probative value of agreement and practice shall be taken into account.[12] According to the ILC, this value depends on, among others, their relation to other means of interpretation, how clear or specifically treaty-related the agreement or practice is, the time when it occurred, the emphasis given to it by the parties themselves, or the applicable burden of proof.[13] Weighing the probative and interpretative value of a subsequent agreement against that of subsequent practice, the balance therefore often (although not necessarily always) tilts in favour of the former when it comes to identifying the parties' agreement regarding the interpretation of the treaty.[14]

In sum, one can best describe subsequent agreements and subsequent practice as two separate but closely related means of interpretation. The difference between these two means is not a substantive or qualitative one but rather one of degree. Acknowledging such different degrees of probative and interpretative value must not be mistaken for re-introducing a hierarchy between subsequent agreements and subsequent practice.[15] Instead, it is important to recall that the exact interpretative value of subsequent agreements and especially subsequent practice, as that of any

---

[11] Commentary on draft conclusion 2 in ILC, 'Report of the International Law Commission on the Work of its 65th Session' (6 May–7 June and 8 July–9 August 2013) UN Doc A/68/10, 23 [9].

[12] This does not mean that the general rules of conflict of laws cannot also help deciding conflicts between subsequent practice and subsequent agreements or even between two or more subsequent agreements. These rules, *mutatis mutandis* applied to subsequent agreements and subsequent practice, include those of *lex specialis derogat legi generali* and *lex posterior derogat legi priori*. As regards the *lex posterior* rule, see in particular the commentary on draft conclusion 9 in ILC, 'Report of the International Law Commission on the Work of its 66th Session' (5 May–6 June and 7 July–8 August 2014) UN Doc A/69/10, 204 [23]. The rule of *lex superior derogat legi inferiori*, in contrast, cannot be applied to subsequent agreements and subsequent practice since art 31 VCLT does not impose any hierarchy upon the elements of the general rule. Generally on these rules, see Erich Vranes, 'Lex Superior, Lex Specialis, Lex Posterior—Zur Rechtsnatur der "Konfliktlösungsregeln"' (2005) 65 ZaöRV 391.

[13] Commentary on draft conclusion 8 in ILC, 'Report of the International Law Commission on the Work of its 66th Session' (5 May–6 June and 7 July–8 August 2014) UN Doc A/69/10, 192 f.

[14] Rahim Moloo, 'When Actions Speak Louder Than Words: The Relevance of Subsequent Party Conduct to Treaty Interpretation' (2013) 31 Berkeley J Int'l L 39, 58, 74; cf also Nolte, 'Report 1—ICJ and Arbitral Tribunals' (n 2) 173 [fn omitted], who notes that the 'evidentiary value is higher in the case of a "subsequent agreement" than in the case of "subsequent practice".' cf also *Kasikili/Sedudu Island* (n 8) 1087 [63].

[15] In fact, subsequent practice was once part of the draft article on subsidiary means of interpretation but was later upgraded to the same status as subsequent agreements. See Sir Humphrey Waldock, 'Third Report on the Law of Treaties' [1964-II] YBILC 5, 52 f and 3.1 of this study.

other means of interpretation, depends on the circumstances of each case and cannot be abstractly defined.

4.2 Subsequent Agreements under Article 31(3)(a) VCLT

Section 4.2 examines the requirements which article 31(3)(a) VCLT imposes on subsequent agreements as a means of interpretation under the general rule. First of all, this provision requires an 'agreement'. Next, article 31(3)(a) VCLT stipulates that the agreement must be one 'between the parties' as well as 'regarding the interpretation of the treaty or the application of its provisions.' And lastly, agreements under article 31(3)(a) VCLT are only those that are 'subsequent'.

4.2.1 'Agreement'

In conventional language, the term 'agreement' implies the existence of a consensus or a concordant will between two or more actors.[16] For the purpose of lits (a) and (b) of article 31(3) VCLT, the ILC similarly defines the term 'agreement' as a 'common understanding' by the parties.[17] Thus, it follows up on the terminology used in the DALT, which referred to 'any subsequent practice … which establishes the understanding of the parties.'[18] The Vienna Conference eventually substituted the term 'agreement' for the term 'understanding'. This change of terminology was not, however, meant to indicate any change of meaning.[19] Denoting a 'common understanding', the term 'agreement' presupposes that the parties are aware of and accept the other parties' positions regarding the interpretation of the treaty.[20] Hence, '[c]onflicting positions expressed by different parties to a treaty preclude the existence of an agreement.'[21]

---

[16] See 'agreement, n' *Oxford English Dictionary Online* (September 2014, OUP) <http://www.oed.com/view/Entry/4159?redirectedFrom=agreement>.

[17] Draft conclusion 9(1) in ILC, 'Report of the International Law Commission on the Work of its 66th Session' (5 May–6 June and 7 July–8 August 2014) UN Doc A/69/10, 197.

[18] ILC, 'Draft Articles on the Law of Treaties with Commentaries' [1966-II] YBILC 187, 218.

[19] UN Conference on the Law of Treaties, 'Summary Records of the Plenary Meetings and of the Meetings of the Committee of the Whole' (First session, Vienna 26 March 1968) UN Doc A/CONF.39/11, 169 [60].

[20] ibid 197 [1], 200 [8].

[21] ibid 198 [3].

4.2.1.1 Agreement and Treaties

Legal language and public international law in particular often use the term 'agreement' in a narrower sense to denote legally binding commitments.[22] This raises the question of whether article 31(3)(a) VCLT uses the term 'agreement' in its broader or narrower sense.

Article 2(1)(a) VCLT, which is part of the context of article 31(3)(a) VCLT, helps to resolve this question. This provision uses the term 'agreement' to define the meaning of 'treaty' for the purpose of the Convention. Thus, article 2(1)(a) VCLT uses the term 'agreement' as a generic term, ie in a broad sense.[23] It presupposes, as the ILC succinctly noted, that, '[w]hile every treaty is an agreement, not every agreement is a treaty.'[24] If article 31(3)(a) VCLT had been meant to cover only treaties, it would have made more sense to employ the term 'treaty' instead of the term 'agreement.'

Moreover, the term 'agreement' pursuant to article 31(3)(a) VCLT serves a different purpose than the term 'treaty' as defined in article 2(1)(a) VCLT. The term 'treaty' is used to demonstrate that the parties have firmly agreed on a legally binding instrument. The term 'agreement' under article 31(3)(a) VCLT, in contrast, indicates that the parties to an existing treaty have agreed on the interpretation of that treaty.[25] Here, the existence of binding obligations is therefore already assumed.[26] The terminological distinction made by the Convention itself speaks for understanding the term 'agreement' in its broader sense. Hence an 'agreement' under article 31(3)(a) VCLT does not necessarily require a treaty but at least the existence of a common understanding.[27]

---

[22] Gardiner, *Treaty Interpretation* (n 3) 243 f.

[23] cf Mark Villiger, *Commentary on the* 1969 *Vienna Convention on the Law of Treaties* (Martinus Nijhoff 2009) 77 [6]. cf also Denys Myers, 'The Names and Scope of Treaties' (1957) 51 AJIL 574, 574. Following Myers' reasoning, this study suggests that a 'treaty' purports to capture the parties' agreement in legally binding terms. Thus, rights and duties under a 'treaty' are stronger than under an agreement that does not amount to a 'treaty'. Yet, it is often difficult in practice to draw a clear-cut distinction between 'treaty' and 'agreement'. This is because the question of whether the parties intended to give binding force to their agreement is open to interpretation.

[24] Commentary on draft conclusion 4 in ILC, 'Report of the International Law Commission on the Work of its 65th Session' (6 May–7 June and 8 July–9 August 2013) UN Doc A/68/10, 32 [6].

[25] cf Gardiner, *Treaty Interpretation* (n 3) 248 f.

[26] ibid 244. See also Wolfram Karl, *Vertrag und spätere Praxis im Völkerrecht—Zum Einfluss der Praxis auf Inhalt und Bestand völkerrechtlicher Verträge* (repr, Springer 2012) 193.

[27] Draft conclusion 9(1) and commentary in ILC, 'Report of the International Law Commission on the Work of its 66th Session' (5 May–6 June and 7 July–8 August 2014) UN Doc A/69/10, 197, 200 [9].

4.2.1.2 Interpretative Treaties

This broader understanding raises the reverse question, namely whether the term 'agreement' under article 31(3)(a) VCLT covers treaties at all. One could also argue that subsequent treaties concerning the interpretation of an earlier treaty either amend or even prevail over the earlier treaty by virtue of the *lex posterior* rule. According to this line of reasoning, a later treaty could not simultaneously function as a means of interpretation anyway. This reasoning, however, disregards that an earlier and later treaty may well exist alongside each other.[28] The later treaty may, for instance, merely supplement the earlier treaty and at the same time contain provisions that define ambiguous terms contained in the earlier treaty.[29]

Besides, one can conceive of cases in which only the earlier and not the later treaty applies to a dispute; here one may argue that it is admissible to take account of the later treaty as a subsequent agreement to the earlier one. Lastly, one needs to remember that the Convention itself acknowledges that the term 'agreement' can encompass the term 'treaty'.[30] Hence it seems inappropriate to categorically exclude treaties from falling under article 31(3)(a) VCLT.[31] In consequence, there is no general answer to the question of whether treaties actually do or do not meet the requirements of article 31(3)(a) VCLT. Instead, it is necessary to consider each treaty's scope of application in the individual case.

4.2.1.3 The Form of Agreement

A more difficult issue relates to the necessary form of subsequent agreements. Does article 31(3)(a) VCLT require subsequent agreements to be in writing or at least somehow formally perpetuated?[32] The ILC and academic literature have unanimously answered this question in the negative.[33]

---

[28] Gardiner, *Treaty Interpretation* (n 3) 250 f.

[29] See Georg Nolte, 'Report 3—Subsequent Agreements and Subsequent Practice of States outside of Judicial or Quasi-Judicial Proceedings' in id (ed), *Treaties and Subsequent Practice* (OUP 2013) 313 f.

[30] See art 2(1)(a) VCLT.

[31] Commentary on draft conclusion 6 in ILC, 'Report of the International Law Commission on the Work of its 66th Session' (5 May–6 June and 7 July–8 August 2014) UN Doc A/69/10, 187 [32]. See also Gardiner, *Treaty Interpretation* (n 3) 242; Nolte, 'Report 3—Practice outside of Judicial Proceedings' (n 29) 309.

[32] cf *European Molecular Biology Laboratory Arbitration (EMBL v Germany)* (Arbitral Tribunal) (1990) 105 ILR 1, 54 f, where the tribunal remarks that subsequent agreements need *not* be contained in one single document.

[33] See in particular the commentary on draft conclusion 4 in ILC, 'Report of the International Law Commission on the Work of its 65th Session' (6 May–7 June and 8 July–9 August 2013) UN Doc A/68/10, 32 [5]. See also eg Georg Nolte, 'First Report on Subsequent Agreements and Subsequent Practice in relation to Treaty Interpretation' (19 March 2013) UN Doc

Indeed, there are good arguments for this view. First of all, the Convention does not explicitly impose any formal requirements upon subsequent agreements. Moreover, Article 2(1)(a) VCLT explicitly requires agreements to be concluded in writing in order to fall under the Convention's definition of 'treaty'. This implies that the Convention does not generally require agreements to be in writing but only if it states so.[34] Article 31(3)(a) VCLT does not call for a treaty or a written agreement but simply for an agreement. If this provision had intended to avoid the evidentiary problems caused by unwritten agreements,[35] it would have made sense to explicitly limit subsequent agreements to agreements in writing. From a more pragmatic perspective, one may further add that requiring subsequent agreements to be in writing could considerably reduce the chances of reaching subsequent agreements and thus deprive article 31(3)(a) VCLT of its practical relevance.

However, there are also arguments that might support the opposite view. The 'Second Report for the ILC Study Group on Treaties over Time', which examined the jurisprudence of courts under special regimes,[36] suggests that subsequent agreements are 'rarely relied on' anyway.[37] Besides, this Report shows that, when courts under special regimes did take account of subsequent agreements, the agreements were in fact written ones.[38] And while the Convention does not explicitly say that

A/CN.4/660, 31 [74]; id, 'Second Report on Subsequent Agreements and Subsequent Practice in relation to Treaty Interpretation' (26 March 2014) UN Doc A/CN.4/671, [54]; Dörr, 'Article 31' (n 9) 554 [75].

[34] See the commentary on draft conclusion 9 in ILC, 'Report of the International Law Commission on the Work of its 66th Session' (5 May–6 June and 7 July–8 August 2014) UN Doc A/69/10, 199 [7], where it was noted that the 'term "agreement' in the Vienna Convention does not imply any particular requirements of form.' This view was subsequently reconfirmed by the PCA in the *Bay of Bengal Maritime Boundary Arbitration (Bangladesh v India)* (7 July 2014) <http://www.pca-cpa.org/showpage.asp?pag_id=1376> [165].

[35] As regards the motives for including the requirement of a written agreement into the Convention's definition of the term 'treaty', see 1.3.1.1.

[36] In this context, the term 'special regime' was used in a non-legal sense to cover regimes that are 'created by treaties which provide for one or more permanent or quasi-permanent bodies of independent members who render (binding or non-binding) assessments on the legal aspects of disputes in individual cases.' See Georg Nolte, 'Report 2—Jurisprudence under Special Regimes relating to Subsequent Agreements and Subsequent Practice' in id (ed), *Treaties and Subsequent Practice* (OUP 2013) 214. The regimes that were covered in this report included: the WTO, the Iran–US Claims Tribunal, ICSID tribunals, the NAFTA, the ECtHR, the IACtHR, the HRC, ITLOS, the International Criminal Court and international criminal tribunals, and the CJEU.

[37] id, 'Report 2—Jurisprudence under Special Regimes relating to Subsequent Agreements and Subsequent Practice' in id (ed), *Treaties and Subsequent Practice* (OUP 2013) 303.

[38] The documents which courts under special regimes considered as subsequent agreements are the interpretative note on art 1105(1) NAFTA that was issued by the Free Trade Commission in 2001 and the 'Elements of Crimes' that were adopted by the Assembly of States Parties to the Rome Statute of the International Criminal Court (9 September 2002) ICC-ASP/1/3, Part II-B. See Georg Nolte, 'Report 2—Jurisprudence under Special Regimes relating to Subsequent Agreements and Subsequent Practice' in id (ed), *Treaties and Subsequent Practice* (OUP 2013) 240 f, 289 f, 303 f.

subsequent agreements must be in writing, it does not explicitly say that they must not. Thus, the text of article 31(3)(a) VCLT is rather ambiguous. If one took the view that article 31(3)(a) VCLT does not require subsequent agreements to be in writing, it would often be difficult or even impossible to distinguish subsequent agreements under lit (a) from subsequent practice under lit (b) of article 31(3) VCLT.[39] In fact, one could even wonder why the Convention considered it necessary to address subsequent agreements and subsequent practice in separate provisions in the first place.

Yet again, the Convention does not *a priori* attach less interpretative weight to subsequent practice under lit (b) than to subsequent agreements under lit (a). For this reason, it is eventually futile to strictly distinguish the former from the latter. Instead of considering subsequent agreements and subsequent practice as two mutually exclusive opposites, one may equally take the view that lits (a) and (b) of article 31(3) VCLT are meant to describe two typical phenotypes of subsequent conduct; relevant subsequent conduct may consequently take a form that is situated on a sliding scale somewhere between lits (a) and (b).[40] In that sense, the ILC acknowledged that 'it is possible that "practice" and "agreement" coincide in specific cases.'[41] Nevertheless, they could be

> distinguished based on whether an agreement of the parties can be identified as such … or whether it is necessary to identify an agreement through individual acts which in their combination demonstrate a common position … [A subsequent agreement under article 31(3)(a) VCLT] must therefore be 'reached' and presupposes *a single common act* by the parties by which they manifest their common understanding.[42]

By requiring only a 'single common act', the Commission thus refused to read any formal requirements into article 31(3)(a) VCLT. The Convention's drafting history

[39] See already Rudolf Bernhardt, 'Interpretation and Implied (Tacit) Modification of Treaties' (1967) 27 ZaöRV 491, 499. Both academic literature and the ILC have acknowledged this problem. See eg Dörr, 'Article 31' (n 9) 554 [75], who remarks that the broad interpretation can lead to a 'potential overlap' between subsequent agreements and subsequent practice. But despite this acknowledgment, he fails to explain why the Convention addresses subsequent agreements and subsequent practice in separate provisions. Moreover, he does not explain how one can distinguish one from the other at all when adopting his understanding of subsequent agreements. According to Moloo, 'The Relevance of Subsequent Party Conduct' (n 14) 58, 'some degree of formality' is required under art 31(3)(a) VCLT as that provision must not cover agreements that are otherwise covered by art 31(3)(b) VCLT. See also Nolte, 'Annex A' (n 9) 375 [24]: 'The boundary between the various means of interpretation provided for in article 31(3) VCLT is not clear … [and] the boundary between subsequent agreement and subsequent practice is rather fluid.'

[40] Rahim Moloo, 'Changing Times, Changing Obligations? The Interpretation of Treaties over Time' (2012) 106 ASIL PROC 261, 262; id, 'The Relevance of Subsequent Party Conduct' (n 14) 58.

[41] Commentary on draft conclusion 4 in ILC, 'Report of the International Law Commission on the Work of its 65th Session' (6 May–7 June and 8 July–9 August 2013) UN Doc A/68/10, 34 [11].

[42] ibid 34 [10] [emphasis added].

eventually lends support to this non-formalistic approach. On the one hand, the Commentary on the ILC's DALT might be read to require subsequent agreements to be in writing. While the Commentary refers to agreements made in connection with a treaty's conclusion as 'documents', it elsewhere implies that such agreements are equivalent to subsequent agreements but for the different point in time at which these are reached.[43] But on the other hand, the delegates to the Vienna Conference did not follow a proposal to clarify that article 31(3)(a) VCLT covered only written agreements, which had been introduced by a delegate from Sierra Leone during the plenary meetings of the Committee of the Whole.[44]

In sum, it is difficult to conclude that article 31(3)(a) VCLT requires subsequent agreements to be somehow formally perpetuated or even laid down in writing. In particular, the silence of the text of article 31(3)(a) VCLT indicates that no formal requirements apply to subsequent agreements. Following the ILC's proposal, this study therefore distinguishes subsequent agreements under lit (a) from subsequent practice under lit (b) of article 31(3) VCLT on whether or not the parties' common understanding is manifested in a single common act.

4.2.2 *'Between the Parties'*

Article 31(3)(a) VCLT further qualifies subsequent agreements in that it requires them to be reached 'between the parties'. At first glance, the term 'party' appears rather straightforward. Nevertheless, it raises two central questions: Firstly, who are 'the parties' for the purpose of article 31(3)(a) VCLT? And secondly, how many parties must have participated in reaching the agreement?

4.2.2.1 Who Are 'the Parties'?

Article 2(1)(g) VCLT assigns a special meaning to the term 'party' for the purpose of the Convention. According to this provision, the term 'party' means a State that has consented to be bound by the treaty and for which the treaty is in force. This definition in principle also applies to article 31(3)(a) VCLT. However, it is important to add that the State parties must be parties to the very treaty to which the subsequent agreement relates. This qualification follows from article 31(3)(a) VCLT, which requires an agreement 'regarding the interpretation of the treaty or

[43] ILC, 'DALT' (n 18) 221 [13] f.

[44] See the Statement by Mr Cole in UN Conference on the Law of Treaties, 'Summary Records of the Plenary Meetings and of the Meetings of the Committee of the Whole' (First session, Vienna 26 March 1968) UN Doc A/CONF.39/11, 174 [29].

the application of its provisions.' Besides, it also lies in the logic of the *pacta tertiis* rule.[45] Hence, the term 'party' under article 31(3)(a) VCLT means those States that have consented to be bound by the very treaty to which their subsequent agreement relates and for whom this treaty is in force.

Being legal entities, States can act only through their organs or other actors. Since article 31(3)(a) VCLT speaks of an agreement 'between' the parties, a subsequent agreement can only be reached by actors whose conduct is attributable to a State party. Article 31(3)(a) VCLT does not address the issue of attribution. Assuming that a subsequent agreement under article 31(3)(a) VCLT presupposes a single common act by the parties by which they manifest their common understanding,[46] attribution will be only seldom controversial. This is because a single common act can only 'manifest' the parties' common understanding if someone clearly acts for the parties.

If one nevertheless sought to establish rules for determining attribution, at least three approaches appear worth considering: firstly, one could consider each State's internal division of competences; secondly, one could consider customary international law rules on attribution as reflected in the 'Articles on the Responsibility of States for Internationally Wrongful Acts' ('Articles on State Responsibility' or ARSIWA);[47] and thirdly, one could, by way of analogy, rely on the rules for the conclusion of treaties under the Convention.

If one took the first approach and considered each State's internal division of competences, every State could independently select the attributable conduct. On the one hand, this approach would entail the advantage that no State would be affected by a subsequent agreement not originating from its corporately organised will. On the other hand, interpreters would have to be familiar with different and often complex internal organisations of State governance. Ultimately diminishing legal certainty at the international level, this approach is therefore impracticable to resolve the issue of attribution under article 31(3)(a) VCLT.[48]

---

[45] The *pacta tertiis* rule under art 34 VCLT provides that a treaty does not create either obligations or rights for a third State without its consent. While art 34 VCLT is only concerned with rights and obligations contained in a treaty, its underlying idea may nevertheless inform the understanding of interpretative agreements, too. For more details on this rule under both customary and treaty law, see Budislav Vukas, 'Treaties, Third-Party Effect' in Rüdiger Wolfrum (ed), *The Max Planck Encyclopedia of Public International Law* (OUP 2012). This does not suggest, however, that participation of States that are not a party to the respective treaty would be incompatible with the *pacta tertiis* rule, at least as long as the agreement (also) remains one between the parties to the respective treaty.

[46] See 4.2.1.3.

[47] The Articles on State Responsibility originate in a draft prepared by the ILC, which was endorsed by and annexed to UNGA Res 56/83 (12 December 2001) UN Doc A/RES/56/83. See generally James Crawford, *State Responsibility—The General Part* (CUP 2013).

[48] cf art 46 VCLT, which shows that the law of treaties does not wish to burden States with a necessity to inform themselves about other States' internal organisation.

The ILC apparently favours the customary international law approach based on the 'Articles on State Responsibility'.[49] However, it did not expressly elaborate on the attribution of conduct for the purpose of article 31(3)(a) VCLT. Instead, the Commission only addressed attribution of subsequent practice under articles 31(3)(b) and 32 VCLT.[50] Besides, it did not explain why the 'Articles on State Responsibility' should be relevant under articles 31(3)(b) and 32 VCLT. Thus, it eventually remains doubtful whether its conclusions were really meant to apply, *mutatis mutandis,* to the attribution of subsequent agreements, too. The advantage of considering customary international law as reflected in the 'Articles on State Responsibility' is that one can find numerous rules on attribution of conduct to a State.[51] These rules are very detailed and also easily accessible to every State.

Nevertheless, it is questionable whether attribution for determining liability for wrongful acts serves the same purpose as attribution in the context of treaty interpretation.[52] The 'Articles on State Responsibility' establish whether a State shall be responsible for a breach of its international obligations. To that end, they very broadly attribute various forms of conduct to a State; among others, they even stipulate attribution for cases of excess of authority or contravention of instructions.[53] By reaching interpretative agreements, which may then influence the treaty's meaning through the process of treaty interpretation, States do not purport to fulfil an obligation but voluntarily exercise a right. This difference between treaty interpretation and liability for wrongful acts suggests that customary international law as reflected in the 'Articles on State Responsibility' is not suitable for determining attribution of conduct under article 31(3)(a) VCLT either.

---

[49] ILC, 'Report of the International Law Commission on the Work of its 65th Session' (6 May–7 June and 8 July–9 August 2013) UN Doc A/68/10, 42 [2].

[50] ibid 41 f.

[51] The actors whose conduct is attributable under the ARSIWA include organs of the State (art 4), persons or entities exercising elements of governmental authority (art 5), organs placed at the disposal of a State by another State (art 6), conduct directed or controlled by a State (art 8), conduct carried out in the absence or default of the official authorities (art 9), conduct of an insurrectional or other movement (art 10), and conduct acknowledged and adopted by a State as its own (art 11).

[52] Sceptical also Nolte, 'First Report' (n 33) 46 [120].

[53] See id, 'Annex A' (n 9) 377 [2], where he suggests that the rules on State responsibility are 'probably too broad' for determining attributable conduct under lits (a) and (b) of art 31(3) VCLT. This criticism has been reiterated in id, 'Report 1—Jurisprudence of the International Court of Justice and Arbitral Tribunals of Ad Hoc Jurisdiction relating to Subsequent Agreements and Subsequent Practice' in id (ed), *Treaties and Subsequent Practice* (OUP 2013) 197 f and id, 'First Report' (n 33) 46 [120]. In its commentary on draft conclusion 5, the ILC accordingly inserted the caveat that attributed conduct not necessarily constituted subsequent practice, see ILC, 'Report of the International Law Commission on the Work of its 65th Session' (6 May–7 June and 8 July–9 August 2013) UN Doc A/68/10, 42 [4]. Thus, it took into account that certain conduct might 'contradict an officially expressed position of the State… and thus contribute to an equivocal conduct by the State.'

The third approach for determining attribution under article 31(3)(a) VCLT draws on articles 7 and 8 VCLT, which deal with the conclusion of treaties. Article 7 VCLT generally considers certain high-ranking government officials to represent their States for the purpose of all acts relating to the conclusion of a treaty.[54] Furthermore, article 8 VCLT stipulates that States can confirm and thus give legal effect to acts performed by someone who is not covered by article 7 VCLT. Relying on these provisions to resolve the issue of attribution under article 31(3)(a) VCLT would entail two advantages. On the one hand, the group of actors covered by these provisions is not as wide as that covered by the 'Articles on State Responsibility'. In other words, these provisions do not excessively attribute conduct to States against their will. On the other hand, these provisions are accessible to everyone who interprets treaties. Therefore, they do not conflict with considerations of legal certainty as does relying on a State's internal division of competences. Apart from that, it is only logical that those who are competent to conclude a treaty should all the more be competent to interpret it.

But in fact, one cannot ignore that a treaty's conclusion considerably differs from its interpretation as regards the range of actors that are potentially involved. While a treaty's conclusion is a singular event in the life of a treaty, interpreting a treaty is closely related to applying it. Interpretation and application of treaties are 'day-to-day businesses' at different levels of State hierarchy and for various State and non-State actors. Against this background, articles 7 and 8 VCLT should be dismissed for being too restrictive for determining attribution under article 31(3)(a) VCLT.[55] However, neither the application of these rules nor the alternative approaches are explicitly prescribed by article 31(3)(a) VCLT. None of these approaches appearing fully suitable, it is worth mentioning that Special Rapporteur Georg Nolte originally made a similar observation as regards attribution of subsequent practice:

> The pertinent rules of attribution for the present purpose of treaty interpretation must therefore be derived from the specific character of the interpretation and the application of treaties by their parties. This suggests that only such conduct which is undertaken or deemed to be accepted by those organs of a State party which are internationally regarded as being responsible for the application of the treaty (as a whole, or of a particular provision of a treaty) may be attributed to a State.[56]

Against this background, this study argues that the attribution of subsequent agreements cannot be satisfactorily determined in the abstract; in particular, rules derived from a different context do not promise to resolve the issue of attribution for the

[54] First of all, these high-ranking government officials include Heads of State, Heads of Government, and Ministers for Foreign Affairs. Furthermore, art 7 VCLT confers limited authority relating to the conclusion of a treaty to a broader group of actors, namely those who can produce a document demonstrating authority to conclude the treaty, those in respect of whom the circumstances imply such authority, as well as heads of diplomatic missions and representatives accredited by States to an international conference or to an IO or one of its organs.

[55] See id, 'Annex A' (n 9) 377 [27], where he rejects art 7 VCLT as 'obviously too narrow'.

[56] id, 'First Report' (n 33) 46 [121].

purpose of article 31(3)(a) VCLT. Where attribution is not uncontroversial but needs to be addressed, it therefore adopts a case-by-case approach, which may be reconsidered in the light of relevant domestic jurisprudence.

4.2.2.2 How Many Parties Are 'the Parties'?

The second question concerning the term 'the parties' relates to the number of parties between whom an agreement under article 31(3)(a) VCLT must be reached. The definite article before 'parties' indicates that 'the parties' means 'all the parties'. Hence the ILC has consistently held that subsequent agreements under article 31(3)(a) VCLT require an agreement between *all* the parties to the treaty.[57] Article 31(3)(a) VCLT, however, neither expressly speaks of an agreement between *all* the parties nor declares that an agreement between only *some* parties suffices. Therefore, a residual ambiguity concerning the correct interpretation of 'the parties' remains.

Notably, this question was hardly debated at all until the adoption of the ILC's DALT. Nonetheless, the Convention's drafting history equally supports the more restrictive interpretation. At its 883rd meeting, the Commission discussed a proposal of its Drafting Committee that aimed at inserting the term 'all parties' in relation to agreements made in connection with the treaty. While this proposal was accepted, the Commission refrained from inserting a similar clarification relating to subsequent agreements. This omission was severely criticised by Commission member Shabtai Rosenne:

> [T]here was a certain ambiguity in paragraphs 3 (a) and (b) which referred to 'the parties', whereas paragraph 2 (a), and by implication paragraph 2 (b), referred to 'all the parties'. In article 69 it was even more important than in article 68 to make it clear that the reference was to all the parties.[58]

This statement suggests that the Commission assumed that subsequent agreements under article 31(3)(a) VCLT had to be reached between all the parties but simply refrained from clarifying this point.

Since both the ordinary meaning of article 31(3)(a) VCLT and its drafting history support the more restrictive interpretation, this study equally maintains that

---

[57] Eg commentary on draft conclusion 4 in ILC, 'Report of the International Law Commission on the Work of its 65th Session' (6 May–7 June and 8 July–9 August 2013) UN Doc A/68/10, 34 [12]; commentary on draft conclusion 10 in id, 'Report of the International Law Commission on the Work of its 66th Session' (5 May–6 June and 7 July–8 August 2014) UN Doc A/69/10, 216 [3].

[58] Shabtai Rosenne in id, 'Summary Records of the 18th Session of the International Law Commission' (4 May–19 July 1966) [1966-I/2] YBILC 1, 268 [100]. Art 69, to which Rosenne refers, is now art 31 VCLT. Art 68 dealt with modification of a treaty by subsequent practice and was eventually deleted during the Vienna Conference, see 3.1.

subsequent agreements must be reached between all the parties to the treaty.[59] As the ILC pointed out, subsequent agreements that fail to satisfy this requirement may be relevant as supplementary means of interpretation under article 32 VCLT;[60] they cannot, however, be taken into account as part of the general rule under article 31(3)(a) VCLT.

4.2.3 *The Object of the Agreement*

Subsequent agreements between the parties under article 31(3)(a) VCLT are only those 'regarding' a particular object, namely either 'the interpretation of the treaty or the application of its provisions.'

4.2.3.1 Sole Purpose v Unintended Side-Effect

The term 'regarding' links the agreement to its object. In conventional language, it means as much as 'in relation to', 'about', and 'concerning'.[61] But these synonyms do not help to elucidate how exactly an agreement and its object must be connected. At least two different interpretations are conceivable. In the one alternative, which this study labels the 'sole purpose alternative', the parties must have reached the agreement with the sole purpose of specifying the interpretation of the treaty or the application of its provisions.[62] This alternative accordingly reads a strong subjective element into the term 'regarding'. In the other alternative, which is referred to as the 'unintended side-effect alternative', it is sufficient if the agreement merely affects the interpretation of the treaty or the application of its provision. The parties

---

[59] Systematic interpretation further corroborates this understanding of art 31(3)(a) VCLT. As argued under 4.3.2.1, art 31(3)(b) VCLT must be interpreted restrictively to the effect that the body of relevant practice, taken together, must be capable of establishing the agreement of *all* parties. Assumed that this interpretation of art 31(3)(b) VCLT is correct, there are good reasons not to impose less stringent requirements upon agreements under art 31(3)(a) VCLT.

[60] Commentary on draft conclusion 4 in ILC, 'Report of the International Law Commission on the Work of its 65th Session' (6 May–7 June and 8 July–9 August 2013) UN Doc A/68/10, 34 [12]; commentary on draft conclusion 6 in id, 'Report of the International Law Commission on the Work of its 66th Session' (5 May–6 June and 7 July–8 August 2014) UN Doc A/69/10, 179 [24]

[61] 'regarding, prep' *Oxford English Dictionary Online* (September 2014, OUP) <http://www.oed.com/view/Entry/248749?rskey=fvpOkS&result=2&isAdvanced=false>.

[62] One commentator who can arguably be understood as having adopted this view is Linderfalk, *On the Interpretation of Treaties* (n 3) 164 [fn omitted]: 'Of course, an agreement "regarding" the interpretation of the treaty or the application of its provisions means an agreement, *the purpose of which* is to clarify the meaning of the treaty or to serve in some other manner as a guide for application.' This statement may, however, as well be understood as endorsing the compromise suggested in the following.

must have neither intended to specify the interpretation of the treaty or the application of its provisions, nor must they have been aware that their agreement may be used for this purpose. Under this alternative, the link between an agreement and its object is purely implicit and will ultimately be established by the interpreter himself.

Read in its context and in the light of the Convention's object and purpose, none of these interpretations is convincing. The 'sole purpose alternative' would ultimately deprive article 31(3)(a) VCLT of most of its relevance. In practice, one or more parties will almost always pursue some additional objectives when reaching a subsequent agreement.[63] The 'unintended side-effect alternative', in contrast, would level both the differences between lits (a) and (b) and between lits (a) and (c) of article 31(3) VCLT. Moreover, it is difficult to speak of an agreement regarding the interpretation of the treaty or the application of its provisions if the parties were unaware that their agreement could have this effect.[64]

A reasonable compromise between the 'sole purpose' and the 'unintended side-effect alternative' would require two things. Firstly, the parties must at least have been aware that their agreement could have the effect of specifying the interpretation of the treaty or the application of its provisions. And secondly, the possible effect of the agreement must be part of the parties' concordant will, albeit not as the sole driving force behind it.[65]

4.2.3.2 Interpretation and Application Distinguished

One possible object of agreements under article 31(3)(a) VCLT is the interpretation of the treaty. Since the meaning of 'interpretation' has already been established in Chap. 1, it is here sufficient to recall these earlier findings. Under the Convention, 'interpretation' is a process that serves to determine a treaty's meaning by ascertaining the objectivised intention of the parties.[66] But what is the difference between an interpretation of the treaty and the application of its provisions? Although the Convention frequently employs the term 'application',[67] it does not define it. In legal terminology, the term 'application' generally describes 'l'opération qui assure le passage de l'abstrait au concret, elle détermine les conséquences de la règle dont

---

[63] And may it be objectives of a political nature at the domestic level.

[64] Commentary on draft conclusion 6 in ILC, 'Report of the International Law Commission on the Work of its 66th Session' (5 May–6 June and 7 July–8 August 2014) UN Doc A/69/10, 172 [7].

[65] cf commentary on draft conclusion 4 in id, 'Report of the International Law Commission on the Work of its 65th Session' (6 May–7 June and 8 July–9 August 2013) UN Doc A/68/10, 35 [13] [emphasis added]: 'The parties must … purport, *possibly among other aims*, to clarify the meaning of a treaty or how it is to be applied.'

[66] See 1.3.1.2.

[67] See eg arts 20(2), 25, 42(2), 43, 63, 66 VCLT.

le sens est dégagé par l'interprétation dans une situation concrète.'[68] As the ILC has noted, interpretation hence 'refers to a mental process, whereas "application" focuses on actual conduct.'[69] This description implies that '"interpretation" is an essential element in the application of treaties.'[70] While a treaty's application can hardly take place without its prior interpretation, a treaty's interpretation not necessarily entails its application.[71] But although this description gives an idea of what the term 'application' may refer to, its meaning nonetheless remains vague.

Some commentators have even argued that 'interpretation' and 'application' could hardly be separated from each other anyway.[72] The ILC acknowledged, on the one hand, that the 'relationship between the terms "interpretation" and "application" is not ... clear-cut' and that the two concepts are 'closely interrelated and build upon each other'[73] But on the other hand, it insisted that the two concepts were distinguishable.[74] The Convention's drafting history does not help to clarify the meaning of the term 'application' either. Originating in a Pakistani proposal,[75] the phrase 'or the application of its provisions' had first been inserted by the Drafting Committee of the Vienna Conference. However, neither the proposal nor the

---

[68] Yasseen, 'L'interprétation des traités' (n 7) 10. In English [translated by the author]: '... the operation which effectuates the transition from the abstract to the concrete, which determines the consequences of the rule whose meaning is determined by the interpretation in a specific situation.' See also Georg Schwarzenberger, 'Myths and Realities of Treaty Interpretation—Articles 27–29 of the Vienna Convention on the Law of Treaties' (1968) 9 Va J Int'l L 1, 7; Serge Sur, *L'interprétation en droit international public* (Pichon & Durand-Auzias 1974) 193 f.

[69] Commentary on draft conclusion 6 in ILC, 'Report of the International Law Commission on the Work of its 66th Session' (5 May–6 June and 7 July–8 August 2014) UN Doc A/69/10, 171 [3].

[70] Waldock, 'Third Report' (n 15) 8 [3]. See also Yasseen, 'L'interprétation des traités' (n 7) 10; Karl, *Vertrag und spätere Praxis* (n 26) 22. As has been pointed out by Maarten Bos, 'Theory and Practice of Treaty Interpretation' (1980) 27 NILR 3, 13, the only case in which interpretation and application do not coincide is when application nullifies the outcome of interpretation, which would then amount to a treaty revision.

[71] Commentary on draft conclusion 6 in ILC, 'Report of the International Law Commission on the Work of its 66th Session' (5 May–6 June and 7 July–8 August 2014) UN Doc A/69/10, 171 [4]; Schwarzenberger, 'Myths and Realities' (n 68) 8; Karl, *Vertrag und spätere Praxis* (n 26) 22.

[72] cf *Applicability of the Obligation to Arbitrate under Section 21 of the United Nations Headquarters Agreement of 26 June 1947* (Advisory Opinion) [1988] ICJ Rep 12, 59 (sep op Judge Shahabuddeen); Distefano, 'La pratique subséquente' (n 3) 44.

[73] Commentary on draft conclusion 6 in ILC, 'Report of the International Law Commission on the Work of its 66th Session' (5 May–6 June and 7 July–8 August 2014) UN Doc A/69/10, 171 [3].

[74] ibid.

[75] For the Pakistani proposal, see UN Conference on the Law of Treaties, 'Reports of the Committee of the Whole' (Vienna, 26 March–24 May 1968 and 9 April–22 May 1969) Official Records: Documents of the Conference, UN Doc A/CONF.39/11/Add2, 150 [269].

Committee's decision was accompanied by an explanation of the meaning of this phrase.[76] Anyway, article 31(3)(a) VCLT indiscriminately considers both agreements regarding the interpretation of a treaty as well as those regarding the application of its provisions as primary means of interpretation. For the purpose of this study, it is therefore ultimately futile to attempt to strictly distinguish 'interpretation' and 'application' under article 31(3)(a) VCLT.

4.2.3.3 Interpretation and Modification Distinguished

A more crucial distinction is the one between subsequent agreements regarding the interpretation of the treaty or the application of its provisions and those regarding the modification of the treaty. On its face, article 31(3)(a) VCLT only covers agreements regarding the *interpretation* of the treaty or the application of its provisions. But does the silence of its text mean that article 31(3)(a) VCLT prevents interpreters from taking account of subsequent agreements regarding the *modification* of the treaty? This question is not meant to dispute the possibility that the parties to a treaty may reach subsequent agreements regarding the treaty's modification. It rather aims at elucidating whether the Vienna rules authorise interpreters to take such agreements into account during the process of interpretation or, more precisely, when applying article 31(3)(a) VCLT.

Agreements regarding the modification of the treaty must not be confused with formal amendments in the form of a treaty. Formal amendments can also include provisions regarding the interpretation of the treaty or the application of its provisions. Albeit only exceptionally, they can be relevant under article 31(3)(a) VCLT.[77] Agreements regarding the modification of the treaty may or may not satisfy the requirements of article 40 VCLT (amendment of multilateral treaties); they may take the form of a treaty or of more informal agreements. This follows from article 39 VCLT (general rule regarding the amendment of treaties), which implies that agreements reached after the treaty's conclusion may amend or modify the treaty without necessarily having to display the same form as the original treaty that is being amended or modified. But these different manifestations are immaterial for deciding whether article 31(3)(a) VCLT or, more generally, articles 31 and 32 VCLT authorise interpreters to take such agreements into account.

Yet, there are good reasons to assume that articles 31 and 32 VCLT do not authorise interpreters to take such agreements into account.[78] Most importantly, the

---

[76] UN Conference on the Law of Treaties, 'Summary Records of the Plenary Meetings and of the Meetings of the Committee of the Whole' (First session, Vienna, 26 March 1968) UN Doc A/CONF.39/11, 422.

[77] See above at 4.2.1.

[78] See Moloo, 'The Interpretation of Treaties over Time' (n 40) 263; id, 'The Relevance of Subsequent Party Conduct' (n 14) 78 f. A different view is apparently held by Dörr, 'Article 31' (n 9) 554 [74], who simply argues that the parties, being the true masters of the treaty, are not limited in making subsequent understandings or agreements but could also, implicitly, modify the treaty. This view, however, proceeds from the wrong perspective. Under art 31(3)

Convention distinguishes between interpretation (and application) on the one hand, and changes of the treaty (amendment and modification) on the other.[79] Identifying the treaty to be interpreted is a process that logically occurs before interpreting this treaty. As has been advocated in Chaps. 1 and 3, interpretation is logically limited by the range of possible meanings that the terms of a treaty may carry.[80] Interpreters and even the parties themselves cross the line to modification if they subsequently assign an ordinary or special meaning to the terms of the treaty which these terms cannot or were not meant to carry. One may object that the line between interpretation and application on the one hand and modification on the other is not only difficult to draw but also irrelevant. Taking that view, it would arguably be immaterial in which order one identified and interpreted a treaty. Either, one could first take account of an agreement regarding the modification of the treaty in order to identify the treaty to be interpreted and then interpret the treaty. Or one could start with the original treaty and take account of the agreement regarding the modification of the treaty when interpreting the original treaty.

The apparent irrelevance of said distinction may explain why international courts and tribunals merely tend to interpret informal modifying agreements in a restrictive fashion instead of refusing to take such agreements into account.[81] According to the ILC,

---

(a) VCLT—Dörr's comment solely refers to lit (a) of art 31(3) VCLT—the question is not so much what the parties can do; instead, the decisive question is what interpreters, in the interpretative process and under the conditions specified in arts 31–33 VCLT, can take into account and which effect their interpretations of the treaty may have.

[79] cf the commentary on draft conclusion 7 in ILC, 'Report of the International Law Commission on the Work of its 66th Session' (5 May–6 June and 7 July–8 August 2014) UN Doc A/69/10, 186 [18].

[80] See 1.3.1.2 and 3.3.1.1. See also, *mutatis mutandis*, Linderfalk, *On the Interpretation of Treaties* (n 3) 169 [fn omitted]: '[A] subsequent practice in the application of a treaty can be said to establish an agreement between the parties regarding the treaty's "interpretation" insofar as practice is consistent with "the ordinary meaning to be given to the terms of the treaty".' More recently, the UK Supreme Court emphasised in *R (ST Eritrea) v Secretary of State for the Home Department* [2012] UKSC 12, [2012] 2 AC 135 [31] (Lord Hope): 'But it must be remembered too that, however generous and purposive its approach to interpretation may be, the court's task remains one of interpreting the document to which the contracting parties have committed themselves by their agreement.... [I]t must interpret what the parties have agreed to. It has no warrant to give effect to what they might, or in an ideal world would, have agreed. One should not overlook the fact that article 31(1) of the Vienna Convention also states that a treaty should be interpreted "in accordance with the ordinary meaning to be given to the terms of the treaty in their context". So the starting point of the construction exercise should be the text of the Convention itself ... A treaty must be interpreted "in good faith". But this is not to be taken to be a source of obligation where none exists ... There is no want of good faith if the Convention is interpreted as meaning what it says and the contracting states decline to do something that its language does not require them to do. Everything depends on what the Convention itself provides.'

[81] cf commentary on draft conclusion 7 in ILC, 'Report of the International Law Commission on the Work of its 66th Session' (5 May–6 June and 7 July–8 August 2014) UN Doc A/69/10, 186 [21].

> States and international courts are generally prepared to accord States parties a rather wide scope for the interpretation of a treaty by way of subsequent agreement. This scope may even go beyond the ordinary meaning of the terms of the treaty. The recognition of this scope for the interpretation of the treaty goes hand in hand with the reluctance by States and courts to recognize that an agreement actually has the effect of amending or modifying the treaty. An agreement to modify a treaty is thus not excluded, but also not to be presumed.[82]

But on closer inspection, said distinction is not at all irrelevant for all types of interpreters.[83] An interpreter's competences may, for example, be expressly limited to interpreting a particular treaty, or the interpreter may be exclusively competent to consider amendments if they satisfy particular procedural requirements.[84] By relying on subsequent agreements regarding the modification of the treaty, such interpreter would circumvent the restrictions upon his competences. This applies, in particular, to interpreters at the national level, whose constitutional law may, for instance, stipulate that State organs are only bound by a treaty after the treaty received parliamentary assent. Under such constitutional order, domestic courts would be prevented from giving effect to agreements regarding the modification of a treaty unless they received parliamentary assent.[85] Although a State's internal law does not, on principle, serve as an argument for the interpretation of treaty law,[86]

---

[82] ibid 187 [21].

[83] See in particular Moloo, 'The Relevance of Subsequent Party Conduct' (n 14) 81, who emphasises the international criminal context, where the principle *nullum crimen sine lege* prohibits interpreters from ignoring the line between interpretation and modification.

[84] ibid 82 f. In this respect, see the dispute concerning art 1131(2) NAFTA and the interpretative note on art 1105(1) NAFTA that was issued by the Free Trade Commission in 2001. The text of this note can be accessed under <http://www.international.gc.ca/trade-agreements-accords-commerciaux>. On said dispute, see eg Charles Brower, 'Investor-State Disputes under NAFTA: The Empire Strikes Back' (2001) 40 Col J Transnat'l L 43, 56 f; id, 'Why the FTC Notes of Interpretation Constitute a Partial Amendment of NAFTA Article 1105' (2006) 46 Va J Int'l L 347; Todd Weiler, 'NAFTA Investment Arbitration and the Growth of International Economic Law' [2002] Bus L Int'l 158, 184 f; id, 'NAFTA Investment Law in 2001: As the Legal Order Starts to Settle, the Bureaucrats Strike Back' (2002) 36 Int'l L 345, 347; Christopher Thomas, 'A Reply to Professor Brower' (2002) 40 Col J Transnat'l L 433, 454; Courtney Kirkman, 'Fair and Equitable Treatment: *Methanex v United States* and the Narrowing Scope of NAFTA Article 1105' (2002) 34 Law & Pol'y Int'l Bus 343, 383. Another example is the dispute concerning interpretations adopted by the Ministerial Conference and the General Council of the WTO under art IX:2 WTO. See eg Joost Pauwelyn, *Conflict of Norms in Public International Law—How WTO Law Relates to other Rules of International Law* (CUP 2003) 112 f; Claus-Dieter Ehlermann and Lothar Ehring, 'The Authoritative Interpretation under Article IX:2 of the Agreement Establishing the World Trade Organization: Current Law, Practice and Possible Improvements' (2005) 8 JIEL 803, 808–12; Frank Biermann, 'The Rising Tide of Green Unilateralism in World Trade Law: Options for Resolving the Emerging North-South Conflict' (2001) 35 JWT 421, 436.

[85] See Chapter 6.

[86] See art 27 VCLT on internal law and observance of treaties.

these considerations nevertheless explain why the pertinent distinction is not at all irrelevant.

In conjunction with the arguments mentioned in the previous paragraphs, this study therefore presumes that subsequent agreements under article 31(3)(a) VCLT do not include agreements regarding the modification of the treaty.[87]

4.2.4 'Subsequent'

Article 31(3)(a) VCLT only covers agreements that are 'subsequent'. This qualification *ratione temporis* ordinarily means as much as 'successive to' or 'later'.[88] To determine whether an agreement is 'subsequent', one needs a temporal point of reference; on its basis, one can then classify the agreement accordingly. The Convention itself, however, does not expressly define this point of reference.

To identify a suitable point of reference, it is helpful to consider article 31(2) VCLT. This provision defines the context in the wider sense for the purpose of the Convention. This wider context includes (a) any agreement relating to the treaty which was made between all the parties in connection with the conclusion of the treaty, and (b) any instrument which was made by one or more parties in connection with the conclusion of the treaty and accepted by the other parties as an instrument related to the treaty. Article 31(2) VCLT thus expressly takes the 'conclusion of the treaty' as the relevant temporal point of reference for instruments falling under this provision. Systematic interpretation suggests that subsequent agreements under article 31(3)(a) VCLT are juxtaposed to agreements and instruments made in connection with the conclusion of the treaty under article 31(2)(a) and (b) VCLT.[89] This, in turn, indicates that subsequent agreements should be considered as agreements made after the conclusion of the treaty.[90]

Hence it becomes necessary to determine what is meant by the 'conclusion' of a treaty. This term is not defined in the Convention either. The ordinary meaning of

[87] See, *mutatis mutandis*, Karl, *Vertrag und spätere Praxis* (n 26) 184 f, who observes that the Convention's rules of interpretation did not envisage modifying agreements. This is not to suggest that subsequent agreements or subsequent practice cannot have the effect of modifying the original treaty. All that is suggested is that art 31(3)(a) and (b) VCLT does not cover modification and, in consequence, does not authorise interpreters to rely on such agreements or practice when engaging in the process of interpretation. Whether an interpreter is competent to interpret only the original treaty or also another (modified) one is a different question.

[88] Maurice Waite (ed), *Oxford Thesaurus of English* (3rd edn, OUP 2009) 852.

[89] See Linderfalk, *On the Interpretation of Treaties* (n 3) 163.

[90] Commentary on draft conclusion 4 in ILC, 'Report of the International Law Commission on the Work of its 65th Session' (6 May–7 June and 8 July–9 August 2013) UN Doc A/68/10, 31 [2]. According to Yasseen, 'L'interprétation des traités' (n 7) 47, the fact that practice under art 31(3)(b) VCLT is practice in the application of the treaty already implied that it must inevitably be subsequent in the sense of taking place after the conclusion of the treaty.

'conclusion' as used throughout the Convention admits several moments in time at which one can regard a treaty as having been 'concluded'.[91] The title of Part II of the Convention, which reads 'Conclusions and entry into force', indicates that the conclusion of a treaty is not identical with but rather occurs before its entry into force.[92] This inference still admits several possible meanings of the term 'conclusion'. One possible interpretation would equate 'conclusion' with a treaty's signature.[93] But Part II of the Convention offers further conceivable interpretations of the term 'conclusion'. Articles 11–15 VCLT, which explain how States consent to be bound by a treaty, expressly refer to a treaty and thus presuppose that such treaty already exists. In consequence, one can assume that the respective treaty has already been concluded at this point in time.[94]

But even if one excludes this very period, the term 'conclusion' will remain ambiguous; it could still be understood as referring either to the drawing up, the authentication, or the signature of the treaty. Recourse to the Convention's *travaux préparatoires* helps to reduce this ambiguity. Special Rapporteur Sir Gerald Fitzmaurice, who first drafted the provisions on the conclusion and entry into force of treaties, originally distinguished between authentication, conclusion, participation, and entry into force of a treaty.[95] In other words, he understood a treaty's conclusion as that moment or period of time when the text of the treaty had already become definite and when States considered this text to be the one by which they would be bound.[96]

Since the ordinary meaning of the term 'conclusion', read in its context, does not lead to an unambiguous interpretation, this study endorses the understanding suggested by Special Rapporteur Sir Gerald Fitzmaurice. In the following, the term 'conclusion' is therefore used to refer to that moment or period of time when the text of a treaty is finally established as definite. In consequence, an agreement is 'subsequent' for the purpose of article 31(3)(a) VCLT if it occurs after the text of the treaty has finally been established as definite.

---

[91] See Egbert Vierdag, 'The Time of the "Conclusion" of a Multilateral Treaty: Article 30 of the Vienna Convention on the Law of Treaties and Related Provisions' (1989) 59 BYIL 75, 75.

[92] ibid 83.

[93] This is because, for the purpose of identifying them, one commonly considers treaties to have been concluded at the date when they were signed. See eg Gardiner, *Treaty Interpretation* (n 3) 232.

[94] ibid 232 f.

[95] Sir Gerald Fitzmaurice, 'First Report on the Law of Treaties' [1956-II] YBILC 104, 121 [48], [52].

[96] ibid 121 [51]. See also ILC, 'Report of the International Law Commission on the Work of its 65th Session' (6 May–7 June and 8 July–9 August 2013) UN Doc A/68/10, 31 [2]; Nolte, 'Report 1—ICJ and Arbitral Tribunals' (n 2) 189; Linderfalk, *On the Interpretation of Treaties* (n 3) 163.

4.3 Subsequent Practice under Article 31(3)(b) VCLT

Section 4.3 focuses on the requirements which article 31(3)(b) VCLT imposes on subsequent practice as a means of interpretation under the general rule. This provision comprises two parts, namely an objective and a subjective one. The objective part includes any subsequent practice in the application of the treaty. The subjective part requires the interpreter to demonstrate that the objective part establishes the agreement of the parties regarding the interpretation of the treaty.

4.3.1 Objective Components of Subsequent Practice

The objective part of article 31(3)(b) VCLT requires 'subsequent practice in the application of the treaty'. As has been shown under 4.2.4, a practice will be 'subsequent' if it occurs after the text of the treaty has finally been established as definite. Hence this objective part still raises three questions: Firstly, what is 'practice'? Secondly, whose practice counts as 'practice'? And thirdly, under which conditions is a certain practice one 'in the application of the treaty'?

4.3.1.1 What Constitutes 'Practice'?

The Convention does not define the term 'practice' within the meaning of article 31(3)(b) VCLT. In conventional language, this term allows for a broad and for a more restrictive interpretation.[97] A prominent proponent of a broad interpretation is Wolfram Karl. In his view, the term 'practice' encompasses any form of conduct, ie active as well as passive[98] and repeated as well as isolated, singular conduct.[99]

[97] cf Gardiner, *Treaty Interpretation* (n 3) 254 f; see also 'practice, n' *Oxford English Dictionary Online* (September 2014, OUP) <http://www.oed.com/view/Entry/149226?rskey=D2CSWk&result=1>.

[98] Karl, *Vertrag und spätere Praxis* (n 26) 112, 114 f; see also the commentary on draft conclusion 4 in ILC, 'Report of the International Law Commission on the Work of its 65th Session' (6 May–7 June and 8 July–9 August 2013) UN Doc A/68/10, 35 [16]; Dörr, 'Article 31' (n 9) 555 [78]; Distefano, 'La pratique subséquente' (n 3) 48.

[99] Karl, *Vertrag und spätere Praxis* (n 26) 112, 114 f. See also Linderfalk, *On the Interpretation of Treaties* (n 3) 166, who convincingly remarks: '[F]rom a principle point of view, I find it difficult to see why *one* application cannot constitute a "practice" if *two* can.' See further Maurice Waite (ed), *Oxford Thesaurus of English* (3rd edn, OUP 2009) 666, where it is at least accepted that the ordinary meaning of the term 'practice' allows both for a broad and a restrictive interpretation. cf also Nolte, 'Report 3—Practice outside of Judicial Proceedings' (n 29) 310 f [fn omitted], where it is cautiously suggested that 'a stand-alone unilateral or bilateral act will normally not be sufficient to constitute a subsequent practice in a multilateral framework. In any event, the VCLT only speaks of practice without formulating any requirement of frequency.' In id, 'First Report' (n 33) 42 [108], the Special Rapporteur more

Richard Gardiner, for example, advocates a more restrictive interpretation. According to him, the very essence of the term 'practice' required that it 'can be shown to have been done systematically or repeatedly in implementation and application of a treaty'.[100]

The ILC only apparently agrees with Gardiner's restrictive understanding of 'practice' by cautiously remarking that

> [t]he distinction between subsequent practice under article 31(3)(b) and subsequent practice under article 32 … contributes to answering the question whether subsequent practice requires repeated action with some frequency or whether a one-time application of the treaty may be enough …. If, however, the concept of subsequent practice as a means of treaty interpretation is distinguished from a possible agreement of the parties, frequency is not a necessary element of the concept of 'subsequent practice' in the broad sense (under article 32).[101]

At first sight, this comment seems to suggest that the term 'practice' should, in principle, be given a narrow reading. Yet, this comment may equally reflect a broader understanding, which is in accordance with this term's context and the Convention's object and purpose. Like subsequent agreements under lit (a), subsequent practice under lit (b) of article 31(3) VCLT derives its interpretative value from the parties' agreement.[102] In the case of subsequent agreements under lit (a), the interpretative value lies in the agreement itself. Subsequent practice under lit (b), in contrast, does not in itself carry this interpretative value. Instead, such practice merely serves as a piece of evidence. Under lit (b), interpreters need to perform the additional intellectual operation of demonstrating that the practice actually establishes the agreement of the parties.

Those who exclude single acts from the meaning of 'practice' typically invoke this term's very 'essence'[103] or 'idea'[104]. The legal consideration behind these

---

clearly endorsed a broad understanding of the term 'practice' by emphasising that art 31(3)(b) VCLT distinguished between (agreed) subsequent practice in the narrow sense and subsequent practice in a broad sense. This led him to conclude that 'frequency is not a necessary element in the definition of the concept of "subsequent practice".' See ibid 43 [109].

[100] Gardiner, *Treaty Interpretation* (n 3) 254. See also Villiger, *Commentary on the VCLT* (n 23) 431 [22]. Yet, the temporal standard which Villiger applies to practice under art 31(3)(b) VCLT appears somewhat inconsistent. This is because he acknowledges, when discussing the formation of customary international law, that 'the duration of practice is a relative requirement, and that customary law may therefore come into being in a comparatively short period of time.' See ibid 9 [13]. See also Yasseen, 'L'interprétation des traités' (n 7) 48; Ian Sinclair, *The Vienna Convention on the Law of Treaties* (2nd edn, MUP 1984) 137; Dörr, 'Article 31' (n 9) 556 [79].

[101] Commentary on draft conclusion 4 in ILC, 'Report of the International Law Commission on the Work of its 65th Session' (6 May–7 June and 8 July–9 August 2013) UN Doc A/68/10, 41 [35].

[102] See 4.1.

[103] Yasseen, 'L'interprétation des traités' (n 7) 48; Sinclair, *The Vienna Convention on the Law of Treaties* (n 100) 137; Gardiner, *Treaty Interpretation* (n 3) 254; Villiger, *Commentary on the VCLT* (n 23) 431 [22].

[104] Yasseen, 'L'interprétation des traités' (n 7) 48.

arguments is that practice under lit (b) must be capable of establishing the parties' agreement.[105] But this reasoning is not convincing. The requirement that practice must be capable of establishing the parties' agreement is not inherent in the term 'practice' itself.[106] Admittedly, repeated practice regularly facilitates establishing the parties' agreement. In that sense, the ILC emphasised that the weight of subsequent practice indeed depended on 'whether and how it is repeated.'[107] Nevertheless, it is not excluded *a priori* that a single act may suffice to establish the parties' agreement, too. This is especially true in respect of bilateral treaties. Nonetheless, the proponents of the restrictive view accept that practice by only some actors and silence by others can fall under article 31(3)(b) VCLT as long as the parties' agreement can be established.[108] Thus, they implicitly acknowledge that the crucial question relates to the notion of agreement and that any practice must be assessed in terms of the parties' agreement anyway.

Another argument supporting a broad understanding of 'practice' can be derived from the formation of customary international law.[109] Asking whether a certain rule of customary international law has come into existence or still exists, one also examines State practice. This is recognised in article 38(1)(b) ICJ Statute, which defines international custom as evidence of a general practice accepted as law. For the purpose of identifying a rule of customary international law, the term 'practice' is commonly understood as referring to 'what the subjects of international law do and say, what they want (or consent to), and what they believe.'[110] In this context, it has been noted that, 'while frequent repetition of a consistent practice would naturally lend it greater weight, "the degree of frequency has to be weighed against the frequency with which the circumstances arise in which the action constituting practice has to be taken, or is appropriate".'[111] In other words, the necessary degree of

---

[105] Gardiner, *Treaty Interpretation* (n 3) 259.

[106] See especially Linderfalk, *On the Interpretation of Treaties* (n 3) 166.

[107] Commentary on draft conclusion 8 in ILC, 'Report of the International Law Commission on the Work of its 66th Session' (5 May–6 June and 7 July–8 August 2014) UN Doc A/69/10, 194 [6].

[108] Gardiner, *Treaty Interpretation* (n 3) 266 f. Those who advocate the broader view, namely that the term 'practice' also includes singles acts, all the more accept that art 31(3)(b) VCLT does not require a practice to which all parties have contributed, see eg Linderfalk, *On the Interpretation of Treaties* (n 3) 167.

[109] See eg Dörr, 'Article 31' (n 9) 555 [78], who also compares practice under art 31(3)(b) VCLT to practice as part of the formation of customary international law, without, however, discussing the differences between the two notions of 'practice'.

[110] Tullio Treves, 'Customary International Law' in Rüdiger Wolfrum (ed), *The Max Planck Encyclopedia of Public International Law* (OUP 2012) [23]. See also Sir Michael Wood, 'State Practice' in Rüdiger Wolfrum (ed), *The Max Planck Encyclopedia of Public International Law* (OUP 2012) [6].

[111] id, 'Second Report on Identification of Customary International Law' (22 May 2014) UN Doc A/CN.4/672 39 [56] quoting Hugh Thirlway, *The Sources of International Law* (OUP 2014) 65.

frequency of relevant practice cannot be determined in the abstract. Related to this pragmatic approach is the observation that 'there is no specific requirement with regard to how long a practice must exist before it can ripen into a rule of customary international law.'[112]

In the end, the prevailing view concerning the formation of customary international law still insists that 'one instance of practice, or a few instances in one occasion, cannot create law.'[113] Nonetheless, the requirements as to frequency and duration are not regarded as absolute. In this respect, it is useful to bear in mind that the concept of 'practice' for the purpose of customary international law is not identical to practice within the meaning of article 31(3)(b) VCLT.[114] Subsequent practice under article 31(3)(b) VCLT does not serve to establish the formation of a new rule of law or its continued existence. It merely helps to interpret an already existing rule of law. This difference, in turn, speaks for applying an even more lenient standard to practice under article 31(3)(b) VCLT than in the context of customary international law.

For these reasons, this study endorses the broader understanding of 'practice' as encompassing any form of conduct. If it is necessary to discard some practice, this can be done when examining whether certain pieces of practice, taken together, establish the parties' agreement regarding the interpretation of the treaty. A danger of using this broad understanding is that one may be tempted—by referring to each of them as 'subsequent practice'—to confuse potentially relevant practice with subsequent practice as a means of interpretation under article 31(3)(b) VCLT. This makes it necessary, for the purpose of terminological clarity, to accurately distinguish between subsequent practice as a means of treaty interpretation and potentially relevant (pieces of) practice. Subsequent practice is regularly used as an abbreviated designation of a means of treaty interpretation pursuant to and satisfying all requirements of article 31(3)(b) VCLT. Potentially relevant (pieces of) practice may or may not satisfy all requirements of article 31(3)(b) VCLT.[115] If potentially relevant practice does not meet all requirements of this provision, interpreters will be precluded from relying on it under the general rule of interpretation.[116]

---

[112] Wood, 'Second Report' (n 111) 40 [58]. cf also the debates about the possibility of 'instant custom', which is said to emerge without further proof of State practice if there is a 'clearly established consensus among States' about the existence of a particular rule. See Niels Petersen, 'Customary Law without Custom?—Rules, Principles, and the Role of State Practice in International Norm Creation' (2007) 23 Am U Int'l L Rev 275, 280 f and Bin Cheng, 'United Nations Resolutions on Outer Space—"Instant" International Customary Law?' (1965) 5 IJIL 23, 23.

[113] Mark Villiger, *Customary International Law and Treaties—A Manual on the Theory and Practice of the Interrelation of Sources* (2nd edn, Kluwer 1997) 19.

[114] Wood, 'State Practice' (n 110) [2].

[115] cf ILC, 'Report of the International Law Commission on the Work of its 65th Session' (6 May–7 June and 8 July–9 August 2013) UN Doc A/68/10, 35 [15]; Nolte, 'First Report' (n 33) 42 [107].

[116] This does not mean, of course, that interpreters cannot consider such practice as a supplementary means of interpretation under art 32 VCLT.

4.3.1.2 Whose Practice Counts as 'Practice'?

Another essential question relating to the term 'practice' is whose practice counts as practice under article 31(3)(b) VCLT. The text of article 31(3)(b) VCLT broadly speaks of 'any practice'. It is neither limited to nor excludes practice originating from certain actors. Once again, this term therefore allows for two opposing interpretations.

In the first alternative, the term 'practice' would be read to cover only those instances of practice that are attributable to a State party.[117] This means that organs of a State party and other actors whose conduct is attributable to the State can produce State practice. Such State practice can originate from all branches of State power and thus include executive, legislative, and judicial practice.[118] Moreover, State practice must not necessarily originate from central government but can stem from all levels of State hierarchy.[119] Examples include national asylum administrations that deny an applicant's claim for non-refoulement under the Refugee Convention because they do not recognise his status as a refugee, a parliament that enacts a law to implement the European Convention on Human Rights, or a court that rejects a passenger's claim for damages against an airline because it does not satisfy the requirements under the Warsaw Convention as implemented into domestic law.

In the second alternative, the term 'practice' under article 31(3)(b) VCLT is not necessarily limited to conduct that is attributable to a State party to the treaty. This broader interpretation of practice hence covers both practice by States that are not a party to the respective treaty and practice by private individuals and private legal entities as well as IOs or other international bodies.[120] In short, the broader reading

---

[117] Gardiner, *Treaty Interpretation* (n 3) 266; Dörr, 'Article 31' (n 9) 557 [82]. Notably, Dörr acknowledges that lit (b) does not explicitly require that practice must be attributable to a contracting party. Yet, he does not explain why lit (b) should be interpreted to implicitly require such attribution. cf also Moloo, 'The Relevance of Subsequent Party Conduct' (n 14) 69, who speaks of 'the conduct of any official tasked to implement the subject matter of a treaty.'

[118] Commentary on draft conclusion 6 in ILC, 'Report of the International Law Commission on the Work of its 66th Session' (5 May–6 June and 7 July–8 August 2014) UN Doc A/69/10, 178 [22]. See also Gardiner, *Treaty Interpretation* (n 3) 257; Dörr, 'Article 31' (n 9) 555 [78]; Distefano, 'La pratique subséquente' (n 3) 42.

[119] Commentary on draft conclusion 5 in ILC, 'Report of the International Law Commission on the Work of its 65th Session' (6 May–7 June and 8 July–9 August 2013) UN Doc A/68/10, 42 [5], 43 [7]. cf Gardiner, *Treaty Interpretation* (n 3) 257.

[120] See Karl, *Vertrag und spätere Praxis* (n 26) 117, who mentions air transport agreements, establishment agreements, and fishing agreements as examples of treaties that are also applied by non-State actors. See also, albeit without going into a detailed statement of reasons for this view, Linderfalk, *On the Interpretation of Treaties* (n 3) 166. Linderfalk instead simply points out that '[a]ll appliers of a treaty are potential creators of "practice".' Some commentators who in principle want to restrict art (31)(3)(b) VCLT to practice that is attributable to a contracting party nevertheless accept that relevant practice may also be produced by IOs, see eg Dörr, 'Article 31' (n 9) 558 [84]: '[W]here States by treaty entrust performance of activities under the treaty to an international organ or organization, the fulfilment of those functions is

of the term ‘practice’ under article 31(3)(b) VCLT covers all possible forms of State party and non-party practice. Examples include decisions of courts that do not belong to a State party, such as decisions by Swiss courts which address questions under the Treaties of the European Union,[121] general comments promulgated by treaty bodies, or an air carrier that has been granted the right to conduct air transport services under an air transport agreement and that subsequently extends its services to routes not explicitly authorised by the parties to the agreement.[122]

The prevailing view in the literature and in the ILC has been that any subsequent conduct—and hence also subsequent practice—must be attributable to a State party.[123] Notably, the Special Rapporteur’s draft conclusion 4 in his ‘First Report’—which relates to the question of whether conduct by private actors or even social developments can be attributed to the State parties—actually suggests that he had originally intended to establish a broader interpretation of article 31(3)(b) VCLT. Following up on his ‘Second Report for the ILC Study Group on Treaties over Time’,[124] he had cautiously contended that ‘[s]ubsequent practice by non-State actors, including social practice, may be taken into account for the purpose of treaty interpretation as far as it is reflected in or adopted by subsequent State practice, or as evidence of such State practice.’[125] The Commission, however, adopted a more restrictive view in its conclusion 5, which reads:

> 1. Subsequent practice under articles 31 and 32 may consist of any conduct in the application of a treaty which is attributable to a party to the treaty under international law.
>
> 2. Other conduct, including by non-State actors, does not constitute subsequent practice under articles 31 and 32. Such conduct may, however, be relevant when assessing the subsequent practice of parties to a treaty.[126]

---

not only attributable to the parties … but can also in itself constitute “subsequent practice” under the treaty.’ This statement suggests that attribution of conduct is not absolutely necessary. Rather, Dörr seems to concentrate on the question of whether an actor fulfils ‘functions’ under a treaty, ie whether it implements the treaty. This, however, raises the question why it should make a difference whether an IO or any other non-party entity implements a treaty.

[121] See eg BGer, Decision of 8 March 2006, BGE 132 III 389, which addresses the ambit of the CJEU’s judgment in Case C–126/97 *Eco Swiss China Time Ltd v Benetton International NV* [1999] ECR I–3055.

[122] See eg *Case concerning the Interpretation of the Air Transport Services Agreement between the United States of America and France, Signed at Paris on 27 March 1946 (France v USA)* (1964) 16 RIAA 5.

[123] See already Nolte, ‘Report 1—ICJ and Arbitral Tribunals’ (n 2) 197 f. See also id, ‘Report 3—Subsequent Agreements and Subsequent Practice of States outside of Judicial or Quasi-Judicial Proceedings’ in id (ed), *Treaties and Subsequent Practice* (OUP 2013) 310.

[124] id, ‘Report 2—Jurisprudence under Special Regimes relating to Subsequent Agreements and Subsequent Practice’ in id (ed), *Treaties and Subsequent Practice* (OUP 2013) 247 f.

[125] id, ‘First Report’ (n 33) 55 [144].

[126] ILC, ‘Report of the International Law Commission on the Work of its 65th Session’ (6 May–7 June and 8 July–9 August 2013) UN Doc A/68/10, 41.

As its commentary explains, the Commission considered whether it should refer, in the text of its draft conclusion, to 'social practice' as an example of non-State practice.[127] Several members, however, expressed concerns 'regarding the meaning and relevance of that notion'.[128] For that reason, the Commission ultimately decided to only 'address the question of the possible relevance of "social practice" in the commentary.'[129] Against this background, it merits attention that the Special Rapporteur's Second Report, which he submitted in 2014, nevertheless contained a more ambitious wording by noting that practice under article 31(3)(b) VCLT 'includes … practices by non-state entities which fall within the scope of what the treaty conveives as forms of its application.'[130]

Despite the ILC's reluctance to embrace a broader understanding of 'practice' within the meaning of article 31(3)(b) VCLT, there are actually good reasons to dismiss the narrower reading. Firstly, article 31(3)(b) VCLT does not speak of the 'practice of the parties'. Had the drafters of the Convention intended such restriction, they could have unambiguously said so. Moreover, systematic considerations do not support a restrictive interpretation either. Lits (a) and (b) of article 31(3) VCLT refer to the agreement between or of the parties. These references to the parties conversely imply that the Convention deliberately refrains from restricting practice to practice attributable to the parties. Besides, the subjective part of article 31(3)(b) VCLT suggests that it is immaterial whether practice is attributable to the parties or not. The decisive question is whether a practice establishes the agreement of the parties. It is this subjective component that links a certain practice to the will of the parties. How interpreters establish this link is, however, left open by the Convention.

The object and purpose of article 31(3)(b) VCLT is to assist in determining the meaning of the terms of the treaty based on the parties' common understanding as it is established through the treaty's application. As a matter of fact, treaties are mostly applied by actors whose conduct is attributable to a State party. Yet, a treaty may exceptionally also conceive other forms of its application, which may equally evidence the parties' common understanding and hence be helpful to determine its meaning.[131] In sum, it is understandable why one may be worried about conceding too much influence on the interpretation of treaties to non-party actors. However,

[127] ibid 47 [19].

[128] ibid.

[129] ibid.

[130] Nolte, 'Second Report' (n 33) [42].

[131] cf the commentary on draft conclusion 6 in ILC, 'Report of the International Law Commission on the Work of its 66th Session' (5 May–6 June and 7 July–8 August 2014) UN Doc A/69/10, 178 [22] [emphasis added], where it is acknowledged that relevant subsequent practice 'may even include conduct by non-state actors which is attributable to one ore more State parties *and which fall within the scope of what the treaty conceives as forms of its application.*' As this quotation shows, the Commission did not adopt the formulation proposed by the Special Rapporteur in his Second Report but again referred to attributable conduct.

article 31(3)(b) VCLT responds to such concerns by requiring that relevant practice must be capable of establishing the agreement of the parties.

Therefore, this study does not follow the prevailing view but advocates a broader interpretation of the term 'practice'. For the purpose of this study, the term 'practice' within the meaning of article 31(3)(b) VCLT is not restricted to practice attributable to a State party but includes any form of conduct irrespective of its origins.

4.3.1.3 'In the Application of the Treaty'

Finally, the objective part of article 31(3)(b) VCLT requires a practice that is 'in the application of the treaty'.[132] This last objective requirement ensures that certain forms of practice cannot be taken into account whereas others can.[133]

On the one hand, the term 'application' excludes accidental practice. The notion 'accidental practice' covers cases of practice originating from actors that not even subconsciously know that their conduct possibly falls within the scope of a treaty.[134] Moreover, the term 'application' excludes deliberate violations of the treaty. Actors who deliberately violate a treaty cannot at the same time produce practice 'in the application' of that treaty.[135] The term 'treaty', on the other hand, clarifies that the practice need not be in the application of the very same provision that is being interpreted. Instead, it is sufficient if it relates to other provisions of the treaty. The definitive article 'the' in front of 'treaty', however, clarifies that the treaty that is being interpreted and the one to which the practice relates must be identical. In consequence, practice in the application of another treaty (and be it one on the same subject matter) does not fall under article 31(3)(b) VCLT.

This does not mean that a given practice cannot constitute practice in the application of two or more treaties. The enactment of domestic legislation may, for instance, aim at implementing a State's obligations under multiple international agreements (eg under the Charter of Fundamental Rights of the European Union,[136] under the ECHR, and under the ICCPR). Article 31(3)(b) VCLT does not require practice that is undertaken in the application of only one treaty. Hence it is possible that practice

---

[132] For the meaning of the term 'application', see 4.2.3.

[133] See eg Karl, *Vertrag und spätere Praxis* (n 26) 118; Gardiner, *Treaty Interpretation* (n 3) 262–66; Dörr, 'Article 31' (n 9) 556 f [80].

[134] cf Nolte, 'Report 1—ICJ and Arbitral Tribunals' (n 2) 175, who suggests that only 'such conduct which the parties consciously relate to the treaty should benefit from being treated as an "authentic" position.' cf also the commentary on draft conclusion 6 in ILC, 'Report of the International Law Commission on the Work of its 66th Session' (5 May–6 June and 7 July–8 August 2014) UN Doc A/69/10, 172 [7].

[135] Commentary on draft conclusion 4 in id, 'Report of the International Law Commission on the Work of its 65th Session' (6 May–7 June and 8 July–9 August 2013) UN Doc A/68/10, 36 [18].

[136] Charter of Fundamental Rights of the European Union [2007] OJ C303/1. Under art 6 TEU, the Charter has the same legal value as the EU Treaties.

in the application of one treaty, and relied on to interpret that treaty in accordance with article 31(3)(b) VCLT, is at the same time also relevant for construing another treaty.

4.3.2 Subjective Components of Subsequent Practice

The subjective part of article 31(3)(b) VCLT requires a practice that is capable of establishing the agreement of the parties regarding the interpretation of the treaty. Thus, practice serves to evidence the existence of an implicit agreement.[137] To establish the necessary link between a given body of practice and the parties' agreement, interpreters need to perform an additional intellectual operation (hence: subjective components). The need for this additional intellectual operation is illustrated by the term 'establish'. Before examining this intellectual operation more closely, this study focuses on that which needs to be established, namely the parties' agreement.

4.3.2.1 The Agreement of the Parties

What the 'agreement of the parties regarding the interpretation of the treaty' means has already been discussed under 4.2. In this context, two central questions were addressed: Does the agreement between the parties require an agreement between all parties? And is it possible and indeed necessary to distinguish agreements regarding the interpretation of a treaty from agreements regarding the modification of a treaty? Having answered both questions in the affirmative, there seems to be no reason to interpret lit (b) differently from lit (a) of article 31(3) VCLT. But since the Convention's drafting history offers some insight into these questions as regards subsequent practice, it may nevertheless be instructive to re-examine the earlier conclusions in the light of this material.

The provision on subsequent agreements basically remained unchanged during the Convention's drafting history and hardly received any attention at all. The draft provision on subsequent practice, in contrast, was repeatedly changed and repeatedly discussed in the Commission. Sir Humphrey Waldock's first draft on treaty interpretation still considered subsequent practice as a subsidiary means of interpretation and simply referred to it as 'subsequent practice of parties in relation to the treaty.'[138] His revised draft, which he presented during the Commission's 769th session, upgraded subsequent practice to become part of the general rule and referred to it as 'any subsequent practice in the application of the treaty which establishes the common understanding of all the parties regarding its interpretation.' This terminology shows that subsequent practice under the general rule required the agreement of all parties. Although the Commission decided to slightly revise

[137] See 4.1.

[138] Waldock, 'Third Report' (n 15) 52.

Waldock's new draft during this session, the wording of the provision on subsequent practice remained unaltered.[139]

Alongside practice that established the agreement of all parties, Sir Humphrey Waldock separately acknowledged another form of subsequent practice. This other form of subsequent practice was practice establishing the agreement of only some parties. In his view, the latter carried less interpretative weight and was 'on a different level' than practice establishing the agreement of all parties.[140] Commission member Grigory Tunkin criticised Waldock for even mentioning such 'inferior' practice.[141] Nevertheless, Waldock emphasised that such 'inferior' practice was not completely irrelevant but could well constitute a subsidiary means of interpretation.[142] Therefore, he insisted on retaining both forms of practice.[143]

In the end, the Commission nevertheless dropped the express reference to 'inferior' practice.[144] Its reasons for doing so, however, remain unclear. As the ILC confirmed in 2013, subsequent practice falling short of the requirements of article 31(3)(b) VCLT may therefore still be taken into account under article 32 VCLT.[145] In any event, it was never doubted that practice under the general rule must be capable of establishing the agreement of all parties. In its final draft of 1969, the Commission suddenly omitted the word 'all' before parties. But in doing so, the Commission

> did not intend to change the rule. It considered that the phrase 'the understanding of the parties' necessarily means 'the parties as a whole.' It omitted the word 'all' merely to avoid any possible misconception that every party must individually have engaged in the practice where it suffices that it should have accepted the practice.[146]

The drafting history therefore supports a restrictive interpretation to the effect that the phrase 'agreement of the parties' under article 31(3)(b) VCLT means the

139 ILC, 'Summary Records of the 16th Session of the International Law Commission' (11 May–24 July 1964) [1964-I] YBILC 1, 313 [55].

140 See Sir Humphrey Waldock's draft in ibid 309 [3].

141 Grigory Tunkin in ibid 314 [72]–[73].

142 Sir Humphrey Waldock in ibid 314 [74]–[76].

143 ibid.

144 Statement by Chairman Roberto Ago, subsequently agreed on by the Commission, in ibid 314 [77].

145 Draft conclusion 1(4) in ILC, 'Report of the International Law Commission on the Work of its 65th Session' (6 May–7 June and 8 July–9 August 2013) UN Doc A/68/10, 11. See also Yasseen, 'L'interprétation des traités' (n 7) 52. For 'other' subsequent agreements and subsequent practice as supplementary means of interpretation, see 4.4.

146 ILC, 'DALT' (n 18) 222 [15]. See also draft conclusion 9(2) and the accompanying commentary in id, 'Report of the International Law Commission on the Work of its 66th Session' UN Doc A/69/10, ILC A/69/10, 197, 201 [13]: '[N]ot all the parties must engage in a particular practice to constitute agreement under art 31(3)(b)… [but] acceptance of such practice by those parties not engaged in the practice can under certain circumstances be brought about by silence or inaction.'

agreement of all parties.[147] As noted earlier, the same conclusion applies, *mutatis mutandis,* to subsequent agreements under article 31(3)(a) VCLT.

4.3.2.2 Interpretation and Modification Distinguished

Both lits (a) and (b) of article 31(3) VCLT only mention the parties' agreement regarding the interpretation of the treaty. As has been argued under 4.2.3, agreements regarding the modification of the treaty are not envisaged by and must therefore not be taken into account under article 31(3)(a) VCLT. Yet, it is questionable whether the same applies to subsequent practice under article 31(3)(a) VCLT.

This is because article 69A of the Commission's draft articles once expressly acknowledged that a treaty may also be modified by subsequent practice.[148] But even at that time, modification by subsequent practice was controversial. Commission member Grigory Tunkin, for instance, warned that 'such an approach was exceedingly dangerous and would jeopardize the stability of treaties by throwing doubt on their status once a practice established by the parties had come into existence.'[149] Moreover, he urged that modification and interpretation should be kept separate because 'any broadening of the concept of interpretation ... would make it possible to disguise the modification of a treaty as an interpretation of its provisions.'[150] Commission member Roberto Ago, in contrast, defended Waldock's draft on modification by subsequent practice. In his view,

> the Commission was considering the very simple case of modification of a treaty by consent of the parties. The only difference was that, instead of modifying the treaty by means of another treaty or another express agreement, the parties did so tacitly by their practice in its application, but there was still consent by the parties. It was true that practice could either merely provide elements for interpreting a treaty or justify its actual modification, but once practice modified a treaty, that showed that the parties were in agreement on the matter.[151]

Since the Vienna Conference eventually deleted the draft provision on modification by subsequent practice,[152] two questions arise: Firstly, whether the Convention now categorically excludes the possibility that a treaty may be modified by subsequent practice. And secondly (if the first question is answered in the negative), whether modification by subsequent practice is now implicitly covered by article 31(3)(b) VCLT so that it can be taken into account during the interpretative process. The

[147] See also Yasseen, 'L'interprétation des traités' (n 7) 48 f; Dörr, 'Article 31' (n 9) 557 f [83].

[148] See n 21 in Chapter 3. This provision became art 68/38 in subsequent drafts.

[149] Griogry Tunkin in ILC, 'Summary Records of the 16th Session of the International Law Commission' (11 May–24 July 1964) [1964-I] YBILC 1, 167 [56].

[150] ibid 164 [15].

[151] ibid 167 [49].

[152] UN Conference on the Law of Treaties, 'Summary Records of the Plenary Meetings and of the Meetings of the Committee of the Whole' (First session, Vienna 26 March 1968) UN Doc A/CONF.39/11, 215. The decision to delete draft art 38 was adopted by 53 votes to 15, with 26 abstentions.

arguments that have been invoked to contend that article 31(3)(a) VCLT does not cover modification also apply to lit (b) of this provision.[153] First of all, the Convention distinguishes between interpretation (and application) on the one hand, and changes of the treaty (amendment and modification) on the other. Although the line between interpretation or application and modification is often blurred, for those who apply a treaty this distinction is nonetheless significant.

These arguments were also mentioned during the Convention's drafting history in respect of draft article 69A. Some of those delegates to the Vienna Conference who favoured its deletion equally emphasised that such modification would entail constitutional problems for many States.[154] Moreover, it was remarked that modification by subsequent practice conflicted with the basic principle of *pacta sunt servanda*.[155] Accepting that flexibility in treaty law was important, it was stressed that the necessary degree of flexibility was guaranteed by subsequent interpretative practice; therefore, modification by subsequent practice could be dispensed with anyway.[156] The Mexican delegate even noted that it was wise to clarify that subsequent interpretative practice 'could be taken into account for purposes of interpretation only if that practice did not openly conflict with the text of the treaty.'[157] Although the Conference did not implement this proposal, it eventually deleted the contentious provision on modification by subsequent practice.[158] This fact may be

---

[153] See 4.2.3.3.

[154] UN Conference on the Law of Treaties, 'Summary Records of the Plenary Meetings and of the Meetings of the Committee of the Whole' (First session, Vienna 26 March 1968) UN Doc A/CONF.39/11, 208 f, esp 208 [63]. See also the commentary on draft conclusion 7 in ILC, 'Report of the International Law Commission on the Work of its 66th Session' (5 May–6 June and 7 July–8 August 2014) UN Doc A/69/10, 191 [34].

[155] UN Conference on the Law of Treaties, 'Summary Records of the Plenary Meetings and of the Meetings of the Committee of the Whole' (First session, Vienna 26 March 1968) UN Doc A/CONF.39/11, 208 f, esp 209 [70] and 210 [75]. See also the commentary on draft conclusion 7 in ILC, 'Report of the International Law Commission on the Work of its 66th Session' (5 May–6 June and 7 July–8 August 2014) UN Doc A/69/10, 191 [34] and Marcelo Kohen, 'Keeping Subsequent Agreements and Practice in Their Right Limits' in Georg Nolte (ed), *Treaties and Subsequent Practice* (OUP 2013) 36, who stresses that 'Treaties… are the most solemn manifestation of the establishment of the coordination of the will of their respective parties. Treaty parties deliberately decided not to keep their agreement informal. What in most cases required lengthy negotiations, the signing of an instrument, parliamentary discussion and approval at the domestic level, ratification by the executive organ, exchange of instruments of ratification or deposit of them, cannot simply be replaced by an interpretation given to some activity on the ground.'

[156] UN Conference on the Law of Treaties, 'Summary Records of the Plenary Meetings and of the Meetings of the Committee of the Whole' (First session, Vienna 26 March 1968) UN Doc A/CONF.39/11, 208 f, esp. 208 [62]. See also the commentary on draft conclusion 7 in ILC, 'Report of the International Law Commission on the Work of its 66th Session' (5 May–6 June and 7 July–8 August 2014) UN Doc A/69/10, 191 [34].

[157] ibid 181 [41].

[158] ibid 215 [69].

taken to suggest that the Conference indeed wished to eliminate any possibility of modifying a treaty by subsequent practice. Nonetheless, it is equally possible that the Conference simply did not wish to address the controversial issue of modification by subsequent practice.[159]

In its commentary on draft conclusion 7, which addresses the possible effects of subsequent practice, the ILC now contends that 'the possibility of amending or modifying a treaty by subsequent practice has not generally been recognized.'[160] In particular, it notes that '[i]nternational courts and tribunals ... have since the adoption of the Vienna Convention mostly refrained from recognozing this possibility' although it still finds much support in the literature.[161] Despite 'some support in international case-law that, absent indications in the treaty to the contrary, the agreed subsequent practice of the parties theoretically may lead to modifications of a treaty', the ILC therefore eventually concludes that 'the actual occurence of that effect is not to be presumed.'[162]

In sum, the Convention's drafting history does not unambiguously demonstrate that the Convention now categorically excludes the possibility of modification through subsequent practice. Nonetheless, it lends support to the view that interpretation and modification should be clearly separated. While it is still conceivable that subsequent practice may have the effect of modifying a treaty, such modifying practice can therefore not be taken into account under article 31(3)(b) VCLT.

4.3.2.3 How to 'Establish' the Agreement?

The parties' agreement under article 31(3)(b) VCLT is not explicit. Instead, interpreters need to establish this agreement by considering the various pieces of relevant practice in the application of the treaty which they identified. Expressly requiring a practice that establishes the parties' agreement would make no sense if any practice in the application of the treaty automatically established this agreement. In consequence, potentially relevant practice must possess certain qualities so that it can justify conclusions as to the parties' agreement.

---

[159] See in particular Yasseen, 'L'interprétation des traités' (n 7) 51 f; Karl, *Vertrag und spätere Praxis* (n 26) 373; Sinclair, *The Vienna Convention on the Law of Treaties* (n 100) 138; Mark Villiger, 'The 1969 Vienna Convention on the Law of Treaties—40 Years After' (2009) 344 RCADI 9, 432 [23]; Dörr, 'Article 31' (n 9) 555 [76]. Disagreeing eg Kohen, 'Keeping Subsequent Agreements and Practice in Their Right Limits' (n 155) 36 f; Sean Murphy, 'The Relevance of Subsequent Agreements and Subsequent Practice for the Interpretation of Treaties' in Georg Nolte (ed), *Treaties and Subsequent Practice* (OUP 2013) 89 f.

[160] Commentary on draft conclusion 7 in ILC, 'Report of the International Law Commission on the Work of its 66th Session' (5 May–6 June and 7 July–8 August 2014) UN Doc A/69/10, 186 [18].

[161] ibid 187 [23].

[162] ibid 192 [35].

These 'qualities' are frequently captured in the catchphrase that subsequent practice must be 'concordant, common and consistent.'[163] However, this catchphrase is misleading and not particularly useful.[164] Firstly, it may tempt interpreters to solely focus on the outward appearance of a given practice and therefore discard pieces of practice that do, taken together with other pieces of practice, establish the parties' agreement.[165] And secondly, this catchphrase may tempt to abstain from closely examining whether all these pieces of practice, taken together, truly establish the parties' agreement. For this reason, this study proposes an alternative, two-step approach. Under this approach, interpreters in a first step identify those pieces of practice that are in the application of the treaty which they interpret. In a second step, interpreters then assess each piece of practice individually and all pieces of practice taken together to determine whether they establish the parties' agreement or not.

Relevant pieces of practice are those which support one particular interpretation (or range of interpretations) of the treaty. To argue that practice must appear to be consistent or sufficiently similar but not identical[166] is therefore imprecise. An exchange of notes, consisting of a request and a reply, or certain action under the treaty accompanied by another State's acquiescence, for example, are pieces of practice that appear rather different. Still, they all may support the same interpretation of the treaty.[167] The decisive factor is not the 'outward appearance' of practice, so to speak, but rather the message that it conveys. But whether the message is the same or sufficiently similar can often only be determined by looking at all potentially relevant pieces of practice without discarding too many pieces in advance. The same applies to single pieces of practice. Hardly establishing the parties' agreement when looked at in isolation, they may well establish this agreement when considered in context.

Another question concerning the parties' agreement relates to the level of certainty with which this agreement needs to be established. Article 31(3)(b) VCLT does not cover cases where the agreement itself is explicit. Hence one cannot achieve absolute certainty on the parties' agreement. If one could, the agreement would instead be one falling under article 31(3)(a) VCLT. However, it is important to remember that the Convention does not consider subsequent practice subordinate

---

[163] See eg Yasseen, 'L'interprétation des traités' (n 7) 48; Sinclair, *The Vienna Convention on the Law of Treaties* (n 100) 137. This formulation has, for instance, been taken up by Dörr, 'Article 31' (n 9) 556 [79] and in WTO, *Japan—Alcoholic Beverages II—Report of the Appellate Body* (4 October 1996) WT/DS8/AB/R-11/AB/R <http://docsonline.wto.org> 13.

[164] cf also the commentary on draft conclusion 8 in ILC, 'Report of the International Law Commission on the Work of its 66th Session' (5 May–6 June and 7 July–8 August 2014) UN Doc A/69/10195 [11], where it is noted that this catchphrase was not 'sufficiently well-established to articulate a minimum threshold for the applicability of article 31, paragraph 3 (b).'

[165] For an example, see the discussion of Justice Scalia's sepatate opinion in the case of *US v Stuart* 489 US 353, 109 S Ct 1183 (1989) at 248 f.

[166] Karl, *Vertrag und spätere Praxis* (n 26) 118.

[167] See eg BGH, Decision of 6 October 2016, I ZB 13/15 <http://www.juris.de> [32].

to subsequent agreements. Subsequent practice is part of the general rule just as subsequent agreements are. Moreover, both means of interpretation derive their interpretative value from the parties' agreement. Taking these considerations together, systematic interpretation suggests that the existence of the parties' agreement under lit (b) must not be considerably less certain than under lit (a) of article 31(3) VCLT. Where the parties' agreement is not reasonably certain, article 31(3)(b) VCLT is not applicable. Yet, interpreters may still take such 'inferior' practice into account under article 32 VCLT, albeit only under the conditions which apply to relying on supplementary means of interpretation.

4.4 'Other' Subsequent Conduct under Article 32 VCLT

Subsequent conduct that does not meet all criteria of article 31(3)(a) and (b) VCLT can still be taken into account as a supplementary means of interpretation under article 32 VCLT.[168] This is because article 32 VCLT does not contain a closed list of admissible supplementary means; although this provision expressly mentions the preparatory work of the treaty and the circumstances of its conclusion, this enumeration is merely exemplary ('including').[169]

The 'other' forms of subsequent conduct that may be taken into account under article 32 VCLT include, in particular, subsequent practice that does not establish an agreement of all parties regarding the treaty's interpretation.[170] Moreover, article

[168] Draft conclusions 1(4) and 4(3) in ILC, 'Report of the International Law Commission on the Work of its 65th Session' (6 May–7 June and 8 July–9 August 2013) UN Doc A/68/10, 13, 31. While these conclusions merely speak of 'other' subsequent practice, the accompanying commentary clarifies that art 32 VCLT may also cover 'other' subsequent agreements. See also Yasseen, 'L'interprétation des traités' (n 7) 52; Sinclair, *The Vienna Convention on the Law of Treaties* (n 100) 138; Villiger, *Commentary on the VCLT* (n 23) 446 [5]; Dörr, 'Article 31' (n 9) 481 [25]; Moloo, 'The Relevance of Subsequent Party Conduct' (n 14) 46, 77; *Kasikili/Sedudu Island* (n 8) 1096 [79] f; ECtHR, *Loizidou v Turkey* (1995) Series A No 310 [79] f; *Demir and Baykara v Turkey [GC]* App no 34503/97 (ECtHR, 12 November 2008) [52]; WTO, *EC—Chicken Cuts—Report of the Appellate Body* (12 September 2005) WT/DS269/AB/R, WT/DS286/AB/R <http://docsonline.wto.org> [305]; WTO, *EC—Computer Equipment—Report of the Appellate Body* (5 June 1998) WT/DS62/AB/R, WT/DS67/AB/R, WT/DS68/AB/R <http://docsonline.wto.org> [90]; *CMS Gas Transmission Company v Argentine Republic* (Decision on Preliminary Objections) (17 July 2003) ICSID Case No ARB/01/8 [47].

[169] See 3.3.2. See also the commentary on draft conclusion 1 in ILC, 'Report of the International Law Commission on the Work of its 65th Session' (6 May–7 June and 8 July–9 August 2013) UN Doc A/68/10, 16 [9]; Gardiner, *Treaty Interpretation* (n 3) 348; Dörr, 'Article 31' (n 9) 574 [9].

[170] Commentary on draft conclusion 1 in ILC, 'Report of the International Law Commission on the Work of its 65th Session' (6 May–7 June and 8 July–9 August 2013) UN Doc A/68/10, 16 [10]. See also the commentary on draft conclusion 7 in id, 'Report of the International Law Commission on the Work of its 66th Session' (5 May–6 June and 7 July–8 August 2014) UN Doc A/69/10, 184 [15].

32 VCLT authorises interpreters to have recourse to subsequent agreements regarding the interpretation of a treaty or the application of its provisions that have been reached between less than all parties.[171] The qualifier 'other' indicates that 'other' subsequent conduct under article 32 VCLT is similar but not identical to subsequent conduct under the general rule.[172] Especially when interpreting multilateral treaties, the recognition of 'other' subsequent conduct as a supplementary means cannot be underestimated. This is because a high number of contracting parties contributes to diminishing the chances of reaching or establishing the agreement of all parties as required by article 31(3)(a) and (b) VCLT.[173]

The potential relevance of 'other' subsequent conduct as a supplementary means of interpretation was already debated during the Convention's drafting history. While Sir Humphrey Waldock's first draft articles on treaty interpretation treated subsequent practice as a supplementary means of interpretation only,[174] subsequent practice establishing the agreement of all parties was subsequently upgraded to become a primary means of interpretation.[175] At the same time, the ILC deleted any reference to practice by individual parties to avoid overemphasising or unduly legitimating such 'other' practice.[176] Nonetheless, Waldock insisted that subsequent practice by only some parties 'could be very important, especially in the case of multilateral treaties.'[177]

Depending on the extent to which an agreement has been reached—between some, between many, or between almost all parties—the distinction between 'other' subsequent conduct and subsequent conduct under the general rule varies and may be more or less subtle. Against this background, the ILC concluded that the weight of 'other' subsequent conduct depends, among others, on the number of 'affected

[171] Commentary on draft conclusion 6 in ibid 179 [24].

[172] To illustrate and uphold the conceptual similarity between the various forms of subsequent conduct, it is expedient to restrict the notion of 'other' subsequent conduct under art 32 VCLT to conduct 'regarding to' or 'in the application of the treaty', see draft conclusion 6(3) and the accompanying commentary in ibid 170, 178 [24]. To the extent that it assists in determining or confirming the meaning of the terms of the treaty, art 32 VCLT arguably also covers conduct that is not 'regarding to' or 'in the application of the treaty'. This includes, for example, practice in the application of a different treaty on the same subject matter, see the Commentary on draft conclusion 1 in id, 'Report of the International Law Commission on the Work of its 65th Session' (6 May–7 June and 8 July–9 August 2013) UN Doc A/68/10, 17 [11]. Yet, such conduct is not sufficiently similar to subsequent agreements and subsequent practice within the meaning of art 31(3)(a) and (b) VCLT. For this reason, it does not fall within the scope of this study.

[173] See 6.1 and 8.2.

[174] Draft article 71(2) in Waldock, 'Third Report' (n 15) 52.

[175] Draft article (70)(3)(b) in ILC, 'Summary Records of the 16th Session of the International Law Commission' (11 May–24 July 1964) [1964-I] YBILC 1, 315 f.

[176] Eg Milan Bartoš and Grigory Tunkin in ibid 314 [72], [75].

[177] Special Rapporteur Sir Humphrey Waldock in ibid 314 [74].

States' that engage in a certain practice.[178] Nonetheless, the Commission has emphasised that 'other' subsequent agreements and subsequent practice 'cannot constitute an "authentic" interpretation of the treaty by all parties and thus will not possess the same weight for the purpose of interpretation.'[179] For this reason, it has called on interpreters to 'always remain conscious of the fact that "the view of one States does not make international law"' so that 'the greater interpretative value should be attributed to' subsequent conduct under the general rule.[180]

However thin the line between subsequent conduct under the general rule and 'other' subsequent conduct under article 32 VCLT may be, it should not be levelled completely. Whereas subsequent agreements and subsequent practice under article 31(3)(a) and (b) VCLT 'shall' be taken into account, recourse to 'other' subsequent conduct is non-mandatory but at the interpreter's discretion.[181] And unless it is merely used to confirm (and not to determine) the meaning resulting from the application of article 31 VCLT, 'other' subsequent conduct can only be taken into account when the general rule leaves the treaty's meaning ambiguous or obscure or leads to a result which is manifestly absurd or unreasonable.

4.5 Conclusion

Chapter 4 aimed at developing a deeper understanding of subsequent agreements and subsequent practice under articles 31 and 32 VCLT. In conclusion, the key findings of this Chapter as well as residual points of controversy, ambiguity, and uncertainty are highlighted.

Subsequent agreements and subsequent practice pursuant to article 31(3)(a) and (b) VCLT are two separate but closely related primary means of interpretation. They are both reached or generated after the text of the treaty has been finally established as definite. Although they are extrinsic to the text of the treaty, subsequent agreements and subsequent practice are to be taken into account in a single combined operation alongside other primary means of interpretation. This means that recourse to subsequent agreements and subsequent practice is not at the interpreter's

[178] See draft conclusion 8 and the accompanying commentary in id, 'Report of the International Law Commission on the Work of its 66th Session' (5 May–6 June and 7 July–8 August 2014) UN Doc A/69/10, 192, 197 [14].

[179] Commentary on draft conclusion 2 in id, 'Report of the International Law Commission on the Work of its 65th Session' (6 May–7 June and 8 July–9 August 2013) UN Doc A/68/10, 23 [11].

[180] Commentary on draft conclusion 4 in ibid 41 [34], quoting *Sempra Energy International v Argentine Republic* (Award) (28 September 2007) ICSID Case No ARB/02/16 [385].

[181] See commentary on draft conclusion 1 in ILC, Report of the International Law Commission on the Work of its 65th Session' (6 May–7 June and 8 July–9 August 2013) UN Doc A/68/10, 16 [9].

discretion but mandatory. Nevertheless, their interpretative weight is not *a priori* superior—nor inferior—to that of other elements of the general rule.

The normative heart of article 31(3)(a) and (b) VCLT is the parties' agreement regarding the interpretation of the treaty (or the application of its provisions). The agreement under lit (a) is an express agreement; practice under lit (b), in contrast, merely serves as a piece of evidence of the parties' implied agreement. The interpretative force of subsequent practice thus varies on a sliding scale depending on how certain the parties' implied agreement can be established. The line between subsequent agreements and subsequent practice, so defined, is only one of degree. This is because article 31(3)(a) VCLT does not expressly require subsequent agreements to be somehow formally perpetuated but merely envisages a 'single common act' that manifests the parties' agreement.

A basic point of controversy relates to the term 'practice'. As argued in this study, potentially relevant practice not only includes active and inactive but also State party and non-party conduct alike. Lit (a) of article 31(3) VCLT expressly requires an agreement between the parties—and hence calls for rules based on which attribution of conduct to a State party can be determined. Lit (b), in contrast, does not expressly require a practice that is attributable to a State party. To qualify as subsequent practice within the meaning of article 31(3)(b) VCLT, such potentially relevant practice must satisfy additional criteria. First and foremost, the body of potentially relevant practice, taken as a whole, must be capable of establishing the parties' agreement. The intellectual operation that links potentially relevant practice to the parties' agreement is not a dispensable add-on but, so to speak, the *sine qua non* of subsequent practice under article 31(3)(b) VCLT.

The term 'agreement' under article 31(3)(a) and (b) VCLT does not denote a legally binding commitment in the sense of a treaty. Instead, it merely presupposes the existence of a common understanding of the parties. Although article 31(3)(a) and (b) VCLT fails to unequivocally say so, the express or implied agreement must have been reached between all parties to the treaty that is being interpreted. Agreements between less than all parties are not sufficient for the purpose of article 31(3)(a) and (b) VCLT. In other words, phenomena below this threshold (ie 'other' subsequent conduct) can only be taken into account as supplementary means of interpretation under article 32 VCLT. Furthermore, agreements under article 31(3)(a) and (b) VCLT are only those regarding the interpretation of the treaty (or the application of its provisions). In consequence, interpreters must not rely on express or implied agreements regarding the modification of the treaty.

Part II
The Jurisprudence of Domestic Courts

In the light of the findings of Part I, Part II of this study is dedicated to subsequent agreements and subsequent practice in the jurisprudence of domestic courts. Articles 31 and 32 VCLT provide for a general legal framework within which these means of interpretation are to be taken into account. Nonetheless, Part I has shown that central aspects about subsequent agreements and subsequent practice remain unclear, leave room for discretion or even misunderstandings.

The jurisprudence of domestic courts may help to gain a better understanding of these means of interpretation by demonstrating how they operate in interpretative practice. This interpretative practice is analysed in the next four chapters. These chapters follow up on, revist, and challenge the findings of Part I. In doing so, they focus on those aspects that have been identified as being either most characteristic of subsequent agreements and subsequent practice or as being particulary controversial and unsettled:

Chapter 5 explores the legal status and effects of subsequent agreements and subsequent practice, Chap. 6 addresses the limited relevance of subsequent agreements, Chap. 7 concentrates on practice by non-party entities, and Chap. 8 elaborates on the notion of 'agreement'. In conclusion, Chap. 9 sums up the findings of Part I and II and gives a brief outlook on the long-term consequences of subsequent agreements and subsequent practice as applied by domestic courts.

Chapter 5
Legal Status and Effects of Subsequent Agreements and Subsequent Practice

Chapter 5 examines the legal status and effects of subsequent agreements and subsequent practice in the jurisprudence of domestic courts. As regards their status (5.1), one may wonder whether domestic courts treat subsequent agreements and subsequent practice like any other primary or supplementary means of interpretation. Do these means perhaps enjoy an 'enhanced' status?[1] Or do domestic courts instead attach less importance to these means than should be given under the Vienna rules? As regards their effects (5.2), one may further ask whether domestic courts rely on subsequent agreements and subsequent practice to support particular types of results. Do State parties need to be afraid that these means of interpretation are used to extend the meaning of the terms of the treaty? And is it correct to primarily associate subsequent agreements and subsequent practice with dynamic interpretation? These questions are discussed to better understand the relative importance of subsequent conduct in interpretative practice. Thus, this Chapter provides a formal background for the ensuing chapters, which focus on substantive issues relating to scope and meaning of subsequent agreements and subsequent practice.

5.1 The Status of Subsequent Agreements and Subsequent Practice

To start with, Chap. 5 concentrates on the status of subsequent agreements and subsequent practice in the jurisprudence of domestic courts. In a first step, it introduces and challenges the popular notion of subsequent agreements and subsequent

[1] Georg Nolte, 'Report 1—Jurisprudence of the International Court of Justice and Arbitral Tribunals of Ad Hoc Jurisdiction relating to Subsequent Agreements and Subsequent Practice' in id (ed), *Treaties and Subsequent Practice* (OUP 2013) 172.

K. Berner, *Subsequent Agreements and Subsequent Practice in Domestic Courts*, Beiträge zum ausländischen öffentlichen Recht und Völkerrecht, https://doi.org/10.1007/978-3-662-54937-7_5

practice as 'authentic' means of interpretation (5.1.1).[2] What does the term 'authentic' mean in the first place? Do domestic courts consider themselves bound by subsequent agreements and subsequent practice due to their status as 'authentic' means of interpretation? In a second step, it more generally analyses the relative weight of subsequent agreements and subsequent practice in the interpretative process (5.1.2). How do domestic courts treat these in relation to other means of interpretation? Do subsequent agreements and subsequent practice form part of the 'single combined operation' under the general rule? Or are they subordinated to other primary means of interpretation and thus effectively degraded to serving merely supplementary purposes?

5.1.1 Authentic Means of Interpretation

Subsequent agreements and subsequent practice are regularly referred to as 'authentic' means of interpretation. The ILC Commentary, for instance, declares that 'subsequent practice ... should be included ... as an authentic means of interpretation alongside interpretative agreements.'[3] The notion of 'authentic' interpretation and 'authentic' means of interpretation has not only been embraced by scholarly literature but also by international courts and tribunals.[4] But despite its popularity, there has been disagreement about what it actually implies. Some commentators contend that subsequent agreements and subsequent practice, being 'authentic' means of

[2] cf 3.3.2.

[3] ILC, 'Draft Articles on the Law of Treaties with Commentaries' [1966-II] YBILC 187, 222 [15].

[4] Eg *Question of Jaworzina (Polish-Czechoslovakian Frontier)* (Advisory Opinion) PCIJ Rep Series B No 8; *Case concerning Kasikili/Sedudu Island (Botswana v Namibia)* [1999] ICJ Rep 1045, 1075 [49], quoting ILC, 'DALT' (n 3) 241 [14]; *Tax Regime Governing Pensions Paid to Retired UNESCO Officials Residing in France (France v UNESCO)* (2003) 25 RIAA 231 [71]; WTO, *EC—Bananas III—Second Recourse to Article 21.5 Report of the Appellate Body* (26 November 2008) WT/DS27/AB/RW2/ECU, WT/DS27/AB/RW/USA <http://docsonline.wto.org> [383], [390]; James Hogg, 'The International Court—Rules of Interpretation II' (1959) 44 Minn L Rev 5, 40 f; Giovanni Distefano, 'La pratique subséquente des états parties à un traité' (1994) 40 AFDI 41, 45; Alexander Feldman, 'Evolving Treaty Obligations: A Proposal for Analyzing Subsequent Practice Derived from WTO Dispute Settlement' (2009) 41 JILP 655, 661, 665; Mark Villiger, *Commentary on the* 1969 *Vienna Convention on the Law of Treaties* (Martinus Nijhoff 2009) 429 [16]; Oliver Dörr, 'Article 31—General Rule of Interpretation' in Oliver Dörr and Kirsten Schmalenbach (eds), *Vienna Convention on the Law of Treaties—A Commentary* (Springer 2012) 554 f [74], 555 [76].

[5] Villiger, *Commentary on the VCLT* (n 4) 429 [16]. For the case of the Charter of the United Nations (signed 26 June 1945, entered into force 24 October 1945) 1 UNTS XVI (UNC), see Krzysztof Skubiszewski, 'Remarks on the Interpretation of the United Nations Charter' in Rudolf Bernhardt (ed), *Völkerrecht als Rechtsordnung, internationale Gerichtsbarkeit, Menschenrechte—Festschrift für Hermann Mosler* (Springer 1983) 898 f; cf György Haraszti,

interpretation, were legally binding.[5] The ILC, in contrast, now maintains that '[t]he character of subsequent agreements and practice of the parties under article 31 (3) (a) and (b) as „authentic means of interpretation" does not … imply that these means necessarily possess a conclusive, or legally binding, effect.'[6]

These opposing positions illustrate that the uncertainty and disagreement about subsequent agreements and subsequent practice as 'authentic' means of interpretation ultimately raise the following question: Do interpretations that are based on *authentic* means of interpretation like subsequent agreements and subsequent practice automatically constitute *legally binding* interpretations?[7] As the meaning of 'authentic interpretation' or 'authentic means of interpretation' is not self-explanatory, this Chapter begins by shortly tracing the origins of authentic interpretation and describes how they re-emerged in connection with subsequent agreements and subsequent practice (5.1.1.1). Against this background, it further examines whether the jurisprudence of domestic courts confirms or refutes that subsequent agreements and subsequent practice are not only *authentic* but also legally binding means of interpretation (5.1.1.2).

5.1.1.1 The Origins and Re-emergence of 'Authentic Interpretation'

Traditionally, the term 'authentic' merely indicates that the lawmaker himself formally and explicitly specifies how the law is to be understood.[8] This idea was captured in the Latin phrase *eius est interpretari legem* cuius *condere.*[9]

Some Fundamental Problems of the Law of Treaties (Akademiai Kiado 1973) 43 f as regards subsequent agreements. See also Hazel Fox, 'Article 31(3)(a) and (b) of the Vienna Convention and the *Kasikili/Sedudu Island* Case' in Malgosia Fitzmaurice, Olufemi Elias, and Panos Merkouris (eds), *Treaty Interpretation and the Vienna Convention on the Law of Treaties—30 Years on* (Martinus Nijhoff 2010) 61 f; Marco Benetar, 'From Probative Value to Authentic Interpretation: The Legal Effect of Interpretative Declarations' (2011) 44 RBDI 170, 194 f; Anthina Chanaki, *L'adaptation des traités dans le temps* (Bruylant 2013) 313–15.

[6] ILC, 'Report of the International Law Commission on the Work of its 65th Session' (6 May–7 June and 8 July–9 August 2013) UN Doc A/68/10, 21 [4].

[7] For more details, see also Katharina Berner, 'Authentic Interpretation in Public International Law' (2016) 76 ZaöRV 845.

[8] Generally on authentic interpretation, see Ioan Voïcu, *De l'interprétation authentique des traités internationaux* (Pédone 1968). See also Wolfram Karl, *Vertrag und spätere Praxis im Völkerrecht—Zum Einfluss der Praxis auf Inhalt und Bestand völkerrechtlicher Verträge* (repr, Springer 2012) 40; Jean-Marc Sorel and Valérie Boré Eveno, 'Article 31—1969 Vienna Convention' in Olivier Corten and Pierre Klein (eds), *The Vienna Conventions on the Law of Treaties—A Commentary* (OUP 2011) 807; cf also Haraszti, *Law of Treaties* (n 5) 43, 142, where he suggests that practical construction (ie subsequent practice) does not qualify as authentic interpretation because of its informal character.

[9] In English [translated by the author]: 'He who makes the law is the one to interpret it.'

Although Roman law had coined this meaning of authentic interpretation, the idea of authentic interpretation did not disappear with the end of the Roman Empire but re-emerged in domestic legal systems of the more recent past.[10] Here, authentic interpretation implied that the lawmaker not only had a right to interpret the law but regularly reserved the *exclusive* right to do so in a legally binding fashion.[11] In short, the traditional meaning of authentic interpretation had three pillars. Firstly, it identified the actor that had issued the interpretation (ie the lawmaker himself). Secondly, it defined the necessary form of this interpretation (ie formal and explicit). And thirdly, it described the legal effect of such interpretation (ie legally binding). In the modern constitutional State, this kind of interpretation became problematic because it encroached upon fundamental principles such as separation of powers and non-retroactivity.[12] For this reason, the traditional idea of authentic interpretation is scarcely relevant to domestic legal systems today.

Nonetheless, authentic interpretation re-emerged in international legal thinking. In particular, the parties' right to interpret their own treaty was invoked by the ILC to explain why subsequent agreements and subsequent practice should be relevant to the interpretation of treaties. But in fact, the ILC not only utilised authentic interpretation to identify the authors of subsequent agreements and subsequent practice. In addition, the Commission also hinted at the legal effect of these means of interpretation. In his 'Third Report', for instance, Sir Humphrey Waldock noted that '[s]ubsequent practice when it is consistent and embraces all the parties would appear to be decisive of the meaning to be attached to the treaty, at any rate when it indicates that the parties consider the interpretation to be binding upon them.'[13] While Waldock recognised that subsequent practice could be binding when it established a tacit agreement of the parties to that effect,[14] the Commission's DALT more cautiously declared that an agreement as to the interpretation of a provision reached after the

---

[10] Hans Schneider, 'Zur authentischen Interpretation von Gesetzen' in Rudolf Bernhardt (ed), *Völkerrecht als Rechtsordnung, internationale Gerichtsbarkeit, Menschenrechte—Festschrift für Hermann Mosler* (Springer 1983) 849; Voïcu, *L'interprétation authentique* (n 8) 74 f.

[11] Schneider, 'Authentische Interpretation' (n 10) 849 f.

[12] Voïcu, *L'interprétation authentique* (n 8) 80; Schneider, 'Authentische Interpretation' (n 10) 852.

[13] Sir Humphrey Waldock, 'Third Report on the Law of Treaties' [1964-II] YBILC 5, 60 [25].

[14] Wolfram Karl puts it in similar terms by regarding only such subsequent conduct as 'authentic' in the sense of legally binding which rests on an implied contract between the parties, see Karl, *Vertrag und spätere Praxis* (n 8) 42, 194. Moreover, Karl also distinguishes the notions 'authentic','quasi-authentic', and 'authoritative'. The latter refers to binding interpretations that are not issued by the parties. 'Authentic' and 'quasi-authentic' interpretations, in contrast, are binding interpretations issued by the parties themselves. The difference between these two notions lies in the fact that 'authentic' interpretations are express and formal in nature whereas 'quasi-authentic' interpretations must be deduced from the parties' conduct, see ibid 40. In consequence, he suggests that subsequent practice under art 31(3)(b) VCLT can only constitute (but does not necessarily have to do so) quasi-authentic interpretation.

[15] ILC, 'DALT' (n 3) 241 [14] [emphasis added].

conclusion of the treaty 'represents an authentic interpretation by the parties which *must be read* into the treaty for purposes of its interpretation'.[15]

Moreover, the Commission 'considered that subsequent practice establishing the understanding of the parties regarding the interpretation of a treaty should be included ... as an authentic means of interpretation alongside interpretative agreements.'[16] It also added that '[s]ubsequent practice in the application of a treaty ... is authoritative evidence as to its interpretation when the practice is consistent, and establishes their understanding regarding the meaning of the provisions of the treaty.'[17] Taken together, these statements apparently suggest that subsequent agreements and subsequent practice are authentic and therefore legally binding means of interpretation. But read more carefully and in their context, these statements equally admit another construction. Instead of asserting that subsequent agreements and subsequent practice were legally binding, Waldock and the ILC may have simply purported to emphasise that they are not inferior to but on a par with the other elements of the general rule.[18]

Nevertheless, the view that subsequent agreements and subsequent practice are both authentic and legally binding means of interpretation has gained support in legal literature. Eugen Villiger, for example, remarked:

> Para 2 and subparas 3(a) and (b) represent forms of authentic interpretation whereby all parties themselves agree on (or at least accept) the interpretation of treaty terms by means which are extrinsic to the treaty. As a result, the parties' authentic interpretation of the treaty terms is not only particularly reliable, it is also endowed with binding force. It provides *ex hypothesi* the 'correct' interpretation among the parties in that it determines which of the various ordinary meanings shall apply.[19]

Similarly, Mustafa Yasseen maintained that '[e]tant un accord entre Etats, elle [l'accord ultérieur] a une force identique à celle du traité initial.'[20]

Such reasoning, however, neglects that the parties often choose subsequent interpretative agreements or subsequent practice to avoid the formalities and legal constraints that come with the conclusion of a treaty. Although it is correct that subsequent conduct derives its interpretative value from the parties' agreement, the contention that this agreement vested subsequent agreements or subsequent practice with binding force raises doctrinal problems. As will be recalled, primary means of interpretation are to be taken into account in a 'single combined operation'.[21] In other words, article 31 VCLT does not establish a hierarchical structure but presupposes that all primary means of interpretation are 'thrown into the crucible'. It is, of

[16] ibid 222 [15].

[17] ibid 236 [1].

[18] ibid 220 [9], 222 [15].

[19] Villiger, *Commentary on the VCLT* (n 4) 429 [16].

[20] Mustafa Yasseen, 'L'interprétation des traités d'après la Convention de Vienne sur le Droit des Traités' (1976) 151 RCADI 1, 45 [explanation added]. In English [translated by the author]: 'Being an agreement between States, it [the subsequent agreement] carries a legal value that is identical to that of the original treaty.'

[21] See 3.3.3.

course, possible to create rules of interpretation that do vest subsequent agreements or subsequent practice with binding force. One example of such divergence from the Vienna rules are the interpretative notes issued by the Free Trade Commission under article 1131(2) NAFTA, which provides that such notes are binding on arbitral tribunals.[22]

The Vienna Convention does not prohibit its parties from agreeing on alternative rules of treaty interpretation. But where its own rules of interpretation apply, the view that subsequent agreements or subsequent practice have binding force and thus *a priori* trump all other means of interpretation is hardly tenable. If one insisted that the term 'authentic' necessarily implied binding force, subsequent agreements and subsequent practice under article 31(3)(a) and (b) VCLT could not be regarded as 'authentic' means of interpretation.[23] If, however, one maintained the notion of subsequent agreements and subsequent practice as 'authentic' means of interpretation to indicate the origin of their interpretative value, one should be mindful not to re-introduce any hierarchical claims.[24]

[22] See generally Gabriele Kaufmann-Kohler, 'Interpretive Powers of the Free Trade Commission and the Rule of Law' in Emmanuel Gaillard and Frédéric Bachand (eds), *Fifteen Years of NAFTA Chapter 11 Arbitration* (Juris 2011).

[23] cf Rudolf Bernhardt, *Die Auslegung völkerrechtlicher Verträge insbesondere in der neueren Rechtsprechung internationaler Gerichte* (Heymann 1963) 44, who argues that the notion 'authentic' should only be used where the outcome of the interpretative process enjoys the same legal force as the instrument that has been interpreted. cf also Ulf Linderfalk, *On the Interpretation of Treaties—The Modern International Law as Expressed in the 1969 Vienna Convention on the Law of Treaties* (Springer 2007) 170, who uses the notion 'authentic interpretation' for those acts that 'do not compete on equal terms with an interpretation arrived at through the application of the rules laid down in the Vienna Convention … [but] always takes precedence.'

[24] As explained in the introduction to 5.1.1, the ILC now seems to take the same view. Yet, its conclusion is the result of a longer deliberative process as an earlier statement by its Special Rapporteur shows. See Nolte, 'Report 1—ICJ and Arbitral Tribunals' (n 1) 171 f, who originally argued that the 'understanding of subsequent agreements and practice as "authentic" means of interpretation suggests that subsequent agreements and subsequent practice possess an enhanced status in the process of treaty interpretation.' Yet, this earlier statement must not necessarily be taken to suggest that subsequent agreements and subsequent practice are superior to all other means of interpretation. Read in its context, it may also merely explain why subsequent agreements and subsequent practice—being objective evidence of the parties' understanding—constitute primary and not just supplementary means of interpretation. See draft conclusion 2 and the accompanying commentary in ILC, 'Report of the International Law Commission on the Work of its 65th Session' (6 May–7 June and 8 July–9 August 2013) UN Doc A/68/10, 20, 21 [3].

5.1.1.2 Authentic Interpretation in Domestic Jurisprudence

References to subsequent agreements and subsequent practice as authentic means of interpretation can also be be found in domestic jurisprudence, although not as numerous as in scholarly literature or international jurisprudence. The German Federal Constitutional Court, for instance, repeatedly discussed the informal development of the NATO Treaty by way of authentic interpretation pursuant to article 31(3)(a) and (b) VCLT.[25] Another example is a decision on the Convention between Italy and Switzerland concerning Frontier Traffic and Grazing,[26] in which the Swiss Federal Supreme Court explicitly referred to and relied on the parties' subsequent conduct as an authentic interpretation of the Convention.[27] In other decisions, the idea behind subsequent agreements and subsequent practice as authentic means of interpretation was rather implicitly referred to. In a decision on the interpretation of article 9 VCDR, for example, the Swiss Federal Supreme Court relied on subsequent practice of the parties 'who, being the „masters of the treaties", influence both interpretation and application of treaty law (Art 31(3)(b) Vienna Convention on the Law of Treaties of 23 May 1969).'[28]

Perhaps the most detailed discussion of the idea behind subsequent agreements and subsequent practice as authentic means of interpretation is contained in a decision of the Supreme Court of India.[29] Although the Court's decision concerned a private law contract, it more generally referred to subsequent agreements and

[25] Eg BVerfGE 90, 286, 362: 'Eine—interpretative—Fortbildung des Vertragsrechts durch sogenannte authentische Interpretation und eine sich auf dieser Grundlage entfaltende oder jene Rechtsfortbildung allererst bewirkende Vertragspraxis… '; in English [translated by the author]: 'An—interpretative—development of treaty law through so-called authentic interpretation and a treaty practice that is either based on this authentic interpretation or itself generates this legal development … '. See also BVerfGE 104, 151, 207: '… authentische Interpretation des NATO-Vertrags durch die Vertragsparteien, aber auch die außervertragliche gemeinsame Verstärkung einer völkerrechtlichen Übung (Art 31 Abs 3 Buchstabe a und b WVRK)… '; in English [translated by the author]: '… authentic interpretation of the NATO Treaty by the contracting parties, but also non-contractual common intensification of a practice under international law (art 31(3)(a) and (b) VCLT)… '. See further BVerwG, Judgment of 21 June 2005, 2 WD 12/04 <http://www.juris.de> [240]: 'Eine explizite authentische Interpretation durch die Vertragsparteien (Art 31 Abs 2 und Abs 3 WVK)…'; in English [translated by the author]: 'An explicit authentic interpretation by the contracting parties (art 31(2) and (3) VCLT)…'.

[26] Convention between Italy and Switzerland concerning Frontier Traffic and Grazing (signed 2 July 1953, entered into force 17 February 1956) 257 UNTS 99.

[27] BGer, Judgment of 19 September 2012, 2C_743/2011, BGE 138 II 524, 527 f.

[28] BGer, Judgment of 8 April 2004, 4C.140/2003, BGE 130 III 430, 439 [translated by the author]. In German: '… welche als "Herren der Verträge" die Auslegung und Anwendung des Völkervertragsrechts mitbestimmen (Art 31 Abs 3 lit b des Wiener Übereinkommens über das Recht der Verträge vom 23. Mai 1969).'

[29] *Godhra Electricity Co Ltd v The State of Gujarat* [1975] AIR 32.

[30] ibid 49.

subsequent practice within the meaning of article 31(3)(a) and (b) VCLT to explain why it should be admissible to consider how a treaty or a contract had been applied by its parties.[30] Taking up the notion of the parties as the 'masters of the treaty', the Court observed:

> Parties can, by mutual agreement, make their own contracts; they can also, by mutual agreement, remake them. The process of practical interpretation application [sic], however, is not regarded by the parties as a remaking of the contract; nor do the courts so regard it. Instead, it is merely further expression by the parties of the meaning that they give and have given to the terms of their contract previously made.
>
> There is no good reason why the courts should not give great weight to these further expressions by the parties, in view of the fact that they still have the same freedom of contract that they had originally … It is true that one party cannot build up his case by making an interpretation in his own favour. It is the concurrence therein that such a party can use against the other party. This concurrence may be evidenced by the other party's express assent thereto, by his acting in accordance with it, by his receipt without objection of performances that indicate it, or by saying nothing when knows that the first party is acting on reliance upon the interpretation.[31]

But despite explicitly or implicitly confirming their status as authentic means of interpretation, domestic courts only seldom inferred from this status that subsequent agreements and subsequent practice were legally binding. A notable exception is a judgment on the 1971 German–Swiss DTA,[32] in which the German Federal Fiscal Court observed that the practice of German and Swiss fiscal authorities constituted an authentic interpretation from which German fiscal authorities could not unilaterally depart.[33] While the Court thus recognised some binding force, it limited its dictum to the effects on German fiscal authorities and did not enlarge upon the effects on other branches of State power.

In a decision on the European Patent Convention, the German Federal Court of Justice more cautiously referred to the potentially binding character of subsequent agreements and subsequent practice. Emphasising that a single State party was unable to authoritatively interpret a multilateral treaty,[34] the Court clarified that a party's interpretation was irrelevant as long as there was no authentic interpretation by all parties to the treaty.[35] Arguably, the use of the term 'authoritative' suggests that the Court wondered whether and under which conditions subsequent conduct could be legally binding. But in the end, the Court stopped short of

---

[31] ibid.

[32] BFHE 215, 237.

[33] ibid 241.

[34] BGHZ 82, 88, 94.

[35] ibid. cf BGer, Judgment of 17 April 2015, 2C_1176/2013, BGE 141 II 233, 242, where the Swiss Federal Court argued that a subsequent agreement within the meaning of art 31(3) VCLT could be qualified as a treaty. Nonetheless, the Court did not consider that 'treaty' as legally binding.

unconditionally recognising that authentic interpretation by all parties was indeed legally binding.

In other cases, German courts took a more differentiated view on the binding nature of subsequent agreements and subsequent practice by distinguishing between the national and the international level. One example is a judgment on the 1959 German–Dutch DTA,[36] in which the German Federal Fiscal Court considered an interpretative agreement between German and Dutch revenue authorities. Notably, the Court held that the agreement fell under article 31(3)(a) VCLT and acknowledged that such agreements may well be binding under international law.[37] Turning to the national level, however, the Court then clarified that the German Basic Law precluded such binding nature.[38] In subsequent rulings, the Court reiterated that it had to distinguish between the legal effects at the international and at the national level and even contemplated extending this distinction to subsequent practice, too.[39] In 2009, the Court confirmed its critical attitude by denying any binding effect to an agreement concluded at the top level of State hierarchy, namely by the German Federal Ministry of Finance and its Belgian counterpart.[40]

Compared to the ambivalent approach of German courts, domestic courts in other jurisdictions more rigorously denied any binding force to subsequent agreements and subsequent practice. In *The Attorney-General v Zaoui (No 2)*, for instance, the Court of Appeal of New Zealand merely recognised that subsequent agreements and subsequent practice within the meaning of article 31(3) VCLT could 'affect the interpretation of treaties'.[41] The Court of Appeal of Hong Kong expressed its critical attitude even more clearly in a case on the Sino–British Joint Declaration.[42] The question here was whether the Court could rely on an agreement that had alledgedly

[36] Agreement between the Kingdom of the Netherlands and the Federal Republic of Germany for the Avoidance of Double Taxation with respect to Taxes on Income and Fortune and Various Other Taxes, and for the Regulation of Other Questions relating to Taxation (signed 16 June 1959, entered into force 18 September 1960) 593 UNTS 43 (1959 Dutch–German DTA), as amended by Additional Protocol (signed 13 March 1980, entered into force 1 January 1981) 1225 UNTS 340.

[37] BFHE 181, 158, 161.

[38] ibid.

[39] BFHE 219, 518, 527 f. See also BFHE 226, 276; 227, 419; 235, 401.

[40] BFHE 226, 267, 271 f. For the agreement, see BMF (Germany), 'Deutsch-belgisches Doppelbesteuerungsabkommen; Verständigungsvereinbarung mit dem belgischen Finanzministerium vom 15. Dezember 2006 über die Zuordnung des Besteuerungsrechts bei Abfindungen an Arbeitnehmer' (10 January 2007) BStBl I 2007, 261.

[41] *Attorney-General v Zaoui (No 2)* [2005] 1 NZLR 690 [130] (Glazebrook J). To the same effect, see BVerwG, Decision of 14 April 1992, 1 C 48/89, [1992] DVBl 844, 845 f.

[42] Joint Declaration of the Government of the United Kingdom of Great Britain and Northern Ireland and the Government of the People's Republic of China on the Question of Hong Kong (signed 19 December 1984, entered into force 27 May 1985) <http://www.cmab.gov.hk/en/issues/joint3.htm> (Sino–British Joint Declaration).

[43] *Ng Ka Ling v The Director of Immigration* [1999] 1 HKLRD 315, 354.

been reached in the Sino–British Joint Liaison Group between the Chinese and UK governments. Doubting that such agreement existed in the first place, the Court clarified that, even if it did, it was not binding anyway because 'art 31(3)(a) only provides that it shall be taken into account. Having done so, the Court can reach a different view.'[43] A similarly critical view was taken by the Austrian Administrative Court in a case on the 1954 Austrian–German DTA.[44] Discussing the effect of an interpretative agreement between Austria and Germany,[45] which in the Court's opinion constituted subsequent practice pursuant to article 31(3)(b) VCLT,[46] the Court firmly emphasised that such practice lacked any binding force in general and did not bind the Court either.[47]

5.1.2 Relative Weight in the Interpretative Process

Subsequent agreements and subsequent practice are not supplementary means of interpretation to be relied on merely in case of ambiguity or obscurity,[48] but of an 'obligatory character and by their very nature … not … norms of interpretation in any way inferior to those which precede them.'[49]

This characterisation by Mustafa Yasseen and Richard Gardiner relates to subsequent agreements and subsequent practice under the general rule. 'Other' subsequent conduct, ie subsequent agreements or subsequent practice that do not meet all criteria of the general rule, is covered by article 32 VCLT. In consequence, such 'other' subsequent conduct can only be taken into account to confirm the meaning resulting from the application of article 31 VCLT or to determine the meaning when the interpretation according to that provision leaves the meaning ambiguous or obscure or leads to a result which is manifestly absurd or unreasonable. These two possible manifestations of subsequent conduct make it difficult to establish its relative weight in the interpretative process.

Subsequent agreements and subsequent practice under the general rule are authentic but not legally binding means of interpretation.[50] This conclusion—instructive as it is—does not sufficiently describe their relative weight vis-à-vis other means of

---

[44] Agreement between the Republic of Austria and the Federal Republic of Germany for the Avoidance of Double Taxation with respect to Taxes on Income and Capital and to Trade and Property Taxes (signed 4 October 1954, entered into force 7 September 1955) 1972 UNTS 277 (1954 Austrian–German DTA).

[45] See BMF (Austria), 'Erlaß Z 1246/1/3-IV/4/86 betreffend die Besteuerung wesentlich beteiligter Gesellschafter-Geschäftsführer nach dem österreichisch-deutschen Doppelbesteuerungsabkommen' (22 December 1986) AÖFV No 32/1987.

[46] VwGH, Judgment of 30 March 2006, 2002/15/0098, 2 f, 5.

[47] ibid 4 f.

[48] Yasseen, 'L'interprétation des traités' (n 20) 49.

[49] Richard Gardiner, *Treaty Interpretation* (2nd edn, OUP 2015) 224.

[50] See 5.1.1.

interpretation. In accordance with the Vienna rules, domestic courts generally do not consider themselves bound by subsequent agreements and subsequent practice. But do domestic courts also respect the relationship between the various means of interpretation under the Vienna rules? Instead of regarding subsequent agreements and subsequent practice as legally binding means of interpretation, domestic courts might as well go to the other extreme. In particular, they might subordinate subsequent agreements and subsequent practice to other primary means of interpretation or even treat them like supplementary ones although the criteria of the general rule are met.

In some cases, domestic courts seemed to treat subsequent agreements and subsequent practice as primary means of interpretation in accordance with the Vienna rules. An example of this end of the spectrum is the judgment of the House of Lords in *R (Mullen) v Secretary of State for the Home Department*.[51] To determine the meaning of article 14(6) ICCPR (compensation for miscarriage of justice), Lord Steyn first examined language and structure of the Covenant.[52] Then he turned to the Covenant's object and purpose and took account of potentially relevant subsequent practice[53] before finally considering the *travaux préparatoires*.[54] Thus, Lord Steyn relied on the various means of interpretation in the very order provided for by the Vienna rules. In particular, he examined subsequent practice together with other elements of the general rule and before considering the Covenant's *travaux préparatoires* as a supplementary means of interpretation.

That subsequent agreements and subsequent practice can qualify as primary means of interpretation was also confirmed by Swiss courts. In a judgment on the interpretation of the 1996 US–Swiss DTA,[55] for example, the Swiss Federal Administrative Court pointed out that the elements listed under article 31(3) VCLT ranked equally with those under article 31(2) VCLT.[56] And in the already-mentioned judgment on the interpretation of article 9(1) VCDR,[57] the Swiss Federal Supreme Court even gave priority to an interpretation supported by subsequent practice over one supported by literal interpretation.[58]

---

[51] *R (Mullen) v Secretary of State for the Home Department* [2004] UKHL 18, [2005] 1 AC 1.

[52] ibid [45] (Lord Steyn).

[53] ibid [45] f (Lord Steyn).

[54] ibid [50] f (Lord Steyn).

[55] BVGer, Judgment of 21 January 2010, BVGE 2010/7.

[56] ibid [3.7.11]. In the same vein, see BVGer, Judgment of 11 March 2011, A-6641/2010 [4.1.2].

[57] BGer, Judgment of 8 April 2004, 4C.140/2003, BGE 130 III 430.

[58] ibid 439. To the same effect, see *SZATV v Minister for Immigration* [2007] HCA 40, (2007) 233 CLR 18 [48] f (Kirby J); BGer, Judgment of 19 September 2012, 2C_743/2011, BGE 138 II 524, 527 f.

[59] *Fothergill v Monarch Airlines Ltd* [1980] UKHL 6, [1981] AC 251.

[60] ibid 290 (Lord Scarman).

[61] ibid.

In other cases, the approach of domestic courts has been more difficult to reconcile with the Vienna rules. In *Fothergill v Monarch Airlines Ltd,*[59] for instance, Lord Scarman accepted that 'British courts should now follow broadly the guidelines declared by the Vienna Convention on the Law of Treaties'.[60] Nonetheless, he maintained that both the *travaux préparatoires* and international case law was 'to be used as aids only' and that such aid was not mandatory.[61] Elaborating on the order in which recourse could be had to the various means of interpretation under the Vienna rules, he added that 'if there be ambiguity or doubt, or if a literal construction appears to conflict with the purpose of the convention, the court must … have recourse to such aids as are admissible and appear to it to be not only relevant but helpful on the point (or points) under consideration.'[62]

Speaking of 'international case law', Lord Scarman's dictum at first sight only included the jurisprudence of international courts, tribunals, and quasi-judicial bodies. Yet, he not only generally juxtaposed literal interpretation to other 'aids' but also included foreign domestic court decisions into his dictum.[63] Viewed in isolation, domestic court decisions are seldom capable of establishing the agreement of all contracting parties. Therefore, Lord Scarman's dictum must not necessarily be read as addressing the status of subsequent agreements and subsequent practice under article 31(3)(a) and (b) VCLT. Still, domestic court decisions may well constitute relevant practice for the purpose of article 31(3)(b) VCLT. For this reason, Lord Scarman's categorical observation *a priori* diminishes the possible weight of domestic court decisions as one possible component of subsequent practice under the general rule.

From this perspective, *Fothergill* may show that the House of Lords did not recognise that subsequent agreements and subsequent practice can qualify as primary means of interpretation. But when the judgment was delivered, the Vienna Convention had not yet entered into force. Even at that date, the Convention may have reflected customary international law rules of treaty interpretation.[64] Yet, it is noteworthy that Lord Scarman did not consider himself bound by the Vienna rules but only acknowledged that British courts should 'follow broadly' their guidelines.[65] Irrespective of the Convention's entry into force, the UK's dualist approach towards international law may have prevented Lord Scarman from considering himself bound by the Vienna rules anyway.[66] For this reason, *Fothergill* is certainly instructive for illustrating the House of Lords' early, and rather reserved approach towards subsequent agreements and subsequent practice. Nonetheless, this decision needs to be read with care.

---

[62] ibid 294 (Lord Scarman).

[63] ibid 295 (Lord Scarman).

[64] For the Vienna rules as a reflection of customary international law, see 3.2.

[65] ibid 290 (Lord Scarman).

[66] For more details on the UK approach towards international law, see 6.3.1.3.

[67] *Deep Vein Thrombosis and Air Travel Group Litigation* [2005] UKHL 72, [2006] 1 All ER 786.

A later, and less ambiguous House of Lords decision is the *Deep Vein Thrombosis and Air Travel Group Litigation.*[67] In this case, it was Lord Steyn who subordinated subsequent agreements and subsequent practice to other elements of the general rule. Noting that article 31 VCLT required treaties to be interpreted in accordance with the ordinary meaning to be given to the terms of the treaty in their context and in the light of its object and purpose, he clarified that this was 'the starting point of treaty interpretation, to which other rules are supplementary: see article 31.2; 31.3; 31.4; and 32.'[68] Thus, Lord Steyn seemed to believe that the general rule of interpretation was not contained in article 31 VCLT as a whole but only in its first paragraph. In consequence, all other means of interpretation, and not only those falling under article 32 VCLT, would constitute supplementary means of interpretation, including subsequent agreements and subsequent practice.[69]

The US Supreme Court, to give another example, generally does not rely on subsequent agreements or subsequent practice as primary means of interpretation either.[70] This can, for instance, be seen in the case of *O'Connor v US,* which concerned the interpretation of an agreement that specified provisions of the Panama Canal Treaty.[71] In a first step, the Court analysed the text of the contentious provision before examining its context and drafting history.[72] In a second step, the Court then additionally referred to the parties' subsequent conduct to confirm the interpretation which it wished to adopt.[73] As argued in Chap. 8, this conduct probably met all criteria of the general rule.[74] Hence, it should have been taken into account as a primary means of interpretation. But while the Court did not expressly attach less weight to the parties' conduct than to other means of interpretation, it nonetheless reversed the sequence envisaged by the Vienna rules. Thus, it blurred the

---

[68] ibid [31] (Lord Steyn).

[69] cf *Trans World Airlines, Inc v Franklin Mint Corp* 466 US 243, 104 S Ct 2691 (1984) 534, where the US Supreme Court considered both drafting history and the parties' subsequent conduct as 'additional aids to construction.'

[70] For examples from other jurisdictions see eg VfGH, Judgment of 14 October 1986, B79/86, VfSlg 11073, 7 f; *Yugraneft Corp v Rexx Management Corp* [2010] 1 SCR 649, 2010 SCC 19 [19] f (Rothstein J); BFHE 144, 483, 484 f; 222, 553, 558.

[71] Agreement in Implementation of Article III of the Panama Canal Treaty (Panama–USA) (signed 7 September 1977, entered into force 1 October 1979) 1280 UNTS 201 (Article III Implementation Agreement).

[72] *O'Connor v US* 479 US 27, 31 f, 107 S Ct 347 (1986).

[73] ibid 33. To the same effect, see eg *US v Stuart* 489 US 353, 368 f, 109 S Ct 1183 (1989), where the Court examined the parties' subsequent conduct after having concluded that none of the other means of interpretation, including the drafting history, supported the respondents' case; *Zicherman v Korean Air Lines Co, Ltd* 516 US 217, 226 f, 116 S Ct 629 (1996), where the Court first examined the treaty's text and its drafting history before referring to the parties' subsequent conduct as 'aids to interpretation' to re-confirm its preferred interpretation of the treaty. cf also *Air France v Saks* 470 US 392, 403, 105 S Ct 1338 (1985).

[74] See 249 f.

distinction between primary and supplementary means of interpretation and rhetorically enhanced the status of the treaty's *travaux préparatoires* vis-à-vis subsequent agreements and subsequent practice.

In other cases, certain US Supreme Court judges did not subordinate subsequent conduct to the *travaux préparatoires* but to an overall textualist approach to interpretation. Thus, they effectively degraded subsequent conduct to a supplementary means of interpretation, too.[75] In *Sumitomo Shoji America, Inc v Avagliano,* which concerned the interpretation of the Japanese–US Treaty on Friendship, Commerce and Navigation,[76] the Court had remarked that interpretation must 'begin with the language of the Treaty itself. The clear import of treaty language controls unless "application of the words of the treaty according to their obvious meaning effects a result inconsistent with the intent or expectations of its signatories".'[77] Based on this remark, the Court relied on the contracting parties' conduct to support its preliminary interpretation of the Treaty.[78] This approach was severely criticised by Justice Scalia in *Stuart,* where the majority had equally relied on '[t]he practice of the treaty signatories.'[79] In Justice Scalia's view, this additional extrinsic evidence had been unnecessarily consulted because when the '[T]reaty's language resolves the issue presented, there is no necessity of looking further … '.[80]

According to him, the majority had mistakenly implied that, '*had* the extrinsic evidence contradicted the plain language of the Treaty it would govern. That is indeed what we mistakenly said in the earlier case that the Court cites as authority for its approach.'[81] In his view, the earlier case (ie *Sumitomo*) had incorrectly quoted the Court's dictum in *Maximov v US* by separating the last clause of a quotation from its context to support the very opposite of what the quotation originally said,[82] namely that 'it is particularly inappropriate for a court to sanction a deviation from

[75] The approach which the US Supreme Court adopted in cases such as *Sumitomo* is reminiscent of the Vattel'ian maxim *in claris non fit interpretatio* (it is not permissible to interpret what has no need of interpretation). See Emer de Vattel, *The Law of Nations or the Principles of Natural Law* (Charles Fenwick tr, repr, Hein 1995) 199.

[76] Treaty of Friendship, Commerce and Navigation (Japan–USA) (signed 2 April 1952, entered into force 30 October 1953) 206 UNTS 143.

[77] *Sumitomo Shoji America, Inc v Avagliano* 457 US 176, 180, 102 S Ct 2375 (1982).

[78] ibid 183 f.

[79] *Stuart* (n 73) 370.

[80] ibid 371.

[81] ibid.

[82] ibid 372.

[83] *Maximov v US* 373 US 49, 54, 83 S Ct 1054 (1963). This statement is difficult to reconcile with arts 31–33 VCLT. Under the Vienna rules, the interpretative process is *not* to be terminated without having applied the general rule as a whole, ie without having considered the (ordinary or special) meaning of the terms of the treaty in their (narrow, broader, and quasi-) context and in the light of the treaty's object and purpose. The fact that the treaty's meaning is (or better: appears to be) obvious does not authorise the interpreter to categorically dismiss extratextual material such as relevant subsequent agreements or subsequent practice.

[84] *Stuart* (n 73) 373.

the clear import of a solemn treaty … when, as here, there is no indication that application of the words of the treaty according to their obvious meaning effects a result inconsistent with the intent or expectations of its signatories.'[83] For this reason, Justice Scalia asserted that the Court had originally meant to say that '[o]nly when a treaty provision is ambiguous have we found it appropriate to give authoritative effect to extratextual materials.'[84]

On the whole, the jurisprudence of domestic courts therefore reveals a disparate picture. In some cases, domestic courts affirmed or denied that subsequent agreements and subsequent practice can qualify as primary means of interpretation. In other cases, they reversed the sequence envisaged by the Vienna rules or relied on subsequent conduct merely to confirm the construction that had been arrived at by applying other means of interpretation. The latter approach resembles that of international courts and tribunals. According to the ILC,

> [i]nternational courts and tribunals ususally begin their reasoning in a given case by determining the 'ordinary meaning' of the terms of a treaty. Subsequent agreements and subsequent practice mostly enter into their reasoning at a later stage when courts asks whether such conduct confirms or modifies the result arrived at by the initial interpretation of the ordinary meaning (or by other means of interpretation).[85]

This approach arguably indicates that domestic courts are sometimes unduly reluctant to classify subsequent agreements and subsequent practice as primary means of interpretation. Yet, this conclusion is not compelling. Moreover, as Chap. 8 reveals,[86] there are equally tendencies in domestic jurisprudence to water down the requirements of the general rule. Hence, there are also cases in which 'other' subsequent conduct is unduly treated as a primary means of interpretation. As regards the relative weight of subsequent agreements and subsequent practice, one may therefore draw the following conclusion. On the whole, 'other' subsequent conduct under article 32 VCLT tends to play a stronger role in the jurisprudence of domestic courts than subsequent agreements and subsequent practice under the general rule—either because domestic courts objectively attach too much weight to such 'other' conduct or because they attach comparatively little weight to conduct that would actually be covered by the general rule.

---

[85] Commentary on draft conclusion 7 in ILC, 'Report of the International Law Commission on the Work of its 66th Session' (5 May–6 June and 7 July–8 August 2014) UN Doc A/69/10, 180 [3].

[86] See in particular 8.2.2.

5.2 The Effects of Subsequent Agreements and Subsequent Practice

Subsequent agreements and subsequent practice primarily serve to determine the meaning of the terms of the treaty. Their impact on the outcome of the interpretative process may, however, differ. In this respect, it is important not to mistake these *results* (ie the effect of applying these means of interpretation) for the *means of interpretation* that are applied. It is well possible that particular means of interpretation—such as subsequent agreements and subsequent practice—are often or even typically relied on to support a particular type of results. Nonetheless, this possibility neither vests the ensuing result with the status of being a means of interpretation; nor does it justify the assumption that the respective means of interpretation exclusively supports that type of results.

It is true that one can conceive of interpretative rules that encourage particular types of results and thus effectively treat these results like means of interpretation. Modelled after the 'living instrument approach' developed by the ECtHR,[87] such rules could, for instance, generally require that treaties be interpreted in an evolutive manner. The Vienna rules, however, do not take this route of favouring or disfavouring particular types of results. But despite their apparent 'neutrality', it cannot be ruled out that interpreters nevertheless tend to identify certain means of interpretation with certain results. Section 5.2 therefore analyses whether reliance on subsequent agreements and subsequent practice by domestic courts favours or disfavours certain types of results, namely extensive and restrictive (5.2.1) and dynamic and static interpretations (5.2.2).

5.2.1 Extensive and Restrictive Interpretation

The ensuing analysis of domestic jurisprudence uses the opposites 'extensive' and 'restrictive' interpretation in their general, purely *linguistic* sense. Nevertheless, it is important to note that public international law distinguishes between two different concepts of 'extensive' and 'restrictive' interpretation. In addition to their linguistic meanings, these opposites are also used in a sense that is closely linked to State sovereignty. Therefore, it is useful to shortly circumscribe these different concepts (5.2.1.1) before turning to domestic jurisprudence (5.2.1.2).

---

[87] See generally Alastair Mowbray, 'The Creativity of the European Court of Human Rights' (2005) 5 Hum Rts L Rev 57.

[88] cf Bernhardt, *Die Auslegung völkerrechtlicher Verträge* (n 23) 177.

5.2.1.1 Different Concepts of Extensive and Restrictive Interpretation

The concepts of 'extensive' and 'restrictive' interpretation in their general, linguistic sense are synonymous with 'broad' and 'narrow' interpretation. As will be recalled, most terms possess not only one but multiple possible ordinary meanings. The opposites 'extensive' and 'restrictive' help to describe the end of this scale of possible meanings at which a particular interpretation is located.[88] A less technical definition has been offered by Judge Dionisio Anzilotti. In the PCIJ's advisory opinion on the *Interpretation of the Convention of 1919 concerning Employment of Women during the Night,* he observed that 'it will be found either that the words have been used in a wider sense than normally attaches to them (broad interpretation) or that they have been used in a narrower sense than normally attaches to them (narrow interpretation).'[89]

In the same vein, the ILC's DALT used the term 'extensive' interpretation in its general sense to describe 'an interpretation going beyond what is expressed or necessarily to be implied in the terms of the treaty.'[90] The Commission's draft conclusions on subsequent agreements and subsequent practice in relation to the interpretation of treaties similarly focus on the 'range of possible interpretations' to characterise an interpretation as being either extensive or restrictive.[91] Taking into account the jurisprudence of international courts and tribunals, it is suggested that subsequent agreements and subsequent practice may 'contribute to the clarification of the meaning of a treaty in the sense of a narrowing down (specifying) of possible meanings ... or ... of confirming a wider interpretation.'[92]

In addition to this general sense, the opposites 'extensive' and 'restrictive' interpretation have also been used in a narrow sense that is closely linked to State sovereignty. This link was most famously established by the PCIJ in the *Lotus Case,*[93] where

[89] *Interpretation of the Convention of 1919 concerning Employment of Women during the Night* (Advisory Opinion) PCIJ Rep Series A/B No 50, 383 (diss op Judge Anzilotti). cf Maarten Bos, 'Theory and Practice of Treaty Interpretation' (1980) 27 NILR 135, 142, who described 'restrictive' interpretation as a '"refining" of the law, ie, the fact of finding new exceptions to existing rules drafted in a broad and comprehensive style.'

[90] ILC, 'DALT' (n 3) 219 [6].

[91] Draft conclusion 7(1) in id, 'Report of the International Law Commission on the Work of its 66th Session' (5 May–6 June and 7 July–8 August 2014) UN Doc A/69/10, 179.

[92] Commentary on draft conclusion 7 in ibid 180 [3].

[93] *Case of the SS 'Lotus' (France v Turkey)* PCIJ Rep Series A No 10.

[94] ibid 18. To the same effect, see Sir Hersch Lauterpacht, 'Restrictive Interpretation and the Principle of Effectiveness in the Interpretation of Treaties' (1949) 26 BYIL 48, 58; Georg Schwarzenberger, *International Law as Applied by International Courts and Tribunals* (3rd edn, Stevens 1957) 509.

[95] Lauterpacht, 'Restrictive Interpretation' (n 94) 59. At 67, Lauterpacht, however, clarifies that he does not recognise restrictive interpretation as a 'principle' of international law.

[96] ibid 56.

[97] Rudolf Bernhardt, 'Evolutive Treaty Interpretation, Especially of the European Convention on Human Rights' (1999) 42 GJIL 11, 14. This observation equally applies to similar 'principles' such as that of *contra proferentem* and effective interpretation.

the Court declared that '[r]estrictions upon the sovereignty of States cannot … be presumed.'[94] Although this dictum related to customary international law only, it has been argued that it contained a 'principle' of restrictive interpretation, which 'lends itself more easily to the application in the field of treaties.'[95] For this reason, some commentators have described the opposites 'restrictive' and 'extensive' interpretation as a choice between either preserving or infringing the sovereignty of that State party which would be affected by the obligation to be interpreted.[96] Yet, the Vienna rules do not mention any such 'principle'. Irrespective of whether the 'principle' of restrictive interpretation has ever been valid at all, one can therefore assume that it no longer applies in the absoluteness with which it has sometimes been proclaimed.[97]

Apart from that, linking the notions of 'extensive' and 'restrictive' interpretation to State sovereignty would hardly promote any analytical purposes either. This is because restrictions to one party's sovereignty may be favourable to the other party's sovereignty—and vice versa. If one used the opposites 'extensive' and 'restrictive' in their narrow sense, many interpretations would therefore be extensive and restrictive at the same time, depending on the individual perspective. For these reasons, the following analysis of case law is based on a general understanding of 'extensive' and 'restrictive' interpretations.

5.2.1.2 Extensive and Restrictive Interpretation in Domestic Jurisprudence

A rare example of how subsequent conduct was used to support an extensive interpretation is the case of *Fothergill v Monarch Airlines Ltd.* This case concerned the interpretation of article 26(2) Warsaw Convention, which stipulated that in the case of damage, the person entitled to delivery must complain to the carrier forthwith after the discovery of the damage, and, at the latest, within seven days from the date of receipt in the case of baggage. Although the plaintiff's luggage had not only been damaged but was even partially lost, the defendant nevertheless asked the House of Lords to apply the time limit in order to dismiss the claim. To determine whether the contentious provision was to be interpreted extensively so as to also cover lost luggage, the House of Lords had recourse to the contracting parties' subsequent conduct in the application of the Warsaw Convention.

In particular, it considered that the parties had, in the course of the 1955 Hague Conference, discussed but finally decided not to amend article 26(2) Warsaw Convention to expressly mention (partial) loss. Since they had also emphasised that they had always understood this provision to apply in case of (partial) loss so that the amendment would have merely been declaratory,[98] two Law Lords agreed with

[98] *Fothergill* (n 59) 260.

[99] ibid 278 (Lord Wilberforce) and 279 (Lord Diplock). Rejecting this view, see however ibid 287 f (Lord Fraser).

[100] BGHZ 84, 339. cf BGH, Judgment of 23 March 1976, VI ZR 150/74, [1976] NJW 1587, 1588, where the question of whether to adopt a broad or a narrow interpretation of the contentious term was still left open.

the defendant and opted for an extensive interpretation.[99] In this respect, it may have been decisive that the events at the 1955 Hague Conference were reliably documented in the minutes of the Conference. Thus, no questions of proof arose as to whether the parties had really agreed on an extensive interpretation. Although this is ultimately a matter of speculation, one may therefore wonder whether this reliable documentation contributed to facilitating the Law Lords' decision to adopt an extensive interpretation.

A German decision on the interpretation of article 28(1) Warsaw Convention illustrates how subsequent practice indirectly served to support an extensive interpretation.[100] The contentious provision stipulated that an action for damages must be brought, at the option of the plaintiff, in the territory of one of the parties, either before the Court having jurisdiction where the carrier is ordinarily resident, or has his principal place of business, or has an establishment by which the contract has been made, or before the Court having jurisdiction at the place of destination. The plaintiffs had advocated an extensive interpretation to the effect that the term 'establishment' included any place where a contract of carriage had been concluded with the consent of the airline.[101] The defendant, in contrast, had argued that the term 'establishment' was to be interpreted restrictively so that it only covered branch offices of the carrier and not independent agencies.[102]

Noting that none of these interpretations was per se incompatible with the ordinary meaning of article 28(1), the Court examined which interpretation foreign domestic courts had favoured.[103] Because some courts had given the contentious term a narrower reading and others a broader one, the Court concluded that this term was, on its face, rather ambiguous. Therefore, it deemed it admissible to apply further means of interpretation to resolve this ambiguity. Resorting to teleological interpretation, the Court eventually construed the contentious term extensively as requested by the plaintiffs.[104] Thus, the practice of some of the parties to the Convention did not, in itself, lead to an extensive interpretation; instead, it facilitated this result in that it called for the application of further means of interpretation which then supported an extensive construction.

Apart from a few exceptions like the ones just mentioned, domestic courts mostly relied on subsequent agreements or subsequent practice to support restrictive interpretations. An example is the Warsaw Convention case *Air France v Saks*, in which the US Supreme Court had to decide whether the term 'accident' pursuant to article 17 encompassed all kinds of unexpected or unusual events or happenings or only those that were external to the injured passenger.[105] Looking for potentially relevant practice, the Court noted that the parties had consistently attempted to restrict the

[101] BGHZ 84, 339, 340.

[102] ibid.

[103] ibid 341 f.

[104] ibid 343 f.

[105] *Saks* (n 73) 395 f.

[106] ibid 403 f.

contentious term so as to exclude passengers' internal reactions, ie injuries that had not been caused by an unexpected or unusual event but solely by the passenger's state of health: Firstly, 'representatives of many of the Warsaw signatories' at the 1971 Guatemala City Conference had approved an amendment that reflected a restrictive understanding. And secondly, several foreign domestic court decisions had embraced a narrower reading of the term 'accident', too.[106] At closer inspection, the material relied on by the Court was insufficient to establish an agreement of all parties to the Convention. Thus, it only qualified as 'other' subsequent practice under article 32 VCLT. Nevertheless, this material eventually led the Court to favour a restrictive interpretation and to conclude that there had been no 'accident' for the purpose of article 17 when the injury had been caused by a passenger's own reaction to a usual operation of the aircraft.[107]

Another example of restrictive interpretation is the case of *R (Mullen) v Secretary of State for the Home Department*, which concerned the meaning of the phrase 'miscarriage of justice' pursuant to article 14(6) ICCPR. The Secretary of State had interpreted this phrase restrictively so that compensation under article 14(6) ICCPR was only due when it was shown beyond reasonable doubt that an innocent person had been convicted. The respondent, who had unsuccessfully claimed compensation, in contrast, argued that the contentious phrase should be interpreted more extensively and cover all cases in which a defendant should not have been convicted. To choose between these competing interpretations, Lord Steyn took account of what he regarded as subsequent practice under article 31(3)(b) VCLT, namely French legislative practice and an Explanatory Report prepared by the Council of Europe's Steering Committee for Human Rights.[108] Noting that these sources unambiguously supported a restrictive interpretation, Lords Steyn finally took the same view and opted for the construction favoured by the Secretary of State.[109]

As is discussed in Chap. 8, Lord Steyn's reasoning in *Mullen* is difficult to reconcile with the requirements which article 31(3)(b) VCLT imposes on the parties' agreement. Notwithstanding that point of criticism, it is remarkable how quickly he decided to adopt a restrictive interpretation although he had identified only few pieces of apparently relevant practice, namely French legislative practice and the Steering Committee's Explanatory Report. On a more abstract level, *Mullen* thus creates the impression that domestic courts like the House of Lords more readily rely on subsequent conduct to adopt restrictive than extensive interpretations.

This impression is reinforced in the case of *Commissioner of the Australian Federal Police and the Commonwealth of Australia v Magno and Almeida,* which concerned the interpretation of the phrase 'impairment of dignity' pursuant to article

[107] ibid.

[108] *Mullen* (n 51) [47] f (Lord Steyn).

[109] ibid.

[110] *Commissioner of the Australian Federal Police and the Commonwealth of Australia v Magno and Almeida* [1992] FCA 566, (1992) 37 FCR 298 [27] (Einfeld J).

[111] ibid [30] f (Einfeld J).

22 VCDR. This provision requires receiving States to take all appropriate steps to protect the premises of diplomatic missions against any intrusion or damage and to prevent any disturbance of the peace of the missions or impairment of their dignity. Interpreted extensively, the phrase 'impairment of dignity' would have included any kind of insult or nuisance whereas its restrictive interpretation would have only covered occurences such as breaches of the peace or disruptions of their essential functions. Since the contentious phrase on its face left room for each alternative,[110] Lord Steyn considered object and purpose of as well as subsequent practice to the VCDR.[111] In particular, he took into account legislative, judicial, and executive practice in the UK and the USA, which finally led him to favour the restrictive alternative.[112]

5.2.2 *Dynamic and Static Interpretation*

The opposites 'dynamic' and 'static' serve to describe the result of an interpretative process from a *temporal perspective*.[113] As has been noted in Chap. 3, treaty interpretation is exacerbated by semantic changes and developments over time.[114] The ordinary or special meaning or meanings prevailing when the treaty was concluded need not be identical with those prevailing at the time when it is being interpreted. In consequence, interpreters often have to choose between different

---

[112] ibid [34] (Einfeld J). See also *De L v Director-General Department of Community Services (NSW)* [1996] HCA 5, (1996) 187 CLR 640.

[113] Instead of juxtaposing static to dynamic interpretation, one may also use the terms 'evolutive' or 'evolutionary'. This alternative terminology is often found in a popular but sometimes misleading academic discourse. Although authors such as Giovanni Distefano, 'L'interprétation evolutive de la norme internationale' (2011) 115 RGDIP 373 have contributed to this discussion in a rather rational way, others have succumbed to the temptation of inflating the discourse and overemphasising the relevance of evolutive interpretation by treating it as a genuine 'means' or 'technique' of interpretation. See in particular Julian Arato, 'Subsequent Practice and Evolutive Interpretation: Techniques of Treaty Interpretation over Time and Their Diverse Consequences' (2010) 9 Law & Prac Int'l Cts & Tribunals 443, who regards both evolutive interpretation and subsequent practice as—so it appears—equally ranked 'techniques' and 'doctrines' of interpretation.

[114] See 3.3.1.1.

[115] cf Martii Koskenniemi, 'Report of the Study Group on Fragmentation of International Law: Difficulties Arising from the Diversification and Expansion of International Law' (13 April 2006) UN Doc A/CN.4/L.682, [475]–[78]. See also Sondre Helmersen, 'Evolutive Treaty Interpretation: Legality, Semantics and Distinctions' (2013) 6 EJLS 127, 129.

[116] cf Ulf Linderfalk, 'Doing the Right Thing for the Right Reason—Why Dynamic or Static Approaches Should Be Taken in the Interpretation of Treaties' (2008) 10 Int'l Comm L Rev 109, 126, who points out that words are not necessarily evolutionary in nature just because they are ambiguous; the fact that a term *can* be interpreted in an dynamic manner does not mean that it has to.

conceivable temporal points of reference for interpreting the treaty. The necessary choice between static and dynamic interpetation is not, however, a separate exercise but rather belongs to the single combined operation of determining the meaning of the terms of the treaty.[115] Hence one should avoid using terms such as 'static', 'dynamic', 'evolutive', or 'evolutionary' to describe the interpretative process itself. These terms can be useful to evaluate the *result* of this process. Applying these terms to describe the interpretative process itself may, however, risk reading into the Vienna rules a principled preference for a particular result which these rules actually do not offer.[116]

5.2.2.1 Defining and Qualifying Dynamic and Static Interpretation

To better understand the difference between static and dynamic interpretation, it is useful to recall the objective of the interpretative process. Under the Vienna rules, 'interpretation' is a process that serves to determine a treaty's meaning by ascertaining the objectivised intention of the parties.[117] Static and dynamic interpretations reveal one or more possible meaning or meanings of the terms of the treaty. To distinguish between 'static' or 'dynamic' results of the interpretative process, one

---

[117] See 1.3.1.2.

[118] See in particular *Case concerning the Dispute regarding Navigational and Related Rights (Costa Rica v Nicaragua)* [2009] ICJ Rep 213, 242 [64]. See also Martin Dawidovicz, 'The Effect of the Passage of Time on the Interpretation of Treaties: Some Reflections on *Costa Rica v Nicaragua*' (2011) 24 LJIL 201, 221; Rahim Moloo, 'Changing Times, Changing Obligations? The Interpretation of Treaties over Time' (2012) 106 ASIL PROC 261, 262; Helmersen, 'Evolutive Treaty Interpretation' (n 115) 128 f; Eirik Bjorge, *The Evolutionary Interpretation of Treaties* (OUP 2014) 1 f.

[119] See eg Sir Gerald Fitzmaurice, 'The Law and Procedure of the International Court of Justice 1951–4: Treaty Interpretation and Certain Other Treaty Points' (1957) 33 BYIL 203, 212.

[120] See eg Feldman, 'Evolving Treaty Obligations' (n 4) 657, who generally remarks: 'Article 31 of the Vienna Convention on the Law of Treaties (VCLT) covers the interpretation of treaties, and, in 31 (3) (a) and (b), designates subsequent agreement and subsequent practice as the main tools for determining the consent of parties to evolving interpretations of treaty obligations.' In this contribution, Feldman soley focuses on the potential of subsequent conduct to support dynamic interpretations and treats subsequent conduct as if its sole purpose was to allow for dynamic interpretation. That subsequent conduct can just as well help to support static interpretations is not even mentioned. For a similarly one-sided view see also Arato, 'Evolutive Interpretation' (n 113) 456 f and Sorel and Boré Eveno, 'Article 31' (n 8) 808 [fn omitted], who maintain that art 31(3) VCLT 'results in an evolutive approach towards treaty interpretation.' For a more more careful formulation see Villiger, *Commentary on the VCLT* (n 4) 432 [23]: 'Authentic interpretation in subpara 3(b) is of a dynamic nature in that it may alter the ordinary meaning of a term.' A more differentiated view has been adopted by Luigi Crema, 'Subsequent Agreements and Practice within and outside the Vienna Convention' in Georg Nolte (ed), *Treaties and Subsequent Practice* (OUP 2013) 23, who emphasised that 'subsequent practice can both display the original meaning of an agreement, and also demonstrate how intentions (and meanings) evolve and are crystallized in real time.'

compares the latest interpretation with the one that would have been adopted upon the treaty's conclusion.[118] A static interpretation is one that reflects that meaning that the contracting parties presumably assigned to the terms of the treaty upon its conclusion.[119] A dynamic interpretation, in contrast, is one that reflects a meaning different from that which the parties presumably assigned to the treaty at its conclusion. In other words, the term 'dynamic' denotes a change or evolution of meaning that occurred since the treaty's conclusion.

Strangely enough, academic discussion has more frequently associated subsequent agreements and subsequent practice with dynamic than with static interpretation.[120] The dominant focus on dynamic interpretation possibly originates in the observation that

> [i]nternational law has a special feature which is designed to ensure that evolving circumstances are taken into account in a way which is compatible with the agreement of the parties. This feature is referred to in articles 31(3)(a) and (b) VCLT.[121]

This observation is extracted from Georg Nolte's proposal that the ILC shall include the topic 'Treaties over Time' in its long-term programme of work. Therefore, it is hardly surprising that it addresses the potential of subsequent agreements and subsequent practice to support dynamic interpretations. The proposal does not, however, maintain that dynamic interpretations are the *only* possible effects of subsequent agreements and subsequent practice. Moreover, the Special Rapporteur later clarified that 'evolutive interpretation does not seem to be a separate method of interpretation but rather the result of a proper application of the usual means of interpretation.'[122]

Nonetheless, the above quotation, when considered out of context, may have created the misleading impression that the drafters of the Convention had included subsequent conduct for the sole purpose of enabling and thus taking a principled decision in favour of evolutive interpretation.[123] Therefore, it is helpful to reiterate

---

[121] Georg Nolte, 'Annex A—Treaties over Time—In Particular: Subsequent Agreement and Practice' in ILC, 'Report of the International Law Commission on the Work of its 60th Session' (5 May–6 June and 7 July–8 August 2008) UN Doc A/63/10 367 [11].

[122] id, 'First Report on Subsequent Agreements and Subsequent Practice in relation to Treaty Interpretation' (19 March 2013) UN Doc A/CN.4/660, 26 [62]. See also draft conclusion 3 and the accompanying commentary in ILC, 'Report of the International Law Commission on the Work of its 65th Session' (6 May–7 June and 8 July–9 August 2013) UN Doc A/68/10, 24, 25 [4] [emphasis added]: 'Subsequent agreements and subsequent practice under articles 31 and 32 may assist in determining *whether or not* the presumed intention of the parties upon the conclusion of the treaty was to give a term used a meaning which is capable of evolving over time.'

[123] See eg Feldman, 'Evolving Treaty Obligations' (n 4) 662, who remarks that the 'concepts of subsequent agreement and subsequent practice are premised on the idea that over time, parties can informally consent to new and different interpretations of treaty obligations.'

[124] See already Nolte, 'Report 1—ICJ and Arbitral Tribunals' (n 1) 188.

[125] These words of caution not only apply to subsequent agreements and subsequent practice but to all other means of interpretation, too. For the Vienna rules' potential to enable dynamic interpretation, see eg Karl, *Vertrag und spätere Praxis* (n 8) 185.

that the Vienna rules do not take such principled decision in favour of dynamic (or static) interpretation.[124] The fact that the Vienna rules admit dynamic interpretation does not mean that treaties always need to be interpreted dynamically or that particular means of interpretation, such as subsequent agreements and subsequent practice, always result in dynamic interpretation.[125]

5.2.2.2 Dynamic and Static Interpretation in Domestic Jurisprudence

When considering domestic jurisprudence, one can hardly deny that subsequent agreements and subsequent practice have been an important instrument to support dynamic interpretations.[126] Several cases in which subsequent agreements and subsequent practice were used to support this type of result were landmark decisions that attracted great attention. Thus, these cases may have created the impression that subsequent agreements and subsequent practice are almost identical to dynamic interpretation. Yet, subsequent agreements and subsequent practice have not solely been used to support dynamic results.

A complete line of decisions that associated subsequent agreements and subsequent practice with dynamic interpretation was delivered by the German Federal Constitutional Court. This line of decisions relates to the development of the NATO Treaty and had been prompted by political changes that took place shortly before and after the Cold War. While the NATO Treaty had originally been concluded to defend the NATO member States against outside attacks, they had subsequently

---

[126] For the international level, cf the jurisprudence of the ECtHR. The following cases ilustrate how the Court discussed subsequent conduct when considering whether or not to interpret the ECHR in a dynamic fashion: *Marckx v Belgium* (1979) Series A No 31 [41]; *Dudgeon v UK* (1981) Series A No 45 [60]; *Lithgow v UK* (1986) Series A No 102 [118]; *Inze v Austria* (1987) Series A No 126 [41]; *Mazurek v France* ECHtR 2000–II [52]; *Goodwin v UK [GC]* ECHtR 2002–VI [85], [90]; *Öcalan v Turkey [GC]* ECHtR 2005–IV [162]–[65]; *Demir and Baykara* [GC] App no 34503/97 (ECtHR, 12 November 2008) [48], [52].

[127] For more details, see 6.3.1.2.2.

[128] BVerfGE 90, 286, 361 f. cf also *King v Bristow Helicopters Ltd (Scotland)* [2002] UKHL 7, [2002] 2 AC 628 [25] (Lord Steyn): '[S]tatutes are generally always speaking, and ought therefore to be interpreted in light of the contemporary social and scientific world. This is not a rule of law but a principle of construction, which may be displaced by a contrary intent revealed by a particular statutory context.... Given that the rationale of the principle is that statutes are generally intended to endure for a long time, one can readily accept that multilateral international trade conventions, which are by statute incorporated in our law, should be approached in a similar way. Indeed one may say that a fortiori they ought to be so interpreted.'

[129] BVerfGE 90, 286, 364. cf also BVerfGE 68, 1, 82; 104, 151, 206 f.

[130] *C v H* [2009] NZCA 100.

[131] Convention on the Civil Aspects of International Child Abduction (signed 25 October 1980, entered into force 1 December 1983) 1343 UNTS 89 (Hague Abduction Convention).

decided to informally adapt the NATO Treaty to the new security framework resulting from these changes.[127] Since none of these adaptations had been based on formal treaty amendments, the Court repeatedly had to decide whether Germany's participation in these adaptations was compatible with the NATO Treaty and still covered by the original Parliamentary assent thereto. However, it not only dismissed any objection against these adaptations and emphasised that treaties such as the NATO Treaty had to be adaptable to changed conditions;[128] what is more, it also recognised that subsequent agreements and subsequent practice were viable means of achieving such adaptation.[129]

The New Zealand case of *C v H*,[130] which concerned the interpretation of the Hague Abduction Convention,[131] is another example of how domestic courts closely linked subsequent conduct to dynamic interpretation. Setting out the nature of the Convention, Chambers J generally remarked:

> The Hague Convention itself is, as Thorpe LJ said in Hunter v Murrow, 'a living instrument' ... His Lordship went on: 'Revision of the text as drafted and agreed in 1980 is simply impracticable, given that any revisions would have to be agreed among such a large body of Contracting States. Therefore evolutions necessary to keep pace with social and other trends must be achieved by evolutions in interpretation and construction. This is a permissible exercise given the terms of the Vienna Convention on the Law of Treaties, which also came into force in 1980. Article 31(3)(b) permits a construction that reflects "any subsequent practice in the application of the treaty which establishes the agreement of the parties regarding its interpretation".'[132]

Putting this general remark into interpretative practice, Baragwanath J then relied on subsequent conduct to interpret the Convention in a dynamic fashion when determining how to construe the notion 'custody rights'.[133] In its traditional understanding, this notion implied that someone had a legal right to custody of a child under the domestic law of the child's State of residence. In a more modern understanding, a person could have 'custody rights' even if he or she exercised de facto rights of custody only.[134] To make a choice between these competing interpretations, Baragwanath J examined judicial and legislative developments in different jurisdictions.[135] Quoting article 31(3)(b) VCLT, he noted that the material which he had examined 'evidence[d] a fundamental change in attitudes' and an 'international change of ethos'.[136] Refusing to 'examine the issue through a 1980 lens', this material led him

[132] *C v H* (n 130) [31] (Chambers J).

[133] ibid [94] f (Baragwanath J).

[134] cf ibid [162] f (Baragwanath J).

[135] ibid [175] f (Baragwanath J).

[136] ibid [176] f (Baragwanath J).

[137] ibid [195] f (Baragwanath J). See also *T v Secretary of State for the Home Secretary* [1996] UKHL 8, [1996] AC 742, 755 (Lord Mustill) and 742 (Lord Slynn).

[138] *Pushpanathan v Canada (Minister of Citizenship and Immigration)* [1998] 1 SCR 982, (1998) 160 DLR (4th) 193.

[139] ibid [130] f (Corry J).

to favour a modern understanding of 'custody rights' and thus to adopt a dynamic interpretation.[137]

An illustrative example of the relationship between subsequent conduct and dynamic interpretation is the case of *Pushpanathan v Canada (Minister of Citizenship and Immigration)*.[138] In this case, the Supreme Court of Canada not merely relied on subsequent conduct to adopt a dynamic interpretation but even subordinated it to a more general 'principle' of dynamic interpretation. At issue was whether trafficking in drugs was 'contrary to the purposes and principles of the United Nations' within the meaning of article 1(F)(c) Refugee Convention. Holding that it was, Cory and Major JJ relied on subsequent practice.[139] But their reasoning did not stop at that. Moreover, they emphasised that

> [i]nternational law is developing continuously. Courts should recognise that the guidance provided by interpretive aids such as the *travaux préparatoires* and subsequent practice must be considered in the light of the current state of the law and international understandings .... [I]nterpretation must be adjusted to take into account evolving ideas and principles in international law. The interpretation of legal instruments is a dynamic process which must take into account the contemporary conditions. To put it another way, the interpretation must respond to the contemporary context.[140]

While the practice which they took into account also served to adapt the Refugee Convention to changed conditions, they also clarified that the 'idea' of dynamic interpretation was broader than that. Thus, they seemed to proclaim a general principle of dynamic interpretation that shaped the interpretative process as a whole. Cory and Major JJ, however, failed to explain how they arrived at the opinion that interpretation 'must' be adjusted to contemporary conditions. As has been argued earlier, the issue whether the result of the interpretative process should be a dynamic one remains, at least under the Vienna rules, an open question that needs to be answered in the interpretative process as well.

The preceding examples illustrate that several courts used subsequent conduct to interpret treaties in a dynamic fashion, or even postulated a general principle of dynamic interpretation. But in fact, there are also cases in which domestic courts relied on subsequent conduct to adopt apparently static interpretations and to convey the impression of continuity in treaty interpretation. One of these cases is *Eastern Airlines, Inc v Floyd*, which concerned the question of whether the notion 'bodily injury' under article 17 Warsaw Convention also covered mental or psychic injuries unaccompanied by any physical manifestation of injury. To resolve this issue, the US Supreme Court took account of the 'post-1929 conduct' and 'interpretations of the signatories'.[141] Noting that some contracting parties had unsuccessfully attempted to substitute a broader wording for the narrow wording limited to bodily unjuries,

[140] ibid [129] (Corry J).

[141] *Eastern Airlines, Inc v Floyd* 499 US 530, 547 f, 111 S Ct 1489 (1991) quoting *Saks* (n 73) 403.

[142] *Floyd* (n 141) 548 f.

[143] ibid 553.

[144] *Bristow Helicopters* (n 128) [82] (Lord Hope).

it emphasised that most parties had always understood the contentious phrase to cover only bodily injuries.[142] Based on these observations, the Court finally refused to adopt a dynamic interpretation and adhered to the traditional understanding of 'bodily injuries' which required some physical manifestation of the injury.[143]

Lord Hope's opinion in the case of *King v Bristow Helicopters Ltd (Scotland)* provides another example of—apparently—static interpretation supported by subsequent conduct. Commenting also on the notion 'bodily injury' within the meaning of article 17 Warsaw Convention, Lord Hope wondered whether the Convention was a document of the so-called 'always speaking type'.[144] Under British law, the peculiarity of this type of document is that interpreters do not have to search for its historical or original meaning but are free to apply the current meaning to present day conditions.[145] In short, documents of the 'always speaking type' are documents that can be interpreted in a dynamic fashion. Lord Hope's response to this question was as follows:

> The search is for the meaning which was to be attributed to the words 'bodily injury' in 1929 when the Convention was entered into. So I think that we should be cautious in the use of subsequent practice. It would not be right to use subsequent practice to show that the meaning of these words has changed. The proper way to change the meaning used in an international convention is by amending the convention. But it would be helpful if there was some evidence of a settled practice on the part of all the contracting parties to show what they have always understood the words to mean.[146]

Later, he added that

> [i]t would be wrong to regard article 17 as limited by the state of medical and scientific knowledge that was current in the 1920s. There is no reason to think that the contracting parties intended that no account should be taken of developments in medical science in determining the question whether a passenger has sustained a bodily injury.[147]

At first glance, Lord Hope not only evaded addressing the dynamic nature of the Warsaw Convention but also seemed to be sceptical about subsequent practice. This scepticism mainly arose from his desire not to promote interpretations that do not 'interpret' a treaty but rather informally amend it. Eventually, he overcame his own scepticism by regarding the parties' subsequent practice not as evidence of a change of meaning. Instead, he emphasised the potential of subsequent practice to show that the parties had always interpreted the treaty in a particular way. By explaining that such apparently static interpretation could also require the interpreter to take into account scientific developments, he eventually blurred the line between static and dynamic interpretation.

---

[145] cf *R v Ireland* [1997] UKHL 34, [1998] AC 147.

[146] *Bristow Helicopters* (n 128) [98] (Lord Hope).

[147] ibid [125] (Lord Hope).

5.3 Conclusion

In conclusion, the jurisprudence of domestic courts suggests that the relative legal importance of subsequent agreements and subsequent practice should not be overestimated. As regards the status of subsequent agreements and subsequent practice, it has been shown that domestic courts have not as wholeheartedly embraced the notion of subsequent agreements and subsequent practice as 'authentic' means of interpretation as international jurisprudence and legal scholarship have done. Some courts recognised the basic idea that the lawmaker should possess the right to interpret the law (or treaty). Yet, domestic courts generally did not use this idea or the notion of 'authentic' means of interpretation to indicate an enhanced legal status but merely for descriptive purposes to hint at the authors of subsequent agreements and subsequent practice. In particular, most courts firmly rejected the claim that authentic interpretation could be equated with legally binding interpretation. Notably, this opposition to any binding effects was not justified by the courts by referring to the Vienna rules and by recalling that such effects would be difficult to reconcile with these rules. Instead, their opposition seemed to be influenced by a general reluctance to grant the authors of subsequent agreements and subsequent practice too much influence on the treaty's interpretation.

However, the jurisprudence of domestic courts not only reaffirmed that subsequent agreements and subsequent practice are not legally binding—a finding which is perfectly compatible with the Vienna rules. On the whole, their jurisprudence even tended to go into the other extreme. In some cases, domestic courts treated subsequent agreements and subsequent practice on a par with other primary means of interpretation. But in others cases, domestic courts were reluctant to concede to subsequent agreements and subsequent practice the same influence on the treaty's interpretation as to intrinsic, text-related means of interpretation. This could be seen when domestic courts did not consider it mandatory to take subsequent agreements and subsequent practice into account; when they declared the ambiguity of the text of the treaty as a necessary prerequisite for considering subsequent agreements and subsequent practice; or when they did not accord them an independent role in the interpretative process but only had recourse to them to confirm an interpretation already arrived at.[148] Sometimes, domestic courts even blurred the line between primary and supplementary means of interpretation by first relying on a treaty's

---

[148] Note, however, that the latter alone does not prove that subsequent conduct is regarded as a supplementary means unless a court clearly points out that considering subsequent conduct is *only* admissible in case of ambiguity or in order to confirm a conclusion reached by other means. See Sorel and Boré Eveno, 'Article 31' (n 8) 826 [43], who observe that the 'idea of confirmation is clearly expressed in the case law of the ICJ.' To the same effect, see also Gerald McGinley, 'Practice as a Guide to Treaty Interpretation' (1995) 9 Fletcher F World Aff 211, 220.

[149] cf Villiger, *Commentary on the VCLT* (n 4) 440 f [37] f, who asserts that the views taken by States and courts alike do not confirm that the structure of the general rule reflects customary international law. In his view, the emerging customary international law on the relationship between the various means of interpretation does not conform to the Vienna rules but has rather modified them.

travaux préparatoires before focusing on subsequent agreements and subsequent practice.[149] Taken together, these observations suggest that 'other' subsequent conduct under article 32 VCLT tends to play a stronger role in the jurisprudence of domestic courts than subsequent agreements and subsequent practice under the general rule.

As regards the effects of subsequent agreements and subsequent practice, the jurisprudence of domestic courts largely reconfirmed the neutral character of these means of interpretation as they were used to support extensive, restrictive, dynamic, and static interpretative results alike. Still, the impression arose that domestic courts more readily relied on subsequent agreements and subsequent practice to adopt restrictive than extensive interpretations. Moreover, it cannot be denied that subsequent agreements and subsequent practice were frequently relied on to support dynamic interpretations and, more generally, to adapt treaties to social, scientific, technical, political, or legal developments. Yet, domestic courts not only considered subsequent conduct as a vehicle for bringing flexibility into treaty law. In addition, their jurisprudence also illustrated the potential of subsequent agreements and subsequent practice to contribute to stability and predictability of treaty law by apparently supporting static interpretations. In fact, it was sometimes difficult to clearly distinguish static and dynamic interpretations based on subsequent conduct. This was because domestic courts treated subsequent conduct as evidencing either the parties' original or their (presumed) evolved intention. Especially when domestic courts relied on subsequent conduct to demonstrate that the parties had always intended that account should be taken of new developments (unforeseen as they may have been at the treaty's conclusion), the line between static and dynamic interpretation thus became blurred.

This blurred line also manifests the special argumentative potential of subsequent agreements and subsequent practice. Where interpreters adopt apparently dynamic (and perhaps even extensive) interpretations to respond to new developments without linking them to objectively discernible arguments, they are easily criticised for absorbing legislative powers by informally amending the treaty. This is especially true for interpretations that are only based on a treaty's object and purpose.[150] By linking progressive or extensive interpretations to the parties' subsequent conduct,

[150] See Schwarzenberger, *International Law* (n 94) 518, who remarks that teleological interpretation 'is apt to degenerate into legislation in disguise.' See also Distefano, 'L'interprétation evolutive' (n 113) 379.

[151] Yasseen, 'L'interprétation des traités' (n 20) 26 f [fn omitted]. In English [translated by the author]: 'Unless the treaty indicates a different intention, the ordinary meaning must be that which prevailed at the time of the conclusion of the treaty. Language can change, the meaning of words can become broader, more precise, and, to some extent, change. From a linguistic point of view, however, words are used in the very sense in which they were used at the time when they were employed. Otherwise one would say to those who have spoken said what they did not mean to and, more importantly, what they could not say. It would be artificial, from a linguistic point of view, to claim that the parties intended to use words in an evolutionary sense. It is indeed difficult to assume, from a linguistic point of view, that the contracting parties attributed to words a meaning that was unknown to them and which these words would perhaps never carry.'

such criticism, however, looses force. Interpreters suddenly do not extend or adapt a treaty at their own discretion but only carry out the intentions of the parties; and perhaps, they even create the impression that their interpretations are not at all as dynamic as they first appeared. Thus, subsequent conduct can help to reduce some of the natural uneasiness about certain types of results, which has most succinctly been captured by Mustafa Yasseen with regard to dynamic interpretations:

> A moins qu'une intention différente ne ressorte du traité, le sens ordinaire doit être celui de l'époque de la conclusion du traité. La langue peut évoluer, le sens des mots peut s'élargir, se préciser et, dans une certaine mesure, changer. Toutefois, du point de vue linguistique, les mots sont employés dans le sens qu'ils ont eu à l'époque de leur emploi, autrement on fera dire à ceux qui ont parlé ce qu'ils n'ont pas voulu dire et plus encore ce qu'ils n'ont pas pu dire. Il serait artificiel de prêter aux parties l'intention d'avoir, du point de vue linguistique, employé des mots dans un sens évolutif. Il est difficile en effet de présumer que les parties aux traités ont employé, du point de vue linguistique, les mots dans le sens inconnu et peut-être imprévisible que les mots pourraient acquérir dans l'avenir.[151]

Chapter 6
The Frequency of Subsequent Agreements

At the international level, subsequent agreements play a significant role in expressing the parties' common understanding regarding the interpretation of a treaty. This is especially true for treaties that establish a meeting of States parties for the purpose of reviewing or implementing the treaty. When Conferences of States Parties (COPs)[1] adopt decisions that seek to address the interpretation of the treaty, these decisions may often qualify as subsequent practice or, in particular, as subsequent agreements.[2] Examples include the 'understandings and additional agreements' adopted by the Biological Weapons Convention[3] Review Conference,[4] resolutions adopted by the Conference of States Parties under the London (Dumping) Convention,[5] or recommendations adopted by the International

[1] More precisely, a COP can be defined as 'a meeting of States parties pursuant to a treaty for the purpose of reviewing or implementing the treaty, except if they act as members of an organ of an international organization.' See draft conclusion 10(1) in ILC, 'Report of the International Law Commission on the Work of its 66th Session' (5 May–6 June and 7 July–8 August 2014) UN Doc A/69/10, 205.

[2] For more details, see draft conclusion 10 and the accompanying commentary in ibid 205 f. See also Georg Nolte, 'Report 3—Subsequent Agreements and Subsequent Practice of States outside of Judicial or Quasi-Judicial Proceedings' in id (ed), *Treaties and Subsequent Practice* (OUP 2013) 364 f.

[3] Convention on the Prohibition of the Development, Production and Stockpiling of Bacteriological (Biological) and Toxin Weapons and on their Destruction (signed 10 April 1972, entered into force 26 March 1975) 1015 UNTS 163 (Biological Weapons Convention; BWC).

[4] See generally Piers Millett, 'The Biological Weapons Convention—Securing Biology in the Twenty-First Century' (2010) 15 J Conflict & Sec L 24, 33 f.

[5] Convention on the Prevention of Marine Pollution by Dumping of Wastes and Other Matter (signed 29 December 1972, entered into force 30 August 1975) 1046 UNTS 120 (London Convention).

K. Berner, *Subsequent Agreements and Subsequent Practice in Domestic Courts*, Beiträge zum ausländischen öffentlichen Recht und Völkerrecht,
https://doi.org/10.1007/978-3-662-54937-7_6

Whaling Commission (IWC) under the International Convention for the Regulation of Whaling.[6]

Notwithstanding their legal relevance at the international level, domestic courts only seldom mentioned subsequent agreements.[7] The reasons for this discrepancy ultimately remain a matter of speculation. Nonetheless, three salient aspects are worth noting. Firstly, domestic courts almost exclusively discussed subsequent agreements when interpreting treaties with only a few parties (6.1). Secondly, domestic courts generally requested solid evidence to establish the existence of subsequent agreements (6.2). And thirdly, some domestic courts faced (perceived or real) constitutional impediments when discussing whether or not to take subsequent agreements into account (6.3).

6.1 The Number of Parties to a Treaty

The cases in which domestic courts mentioned subsequent agreements concerned the interpretation of treaties on various subject matters. Among others, they concerned DTAs,[8] an agreement on joint infrastructure projects,[9] the Gasoil Agreement between the Rhine River States and Belgium,[10] the NATO Treaty,[11] the Sino–British Joint Declaration,[12] and the Refugee Convention.[13] Despite their thematic diversity, these treaties have one thing in common: except for the NATO Treaty and the Refugee Convention, all of them have only a few parties.

This is an interesting observation because articles 31–33 VCLT do not on their face distinguish treaties according to the numbers of their parties. Such distinction is not at all uncommon to the law of treaties. Among others, the Vienna Convention

---

[6] International Convention for the Regulation of Whaling (signed 2 December 1946, entered into force 10 November 1948) 161 UNTS 72 (Whaling Convention; ICRW). As regards the role of the IWC, see ICJ, *Whaling in the Antarctic (Australia v Japan)* Judgment of 31 March 2014 <http://www.icj-cij.org/docket/files/148/18136.pdf> [46].

[7] As regards international courts and tribunals under special regimes, see Georg Nolte, 'Report 2—Jurisprudence under Special Regimes relating to Subsequent Agreements and Subsequent Practice' in id (ed), *Treaties and Subsequent Practice* (OUP 2013) 303.

[8] See eg VwGH, Judgment of 30 March 2006, 2002/15/0098; Cour de Cassation de Belgique, Decision of 9 May 2008, F.06.0124.F <http://jure.juridat.just.fgov.be>; BFHE 157, 39; 181, 158; 226, 276; 226, 267; 227, 419; 235, 401; BVGer, Judgment of 21 January 2010, BVGE 2010/7.

[9] VfGH, Judgment of 15 October 1998, A13/96, VfSlg 15309.

[10] BFHE 144, 483.

[11] See eg BVerfGE 90, 286; 104, 151.

[12] *Ng Ka Ling v The Director of Immigration* [1999] 1 HKLRD 315.

[13] *Diatlov v Minister for Immigration and Multicultural Affairs* [1999] FCA 468, (1999) 167 ALR 313.

stipulates special rules for the amendment of multilateral treaties,[14] for the suspension of the operation of a multilateral treaty by agreement between certain of the parties only,[15] and for material breaches of bilateral and multilateral treaties.[16] The Vienna rules of interpretation and article 31(3)(a) VCLT in particular, however, apply to bilateral, plurilateral, and multilateral treaties alike. On the one hand, the Convention thus presupposes that distinguishing between bilateral and multilateral treaties is expedient or even necessary in some areas. On the other hand, it presumes that such distinction is not necessary when it comes to treaty interpretation. In spite of that, the jurisprudence of domestic courts apparently demonstrates that the chances of reaching subsequent agreements diminish as the number of contracting parties increases.[17]

But on closer inspection, it is not that easy to draw reliable conclusions from the numerical importance of subsequent agreements. First of all, most cases in which subsequent agreements have been discussed concerned the interpretation of DTAs. DTAs, however, represent a special case even among other bilateral treaties. This is because DTAs regularly expressly provide for the conclusion of interpretative agreements.[18] It is therefore possible that fiscal authorities quite naturally enter into

---

[14] See art 40 VCLT.

[15] See art 58 VCLT.

[16] See art 60(1) and (2) VCLT.

[17] Thus, the jurisprudence of domestic courts may confirm assumptions that were voiced by Sean Murphy, 'The Relevance of Subsequent Agreements and Subsequent Practice for the Interpretation of Treaties' in Georg Nolte (ed), *Treaties and Subsequent Practice* (OUP 2013) 92 f and Ole Fauchald, 'The Legal Reasoning of ICSID Tribunals—An Empirical Analysis' (2008) 19 EJIL 301, 328.

[18] Eg art 21(1) and (2) of the Agreement between the Republic of Austria and the Federal Republic of Germany for the Avoidance of Double Taxation with respect to Taxes on Income and Capital and to Trade and Property Taxes (signed 4 October 1954, entered into force 7 September 1955) 1972 UNTS 277 (1954 Austrian–German DTA); art 25(1) and (2) of the Agreement between the Kingdom of the Netherlands and the Federal Republic of Germany for the Avoidance of Double Taxation with respect to Taxes on Income and Fortune and Various Other Taxes, and for the Regulation of Other Questions relating to Taxation (signed 16 June 1959, entered into force 18 September 1960) 593 UNTS 43 (1959 Dutch–German DTA); art 24(2) of the Convention between the Government of Australia and the Government of the United States of America for the Avoidance of Double Taxation and the Prevention of Fiscal Evasion with respect to Taxes on Income (signed 6 August 1982, entered into force 31 October 1983) 1424 UNTS 37 (1982 Australian–US DTA), as amended by Protocol (signed 27 September 2001, entered into force 12 May 2003) 2260 UNTS 117; art 25(3) of the Convention between the United States of America and the Federal Republic of Germany for the Avoidance of Double Taxation and the Prevention of Fiscal Evasion with respect to Taxes on Income and Capital and to Certain Other Taxes (signed 29 August 1989, entered into force 21 August 1991) 1708 UNTS 52 (1989 US–German DTA); art 25(3) of the Convention between the United States of America and the Swiss Confederation for the Avoidance of Double Taxation with respect to Taxes on Income (signed 2 October 1996, entered into force 1 January 1998) BBl 1997 II 1104 (1996 US–Swiss DTA).

such agreements because they are familiar with these interpretative instruments and not because of the bilateral nature of DTAs. Furthermore, the jurisprudence of domestic courts must not necessarily reflect the true relevance of subsequent agreements. In fact, numerous multilateral treaties provide for institutional frameworks within which subsequent agreements may be reached.[19] Against this background, it is conceivable that there exist more subsequent agreements regarding the interpretation of multilateral treaties than domestic jurisprudence exhibits.

To corroborate the assumption that the number of contracting parties influences the chances of reaching subsequent agreements, one may compare the overall number of references to subsequent agreements and subsequent practice respectively. On the whole, domestic courts more often addressed practice-based arguments than arguments based on subsequent agreements. But while domestic courts comparatively rarely considered subsequent agreements regarding the interpretation of bilateral treaties, references to agreements regarding the interpretation of multilateral treaties were even more exceptional. In sum, and notwithstanding other possible factors, the jurisprudence of domestic courts therefore indeed suggests that the number of contracting parties to some extent influences the numerical importance of subsequent agreements as a means of treaty interpretation.

6.2 Solid Evidence of Subsequent Agreements

Another possible reason why domestic courts only seldom mentioned subsequent agreements is their insistence on solid evidence to establish their existence. This insistence on solid evidence may or may not reveal tendencies among domestic courts to favour a formalistic understanding of subsequent agreements.

The Vienna rules do not stipulate formal requirements for subsequent agreements under article 31(3)(a) VCLT.[20] Instead of declaring that subsequent agreements must be somehow formally perpetuated, they seem to distinguish subsequent agreements from subsequent practice based on these means' probative value. Whereas subsequent agreements *ipso facto* form the basis of a particular interpretation, potentially relevant practice merely serves as a piece of evidence for establishing the parties' agreement. This non-formalistic understanding of subsequent agreements, which merely presupposes a 'single common act',[21] on the one hand facilitates the conclusion of subsequent agreements. In consequence, subsequent agreements are an

[19] See in particular the commentary on draft conclusion 10 in ILC, 'Report of the International Law Commission on the Work of its 66th Session' (5 May–6 June and 7 July–8 August 2014) UN Doc A/69/10, 205 f; see also Nolte, 'Report 3—Practice outside of Judicial Proceedings' (n 2) 364 f.

[20] See 4.2.1.3.

[21] See 4.2.1.3 and the commentary on draft conclusion 4 in ILC, 'Report of the International Law Commission on the Work of its 65th Session' (6 May–7 June and 8 July–9 August 2013) UN Doc A/68/10, 34 [10].

attractive option for State parties to influence the interpretation of their treaty. But on the other hand, such non-formalistic understanding of subsequent agreements blurs the line between subsequent agreements and subsequent practice and may entail evidentiary problems as to whether or not a subsequent agreement has been reached.

The difficulties in identifying subsequent agreements and in keeping apart the various means of interpretation under article 31(3) VCLT become evident, for instance, in the case of *Diatlov v Minister for Immigration and Multicultural Affairs*. To interpret the Refugee Convention, one of the judges relied on the 1954 Stateless Persons Convention.[22] Explaining why it should be admissible to take this instrument into account, he remarked: 'It seems clear enough that the Stateless Persons Convention forms part of the context for the purpose of construing the Refugees Convention: see Vienna Convention, article 31(3)(a),(c).'[23] This statement is peculiar because it is difficult to see why the Stateless Persons Convention should actually fall under any one of these provisions. Since not all parties to the Refugee Convention had hitherto ratified the Stateless Persons Convention, the latter is not a relevant rule applicable in the relations between all the parties to the former as required by article 31(3)(c) VCLT.[24] For the same reason and because the Stateless Persons Convention had not been concluded with a view to interpreting the Refugee Convention,[25] one may equally question whether the former satisfies the requirements under article 31(3)(a) VCLT. Instead, there are good reasons to conclude that the Stateless Persons Convention would not have been admissible at all under article 31 VCLT. By citing two provisions and thus avoiding any specification, the judge therefore conveyed the impression that he was either unable or unwilling to explain which provision actually applied.

An Austrian judgment on the 1954 Austrian–German DTA similarly illustrates the difficulties in identifying subsequent agreements. This case raised the question of how to distinguish independent from employed work when the taxpayer, whose work had to be classified, worked for a German company that held a 100 per cent share in an Austrian company. To specify the meaning of 'independent' and

[22] Convention relating to the Status of Stateless Persons (signed 28 September 1964, entered into force 6 June 1960) 360 UNTS 117 (Stateless Persons Convention).

[23] *Diatlov* (n 13) 313 [28] (Sackville J). The German Federal Court of Justice, in contrast, expressly dismissed a later treaty as irrelevant under art 31(3)(a) VCLT: Firstly, because the later treaty had not been concluded with a view to interpreting the earlier treaty; and secondly, because not all parties to the earlier treaty had also ratified the later treaty. See BGH, Judgment of 21 April 2016, I ZR 43/14 <http://www.juris.de> [86]–[87].

[24] For the question of whether art 31(3)(c) VCLT requires relevant rules applicable in the relation between *all* the parties, see generally Campbell McLachlan, 'The Principle of Systemic Integration and Article 31(3)(c) of the Vienna Convention' (2005) 54 ICLQ 279; ILC, 'Report of the International Law Commission on the Work of its 58th Session' (1 May–9 June and 3 July–11 August 2006) UN Doc A/61/10, 414–15 [21].

[25] For the question under which conditions a subsequent agreement is one 'regarding' the interpretation of the treaty as required by art 31(3)(a) VCLT, see 4.2.3.

'employed' work in this borderline case, the Austrian revenue authority had relied on an interpretative agreement between Austrian and German revenue authorities.[26] The existence of this agreement was established beyond doubt because it had been published in the Official Gazette of the Austrian Fiscal Administration.[27] Given this clear documentation, one would have probably expected the authority to regard this agreement as a subsequent agreement in the sense of article 31(3)(a) VCLT. But surprisingly, the authority referred to the interpretative agreement as a case of subsequent practice pursuant to article 31(3)(b) VCLT. Although the Austrian Administrative Court ultimately upheld the authority's view and discussed the legal effects of the interpretative agreement, it did not object to its classification as subsequent practice.[28] Since Austrian courts had cited article 31(3)(a) VCLT on other occasions, one may only suspect that the Austrian Administrative Court was to some extent unsure as to the agreement's correct classification under the Vienna rules.[29]

A judgment on the International School in Vienna is one of those cases in which Austrian courts cited article 31(3)(a) VCLT.[30] The School's foundation dates back until 1979 when the Federal State and the province of Vienna agreed on a number of joint projects and infrastructural measures.[31] Because the Federal State and the province of Vienna disagreed about the allocation of costs for the International School, the case was brought before the Austrian Constitutional Court. In its judgment, the Court relied on an agreement between the Vienna Executive Councillor for Financial Affairs on the one hand and the Federal Ministers for Finance and Economic Affairs on the other.[32] This agreement, which had been reached in 1993, aimed at determining the applicable terms of payment for the School in a legally binding way. The agreement did not constitute a treaty within the meaning of article 2(1)(a) VCLT. However, article 15(a) of the Austrian Federal Constitutional Law (B-VG), pursuant to which it had been concluded, declared that the Vienna Convention should be applicable to agreements like this. Notably, the Court expressly referred to the settlement agreement as an agreement within the meaning of article 31(3)(a) VCLT.[33] This is remarkable because under Austrian domestic law, both agreements were legally binding instruments. Nevertheless, the Court did not ask whether the

[26] VwGH, Judgment of 30 March 2006, 2002/15/0098, 2 f, 5.

[27] BMF (Austria), 'Erlaß Z 1246/1/3-IV/4/86 betreffend die Besteuerung wesentlich beteiligter Gesellschafter-Geschäftsführer nach dem österreichisch-deutschen Doppelbesteuerungsabkommen' (22 December 1986) AÖFV No 32/1987.

[28] VwGH, Judgment of 30 March 2006, 2002/15/0098, 6.

[29] Thus, not all courts that fail to identify subsequent agreements must have been influenced by a formalistic approach to subsequent agreements. In the alternative, these courts may also be unfamiliar with the requirements of the Vienna rules.

[30] VfGH, Judgment of 15 October 1998, A13/96, VfSlg 15309.

[31] Vereinbarung gemäß Art 15a B-VG über Vorhaben in der Bundeshauptstadt Wien, an welchen der Bund und das Land Wien interessiert sind (Austria–Vienna) (signed 9 May 1979, entered into force 20 December 1979) BGBl (Austria) 18/1980 (Art 15a B-VG Agreement).

[32] VfGH, Judgment of 15 October 1998, A13/96, VfSlg 15309, 11.

[33] ibid.

later agreement merely interpreted or even amended or superseded the earlier one. Instead, it quite naturally assumed that legally binding instruments could be taken into account under article 31(3)(a) VCLT.

Compared to other manifestations of subsequent agreements, such legally binding instruments entail the advantage of being easy to identify since they are commonly laid down in writing. The same advantage in terms of evidence applies to written but non-binding agreements. Despite these advantages, discussions on whether to read any formal requirements into article 31(3)(a) VCLT quickly raise concerns about unintentionally limiting the relevance of subsequent agreements.[34] The jurisprudence of domestic courts, however, suggests that such concerns are ill-founded. Domestic courts have only rarely relied on subsequent agreements anyway and tended to dismiss poorly documented ones. This can be seen in the case of *Ng Ka Ling v Director of Immigration,* which concerned the interpretation of the Sino–British Joint Declaration.[35] One of the claimants had relied on an interpretative agreement that had allegedly been reached in the Sino–British Joint Liaison Group and that, so the claimant, satisfied the requirements of article 31(3)(a) VCLT.[36] This Joint Liaison Group, which was established under article 5 of the Joint Declaration, consisted of Chinese and British representatives of ambassadorial rank and four other members to be designated by each party.[37] One of the functions of the Joint Liaison Group was to conduct consultations on the Joint Declaration's implementation and on such subjects as may be agreed by the two sides.[38] Hence one may well argue that decisions taken by that Group could constitute subsequent agreements within the meaning of article 31(3)(a) VCLT. Still, the claimant could not reliably prove that the agreement really existed. Instead, he merely presented a booklet allegedly 'compiled "on the basis of the existing immigration regulations and practices and the common view of the British and Chinese sides in the [Joint Liaison Group]".'[39] Therefore, the Court doubted the agreement's existence and ultimately refused to take account of it, not even discussing it as potentially relevant practice instead.[40]

Another example of how a domestic court may establish the existence of subsequent agreements is a decision on the 1965 Belgian–French DTA.[41] To demonstrate

---

[34] See 4.2.1.

[35] *Ng Ka Ling* (n 12) 353 f.

[36] ibid.

[37] See art 7 of Annex II to the Joint Declaration of the Government of the United Kingdom of Great Britain and Northern Ireland and the Government of the People's Republic of China on the Question of Hong Kong (signed 19 December 1984, entered into force 27 May 1985) <http://www.cmab.gov.hk/en/issues/joint3.htm> (Sino–British Joint Declaration).

[38] See art 3(a) and (b) of Annex II to the Sino–British Joint Declaration.

[39] *Ng Ka Ling* (n 12) 353 [explanation added].

[40] ibid 354.

[41] Convention between Belgium and France for the Avoidance of Double Taxation and the Establishment of Rules of Reciprocal Administrative and Legal Assistance with respect to Taxes on Income (signed 10 March 1964, entered into force 17 June 1965) 557 UNTS 13 (1964 Belgian–French DTA).

that there had been some communication between Belgium and France regarding the interpretation of the DTA, the Belgian Cour de Cassation simply relied on a letter sent by a French tax authority.[42] In the Court's view, this was sufficient evidence to conclude that the contracting parties had actually reached an interpretative agreement.[43] Although German courts frequently refused to take subsequent agreements into account, they have equally preferred straightforward cases of subsequent agreements not raising any questions of evidence. This can be seen in a judgment on the interpretation of the Gasoil Agreement between the Rhine River States and Belgium.[44] Here the question was whether the Agreement, which provided for a duty exemption for gasoil used by ships, applied both to commercial shipping and to ships used for a non-commercial purpose.[45] Article 1(1) of the Agreement merely provided that '[l]es Etats riverains du Rhin et la Belgique ne percevront ni droit de douane ni autres taxes sur le gasoil consommé régulièrement comme avitaillement des bateaux naviguant sur le Rhin et ses affluents ou sur les voies d'eau visées à l'article 2 de l'Acte de Mannheim.'[46]

Taking the view that ships used for commercial purposes were not covered by this exemption, the German Federal Fiscal Court relied on a decision of the Central Commission for the Navigation of the Rhine (CCNR). This decision, which had been adopted on 29 November 1982, clarified that the Gasoil Agreement did not exempt sports and leisure boats from any duty.[47] Since this decision had described itself as one falling under article 31(3)(a) VCLT, the Court equally held that it was a subsequent agreement within the meaning of said provision.[48] In this respect, it is useful to recall that the CCNR is an IO and thus legally separate from its contracting parties. Therefore, it is not that obvious why a decision taken by the CCNR should constitute an agreement between the parties to the Gasoil Agreement. Hence one

---

[42] Cour de Cassation de Belgique, Decision of 9 May 2008, F.06.0124.F <http://jure.juridat.just.fgov.be>.

[43] ibid 8: '[C]onformément à l'article 31, 3°, a), de la Convention de Vienne sur le droit des traités, il y a lieu de tenir compte pour l'interprétation d'un traité, "de tout accord ultérieur intervenu entre les parties au sujet de l'interprétation du traité ou de l'application de ses dispositions".' In English [translated by the author]: '[I]n accordance with art 31(3)(a) of the Vienna Convention on the Law of Treaties, account may be taken for the interpretation of a treaty of "any subsequent agreement between the parties regarding the interpretation of the treaty or the application of its provisions".'

[44] Agreement on the Taxation and Customs Regime for Gasoil Consumed as Board Supply in the Navigation on the Rhine (signed 16 May 1952, entered into force 28 January 1954) BGBl (Germany) 1953 II 532 (Gasoil Agreement).

[45] BFHE 144, 483, 483.

[46] In English [translated by the author]: 'The Rhine River States and Belgium shall not impose any customs duties or other taxes on gasoil that is used for refuelling vessels navigating on the Rhine River and its tributaries or on those waterways that are referred to in Article 2 of the Act of Mannheim.'

[47] BFHE 144, 483, 485 f.

[48] ibid 486.

may suspect that the Court quite naturally adopted the CCNR's view for reasons of convenience and without having critically reflected upon it.

In sum, domestic jurisprudence does not unequivocally demonstrate that domestic courts tended to favour a formalistic understanding of subsequent agreements. Hence it cannot refute the conclusion arrived at in Chap. 4, namely that article 31(3)(a) VCLT does not implicitly stipulate any formal requirements for subsequent agreements.[49] Nonetheless, it could be seen that domestic courts mostly took note of agreements that were laid down in writing or were otherwise reliably documented. In other words, domestic courts tended to require rather solid evidence of potentially relevant subsequent agreements. Moreover, they sometimes had difficulties in distinguishing subsequent agreements from subsequent practice under lit (b) or from other rules of international law under lit (c) of article 31(3) VCLT. These observations suggest that it is ultimately immaterial whether one reads formal requirements into article 31(3)(a) VCLT or not. Interpreters such as domestic courts, so it seems, only reluctantly rely on subsequent agreements that are not formally perpetuated. This may either indicate an underlying tendency to formalism, some unfamiliarity with the Vienna rules, or simply an increased awareness towards questions of evidence. In any case, the degree of formalisation seems to be another factor that influences the margin for subsequent agreements in domestic jurisprudence.

6.3 Constitutional Impediments

In some way, it is remarkable that domestic courts only rarely base their interpretations on subsequent agreements. This is because there are indeed several cases in which they deliberated whether they could take such agreements into account. Yet, these deliberations often led them to conclude that constitutional reasons prevented them from giving weight to potentially relevant agreements. In addition to such perceived or real constitutional concerns, the jurisprudence of domestic courts also reveals a more deep-rooted uneasiness about subsequent agreements. The foregoing observations apply in particular to the German Federal Fiscal Court, which produced a long line of cases on subsequent agreements regarding the interpretation of DTAs. These cases form the starting point for the following analysis, which purports to illustrate why domestic courts may conceive of subsequent agreements as two-edged swords.

6.3.1 Negative Impact on Parliamentary Participation Rights

Domestic courts in Germany frequently identified potentially relevant subsequent agreements. But in the end, several courts refused to take these agreements into account for constitutional reasons. More precisely, these courts were concerned not

---

[49] See 4.2.1.3.

to circumvent Parliamentary participation rights in foreign affairs and thus violate the German Basic Law. Although courts in other jurisdictions did not specifically address constitutional concerns relating to subsequent agreements, their jurisprudence occasionally revealed similar considerations on subsequent practice and parliamentary rights.

6.3.1.1 Parliamentary Participation in Foreign Affairs in Germany

Parliamentary participation rights in foreign affairs in Germany are mainly laid down in article 59(2) of the German Basic Law (*Grundgesetz*; GG). Under this provision, treaties that regulate the political relations of the Federation or relate to subjects of federal legislation require the consent or participation, in the form of a federal law, of the bodies responsible in such a case for the enactment of federal law. Article 59(2) GG thus stipulates a ratification requirement for certain types of treaties that are sufficiently important in one way or another.[50] The first category of treaties, ie those regulating the political relations of the Federation, is commonly interpreted restrictively. According to the German Federal Constitutional Court,

> [a] treaty does not become a political treaty within the meaning of Art 59(2) of the Basic Law simply by way of the fact that it deals quite generally with public affairs, the good of the community or affairs of state. If this were the case, then every treaty would be a political treaty, such that the limitation found in Art 59(2) would be devoid of meaning. Instead, in addition to the above-mentioned conditions, such a treaty must also directly affect the existence of the state, its territorial integrity, its independence and its position or prominent weight within the community of states.[51]

The first category of treaties that are subject to a ratification requirement therefore only covers those of a highly political nature.[52] The second category of treaties, ie those relating to subjects of federal legislation, is described in somewhat misleading terms. Contrary to what one would expect, it does not mean to juxtapose federal legislation to legislation of the *Länder*. Instead, this category juxtaposes federal

[50] These elaborations draw on Katharina Berner, '"Sovereignty of Parliament" under the Grundgesetz—How the German Constitutional Court Discovers Parliamentary Participation as a Means of Controlling European Integration' (2013) 19 EPL 249.

[51] BVerfGE 1, 372, 380 f. In German: 'Ein Staatsvertrag wird noch nicht dadurch zu einem politischen im Sinne des Art 59 Abs 2 GG, daß er sich ganz allgemein mit öffentlichen Angelegenheiten, dem Gemeinwohl oder den Staatsgeschäften befaßt. Wäre dies der Fall, so wäre jeder Staatsvertrag politisch, so daß die im Art 59 Abs 2 vorgesehene Begrenzung ihres Sinnes entbehren würde. Hinzukommen muß vielmehr, daß die Existenz des Staates, seine territoriale Integrität, seine Unabhängigkeit, seine Stellung oder sein maßgebliches Gewicht in der Staatengemeinschaft durch den Vertrag selbst berührt werden.' The English translation is available at <http://www.utexas.edu/law/academics/centers/transnational/work_new/german>.

[52] Rudolf Streinz, 'Artikel 59' in Michael Sachs and others (eds), *Grundgesetz—Kommentar* (7th edn, CH Beck 2014) [2].

legislation to acts adopted by the executive. In consequence, '[t]he content of a treaty is only a matter of federal legislation when a federal law is required in order to implement the treaty, ie, when the Federation assumes obligations under the treaty that can only be fulfilled via the enactment of a federal law.'[53] Under German constitutional law, a legislative act is necessary if, for instance, a certain measure interferes with fundamental rights.[54] This reflects the so-called *Wesentlickeitsprinzip*, according to which essential decisions (*wesentliche Entscheidungen*), which affect the foundations of the State and its citizens, must be taken by Parliament itself and cannot be delegated to the executive.

Typical examples of the latter category, ie treaties that can only be implemented by enacting a federal law, are treaties dealing with taxation matters. This is because taxation easily impairs fundamental rights such as the general principle of equality or the principle of non-retroactivity.[55] Examples of the former category, ie treaties of a highly political nature, are treaties of alliance such as the NATO Treaty. Once the ratification requirement under article 59(2) GG applies, the German Federal Parliament (*Bundestag*) must formally express its consent to the respective treaty by enacting a federal law.[56] Contrary to the wording of article 59(2) GG, such consent is both necessary when a treaty is concluded and when it is amended in a way that falls under the ratification requirement.[57] When German courts need to decide whether a ratification requirement applies, it is crucial for them to determine whether a certain conduct or instrument merely interprets or actually amends the treaty.

---

[53] BVerfGE 1, 372, 389.

[54] Ondolf Rojahn, 'Artikel 59' in Ingo von Münch and others (eds), *Grundgesetz—Kommentar* (6th edn, CH Beck 2012) [24].

[55] Andreas Musil, 'Steuergerechtigkeit im Verfassungsstaat—Über die Bedeutung der Grundrechte im Steuerrecht' in Marten Breuer (ed), *Der Staat im Recht—Festschrift für Eckart Klein zum 70. Geburtstag* (Duncker & Humblot 2013) esp 238, 243. See also Christoph Schreuer, 'Wechselwirkungen zwischen Völkerrecht und Verfassung bei der Auslegung völkerrechtlicher Verträge' in Georg Ress and Christoph Schreuer (eds), *Wechselwirkungen zwischen Völkerrecht und Verfassung bei der Auslegung völkerrechtlicher Verträge* (CF Müller 1982) 73 f, who emphasised that informal, unpublished agreements regarding the interpretation of treaties such as DTAs may raise serious concerns from a rule of law State perspective when they affect individual rights.

[56] To be enacted, a federal law normally requires a simple majority of the votes cast, see art 42(2) GG. In addition, such federal law must also pass through either a consent or an objection procedure in the Federal Council (*Bundesrat*), see art 59(2) in conjunction with arts 77, 78 GG.

[57] Christian Hillgruber, 'Die Fortentwicklung völkerrechtlicher Verträge als staatsrechtliches Problem: Wie weit trägt der Rechtsanwendungsbefehl des Zustimmungsgesetzes nach Art 59 Abs 2 Satz 1 GG?' in Josef Isensee and Helmut Lecheler (eds), *Freiheit und Eigentum—Festschrift für Walter Leisner zum 70. Geburtstag* (Duncker & Humblot 1999) 64 f; Streinz, 'Artikel 59' (n 52) [38] f.

6.3.1.2 Different Approaches to the Ratification Requirement

Admittedly, it is often difficult to distinguish subsequent interpretative agreements or subsequent practice from informal amendments of a treaty. Nonetheless, this distinction is crucial from a constitutional perspective.[58] Interpreters acting at the international level may perhaps choose the easy way by silently ignoring this distinction. National actors that must respect parliamentary rights similar to those in Germany, however, cannot do so. Hence it is not surprising that domestic courts, and in particular the German Federal Fiscal Court, repeatedly discussed this distinction.

6.3.1.2.1 Objective Approach

On the whole, the German Federal Fiscal Court has adopted an objective approach to distinguish interpretative agreements from informal amendments. More generally and corresponding to that, the Court's reasoning has been premised on a predominantly literal approach to interpretation.

This can be seen in a judgment on the 1925 German–Italian DTA, whose article 7(2) exempted income from taxation in Germany when the employee had been working for a public legal entity in Italy.[59] The Hessian Minister of Finance had taken the view that this provision did not apply to someone who worked for the German branch of a bank established under Italian public law.[60] In support, he had relied on a letter by the German Federal Minister of Finance.[61] This document evidenced that German and Italian fiscal authorities had agreed to apply the contentious provision to activities performed in the public sector only.[62] The Court, however, refused to interpret the exemption under article 7(2) that restrictively because this provision was, on its face, not limited to activities performed in the public sector.[63]

By restricting the general exemption under article 7(2), the fiscal authorities' agreement did not merely interpret the DTA but had the effect of actually changing its meaning, so the Court argued.[64] Emphasising that the DTA had been incorporated into German law by an Act of Parliament, it therefore held that the agreement in effect overrode Parliamentary assent.[65] But in fact, article 7(2) did not unambiguously answer the contentious issue in one way or the other. Under the Vienna rules, one may have therefore argued that the text of the contentious provision was open to different interpretations. Consequently, other means of interpretation, such as the

[58] See 4.2.3.

[59] BFHE 157, 39.

[60] ibid 40.

[61] ibid.

[62] ibid.

[63] ibid 41.

[64] ibid.

[65] ibid 43.

fiscal authorities' agreement, would not have constituted an informal amendment but would have merely helped to determine the meaning of an ambiguous provision.

The Court's objective and rather textualist approach has been confirmed in subsequent decisions.[66] In a judgment on the 1967 German–Belgian DTA,[67] for instance, the German Federal Fiscal Court emphasised the text of the contentious provision to refuse relying on a subsequent agreement between the German Federal Ministry of Finance and its Belgian counterpart.[68] This case raised the question of whether German revenue authorities could impose a tax on a severance payment received by a Belgian resident from his former German employer. In the Court's view, the clear wording of the DTA suggested that the taxpayer's State of residence and not his State of employment was competent to tax such severance payment.[69] Taking the opposite view, the German revenue authority had invoked said agreement between the German and Belgian ministries of finance.

Although article 25(3) of the DTA expressly envisaged such agreements, the Court pointed out that their legal effects were subject to constitutional restrictions.[70] This meant, so the Court continued, that such agreements were subject to the same Parliamentary participation requirements as the respective treaty itself.[71] Acknowledging that subsequent agreements were part of the Vienna rules of interpretation, the Court clarified that it may well take such agreements into account irrespective of

---

[66] See also BFHE 227, 419, 426. Here the Court asked whether a subsequent agreement in effect led to an amendment of the original treaty. The answer to this question depended, so the Court, on whether or not the agreement contradicted the ordinary meaning of the terms of the treaty.

[67] BFHE 226, 267. cf also BFHE 226, 276; 227, 419; 235, 401; BFH, Judgment of 10 June 2015, I R 79/13 <http://www.juris.de>; id, Judgment of 25 November 2015, I R 50/14 <http://www.juris.de>.

[68] For the agreement, see BMF (Germany), 'Deutsch-belgisches Doppelbesteuerungsabkommen; Verständigungsvereinbarung mit dem belgischen Finanzministerium vom 15. Dezember 2006 über die Zuordnung des Besteuerungsrechts bei Abfindungen an Arbeitnehmer' (10 January 2007) BStBl I 2007, 261.

[69] BFHE 226, 267, 270. See art 15(1) of the Agreement between the Federal Republic of Germany and the Kingdom of Belgium for the Avoidance of Double Taxation and the Regulation of Certain Other Matters with respect to Taxes on Income and Fortune, Including the Business Tax and Land Taxes (signed 11 April 1967, entered into force 30 July 1969) 704 UNTS 361 (1967 German–Belgian DTA): '… Gehälter, Löhne und ähnliche Vergütungen, die eine in einem Vertragsstaat ansässige Person aus unselbständiger Arbeit bezieht, [können] nur in diesem Staat besteuert werden, es sei denn, dass die Arbeit in dem anderen Vertragsstaat ausgeübt wird. Wird die Arbeit dort ausgeübt, so können die dafür bezogenen Vergütungen in dem anderen Staat besteuert werden.' In English [official translation]: 'Salaries, wages and other similar remuneration derived by a resident of a Contracting State in respect of an employment shall be taxable only in that State unless the employment is exercised in the other Contracting State. If the employment is so exercised, such remuneration as is derived therefrom may be taxed in that other State.'

[70] BFHE 226, 267, 271 f.

[71] ibid.

whether they had received Parliamentary assent or not.[72] But unless this assent had been given, it could only take these agreements into account in order to confirm the ordinary meaning of the respective treaty but not to support informal amendments thereof.[73]

Insofar as the German Federal Fiscal Court merely reaffirms the distinction between amendment and interpretation, its approach is well in line with the Vienna rules of interpretation. In some decisions, however, the Court seems to not only insist on this absolute limit and to respond to legitimate constitutional concerns. Instead, it more categorically dismisses potentially relevant agreements irrespective of whether or not they are compatible with the ordinary meaning of the terms of the treaty. These decisions create the impression that the Court occasionally cultivates and succumbs to a more general sentiment of uneasiness about subsequent agreements as means of interpretation.[74] In a judgment on the German–Dutch DTA, for instance, the Court generally refused to take a subsequent agreement into account without even discussing whether it conflicted with a literal construction of the DTA.[75] This case raised the question under which conditions one party's national was 'present' within the other party's territory.

German and Dutch revenue authorities had reached an agreement which,[76] in the Court's view, constituted a subsequent agreement within the meaning of article 31(3)(a) VCLT. Yet, the Court flatly declared that, for constitutional reasons, such agreement did not entail any legally binding effect at the national level.[77] As will be recalled, the Vienna rules do not regard subsequent agreements as legally binding either so that this dictum is, in itself, not surprising.[78] But in addition, the Court categorically refused to take the agreement into account and dismissed it as completely irrelevant for interpreting the DTA.[79] In a later decision, the Court noted in an obiter dictum that 'even a formal agreement on the interpretation of a treaty could only affect the respective case at hand and not generally influence the interpretation of the treaty beyond this particular case.'[80] At first sight, these dicta merely refused to recognise

---

[72] ibid 272 f.

[73] ibid. See also BFHE 237, 360, 366, where the Court reiterated that the ordinary meaning of a DTA and not an interpretative agreement constituted an absolute limit within which a correct and admissible interpretation had to be situated.

[74] cf also BFHE 145, 341, 348 on the Convention between the United States of America and the Federal Republic of Germany for the Avoidance of Double Taxation with respect to Taxes on Income (signed 22 July 1954, entered into force 20 December 1954) 239 UNTS 135 (1954 US–German DTA), where the Court pointed out that an interpretation arrived at in accordance with general principles of interpretation may not be rejected by simply referring to the other contracting party's treaty practice.

[75] BFHE 181, 158.

[76] ibid 161.

[77] ibid. cf also VwGH, Judgment of 23 February 2010, 2008/15/0148, 2.

[78] See 5.1.1.

[79] BFHE 181, 158, 161.

[80] BFHE 219, 518, 527 f.

any legally binding effect of subsequent agreements. However, these correct observations were then used to explain why the Court would not even take a potentially relevant agreement into account. In this respect, the Court no longer asked whether or not the agreement was compatible with a literal interpretation of the respective DTAs.

That the German Federal Fiscal Court has not always been genuinely concerned with literal interpretation can also be seen in a judgment on the 1971 German–Swiss DTA. In this case, the Court quite readily relied on several interpretative agreements between German and Swiss revenue authorities to confirm an interpretation which it had arrived at by relying on the DTA's *travaux préparatoires*.[81] This merits attention because the Court obviously did not bother whether its interpretation supported by the *travaux* was compatible with a literal interpretation of the DTA. Although the same constitutional concerns about Parliamentary participation may be invoked when historical interpretation informally amends a treaty, these concerns did not surface here. Irrespective of whether constitutional concerns are legitimate or not, the Court's reluctance towards subsequent agreements seems to be partly based on other reasons. In this respect, it is instructive to compare the Court's critical attitude towards subsequent agreements to its rather benevolent attitude towards subsequent practice.[82]

In a judgment on the 1992 German–Swiss DTA, for instance, the Court readily relied on the 'longstanding practice of the contracting parties'[83] under article 31(3)(b) VCLT without discussing whether its interpretation was compatible with German constitutional law. The legal issue of the case was as follows: Article 15(4) of the DTA expressly stipulated that the location of a particular activity should always be considered as being Switzerland irrespective of where the activity had really been performed. Article 24(1), in contrast, did not expressly stipulate a similar presumption although its wording was otherwise similar. The German Federal Ministry of Finance had therefore argued that the presumption under article 15(4) could not be read into article 24(1) so that the latter could only be interpreted as referring to the location where the activity had really been performed.[84] Disagreeing with this interpretation, the Court noted that both German and Swiss fiscal authorities had, for more than 20 years, read the presumption under article 15(4) into article 24(1), too.[85] In the Court's view, this practice was

> a material and objectively identifiable indicator of how the parties understand the treaty or, at least, how they understood it when concluding the treaty and in the years immediately thereafter. This common understanding constitutes an authoritative interpretation by the parties decisive for the interpretation of the Agreement, one from which German fiscal authorities may not unilaterally depart.[86]

---

[81] BFHE 222, 553, 556 f, 558.

[82] See, however, BFHE 145, 341, 348 and BFHE 219, 518, 527 f as exceptions to the Court's benevolent attitude towards subsequent practice. In these cases, the Court considered whether or not it should adopt a more reserved approach towards subsequent practice, too.

[83] BFHE 215, 237, 240 f.

[84] ibid.

[85] ibid 241.

[86] ibid [translated by the author]. In the German original, the quotation reads: 'Sie [die nachfolgende Praxis] ist ein gewichtiges und objektiv feststellbares Indiz dafür, wie die Parteien

This dictum is all the more remarkable if one compares it to the Court's judgment on the 1925 German–Italian DTA, where it had refused to interpret a provision restrictively when a literal interpretation of said provision did not support such restriction.[87] However, the Court's objective approach to distinguishing interpretation from amendment sometimes also prevented it from relying on subsequent practice. This can be seen in a judgment on the interpretation of article 15(3) of the 1971 German–Swiss DTA,[88] which regulated taxation of employed work that was performed aboard a ship. As in the Court's 2006 judgment, the question arose whether the location where the employed activity was performed should always be considered as being the location where the employing company was resident. But unlike in 2006, the Court now concluded that this presumption did not apply although German and Swiss tax authorities had, until 1995, consistently interpreted article 15(3) in this way.[89] This was because article 31(3)(b) VCLT did not, according to the Court, authorise interpreters to rely on subsequent conduct that lacked sufficient support in the text of the pertinent treaty.[90]

6.3.1.2.2 Mixed Approach

Unlike the German Federal Fiscal Court, the German Federal Constitutional Court has not produced such an exceptionally long line of cases dealing exclusively with subsequent agreements. This is not astonishing as international tax law comparatively often envisages the adoption of subsequent interpretive agreements in express terms. However, the Constitutional Court's case law on the development of the NATO Treaty after the Cold War, which concerned both subsequent agreements and subsequent practice,[91] is no less instructive as an alternative approach to distinguishing

den Vertrag einvernehmlich verstehen bzw. zumindest im Zeitpunkt des Vertragsschlusses und in den darauf folgenden Jahren verstanden haben. Dieses einvernehmliche Verständnis enthält eine für die Abkommensauslegung maßgebliche authentische Interpretation durch die Vertragsparteien, von der sich die deutsche Finanzverwaltung nicht einseitig durch eine abweichende Deutung des Art 15 Abs 4 DBA Schweiz 1992 lösen kann.'

[87] BFHE 157, 39.

[88] Agreement between the Federal Republic of Germany and the Swiss Confederation for the Avoidance of Double Taxation with Respect to Taxes on Income and on Capital (signed 11 August 1971, entered into force 29 December 1972) 2545 UNTS 207 (1971 German–Swiss DTA).

[89] BFH, Judgment of 10 January 2012, I R 36/11 <http://www.juris.de> [21].

[90] ibid.

[91] Especially the decisions by which the NATO member States adopted the New Strategic Concepts may be qualified as subsequent agreements, see eg Dietrich Murswiek, 'Die Fortentwicklung völkerrechtlicher Verträge: Verfassungsrechtliche Grenzen und Kontrolle im Organstreit' [2007] NVwZ 1130, 1133. The 1991 Strategic Concept was discussed in BVerfGE 90, 286 and the 1999 Strategic Concept in BVerfGE 104, 151.

informal amendments from interpretation.[92] This alternative approach differs from that preferred by the German Federal Fiscal Court in that it combines subjective with objective criteria. Thus, it leaves more room for subsequent agreements and subsequent practice alike.

In each of these decisions on the NATO Treaty, the claimants had challenged governmental action for violating Parliamentary rights under article 59(2) GG. In the claimants' view, the impugned acts and the respective NATO measures, in which the German government had participated in, did not merely interpret but in fact informally amended the NATO Treaty. Therefore, so the claimants' reasoning continued, the German government would have had to seek Parliamentary consent. The various proceedings that had been brought before the Court concerned, among others: the German government's assent to equipping US forces in Germany with nuclear equipped rockets (the so-called NATO double-track decision);[93] the participation of armed German forces in the deployment of an International Security Assistance Force (ISAF) in Afghanistan;[94] the German government's assent, within the respective NATO and Western European Union (WEU) bodies, to deploy German armed forces to participate in NATO and WEU missions monitoring embargoes and enforcing flight bans imposed by the UN on the former Federal Republic of Yugoslavia;[95] the deployment of German troops in NATO Airborne Early Warning and Control System (AWACS) aircraft to monitor airspace above Turkish territory;[96] and the German government's assent to NATO's New Strategic Concept in 1999.[97]

To fully comprehend the Court's alternative approach, it is important to briefly mention its view on the separation of powers in foreign affairs. As the Court pointed out in its judgment on the NATO double-track decision, article 59(2) GG requires Parliamentary assent to a treaty's conclusion but not, as a rule, to acts other than the conclusion of treaties irrespective of whether or not such other acts entailed legal obligations for Germany.[98] In its judgment on flight bans and embargoes, the Court further clarified that Parliamentary competences in foreign affairs were an exception to the principal competence that was assigned to the German executive.[99] Like the German Federal Fiscal Court, the German Federal Constitutional Court has acknowledged that the question if article 59(2) GG applied depended on whether the original treaty had been amended.

---

[92] For a critical analysis of this line of cases, see, among others, Hillgruber, 'Die Fortentwicklung völkerrechtlicher Verträge' (n 57); Murswiek, 'Die Fortentwicklung völkerrechtlicher Verträge' (n 91).

[93] BVerfGE 68, 1.

[94] BVerfGE 118, 244.

[95] BVerfGE 90, 286.

[96] BVerfGE 121, 135.

[97] BVerfGE 104, 151, 151.

[98] BVerfGE 68, 1, 88.

[99] BVerfGE 90, 286, 357 f.

Based on its view on the separation of powers in foreign affairs, and contrary to the objective approach adopted by the German Federal Fiscal Court—under which a construction amounted to an amendment once it exceeded a literal interpretation of the terms of the treaty—the German Federal Constitutional Court introduced the parties' intention to amend the treaty as the decisive criterion for distinguishing interpretation from amendment:[100]

> There may be nothing indicating the intention to conclude a treaty when the parties to an existing treaty find themselves in a process of reorientation, a process in which they merely adjust steps aiming at reforms and in which they declare their intentions to implement these reforms at successive conferences. In such situation, the parties will hardly be able to arrive at final conclusions which may take the form of a treaty but only to formulate planning guidelines for a certain development.[101]

Although the Court admitted that it may be difficult to identify the line between amendments and interpretation, it further added that it was immaterial whether an interpretation in effect constituted an amendment and even entailed new rights and duties for the parties as long as the parties did not mean to amend the treaty.[102]

While the distinction between amendment and interpretation remained central to the Court, it later introduced a two-pronged test to determine whether Parliamentary participation under article 59(2) GG was necessary. In addition to asking whether the original treaty had been amended (a question that mainly focused on the parties' intention), the Court further emphasised that governmental action to adapt a treaty to changing conditions must also not exceed the so-called 'integration programme' of the original domestic act of approval.[103] This vague concept is not mentioned in the Basic Law but has been introduced by the Court in its 1981 decision[104] on

[100] ibid 359 f. Critically Georg Nolte, 'Bundeswehreinsätze im kollektiven Sicherheitssystem—Zum Urteil des Bundesverfassungsgerichts vom 12. Juli 1994' (1994) 54 ZaöRV 652, 666 f. See also Rojahn, 'Artikel 59' (n 54) [48], [66], who emphasised that the distinction between interpretation and amendment should be based on objective criteria.

[101] BVerfGE 90, 286, 361 [translated by the author]. In German: 'An Anhaltspunkten für einen Vertragsabschlußwillen kann es etwa fehlen, wenn Partner eines bestehenden Vertrages sich in einem Prozeß der Neuorientierung befinden, in dem sie in aufeinanderfolgenden Konferenzen die jeweiligen Schritte einer Reformplanung abstimmen und auch ihre Bereitschaft zur Durchführung von Reformen bekunden. In einer solchen Situation werden regelmäßig noch keine endgültigen, zur Vertragsreife ausformulierten Lösungen gefunden, vielmehr nur Planungsrichtlinien und Entwicklungsvorhaben formuliert werden.' cf BVerfG, Decision of 15 December 2015, 2 BvL 1/12, [2016] NJW 1295, 1302 f, where the Court recognised that subsequent practice under art 31(3)(b) VCLT may amend the content or at least the interpretation of the treaty.

[102] BVerfGE 90, 286, 362 f. The importance of the parties' intention for distinguishing interpretation and amendment was subsequently reconfirmed in BVerfGE 104, 151, 201.

[103] BVerfGE 121, 135, 157–59.

[104] BVerfGE 58, 1, 37 f. Since this concept has first been introduced by the Court, it has been further elaborated on mainly in the context of European integration. See eg BVerfGE 75, 223, 240; 89, 155, 187 f; 123, 267, 347–52; 131, 152, 215–25; 132, 195, 243 f, 259.

the EUROCONTROL Convention.[105] According to the Court, a treaty aims at integration if it envisages a stable and ever closer co-operation among State parties in implementing the treaty.[106] Because integration is necessarily dynamic, the Court has emphasised that 'Parliament's legal and political responsibility is not limited to a single act of approval, but also extends to the further execution of the treaty.'[107]

The problem about this construction is that it deals with an anticipatory and hence somewhat fictitious kind of Parliamentary assent.[108] In spite of that, the Court has not overstretched its requirements as to which developments Parliament must have foreseen in order to be able to assent to them. According to the Court, government 'does not act beyond the framework of authorisation established by Parliament's Act of Assent … merely because individual provisions … are violated,' but only if it infringes essential structural decisions under the original treaty.[109] The question of whether essential structural decisions have been infringed is more objective than one aiming at the parties' intention. However, it also leaves much space for future developments through informal mechanisms.[110]

Unlike the predominantly textualist approach adopted by the German Federal Fiscal Court, such mixed approach concedes a greater role to subsequent agreements and subsequent practice. Yet, one may critically wonder whether this alternative approach does not perhaps go too far in that it seriously threatens Parliamentary participation rights. Pointing out that Parliament had some means at its disposal to control government,[111] the German Federal Constitutional Court itself admitted that these control mechanisms were hampered by the way in which informal developments of treaties took place, ie by coordinated decision-making in international forums.[112] More precisely, the Court acknowledged that '[t]here is a danger that conduct which is legally relevant but beyond formal amendments may lead to gradual changes of a treaty's content. This is especially true if the governments of

---

[105] EUROCONTROL International Convention relating to Cooperation for the Safety of Air Navigation (signed 13 December 1960, entered into force 1 March 1963) 523 UNTS 117 (EUROCONTROL Convention).

[106] BVerfGE 104, 151, 195.

[107] ibid 209 [translated by the author]. In German: 'Die rechtliche und politische Verantwortung des Parlaments erschöpft sich nicht in einem einmaligen Zustimmungsakt, sie erstreckt sich auch auf den weiteren Vertragsvollzug.'

[108] Critically Georg Nolte, 'Die "neuen Aufgaben" von NATO und WEU—Völker- und verfassungsrechtliche Fragen' (1994) 54 ZaöRV 95, esp 119 f.

[109] BVerfGE 104, 151, 210 [translated by the author]. In German: 'Die Bundesregierung handelt nicht schon dann außerhalb des vom Zustimmungsgesetz … gezogenen Ermächtigungsrahmens, wenn gegen einzelne Bestimmungen des … Vertrags verstoßen wird.'

[110] See Johannes Rux, 'Das neue "NATO-Konzept"—Anmerkung zum Urteil des BVerfG vom 22.11.2001—2 BvE 6/99' [2002] JA 461, 463 f, who suspects that the Court's decision to preserve the German government's wide room for manoeuvre in foreign affairs was to some extent a reaction to the terrorist attacks of 11 September 2001.

[111] BVerfGE 121, 135, 159.

[112] ibid.

the contracting parties confess to a particular understanding of the treaty.'[113] Judges Limbach, Böckenförde, Kruis, and Sommer, who disagreed with the majority of the Court in its judgment on flight bans and embargoes in that they found article 59(2) GG to be violated, more harshly criticised the Court's mixed subjective approach.[114] In their view, it was dangerous to let Parliamentary participation rights be excluded by deliberately opting for a gradual development which could not be clearly characterised as amendment or conclusion of a new treaty.[115] Quoting Georg Ress, they warned in vivid terms that such informal adaptions in effect 'set the treaties on wheels'.[116]

6.3.1.3 Parliamentary Participation and Subsequent Practice in Other States

Domestic courts in other States do not seem to have addressed constitutional concerns relating to subsequent agreements.[117] Yet, a few of them, such as the House of Lords and the High Court of Australia, were concerned about engaging in judicial activism and eroding Parliamentary rights by relying on subsequent practice.

In the House of Lords case *James Buchanan & Co Ltd v Babco Forwarding and Shipping (UK) Ltd*, for instance, Lord Dilhorne refused to engage in what he considered as filling lacunae in the CMR based on the parties' subsequent practice thereto. At issue was whether excise duties were covered by article 23(4) CMR. This provision stipulated that the carriage charges, customs duties, and other charges incurred in respect of the carriage of the goods shall be refunded in full in case of total loss, but no further damages shall be payable.[118] To explain why he did not mean to rely on certain foreign court decisions to interpret this provision, Lord Dilhorne pointed

[113] BVerfGE 104, 151, 208 [translated by the author]. In German: 'Es besteht zwar die Gefahr, dass durch rechtserhebliches Handeln unterhalb der förmlichen Vertragsänderung eine allmähliche Inhaltsveränderung des Vertrags eintritt … Das gilt insbesondere, wenn sich die Exekutivspitzen der Mitgliedstaaten in einer wichtigen Frage zu einem bestimmten Vertragsverständnis bekennen.'

[114] BVerfGE 90, 286, 372–78.

[115] ibid 376 f.

[116] ibid 273 f, quoting Georg Ress, 'Verfassungsrechtliche Auswirkungen der Fortentwicklung völkerrechtlicher Verträge—Überlegungen zum Verhältnis des Grundgesetzes zur Europäischen Wirtschaftsgemeinschaft und zur Europäischen Menschenrechtskonvention' in Walther Fürst, Roman Herzog, and Dieter Umbach (eds), *Festschrift für Wolfgang Zeidler* (de Gruyter 1987) 1179 [translated by the author]. In German: '… der Vertrag damit gleichsam auf Räder gesetzt werde.'

[117] An exception is a judgment on the 1996 US–Swiss DTA, in which the Swiss Federal Administrative Court emphasised that interpretative subsequent agreements may neither supplement nor amend the 'mother agreement', see BVGer, Judgment of 21 January 2010, BVGE 2010/7, 102.

[118] *James Buchanan & Co Ltd v Babco Forwarding and Shipping (UK) Ltd* [1978] AC 141 (HL) 151 (Lord Wilberforce).

out that he was 'reluctant to conclude that there was any gap in the Convention to the drawing up of which no less than 30 countries were parties',[119] adding that '[t]he courts have rightly refused to encroach on the province of Parliament and have refused to engage in legislation'.[120]

These dicta are instructive in that they apparently explain why the House of Lords should be reluctant to rely on subsequent practice or subsequent agreements when interpreting general and vague treaty provisions. To take effect in the British legal system, treaties traditionally required an Act of Parliament.[121] Once Parliament had incorporated a treaty into the British legal system, British courts would, as a rule, only apply and interpret the respective statute and not the treaty itself.[122] Therefore, any subsequent agreement or subsequent practice could potentially encroach upon Parliamentary sovereignty if going beyond the content which Parliament once enacted. As Dicey famously explained, the doctrine of Parliamentary sovereignty means that Parliament 'has ... the right to make or unmake any law whatever; and, further, that no person or body is recognised by the law of England as having a right to override or set aside the legislation of Parliament.'[123] In consequence, British courts must be careful, like their German counterparts, not to rely on a certain practice or agreement that does not merely interpret but in fact amend the treaty.

What is interesting about this line of reasoning is that it only works under softened variants of dualism like the modern British approach to international law. Under the traditional, strictly dualist approach, there would have been no reason for British courts to apply international law rules of the interpretation of treaties in the first place.[124] Traditionally, they would have never referred to a treaty directly but only taken the 'indirect

[119] ibid 156 (Lord Dilhorne).

[120] ibid.

[121] Eg *The Parlement Belge* (1879) 4 PD 129 154 f; *Attorney General for Canada v Attorney General for Ontario* [1937] AC 326 (PC) 347 (Lord Atkin); *Hoani Te Heuheu Tukino v Aotea District Maori Land Board* [1941] UKPC 6, [1941] AC 308, 324; *Thomas v Baptiste* [1999] UKPC 13, [2000] 2 AC 1 [26] (Lord Millett); cf *Malone v Metropolitan Police Commissioner* [1979] ch 344; Kenneth Keith, 'Treaties and Legislation—Based on *Corocraft Ltd v Pan American Airways Inc*' [1970] ICLQ 127, 129. See also Francis Mann, 'The Enforcement of Treaties by English Courts' (1958) 44 Transactions of the Grotius Society 29, 30; Ian Sinclair, 'The Principles of Treaty Interpretation and their Application by the English Courts' (1963) 12 ICLQ 508, 525.

[122] Christoph Schreuer, 'The Interpretation of Treaties by Domestic Courts' (1971) 45 BYIL 255, 257; Shaheed Fatima, 'Using International Law in Domestic Courts—Part I: Domesticated Treaties' (2003) 8 JR 81, 86.

[123] Albert Dicey, *Introduction to the Study of the Law of the Constitution* (8th edn, Macmillan 1915) 38.

[124] Eg *Barras v Aberdeen Steam Trawling & Fishing Co* [1933] UKHL 3, [1933] AC 402; *British Airways Board v Laker Airways Ltd* [1984] UKHL 7, [1985] AC 58; *JH Rayner (Minsinc Lane) Ltd v Department of Trade and Industry* [1990] 2 AC 418 (HL). See also Schreuer, 'Wechselwirkungen zwischen Völkerrecht und Verfassung' (n 55) 67 f. See generally Francis Mann, 'The Interpretation of Uniform Statutes' (1946) 62 LQR 278.

route' via domestic legislation, which would then have to be interpreted according to domestic rules for construction.[125] Today, however, British courts often apply treaties directly and use international rules of treaty interpretation.[126] Thus, they show tendencies of watering down Britain's dualist tradition. From the perspective of international law, this may be a positive development because, by each applying the same rules of treaty interpretation, domestic courts to some extent contribute to ensuring uniform interpretation of that treaty. For domestic courts like the British ones, however, this development entails formerly unknown challenges in terms of safeguarding parliamentary sovereignty, which were considerably less acute in the past.

Another example of a softened dualist approach to international law is Australia. The approach of Australian courts towards treaty law has succinctly been described by Mason CJ and Deane J in *Minister of State for Immigration and Ethnic Affairs v Teoh:*

> [T]he provisions of an international treaty to which Australia is a party do not form part of Australian law unless those provisions have been validly incorporated in our municipal system by statute. This principle has the foundation in our constitutional system that the making and ratification of treaties falls within the province of the Executive in the exercise of its prerogative power whereas the making and alteration of the law fall within the province of Parliament and not the Executive….
>
> But the fact that the Convention has not been incorporated into Australian law does not mean that its ratification holds no significance for Australian law. Where a statute or subordinate legislation is ambiguous, the courts should favour that construction which accords with Australia's obligations under a treaty or international convention to which Australia is a party, at least in those cases in which the legislation is enacted after, or in contemplation of, entry into, or ratification of, the relevant international instrument. That is because Parliament, prima facie, intends to give effect to Australia's obligations under international law.[127]

Corresponding to this softened variant of dualism, Australian courts have often relied on the Vienna rules in general and subsequent conduct in particular to interpret treaties to cast light on the meaning of domestic legislation. Nonetheless, they have been mindful not to circumvent Parliamentary rights by interpreting treaty provisions in a way that had not been envisaged by Parliament when implementing the treaty into domestic law. Like the House of Lords, the High Court of Australia

[125] Schreuer, 'Wechselwirkungen zwischen Völkerrecht und Verfassung' (n 55) 68.

[126] Eg *Kramer v Attorney General* [1923] AC 528 (HL); *Philippson v Imperial Airways Ltd* [1939] AC 332 (HL); *Salomon v Customs and Excise Commissioners* [1967] 2 QB 116; *Owners of Cargo Lately Laden on Board the MV Erkowit v Owners of the Eschersheim (The Eschersheim, the Jade and the Erkowit)* [1976] 1 WLR 430 (HL); *Buchanan* (n 118); *Rio Tinto Zinc Corp v Westinghouse Electric Corp (Nos 1 and 2)* [1978] AC 547 (HL); *Quazi v Quazi* [1980] AC 744 (HL); *Fothergill v Monarch Airlines Ltd* [1980] UKHL 6, [1981] AC 251. See also Schreuer, 'Wechselwirkungen zwischen Völkerrecht und Verfassung' (n 55) 68; id, 'The Interpretation of Treaties by Domestic Courts' (n 122) 257 f. For a general overview of how British courts still waver between applying and not applying international rules of interpretation, see Richard Gardiner, 'Treaty Interpretation in the English Courts Since *Fothergill v Monarch Airlines* (1980)' (1995) 44 ICLQ 920.

[127] *Minister of State for Immigration and Ethnic Affairs v Teoh* [1995] HCA 20, (1995) 183 CLR 273 [25], [26] (Mason CJ and Deane J) [fn omitted].

therefore emphasised in *Maloney v The Queen* that subsequent conduct which in effect altered a treaty's text could not be taken into account by Australian courts:

> The application in a court of criteria derived from an international instrument may require consideration by the court of whether it is constitutionally competent to apply the criteria and, if so, to what extent. Obligations imposed by international instruments on States do not necessarily take account of the division of functions between their branches of government. The difficulty is compounded when the interpretation of the international instrument is said to have been subject to change by reference to practices occurring since the enactment of legislative provisions implementing it into domestic law. Such practices may, by operation of Art 31(3) of the Vienna Convention, be taken into account in interpretation of the treaty or convention for the purposes of international law. They may lead to its informal modification. However, they cannot be invoked, in this country, so as to authorise a court to alter the meaning of a domestic law implementing a provision of a treaty or convention.[128]

6.3.2 Legal Advantages over Other Means of Interpretation

Having depicting the reputed negative effects of subsequent agreements, one may wonder whether this means of interpretation also entails legal advantages over other means. Some of these advantages were alluded to in a judgment on the 1925 German–Italian DTA.[129] In this decision, the German Federal Fiscal Court explained that it was not for the judiciary to fill lacunae in a treaty but for the contracting parties themselves by way of reaching, for example, subsequent agreements within the meaning of article 31(3)(a) VCLT.[130] This statement contrasts subsequent agreements with unilateral judicial constructions that are based on other means of interpretation. However, it is difficult to understand what exactly the Court meant to say.

One possible reading of the Court's dictum relates to the division of competences between the contracting parties at the international level on the one hand and domestic courts at the national level on the other. Understood this way, the Court's dictum would recall that, unlike most other means of interpretation, subsequent agreements are closely linked to the idea of the contracting parties as the true masters of the treaty. Under the Vienna rules, however, this reading does not fully make sense.

---

[128] *Maloney v The Queen* [2013] HCA 28, (2013) 298 ALR 308 [15] (French J) [fn omitted]. See also *Minister for Home Affairs of the Commonwealth v Zentai* [2012] HCA 28, (2012) 289 ALR 644 [35]–[36] (French J); *Commonwealth Minister for Justice v Adamas* [2013] HCA 59, (2013) 304 ALR 305 [31] (French CJ, Hayne, Crennan, Kiefel, Bell, Gageler, and Keane JJ).

[129] Convention for the Avoidance of Double Taxation and the Settlement of Other Questions Connected with Direct Taxes (Germany–Italy) (signed 31 October 1925, entered into force 1 January 1926) 53 LNTS 245 (1925 German–Italian DTA).

[130] BFHE 155, 374, 378 f.

This is because the Court only juxtaposed interpretations supported by subsequent agreements to other, so to speak unilateral judicial interpretations. It is certainly true that an individual court is better insulated against accusations of judicial activism if it invokes agreements reached between all parties.

But apart from conferring on interpretations the *impression* of greater legitimacy, the effects of subsequent agreements do not exceed those which an individual court can achieve by relying on any other means of interpretation.[131] So it is difficult to see how courts may, under the Vienna rules, rely on subsequent agreements to support interpretations which they did not consider themselves competent to arrive at by relying on other means of interpretation. As regards the division of competences between the contracting parties at the international and domestic courts at the national level, subsequent agreements therefore do not—in the abstract—possess any legal advantages over other means of interpretation. From that perspective, the Court's dictum exhausts itself in presenting subsequent agreements as a protection against unilateral judicial activism that risks transgressing the meaning of the terms of the treaty as agreed on by its parties.

Another possible reading of the Court's dictum relates to the principle of separation of powers at the national level. To start with, it is expedient to recall that subsequent agreements are mostly the product of executive action.[132] Looking at the division of competences between the various State actors in treaty-related matters, one may at first sight conclude that interpretations supported by subsequent agreements positively strengthen the principle of separation of powers between executive

[131] The same applies to interpretations adopted by executive or legislative bodies. Interpretations which these bodies may adopt by taking account of subsequent agreements within the meaning of art 31(3)(a) VCLT in no way differ from interpretations adopted by relying on other means of interpretation.

[132] See Ingrid Wuerth, 'Treaty Interpretation, Subsequent Agreements and Practice, and Domestic Constitutions' in Georg Nolte (ed), *Treaties and Subsequent Practice* (OUP 2013) 158.

[133] In the UK and Belgium, treaty-making powers are part of the Royal prerogative, see Rosalyn Higgins, 'United Kingdom' in Francis Jacobs and Shelley Roberts (eds), *The Effect of Treaties in Domestic Law* (Sweet & Maxwell 1987) 123; Ian Sinclair and Susan Dickson, 'Chapter 6—National Treaty Law and Practice: United Kingdom' (1995) 27 Stud Transnat'l Legal Pol'y 223, 223; Arnold McNair, *The Law of Treaties* (repr, Clarendon Press 2003) 68; Marc Maresceau, 'Belgium' in Francis Jacobs and Shelley Roberts (eds), *The Effect of Treaties in Domestic Law* (Sweet & Maxwell 1987) 2. Similarly, treaty-making is essentially an executive function in Australia, Austria, Canada, India, and the USA, too, see David Sloss, 'Treaty Enforcement in Domestic Courts—A Comparative Analysis' in id (ed), *The Role of Domestic Courts in Treaty Enforcement—A Comparative Study* (CUP 2009) 17; Ignaz Seidl-Hohenveldern, 'Relation of International Law to Internal Law in Austria ' (1955) 49 AJIL 451, 456 f; Gibran van Ert, 'Dubious Dualism: The Reception of International Law in Canada' (2010) 44 Val UL Rev 927, 927 f; Kuljit Thakore, 'Chapter 3—National Treaty Law and Practice: India' (1995) 27 Stud Transnat'l Legal Pol'y 79, 82 f; David Bederman, 'Revivalist Canons and Treaty Interpretation' (1993) 41 UCLA L Rev 953, 957, and US Const art II(2). In Switzerland, some treaties are subject to the approval of the Federal Assembly;

and judiciary. This is because treaty-making powers are regularly vested in the executive branch of the State.[133] In Germany, for example, article 59(1) of the Basic Law provides that treaties concluded for the Federal State are concluded by the Federal President *(Bundespräsident);* in practice, however, most treaties are concluded by the Federal Government or individual Federal Ministers.[134] Although the German legislature is sometimes vested with participation rights (which may well have some de facto influence), these participation rights do not extend to legally influencing the content of the future treaty.[135] The judicial branch of the State, in contrast, possesses no competences in treaty-related matters at all. By basing their interpretations on subsequent agreements between the parties, courts therefore only help to enforce the intention of the parties instead of independently determining the meaning of the terms of the treaty, so it appears.

But this line of reasoning forgets that the competences for making a treaty are not identical with those for interpreting it. Treaty-making powers are vested in very few actors. The power to interpret treaties, in contrast, is evenly vested in numerous actors. To maintain that interpretations supported by subsequent agreements are nevertheless beneficial to the principle of separation of powers, it is therefore necessary to resort to the following *a fortiori* argument: Because it is the executive that holds treaty-making powers, it is all the more competent to interpret treaties by way of subsequent agreements. This reasoning has an appealing logic. Nonetheless, it is not compelling but merely the result of a stylistic device. For this reason, the question between which actors a subsequent agreement has been reached should not influence an intepreter's decision whether or not such an agreement should be taken into account. In sum, one must therefore conclude that subsequent agreements do not possess any legal advantages over other means of interpretation.

---

apart from that, however, treaty-making powers are vested in the Federal Council, see Luzius Wildhaber, 'Parliamentary Participation in Treaty-Making, Report on Swiss Law' (1991) 67 Chi-Kent L Rev 437, 440 f.

[134] The Federal Government consists of the Federal Chancellor *(Bundeskanzler)* and the Federal Ministers, see art 62 GG. Whether this practice is compatible with the Basic Law is a question of controversy, see eg Streinz, 'Artikel 59' (n 52) [10]–[12]. Under art 32(3) GG, the *Länder* may conclude treaties in their own name insofar as they have the power to legislate; yet, such treaties must be approved by the Federal State. Within the *Länder*, the treaty-making powers also lie with the executive branches, see eg art 57 of the North Rhine-Westphalian Constitution, arts 47(3), 72(2) of the Bavarian Constitution, art 50 of the Constitution of Baden-Wuerttemberg, art 35 of the Constitution of Lower Saxony, and art 103 of the Hessian Constitution. For a general overview of competences and procedures in treaty-related matters under the German Basic Law, see Hans Treviranus and Hubert Beemelmans, 'Chapter 2—National Treaty Law and Practice: Federal Republic of Germany' (1995) 27 Stud Transnat'l Legal Pol'y 43.

[135] Hillgruber, 'Die Fortentwicklung völkerrechtlicher Verträge' (n 57) 65; Christian Calliess, 'Auswärtige Gewalt, § 83' in Peter Axer, Josef Isensee, and Paul Kirchhof (eds), *Aufgaben des Staates* (3rd edn, CF Müller 2006) 605. See also § 82(2) of the Rules of Procedure of the German Bundestag, which provides that the Bundestag cannot introduce amendments relating to treaties falling under art 59(2) GG.

6.4 Conclusion

Chapter 6 followed up on the observation that domestic courts only rarely based their interpretations on subsequent agreements. Without pretending to exhaustively explain why that has been the cases, it nevertheless closes with three interrelated propositions.

First of all, the jurisprudence of domestic courts suggests that the number of parties to a treaty is diametrically opposed to the numerical relevance of subsequent agreements. In other words, the more parties a treaty has, the more unlikely it is that domestic courts interpret the treaty by relying on subsequent agreements. Notwithstanding the fact that several multilateral instruments provide for institutional frameworks within which subsequent agreements may be reached, domestic courts rarely discussed subsequent agreements regarding the interpretation of multilateral agreements. Subsequent agreements to bilateral agreements, and especially DTAs, in contrast, have played a more important role in the jurisprudence of domestic courts.

This may be partly due to the fact that domestic courts generally insisted on solid evidence to establish the existence of such agreements. In other words, domestic courts have only taken note of those agreements that were laid down in writing or were otherwise reliably documented. Corresponding to that, they have been less inclined to take subsequent agreements into account where it was doubtful whether the respective agreement had really been reached. If one assumes that it is easier to reliably document agreements between only few parties, it is probably not surprising that domestic courts only rarely discussed subsequent agreements regarding the interpretation of multilateral agreements.

Furthermore, the jurisprudence of domestic courts depicts subsequent agreements as two-edged swords. On the one hand, subsequent agreements were sometimes regarded as counteracting undue unilateral judicial activism by linking interpretation to the agreement of all parties. In this connection, subsequent agreements were referred back to the general idea of the parties as the true masters of the treaty, thus creating the impression that interpretations supported by subsequent agreements carried more legitimacy than interpretations arrived at by relying on other means. Yet, it is important to emphasise that these apparent advantages are largely based on rhetoric. On the other hand, it is often difficult to distinguish interpretative agreements from those constituting informal amendments of the treaty. Therefore, domestic courts were divided on whether subsequent agreements should be perceived as a threat to parliamentary participation rights and therefore not be taken into account.

The jurisprudence of the German Federal Fiscal Court on the one hand and the German Federal Constitutional Court on the other exemplify two alternative approaches to this difficult distinction. The German Federal Fiscal Court tended to distinguish interpretations from informal amendments based on an objective approach. Under this objective approach, a construction amounts to an amendment once it exceeds a literal interpretation of the terms of the treaty. The German

Federal Constitutional Court, in contrast, utilised a mixed approach. This mixed approach focuses on the intentions of the parties but also asks whether a particular development exceeds the 'integration programme' of the original domestic act of approval. However, none of these approaches appears truly satisfactory. The objective approach deprives subsequent agreements of most of their relevance by subordinating them to any literal interpretation of the terms of a treaty. The mixed approach, in contrast, fails to ensure that Parliamentary participation rights are not circumvented by amendments disguised as interpretations.

It merits attention that domestic courts across various jurisdictions have been less reluctant to rely on subsequent practice although the same challenge of distinguishing interpretations from amendments arises here. Only few courts, like the House of Lords and the High Court of Australia, refused to rely on subsequent practice when they were concerned that the resultant interpretation would go beyond legislation that had been enacted by parliament to give effect to the treaty. In the end, the difficult distinction between interpretations and amendments is not even peculiar to subsequent agreements and subsequent practice but may arise in respect to any other means of interpretation as well. What distinguishes subsequent agreements and subsequent practice from other means of interpretation is the fact that they involve other actors, namely the contracting parties as whole and those individual actors who generate practice or reach agreements. Subsequent agreements and subsequent practice are attractive options for these other actors to deliberately adapt a treaty to changing conditions and to informally amend it instead of pursuing more complicated, formal amendment mechanisms. For this reason, some courts seem to be more critical of subsequent agreements and subsequent practice than of other means of interpretation. This aspect may further help to explain the discrepancy between subsequent agreements and subsequent practice because the former often take a form that more closely resembles genuine amendments than the latter; and whereas subsequent practice frequently comprises judicial conduct, subsequent agreements are more often reached between other actors than national judiciaries or legislatures, namely national executives.[136]

To some extent, the snake therefore bites its own tail. On the one hand, domestic courts seem to prefer agreements of a more formalised nature. On the other, such formalised agreements more easily raise suspicions of being meant to evade formal amendment mechanisms. In the end, the way in which domestic courts approach subsequent agreements and subsequent practice also reveals how they understand their own role when delivering decisions that raise issues of treaty interpretation. This can be seen if one compares the jurisprudence of the German Federal Fiscal Court, the House of Lords, and the High Court of Australia to that of the German Federal Constitutional Court. The latter adopted a more distant perspective in that

[136] See already Wuerth, 'Treaty Interpretation' (n 132) 158, who assumed—without substantiating this assumption—that subsequent agreements might raise more constitutional concerns because 'the role of the executive branches is likely to be much stronger in the art 31(3)(a) context.'

it merely balanced legislative and executive competences in foreign affairs. The former courts, in contrast, seemed to be more sensitive towards their own competences and responsibilities as regards treaty interpretation. In consequence, they recognised that they would themselves exceed their competences and interfere with legislative competences if they relied on practice or agreements that in effect informally amended the treaty; or, in other words, they sought not to increase interpretative powers of national executives in relation to legislatures and judiciaries.

Chapter 7
Practice by Non-Party Entities

Chapter 7 examines whether and in which way practice that is not attributable to a State party can be relevant under article 31(3)(b) VCLT. On its face, article 31(3)(b) VCLT does not distinguish between practice that is attributable to and practice that is not attributable to a State party (in short: 'practice by non-party entities' or 'non-party practice'). Nonetheless, this distinction has given rise to some debate.[1]

The ILC and many commentators have argued that the term 'practice' under article 31(3)(b) VCLT does *not* cover non-party practice.[2] The proponents of this view do not need to discuss whether non-party practice is capable of satisfying the other requirements under article 31(3)(b) VCLT. If one did not share this view and maintained that such restrictive interpretation was neither necessary nor legally convincing, one could not, however, avoid asking whether non-party entities can 'apply' a treaty and, in particular, whether their practice may establish the agreement of the parties regarding the interpretation of the treaty.

Because it is more difficult to establish this agreement in the case of non-party practice than in the case of practice attributable to a State party, the restrictive and the extensive interpretation of the term 'practice' often lead to the same result in the end, namely the exclusion of non-party practice. If a given non-party practice does not satisfy *all* requirements of article 31(3)(b) VCLT, it does not constitute a

[1] See 4.3.1.2.

[2] See in particular draft conclusion 5(1) and the accompanying commentary in ILC, 'Report of the International Law Commission on the Work of its 65th Session' (6 May–7 June and 8 July–9 August 2013) UN Doc A/68/10, 41 f. See also Mark Villiger, *Commentary on the 1969 Vienna Convention on the Law of Treaties* (Martinus Nijhoff 2009) 431 [22]; Richard Gardiner, *Treaty Interpretation* (2nd edn, OUP 2015) 266 f; Oliver Dörr, 'Article 31—General Rule of Interpretation' in Oliver Dörr and Kirsten Schmalenbach (eds), *Vienna Convention on the Law of Treaties—A Commentary* (Springer 2012) 557 [82].

K. Berner, *Subsequent Agreements and Subsequent Practice in Domestic Courts*, Beiträge zum ausländischen öffentlichen Recht und Völkerrecht,
https://doi.org/10.1007/978-3-662-54937-7_7

primary means of interpretation unless it falls under another element of the general rule. But in this case, the proponents of a restrictive interpretation as well as those of an extensive interpretation still need to ask whether this non-party practice may become indirectly relevant under article 31(3)(b) VCLT by reflecting or inducing relevant practice of a State party.

Against this background, Chap. 7 takes a step back from the controversy about the term 'practice'. It more generally asks how domestic courts have dealt with non-party practice to understand whether and in which way such practice can be directly or indirectly relevant under article 31(3)(b) VCLT. For that purpose, it concentrates on three distinct kinds of non-party practice, namely the output of treaty bodies (7.1), publications issued by the UNHCR (7.2), and the Model Convention on Income and Capital and related documents published by the OECD (7.3). Unlike practice by private individuals and private legal entities ('non-State practice'), which has played no role at all in the jurisprudence of domestic courts, these kinds of non-party practice have been frequently mentioned in domestic court decisions.

7.1 The Output of Treaty Bodies

Various treaty regimes, especially in the field of human rights, not only create rights and obligations for their parties. In addition, they also establish a 'treaty body', ie a committee of independent experts, to monitor the treaty's implementation.[3] Examples of human rights treaty bodies include:

- the Committee on the Elimination of Discrimination against Women (CEDAW Committee),[4]
- the Human Rights Committee (HRC),[5]
- the Committee on Economic, Social and Cultural Rights (ICESCR Committee),[6]

---

[3] See Georg Nolte, 'Report 3—Subsequent Agreements and Subsequent Practice of States outside of Judicial or Quasi-Judicial Proceedings' in id (ed), *Treaties and Subsequent Practice* (OUP 2013) 378 f. For a general overview, see also Geir Ulfstein, 'Treaty Bodies and Regimes' in Duncan Hollis (ed), *The Oxford Guide to Treaties* (OUP 2012).

[4] The CEDAW Committee monitors the implementation of the Convention on the Elimination of All Forms of Discrimination against Women (signed 18 December 1979, entered into force 3 September 1981) 1249 UNTS 13 (CEDAW) and the Optional Protocol to the Convention on the Elimination of All Forms of Discrimination against Women (signed 6 October 1999, entered into force 22 December 2000) 2131 UNTS 83 (CEDAW-OP). It has been established under art 17 CEDAW.

[5] The HRC monitors the implementation of the International Covenant on Civil and Political Rights (signed 16 December 1966, entered into force 23 March 1976) 999 UNTS 171 (ICCPR) and its optional protocols. It has been established under art 28 ICCPR.

[6] The ICESCR Committee monitors the implementation of the International Covenant on Economic, Social and Cultural Rights (signed 16 December 1966, entered into force 3 January 1976) 993 UNTS 3 (ICESCR). It has been established under ECOSOC Res 1985/17 (28 May

- the Committee against Torture (CAT Committee),[7]
- and the Committee on the Rights of the Child (CRC Committee).[8]

As one commentator explained, '[e]xpertise, impartiality, and independence of its members, which act in their personal capacity, are key for the functions of the bodies.'[9] Although each party to the respective treaty can normally nominate one or more candidates,[10] the elected members neither represent a particular State nor do they act for a higher institution.[11] This distinguishes treaty bodies both from COPs and from IOs and their organs.[12] Because their monitoring work inevitably goes hand in hand with interpreting the respective treaty,[13] the output of treaty bodies provides practical guidance to other actors such as domestic courts. But notwithstanding their practical relevance, the question arises on which legal basis domestic

1985) UN Doc E/RES/1985/17. Although it has not been established under the Covenant itself, it is generally regarded as a treaty body, too. See eg International Human Rights Instruments, 'Report on the Working Methods of the Human Rights Treaty Bodies relating to the State Party Reporting Process' (25 May 2005) UN Doc HRI/MC/2005/4, [4].

[7] The CAT Committee monitors the implementation of the Convention against Torture and Other Cruel, Inhuman or Degrading Treatment (signed 10 December 1984, entered into force 26 June 1987) 1465 UNTS 85 (CAT). It has been established under art 17 CAT.

[8] The CRC Committee monitors the implementation of the Convention on the Rights of the Child (signed 20 November 1989, entered into force 2 September 1990) 1577 UNTS 3 (CRC) and its optional protocols. It has been established under art 43 CRC.

[9] Peter-Tobias Stoll, 'Human Rights, Treaty Bodies' in Rüdiger Wolfrum (ed), *The Max Planck Encyclopedia of Public International Law* (OUP 2012) [1].

[10] Eg art 17(2) CAT; art 17(2) CEDAW; art 43(3) CRC; art 29(2) ICCPR; ECOSOC Res 1985/17 (28 May 1985) UN Doc E/RES/1985/17 at (c).

[11] See in particular International Human Rights Instruments, 'Guidelines on the Independence and Impartiality of Members of the Human Rights Treaty Bodies (Addis Ababa Guidelines)' (2012) UN Doc HRI/MC/2012. See further art 17(1) CAT; art 17(1) CEDAW; art 43(2) CRC; art 28(3) ICCPR; ECOSOC Res 1985/17 (28 May 1985) UN Doc E/RES/1985/17 at (b). See also rules 14–15 of the CAT Committee, 'Rules of Procedure of the Committee against Torture' (13 August 2013) UN Doc CAT/C/3/Rev.6 (CAT Committee Rules of Procedure); rule 15 of the CEDAW Committee, 'Rules of Procedure of the Committee on the Elimination of Discrimination against Women' (28 May 2008) UN Doc HRI/GEN/3/Rev.3 (CEDAW Committee Rules of Procedure); rules 11–11bis of the CRC Committee, 'Rules of Procedure of the Committee on the Rights of the Child' (16 April 2013) UN Doc CRC/C/4/Rev.3 (CRC Committee Rules of Procedure); rule 16 HRC, 'Rules of Procedure of the Human Rights Committee' (11 January 2012) UN Doc CCPR/C/3/Rev.10 (HRC Rules of Procedure).

[12] For more details on this distinction, see Nolte, 'Report 3—Practice outside of Judicial Proceedings' (n 3) 364 f, 379.

[13] Committee on Human Rights Law and Practice, 'Final Report on the Impact of Findings of the United Nations Human Rights Treaty Bodies' (2004) 71 Int'l L Ass'n Rep Conf 621, 627.

courts can actually take this output into account. In particular, one may wonder whether recourse may be had to this output under article 31(3)(b) VCLT.[14]

To answer this question, this subchapter briefly circumscribes the different types of treaty body output as well as the debate about their interpretative value (7.1.1). Next, it more closely examines how domestic courts have actually used treaty body output. In doing so, it focuses in particular on those decisions that help to cast a light on the legal status of this output (7.1.2). Based on this examination, this subchapter concludes by critically evaluating whether the jurisprudence of domestic courts supports the proposition that treaty body output is covered by article 31(3)(b) VCLT (7.1.3).

7.1.1 The Interpretative Value of Treaty Body Output

Treaty bodies monitor the implementation of 'their' treaty through different procedures. The monitoring procedures, which treaty bodies typically have at their disposal, are State reporting procedures, complaints procedures, and procedures for adopting general comments.[15] Each of these procedures generates a different type of output. What these types of output have in common is that they are legally non-binding,[16] that they process and provoke practice from contracting parties and non-parties alike,[17] and that their interpretative value is highly controversial.

[14] For the arguments that have been advanced to justify the relevance of treaty body output under art 31(3)(b) VCLT, see below at 205 f. As regards the status of treaty body output under *national* law, see Rosanne van Alebeek and André Nollkaemper, 'The Legal Status of Decisions by Human Rights Treaty Bodies in National Law' in Helen Keller and Geir Ulfstein (eds), *UN Human Rights Treaty Bodies—Law and Legitimacy* (CUP 2012) 356 f.

[15] Eg Kerstin Mechlem, 'Treaty Bodies and the Interpretation of Human Rights' (2009) 42 Vand J Transnat'l L 905, 922. In addition, some treaty bodies may also conduct independent inquiries if they have received information about serious, grave or systematic violations of the treaty by a State party. See eg art 20 CAT; art 8 CEDAW-OP; art 11 of the Optional Protocol to the International Covenant on Economic, Social and Cultural Rights (signed 5 May 2013, entered into force 10 December 2008) UN Doc A/63/435 (ICESCR-OP); art 13 of the Optional Protocol to the Convention on the Rights of the Child on a Communications Procedure (signed 19 December 2011, entered into force 14 April 2014) UN Doc A/RES/66/138 (CRC-OP 3).

[16] Committee on Human Rights Law and Practice, 'Final Report' (n 13) 626. See also Michael O'Flaherty, 'The Concluding Observations of United Nations Human Rights Treaty Bodies' (2006) 6 Hum Rts L Rev 27, 33 f; Dinah Shelton, 'The Legal Status of Normative Pronouncements of Human Rights Treaty Bodies' in Holger Hestermeyer (ed), *Coexistence, Cooperation and Solidarity—Liber Amicorum Rüdiger Wolfrum* (Martinus Nijhoff 2012) 559.

[17] Eg art 45(a) CRC; rules 63, 69 CAT Committee Rules of Procedure; rules 45–47 CEDAW Committee Rules of Procedure; rules 68–69 of the CESCR, 'Rules of Procedure of the Committee on Economic, Social and Cultural Rights' (1 September 1993) UN Doc E/C.12/1990/4/Rev.1 (CESCR Rules of Procedures); rules 67(2), 71(2) HRC Rules of Procedure.

Under the reporting procedures, States are required to submit initial and periodic reports on how they have implemented the treaty.[18] After considering these reports, treaty bodies normally formulate concluding observations. These concluding observations are designed to advise the reporting State on how to improve the treaty's implementation.[19] Treaty bodies do not adopt these observations on the basis of the State report only. Instead, they may also take into account additional information from the reporting State, from other UN entities, and sometimes even from NGOs.[20] Moreover, treaty bodies normally examine State reports together with government representatives. Thus, the reporting procedure is not adversarial in nature but rather invites State parties and other actors to engage in a 'constructive dialogue'.[21] Nevertheless, the concluding observations of treaty bodies have also attracted criticism. Some commentators deplored that they were not always of a high quality,[22] that there was 'only a very inexact correlation between concluding observations and the actual dialogue and exchanges with the State party',[23] and that several treaty bodies expressed concerns and made recommendations 'regarding matters which clearly cannot be considered treaty obligations'.[24]

Under individual complaints procedures, treaty bodies may formulate their 'views' on complaints from individuals who claim to be victims of a violation by

[18] Eg art 19(3) CAT; art 18 CEDAW; arts 44, 45(d) CRC; art 40 ICCPR; art 16 ICESCR. See further eg rule 71 CAT Committee Rules of Procedure; rules 52–53 CEDAW Committee Rules of Procedure; rule 75 CRC Committee Rules of Procedure; rule 71(3) HRC Rules of Procedure; rules 58, 64 CESCR Rules of Procedures. On the development of concluding observations, see generally O'Flaherty, 'Concluding Observations' (n 16).

[19] ibid 33.

[20] See generally International Human Rights Instruments, 'Report on the Working Methods of the Human Rights Treaty Bodies relating to the State Party Reporting Process' (25 May 2005) UN Doc HRI/MC/2005/4, [88]–[104]. See also art 45(a) CRC; rules 63, 69 CAT Committee Rules of Procedure; rules 45–47 CEDAW Committee Rules of Procedure; rules 68–69 CESCR Rules of Procedures; rules 67(2), 71(2) HRC Rules of Procedure.

[21] Nolte, 'Report 3—Practice outside of Judicial Proceedings' (n 3) 380. See generally International Human Rights Instruments, 'Report on the Working Methods of the Human Rights Treaty Bodies relating to the State Party Reporting Process' (25 May 2005) UN Doc HRI/MC/2005/4, [50] f. See further rules 68, 70 CAT Committee Rules of Procedure; rule 51(4) CEDAW Committee Rules of Procedure; rule 62 CESCR Rules of Procedures; rule 72 CRC Committee Rules of Procedure; rule 68 HRC Rules of Procedure.

[22] Philip Alston, 'Final Report on Enhancing the Long-term Effectiveness of the United Nations Human Rights Treaty System' (27 March 1997) UN Doc E/CN.4/1997/74, [109]. See also O'Flaherty, 'Concluding Observations' (n 16) 37 f; Shelton, 'Normative Pronouncements' (n 16) 566.

[23] O'Flaherty, 'Concluding Observations' (n 16) 41.

[24] ibid 42.

a State party.[25] Last but not least, many treaty bodies also adopt general comments (sometimes referred to as general recommendations), in which they either address a particular thematic issue or a particular provision of the respective treaty.[26] Like the reporting procedures, this monitoring procedure draws on various external sources such as submissions by other UN entities or by NGOs.[27]

This brief overview shows that concluding observations, views on individual complaints, and general comments reflect a treaty body's understanding of the treaty—be it as regards a particular situation or *in abstracto*. Although they are legally non-binding, these various forms of output undeniably possess a high power of persuasion because, as Christian Tomuschat explained, '[n]o better expertise as to the scope and meaning of any of the human rights treaties can be found than in the expert bodies set up to monitor their observance by states.'[28] Against this background, the question arises as to what the *legal* value of treaty body output as a means of treaty interpretation is. Can interpreters rely on treaty body output, and are they perhaps even obliged to do so, under international law rules of treaty interpretation as they are laid down and reflected in the Vienna rules? A partial reply to this question would be that treaty body output is at least admissible as a supplementary means of interpretation under the conditions specified in article 32 VCLT.[29] However, if treaty body output could solely be taken into account as a supplementary means of interpretation, interpreters could consider or ignore this output at their discretion. Hence the key question is whether this output can be regarded as a primary means of interpretation under article 31 VCLT.

Those commentators who suggest that treaty body output might be regarded as a primary means of interpretation usually refer to article 31(3)(b) VCLT or some

---

[25] Eg art 22 CAT; art 1 CEDAW-OP; art 5 CRC-OP 3; art 2 ICESCR-OP; art 1 of the Optional Protocol to the International Covenant on Civil and Political Rights (signed 16 December 1966, entered into force 23 March 1976) 999 UNTS 171 (ICCPR-OP 1). Several treaty bodies may also consider complaints by one party about alleged violations of the treaty by another party, see eg arts 21, 30 CAT; art 29 CEDAW; art 12 CRC-OP 3; art 10 ICESCR-OP; arts 41–43 ICCPR. Yet, no such inter-State complaint has been lodged so far.

[26] Eg art 21(1) CEDAW; art 40(4) ICCPR. See further rule 74 CAT Committee Rules of Procedure; rule 65 CESCR Rules of Procedures; rule 77 CRC Committee Rules of Procedure.

[27] Eg art 45(a) CRC; rules 45–47 CEDAW Committee Rules of Procedure; rules 68–69 CESCR Rules of Procedures. See also Philip Alston, 'Final Report on Enhancing the Long-term Effectiveness of the United Nations Human Rights Treaty System' (27 March 1997) UN Doc E/CN.4/1997/74, [107].

[28] Christian Tomuschat, *Human Rights—Between Idealism and Realism* (3rd edn, OUP 2014) 267. See also id, 'National Implementation of International Standards on Human Rights' [1984] CHRYB 31, 36.

[29] See Nolte, 'Report 3—Practice outside of Judicial Proceedings' (n 3) 384, where it is noted that treaty body output does not, 'as such, constitute subsequent agreements or practice in the sense of Art 31(3)(a) and (b) VCLT.' This observation does not, however, exclude that treaty body output may be taken into account under art 32 VCLT. cf Committee on Human Rights Law and Practice, 'Final Report on the Impact of Findings of the United Nations Human Rights Treaty Bodies' (2004) 71 Int'l L Ass'n Rep Conf 621, 628.

modified concept of subsequent practice under customary international law.[30] The main argument that is used to enhance the legal status of treaty body output is the 'special characteristics of human rights law.'[31] Most prominently, the International Law Association (ILA) remarked:

> The reference in article 31 to subsequent practice—as with so many other provisions in the VCLT—is written as if no monitoring body had been established by a treaty, as if no third-party interests existed, and as if it were only for other States to monitor each other's compliance and to react to non-compliance. Human rights treaties are different in some important respects from the presumed ideal type of a multilateral treaty which underpins the formulation of the individual provisions of the VCLT. Given these differences, it appears arguable that in interpreting these types of treaties (with third-party beneficiaries and an independent monitoring mechanism), relevant subsequent practice might be broader than subsequent State practice and include the considered views of the treaty bodies adopted in the performance of the functions conferred on them by the States parties.[32]

If one maintained that article 31(3)(b) VCLT does not require practice that is attributable to a State party, it would appear only logical to conclude that treaty body output constitutes practice within the meaning of this provision. But even if one proceeded from that assumption, treaty body output would still need to satisfy the other requirements of article 31(3)(b) VCLT. In particular—provided one did not dispense with this requirement either—interpreters would have to demonstrate that such output is capable of establishing the parties' agreement regarding the interpretation of the treaty. But unless the parties somehow react to a treaty body's output (here the reaction would in itself constitute potentially relevant practice), it is very difficult to establish this link between the treaty body's output and the parties' agreement.

To solve this problem, one can think of two alternative lines of reasoning. In the one alternative, one might argue that State parties in advance agree to any future interpretation by the treaty body which they established. In consequence, they can be presumed to have acquiesced in a particular interpretation by that treaty body

[30] Christopher Hall, 'The Duty of States Parties to the Convention against Torture to Provide Procedures Permitting Victims to Recover Reparations for Torture Committed Abroad' (2007) 18 EJIL 921, 927; Martin Scheinin, 'Human Rights Treaties and the Vienna Convention on the Law of Treaties—Conflicts or Harmony' in Venice Commission (ed), *The Status of International Treaties on Human Rights* (Council of Europe Publ 2006) 52; cf also Mechlem, 'Treaty Bodies' (n 15) 920, who cautiously remarks that 'treaty bodies … are also the principal generators of "subsequent practice" in the sense of Article 31(3)(b) of the Vienna Convention …. Given the special role of the committees as compared with other multilateral treaties, it would be inappropriate to limit "practice" to subsequent *state* practice alone.' Matthias Herdegen, *Völkerrecht* (15th edn, Beck 2016) 140. See also Ulfstein, 'Treaty Bodies and Regimes' (n 3) 438, who mistakenly refers to 31(2)(b) VCLT.

[31] Scheinin, 'Human Rights Treaties' (n 30) 46.

[32] Committee on Human Rights Law and Practice, 'Final Report on the Impact of Findings of the United Nations Human Rights Treaty Bodies' (2004) 71 Int'l L Ass'n Rep Conf 621, 629 [22] [fn omitted].

unless there is specific evidence to the contrary.[33] In the other alternative, one might say that the parties' agreement is superfluous because the 'special characteristics of human rights treaties' call for a modification of the international law rules of treaty interpretation.[34] The objective of this subchapter is not to take up theoretical discussions about whether these lines of reasoning are convincing. Instead, it examines how domestic courts have actually used treaty body output as a means of interpretation.

Sure enough, domestic courts are just one among many types of actors that interpret treaties. Nevertheless, their practice also influences the understanding of the Vienna rules. Thus, it can help to appraise whether the proposition that treaty body output falls under article 31(3)(b) VCLT (or some modified concept of subsequent practice) is realistically tenable or not.

7.1.2 Treaty Body Output in the Jurisprudence of Domestic Courts

To interpret international human rights instruments, domestic courts frequently cite the various types of treaty body output such as concluding observations, views, or general comments. Still, one can hardly ignore that they do so in a 'pick-and-choose manner'.[35] While they readily rely on treaty body output in some cases, they dismiss or even ignore it in other cases. When domestic courts refer to treaty body output, they mostly do so in passing and without discussing how it fits into the Vienna rules.[36] Hence, domestic courts obviously consider it admissible to use treaty body output as a means of interpretation.

---

[33] Scheinin, 'Human Rights Treaties' (n 30) 52.

[34] Critically Georg Nolte, 'Fourth Report on Subsequent Agreements and Subsequent Practice in Relation to the Interpretation of Treaties' (7 March 2016) UN Doc A/CN.4/694, 18, who sees 'no reason why articles 31 and 32 would be insufficient to deal with particular aspects of human rights treaties.'

[35] van Alebeek and Nollkaemper, 'Decisions by Human Rights Treaty Bodies' (n 14) 409.

[36] See eg *Ye v Minister of Immigration* [2009] 2 NZLR 596 [74]–[79] (Glazebrook J) citing CRC Committee, 'General Comment No 5' (27 November 2003) UN Doc CRC/GC/2003/5, CRC Committee, 'General Comment No 6' (1 September 2005) UN Doc CRC/GC/2005/6, CRC Committee, 'General Comment No 7' (20 September 2006) UN Doc CRC/C/GC/7/Rev.1; *Minister for Immigration and Citizenship v MZYYL* [2012] FCAFC 147, (2012) 207 FCR 211 [19] citing HRC, 'General Comment No 31' (26 May 2004) UN Doc CCPR/C/21/Rev.1/Add.13; BGH, Decision of 29 May 2013, XII ZB 530/11, [2013] NJW 3095, 3097 citing CRC Committee, 'General Comment No 6' (1 September 2005) UN Doc CRC/GC/2005/6; BVerfG, Decision of 5 July 2013, 2 BvR 708/12 <http://www.juris.de> [24] citing CRC Committee, 'General Comment No 10' (25 April 2007) UN Doc CRC/C/GC/10; BVerfG, Decision of 23 October 2013, 1 BvR 1842/11, [2014] NJW 46, 48 f citing CESCR, 'General Comment No 17' (12 January 2006) UN Doc E/C.12/GC/17; BGHSt 39,

The more interesting question is whether domestic courts regard treaty body output as being covered by article 31(3)(b) VCLT or some modified concept of mandatory subsequent practice. For this reason, it is useful to focus on those cases in which domestic courts addressed the interpretative value of treaty body output. Indeed, a judgment by the Swiss Federal Court on the interpretation of article 2 CEDAW can be read as supporting this proposition. At issue in this case was whether article 2 CEDAW obliged State parties to create some kind of equal opportunity commission. To specify the content of this provision, the Court relied on the CEDAW Committee's General Recommendations Nos 6[37] and 28[38] and on its conclusions[39] on Switzerland's periodic reports.[40]

Conceding that neither these recommendations nor the concluding observations were legally binding,[41] the Court emphasised that these pronouncements were nevertheless of legal value and an important source for interpreting the Convention.

1, 21 citing HRC, 'General Comment No 6' (27 May 2008) UN Doc HRI/GEN/1/Rev.9 (Vol I); BVGer, Judgment of 20 September 2011, E-5012/2006 [5.2.1] citing CAT Committee, 'General Comment No 2' (24 January 2008) UN Doc CAT/C/GC/2; BVGer, Judgment of 18 December 2007, C-2019/2007 [3.3.2] citing HRC, 'General Comment No 27' (1 November 1999) UN Doc CCPR/C/21/Rev.1/Add.9; BVGer, Judgment of 3 January 2014, D-6370/2013 [5.2.1] citing CAT Committee, 'General Comment No 2' (24 January 2008) UN Doc CAT/C/GC/2; *Sepet v Secretary of State for the Home Department* [2003] UKHL 15, [2003] 3 All ER 304 [48]–[49] (Lord Hoffmann) citing HRC, 'General Comment No 22' (27 September 1993) UN Doc CCPR/C/21/Rev.1/Add.4; *R (European Roma Rights Centre) v Immigration Officer at Prague Airport* [2004] UKHL 55, [2005] 2 AC 1 [24] (Lord Bingham) citing HRC, 'General Comment No 31' (26 May 2004) UN Doc CCPR/C/21/Rev.1/Add.13; *ZH (Tanzania) v Secretary of State for the Home Department* [2011] UKSC 4, [2011] 2 AC 166 [27] (Lady Hale) citing CRC Committee, 'General Comment No 6' (1 September 2005) UN Doc CRC/GC/2005/6; *RT (Zimbabwe) v Secretary of State for the Home Department* [2012] UKSC 38, [2013] 1 AC 152 [33] (Lord Dyson) citing HRC, 'General Comment No 22' (27 September 1993) UN Doc CCPR/C/21/Rev.1/Add.4 and HRC, 'General Comment No 34' (12 September 2011) UN Doc CCPR/C/GC/34; *HH v Deputy Prosecutor of the Italian Republic, Genoa* [2012] UKSC 25, [2013] 1 AC 338 [85] (Lady Hale) citing CRC Committee, 'General Comment No 12' (20 July 2009) UN Doc CRC/C/GC/12. For further examples, see Committee on Human Rights Law and Practice, 'Interim Report on the Impact of the Work of the United Nations Human Rights Treaty Bodies on National Courts and Tribunals' (2002) 70 Int'l L Ass'n Rep Conf 508, 526 f and id, 'Final Report' (n 13) 631 f.

[37] CEDAW Committee, 'General Recommendation No 6' (1988) UN Doc A/43/38.

[38] CEDAW Committee, 'General Recommendation No 28' (16 December 2010) UN Doc CEDAW/C/GC/28.

[39] CEDAW Committee, 'Concluding Observations on Switzerland's First and Second Periodic Report on Implementation of the CEDAW' (18 August 2003) UN Doc A/58/38(SUPP) [113] and 'Concluding Observations on Switzerland's Third Periodic Report on Implementation of the CEDAW' (14 August 2009) UN Doc CEDAW/C/CHE/CO/3, [22].

[40] BGer, Judgment of 21 November 2011, 1C 549/2010, BGE 137 I 305, 323 f.

[41] ibid 325.

According to the Court, this was because they reflected the common agreement of the Committee—a body established by the contracting parties and vested with special authority—regarding the parties' obligations under the Convention.[42] Although the Court did not cite article 31(3)(b) VCLT, its choice of words might suggest that it considered the CEDAW's Committee's pronouncements as a special form of subsequent practice.

Yet, the Swiss court's reasoning must not necessarily be understood this way. In *Minister for Immigration & Multicultural & Indigenous Affairs v Al Masri,* the Federal Court of Australia similarly remarked that it was legitimate to have regard to the views adopted by the HRC 'as the opinions of an expert body established by the treaty to further its objects by performing functions that include reporting, receiving reports, conciliating and considering claims that a State Party is not fulfilling its obligations.'[43] Taken in isolation, this reasoning might well have served to attach a higher weight to the Committee's views. Nonetheless, it appears likely that the Court did not mean to do so since it examined these views only after it had taken recourse to the Covenant's *travaux préparatoires* and to confirm a literal interpretation of the Covenant. The sequence in which the various means of interpretation were used does not, in itself, indicate the legal status assigned to the Committee's views. But in addition, the Court had recourse to them only to confirm an interpretation already arrived at by relying on other means. These aspects, taken together, create the impression that the Court treated the views more as a supplementary means of interpretation and not as part of the general rule.

The view that treaty body pronouncements constitute nothing more than supplementary means of interpretation was subsequently confirmed in *Minister for Immigration and Citizenship v Anochie,* which raised the question of whether the ICCPR implicity prohibited refoulement. Questioning whether treaty body pronouncements could be relied on to interpret the Covenant, Perram J remarked:

> Additionally, recourse may be had to 'supplementary means of interpretation', according to art 32 of the VCLT, 'in order to confirm [*inter alia*] the meaning resulting from the application of article 31'. In *Thiel* at 357, McHugh J (with whom Mason CJ, Brennan and Gaudron JJ agreed on this point at 344) held that the commentary prepared by the Organisation for Economic Co-operation and Development ('the OECD') on its 'Model Convention for the Avoidance of Double Taxation with Respect to Taxes on Income and on Capital' (and,

[42] ibid: 'Dies bedeutet jedoch nicht, dass den Empfehlungen des Ausschusses keinerlei rechtliche Bedeutung zukäme: Sie bringen die übereinstimmende Auffassung des Ausschusses als eines von den Vertragsstaaten eingesetzten und mit besonderer Autorität ausgestatteten Expertengremiusms über die sich aus dem Übereinkommen ergebenden Verpflichtungen eines Staates zum Ausdruck und sind insofern eine wichtige Erkenntnisquelle für die Auslegung der Konvention…' In English [translated by the author]: 'This is not to say that recommendations of the Committee were legally irrelevant. They reflect the common intention of the Committee, which is an expert body that is set up by the contracting parties and vested with a special authority as regards the parties' obligations under the treaty. Thus, its recommendations are an important source of information for interpreting the Convention.'

[43] *Minister for Immigration & Multicultural & Indigenous Affairs v Al Masri* [2003] FCAFC 70, (2003) 197 ALR 241 [148] (Black CJ, Sundberg, and Weinberg JJ).

indeed, the Model Convention itself) were supplementary means of interpretation within the meaning of art 32. Dawson J reached the same conclusion (at 350).

This suggests that a commentary or other interpretive statement prepared by an equivalent body on the ICCPR will itself be a supplementary means of interpretation to which regard may legitimately be had. Article 28 of the ICCPR establishes the Committee, which has a membership elected by the States who have acceded to the Convention: art 30(4).

To my mind, there is potentially one distinguishing feature from the situation in *Thiel*. In that case, the *Convention on the Organisation for Economic Cooperation and Development* [1971] ATS 11 reconstituted the Organisation for European Economic Co-operation as the OECD and, as part of its work, the OECD developed the Model Convention on Double Taxation. At the same time, it wrote a commentary on the Model Convention and has continued to update both documents. The commentary thereby prepared was material created by the author of the Model Convention. Its ability to assist in the interpretation of the Model Convention is obvious.

This may not be so in the case of the Committee. It did not create the ICCPR but was instead created by it. It is not self-evident that the opinions of a body constituted by a treaty on what the substantive (as opposed to constitutive) provisions of that treaty mean is necessarily useful material in the process of interpretation. Nevertheless, upon reflection, I accept that the Committee's interpretation of the ICCPR is admissible in its construction. This is because, in the first place, art 40(4) expressly authorises the Committee to issue General Comments about the ICCPR ....[44]

Thus, Perram J reluctantly acknowledged that treaty body pronouncements may at least be relevant under article 32 VCLT. The Court of Appeal of Hong Kong, in contrast, went even further in that it denied them any interpretative weight. This can be seen in the case of *Ubamaka v Secretary for Security*. This case concerned a deportation order against a Nigerian national that allegedly violated articles 7 and 14(7) ICCPR. Although it finally denied any violation, the Court examined whether the complaint would have also been precluded by the UK's immigration reservation to the Covenant. The reservation reads:

The Government of the United Kingdom reserve the right to continue to apply such immigration legislation governing entry into, stay in and departure from the United Kingdom as they may deem necessary from time to time and, accordingly, the acceptance of art. 12.4 and of other provisions of the Covenant is subject to the provisions of any such legislation as regards persons not at the time having the right under the law of the United Kingdom to enter and remain in the United Kingdom. The United Kingdom also reserves a similar right in regard to each of its dependent territories.[45]

Because the Sino–British Joint Declaration stipulated that the ICCPR 'as applied to Hong Kong' was to remain in force, the Covenant continued to apply to Hong Kong as it originally applied to the UK, ie including the reservation.[46] The respondent,

---

[44] *Minister for Immigration and Citizenship v Anochie* [2012] FCA 1440, (2012) 209 FCR 497 [42]–[45] (Perram J).

[45] *Ubamaka v Secretary for Security* [2011] 1 HKLRD 359 [125] (Fok J).

[46] Joint Declaration of the Government of the United Kingdom of Great Britain and Northern Ireland and the Government of the People's Republic of China on the Question of Hong Kong (signed 19 December 1984, entered into force 27 May 1985) <http://www.cmab.gov.hk/en/issues/joint3.htm> (Sino–British Joint Declaration), Annex I Sec III.

however, argued that the whole reservation was unlawful and invalid because it was generally inconsistent with the Covenant's object and purpose. In consequence, so his reasoning continued, the whole reservation was severed from the orginal ratification and entailed no legal effect.[47] To support his reasoning, he relied on the HRC's General Comment No 24.[48] Recalling that a reserving party would normally not be bound by a treaty when its reservation was unacceptable, the Comment maintained that this rule did not apply to unacceptable reservations to the Covenent. Due to its special character as a human rights treaty, so the Comment argued, 'the Covenant will be operative for the reserving party without benefit of the reservation.' But the Court refused to follow the Comment's interpretation of the Covenant because it had received considerable criticism from both the UK and US governments.[49] Consequently, it held that the immigration reservation was not invalid so that the claims as regards the Covenant would have been precluded anyway.[50]

A judgment by German Federal Administrative Court further suggests that the interpretative value of treaty body output is at most an indirect one. To determine whether the re-introduction of tuition fees in North-Rhine Westpalia was compatible with article 13(2) ICESCR, the Court among others examined concluding observations on State reports[51] as well as General Comments[52] by the ICESCR Committee. As a starting point, the Court emphasised that such pronouncenments were not legally binding.[53] Their relevance, so the Court continued, instead lay in the fact that they could be taken as either reflecting existing or influencing future practice of the

[47] *Ubamaka* (n 45) [128]–[29] (Fok J).

[48] HRC, 'General Comment No 24' (11 November 1994) UN Doc CCPR/C/21/Rev.1/Add.6.

[49] *Ubamaka* (n 45) [143] f (Fok J).

[50] ibid [148] (Fok J). Interestingly, the Court even held that the reservation also precluded the incorporation of those rules of customary international law that corresponded to the allegedly violated rights under the Covenant, see ibid [150] f (Fok J). Thus, the rights under the Covenant had no direct or indirect effect on the outcome of the case.

[51] CESCR, 'Concluding Observations on Germany's Third Periodic Report on Implementation of the ICESCR' (4 December 1998) UN Doc E/C.12/1/Add.29, [37]; CESCR, 'Concluding Observations on Germany's Fourth Periodic Report on Implementation of the ICESCR' (24 September 2001) UN Doc E/C.12/1/Add.68, [47]; CESCR, 'Concluding Observations on the United Kingdom's Fourth Periodic Report on Implementation of the ICESCR' (5 June 2002) UN Doc E/C.12/1/Add.79, [41]; CESCR, 'Concluding Observations on Canada's Third Periodic Report on Implementation of the ICESCR' (10 December 1998) UN Doc E/C.12/1/Add.31, [49]; CESCR, 'Concluding Observations on Canada's Fourth and Fifth Periodic Report on Implementation of the ICESCR' (22 May 2006) UN Docs E/C.12/CAN/CO/4 and E/C.12/CAN/CO/5, [65]; CESCR, 'Concluding Observations on the Netherlands' Second Periodic Report on Implementation of the ICESCR' (16 June 1998) UN Doc E/C.12/1/Add.25, [27]; CESCR, 'Concluding Observations on Austria's Third Periodic Report on Implementation of the ICESCR' (25 January 2006) UN Doc E/C.12/AUT/CO/3, [31].

[52] CESCR, 'General Comment No 11' (11 May 1999) UN Doc E/C.12/1999/5; CESCR, 'General Comment No 13' (8 December 1999) UN Doc E/C.12/1999/10.

[53] BVerwGE 134, 1, 21 f. See also BVerfG, Decision of 26 July 2016, 1 BvL 8/15, [2017] NJW 53, 58.

contracting parties in the application of the Covenant.[54] Based on these observations, the Court then considered concrete examples of State practice and related statements by the Committee. On the one hand, it noted that several parties had introduced tuition fees and that the Committee had even approved such fees where they had been designed in a socially acceptable way.[55] On the other hand, the Court remarked that other German *Länder* had actually been criticised by the Committee for introducing similar fees.[56] Taking everything into account, the Court finally held that the parties' practice allowed the conclusion that the contentious re-introduction of tuition fees was compatible with the ICESCR.[57]

This indirect relevance of treaty body output was also acknowledged by the House of Lords in the case of *R (Mullen) v Secretary of State for the Home Department.* Although the case concerned the interpretation of the ICCPR, Lord Steyn took note of an Explanatory Report from the Committee of Experts on Human Rights.[58] Noting that the Report had a 'great persuasive value in the process of interpretation,'[59] he explained that

> it is a basis on which states sign and ratify the Protocol [ie Protocol 7 to the ECHR]. Inevitably, state practice will be based on the Explanatory Report, and in this way it becomes directly relevant to the interpretation of article 14(6): article 31(3)(b) of the Vienna Convention on the Law of Treaties.[60]

Mullen and the judgment of the German Federal Administrative Court on tuition fees thus clarify that interpreters must carefully distinguish between relevant practice as such and material which is capably of either reflecting or inducing such practice. According to the German Federal Administrative Court and Lord Steyn,

[54] BVerwGE 134, 1, 21 f.

[55] ibid 25 f.

[56] ibid.

[57] ibid 26 f.

[58] The Committee of Experts on Human Rights (which preceeded the Steering Committee for Human Rights) was not a treaty body strictly speaking as it was composed of representatives of the 47 member States of the Council of Europe. Moreover, the Committee was not established under the ECHR but more generally tasked with developing and promoting human rights in Europe, see Martyn Bond, *The Council of Europe and Human Rights—An Introduction to the European Convention on Human Rights* (Council of Europe Publ 2010) 69.

[59] *R (Mullen) v Secretary of State for the Home Department* [2004] UKHL 18, [2005] 1 AC 1 [48] (Lord Steyn).

[60] ibid [48] (Lord Steyn) [explanation added]. In a later decision, however, the UK Supreme Court blurred the line between potential catalysts for subsequent conduct and conduct that was in itself relevant under art 31 VCLT. In *Smith v The Ministry of Defence,* it contended that intrinsically non-binding instruments of Council of Europe organs, in particular recommendations and resolutions of the Committee of Ministers and the Parliamentary Assembly, 'constitute agreements within the meaning of article 31(3)(a) of the Vienna Convention, account of which may be taken in the interpretation of a treaty or the application of its provisions.' See *Smith v The Ministry of Defence* [2013] UKSC 41, [2014] 1 AC 52 [53] (Lord Hope).

pronouncements of treaty bodies such as the ICESCR Committee or the Committee of Experts on Human Rights do not in themselves constitute relevant practice. In consequence, it is only logical to conclude that such pronouncements may not only indirectly influence the interpretation of the treaty for which the respective body is responsible but also of related treaties, provided that they also generate practice in the application of these other treaties.

In the case of Jones *v Ministry of Interior for the Kingdom of Saudi Arabia,* the House of Lords more clearly emphasised that treaty body output as such carried only little interpretative value. This case raised the question of whether article 14 CAT created an exception to the general principle of State immunity in civil proceedings. The CAT Committee seemed to have taken the view that such exception existed as it had recommended, after considering its periodic reports from 2002 and 2004, that Canada should ensure the provision of compensation through its civil jurisdiction to all victims of torture. The House of Lords, however, did not share this view and even doubted the Committee's authority to influence the interpretation of the CAT. Lord Bingham, for example, remarked:

> But the Committee is not an exclusively legal and not an adjudicative body; its power under article 19 is to make general comments; the Committee did not, in making this recommendation, advance any analysis or interpretation of article 14 of the Convention; and it was no more than a recommendation. Whatever its value in influencing the trend of international thinking, the legal authority of this recommendation is slight.[61]

Lord Hoffmann rejected the Committee's legal point of view in even clearer words. He pointed out that the Committee's view was not shared by the parties to the Convention but had rather been objected to. In their own periodic reports and during the debates on the Canadian reports, the parties had constantly insisted that article 14 CAT did not require them to provide a civil remedy for victims of torture in foreign States.[62] In consequence, Lord Hoffmann matter-of-factly concluded that the Committee's recommendation, 'as an interpretation of article 14 or a statement of international law' had 'no value.'[63]

7.1.3 Evaluation

On the whole, the jurisprudence of domestic courts does not support the oft-repeated proposition that treaty body output might be covered either by article 31(3)(b) VCLT or by some modified concept of mandatory subsequent practice. In particular, domestic courts are not willing to accept that State parties agreed to any

[61] *Jones v Ministry of Interior for the Kingdom of Saudi Arabia* [2006] UKHL 26, [2007] 1 AC 27 [23] (Lord Bingham).

[62] ibid [56] f (Lord Hoffmann).

[63] ibid [57] (Lord Hoffmann).

interpretation that a treaty body recommends. By emphasising that the output of treaty bodies is not legally binding and by insisting that it is, at the most, a supplementary means of interpretation, they rather recall that State parties retained their interpretative authority over the treaty.[64] That domestic courts sometimes follow and sometimes reject interpretations recommended by treaty bodies is not at all inconsistent but a logical consequence of regarding treaty body output as a supplementary means of interpretation.

In spite of that, the jurisprudence of domestic courts also illustrates that treaty body output can indirectly influence a treaty's interpretation by either reflecting existing or inducing future subsequent State practice or agreements.[65] On the one hand, the interpretation of the treaty that is contained in a treaty body's concluding observations, general comments, or views also takes into account and hence to some extent reflects existing State practice. On the other hand, State parties often react to a treaty body's output by, for example, expressing their agreement with or objecting to a general comment or concluding observations, or by complying with or refusing to comply with a treaty body's view on a complaint.

However, these various forms of reaction or earlier input from State parties also reconfirm that the parties not always agree with a treaty body's output, even if the treaty body maintains that they do. For example, a State party's conduct, which a treaty body criticises in its concluding observations or its view on a complaint, may indeed constitute a deliberate violation of the treaty.[66] But just as well, the State may genuinely believe that its conduct is in conformity with the treaty whereas the treaty body's interpretation in fact exceeds the terms of the treaty. Moreover, one must not forget that treaty bodies also receive information from other sources such as UN entities and NGOs.

In consequence, treaty body output may be a valuable starting point for interpreters in order to detect potentially relevant practice for the purpose of article 31(3)(b) VCLT. However, interpreters should not just blindly assume that the State parties have generated (or will generate) relevant practice that confirms the interpretation advocated by the treaty body. While the jurisprudence of domestic courts largely confirms that treaty body output may be taken into account under article 32 VCLT,[67] it also shows that relevant State practice under article 31(3)(b) VCLT is still superior to and hence ultimately overrides a treaty body's recommendations.

---

[64] cf also Ulfstein, 'Treaty Bodies and Regimes' (n 3) 439 f; Joanne Pedone and Andrew Kloster, 'New Proposals for Human Rights Treaty Body Reform' (2013) 22 J Transnat'l L & Pol'y 29, 37.

[65] See also Nolte, 'Report 3—Practice outside of Judicial Proceedings' (n 3) 381 f and id, 'Fourth Report' (n 34) 19.

[66] Hall, 'The Duty of States Parties to the CAT' (n 30) 929.

[67] See also Nolte, 'Fourth Report' (n 34) 26.

7.2 The Office of the UN High Commissioner for Refugees

To interpret the Refugee Convention and the Refugee Protocol, domestic courts frequently rely on publications issued by the UNHCR. Although its functions are closely linked to these instruments, the UNHCR is not a treaty body strictly speaking but a subsidiary organ of the UNGA.[68] All the same, the interpretative value of its pronouncements raises familiar questions: How do they fit into the Vienna rules? Do interpreters unduly frustrate their practical relevance by regarding them as supplementary means of interpretation only? Or do they constitute primary means of interpretation under the general rule of interpretation? Indeed, some commentators have vaguely suggested that UNHCR publications 'take into account State practice and, while not legally binding, serve as an authoritative interpretation of current refugee law.'[69] Others, in contrast, object that UNHCR's supervisory role 'does not extend to a mandate to provide authoritative rulings or opinions on the meaning of particular treaty terms, and accordingly UNHCR can issue only *guidance* on the 1951 Convention's interpretation.'[70]

Following up on this uncertainty, this subchapter elucidates whether and in which way UNHCR publications may indeed be relevant under article 31(3)(b) VCLT. For that purpose, it briefly describes the link between the Refugee Convention and the Refugee Protocol, on the one hand, and UNHCR on the other (7.2.1). This overview is followed by an exemplary analysis of domestic court decisions in cases under the Refugee Convention and the Refugee Protocol (7.2.2). Based on this analysis, this subchapter concludes by evaluating the legal status of UNHCR publications both from a doctrinal perspective and in the light of this interpretative practice (7.2.3).

7.2.1 The Link between the Refugee Convention, the Refugee Protocol, and the UNHCR

Having been adopted in 1951 as a post-Second World War instrument, the Refugee Convention was originally limited in scope to persons fleeing events occurring before 1 January 1951 and within Europe.[71] These limitations were removed by

[68] See art 22 Charter of the United Nations (signed 26 June 1945, entered into force 24 October 1945) 1 UNTS XVI (UNC) and UNGA Res 319 (IV) (3 December 1949) UN Doc A/RES/319(IV).

[69] Erika Feller and Anja Klug, 'Refugees, United Nations High Commissioner (UNHCR)' in Rüdiger Wolfrum (ed), *The Max Planck Encyclopedia of Public International Law* (OUP 2012) [82]. See also James Hathaway, *The Rights of Refugees under International Law* (reprint, CUP 2011) 54, who notes that 'the UNHCR's *Handbook on Procedures and Criteria for Determining Refugee Status* … [is] to be taken into account as evidence of "subsequent agreement between the parties" on the meaning of the treaty.'

[70] Jane McAdam, 'Interpretation of the 1951 Convention' in Andreas Zimmermann (ed), *The* 1951 *Convention relating to the Status of Refugees and its* 1967 *Protocol—A Commentary* (OUP 2011) 79 [4].

[71] Art 1(A)(2) and (B)(1) Convention relating to the Status of Refugees (signed 28 July 1951, entered into force 22 April 1954) 189 UNTS 137 (Refugee Convention).

the Refugee Protocol in 1967.[72] Although the Protocol obliges its parties to apply the substantive provisions of the Refugee Convention,[73] it is an independent legal instrument. Therefore, States may accede to the Refugee Protocol irrespective of whether they are a party to the Refugee Convention.[74] Unlike many human rights law instruments, neither the Refugee Convention nor the Protocol establish a committee of independent experts to monitor their implementation. Instead, the parties to these instruments undertake to cooperate with UNHCR in the exercise of its functions and to facilitate its duty of supervising the application of their provisions.[75]

Thus, the Refugee Convention and the Refugee Protocol complement the 'Statute of the Office of the High Commissioner for Refugees',[76] whose subpara 8(a) calls on UNHCR to supervise the application of international conventions for the protection of refugees. To carry out this supervisory function, UNHCR has issued various documents which purport to provide guidance to governments as regards the interpretation of the Refugee Convention and the Refugee Protocol.[77] These documents include, most importantly, its 'Handbook on Procedures and Criteria for Determining Refugee Status under the 1951 Convention and the 1967 Protocol relating to the Status of Refugees'[78] and its 'Guidelines on International Protection'.[79] In the light of the debates about the interpretative value of treaty body output, their self-defined objective to guide the interpretation of the Refugee Convention and the Refugee Protocol raises the question of whether and to which extent UNHCR publications may be regarded as potentially relevant non-party practice or at least as reflections of existing practice by contracting parties. If that were the cases, UNHCR publications would be either directly or indirectly relevant under article 31(3)(b) VCLT. Thus, they could more strongly influence the interpretation of the Refugee Convention

---

[72] Art I(2) and (3) Protocol relating to the Status of Refugees (signed 31 January 1967, entered into force 4 October 1967) 606 UNTS 267 (Refugee Protocol).

[73] Art I(1) Refugee Protocol.

[74] Art V Refugee Protocol.

[75] Art 35(1) Refugee Convention and art II(1) Refugee Protocol.

[76] UNGA, 'Statute of the Office of the United Nations High Commissioner for Refugees' Annex to UNGA Res 428 (V) (14 December 1950) UN Doc A/RES/428(V) (UNHCR Statute).

[77] UNHCR, 'Handbook on Procedures and Criteria for Determining Refugee Status under the 1951 Convention and the 1967 Protocol relating to the Status of Refugees' (December 2011) UN Doc HCR/1P/4/ENG/REV.3 (UNHCR Handbook) 6; see also UNHCR ExCom Conclusion No 8 (XXVIII), 'Determination of Refugee Status' (12 October 1977) at (g) as well as the preambles to UNHCR's 'Guidelines on International Protection'.

[78] The Handbook had first been published in September 1979 and was re-edited in January 1992. In 2011, the Handbook was re-issued but its content remained unchanged.

[79] As of today, UNHCR has issued ten 'Guidelines on International Protection' covering topics such as gender-related persecution, the meaning of 'membership of a particular social group', cessation of refugee status, the application of the exclusion clauses, and refugee claims based on religious belief or sexual orientation. All UNHCR Guidelines are available at <http://www.refworld.org>.

and the Refugee Protocol than as a non-mandatory supplementary means of interpretation under article 32 VCLT.

As regards treaty body output, Section 7.1 noted that domestic courts are hesitant to equate supervisory competences with interpretative authority. In addition, they also frequently questioned that such output faithfully reflected existing State practice capable of establishing the parties' agreement regarding the interpretation of the respective treaty. In this respect, domestic courts largely acknowledged that treaty body output can be indirectly relevant under article 31(3)(b) VCLT. Yet, their jurisprudence also cautions against believing that this was always the case. The arguments by which domestic courts sought to deny the direct interpretative value of treaty body output under article 31(3)(b) VCLT are instructive to assess the interpretative value of UNHCR pronouncements, too. In addition, it is important to consider that UNHCR has a much broader mandate than treaty bodies. Unlike treaty bodies, which monitor the implementation of a particular instrument, UNHCR's mandate is not limited to supervising the implementation of the Refugee Convention and the Refugee Protocol. Instead, it is established without exclusively referring to these instruments.

When UNHCR was established in 1949, its mission was defined broadly and without reference to the Refugee Convention and the Refugee Protocol, namely to provide international protection to refugees falling within the competence of the Office and to seek permanent solutions to the problem of refugees.[80] Under its Statute, UNHCR's mandate is circumscribed by the term 'refugee', whose meaning is similar but not identical to the term 'refugee' as used in the Refugee Convention and the Refugee Protocol.[81] Moreover, ECOSOC and the UNGA have constantly extended UNHCR's mandate to 'additional activities'[82] relating to other persons in need of international protection such as internally displaced persons or stateless people who are not refugees.[83] Since its mandate exceedes the Refugee Convention and the Refugee Protocol, even publications on refugee protection are susceptible

[80] UNGA Res 319 (IV) (3 December 1949) UN Doc A/RES/319(IV) and UNHCR Statute, para 1.

[81] Volker Türk, 'UNHCR's Supervisory Responsibility' (2001) 14 RQDI 135, 142; Feller and Klug, 'UNHCR' (n 69) [45].

[82] See UNHCR Statute, para 9.

[83] As regards internally displaced persons, see in particular UNGA Res 48/116 (18 February 1994) UN Doc A/RES/48/116. See further UNGA Res 2958 (XXVII) (12 December 1972) UN Doc A/RES/2958(XXVII); UNGA Res 48/118 (24 March 1994) UN Doc A/RES/48/118; ECOSOC Res 1655 (LII) (1 June 1972) UN Doc E/RES/1655(LII); ECOSOC Res 1705 (LIII) (27 July 1972) UN Doc E/RES/1705(LIII). As regards stateless persons, see in particular art 11 of the Convention on the Reduction of Statelessness (signed 30 August 1961, entered into force 13 December 1975) 989 UNTS 175 (Statelessness Convention). See further UNGA Res 3274 (XXIX) (10 December 1974) UN Doc A/RES/3274(XXIX); UNGA Res 31/36 (30 November 1976) UN Doc A/RES/31/36; UNGA Res 50/152 (9 February 1996) UN Doc A/RES/50/152.

to reflecting an understanding of the law that goes beyond the boundaries of these instruments.

Two factors render it even more likely that UNHCR publications not only reflect State practice in the application of the Refugee Convention and the Refugee Protocol but consciously or subconsciously advocate informal amendments of these instruments. Firstly, UNHCR publications often do not reveal whether and to which extent a particular interpretation of the Convention and Protocol is based on State practice in the application of these instruments, on 'complementary protection',[84] on the views of UNHCR, on UNHCR ExCom Conclusions, or on academic literature.[85] And secondly, UNHCR publications are not intended to just faithfully reflect existing State practice in the first place but also purport to continuously develop existing refugee law.[86] But once UNHCR publications intend to reflect existing State practice and to develop refugee law at the same time, it may, of course, be difficult if not impossible to distinguish passages motivated by the former from passages motivated by the latter intention.

7.2.2 UNHCR Publications in Domestic Jurisprudence

At first sight, the jurisprudence of domestic courts certifies UNHCR publications 'high persuasive authority'.[87] Domestic courts habitually refer to UNHCR publications and usually take it for granted that recourse may be had to this material to

[84] The notion 'complementary protection' refers to protection that is granted on the basis of an international protection need outside the Refugee Convention framework. See generally Jane McAdam, *Complementary Protection in International Refugee Law* (OUP 2007).

[85] Eg UNHCR, 'Handbook on Procedures and Criteria for Determining Refugee Status under the 1951 Convention and the 1967 Protocol relating to the Status of Refugees' (December 2011) UN Doc HCR/1P/4/ENG/REV.3 (UNHCR Handbook), 2; UNHCR, 'Guidelines on International Protection No 3: Cessation of Refugee Status under Article 1C(5) and (6) of the 1951 Convention relating to the Status of Refugees (the "Ceased Circumstances" Clauses)' (10 February 2003) UN Doc HCR/GIP/03/03, [5]; UNHCR, 'Guidelines on International Protection No 6: Religion-Based Refugee Claims under Article 1A(2) of the 1951 Convention and/or the 1967 Protocol relating to the Status of Refugees' (28 April 2004) UN Doc HCR/GIP/04/06, 1. See also Corinne Lewis, *UNHCR and International Refugee Law—From Treaties to Innovation* (Routledge 2012) 61 f, 66 f.

[86] Eg UNHCR ExCom Conclusion No 25 (XXXIII), 'General Conclusion on International Protection' (20 October 1982) at (i); UNHCR ExCom Conclusion No 77 (XLVI), 'General Conclusion on International Protection' (20 October 1995) at (o); UNHCR ExCom Conclusion No 81 (XLVIII), 'General Conclusion on International Protection' (17 October 1997) at (p), endorsed by UNGA Res 52/103 (9 February 1998) UN Doc A/RES/52/103. See also Corinne Lewis, 'UNHCR's Contribution to the Development of International Refugee Law—Its Foundations and Evolution' (2006) 17 IJRL 67, 80 f.

[87] *R (Adan) v Secretary of State for the Home Department* [2000] UKHL 67, [2001] 2 AC 477, 520 (Lord Steyn). See also BVerfG, Decision of 12 March 2008, 2 BvR 378/05 <http://www.juris.de> [38].

interpret the Refugee Convention and the Refugee Protocol.[88] But this first impression is false. Domestic courts have been mindful not to overemphasise the legal status of UNHCR publications. They have noted that UNHCR publications had no binding force in international and national law and even warned that there was a danger of regarding this material as if it had the same force as the Refugee Convention itself.[89] Besides, domestic courts have been reluctant to regard this material as primary means of interpretation. In particular, their jurisprudence widely indicates that UNHCR publications cannot be taken into account as potentially relevant non-party practice under article 31(3)(b) VCLT.

A noteworthy exception is the case of *Rishmawi v Minister for Immigration & Multicultural Affairs,* where the Federal Court of Australia maintained that '[r]ecourse to the Travaux and the Handbook is permitted as part of the context (Article 31(2)) and subsequent international practice (Article 31(3)(b)) which Article 31 of the Vienna Convention requires to be taken into account.'[90] In *Semunigus v Minister for Immigration & Multicultural Affairs*,[91] in contrast, the Court denied that UNHCR publications were covered by article 31(3)(b) VCLT. In this case, the appellant had submitted that '[t]he Handbook … embodies "subsequent practice in the application of the [Convention] which establishes the agreement of the parties regarding its interpretation" and this is to be taken into account in its interpretation.'[92] The Court, however, rejected this assertion and emphasised that it was 'not possible to regard the Handbook as having or as being intended to have binding force, or as being capable of being given such character'.[93]

---

[88] Eg VfGH, Judgment of 12 September 2013, U 1053/2012-14 [2.2]; VwGH, Judgment of 18 December 1996, 96/20/0793, 1; VwGH, Judgment of 10 December 1997, 94/20/0002, 2; VwGH, Judgment of 21 March 2003, 2000/20/0189, 2; VwGH, Judgment of 20 February 2009, 2007/19/0535, 2 f; BVerwGE 120, 16, 22; 133, 203, 217; 146, 67, 84; BVGer, Judgment of 18 June 2010, D-1308/2010 [3.2], [5]; BVGer, Judgment of 25 August 2010, E-2190/2010 [5.1], [5.2.1]; BVGer, Judgment of 20 September 2011, E-7449/2009, BVGE 2011/29 [6], [8.1.2]–[8.1.4], [8.3.3.1]; *T v Secretary of State for the Home Secretary* [1996] UKHL 8, [1996] AC 742 768 (Lord Mustill); *Secretary of State for the Home Department v K* [2006] UKHL 46, [2007] 1 AC 412 [15] (Lord Bingham), [45] and [52] (Lord Hope), [100] and [109] (Lady Hale), [118] and [120] [Lord Brown]; *HJ (Iran) v Secretary of State for the Home Department* [2010] UKSC 31, [2011] 1 AC 596 [19] (Lord Hope); *Al-Sirri v Secretary of State for the Home Department* [2012] UKSC 54, [2013] 1 AC 745 [36] and [38] (Lady Hale and Lord Dyson).

[89] Eg VwGH, Judgment of 8 November 1995, 95/01/0070, 2; VwGH, Judgment of 20 December 1995, 95/01/0104, 2; VwGH, Judgment of 17 December 1996, 95/01/0127, 3; *T* (n 88) 768 (Lord Mustill); *Horvath v Secretary of State for the Home Department* [2000] UKHL 37, [2001] 1 AC 489, 506 (Lord Lloyd); *Adan* (n 87) 520 (Lord Steyn); *Al-Sirri* (n 88) [36] (Lady Hale and Lord Dyson).

[90] *Rishmawi v Minister for Immigration & Multicultural Affairs* [1997] FCA 829, (1997) 77 FCR 421, 424 (Cooper J.)

[91] *Semunigus v Minister for Immigration & Multicultural Affairs* [1999] FCA 422.

[92] ibid [7] (Finn J).

[93] ibid [8] (Finn J).

Acknowledging that the Handbook was a useful guide to interpreting the Refugee Convention and the Refugee Protocol, it clarified that this material 'on its face purports to do no more than provide a source of guidance and assistance to contracting States'.[94] Still, the Court apparently felt uncomfortable with denying UNHCR publications any interpretative value. In the case of *Rezaei v Minister for Immigration and Multicultural Affairs,* it 'backpedalled' from its more critical attitude in *Semunigus* by vaguely noting that it was at least 'arguable that the Handbook is a piece of extrinsic material (yet of later production) which can be used to interpret the Convention: Article 31 of the Vienna Convention on the Law of Treaties'.[95] Although the Court did not cite article 31(3)(b) VCLT, this statement can be read to suggest that the Handbook may constitute a relevant form of subsequent practice.

Another, although more ambiguous exception is the case of *Pushpanathan v Canada (Minister of Citizenship and Immigration)*, which concerned the question of whether trafficking in drugs was 'contrary to the purposes and principles of the United Nations' in the sense of article 1(F)(c) Refugee Convention. On appeal, the Supreme Court of Canada approached this question rather sweepingly by trying to identify a 'consensus in international law' as to which acts may be contrary to the purposes and principles of the United Nations.[96] Although the Supreme Court examined the Handbook,[97] it refrained from citing article 31(3)(b) VCLT to explain why it should be admissible to consider this material. Yet, it incorrectly assumed that the lower instance court, the Federal Court of Canada, had referred to the Handbook as an interpretative source that was admissible under article 31(3)(b) VCLT.[98]

In fact, the Federal Court had not cited article 31(3)(b) VCLT[99] and the judgments invoked by the Federal Court had not mentioned article 31(3)(b) VCLT either.[100] Instead, one of these judgments merely remarked that, '[w]hile not formally binding on signatory states, the Handbook has been endorsed by the states which are members of the Executive Committee of the UNHCR, including Canada, and has

---

[94] ibid [10] (Finn J). See also *Minister for Immigration and Multicultural and Indigenous Affairs v QAAH of 2004* [2006] HCA 53, (2006) 231 ALR 340 [76] (Kirby J), where the Court remarked that 'due weight should therefore be given to the guidance provided by relevant UNHCR publications, including the UNHCR Handbook and the Guidelines. This does not mean that such sources are binding on this or any other court. But it does mean that, like other final courts, this Court will often derive great assistance by having access to such materials.'

[95] *Rezaei v Minister for Immigration and Multicultural Affairs* [2001] FCA 1294 [50] (Allsop J).

[96] *Pushpanathan v Canada (Minister of Citizenship and Immigration)* [1998] 1 SCR 982, (1998) 160 DLR (4th) 193 [65] f (Bastarache J).

[97] ibid [66] f (Bastarache J).

[98] ibid [54] (Bastarache J).

[99] *Pushpanathan v Canada (Minister of Citizenship and Immigration)* [1996] 2 FC 49, 191 NR 247.

[100] *Ward v Canada (Minister of Employment & Immigration)* [1993] 2 SCR 689, 103 DLR (4th) 1; *Chan v Canada* [1995] 3 SCR 593, 128 DLR (4th) 213.

been relied upon by the courts of signatory states.'[101] On its face, this remark is rather ambiguous. Ordinarily, the term 'endorse' means as much as 'to confirm' or 'to approve'.[102] Therefore, the lower court arguably observed that the UNHCR ExCom had welcomed either the compilation of the Handbook as such or even agreed with the interpretations advocated therein. Nonetheless, it should be borne in mind that the UNHCR ExCom does not comprise all parties to the Refugee Convention.[103] For this reason, even an approval by all UNHCR ExCom members will only rarely establish the agreement of all parties to the Convention. Besides, the lower court did not expressly address the legal status of the Handbook as a means of interpretation. In sum, the Supreme Court therefore seems to have read more into the earlier judgments than they objectively supported. This arguably suggests that the Supreme Court itself wondered whether the Handbook might be admissible under article 31(3)(b) VCLT.

In most cases, domestic courts denied that UNHCR publications, in themselves, carried any interpretative value under the general rule. Instead, they merely considered this material as one among other possible aids to discover potentially relevant practice for the purpose of article 31(3)(b) VCLT.[104] In that sense, the House of Lords, for instance, remarked:

> While the Handbook is not by any means itself a source of law, many signatory states have accepted the guidance which on their behalf the UNHCR was asked to provide, and in those circumstances it constitutes, in our judgment, good evidence of what has come to be international practice within article 31(3)(b) of the Vienna Convention.[105]

Similarly, the High Court of Australia noted:

> In 1979, the United Nations' High Commissioner for Refugees published the Handbook on Procedures and Criteria for Determining Refugee Status … Its purpose was to assist parties to the Convention and Protocol in determining claims to refugee status. It drew on the experience of the High Commissioner's office as well as the practices of contracting states after the Convention came into force in 1954 …. It may be used in Australia to assist in the interpretation of the Convention so long as it does not purport to usurp the function of the court or tribunal in giving meaning to the words of the Convention definition.[106]

In accordance with considering UNHCR publications as only one among other aids to discover practice, domestic courts have often scrutinised whether the alleged practice actually exists. Even where UNHCR had claimed to faithfully reflect State

---

[101] *Ward* (n 100) [34] (La Forest J). In the same vein, see *Chan* (n 100) [46] (La Forest J).

[102] See 'endorse | indorse, v' *Oxford English Dictionary Online* (September 2014, OUP) <http://www.oed.com/view/Entry/61987?rskey=kdDrJe&result=2>.

[103] The Refugee Convention has 145 parties whereas the UNHCR ExCom currently consists of 101 members. For membership in the UNHCR ExCom, see <http://www.unhcr.org>.

[104] See also BVerfGE 94, 49, 91; BVerwGE 124, 276, 289 f; 132, 79, 92 f; BVGer, Judgment of 11 September 2008, E-4207/2006, BVGE 2008/34, 501 [6.1] f.

[105] *Adan* (n 87) 500 (Lord Woolf).

[106] *A v Minister for Immigration & Ethnic Affairs* [1997] HCA 4, (1997) 190 CLR 225, 302 (Kirby J) [fn omitted].

practice, domestic courts have not always trusted in this claim's correctness.[107] This can be seen in a decision of the German Federal Administrative Court on the interpretation of article 1(C)(5) Refugee Convention. To support its reading of this provision, the Court sought to show that no contrary practice within the meaning of article 31(3)(b) VCLT existed.[108] As 'auxiliary means' to identify such practice, the Court examined UNHCR's Guidelines on the Cessation of Refugee Status.[109] Notably, the Guidelines themselves and an additional statement by UNHCR[110] asserted that this material was based on and reflected existing State practice.[111] The Court, however, did not attach any weight to these assertions. Instead, it critically examined whether the alleged State practice really existed.[112] And since it discovered no evidence of it, the Court ultimately found its reading of the contentious provision confirmed.[113]

Another example of how courts sought to verify whether the interpretation advocated by UNHCR was actually supported by State practice is *R v Asfaw*. By way of introduction, Lord Hope acknowledged that 'weight must be attached to the views of UNHCR in the light of its functions under article 35 of the Convention and to those academics who specialise in this field.'[114] Emphasising that UNHCR's assertions 'appear never to have been tested judicially elsewhere in the courts of the states parties', he then concluded that there was no relevant (judicial) State practice upon which he could rely.[115] In the same vein, Lord Mance remarked that

> [t]here is no suggestion in this case of any relevant agreement or other instrument made between any of the Contracting States in connection with or subsequent to the conclusion of the Convention. Nor was there made to the House any explicit suggestion of subsequent state practice establishing the meaning of the parties regarding the Convention's interpretation, although reference was made to views expressed by the United Nations High Commissioner for Refugees and by certain commentators which mention inter alia the practice of 'some states'.[116]

---

[107] cf also *Ezokola v Canada (Citizenship and Immigration)* [2013] SCC 40, 361 DLR (4th) 1 [77] (LeBel and Fish JJ), where the Court distinguished between UNHCR's interpretation of the Refugee Convention and the contracting parties' reaction thereto.

[108] BVerwG, Decision of 7 February 2008, 10 C 33/07 <http://www.juris.de> [31].

[109] UNHCR, 'Guidelines on International Protection No 3: Cessation of Refugee Status under Article 1C(5) and (6) of the 1951 Convention relating to the Status of Refugees (the "Ceased Circumstances" Clauses)' (10 February 2003) UN Doc HCR/GIP/03/03. See BVerwG, Decision of 7 February 2008, 10 C 33/07 <http://www.juris.dc> [32] and [34].

[110] UNHCR, 'Ergänzende Stellungnahme des UNHCR zu den Voraussetzungen der Beendigung der Flüchtlingseigenschaft nach Art 1 C (5) 1 des Abkommens von 1951 über die Rechtsstellung der Flüchtlinge (Genfer Flüchtlingskonvention)' (October 2005) <http://www.refworld.org/docid/48abd5570.html>.

[111] UNHCR, 'Guidelines on International Protection No 3: Cessation of Refugee Status under Article 1C(5) and (6) of the 1951 Convention relating to the Status of Refugees (the "Ceased Circumstances" Clauses)' (10 February 2003) UN Doc HCR/GIP/03/03, [5].

[112] BVerwG, Decision of 7 February 2008, 10 C 33/07 <http://www.juris.de> [34].

[113] ibid [31].

[114] *R v Asfaw* [2008] UKHL 31, [2008] 1 AC 1061 [53] (Lord Hope).

[115] ibid.

[116] ibid [126] (Lord Mance).

In other cases, domestic courts were less critical towards the reliability of UNHCR publications. In the case of *Németh v Canada (Justice)*, for instance, the Supreme Court of Canada mentioned UNHCR's 'Guidance Note on Extradition and International Refugee Protection'[117] to show that extradition authorities in some countries did not consider themselves bound by a previous formal conferral of refugee status by an immigration or asylum authority.[118] Based on this Note, the Court concluded that the Refugee Convention as interpreted in State practice did not prohibit extradition where a previous finding that a person was a refugee had been formally set aside.[119] Although the Court did not treat the Note as a means of interpretation in its own right, it did not conduct its own research on potentially relevant State practice but simply embraced the assessment made by UNHCR.

Similarly, Lord Clyde rather uncritically noted in *Horvath* that UNHCR's Handbook had 'the weight of accumulated practice behind it.'[120] Based on this observation, he relied on the Handbook's recommendation as to when offensive acts committed by a local populace may constitute persecution within the meaning of the Refugee Convention.[121] In addition, he also briefly referred to domestic and foreign case law on that issue.[122] This reference, however, did not serve to seriously question the Handbook's authority but merely underlined UNHCR's recommendation.

In sum, most cases confirm that UNHCR publications are not directly relevant under article 31(3)(b) VCLT. But sometimes, domestic courts displayed an even more critical attitude towards this material. This applies in particular to the Federal Court of Australia. In the case of *SRYYY v Minister for Immigration & Multicultural & Indigenous Affairs*, for instance, the Court remarked:

> Article 31(1) of the Vienna Convention provides that a treaty is to be interpreted in good faith, 'in accordance with the ordinary meaning to be given to the terms of the treaty in their context and in the light of its object and purpose'. Articles 31(3) and 32 of the Vienna Convention permit recourse to matters external to the treaty, including 'subsequent practice in the application of the treaty', 'relevant rules of international law applicable in the relations between the parties' to the treaty and the *travaux preparatoires* of the treaty. Recourse may also be had to relevant decisions in other jurisdictions … and the views of eminent academic commentators in the relevant field … Finally, publications of the UNHCR such as its Handbook on Procedures and Criteria for Determining Refugee Status under the 1951 Convention and the 1967 Protocol relating to the Status of Refugees ('UNHCR Handbook') may also be of assistance in interpreting the meaning of the Refugees Convention.[123]

[117] UNHCR, 'Guidance Note on Extradition and International Refugee Protection' (April 2008) <http://www.refworld.org/docid/481ec7d92.html>.

[118] *Németh v Canada (Justice)* [2010] 3 SCR 281, 2010 SCC 56 [52] (Cromwell J).

[119] ibid [49], [52] (Cromwell J).

[120] *Horvath* (n 89) 515 (Lord Clyde).

[121] ibid.

[122] ibid 515 f (Lord Clyde).

[123] *SRYYY v Minister for Immigration & Multicultural & Indigenous Affairs* [2005] FCAFC 42, (2005) 147 FCR 1 [18] (Merkel, Finkelstein, and Weinberg JJ).

This statement illustrates that the Court did not regard UNHCR publications as relevant under article 31(1) VCLT. Furthermore, the Court even mentioned this material only after supplementary means of interpretation such as foreign court decisions and academic publications. Thus, it attributed very little interpretative weight to this material. This impression was reinforced in *NBGM v Minister for Immigration & Multicultural & Indigenous Affairs,* where the Court explained:

> One clear basis for that consideration is to treat the Handbook as one would the work of learned jurists. On this basis, a court may have regard not only to the Handbook, but also guidelines issued by the same Office, for interpretive guidance. Relevant in this respect are the Guidelines on the Cessation of Refugee Status Under Article 1C(5) and (6) issued in 1999 and, in a superseding form, issued in 2003 (the 'Guidelines'). Another possible basis for the use of such material is the understanding of state practice in the application of the Convention. (See Article 31(3)(b) of the Vienna Convention, in particular in the light of the terms of Article 35 of the Convention.) .... It is sufficient for present purposes to recognise the former basis for the assistance of such material.
>
> Caution has been expressed by some as to the use of the Handbook ... Such caution can be seen to be directed to ensuring that reference to the Handbook is not taken to be determinative of any question of interpretation, or as a substitute for the words of the Convention interpreted in the liberal fashion referred to earlier, or to be more than a secondary source as an aid to interpretation akin to the work of jurists.[124]

Although the Court suggested that UNHCR publications might be relevant under article 31(3)(b) VCLT, it ultimately refused to unreservedly embrace this view. Instead, it regarded this material as a supplementary means of interpretation ('secondary source') only.

The House of Lords once questioned the interpretative value of UNHCR publications in even clearer terms. In the case of *R (Sivakumuran) v Secretary of State for the Home Department,* UNHCR had been granted leave to intervene and vaguely asserted that its Handbook, 'prepared for and at the request of states, provides guidance to states' on the interpretation of the Refugee Convention.[125] Assuming that UNHCR regarded its Handbook as part of the Convention's *travaux préparatoires,* the House of Lords pressed on UNHCR to specify on which basis it may have regard to the Handbook.[126] Interestingly, UNHCR insisted that its Handbook should not merely be taken into account under article 32 VCLT but

> as evidence of state practice in the interpretation and application of the Convention: see article 31 of the Vienna Convention on the Law of Treaties. It was prepared for and at the request of states members of the Executive Committee of the High Commissioner's Programme for the guidance of governments. The Handbook is based on the intervener's experience, including the practice of states with regard to the determination of refugee status, diplomatic exchanges of views between the intervener's Office and the competent authorities of contracting states and the academic literature devoted to the subject over the

---

[124] *NBGM v Minister for Immigration & Multicultural & Indigenous Affairs* [2006] FCAFC 60 [161]–[62] (Allsop J).

[125] *R (Sivakumuran) v Secretary of State for the Home Department* [1987] UKHL 1, [1988] AC 958.

[126] ibid 981 (Lord Bridge).

> last quarter of a century. It has since been widely circulated and utilised by governments and cited in many judicial decisions.[127]

Hence, UNHCR did not assert that its publications were, in themselves, relevant under article 31(3)(b) VCLT. Instead, it endorsed the view adopted in many domestic court cases, namely that its publications could provide evidence of State practice and thus become indirectly relevant under article 31(3)(b) VCLT. Although UNHCR did not overemphasise the interpretative value of its publications, the House of Lords nonetheless firmly objected: '[T]he Handbook amounts to a statement of the point of view espoused by the High Commissioner, but provides no justification for that point of view, as a matter of construction.'[128]

Radical as this statement appears at first sight, it is, however, important to recall that it neither corresponds to the view adopted by the House of Lords in other cases nor to that adopted by other domestic courts. Nonetheless, it illustrates that domestic courts have ambivalent feelings towards UNHCR publications. Appreciating the usefulness of this material in some cases, they seek to counteract the impression that this material and eventually UNHCR itself could claim interpretative instead of merely persuasive authority.

7.2.3 Evaluation

On the whole, domestic courts have approached UNHCR publications even more critically than treaty body output, although the overall impression was similarly ambivalent. In most cases, domestic courts assigned 'high persuasive authority'[129] to UNHCR publications and referred to them to interpret the Refugee Convention and the Refugee Protocol without discussing the legal basis for taking this material into account. As UNHCR publications are at least covered by article 32 VCLT as supplementary means of interpretation, this in itself does not say much about their exact legal status. In those cases, however, in which their legal basis was addressed, domestic courts were mindful not to overemphasise the legal status of UNHCR publications.

In a few cases, domestic courts vaguely referred to article 31(3)(b) VCLT in connection with UNHCR publications. Yet, they avoided clear and unambiguous statements to the effect that this material constituted relevant non-party practice under this provision. Morevover, such vague references were not reconfirmed in subsequent decisions. Most cases, on the contrary, indicate that domestic courts do not regard UNHCR publications as directly relevant under article 31(3)(b) VCLT. Instead, they generally treated this material as one among other possible aids to discover potentially relevant State practice for the purpose of article 31(3)(b) VCLT.

---

[127] ibid 981.

[128] ibid 1000 (Lord Goff).

[129] See in particular *Adan* (n 87), 520 (Lord Steyn).

In this respect, several domestic courts even took note of UNHCR's claim to reflect State practice under the Refugee Convention and the Refugee Protocol.

Nonetheless, domestic courts regularly doubted that this claim was correct in the case at hand. In consequence, they conducted their own research for potentially relevant State practice and, based on their own research, even rejected the interpretation advocated by UNHCR because it lacked sufficient support in State practice. This reconfirms the overall impression that domestic courts do not consider UNCHR publications as primary means of interpretation. But whereas some courts critically asked whether and to which extent UNHCR publications reflected or induced relevant State practice, others were less critical towards the reliability of UNHCR publications. These courts did not recognise this material as directly relevant under article 31(3)(b) VCLT either. Still, they unreservedly accepted UNHCR's claim that its publications had 'the weight of accumulated practice' behind them.[130] Thus, their reasoning somewhat blurred the difference between relevant State practice on the one hand and useful tools to identify such practice on the other.

Notably, domestic courts did not address the fact that UNHCR's mandate exceeds the Refugee Convention and the Refugee Protocol. Hence one may wonder whether domestic courts are even aware that UNHCR's mandate is broader than that of treaty bodies. Notwithstanding their indirect relevance under article 31(3)(b) VCLT, the jurisprudence of domestic courts suggests that recourse may be had to UNHCR publications and treaty body output alike as supplementary means of interpretation under article 32 VCLT.

7.3 The OECD 'Model Convention on Income and Capital'

Section 7.3 deals with a specific cooperative context of treaty interpretation,[131] namely the regulation of international juridical double taxation. International juridical double taxation can be defined as 'the imposition of comparable taxes in two (or more) States on the same taxpayer in respect of the same subject matter for identical periods.'[132] To eliminate the harmful economic effects of double taxation, States have gradually created a network of more than 3000, mostly bilateral, DTAs.[133]

---

[130] See in particular *Horvath* (n 89) 515 (Lord Clyde).

[131] For this terminology, see Nolte, 'Report 3—Practice outside of Judicial Proceedings' (n 3) 360.

[132] See OECD, *Model Tax Convention on Income and on Capital 2010* (OECD Pub 2012) I-1 [1]. cf also Yoram Margalioth, 'Double Taxation' in Rüdiger Wolfrum (ed), *The Max Planck Encyclopedia of Public International Law* (OUP 2012) [1].

[133] id, 'International Taxation' in Rüdiger Wolfrum (ed), *The Max Planck Encyclopedia of Public International Law* (OUP 2012) [82]. To appreciate the countless number of DTAs, see eg the overview of DTAs that have been concluded by the following States: Australia <http://www.ato.gov.au/General/International-tax-agreements/In-detail/Tax-treaties/Countries-that-have-a-tax-treaty-with-Australia>; Austria <https://www.bmf.gv.at/steuern/int-steuerrecht/oesterreichische-doppelbesteuerungsabkommen.html>; Canada <http://www.fin.gc.ca/treaties-conventions/

Although each agreement is an independent treaty between two (or more) States, an overwhelming number of these agreements is based on or even replicates the provisions of the OECD 'Model Convention on Income and Capital'.[134] This document is not the only model for DTAs but has been by far the most successful one.[135]

Therefore, it is not surprising that the Model Convention and related documents, such as the Commentaries thereon or the OECD 'Transfer Pricing Guidelines for Multinational Enterprises and Tax Administrations',[136] have played a special role in the jurisprudence of domestic courts.[137] As the OECD itself noted, '[b]ilateral tax treaties are receiving more and more judicial attention as well. The courts are increasingly using the Commentaries in reaching their decisions … [and] the Commentaries have been cited in the published decisions of the courts of the great majority of member countries.'[138] Although no one denies that the Model Convention and related documents are de facto highly relevant to the interpretation of DTAs, it has been rather controversial whether and to which extent these documents are also legally relevant under the Vienna rules of interpretation.

In the following, this subchapter focuses on a specific part of this controversy by asking whether the Model Convention and related documents are relevant under article 31(3)(a) or (b) VCLT. As the answer to this question is complicated by the specific cooperative context of DTAs, it is useful to firstly set out the institutional framework of the OECD (7.3.1). This outline is supplemented by a cursory overview of the debates on how the Model Convention and related documents fit into the Vienna rules (7.3.2). Against this background, this subchapter then examines

treatystatus_-eng.asp>; Germany <http://www.bundesfinanzministerium.de/Web/DE/Themen/Steuern/Internationales_Steuerrecht/Staatenbezogene_Informationen/staatenbezogene_info.html>; New Zealand <http://taxpolicy.ird.govt.nz/tax-treaties#dta>; Switzerland <http://www.admin.ch/opc/de/classified-compilation/0.67.html#0.67>; UK <http://www.hmrc.gov.uk/tax-treaties/in-force/index.htm>; USA <http://www.irs.gov/Businesses/International-Businesses/United-States-Income-Tax-Treaties---A-to-Z>.

[134] OECD, *Model Tax Convention on Income and on Capital* 2010 (n 132).

[135] Margalioth, 'Double Taxation' (n 132) [6]; id, 'International Taxation' in Rüdiger Wolfrum (ed), *The Max Planck Encyclopedia of Public International Law* (OUP 2012) [5], [88]. Alternative models include: UN, 'Model Double Taxation Convention between Developed and Developing Countries' (2011) UN Doc ST/ESA/PAD/SER.E/21; USA, 'Model Income Tax Convention' (15 November 2006) <http://www.irs.gov/pub/irs-trty/model006.pdf>.

[136] OECD, *Transfer Pricing Guidelines for Multinational Enterprises and Tax Administrations* (OECD Pub 2010).

[137] Edwin van der Bruggen, 'The Power of Persuasion: Notes on the Sources of International Law and the OECD Commentary' (2003) 31 Intertax 259, 259; Michael Lang and Florian Brugger, 'The Role of the OECD Commentary in Tax Treaty Interpretation' (2008) 23 ATF 95, 95; Nicola Bonucci and Gita Kothari, 'Organization for Economic Cooperation and Development (OECD)' in Rüdiger Wolfrum (ed), *The Max Planck Encyclopedia of Public International Law* (OUP 2012) [53].

[138] OECD, *Model Tax Convention on Income and on Capital* 2010 (n 132) I-9 [29.3].

whether domestic courts have discussed these documents in a way that helps to cast light on their legal status under the Vienna rules and article 31(3)(a) or (b) VCLT in particular (7.3.3).

7.3.1 The OECD, its Model Convention, and Related Documents

The OECD is an IO whose origins go back until 1949.[139] In that year, the Organisation for European Economic Co-operation (OEEC) was established to administer the implementation of the Marshall Plan and to strengthen cooperation between European economies.[140] With the accession of Canada and the USA in 1961, the OEEC was reconstituted as the OECD in order to carry out its objectives at a global level.[141] According to article 1 OECD Convention, the organisation aims at promoting policies that are designed to achieving the highest sustainable growth, to contribute to sound economic expansion, and to contribute to the expansion of world trade. Today, the OECD has 35 member States.[142]

The body from which all acts of the organisation derive is the OECD Council.[143] The Council consists of one representative per member State plus a representative of the European Commission.[144] To achieve its aims, the OECD may, apart from entering into agreements with member States, non-member States, and other IOs, either adopt decisions or recommendations.[145] Both decisions and recommendations are generally taken by consensus.[146] Yet, only decisions are legally binding on OECD member States.[147] To facilitate its work, the OECD has set up numerous committees on specific policy areas. These committees are, among others, involved in the drafting process of decisions and recommendations before they are finally adopted by the OECD Council.[148] One of these committees is the Committee on Fiscal Affairs

[139] See generally on the origins of the OECD Richard Woodward, *The Organisation for Economic Cooperation and Development* (Routledge 2009).

[140] ibid 14 f; Bonucci and Kothari, 'OECD' (n 137) [4]. The OEEC was established by the Convention for European Economic Co-operation (signed 16 April 1948, entered into force 28 July 1948) 888 UNTS 141 (OEEC Convention).

[141] Woodward, *OECD* (n 139) 16 f; Bonucci and Kothari, 'OECD' (n 137) [6]. The OECD was established by the Protocol on the Revision of the Convention for European Economic Co-operation of 16 April 1948 (signed 14 December 1960, entered into force 30 September 1961) 888 UNTS 179 (OECD Convention).

[142] See <http://www.oecd.org/about/membersandpartners>.

[143] Art 7 OECD Convention.

[144] Art 7 OECD Convention and Supplementary Protocol No 1.

[145] Art 5 OECD Convention.

[146] Art 6(1) OECD Convention.

[147] Art 5(a) and (b) OECD Convention; see also rule 18(a) and (b) of the OECD Council, 'Rules of Procedure of the Organisation for Economic Co-operation and Development' (30 September 1961) Doc OECD/C(61)21 (OECD Rules of Procedure).

[148] cf rules 22–26 OECD Rules of Procedure.

(CFA).[149] As its name indicates, the CFA is the OECD's main tax policy body. Its work is intended to enable governments to 'improve the design and operation of their national tax systems, to promote co-operation and co-ordination among them in the area of taxation and to reduce tax barriers to international trade and investment' by creating, among others, standards, guidelines, and best practices.[150]

In 1963, the OECD promulgated its 'Draft Double Taxation Convention on Income and Capital'.[151] A revised version of this document was published in 1977 as the final 'Model Tax Convention on Income and Capital'.[152] Each of these Model Conventions was accompanied by extensive Commentaries, which illustrate and interpret the provisions of the Model Convention. Since 1992, both the Model Convention and the Commentaries have been updated on a regular basis.[153] But while these regular updates helped to keep pace with changing international developments, the resulting 'ambulatory' nature of Model Convention and Commentaries has entailed much uncertainty as regards the application of the Vienna rules. Because Model Convention and Commentaries have been adopted pursuant to article 5(b) OECD Convention, they are not legally binding as such but merely recommendations.[154] Although the OECD Council has repeatedly recommended its member States to conform to the Model Convention as interpreted by the Commentaries thereon,[155] there is no need to say that these recommendations—not being legally binding themselves—are incapable of vesting the Model Convention and the Commentaries with higher legal force.

In addition to its Model Convention and the Commentaries, the OECD has also published reports and guidelines on specific problems in the application of its Model. An important example of such guidelines are the 'Transfer Pricing Guidelines for Multinational Enterprises and Tax Administrations'.[156] These guidelines, which

---

[149] The CFA, formerly known as the 'Fiscal Committee', was established by the OEEC, 'Resolution of the Council Creating a Fiscal Committee' (19 March 1956) Doc C(56)49/Final.

[150] See OECD, 'Resolution of the OECD Concil Revising the Mandate of the Committee on Fiscal Affairs' (13 November 2008) Docs C(2008)147 and C/M(2008)20, item 285.

[151] OECD, *Draft Double Taxation Convention on Income and Capital* (OECD Pub 1963).

[152] OECD, *Double Taxation of Income and Capital: Revised Texts of Certain Articles of the* 1963 *OECD Draft Convention and of the Commentary Thereon* (OECD Pub 1977).

[153] See <http://www.oecd.org/tax/treaties/oecdmtcavailableproducts.htm>; see further David Ward, *The Interpretation of Income Tax Treaties with Particular Reference to the Commentaries on the OECD Model* (IFA 2005) 4 f; Stefan Oesterhelt, 'Bedeutung des OECD-Kommentars für die Auslegung von Doppelbesteuerungsabkommen' (2011/2012) 80 ASA 373, 375.

[154] van der Bruggen, 'OECD Commentary' (n 137) 261 f. See also OECD, *Model Tax Convention on Income and on Capital 2010* (n 132) I-9 [29].

[155] Such recommendation was adopted for the first time in 1963. For the latest recommendation, see OECD, 'Recommendation of the OECD Council concerning the Model Tax Convention on Income and Capital' (23 October 1997) Doc C(97)195/FINAL.

[156] OECD, *Transfer Pricing Guidelines for Multinational Enterprises and Tax Administrations* (n 136).

were first published in 1979, elaborate on the so-called arm's length principle.[157] Although not expressly laid down in the Model Convention, this principle is implicitly envisaged in article 9 (associated enterprises).[158] As the Commentaries explain, article 9 deals with 'adjustments to profits that may be made for tax purposes where transactions have been entered into between associated enterprises (parent and subsidiary company) on other than arm's length terms.'[159] The notion 'arm's length terms' thus serves as a catchphrase to describe a transaction that has been entered into between two independent enterprises, ie on normal open market commercial terms. In other words, the arm's length principle is central for determining whether taxation authorities may or may not re-write the accounts of an enterprise in order to calculate tax liabilities.

Before turning to the ongoing controversies about how the Model Convention and related documents such as the Commentaries or the Transfer Pricing Guidelines fit into the Vienna rules, it must be emphasised that these rules govern the interpretation of DTAs as they govern the interpretation of any other treaty.[160] In light of

---

[157] See generally Jens Wittendorff, *Transfer Pricing and the Arm's Length Principle in International Tax Law* (Kluwer 2010).

[158] Art 9 of the 2010 Model Tax Convention reads:

1. Where

(a) an enterprise of a Contracting State participates directly or indirectly in the management, control or capital of an enterprise of the other Contracting State, or

(b) the same persons participate directly or indirectly in the management, control or capital of an enterprise of a Contracting State and an enterprise of the other Contracting State,

and in either case conditions are made or imposed between the two enterprises in their commercial or fiscal relations which differ from those which would be made between independent enterprises, then any profits which would, but for those conditions, have accrued to one of the enterprises, but, by reasons of those conditions, have not accrued, may be included in the profits of that enterprise and taxed accordingly.

2. Where a Contracting State includes in the profits of an enterprise of that State—and taxes accordingly—profits on which an enterprise of the other Contracting State has been charged to tax in that other State and the profits so included are profits which would have accrued to the enterprise of the first-mentioned State if the conditions made between the two enterprises had been those which would have been made between independent enterprises, then the other Contracting State shall make an appropriate adjustment to the amount of the tax charged therein on those profits. In determining such adjustment, due regard shall be had to the other provisions of this Convention and the competent authorities of the Contracting States shall if necessary consult each other.

[159] OECD, *Model Tax Convention on Income and on Capital 2010* (n 132) C(9)-1 [1].

[160] Franciscus Engelen, *Interpretation of Tax Treaties under International Law—A Study of Articles 31, 32 and 33 of the Vienna Convention on the Law of Treaties and Their Application to Tax Treaties* (IBFD 2004) 426 f; David Lai, 'Interpretation of Double Taxation Agreements in Hong Kong' (2007) 37 HKLJ 137, 141 f; Lang and Brugger, 'OECD Commentary' (n 137) 97. See also *Thiel v Federal Commissioner of Taxation* [1990] HCA 37, (1990) 171 CLR 338 [12] (McHugh J), [8] (Dawson J); BVGer, Judgment of 21 January 2010, BVGE 2010/7, 98 [3.6.1]; Klaus Vogel, 'Double Tax Treaties and Their Interpretation' (1986) 4 Int'l Tax & Bus Law 1, 15.

their practical relevance, it is understandable why legal literature largely agrees that these documents should be taken into account when interpreting DTAs.[161] Still, the conditions under which it is admissible to consider these documents—and, in consequence, the limits for doing so—cannot (solely) be deduced from the exigencies of international tax law but from the Vienna rules themselves.[162] Since the Vienna rules inevitably circumscribe and thus limit when and how these documents may be taken into account to interpret DTAs, close adherence to the Vienna rules must not necessarily be to the liking of international tax lawyers.[163] But as one author pointedly remarked, it 'would be a good idea for international tax lawyers to study the VCLT' because '[a] lot of hard thinking went into that treaty, and it should not be lightly ignored.'[164] That is not to say that there have been no attempts to justify why the Model Convention and related documents can be taken into account under the Vienna rules. In fact, almost any provision of the Vienna rules has once been invoked to provide this justification.

Some commentators have noted that the Model Convention and related documents could *at least* be taken into account as supplementary means of interpretation under article 32 VCLT.[165] Since article 32 VCLT does not contain a closed list of admissible material, this view is hardly controversial. However, supplementary means of interpretation are subject to additional conditions and recourse to them is not mandatory. If the Model Convention and related documents were only covered by article 32 VCLT, their relevance would be diminished.[166] Therefore, many commentators have advocated that these documents were also covered by the general rule of interpretation under article 31 VCLT. One line of reasoning follows up on the observation that numerous DTAs are drafted in similar or even identical terms like the Model Convention. This, so the argument continues, gave rise to the assumption

---

[161] Eg Ward, *Interpretation of Income Tax Treaties* (n 153) 29 f; van der Bruggen, 'OECD Commentary' (n 137) 269; Lang and Brugger, 'OECD Commentary' (n 137) 98 f; Vogel, 'Double Tax Treaties' (n 160) 39 f; Engelen, *Interpretation of Tax Treaties* (n 160) 439 f.

[162] Some commentators have even suggested that it was not necessary to fit OECD documents into the Vienna rules, see eg Ward, *Interpretation of Income Tax Treaties* (n 153) 18, 29 f. cf also van der Bruggen, 'OECD Commentary' (n 137) 270.

[163] cf Jose Calderón, 'The OECD Transfer Pricing Guidelines as a Source of Tax Law: Is Globalization Reaching the Tax Law?' (2007) 35 Intertax 4, 20, who boldly claims that the Transfer Pricing Guidelines, had 'evolved, to a degree, into an instrument of hard law.'

[164] Reuven Avi-Yonah, 'International Tax as International Law' (2004) 57 Tax L Rev 483, 493.

[165] Ines Hofbauer, 'Tax Treaty Interpretation in Austria' in Michael Lang (ed), *Tax Treaty Interpretation* (Kluwer 2001) 25; Lang and Brugger, 'OECD Commentary' (n 137) 98 f; Oesterhelt, 'Bedeutung des OECD-Kommentars' (n 153) 379; Vogel, 'Double Tax Treaties' (n 160) 40; Engelen, *Interpretation of Tax Treaties* (n 160) 460. See also *Thiel* (n 160) [10] (Dawson J). Critically, however, Ward, *Interpretation of Income Tax Treaties* (n 153) 24 f.

[166] cf Vogel, 'Double Tax Treaties' (n 160) 40, who notes with concern that '[n]o reason exists … to refer to these sources only as secondary means of interpretation, as is the case for "preparatory work" within the meaning of Article 32.'

that the respective DTA was intended to have the same meaning as the Model Convention as interpreted by the Commentaries and other related documents. Notwithstanding the possibility of rebutting this presumption,[167] the Model Convention and related documents would therefore be relevant as reflecting the DTA's ordinary or special meaning under article 31(1) or (4) VCLT.[168] An alternative, more controversial view maintains that the Model Convention and related documents formed part of the context within the meaning of article 31(2) VCLT.[169]

Irrespective of whether these different lines of reasoning are convincing, it is important to see that they are only capable of justifying references to those OECD documents that had been published before or at the same time when the respective DTA was concluded.[170] Because OECD documents are being frequently amended so that many DTAs predate the currently applicable versions, critical voices have begun to doubt that these amendments could that easily affect the interpretation of earlier DTAs.[171] The OECD itself has tried to authoritatively silence these concerns by claiming that amendments to the Model Convention and the Commentaries that do not differ in substance from the amended articles 'are normally applicable to the interpretation and application of conventions concluded before their adoption because they reflect the consensus of OECD member countries as to the proper interpretation of existing provisions and their application to specific situations.'[172]

Although the OECD even maintained that tax authorities in the OECD member States apply the Model Convention and the Commentaries to earlier DTAs,[173] its 'self-authorisation'—which is in itself nothing more than a recommendation—does not automatically mean that later OECD documents are covered by the general rule

---

[167] cf Lang and Brugger, 'OECD Commentary' (n 137) 100.

[168] Eg Hofbauer, 'Tax Treaty Interpretation in Austria' (n 165) 26; John Avery Jones, 'Tax Treaty Interpretation in the United Kingdom' in Michael Lang (ed), *Tax Treaty Interpretation* (Kluwer 2001) 364; Lang and Brugger, 'OECD Commentary' (n 137) 99 f; Oesterhelt, 'Bedeutung des OECD-Kommentars' (n 153) 379 f; see also *UBS AG v Revenue and Customs Commissioners* [2005] STC (SCD) 589 [10].

[169] See in particular Kees van Raad, 'Interpretatie van belastingverdragen' (1978) 47 MBB 49, 55; Lai, 'Interpretation of DTAs in Hong Kong' (n 160) 147 f. cf *Thiel* (n 160) [9] (Dawson J). Critically eg Hofbauer, 'Tax Treaty Interpretation in Austria' (n 165) 25 and Ekkehart Reimer, 'Tax Treaty Interpretation in Germany' in Michael Lang (ed), *Tax Treaty Interpretation* (Kluwer 2001) 135.

[170] Vogel, 'Double Tax Treaties' (n 160) 41.

[171] At least sceptical Ward, *Interpretation of Income Tax Treaties* (n 153) 78 f, 110 f. More critically eg Michael Lang, 'Later Commentaries of the OECD Committee on Fiscal Affairs, Not to Affect the Interpretation of Previously Concluded Tax Treaties' (1997) 25 Intertax 7, 7 f; Lang and Brugger, 'OECD Commentary' (n 137) 101 f; Lang, 'Later OECD Commentaries' (n 171) 7 f; Oesterhelt, 'Bedeutung des OECD-Kommentars' (n 153) 380 f; Steffen Lampert, 'Germany' in Michael Lang (ed), *The Impact of the OECD and UN Model Conventions on Bilateral Tax Treaties* (CUP 2012) 469 f.

[172] See OECD, *Model Tax Convention on Income and on Capital 2010* (n 132) I-10 f [35].

[173] See ibid I-11 [36.1].

of interpretation under article 31 VCLT.[174] In fact, such statements by the OECD on the legal status of its publications are only recommendations themselves and therefore incapable of vesting these publications with a legal status which they do not enjoy under the OECD Convention. Therefore, some commentators have attempted to clothe this 'self-authorisation' in legal terms. More precisely, there has been some debate about whether later OECD documents may fall under article 31(3)(a) or (b) VCLT and thus acquire the status of primary means of interpretation.[175]

7.3.2 *The OECD Model Convention in Domestic Jurisprudence*

Unlike legal literature, domestic courts have only rarely addressed the problem of later OECD documents at all. Instead, they mostly mentioned later OECD documents en passant without explaining on which legal basis these documents may be taken into account.[176] In some cases, domestic courts merely touched upon this issue without outlining the legal consequences for the interpretation of DTAs. In *McDermott Industries (Aust) Pty Ltd v Commissioner of Taxation*, for instance, the Federal Court of Australia remarked:

> A useful starting point is the commentary to the draft OECD Model Convention for the Avoidance of Double Taxation with respect to Taxes on Income and on Capital, presented in 1963 ('OECD Model Convention'), which has served as a model for many although

[174] cf Oesterhelt, 'Bedeutung des OECD-Kommentars' (n 153) 380.

[175] This position has, eg, been taken by Mike Waters, 'The Relevance of OECD Commentaries in the Interpretation of Tax Treaties' in Michael Lang and Heinz Jirousek (eds), *Praxis des Internationalen Steuerrechts—Festschrift für Helmut Loukota zum 65. Geburtstag* (Linde 2005) 680 f; Reimer, 'Tax Treaty Interpretation in Germany' (n 169) 137. cf also Nolte, 'Report 3—Practice outside of Judicial Proceedings' (n 3) 363, who suggested that it was a promising approach to 'consider whether the amended Model Convention or Commentaries are a form of subsequent practice of the parties which should be taken into account according to Art. 31 (3)(b) VCLT.' Later, he clarified, however, that the amended Model Convention or Commentaries do not automatically amount to relevant practice but only if the parties to the respective DTA 'apply a treaty according to the amended Commentary or the amended Model Convention.'

[176] Eg VwGH, Judgment of 21 March 1996, 94/15/0128 on the interpretation of the Agreement between the Principality of Liechtenstein and the Republic of Austria for the Avoidance of Double Taxation with respect to Taxes on Income and Fortune (signed 5 November 1969, entered into force 7 December 1970) 771 UNTS 149 (1969 Liechtenstein–Austrian DTA); VfGH, Judgment of 15 March 1990, B758/88, VfSlg 12326 on the Convention between the Republic of Austria and the Portuguese Republic for the Avoidance of Double Taxation with respect to Taxes on Income and Fortune (signed 29 December 1970, entered into force 27 February 1972) 823 UNTS 277 (1970 Austrian–Portuguese DTA); BVGer, Judgment of 12 May 2011, A-4683/2010, 17 f [6.3.4] on the interpretation of the Convention between the Government of the Republic of Singapore and the Swiss Confederation for the Avoidance of Double Taxation with respect to Taxes on Income and on Capital (signed 25 November 1975, entered into force 17 December 1976) SR 0.672.968.91 (1975 Singaporean–Swiss DTA).

> not all of Australia's double tax agreements. Certainly the commentary has been used to assist in the interpretation of double tax agreements based upon it, although there may be a theoretical difficulty in using commentary published after the adoption of a double taxation agreement as relevant to the construction of that agreement.[177]

Since the case arose under the amended 1969 Australian–Singaporean DTA,[178] there was no necessity for the Court to further elaborate on the difficulty of using later Commentaries as it referred to the Commentaries on the 1963 Model Convention. Yet, this decision illustrates that the Court was very well aware that such difficulties, albeit merely 'theoretical' according to the Court, existed.[179] But even if later OECD documents were used to interpret earlier DTAs, domestic courts would hardly face any difficulties if they regarded both earlier and later OECD documents as supplementary means of interpretation only. Taking the view that earlier documents are supplementary means of interpretation *only*,[180] one can hardly think of reasons to justify why later documents should be more than that.

Where domestic courts nonetheless took a stance on the doctrinal difficulties resulting from later OECD documents, they expressed very different views on that matter. The German Federal Fiscal Court, for instance, refused to rely on later OECD documents to interpret earlier DTAs. This can be seen in a judgment on the 1977 German–Hungarian DTA. This case raised the question of whether the taxpayer's residence country (here: Germany) was competent to determine the income that would be attributable to that taxpayer for tax reasons or whether the attributable income was to be determined by the country in which the taxpayer had his place of work and where the income originated from. Because the 1999 OECD Partnership

---

[177] *McDermott Industries (Aust) Pty Ltd v Commissioner of Taxation* [2005] FCAFC 67, (2005) 142 FCR 134 [42] (Hill, Sundberg, and Stone JJ).

[178] Agreement between the Government of the Commonwealth of Australia and the Government of the Republic of Singapore for the Avoidance of Double Taxation and the Prevention of Fiscal Evasion with respect to Taxes on Income (signed 11 February 1969, entered into force 4 June 1969) 708 UNTS 228 (1969 Australian–Singaporean DTA) as amended by Protocol (signed 16 October 1989, entered into force 5 January 1990) 1571 UNTS 500.

[179] cf VwGH, Judgment of 31 July 1996, 92/13/0172, 3 f on the interpretation of the Agreement between the Republic of Austria and the Swiss Confederation for the Avoidance of Double Taxation in the Field of Taxes on Income and on Capital (signed 30 January 1974, entered into force 4 December 1974) 2176 UNTS 297 (1974 Austrian–Swiss DTA); cf also VwGH, Judgment of 21 May 1997, 96/14/0084, 3 f on the interpretation of the 1974 Austrian–Swiss DTA. In these cases, the Austrian Court emphasised that Commentaries existing *at the time* when the respective DTA was concluded were relevant to the interpretation of that DTA.

[180] Eg BVGer, Judgment of 21 January 2010, BVGE 2010/7, 100 [3.6.2], where the Court remarked that the Model Convention and the Commentaries were supplementary means of interpretation only since they addressed the governments of the OECD member States but not the member States' courts or their taxpayers. To the same effect, see BVGer, Judgment of 23 July 2012, A-1246/2011 [3.3.4].

Report recommended the latter interpretation,[181] the Court, which disagreed with this view, discussed under which conditions such reports could be legally relevant to the interpretation of DTAs.[182] By way of introduction, the Court acknowledged that recommendations issued by the OECD, such as those contained in the pertinent report, may well constitute a guide to interpretation.[183] However, this was only the case where the respective DTA had entered into force *after* the updated version of the OECD Model Convention and the Commentaries thereon.[184] If, in contrast, a DTA had entered into force before the Model Convention and Commentaries, OECD recommendations relating to the updated versions could not, so the Court continued, reflect the intention of the parties regarding the interpretation of the earlier DTA.[185]

Although it did not say so, the Court thus implicitly refused to acknowledge that later OECD documents may be relevant under article 31(3)(a) or (b) VCLT. That the Court requires some sort of evidence of the parties' intention to read OECD documents into their DTA can also be seen in a judgment on the 1959 German–French DTA,[186] as amended in 2001.[187] The case raised the question of whether a taxpayer's 'stay' in his country of work in the sense of article 13(4) of the DTA included only those days on which he was physically present on the territory, or whether it covered the whole period of employment irrespective of short returns to his residence country due to weekends, illnesses, etc.[188] To resolve this issue, the Court relied on the Commentaries to the 1977 OECD Model Convention. In the Court's view, this was admissible because the DTA had been amended in 2001, ie after the 1977 OECD Model Convention had been published, and because the amendment had aimed at bringing the DTA in line with the Model Convention.[189] This amendment, so the Court argued, indicated that the parties to the DTA had intended to embrace the understanding underlying the Model Convention.[190] In a later judgment, the Court more clearly

---

[181] OECD, *The Application of the OECD Model Tax Convention to Partnerships* (OECD Pub 1999).

[182] BFHE 234, 63, 67.

[183] ibid 69.

[184] ibid. To the same effect, see BFHE 229, 322, 334; 232, 476, 483.

[185] BFHE 234, 63, 69.

[186] Convention between the French Republic and the Federal Republic of Germany for the Avoidance of Double Taxation and the Establishment of Principles for Reciprocal Administrative and Legal Assistance with respect to Taxes on Income and Fortune, Business Taxes and Land Taxes (signed 21 July 1959, entered into force 4 November 1961) 770 UNTS 325 (1959 French–German DTA).

[187] Additional Protocol to the Convention between the French Republic and the Federal Republic of Germany for the Avoidance of Double Taxation and the Establishment of Principles for Reciprocal Administrative and Legal Assistance with respect to Taxes on Income and Fortune, Business Taxes and Land Taxes of 21 July 1959 (signed 20 December 2001, entered into force 1 June 2003) BGBl (Germany) 2002 II 2370.

[188] BFHE 235, 401, 402.

[189] ibid 405.

[190] ibid.

remarked that later Commentaries did not, in themselves, reflect the parties' agreement as regards the interpretation of their DTA.[191] Instead, they only expressed the opinion of those who drafted them but did not constitute an application of a DTA that was capable of indicating a particular interpretation of that instrument.[192]

The Belgian Cour de Cassation, in contrast, adopted a different approach. In a judgment on the 1970 Belgian–Luxembourg DTA,[193] the Court acknowledged that the Model Convention and the Commentaries formed part of the context within the meaning of article 31(3)(a) VCLT, provided that the pertinent DTA did not considerably differ from the Model Convention.[194] It is remarkable that the Court neither explained why these OECD documents—which had been adopted by an IO whose legal identity is separate from that of its member States—should either constitute an 'agreement between the parties regarding the interpretation of the treaty' (article 31(3)(a) VCLT) or at least a 'practice in the application of the treaty which establishes the agreement of the parties regarding its interpretation' (article 31(3)(b) VCLT). Instead, the Court suggested that an identical or sufficiently identical wording was enough to link these documents to the respective DTA as required by article 31(3)(a) or (b) VCLT. Whether the Court's legal assessment would differ in cases where non-OECD member States are concerned, remains, however, unclear.

An at least partly convincing approach was adopted by the Federal Court of Australia in the case of *Commissioner of Taxation v SNF (Australia) Pty Ltd.*[195] This case concerned the interpretation of provisions on transfer pricing that were contained, in identical terms, in the 1976 Australian–French DTA,[196] the 1982 Australian–US DTA,[197] and the 1988 Australian–Chinese DTA.[198] These provisions, in

---

[191] BFH, Judgment of 16 January 2014, I R 30/12 <http://www.juris.de> [19].

[192] ibid. To the same effect, see BFH, Decision of 11 December 2013, I R 4/13 <http://www.juris.de> [15].

[193] Agreement between Belgium and Luxembourg for the Avoidance of Double Taxation and the Regulation of Certain Other Matters with respect to Taxes on Income and Fortune (signed 17 September 1970, entered into force 30 December 1972) 870 UNTS 167 (1970 Belgian–Luxembourg DTA).

[194] Cour de Cassation de Belgique, Decision of 28 May 2004, F.02.0078.F <http://jure.juridat.just.fgov.be>.

[195] *Commissioner of Taxation v SNF (Australia) Pty Ltd* [2011] FCAFC 74, (2011) 193 FCR 149.

[196] Agreement between the Government of Australia and the Government of the French Republic for the Avoidance of Double Taxation and the Prevention of Fiscal Evasion with respect to Taxes on Income (signed 13 April 1976, entered into force 21 September 1977) 1072 UNTS 379 (1976 Australian–French DTA), as amended by Protocol (signed 19 June 1989, entered into force 19 July 1990) 1583 UNTS 491.

[197] Convention between the Government of Australia and the Government of the United States of America for the Avoidance of Double Taxation and the Prevention of Fiscal Evasion with respect to Taxes on Income (signed 6 August 1982, entered into force 31 October 1983) 1424 UNTS 37 (1982 Australian–US DTA), as amended by Protocol (signed 27 September 2001, entered into force 12 May 2003) 2260 UNTS 117.

[198] Agreement between the Government of Australia and the Government of the People's Republic of China for the Avoidance of Double Taxation and the Prevention of Fiscal Evasion with respect to Taxes on Income (signed 17 November 1988, entered into force 28 November 1990) 1642 UNTS 3 (1988 Australian–Chinese DTA).

turn, were identical to article 9 of the OECD Model Convention. This case raised the question of whether and to which extent the Model Convention and the accompanying Commentaries as well as the Transfer Pricing Guidelines were relevant to the interpretation of these DTAs.[199] As a starting point, the Court maintained that the Model Convention and the Commentaries may either be considered as part of the context under article 31(3)(2) VCLT or as part of the drafting history of the DTAs under article 32 VCLT.[200]

However, the Court failed to indicate which version of the Model Convention and the Commentaries it actually referred to. Since the judgment was delivered in 2011 and because the Court acknowledged that the Commentaries had been 'modified from time to time,'[201] it presumably referred to the updates from 2010. Therefore, it is surprising that the Court unreservedly held that the Model Convention and the Commentaries were covered by article 31(2) VCLT as part of the context or by article 32 VCLT as part of the drafting history. Especially the former alternative is difficult to reconcile with the Vienna rules. This is because the Model Convention and Commentaries do not qualify as text, preambles, or annexes; nor do they qualify as agreements or instruments relating to and made in connection with the DTAs. Even more surprisingly, the Court did not bother either that China was (and still is) not an OECD member State. Instead, the Court considered it sufficient to point out that the contentious provisions of the DTAs were identical to the respective provision of the Model Convention.

This rather uncritical approach stands in stark contrast to the way in which the Court then approached the Transfer Pricing Guidelines. Referring to the language of the Guidelines' preface, the Court first emphasised that they were not legally binding.[202] Based on this observation, it further clarified:

> Under Article 31(3) they can be examined only if they reflect the subsequent agreement of the States in question or, under Article 31(3)(b), 'any subsequent practice in the application of the treaty which establishes the agreement of the parties regarding its interpretation'. In order to permit recourse to the guidelines it would therefore be necessary to show that Australia and each of China, the US and France had either agreed to apply the portion of the guidelines relied upon in their performance of the equivalent of Article 9 of each agreement or that it was their practice to do so.
>
> There was no evidence that any of the States in question had adopted the practice of applying the guidelines to any of the circumstances in which Article 9 of the Model Law might obtain in their jurisdictions. It must therefore follow that they may not be examined … The guidelines then are not a legitimate aid to the construction of the double taxation treaties.[203]

This quotation shows that the Court did not consider the Guidelines themselves as an agreement or practice that could come under article 31(3)(a) or (b) VCLT.

[199] *SNF (Australia)* (n 195) [101] f, [110] f (Ryan, Jessup, and Perram JJ).

[200] ibid [114] (Ryan, Jessup, and Perram JJ).

[201] ibid [107] (Ryan, Jessup, and Perram JJ).

[202] ibid [116] (Ryan, Jessup, and Perram JJ).

[203] ibid [116] f (Ryan, Jessup, and Perram JJ).

Instead, the Court required additional evidence that the parties to the DTAs had either agreed to apply the Guidelines or that it had been their practice to do so. Viewed in isolation, the Guidelines thus did not carry any interpretative weight in the Court's opinion. While the Court considered it possible that the Guidelines could generate a certain practice or be the object of an agreement between or of the parties, it would have been this practice or agreement which would have become relevant under article 31(3)(a) or (b) VCLT.

7.3.3 *Evaluation*

In sum, domestic courts have not taken a uniform approach to later OECD documents. In fact, they only rarely addressed this problem in the first place. Still, a few valuable ideas can be drawn from their jurisprudence. First of all, the view that OECD documents themselves constitute subsequent agreements or subsequent practice finds only little explicit support in the jurisprudence of domestic courts. The fact that domestic courts have only rarely referred to later OECD documents as subsequent agreements or subsequent practice can therefore be interpreted as a kind of 'eloquent silence'. Yet, they have not discussed the various arguments against this view, such as the fact that the OECD is an IO and therefore possesses a legal identity separate from that of its member States.[204]

Because of its separate legal identity, one needs to explain why a recommendation adopted by the OECD Council, or a document adopted by the CFA, should at the same time constitute an agreement between the parties to the respective DTA or a practice in the application of the DTA that establishes the parties' agreement. Since IOs can generate their own 'established practice', which may lead to so-called 'rules of the organisation',[205] there is little room for arguing that the same practice was capable of 'piercing the organisational veil' and of affecting treaties concluded between the organisation's member States. Admittedly, one might object that both the OECD Council and the CFA are composed of representatives of all OECD member States, and that decisions by these bodies normally require the consent of all of their members. Hence one might argue that the members in these bodies actually act in two separate capacities, ie, firstly, as a member of the respective OECD body and, secondly, as a representative of a particular OECD member State. In the latter capacity, a member's vote could then be seen as not only contributing to consensual decision-making but also as expressing the agreement of or generating practice attributable to a particular member State.

Taking the case of the EU, one may well accept that one person can act in two capacities: under EU law, the representatives of the governments of the Member States meeting within the Council regularly act as representatives of their governments

[204] cf Oesterhelt, 'Bedeutung des OECD-Kommentars' (n 153) 381 at fn 41.

[205] Art 5 VCLT; see further Christopher Peters, 'Subsequent Practice and Established Practice of International Organizations—Two Sides of the Same Coin?' (2011) 3 GOJIL 617.

on the occasion of meetings of the Council of the European Union, which is an organ of the EU. But irrespective of whether OECD Council or CFA members can equally wear 'two hats'—their conduct, first of all, relates to OECD documents and not DTAs concluded by an OECD member State. Although the OECD itself claims that an amended Model Convention or Commentaries can impact on earlier DTAs, this does not automatically mean that a particular member States actually wishes to follow this recommendation when it comes to its own agreements. After all, the Model Convention is merely a model that, like other OECD recommendations, lacks binding force. OECD member States may wish to contribute to OECD's work, and to adopt recommendations on tax issues, for various reasons. Hence one can hardly assume that they automatically agree that any amendment should also affect their own treaties.

While it is true that each member State can abstain from voting,[206] enter reservations, or submit interpretative declarations,[207] member States could have adopted their recommentions in tax matters as legally binding decisions if they had unreservedly wished to follow the respective recommendation. If one still rejected all of these objections and assumed, like the Belgian Cour de Cassation did, that later OECD documents can fall under article 31(3)(a) or (b) VCLT, it would still remain questionable whether this should also be true as regards the interpretation of treaties between non-OECD member States.[208] Here, at the latest, any claim that later OECD documents constitute subsequent agreements or subsequent practice reaches its argumentative limits, especially if a non-member State is not entitled to participate in the work of OECD bodies at all.[209]

As a 'lowest common denominator', the jurisprudence of domestic courts confirms that later OECD documents can be indirectly relevant under article 31(3)(a) or (b) VCLT if they are the object of an agreement between or of the parties or if they generate relevant practice in the application of a DTA.[210] In that sense, later OECD documents may certainly serve as a catalyst for subsequent agreements or subsequent practice in the same way as treaty body output and UNHCR publications do. In this context, it does not matter whether the parties to the DTA are or are not OECD member States. Yet, as the judgment of the Federal Court of Australia in the case of *Commissioner of Taxation v SNF (Australia) Pty Ltd* illustrated, such indirect relevance needs to be established in every single case. Irrespective of the OECD claiming a certain interpretative impact of its documents, this impact is in no way guaranteed. Nevertheless, acknowledging this catalyst function may offer

---

[206] Art 6(2) OECD Convention.

[207] Rule 20 OECD Rules of Procedure; see also OECD, *Model Tax Convention on Income and on Capital 2010* (n 132) I-9 [30]–[32].

[208] Lang, 'Later OECD Commentaries' (n 171) 8.

[209] As regards the different levels of participation beyond that of full membership, see rules 8–10 OECD Rules of Procedure; see also OECD, 'Resolution of the Council concerning the Participation of Non-Members in the Work of Subsidiary Bodies of the Organisation' (8 July 2004) Doc C(2004)132/FINAL.

[210] Lang and Brugger, 'OECD Commentary' (n 137) 103.

an acceptable solution in cases where OECD documents would otherwise be denied any relevance.

7.4 Conclusion

Taking treaty body output, UNHCR publications, and the OECD Model Convention as examples, this Chapter examined how domestic courts have dealt with non-party practice. In doing so, Chap. 7 aimed at understanding whether and in which way non-party practice may be directly or indirectly relevant under article 31(3)(b) VCLT. In sum, domestic courts held that non-party practice may be indirectly but not directly relevant under this provision. Thus, they distinguished between the 'persuasive' authority enjoyed by non-party practice due to its practical relevance or the special expertise of those who generated it, on the one hand, and the ultimate interpretative authority of the contracting parties, on the other.

As regards 'persuasive' authority, it is remarkable how frequently domestic courts have had recourse to non-party practice such as treaty body output, UNHCR publications, and the OECD Model Convention. Hence, the usefulness and practical relevance of this material can hardly be denied. It is widely accepted and also finds support in the jurisprudence of domestic courts that treaty body output, UNHCR publications, the OECD Model Convention, or other non-party practice can at least be taken into account under article 32 VCLT. However, this option seems like the 'second-best solution' if an interpreter is concerned that this would not do justice to the practical relevance of this material. This is in particular the case if this material is vested with a kind of 'official' nature and if its author even claims a certain interpretative authority to indicate the correct meaning of the respective treaty. As will be recalled, treaty body output, UNHCR publications, and the OECD Model Convention are extrinsic to the text of the respective treaty and regularly promulgated after the treaty having entered into force.

Therefore, it is not surprising that attempts have been made to invoke article 31(3)(b) VCLT to explain why this material should be classified as a primary means of interpretation. The jurisprudence of domestic courts, however, shows that any reasoning that aims at enhancing the legal status of this material ignores interpretative practice. Occasionally, domestic courts indeed discussed whether treaty body output, UNHCR publications, or the OECD Model Convention were directly relevant under article 31(3)(b) VCLT. Yet, they generally concluded that they were not. As regards the controversy about the meaning of the term 'practice', it is noteworthy that the reasoning of domestic courts supports neither the view that this term *does include* nor that it *does not include* non-party practice.

But while they generally refused to regard non-party practice as directly relevant under article 31(3)(b) VCLT, domestic courts frequently emphasised that such practice could be indirectly relevant under this provision by reflecting or inducing potentially relevant State practice. Treating such practice as aids to discover potentially relevant State practice (often alongside other aids such as legal literature), domestic courts thus sometimes blurred the line between these aids and the relevant practice as such. In some cases, they actually took it for granted that treaty body output, UNHCR publications, or the OECD Model Convention faithfully reflected existing State practice or had not been objected to by the parties to the respective treaty. In other cases, they accurately distinguished between the self-asserted claim by non-party entities to reflect practice of State parties, on the one hand, and the question of whether such practice really existed, on the other. In doing so, they took into consideration that much non-party practice draws on other sources than just practice of State parties, is produced under a mandate that is broader than the respective treaty, or purports to develop the meaning of the treaty instead of merely interpreting it.

On the one hand, this critical approach to non-party practice certainly diminishes its interpretative value even further. On the other hand, domestic courts thus reconfirm that the parties to the treaty have retained ultimate interpretative authority over their treaty.

Chapter 8
The Notion of 'Agreement'

Chapter 8 is dedicated to the normative heart of subsequent practice,[1] namely the notion of 'agreement'. A single instance of practice and even an accumulated body of practice do not, in themselves, satisfy the requirements under article 31(3)(b) VCLT. To acquire the status of a primary means of interpretation, subsequent practice in the application of the treaty must be capable of establishing the agreement of all parties regarding the treaties' interpretation.[2] Unlike under article 31(3)(a) VCLT, the parties' agreement under article 31(3)(b) VCLT is not manifest. The interpreter therefore needs to assess all potentially relevant practice to determine whether this practice, taken as a whole, actually establishes the parties' agreement. This additional intellectual operation is not a dispensable add-on. It is, on the contrary, the *sine qua non* that justifies the status of subsequent practice as a primary means of interpretation by linking it to the agreement of the parties as the true masters of the treaty.

Despite its importance, the notion of 'agreement' is not clearly defined in the Vienna rules. This Chapter therefore analyses relevant case law of domestic courts to refine the contours of the parties' 'agreement'. In a first step, it is examined how one or more parties' inaction or silence may be dealt with when trying to establish the parties' agreement under article 31(3)(b) VCLT (8.1). Establishing the parties' agreement is more difficult if there is no active conduct by all parties. This Chapter therefore outlines the circumstances in which public international law regards silence or inaction as 'eloquent silence' signalling consent instead of ignorance, indifference, or even objection. Against this theoretical background, it describes typical cases in which domestic courts have attached interpretative value to inaction or silence when relying on subsequent practice as a means of interpretation.

---

[1] See 4.1.

[2] See 4.3.2.1.

K. Berner, *Subsequent Agreements and Subsequent Practice in Domestic Courts*, Beiträge zum ausländischen öffentlichen Recht und Völkerrecht,
https://doi.org/10.1007/978-3-662-54937-7_8

In a second step, Chap. 8 focuses on the more general issue of agreement and selected practice (8.2). The starting point is the observation that domestic courts hardly ever discuss whether a certain practice actually establishes the parties' agreement. Since domestic courts thus tend to blur the line between practice and agreement, this Chapter critically assesses the spectrum of selectivity (ie reliance on active conduct of only some parties) that characterises their approach to subsequent practice. By addressing silence and selected practice separately, Chap. 8 takes into account that interpreters have two options for dealing with silence. In the one alternative, interpreters search for relevant conduct of all parties. If their search reveals active conduct of only some parties, they should then openly address this outcome. In particular, they should discuss whether active and inactive conduct alike carry interpretative value so that the parties' agreement can be established. In the other alternative, interpreters solely rely on active conduct of only some parties without even mentioning the other parties' conduct.

A benevolent explanation for selected practice may be that there truly was active conduct of only some parties. Moreover, domestic courts may have been motivated by a legitimate desire to interpret treaties in a uniform fashion; hence reliance on selected practice might arguably have to be welcomed instead of being discouraged. Such considerations may reasonably guide the way in which domestic courts approach 'other' subsequent conduct under article 32 VCLT. The general rule, however, does not exempt interpreters from assessing whether silence signals consent. More generally, it does not encourage interpreters to pursue ulterior motives at the expense of the parties' agreement. Besides, there is also a less benevolent explanation for reliance on active conduct of only some parties. Where interpreters do not mention the conduct of all parties, it is equally possible that they did not search for relevant conduct of all parties or even deliberately concealed less suitable conduct that would not have supported their preferred interpretation.

In conclusion, Chap. 8 assesses whether domestic courts unduly approached the notion of 'agreement' in a way that may eventually risk rendering it meaningless (8.3). In particular, it asks whether their previously described selectivity may not only be an imperfect way of dealing with silence but may also reflect more serious deficiencies relating to the notion of 'agreement'.

8.1 Agreement and Silence

As noted earlier, article 31(3)(b) VCLT does not require active conduct by all parties.[3] Nonetheless, the accumulated body of practice that is being relied on must establish the agreement of all the parties regarding the treaty's interpretation. This raises the question of whether silence or inaction automatically signal ignorance, indifference, or even objection or whether interpreters may also regard such omissions to act as implicit consent.

[3] See 4.3.2.1 and draft conclusion 9(2) and the accompanying commentary in ILC, 'Report of the International Law Commission on the Work of its 66th Session' (5 May–6 June and 7 July–8 August 2014) UN Doc A/69/10, 197, 201 [13].

8.1.1 *Eloquent Silence in International Law*

This question implies, as one commentator observed, that 'silence or inaction is seldom an adequate manifestation of consent.'[4] With respect to article 31(3)(b) VCLT, this caveat contributes to safeguarding the parties' agreement from being negated. Taking this agreement seriously is all the more important if one conceives it as a specific manifestation of the principle of consent. This principle is rooted in the sovereign equality of States and thus constitutes one of the bedrocks of public international law.[5] As the PCIJ famously remarked in its *Lotus* judgment in 1927,

> [i]nternational law governs relations between independent States. The rules of law binding upon States therefore emanate from their own free will as expressed in conventions or by usages generally accepted as expressing principles of law and established in order to regulate the relations between these co-existing independent communities or with a view to the achievement of common aims.[6]

Irrespective of whether or not the principle of State consent has begun to erode or fallen into 'decay' in other contexts,[7] the law of treaties to a large extent 'continues to be pre-conditioned on the presence of state consent.'[8] Yet, States must not

---

[4] Nuno Sérgio Marques Antunes, 'Acquiescence' in Rüdiger Wolfrum (ed), *The Max Planck Encyclopedia of Public International Law* (OUP 2012) [26].

[5] James Crawford, *Brownlie's Principles of Public International Law* (8th edn, OUP 2012) 449. See also Jutta Brunnée, 'Consent' in Rüdiger Wolfrum (ed), *The Max Planck Encyclopedia of Public International Law* (OUP 2012) [1].

[6] *Case of the SS 'Lotus' (France v Turkey)* PCIJ Rep Series A No 10 18. For this reading of the *Lotus* judgment, see eg Prosper Weil, 'Towards Relative Normativity in International Law?' (1993) 77 AJIL 413, 420 f; Brunnée, 'Consent' (n 5) [1]. Anthony d'Amato, 'Consent, Estoppel and Reasonableness: Three Challenges to Universal International Law' (1969) 10 Va J Int'l L 1, 3, in contrast, submits that the *Lotus* judgment may also 'be seen to stand more for a limitation on the idea of consent than a reinforcement of it.' Similarly critically Hugh Handeyside, 'The *Lotus* Principle in ICJ Jurisprudence: Was the Ship ever Afloat?' (2007) 29 Mich J Int'l L 71, 75 f.

[7] See in particular Nico Krisch, 'The Decay of Consent: International Law in an Age of Global Public Goods' (2014) 108 AJIL 1. On the relevance of State consent in public international law, see also d'Amato, 'Consent, Estoppel and Reasonableness: Three Challenges to Universal International Law' (n 6) 3 f; Alain Pellet, 'The Normative Dilemma: Will and Consent in International Law-Making' (1988) 12 AYBIL 22, 33 f; Christian Tomuschat, 'Obligations Arising for States without or against Their Will' (1993) 241 RCADI 195, 290; Brunnée, 'Consent' (n 5) [15]–[18].

[8] cf arts 11–17 (Conclusion of treaties), 34–37 (Treaties and third States), and 39–41 (Amendment and modification) VCLT. See also Duncan Hollis, 'Why State Consent Still Matters—Non-State Actors, Treaties, and the Changing Sources of International Law' (2005) 23 Berkeley J Int'l L 137, 140; Brunnée, 'Consent' (n 5) [5].

necessarily express their consent explicitly but may also do so by implication.[9] A special case of consent by implication is provided for by several multilateral treaties, namely so-called 'tacit consent' or 'opting out procedures'.[10] These procedures are primarily used to facilitate adjusting or amending annexes or appendixes of a technical nature. For this purpose, an organ of an IO, a COP, or a treaty body typically adopts a decision which then becomes binding on all parties to the treaty unless they explicitly object within a certain period of time.[11] Strictly speaking, tacit consent or opting out procedures therefore do not provide for consent by implication but rather shift the moment at which States express their consent. To be precise, tacit consent or opting out procedures thus rest on anticipated consent that is expressed upon ratification of the respective treaty.[12]

In the case of 'acquiescence', public international law recognises tacit consent in the true sense.[13] On balance, international courts and tribunals largely concede that

> [a]cquiescence only emerges where it refers to facts that are (or ought to be) known by the aqcuiescing State (*notoriety*), where such facts are of direct interest for the acquiescing State (*interest*), when these facts have existed for a significant period (*lapse of time*) without significant change of context and the meaning conveyed (*consistency*), and in cases in which the conduct is attributable to a relevant representative of the State (*provenance*).[14]

---

[9] Anthony Aust, *Modern Treaty Law and Practice* (3rd edn, CUP 2013) 104; Krisch, 'The Decay of Consent' (n 7) 26.

[10] See generally Malgosia Fitzmaurice, 'Consent to Be Bound—Anything New under the Sun?' (2005) 74 NJIL 483.

[11] Eg arts 38 and 90(a) of the Convention on International Civil Aviation (signed 7 December 1944, entered into force 4 April 1947) 15 UNTS 295 (ICAO Convention); art 22 of the Constitution of the World Health Organization (signed 22 July 1946, entered into force 7 April 1948) 14 UNTS 185 (WHO Constitution); art 8(b) of the Convention of the World Meteorological Organization (signed 11 October 1947, entered into force 23 March 1950) 77 UNTS 143 (WMO Convention); art XV(8) of the Maritime Labour Convention (signed 23 February 2006, entered into force 20 August 2013) (2006) 45 ILM 792 (MLC); art XV of the Convention on International Trade in Endangered Species of Wild Fauna and Flora (signed 3 March 1973, entered into force 1 July 1975) 993 UNTS 243 (CITES); arts X–XI of the Convention on the Conservation of Migratory Species of Wild Animals (signed 23 June 1979, entered into force 1 November 1983) 1651 UNTS 333 (CMS); arts 9–10 of the Vienna Convention for the Protection of the Ozone Layer (signed 22 March 1985, entered into force 22 September 1988) 1513 UNTS 293 (Ozone Convention).

[12] Fitzmaurice, 'Consent to Be Bound' (n 10) 489.

[13] Acquiescence needs to be distinguished from the related doctrine of estoppel, which protects legitimate expectations that have been induced by the conduct of another actor. Although both acquiescence and estoppel are founded on the principle of good faith, the latter necessarily requires an element of detriment or prejudice. See generally Thomas Cottier and Jörg Müller, 'Estoppel' in Rüdiger Wolfrum (ed), *The Max Planck Encyclopedia of Public International Law* (OUP 2012); Crawford, *Brownlie's Principles* (n 5) 422.

[14] Marques Antunes, 'Acquiescence' (n 4) [21]. See also Ian MacGibbon, 'The Scope of Acquiescence in International Law' (1954) 31 BYIL 143, esp 143, 172; *Fisheries Case (UK*

Once a State's silence or inaction is held to satisfy the above conditions, its conduct may not only contribute to constituting, modifying, disposing of, or terminating rights and duties.[15] Furthermore, its tacit consent may also relate to issues of treaty interpretation.[16] As Ian MacGibbon noted as early as 1954, '[t]he failure of one party to a treaty to protest against acts of the other party in which a particular interpretation of the terms of the treaty is clearly asserted affords cogent evidence of

---

v Norway) [1951] ICJ Rep 116, 134–39: 'The notoriety of the facts, the general toleration of the international community, Great Britain's position in the North Sea, her own interest in the question, and her prolonged abstention would in any case warrant Norway's enforcement of her system against the United Kingdom'; *Case concerning the Right of Passage over Indian Territory (Portugal v India)* (Merits) [1960] ICJ Rep 6, 39–44: 'practice having continued over a period extending beyond a century and a quarter'; *Case concerning the Arbitral Award Made by the King of Spain on 23 December 1906 (Honduras v Nicaragua)* [1960] ICJ Rep 192, 210–14: 'failure to raise any question with regard to the validity of the Award for several years after the full terms of the Award had become known to it'; *Case concerning the Temple of Preah Vihear (Cambodia v Thailand)* (Merits) [1962] ICJ Rep 6, 27–33: 'where it is clear that the circumstances were such as called for some reaction, within a reasonable period'; *Sovereignty over Pedra Branca/Pulau Batu Puteh, Middle Rocks and South Ledge (Malaysia v Singapore)* [2008] ICJ Rep 12, 50–51 [121]: 'silence may also speak, but only if the conduct of the other State calls for a response'; *Military and Paramilitary Activities in and against Nicaragua (Nicaragua v USA)* (Merits) [1986] ICJ Rep, 14, 410 [39]: 'Having regard to the public and unchanging nature of the official statements concerning Nicaragua's commitment under the Optional-Clause system, the silence of its Government can only be interpreted as an acceptance of the classification thus assigned to it'; *EC—Chicken Cuts—Report of the Appellate Body* (12 September 2005) WT/DS269/AB/R, WT/DS286/AB/R <http://docsonline.wto.org> [272]: acquiescence 'may occur when a party that has not engaged in a practice has become or has been made aware of the practice of other parties… but does not react to it. However, we disagree with the Panel that "lack of protest" against one Member's classification practice by other WTO Members may be understood, on its own, as establishing agreement with that practice by those other Members. Therefore, the fact that Brazil and Thailand, having actually exported the products at issue, may have accepted the European Communities' import classification practice under heading 02.10, is not dispositive of whether other Members with actual or potential trade interests have also accepted that practice'; *Young Loan Arbitration on German External Debts (Belgium, France, Switzerland, UK, and USA v Germany)* (1980) 19 RIAA 67, 104 [31]: 'clearly without realising'; *Case concerning a Dispute between Argentina and Chile concerning the Beagle Channel (Argentina v Chile)* (1977) 21 RIAA 53, 187 [169], 188 [172]: 'public and well-known to Argentina', 'the important point is that her continued failure to react to acts openly performed, ostensibly by virtue of the Treaty, tended to give some support to that interpretation of it which alone could justify such acts'. See the commentary on draft conclusion 9 in ILC, 'Report of the International Law Commission on the Work of its 66th Session' (5 May–6 June and 7 July–8 August 2014) UN Doc A/69/10, 203 [19]–204 [21] with further references.

[15] Marques Antunes, 'Acquiescence' (n 4) [11].

[16] id, 'Acquiescence' in Rüdiger Wolfrum (ed), *The Max Planck Encyclopedia of Public International Law* (OUP 2012) [14]. cf also Aust, *Modern Treaty Law* (n 9) 214 f.

the understanding of the parties of their respective rights and obligations under the treaty.'[17] Although scholars and practitioners largely agree on the requirements for acquiescence in the abstract, these requirements are rather vague and strongly dependent on the circumstances *in casu*.[18] For this reason, critical voices have insisted that acquiescence must not become a mere construct but should 'correspond[s] accurately with the implied intention of the acquiescing State.'[19]

To recapitulate the circumstances in which public international law regards silence or inaction as 'eloquent silence', it is helpful to re-emphasise that 'eloquent silence' constitutes an exception. At least in matters relating to treaty law, State consent is still so essential that interpreters should be mindful not to negate the parties' agreement under article 31(3)(b) VCLT by equating any inaction or silence with consent. True acquiescence, first and foremost, requires that the acquiescing State knew or should have known the circumstances to which its implicit consent relates. To avoid that State consent becomes an empty phrase, one may further argue that constructed knowledge must come close to actual knowledge. In addition, it requires special reasons to assume that that acquiescing State would and should have objected if it had meant to withhold its consent. As the tacit consent or opting out procedures provided for by several multilateral treaties illustrate, States may, for instance, expressly anticipate their consent while retaining the option to object in individual cases. Hence, one can assume that the special reasons that are necessary to demonstrate acquiescence must be more than actual or constructed knowledge of the circumstance to which the State is deemed to consent, and also more than the mere existence of a contractual relationship.

8.1.2 How Domestic Courts Interpret Silence or Inaction

Without explicitly addressing this issue, the jurisprudence of domestic courts has been largely unanimous in dealing with silence or inaction by one or more States when using subsequent practice as a means of interpretation. On the whole, domestic courts readily relied on active conduct by only some parties irrespective of whether there was any reason to assume that the other parties had acquiesced in the interpretation reflected therein. Thus, the jurisprudence of domestic courts seems to deviate from the requirements for acquiescence under public international law.

The German Federal Administrative Court, for instance, treated one State party's silence as tacit consent to another party's active conduct when interpreting a bilateral treaty. This can be seen in one of its judgments on the 1929 German–Persian

[17] MacGibbon, 'Acquiescence' (n 14) 146.

[18] Víctor Cedeño and Maria Torres Cazorla, 'Unilateral Acts of States in International Law' in Rüdiger Wolfrum (ed), *The Max Planck Encyclopedia of Public International Law* (OUP 2012) [37]; Marques Antunes, 'Acquiescence' (n 4) [19].

[19] MacGibbon, 'Acquiescence' (n 14) 169.

Establishment Agreement.[20] At issue was the interpretation of the term 'immigration' which, in the Court's view, meant any residence on German territory for an indefinite period of time for more than just a limited purpose.[21] To support this construction, the Court relied on German administrative and judicial practice, to which Iran (as the legal successor of the Persian Empire) had apparently never objected.[22] Although the Court cited article 31(3)(b) VCLT, it neither addressed Iran's omission to respond to this practice in greater detail nor explained how Iran could be taken to have acquiesced in this practice. In particular, the Court did not even indicate whether Iran had been aware of how the Establishment Agreement had been applied in Germany. Hence the Court seemed to assume that active conduct by one party—at least in a bilateral relationship—sufficed to satisfy the requirements under article 31(3)(b) VCLT. Moreover, the Court's reasoning also suggests that Iran should have objected to Germany's practice to avoid the impression of having acquiesced in it. But apart from the fact that Iran had entered into a bilateral contractual relationship with Germany, it is difficult to see why it should have been obliged to do so. In particular, Germany had neither contacted Iran in a way that obviously called for a response nor otherwise brought its application of the Agreement to Iran's attention.[23]

Reading, like the German Federal Administrative Court did, an 'obligation to object' into a bilateral contractual relationship appears all the more questionable if one considers the following judgment of the Swiss Federal Supreme Court on the interpretation of the 1858 Baden–Swiss Railway Treaty.[24] This judgment illustrates that even a State's active conduct does not automatically reflect its consent to a particular construction. Article 4 of the Treaty, which regulated the extension of the Baden railway over the territory of the canton of Schaffhausen, stipulated that the Grand-Duchy of Baden was exempt from paying any tax or duty to the canton or its municipalities for the acquisition of property for the railway or its members or for the operation of the railway in particular and from paying any tax or duty at

---

[20] Convention between Germany and the Persian Empire regarding Conditions of Residence (signed 17 February 1929, entered into force 11 January 1931) 111 LNTS 241 (1929 German–Persian Establishment Agreement).

[21] BVerwG, Judgment of 29 November 1988, 1 C 75/86, [1989] NVwZ 765, 766.

[22] ibid.

[23] cf, by way of contrast, BVerwG, Judgment of 10 July 1984, 1 C 30/81, [1985] DVBl 242, 243, where the Court emphasised that German authorities had, through diplomatic channels, sought Iran's approval to giving German citizenship to an Iranian refugee. This unilateral conduct evidenced, in the Court's view, the parties' agreement that a person's refugee status did not eliminate the general duty under the 1929 German–Persian Establishment Agreement to seek the other party's approval before naturalising one of its citizens.

[24] Treaty between the Grand Duchy of Baden and the Swiss Confederation Acting in Particular on Behalf of the Canton of Schaffhausen in Respect of the Continuation of the State Railways of the Grand Duchy of Baden through the Territory of the Canton of Schaffhausen (signed 30 December 1858, entered into force 28 February 1859) SR 0.742.140.313.62 (1858 Baden–Swiss Railway Treaty).

all. The question before the Court was whether Germany, the present owner of the Grand-Duchy's railway, could still invoke the general exemption from taxes and duties provided for in the 1858 Treaty. Taking into account how the Treaty had been applied in practice, the Court noted that Swiss cantons had for years imposed State and municipal taxes on German railway property.[25] Although Germany had never objected to this practice, the Court nonetheless concluded that Germany had not consented to the Swiss canton's interpretation. Instead, the Court considered it more likely that Germany had simply paid these taxes and duties to ensure good neighbourly relations but not because it recognised its legal obligation to do so.[26]

This reasoning is noteworthy. By uncritically relying on Swiss and German practice, it would have been easy for the Court to justify why the tay exemption should not apply. The Court's caveat concerning the interpretative value of active conduct applies all the more in case of silence or inaction. Unless there is reason to believe that an inactive State actually consented to another party's active conduct, its passivity may have been motivated by various reasons and need not necessarily signal acquiescence. To elucidate a State's motives for remaining silent, it is important to take a broader perspective beyond the case at hand. This can be seen in the US Supreme Court case *US v Stuart,* which concerned the interpretation of the 1942 US–Canadian DTA.[27] The DTA obliged each contracting party to furnish the other party that information which its competent authorities had at their disposal or were in a position to obtain under its revenue laws. To explain why the DTA authorised US authorities to furnish Canadian authorities with bank records which they were not allowed to obtain themselves under US tax law, the Court relied on the fact that the US government had regularly complied with similar requests in the past without reassuring itself that it would have been allowed to obtain this information under domestic law.[28] This reasoning was severely criticised by Justice Scalia. Among others, he recalled that courts must not rely on 'unilateral' conduct but only on such extratextual material that reflected a mutual agreement of the parties.[29]

Although Scalia was correct in emphasising the parties' agreement, his criticism is not fully convincing. First of all, he implied that Canada's requests could not be considered as a practice in the application of the DTA. This view, however, ignores that Canada had apparently requested information from the USA and received and used this information in the past. But even if one agreed with Scalia in that there was an omission to act on the Canadian side, this would not mean that Canada's conduct was incapable of casting any light on the parties' agreement regarding the interpretation of the DTA. To exclude Canada's requests, when assessing the US government's practice, would considerably distort the overall impression of the case. The

---

[25] BGer, Judgment of 17 February 1971, BGE 97 I 359, 370 f.

[26] ibid 371.

[27] Convention between the United States of America and Canada relating to the Avoidance of Double Taxation and Fiscal Evasion in the Case of Income Taxes (signed 4 March 1942, entered into force 15 June 1942) 124 UNTS 271 (1942 US–Canadian DTA).

[28] *US v Stuart* 489 US 353, 370, 109 S Ct 1183 (1989).

[29] ibid 375.

US government had not furnished Canada with information *ex proprio motu* but only in compliance with requests by Canada. Assuming that Canada did not wish to act in bad faith by inducing the USA to violate the DTA, these requests suggest that Canada had equally believed that the DTA did not prohibit the USA from providing the requested information.

Situations in which one party induced another party's active conduct may be compared to silence or inaction in institutionalised or cooperative contexts. In both situations, a party's silence or inaction in a particular situation may conceal active conduct at an earlier date. An illustrative example of how courts dealt with silence in cooperative contexts is the case *O'Connor v US.* At issue was whether US taxpayers employed by the Panama Canal Commission were exempt from US taxation on their salaries paid by the Commission. According to the petitioner, this exemption was provided for by article XV(2) of a US–Panamanian agreement,[30] which stipulated that US citizen employees and dependents shall be exempt from any taxes, fees, or other charges on income received as a result of their work for the Commission as well as on income derived from sources outside the Republic of Panama. Favouring a more restrictive interpretation to the effect that article XV(2) exempted from Panamanian but not from US taxation,[31] the US Supreme Court relied on the contracting parties' conduct after the treaty had entered into force.[32] In particular, it emphasised that the Panama Commission—a US agency[33]—had for years withheld US income taxes from US employees.[34] The Board of the Commission, however, which was composed of both US and Panamanian members and which was meant to control the Commission's practice,[35] had never objected to this practice.[36] In the Court's view, this meant that the Commission's practice had 'gone unchallenged by Panama.'[37]

In a non-cooperative context, one may have objected that Panama had not been obliged to react to the Commission's practice to avoid the impression of having acquiesced in it. Standing on its own, Panama's omission to act would not have carried any interpretative value at all. In fact, one may have even wondered whether Panama was aware that the Commission, being a US agency, had withheld income in the first place. But in this case, Panama had representatives on a supervisory

[30] Agreement in Implementation of Article III of the Panama Canal Treaty (Panama–USA) (signed 7 September 1977, entered into force 1 October 1979) 1280 UNTS 201 (Article III Implementation Agreement).

[31] *O'Connor v US* 479 US 27, 31 f, 107 S Ct 347 (1986).

[32] ibid 34.

[33] See art III(3) of the Panama Canal Treaty (Panama–USA) (signed 7 September 1977, entered into force 1 October 1979) 1280 UNTS 3 (Panama Canal Treaty).

[34] *O'Connor* (n 31) 33.

[35] See art III(3) Panama Canal Treaty. While all members of the Board were appointed by the USA, the Panamanian members were proposed by Panama for appointment by the USA, see art III(3)(a) Panama Canal Treaty.

[36] *O'Connor* (n 31) 33.

[37] ibid.

board tasked with monitoring the Commission. Provided that these representatives complied with their assigned supervisory tasks, one may assume that they knew or should have known of the Commission's practice. In addition, one may even argue that Panama would have acted in bad faith if it had subsequently objected to the Commission's practice although its representatives should have been capable of reacting immediately.

Similar considerations may have also influenced the German Federal Constitutional Court in its decision on the EUROCONTROL Convention. In this case, the Court had to determine whether the exclusive competence for determining legal disputes between EUROCONTROL and its employees was held by the agency's Director General and the Administrative Tribunal of the ILO as envisaged by articles 91 and 92 of the Staff Regulations.[38] The Protocol to the Convention unconditionally guaranteed that national courts should be competent to decide such disputes. Nevertheless, the Court finally took the view that this guarantee was merely transitional and therefore did not preclude the contested exclusive jurisdiction. To support this interpretation, the Court relied on the contracting parties' subsequent practice in the application of the Protocol:

> As elements in this practice, in the present case one may assess the facts that the Contracting Parties objected neither to adoption of the relevant provisions in the Conditions of Employment nor to the establishment of the international competence of the ILO Administrative Tribunal for legal disputes arising therefrom, even a short time after the entry into force of the Eurocontrol Convention and associated documents, particularly since such an arrangement is usual in the case of a number of international organizations.[39]

This dictum illustrates that the Court did not, strictly speaking, rely on the parties' active conduct but merely on their omission to react to the new jurisdictional arrangement. Notably, the Court emphasised that the new arrangement was not unusual for IOs. This implies that it was irrelevant for the parties' acquiescence whether they foresaw the effects on the original arrangement under the Protocol.

A more controversial example of silence in an institutionalised context is the UK Supreme Court's judgment in the case of *Assange v The Swedish Prosecution Authority*. At issue was whether public prosecutors could be regarded as judicial authorities for the purpose of the European Arrest Warrant Framework Decision.[40] Arguing that they could, the majority of the Court relied on the fact that several European Union (EU) Member States had designated a prosecutor as the issuing and executing authority of arrest warrants, and that the other Member States had not

---

[38] EUROCONTROL, 'General Conditions of Employment Governing Servants at the EUROCONTROL Maastricht Centre' (1 August 2013) <http://www.eurocontrol.int/sites/default/files/publication/files/general-conditions-employment-maastricht.pdf>.

[39] BVerfGE 59, 63, 94 f.

[40] Council Framework Decision 2002/584/JHA of 13 June 2002 on the European Arrest Warrant and the Sur-render Procedures between Member States [2002] OJ L190/1 (Framework Decision).

objected to this practice.[41] In *Bucnys v Ministry of Justice, Lithuania*,[42] this reasoning was criticised since it was considered inadmissible to rely on subsequent State practice to interpret Framework Decisions. According to Lord Mance, who gave the opinion for a unanimous Supreme Court, it was unlikely that the Framework Decision could be interpreted by applying the Vienna rules. This was because, so Lord Mance argued, the Vienna Convention only applied to treaties and the Framework Decision did not qualify as a treaty but as a subsidiary measure under EU law.[43] In addition, he emphasised that the CJEU was very unlikely to accept 'that the member states could by agreement between themselves alter or influence the meaning of Community measures arrived at under the Treaties.'[44]

If one questioned the validity of this criticism, one could object that articles 31 and 32 VCLT reflect customary international law so that subsequent practice might be used to interpret both treaties and other international legal instruments. Moreover, one could point out that the Framework Decision was a 'third pillar' and hence intergovernmental measure under Title VI of the Treaty on European Union (Treaty of Nice),[45] whose nature differed from supranational EU law and therefore justified applying different interpretative principles. And finally, one might add that subsequent practice within the meaning of article 31(3)(b) VCLT cannot be used to 'change' a treaty anyway but merely helps to cast light on its meaning.

But notwithstanding this controversy, the UK Supreme Court's judgment in *Assange* is also instructive for another reason, namely as regards its approach to agreement and silence by some parties. Notably, the majority acknowledged that active conduct by some parties alone was 'not a conclusive factor' because article 31(3)(b) VCLT required practice that established the agreement of the parties.[46] Therefore, 'what is required to establish the agreement of the parties is that there should be active practice on the part of at least some of the parties to the treaty … and it must have been acquiesced in or—at least—not objected to by the other parties.'[47] Hence, the majority of the Court did not ask whether the other Member States had acquiesced in the practice of those States who had appointed public prosecutors. Furthermore, it assumed that it was sufficient that the other Member States had not objected to this practice. This low threshold for establishing the parties' agreement is all the more surprising since several Member States had only appointed judges as

---

[41] *Assange v The Swedish Prosecution Authority* [2012] UKSC 22, [2012] 2 AC 471 [68]–[71] (Lord Phillips).

[42] *Bucnys v Ministry of Justice, Lithuania* [2013] UKSC 71, [2013] 3 WLR 1485.

[43] ibid [39]–[43] (Lord Mance).

[44] ibid [42] (Lord Mance).

[45] Treaty on European Union (signed 7 February 1992, entered into force 1 November 1993) 1759 UNTS 3 (TEU) in the version resulting from the Treaty of Nice Amending the Treaty on European Union, the Treaties Establishing the European Communities and Certain Related Acts (signed 26 February 2001, entered into force 1 February 2003) 2701 UNTS No 47937 (Treaty of Nice).

[46] *Assange* (n 41) [106] (Lord Kerr).

[47] ibid [107] (Lord Kerr).

judicial authorities for the purpose of the Framework Directive. But for the majority, this was not 'inconsistent with the existence of an agreement established by subsequent practice.'[48] Lady Hale, however, vehemently criticised this understanding of article 31(3)(b) VCLT. In her dissenting opinion, she emphasised that

> the practice has to be such as to establish the *agreement* of all the parties as to its interpretation. Given the lack of a common or concordant practice between the parties, is the failure to date of those countries which do not authorise prosecutors and other bodies to object to those who do sufficient to establish their agreement? … Failure to address minds to an issue is not the same as acquiescence in a particular state of affairs.[49]

However, the majority did not explain why it considered it sufficient for establishing the parties' agreement that some parties had not objected to the practice that was relied on. Hence one can only wonder about the majority's reasons for not requiring genuine acquiescence. One conceivable argument could have been the close relationship between the EU Member States. Yet, article 34(2) TEU (Treaty of Nice), pursuant to which Framework Decisions were adopted before the entering into force of the Lisbon Treaty,[50] expressly required unanimity of the EU Council. Therefore, this argument does not appear very strong.

As the aforementioned cases illustrated, several domestic courts readily relied on active conduct by only some parties. An exception to this permissive approach is a decision of the German Federal Constitutional Court on the constitutionality of a domestic law that gave effect to a Protocol[51] amending the 1931 German–Swiss DTA.[52] The Protocol authorised each State party to take income otherwise exempted from taxation into account for determining a taxpayer's tax rate. For this reason, it seemed to conflict with the DTA, which generally provided that income was subject to taxation only in that State in which the activity that had generated the income had been undertaken. Due to late ratification by the German legislature, the Protocol had not entered into force until 20 April 1959 although it was to apply to any tax imposed after 31 December 1956. In consequence, the Court had to determine

---

[48] ibid [131] (Lord Dyson).

[49] ibid [191] (Lady Hale). cf *Al-Waheed v Ministry of Defence* [2017] UKSC 2, [2017] WLR(D) 50 [310]–[311] (Lord Reed).

[50] Treaty of Lisbon Amending the Treaty on European Union and the Treaty Establishing the European Community (signed 13 December 2007, entered into force 1 December 2009) 2702 UNTS No 47938 (Lisbon Treaty).

[51] Additional Protocol to the Agreement between the German Reich and the Swiss Confederation for the Avoidance of Double Taxation in the Area of Direct Tax and Inheritance Tax of 15 June 1931 (signed 9 September 1957, entered into force 20 April 1959) BGBl (Germany) 1959 II 408.

[52] Convention between the German Reich and the Swiss Confederation for the Prevention of Double Taxation in the Matter of Direct Taxes and Succession Duties (signed 15 July 1931, entered into force 29 January 1934) 144 LNTS 389 (1931 German–Swiss DTA) as amended by Additional Agreement (signed 11 January 1934, entered into force 29 January 1934) 144 LNTS 449.

whether the act that had been adopted to implement the Protocol had retroactive effect and therefore violated the German Basic Law. Denying any retroactitity, the German Minister of Finance argued that German tax authorities had already been competent to consider income otherwise exempted from taxation by virtue of the 1931 German–Swiss DTA.[53] In particular, he emphasised that Switzerland had 'always' taken such income into account when determining the applicable tax rate and that Germany had never objected to this practice. This evidenced, in the Minister's view, that the 1957 Protocol was merely declaratory and without retroactive effect.[54]

The Court, however, did not follow the Minister's reasoning. Leaving it open why Switzerland might have considered itself entitled to take exempted income into account, it clarified that German law would have required a formal amendment to the DTA to authorise such interpretation.[55] In addition, the Court further remarked that German tax authorities had refrained from taking exempted income into account until the 1957 Protocol entered into force.[56] Based on these observations, the Court finally concluded that the 1957 Protocol did have retroactive effect and therefore violated the German Basic Law.[57] As could be seen, the Court pursued two lines of argument. The first one focused on domestic constitutional law whereas the second addressed Switzerland's and Germany's conduct from an international law perspective. This second line of argument implied that unilateral conduct was not, in itself, sufficient to support a particular interpretation of a bilateral treaty. Stressing that German authorities had not engaged in the same conduct as their Swiss counterparts, the Court refused to acknowledge that Germany had, by not objecting to the Swiss practice, acquiesced in the interpretation that was reflected therein.

8.1.3 Evaluation

Adequately dealing with a party's silence constitutes a major problem under article 31(3)(b) VCLT. Although article 31(3)(b) VCLT does not require active conduct of all parties, the practice that is taken into account must nonetheless be capable of establishing the agreement of all parties. Where parties did not generate active conduct, interpreters must decide whether their silence carries any interpretative value. On its face, silence may signal ignorance or indifference, but also objection or consent. In matters relating to treaty law, it is difficult to establish agreement by way of silence.[58]

---

[53] BVerfGE 30, 272, 276, 278.

[54] ibid 278 f.

[55] ibid 283.

[56] ibid 283 f.

[57] ibid 286 f.

[58] See the commentary on draft conclusion 9 in ILC, 'Report of the International Law Commission on the Work of its 66th Session' (5 May–6 June and 7 July–8 August 2014) UN Doc A/69/10, 203 [19].

The rare situations in which general public international law equates silence with consent are covered by the notion of 'acquiescence'. Besides, several multilateral treaties provide for so-called tacit consent or opting out procedures, which anticipate and thus constitute a special form of implied consent. These procedures as well as the requirements for acquiescence under general public international law offer valuable guidance for interpreters to assess the interpretative value of silence for the purpose of article 31(3)(b) VCLT. First of all, interpreters should only infer consent from silence if the allegedly acquiescing State knew or ought to have known the facts to which its acquiescence relates. And secondly, interpreters should have veritable reasons to believe that the alledgedly acquiescing State would and should have objected to these facts if it had meant to withhold its consent.

These considerations suggest that silence will only exceptionally lead to establishing agreement for the purpose of article 31(3)(b) VCLT. Nevertheless, domestic courts indiscriminately considered active and inactive conduct alike. In fact, only few courts unreservedly proceeded on the assumption that silence, in itself, does not carry interpretative value or even indicate consent. But not any reliance on silence by domestic courts actually belied their attempts to establish the parties' agreement. In several cases, domestic courts treated silence as acquiescence because it occurred in a cooperative or institutionalised context that justified imposing stricter standards on what States ought to have known and on when they should have voiced their disagreement. Reminiscent of the tacit consent or opting out procedures to simplify amendment mechanisms, the parties in these cases had explicitly agreed to circumstances which modified the usual way of applying a treaty and of supervising its application.

In other cases, domestic courts treated silence as acquiescence although the only apparent reason for doing so was the existence of a bilateral contractual relationship. Apart from that, these cases offered no indication why the parties should have been willing to agree to any application of their treaty unless explicitly voicing their disagreement. If the parties' agreement under article 31(3)(b) VCLT was taken seriously, such extensive understanding of acquiescence imposes burdens on States that are hardly manageable. To avoid a finding of acquiescence, States would have to object to any practice of which they disapprove. Therefore, they should always be informed of how the other party applies their treaty. Still, there may be situations in which such constant and comprehensive knowledge is difficult or even impossible to obtain. In the extreme, such extensive understanding of acquiescence may eventually frustrate the requirements of article 31(3)(b) VCLT in that it claims to establish agreement where in reality only disagreement exists.

8.2 Agreement and Selected Practice

Article 31(3)(b) VCLT distinguishes between practice in the application of the treaty and the parties' agreement regarding its interpretation. This distinction must not be mistaken for a subtlety. It rather illustrates that it is the parties' agreement and not a single instance of practice or even an accumulated body of practice that carries interpretative value under the general rule. In other words, interpreters must not rely on any practice but only on that which is capable of establishing the parties' agreement. Hence it is essential to determine how interpreters may ascertain whether practice actually establishes the necessary agreement for the purpose of article 31(3)(b) VCLT. The parties' agreement under article 31(3)(b) VCLT denotes the agreement of all parties to the treaty.[59] This raises the question—closely linked to but separate from the difficulties concerning silence—whether interpreters may be selective in their examination of potentially relevant practice or whether such selectivity is incompatible with the general rule.[60]

8.2.1 Ascertaining the Parties' Agreement

The process of ascertaining the parties' agreement should not be underestimated. Having accumulated various potentially relevant pieces of practice, interpreters ought to scrutinise whether these pieces, taken as a whole, actually possess sufficient probative value to establish the parties' agreement.

In few cases, domestic courts at least superficially confirmed the distinction between practice and agreement, albeit without openly ascertaining the latter. In *Deep Vein Thrombosis and Air Travel Group Litigation*, for instance, Lord Mance introduced his examination of State practice in the application of article 17 Warsaw Convention by noting that '[i]t is also legitimate to have regard to any subsequent practice among the parties which is capable of establishing their agreement regarding interpretation.'[61] At first sight, this dictum seems to confirm the distinction between practice and agreement. Yet, Lord Mance then simply listed several decisions by Australian, Canadian, and especially US courts without linking them to the parties' agreement.[62] Thus, Lord Mance apparently disregarded the very standard which he had just embraced. But this conclusion is not compelling. Arguably, he did not mean to recognise the parties' agreement as a *separate requirement* under article 31(3)(b) VCLT. Instead, he may have also remarked that—as a *general*

[59] 4.3.2.1.

[60] For more details, see also Katharina Berner, 'Judicial Dialogue and Treaty Interpretation—Revisiting the "Cocktail Party" of International Law' (2016) 54 AVR 67.

[61] *Deep Vein Thrombosis and Air Travel Group Litigation* [2005] UKHL 72, [2006] 1 All ER 786 [54]–[55] (Lord Mance).

[62] ibid [66]–[81] (Lord Mance). In the same vein, see *King v Bristow Helicopters Ltd (Scotland)* [2002] UKHL 7, [2002] 2 AC 628 [80] (Lord Hope), where it was acknowledged that 'it is also legitimate to have regard to subsequent practice in the application of the Convention, if this shows that the contracting parties were in agreement as to its interpretation when it was entered into.' Yet, Lord Hope did not suit the action to the word because his analysis of practice was in fact highly selective and lacked any attempt to establish the parties' agreement.

assumption—subsequent practice under article 31(3)(b) VCLT is per se capable of establishing the parties' agreement.

By and large, domestic courts not even upheld the distinction between practice and the parties' agreement pro forma. In accordance with the alternative reading of Lord Mance's dictum, many courts presupposed that potentially relevant practice reflected the parties' agreement anyway. In that sense, the US Supreme Court noted in *Stuart* that '[t]he practice of the treaty signatories counts as evidence of the treaty's proper interpretation, since their conduct generally evidences their understanding of the agreement they signed.'[63] Where courts did not cite article 31(3)(b) VCLT—as was the case in *Stuart*—such statements need not necessarily refer to subsequent practice as envisaged by the general rule. Instead, they may also be understood as referring to 'other' practice as a supplementary means of interpretation.[64] But where courts did cite article 31(3)(b) VCLT, they most likely meant to rely on practice as a primary means of interpretation. In these cases, it would be opportune to not only accumulate various pieces of practice but also to ascertain the parties' agreement.

The case of *R (Al-Jedda) v Secretary of State for Defence* illustrates how domestic courts regularly blurred the line between practice and agreement.[65] This case had been brought by a British-Iraqi national who had been held in custody by British troops at detention facilities in Iraq. As Al-Jedda had not been charged with any offence and neither charge nor trial were in sight, he claimed that his right to liberty under article 5(1) ECHR had been infringed. In contrast to the other Law Lords, Lord Bingham wondered whether article 5(1) ECHR had been derogated from. For this reason, he shortly discussed whether article 15(1) ECHR (derogations from Convention rights) covered overseas peacekeeping operations in the first place.[66] This was doubtful because article 15(1) ECHR required a public emergency threatening the life of the nation. Moreover, this provision limited the admissible derogating measures to those strictly required by the exigencies of the situation.

According to Lord Bingham, '[i]t has not been the practice of states to derogate in such situations, and since subsequent practice in the application of a treaty may (under article 31(3)(b) of the Vienna Convention) be taken into account in interpreting the treaty it seems proper to regard article 15 as inapplicable.'[67] This interpretation was subsequently reconfirmed in *Hassan v UK,* where the ECtHR noted that the 'practice of the High Contracting Parties is not to derogate from their obligations under Article 5 in order to detain persons … during international armed

[63] *Stuart* (n 28) 369. See also *Zicherman v Korean Air Lines Co, Ltd* 516 US 217, 226–27, 116 S Ct 629 (1996).

[64] To the same effect, see BVerfGE 112, 1, 33; 59, 63, 94 f; *SZATV v Minister for Immigration* [2007] HCA 40, (2007) 233 CLR 18 [68]–[74] (Kirby J).

[65] See also eg BVerwG, Decision of 14 April 1992, 1 C 48/89, [1992] DVBl 844, 845 f.

[66] *R (Al-Jedda) v Secretary of State for Defence* [2007] UKHL 58, [2008] 1 AC 332 [38] (Lord Bingham).

[67] ibid. Similarly, see *Medellin v Texas* 552 US 491, 128 S Ct 1346, 1363 (2008), where the Court regarded the non-existence of State practice as an argument.

conflicts.'[68] In this case, the ECtHR maintained that 'consistent practice on the part of the High Contracting Parties, subsequent to their ratification of the Convention, could be taken as establishing their agreement.'[69] In contrast to the ECtHR, which examined the practice under the Convention in greater detail to determine its consistency, Lord Bingham did not further elaborate on his practice-based argument. In particular, he did not indicate whether the practice which he had sweepingly referred to was actually capable of establishing the parties' agreement.

A different approach to the parties' agreement was adopted by the Court of Appeal of New Zealand in the case of *Lena-Jane Punter v Secretary for Justice, ex p Adam Punter*, which concerned the interpretation of the Hague Abduction Convention. Setting out his approach to treaty interpretation, Glazebrook J explained that 'under article 31(3)(b) of that Convention … subsequent practice in the application of a treaty is regarded as establishing the agreement of the parties regarding the interpretation and is to be taken into account in the interpretation of the treaty.'[70] In accordance with this explanation, Glazebrook J thereafter relied on subsequent practice in the form of foreign court decisions without asking whether this practice was capable of establishing the parties' agreement.[71] Reminiscent of Lord Mance's comment in *Deep Vein Thrombosis,* this dictum suggests that Glazebrook J did not consider it necessary to ascertain the parties' agreement. Instead, he seemed to believe that any practice in the application of the treaty *automatically* established the necessary agreement.[72]

The abovementioned cases illustrate how domestic courts regularly blurred the line between practice and agreement. A rare exception is the German Federal Administrative Court's decision on the interpretation of article 1(C)(5) Refugee Convention.[73] This case discussed whether refugee status could be withdrawn once a change of circumstances eliminated a previously reasonable fear of persecution. Interpreting article 1(C)(5) more broadly, a change of circumstances would not be sufficient. Instead, other circumstances such as a minimum level of human rights protection in the refugee's home State would have to be taken into account, too. The German Federal Administrative Court, however, dismissed the broader interpretation. In the

[68] *Hassan v UK [GC]* App no 29750/09 (ECtHR, 16 September 2014) [101].

[69] ibid [101].

[70] *Lena-Jane Punter v Secretary for Justice, ex p Adam Punter* [2004] 2 NZLR 28 [61] (Glazebrook J).

[71] ibid [66]–[75], [87]–[124] (Glazebrook J).

[72] In the same vein, see BFHE 215, 237, 241, where the German Federal Fiscal Court noted that State practice constituted a material and objectively identifiable indicator of how the parties understand the treaty or, at least, how they understood it when concluding the treaty and in the years immediately thereafter.

[73] BVerwG, Decision of 7 February 2008, 10 C 33/07 <http://www.juris.de>. See also VfGH, Judgment of 25 September 2015, V 41/2015-11 [46], where the Court could not even make out an agreement between Austrian courts and the Austrian government. For this reason, it dismissed the Austrian Minister of Finance's line of reasoning, which strongly relied on art 31(3)(b) VCLT.

Court's view, such other circumstances were irrelevant under the Refugee Convention. This was because the Convention was only meant to protect against persecution and not to ensure human rights in general.[74]

To support this reading, the Court emphasised that there was no common and concordant subsequent State practice supporting any other construction.[75] Having said so, it clarified that article 31(3)(b) VCLT did not simply envisage some practice in the application of the treaty.[76] Instead, potentially relevant practice also had to be capable of establishing the agreement of all State parties regarding the treaty's interpretation.[77] Based on this observation, the Court then discussed and dismissed several pieces of practice.[78] In doing so, it very accurately distinguished between practice on the one hand and the parties' agreement on the other. In addition, it even sought to explain why this practice, which it had identified as potentially relevant, was incapable of establishing the parties' agreement regarding the interpretation of the Refugee Convention.

In summary—and notwithstanding the previous example—domestic courts hardly ever openly examine whether potentially relevant practice actually rests on the parties' agreement. Instead, they mostly seem to take it for granted that it does. But why should this approach be problematic under article 31(3)(b) VCLT? Subsequent practice serves as a piece of evidence demonstrating the existence of a non-manifest agreement. For this reason, article 31(3)(b) VCLT requires interpreters to perform an additional intellectual operation to establish a link between a given practice and the parties' agreement.[79] As the parties' agreement is non-manifest, interpreters cannot but draw inferences. But these inferences have to be drawn and they have to be drawn reasonably. Article 31(3)(b) VCLT does not establish the presumption—as many domestic courts seemed to believe—that practice does establish the parties' agreement.

One case in which it is indispensable to ascertain the parties' agreement is reliance on non-party practice. Regarded in isolation, it is far-fetched to argue that any non-party practice in the application of a treaty automatically establishes the parties' agreement. Domestic courts, however, tend not to regard non-party conduct as directly relevant under article 31(3)(b) VCLT. Therefore, this situation is of a rather theoretical nature. A more common and more problematic situation is that in which interpreters do not ascertain the parties' agreement although there is active conduct by only some State parties. The term 'practice' under article 31(3)(b) VCLT

---

[74] BVerwG, Decision of 7 February 2008, 10 C 33/07 <http://www.juris.de> [29].

[75] ibid [31]. cf also *Macoun v Commissioner of Taxation* [2015] HCA 44, (2015) 326 ALR 452 [80] (French CJ, Bell, Gageler, Nettle and Gordon JJ).

[76] BVerwG, Decision of 7 February 2008, 10 C 33/07 <http://www.juris.de> [31].

[77] ibid. cf also *Minister for Immigration v Ibrahim* [2000] HCA 55, (2000) 204 CLR 1 [140] (Gummow J): '[W]hile Art 31(3)(b) of the Vienna Convention on the Law of Treaties recognises the significance of "subsequent practice in the application of the treaty", there must be at least a tacit or implicit agreement of the parties regarding its interpretation.'

[78] BVerwG, Decision of 7 February 2008, 10 C 33/07 <http://www.juris.de> [32], [34].

[79] See 4.1.

also covers omissions to act.[80] Yet it would be wrong to generally assume that omissions to act reflect a particular understanding of the treaty or even signal a State's acquiescence in another party's active conduct.[81]

Even where interpreters rely on active conduct by all parties, they had better uphold the distinction between practice and agreement. This is because States do not always 'speak with one voice' when it comes to treaty interpretation. Different actors from different levels of State hierarchy may well take different views on interpreting a treaty. Therefore, it is often necessary to identify the actor(s) that possess ultimate interpretative authority in the case at hand. By blurring the line between practice and agreement, interpreters will risk overlooking inconsistent practice and a lack of agreement at the intra-State level. And what is more, they will even risk disregarding a legal position taken by the State as a whole by unduly overemphasising single aberrations.

However, blurring the line between practice and agreement creates yet another danger. This danger is even greater than those just mentioned. Consciously or unconsciously, interpreters may select the practice upon which they rely.

8.2.2 *The Spectrum of Selectivity*

Where interpreters do not ascertain the parties' agreement, they may be tempted not to identify and to consider all instances of relevant practice. Instead, they may—consciously or unconsciously—pick and choose those instances of practice which support the desired result. As regards the jurisprudence of domestic courts, concerns about selectivity are not hypothetical but well-founded. The way in which domestic courts utilise subsequent practice as a means of interpretation is highly selective. In some cases, however, domestic courts were markedly less selective than in others. Less selective means that the court sought to identify practice by all or at least most parties to the treaty. Moreover, one can distinguish different types of selectivity, namely purely quantitative (8.2.2.1), regional (8.2.2.2), and qualitative selectivity (8.2.2.3).

The cases in which domestic courts were less selective usually concerned treaties with only few parties. An example is the judgment of the German Federal Fiscal Court on the interpretation of the Gasoil Agreement.[82] In this case, the Court examined executive practice in Germany, Switzerland, and France and legislative practice in the Netherlands.[83] This judgment analyses State practice in a comparatively detailed fashion. Instead of examining the practice of only some parties, the Court thoroughly discussed how each contracting party had applied the contentious

[80] See 4.3.1.1.

[81] See 8.1.

[82] BFHE 144, 483.

[83] ibid 486 f.

provision. But this thorough discussion is not solely due to the Court's own diligence. A comprehensive discussion of State practice was considerably facilitated because the case concerned a treaty with only a few parties. Furthermore, the respondent had brought the relevant practice to the Court's attention.[84] Therefore, the Court did not need to conduct its own research on how the Gasoil Agreement had been applied.

Treaties with many parties render it more difficult to identify relevant practice by all parties. Interpreters that take the Vienna rules seriously therefore regularly conclude that the requirements of article 31(3)(b) VLCT are not met. This can be seen in the already mentioned decision of the German Federal Administrative Court on the interpretation of article 1(C)(5) Refugee Convention.[85] In this case, the high number of parties explained why the Court refused to consider the practice of only few parties sufficient for the purpose of article 31(3)(b) VCLT.[86] Another example is the judgment of the German Federal Court of Justice on the European Patent Convention.[87] Refusing to base its interpretation of the Convention on a unilateral statement by the German government, the Court objected that

> the government of a single contracting party cannot authoritatively interpret a multilateral treaty such as the European Patent Convention. So long as there is no authentic interpretation by all contracting parties, it is legally immaterial whether further governments of some of the contracting parties shared the view expressed by the government of the Federal Republic of Germany.[88]

However, individual pieces of practice beyond the scope of article 31(3)(b) VCLT are not completely irrelevant. Interpreters can rely on such 'other' conduct as a supplementary means of interpretation under article 32 VCLT.[89] Article 32 VCLT does not distinguish between admissible and inadmissible practice. For this reason, interpreters can feel free to consider single instances of practice or an accumulated body of practice which do not establish the agreement of all or at least most parties to the treaty.

The relevance of 'other' subsequent conduct has been explicitly acknowledged by the Court of Appeal of New Zealand. In *Ye v Minister of Immigration*, it discussed

---

[84] ibid.

[85] BVerwG, Decision of 7 February 2008, 10 C 33/07 <http://www.juris.de>.

[86] ibid [31] f.

[87] Convention on the Grant of European Patents (signed 5 October 1973, entered into force 7 October 1977) 1065 UNTS 199 (European Patent Convention).

[88] BGHZ 82, 88, 93 f [translated by the author]. In German: 'Die Regierung eines einzelnen Staates ist gar nicht in der Lage, einen mehrseitigen völkerrechtlichen Vertrag wie das Europäische Patentübereinkommen verbindlich auszulegen. Solange keine authentische Interpretation des Vertrages durch alle Vertragsstaaten erfolgt ist, ist es auch ohne rechtliche Bedeutung, ob weitere Regierungen einzelner Vertragsstaaten denselben Standpunkt eingenommen haben wie die Bundesregierung der Bundesrepublik Deutschland.'

[89] See 4.4. See also draft conclusion 4(3) and the accompanying commentary in ILC, 'Report of the International Law Commission on the Work of its 65th Session' (6 May–7 June and 8 July–9 August 2013) UN Doc A/68/10, 31, 37–41.

whether the so-called *Puli'uvea* test was compatible with article 3(1) UNCROC. The test requires a child's best interest to be a primary but not a paramount consideration when removing its parents from New Zealand. Article 3(1) UNCROC, in contrast, stipulates that the best interests of the child shall be a primary consideration in all actions concerning children.[90] Affirming their compatibility, Glazebrook J relied on a decision of the Canadian Supreme Court,[91] in which it had held that a child's best interest did not outweigh any other consideration. According to Glazebrook J, it was admissible to take this decision into account because '[t]he Vienna Convention also permits supplementary means of interpretation to be used under art 32 such as decisions from other jurisdictions.'[92] Thus, he effectively distinguished between subsequent practice under article 31(3)(b) VCLT and 'other' subsequent conduct under article 32 VCLT.

Practice can be relevant as subsequent practice under article 31(3)(b) VCLT and as 'other' conduct under article 32 VCLT. Where courts have recourse to selected practice without citing article 31 or 32 VCLT, it remains doubtful whether they regarded that practice as a primary or supplementary means of interpretation. But irrespective of that, selected practice that does not establish the parties' agreement can only be relied on for the purpose and under the conditions specified in article 32 VCLT, ie in order to confirm the meaning resulting from the application of article 31 VCLT or to determine the meaning when the interpretation according to article 31 VCLT leaves the meaning ambiguous or obscure or leads to a result which is manifestly absurd or unreasonable. Unless a court expressly clothes selected practice with the greater interpretative weight of a primary means of interpretation, the decisive question is whether it uses that practice in contravention of article 32 VCLT.

In the Warsaw Convention case *Air France v Saks*,[93] for example, the US Supreme Court used the conduct of 'many' signatories merely to reconfirm and refine an interpretation of article 17 Warsaw Convention which it had arrived at by applying primary means of interpetation.[94] Because the Court did not cite the Vienna rules, it

---

[90] *Ye v Minister of Immigration* [2009] 2 NZLR 596 [61] f (Glazebrook J).

[91] ibid [71] f (Glazebrook J).

[92] ibid.

[93] *Air France v Saks* 470 US 392, 105 S Ct 1338 (1985).

[94] ibid 397 f, 401, 404–7. cf also *El Al Israel Airlines, Ltd v Tsui Yuan Tseng* 525 US 155, 175, 119 S Ct 662 (1999); *Victrawl Pty Ltd v Telstra Corporation Ltd* [1995] HCA 51, (1995) 183 CLR 595 [15] f (Brennan J); *Lozano v Montoya Alvarez* 134 S Ct 1224, 1127 (2014); BVerwGE 139, 272, 288 f; *Abbott v Abbott* 560 US 1, 130 S Ct 1983, 1993 f (2010). Notably, the selective approach of the majority in *Abbott* was criticised by Stevens, Thomas, and Breyer JJ in a dissenting opinion, who 'fail[ed] to see the international consensus—let alone the "broad acceptance" … that the Court finds among those varied decisions from foreign courts that have considered the effect of a similar travel restriction within the Convention's remedial scheme. The various decisions of the international courts are, at best, in equipoise. Indeed, the Court recognizes that courts in Canada and France have concluded that travel restrictions are not "rights of custody" within the meaning of the Convention.' See ibid 2009 (diss op Stevens, Thomas, and Breyer JJ).

eventually remains unclear whether it regarded that practice as a primary or supplementary means of interpretation. On the one hand, the practice was not decisive for arriving at the Court's interpretation.[95] But on the other hand, article 31 VCLT does not require each primary means of interpretation to be decisive in each and every case. A primary means of interpretation may cast doubt on a provisional interpretation of the terms of the treaty; it may not be instructive at all; or it may support the same and thus 'confirm' a provisional interpretation supported by other primary means.

In *Saks,* the US Supreme Court did not ignore mandatory practice within the meaning of article 31(3)(b) VCLT; it did not attach decisive weight to the practice by 'many' signatories; and it did not unduly vest this practice with the interpretative weight of a primary means of intepretation. For this reason, the Court's selectivity did not infringe the Vienna rules. Cases like *Saks* need to be distinguished from those cases in which selected instances of practice were obviously regarded as a primary means of interpretation. These cases are more difficult to reconcile with the Vienna rules.

8.2.2.1 Quantitative Selectivity

An unequivocal example of selectivity under article 31(3)(b) VCLT is Lord Steyn's examination of French legislative practice in the case of *R (Mullen) v Secretary of State for the Home Department.* In his view, this isolated practice was an admissible guide to interpreting the ICCPR because, 'the French dimension established state practice, which is relevant to treaty construction: article 31(3)(B) of the Vienna Convention on the Law of Treaties'.[96] This dictum was severely criticised by Lord Phillips in *R (Adams) v Secretary of State for Justice*, who remarked that '[t]his practice on the part of only one of the many signatories to the ICCPR does not provide a guide to the meaning of article 14(6).... It has not been suggested that there is any consistency of practice on the part of the signatories that assists in determining the meaning of article 14(6).'[97]

---

[95] Further examples of subsequent practice used as a supplementary means of interpretation include BGHZ 145, 97, 101 f, where the Court relied on decisions by Canadian, Austrian, Italian, and UK courts as well as Dutch and UK legislation to reconform its interpretation of art 16 of the Convention on the Civil Aspects of International Child Abduction (signed 25 October 1980, entered into force 1 December 1983) 1343 UNTS 89 (Hague Abduction Convention); *T v Secretary of State for the Home Secretary* [1996] UKHL 8, [1996] AC 742 779 (Lord Loyd), where Canadian and US decisions were taken into account to interpret the Refugee Convention because '[i]n a case concerning an international convention it is obviously desirable that decisions in different jurisdictions should, so far possible, be kept in line with each other.' See further *Fothergill v Monarch Airlines Ltd* [1980] UKHL 6, [1981] AC 251 278 (Lord Wilberforce), where French and US court decisions were taken into account to explain why it was admissibe to consider the Warsaw Convention's *travaux préparatoires*.

[96] *R (Mullen) v Secretary of State for the Home Department* [2004] UKHL 18, [2005] 1 AC 1 [47] (Lord Steyn).

[97] *R (Adams) v Secretary of State for Justice* [2011] UKSC 18, [2012] 1 AC 48 [17] (Lord Phillips).

Another example of selectivity is the case of *Attorney-General v Zaoui (No 2)*, which concerned the interpretation of the phrase 'danger to the security of the country' within the meaning of article 33(2) Refugee Convention. Having acknowledged that subsequent practice could, under article 31(3)(b) VCLT, affect the interpretation of treaties,[98] Glazebrook J superficially referred to few Canadian and UK court decisions to determine the meaning of the contentious phrase.[99] A similarly high degree of selectivity can be seen in the case of *King v Bristow Helicopters Ltd (Scotland)*, which concerned the interpretation of the phrase 'bodily injury' under article 17 Warsaw Convention (as amended).[100] Notably, all Law Lords stressed the importance of US Supreme Court decisions for casting light on the meaning of this phrase.[101] Yet, only Lord Hope explained why these decisions were so important, namely because 'it is also legitimate to have regard to subsequent practice in the application of the Convention, if this shows that the contracting parties were in agreement as to its interpretation when it was entered into'.[102] Citing the Vienna rules, he continued:

> In an ideal world the Convention should be accorded the same meaning by all who are party to it. So case law provides a further potential source of evidence. Careful consideration needs to be given to the reasoning of courts of other jurisdictions which have been called upon to deal with the point at issue, particularly those which are of high standing. Considerable weight should be given to an interpretation which has received general acceptance in other jurisdictions. On the other hand a discriminating approach is required if the decisions conflict, or if there is no clear agreement between them.[103]

At first sight, these statements suggest that Lord Hope was truly concerned with identifying the parties' agreement. Moreover, they seem to imply that foreign court decisions should not be relied on in the absence of true agreement. Nevertheless, Lords Hope then referred to the same 'consistent body of judicial opinion in the United States' that his fellow judges had already taken note of.[104] Next, he quickly referred to few Australian and Israeli decisions—as he explained because no other cases outside the USA had been referred to the Court's attention—to reconfirm the

---

[98] *Attorney-General v Zaoui (No 2)* [2005] 1 NZLR 690 [130] (Glazebrook J).

[99] ibid [134] (Glazebrook J).

[100] Protocol to Amend the Convention for the Unification of Certain Rules relating to International Carriage by Air Signed at Warsaw on October 12, 1929 (signed 28 September 1955, entered into force 1 August 1963) 478 UNTS 371 (Hague Protocol)

[101] *Bristow Helicopters* (n 62) [7] (Lord Mackay): 'Because I consider it important that the Warsaw Convention should have a common construction in all the jurisdictions of the countries that have adopted the Convention, I attach crucial importance to the decisions of the United States Supreme Court.' cf also ibid [18]–[20] (Lord Steyn).

[102] ibid [80] (Lord Hope).

[103] ibid [80]–[81] (Lord Hope).

[104] ibid [80], [107]–[18] (Lord Hope).

interpretation arrived at after looking at US cases.[105] In sum, Lord Hope therefore relied on practice that was far from reliably establishing the parties' agreement. An absence of obvious disagreement, like in this case, may increase the interpretative weight of 'other' subsequent conduct under article 32 VCLT; yet it is not synonymous with the parties' agreement as envisaged by article 31(3)(b) VCLT.

8.2.2.2 Regional Selectivity

A special, and perhaps even more questionable type of selectivity is regional selectivity. The notion 'regional selectivity' describes those cases in which interpreters do not consider all potentially relevant practice but focus on practice from a particular region. It often relates to universal treaties that have a regional counterpart or in the implementation of which a particular group of States takes coordinated action.

How regional implementation measures are relied on as regional practice can be seen in a judgment of the German Federal Administrative Court on the interpretation of article 1(A)(2) Refugee Convention. Expressly citing article 31(3)(b) VCLT, the Court remarked that there was no uniform State practice conflicting with its preferred interpretation. For this reason and

> [i]n the light of the 'Joint Position' of the Council of the European Union of 4 March 1996 … this Senate considers itself confirmed in its view that its interpretation is still shared by a majority of the governments of the contracting parties and in accordance with prevailing state practice.[106]

This dictum is important because it seemed to reverse the ordinary 'burden of proof' under article 31(3)(b) VCLT.[107] Article 31(3)(b) VCLT attaches interpretative

---

[105] ibid [80], [119]–[27] (Lord Hope); see also ibid [178] (Lord Hophouse), who embraced Lord Hope's interpretation of the Warsaw Convention because it reflected, in this view, the 'direction in which the jurisdiction which has to deal with the greatest volume of air passenger litigation, the United States, has moved'. In the same vein, see BGer, Judgment of 25 September 2012, 4A_284/2012, BGE 138 III 708, 709 f, where the Court first acknowledged that it may only rely on subsequent practice pursuant to art 31(3)(b) VCLT where such practice reflected the agreement of the parties regarding a treaty's interpretation. Then, however, the Court relied on one Austrian and two German court decisions without discussing how these decisions could establish the parties' agreement.

[106] BVerwGE 104, 254, 256 f [translated by the author], referring to Joint Position 96/196/JHA of 4 March 1996 Defined by the Council on the Basis of Article K.3 of the Treaty on European Union on the Harmonised Application of the Definition of the Term 'Refugee' in Article 1 of the Geneva Convention of 28 July 1951 relating to the Status of Refugees [1996] OJ L63/2. In German: 'Der Senat sieht sich in seiner Ansicht, daß das von ihm gefundene Auslegungsergebnis auch heute noch der Auffassung der Regierungen der meisten Vertragsstaaten und der überwiegenden Staatenpraxis entspricht, schließlich durch den "Gemeinsamen Standpunkt" des Rates der Europäischen Union vom 4. März 1996… bestätigt.'

[107] To 'reverse the burden of proof' under art 31(3)(b) VCLT, the Court used the following reasoning. Firstly, it asserted that there was no uniform practice that was capable of refuting

weight to practice that establishes the parties' agreement; it does not attach weight to the opposite phenomenon, namely an absence of such practice. Moreover, the only practice which the Court could rely on was a EU document. First of all, this document qualifies as organisational practice and not as State practice. 'Joint Positions' were adopted by the Council of the European Union and not by the European Council or the representatives of the governments of the Member States meeting within the Council.[108] But apart from that, it is difficult to see how such regional practice may cast a light on anything but a European understanding of the Refugee Convention.

The case *R (Mullen) v Secretary of State for the Home Department* illustrates how courts select regional practice to a universal treaty when considering a related regional instrument. This case concerned the interpretation of article 14(6) ICCPR, which secures a right to compensation in cases of miscarriage of justice. Its regional counterpart, so to speak, is article 3 of Protocol 7 ECHR.[109] This provision equally provides for compensation for wrongful conviction and was adopted to bring the Convention into line with the ICCPR.[110] In contrast to his fellow judges,[111] Lord Steyn was less reluctant to rely on the ECHR context to interpret the ICCPR. In his view, this context could add something to understanding European jurisprudence.[112] Examining the already mentioned Explanatory Report prepared by the Steering Committee for Human Rights as 'a basis on which states sign and ratify the Protocol', he argued that State practice would be based on the Report and, by virtue of article 31(3)(b) VCLT, become 'directly relevant to the interpretation of article 14(6)' ICCPR.[113]

This reasoning is noteworthy because Lord Steyn relied on article 31(3)(b) VCLT despite considering regional practice only. Since article 3 of Protocol 7 ECHR had been adopted to comply with the requirements under article 14(6) ICCPR, one may well argue that practice in the application of the former provision also constitutes practice in the application of the latter. Nonetheless, Lord Steyn's reasoning is difficult to reconcile with article 31(3)(b) VCLT. A practice in the application of a

---

its own construction. And secondly, the Court took the lack of contrary practice as an argument to conclude that its own construction was actually shared by the majority of the governments of the contracting parties.

[108] Art 15 TEU (Treaty of Amsterdam). See also Elfriede Regelsberger and Dieter Kugelmann, 'Artikel 15—Gemeinsame Standpunkte' in Rudolf Streinz (ed), *EUV/EGV—Vertrag über die Europäische Union und Vertrag zur Gründung der Europäischen Gemeinschaft* (CH Beck 2003) [1]–[3].

[109] Protocol 7 to the European Convention for the Protection of Human Rights and Fundamental Freedoms (signed 22 November 1984, entered into force 1 November 1988) ETS No 117 (Protocol 7 ECHR).

[110] cf *Mullen* (n 96) [9] (Lord Bingham).

[111] ibid.

[112] ibid [38]–[44] (Lord Steyn).

[113] ibid [48] (Lord Steyn).

regional instrument may perhaps cast light on how its parties understand an equivalent universal instrument like the ICCPR. Yet, it is difficult to see how such regional practice can establish the agreement of other parties to the universal instrument. This is especially true as regards treaties such as the ECHR and the ICCPR because the way in which States interpret scope and meaning of the rights granted therein also depends on and varies according to their cultural-regional background.

Curiously, domestic courts do not seem to consider regional selectivity problematic at all. This can be seen in the case of *Itel Containers Intern Corp v Huddleston,*[114] in which the US Supreme Court had to determine whether a sales tax imposed by Tenessee law was prohibited by the 1956[115] and 1972[116] Container Conventions. In its reasoning, Itel had invoked the 'consistent practice' of other contracting parties to the Conventions not to impose any tax on containers within their borders.[117] In addition to statements of 11 other signatories objecting to the Tennessee tax,[118] Itel had also relied on the European Value Added Tax (VAT) system.[119] While the Court rejected Itel's practice-based arguments,[120] it did not mind Itel's emphasis on regional practice. But judged against the Vienna rules, the Court may have also criticised that the European VAT system was insufficient to demonstrate consistent (legislative) practice of EU and non-EU signatories of the Container Conventions alike. Even taken together with the objections to the Tennessee tax, there remains a regional selectivity in Itel's reasoning, which does not correspond to the universal nature of the Container Conventions.

8.2.2.3 Qualitative Selectivity

Regional selectivity often not only means that interpreters consider practice of a limited number of States. In addition, regional selectivity may also—deliberately or not—entail a selection as regards the quality of practice. States belonging to a particular geographical region are more likely to share certain values (cultural, political, religious ones, etc) that affect their understanding of the treaty.

The jurisprudence of domestic courts offers various other examples of qualitative selectivity. In *Yugraneft Corp v Rexx Management Corp*, for instance, the Supreme Court of Canada highlighted the different legal traditions of those States upon whose practice it relied. This case concerned the interpretation of article III of the New

114 *Itel Containers Intern Corp v Huddleston* 507 US 60, 113 S Ct 1095 (1993).

115 Customs Convention on Containers (signed 18 May 1956, entered into force 4 August 1959) 338 UNTS 103 (1956 Containers Convention).

116 Customs Convention on Containers (signed 2 December 1972, entered into force 6 December 1975) 988 UNTS 43 (1972 Containers Convention).

117 *Itel* (n 114) 67.

118 ibid 68.

119 ibid 67.

120 ibid 66 f.

York Convention,[121] which provides that recognition and enforcement of foreign arbitral awards shall be in accordance with the rules of procedure of the territory where the award was relied on. At issue was whether local limitation periods were 'rules of procedure' and therefore permitted under article III. To outline the different views on this issue, Rothstein J first noted that several common law countries had considered such periods procedural in nature whereas several civil law countries had regarded them as part of substantive law.[122] Citing article 31(3)(b) VCLT,[123] he then referred to a 'recent study' conducted by the International Chamber of Commerce and a report prepared by the UN Commission on International Trade Law (UNCITRAL).

These documents asserted that 53 State parties to the New York Convention imposed some kind of time limit on the enforcement of foreign arbitral awards.[124] According to Rothstein J, the documents thus evidenced that local limitation periods had to be considered as procedural in nature and therefore permitted under the Convention. In this respect, he stressed that the States imposing such time limits comprised both common law and civil law countries.[125] Because Rothstein J had ealier noted that as many as 140 States had so far ratified the Convention,[126] this emphasis on the States' legal systems is particularly interesting. In purely numerical terms, it is difficult to see how practice of 53 State parties can establish the agreement of most or even all parties to the Convention. Thus, the distribution of practice across different legal traditions (a qualitative criterion) was effectively treated as compensating for the fragmentary—albeit comparatively large—body of relevant practice.

A different qualitative criterion was applied in the Warsaw Convention case *Fothergill v Monarch Airlines Ltd*. This case concerned the time limit under article 26(2) Warsaw Convention. On its face, the limit only applied to damaged baggage. Counsel for the defendant, however, sought to demonstrate that the limit also applied to (partially) lost baggage and invoked various foreign court decisions. Yet, the House of Lords refused to take these decisions into account. As Lord Wilberforce explained, 'they are not decisions of the highest courts; secondly, the process of law reporting varies from country to country and they may not be exhaustive.'[127] And Lord Diplock more generally pointed out that 'the persuasive value of a particular court's decision must depend upon its reputation and its status, the extent to which its decisions are binding upon courts of co-ordinate and inferior jurisdiction in its own country, and the coverage of the national law reporting system.'[128]

---

[121] Convention on the Recognition and Enforcement of Foreign Arbitral Awards (signed 10 June 1958, entered into force 7 June 1959) 330 UNTS 3 (New York Convention).

[122] *Yugraneft Corp v Rexx Management Corp* [2010] 1 SCR 649, 2010 SCC 19 [16] (Rothstein J).

[123] ibid [21] (Rothstein J).

[124] ibid.

[125] ibid.

[126] ibid [10] (Rothstein J).

[127] *Fothergill* (n 95) 275 f (Lord Wilberforce).

[128] ibid 284 (Lord Diplock).

These words of caution were reconfirmed in *Sidhu v British Airways*. This case raised the question of whether the Warsaw Convention provided an exclusive cause of action and remedy once it was applicable. The parties to the case had brought several foreign court decisions to the House of Lords' attention that allegedly supported their positions. Against this background, Lord Hope reiterated that 'much must depend upon the status of each court and the extent to which the point of issue has been subjected to careful analysis.'[129] Looking at a French case that had been mentioned by one of the parties, he then refused to take this case into account because, being a decision of a first instance court only, it lacked the necessary persuasive value.[130] This dictum illustrates that selectivity must not necessarily be incompatible with the Vienna rules. Individual pieces of practice sometimes cannot reliably establish the parties' agreement. Dismissing such practice does not discriminate against individual States as such but rather upholds the distinction between practice and agreement.

A different kind of qualitative selectivity is illustrated in *Commissioner of the Australian Federal Police and the Commonwealth of Australia v Magno and Almeida*. This case concerned the interpretation of the phrase 'impairment of dignity' pursuant to article 22 VCDR. To circumscribe the conduct that might actually impair a mission's dignity, Einfeld J relied on UK and US practice because the 'international application of the Convention by democratic countries indicates that another significant consideration is freedom of speech in the host country'.[131] While admitting that his examples of US and UK practice may be 'insufficient as to what ought to be the Australian interpretation of the Convention', he clarified that this practice

> certainly provide[d] influential examples of how two important democratic countries with experience in the field have interpreted it. Considering the very different constitutional frameworks of these two exemplifying nations, I can think of no reason why, and have found no authority suggesting that, Australia should apply the Convention differently.[132]

Since Einfeld J introduced his examination of State practice by citing article 31(3)(b) VCLT,[133] he obviously meant to apply this provision. Yet, his interpretative approach is difficult to reconcile with the Vienna rules. Firstly, he relied on the practice of only two parties. In other words, Einfeld J simply assumed that the practice of only two parties established the agreement of 190. And secondly, Einfeld J attached special weight to practice by democratic countries. Thus, he seemed to

---

[129] *Sidhu v British Airways* [1997] AC 430 (HL) 443 (Lord Hope). cf *Eastern Airlines, Inc v Floyd* 499 US 530, 551 f, 111 S Ct 1489 (1991), where the US Supreme Court refused to take an Israeli decision into account because this decision had, in the Court's view, been based on political considerations.

[130] *Sidhu* (n 129) 453 (Lord Hope).

[131] *Commissioner of the Australian Federal Police and the Commonwealth of Australia v Magno and Almeida* [1992] FCA 566, (1992) 37 FCR 298 [30] (Einfeld J).

[132] ibid [35] (Einfeld J).

[133] ibid [26] (Einfeld J).

imply that a self-defined qualitative criterion was capable of compensating for a marked lack of quantity.

8.2.3 *Selected Practice and Uniform Interpretation*

Some treaties expressly call on interpreters to promote uniformity in their application. Most of these treaties aim at harmonising private law, such as the UN Convention on Contracts for the International Sale of Goods,[134] the Convention on the Limitation Period in the International Sale of Goods,[135] and the UN Convention on the Carriage of Goods by Sea.[136] Besides, treaties 'typically create common and reciprocal obligations for treaty parties'.[137] At first sight, it therefore appears obvious that interpreters ought to construe and apply treaties in a uniform fashion.

In that sense, Lord Hope recognised in *R (Pinochet) v Commissioner of Police for the Metropolis* 'that international treaties should, so far as possible, be construed uniformly by the national courts of all states.'[138] This dictum was subsequently reconfirmed in the Warsaw Convention case of *Deep Vein Thrombosis and Air Travel Group Litigation.* Lord Steyn, for instance, noted that '[i]n interpretation of a trade law treaty, like the Warsaw Convention, it is of great importance that the courts of treaty states, and particular their higher courts, should strive for uniform interpretation on debatable issues. Such uniformity is not always attainable but must be the constant aim.'[139] And Lord Mance pointed out:

> It is also legitimate to have regard to any subsequent practice among the parties which is capable of establishing their agreement regarding interpretation ... Allied to the legitimacy of having regard to subsequent practice is the significant consideration that a convention like the Warsaw Convention as amended is aimed at achieving conformity of law and practice in its field, and that uniformity in its interpretation is highly desirable.[140]

---

[134] Art 7(1) of the United Nations Convention on Contracts for the International Sale of Goods (signed 11 April 1980, entered into force 1 January 1988) 1489 UNTS 3 (CISG).

[135] Art 7 of the Convention on the Limitation Period in the International Sale of Goods (signed 14 June 1974, entered into force 1 August 1988) 1511 UNTS 3 (Limitation Convention).

[136] Art 3 of the United Nations Convention on the Carriage of Goods by Sea (signed 31 March 1978, entered into force 1 November 1992) 1695 UNTS 3 (Hamburg Rules). See also art 18 of the Convention on the Law Applicable to Contractual Obligations (signed 19 June 1980, entered into force 1 April 1991) 1605 UNTS 59 (Rome Convention); art 4(1) of the UNIDROIT Convention on International Factoring (signed 28 May 1988, entered into force 1 May 1995) 2323 UNTS 373; art 6(1) of the UNIDROIT Convention on International Financial Leasing (signed 28 May 1988, entered into force 1 May 1995) 2321 UNTS 195.

[137] Anthea Roberts, 'Comparative International Law? The Role of National Courts in Creating and Enforcing International Law' (2011) 60 ICLQ 57, 83.

[138] *R (Pinochet) v Commissioner of Police for the Metropolis* [2000] 1 AC 147, [1999] UKHL 17, 244 (Lord Hope).

[139] *Deep Vein Thrombosis* (n 61) [35] (Lord Steyn).

[140] ibid [54]–[55] (Lord Mance).

Thus, Lord Mance expressly linked the general objective of uniform interpretation to subsequent practice as a primary means of interpretation. But like his fellow judges, he then only referred to decisions by Australian, Canadian, and especially US courts to demonstrate that 'there is a substantial body of international authority consistent with the views I have expressed'.[141]

On the one hand, *Deep Vein Thrombosis* illustrates that the objective of uniform interpretation may well encourage references to subsequent practice (in a wider sense). On the other hand, it also shows that domestic courts do not necessarily refer to potentially relevant practice in a less selective fashion just because they strive for uniform interpretation. Firstly, the House of Lords only relied on decisions from few English speaking countries. Secondly, it only mentioned judicial practice and did not discuss whether there was any other relevant practice in the application of the Warsaw Convention. And thirdly, the predominance of US jurisprudence suggests that selective reliance on judicial practice may grant certain State parties (or their courts and individual judges) considerably more influence on the interpretation of the treaty than others.

That the objective of uniform interpretation does not necessarily reduce selectivity can also be seen in Justice Scalia's dissenting opinion in *Olympic Airways v Husain*.[142] Having failed to consider apparently relevant UK and Australian court decisions, Scalia dismissed the majority's reasoning as unconvincing. In his view, the US Supreme Court should 'accord the judgments of our sister signatories "considerable weight"' when interpreting an international treaty such as the Warsaw Convention.[143] As the Court had hitherto examined foreign legal material more readily when interpreting constitutional law,[144] Scalia considered that 'sudden insularity' rather 'striking'.[145] At his point, it is instructive to briefly delineate Scalia's attitude as regards the use of foreign legal material in constitutional interpretation.

The US Supreme Court's invocation of foreign legal material in constitutional interpretation had sparked intense debates between 'nationalists' and 'transnationalists'[146] in

[141] ibid [66]–[81] (Lord Mance).

[142] *Olympic Airways v Husain* 540 US 644, 124 S Ct 1221 (2004).

[143] ibid 658 (diss op Scalia J), citing *Saks* (n 93) 404.

[144] Eg *Thompson v Oklahoma* 487 US 815, 830 f, 108 S Ct 2687 (1988); *Atkins v Virginia* 536 US 304, 316 f, 122 S Ct 2242 (2002); *Lawrence v Texas* 539 US 558, 572–73, 123 S Ct 2472 (2003); *Roper v Simmons* 543 US 551, 564 f, 125 S Ct 1183 (2005). For further references, see Rex Glensy, 'Which Countries Count?: *Lawrence v Texas* and the Selection of Foreign Persuasive Authority' (2005) 45 Va J Int'l L 357.

[145] *Husain* (n 142) 658 (diss op Scalia J).

[146] For this nomenclature see in particular Harold Koh, 'The Ninth Annual John W Hager Lecture, the 2004 Term: The Supreme Court Meets International Law' (2004) 12 Tulsa J Comp & Int'l L 1.

academia and among the justices.[147] Whereas 'transnationalists' such as Justice Breyer advocated the use of foreign legal material, 'nationalists' such as Justice Scalia repeatedly criticised its use. First of all, Scalia contended that foreign legal material was legally irrelevant when interpreting the US Constitution. In his view, it could neither contribute to US originalist constitutional interpretation nor determine modern day American views.[148] Secondly, he argued that references to foreign legal material tended to be illegitimate because they were highly selective and self-serving.[149] To emphasise the latter argument, he pointedly remarked in *Roper v Simmons* that 'all the Court has done today … is to look over the heads of the crowd and pick out its friends.'[150]

In *Husain,* Scalia therefore contrasted constitutional interpretation with treaty interpretation: 'One would have thought that foreign courts' interpretations of a treaty that their governments adopted jointly with ours, and that they have an actual role in applying, would be (to put it mildly) all the more relevant.'[151] Speaking extra-judicially, he further clarified this dictum. According to him, 'we should defer to the views of other signatories, much as we defer to the views of agencies—that is to say defer if it's within the ballpark, if it's a reasonable interpretation, though not necessarily the very best.'[152] In his view, US courts 'should give considerable respect to the interpretation of the same treaty by the courts of other signatories' because '[o]therwise the whole object of the treaty, which is to establish a single, agreed-upon regime governing the actions of all the signatories, will be frustrated'.[153]

As regards constitutional interpretation, Scalia has repeatedly warned against using foreign legal material in a selective fashion. In *Husain*, in contrast, he was 'easily convinced by the decisions of two States out of more than 150 treaty parties.'[154] This apparent contradiction might be resolved by invoking the justificatory potential of uniform interpretation. The objective of uniform interpretation

---

[147] See eg Antonin Scalia, 'Keynote Address: Foreign Legal Authority in the Federal Courts' (2004) 98 ASIL PROC 305; Melissa Waters, 'Justice Scalia on the Use of Foreign Law in Constitutional Interpretation: Unidirectional Monologue or Co-Constitutive Dialogue?' (2004) 12 Tulsa J Comp & Int'l L 149; Normen Dorsen, 'The Relevance of Foreign Legal Materials in US Constitutional Cases: A Conversation between Justice Antonin Scalia and Justice Stephen Breyer' (2005) 3 ICON 519; Glensy, 'Which Countries Count?' (n 144); Melissa Waters, 'Treaty Dialogue in *Sanchez-Llamas*: Is Chief Justice Roberts a Transnationalist, after All?' (2007) 11 LCLR 89; Roberts, 'Comparative International Law' (n 137).

[148] Eg *Thompson* (n 144) 868 (diss op Scalia J); *Atkins* (n 144) 348 (diss op Scalia J); *Lawrence* (n 144) 598 (diss op Scalia J); *Roper* (n 144) 608 f (diss op Scalia J).

[149] Eg *Thompson* (n 144) 868 f (diss op Scalia J); *Lawrence* (n 144) 598 (diss op Scalia J); *Roper* (n 144) 609 f (diss op Scalia J).

[150] ibid 617 (diss op Scalia J).

[151] *Husain* (n 142) 658.

[152] Dorsen, 'Foreign Legal Materials' (n 147) 521.

[153] Scalia, 'Foreign Legal Authority' (n 147) 305.

[154] Roberts, 'Comparative International Law' (n 137) 87 f.

of treaty law arguably not only encourages references to subsequent practice. In addition, it might also explain why selective references to foreign practice might be better than no references at all. By taking into account how a treaty has been interpreted and applied in other States—albeit only selectively—domestic courts arguably minimise the risk of inconsistent interpretations.[155] But appealing as it may seem, this reasoning is flawed in two respects.

Firstly, articles 31–33 VCLT are not primarily concerned with interpreting treaties in a uniform fashion but with interpreting treaties correctly.[156] Ideally, all interpreters interpret a treaty correctly so that uniform and correct interpretations coincide. However, uniform interpretation does not guarantee a treaty's correct interpretation. Because subsequent practice requires the parties' agreement, the general rule implicitly recognises the relevance of uniform interpretation. Yet, subsequent practice under article 31(3)(b) VCLT does not *a priori* trump other primary means of interpretation.[157] Irrespective of whether the interpretative result conforms to interpretations adopted elsewhere, the correct interpretation of the treaty can only be established by applying all elements of the general rule in a single combined operation.[158]

Secondly, the objective of uniform interpretation does not authorise interpreters to disregard the requirements of articles 31–33 VCLT. Subsequent practice within the meaning of article 31(3)(b) VCLT must be capable of establishing the parties' agreement. In other words, the fact that an interpretation has been adopted elsewhere cannot compensate for a lack of agreement. If the criteria of article 31(3)(b) VCLT are not meet, the objective of uniform interpretation may explain why 'other' subsequent conduct might be taken into account as a supplementary means of interpretation under article 32 VCLT. Yet, it must not be forgotten that interpreters sometimes invoke such 'other' conduct in a selective and self-serving fashion. In that sense, one commentator noted:

> If a comparative survey produces cases that the decision maker likes, the temptation will be to characterize these judgments as impartial evidence of the existence or meaning of international law. If the survey produces cases that the decision maker dislikes, these decisions are likely to be discounted as unpersuasive on the basis that they reflect the practice of only a few States.[159]

In sum, the Vienna rules do not dictate the objective of uniform interpretation. If the interpretative process results in uniform *and* correct interpretations, this outcome

[155] cf ibid 83.

[156] cf Martin Gebauer, 'Uniform Law, General Principles and Autonomous Interpretation' (2000) 5 ULR 683, 692; Roberts, 'Comparative International Law' (n 137) 84. Disagreeing Roderick Munday, 'The Uniform Interpretation of International Conventions' (1978) 27 ICLQ 450, 450: 'The principal objective of an international convention is to achieve uniformity of legal rules within the various States party to it.'

[157] See 5.1.1.

[158] See 3.3.3.

[159] Roberts, 'Comparative International Law' (n 137) 90

is to be welcomed. Yet, the desire to interpret treaties in a uniform fashion does not exempt from the requirements of articles 31–33 VCLT. Unless interpretations adopted elsewhere can be linked to the parties' agreement, they should be treated with caution. Under article 32 VCLT, interpreters can rely on selected practice that does not establish the parties' agreement. In doing so, they should, however, try to counteract the impression that reliance on selected practice is self-serving. This cannot be achieved by treating apparent uniformity as a justification for reliance on selected practice. Not uniformity but identifying the parties agreement should be the constant—albeit not always attainable—aim.

8.2.4 Evaluation

The distinction between practice and agreement is fundamentally important to the idea of subsequent practice under article 31(3)(b) VCLT. But despite its importance, domestic courts hardly mention the parties' agreement at all. Moreover, they seldom openly ascertain the parties' agreement once they identified potentially relevant subsequent practice in the application of the treaty.

Sometimes, domestic courts at least superficially uphold the distinction between practice and agreement. But even then, they tend to refrain from ascertaining the parties' agreement. More often, domestic courts implicitly take it for granted that potentially relevant practice also establishes the parties' agreement. This approach is not convincing. Doubts as to whether practice really establishes the parties' agreement may arise in various situations. Such doubts are especially justified where the interpreter relies on non-party practice (which is, however, very uncommon for domestic courts); furthermore, they are justified where the interpreter needs to determine whether a party's omission to act can contribute to establishing the parties' agreement. But doubts may also arise where different State actors do not 'speak with one voice'. Here, interpreters should ask themselves whose interpretation ought to prevail at the intra-State level. And most importantly, such doubts are justified where interpreters—deliberately or not—select the practice upon which they rely.

Selectivity implies that interpreters identify or mention only some pieces of potentially relevant practice. Treaties with few parties seem to minimise the risk of selectivity. Similarly, this risk is lower if potentially relevant practice has been brought to the interpreter's attention. Although selectivity is a widespread phenomenon, not all types of selectivity necessarily negate the parties' agreement as envisaged by article 31(3)(b) VCLT. In cases such as *Fothergill* and *Sidhu,* the House of Lords convincingly explained why interpreters should carefully assess the interpretative value of each instance of practice. On the one hand, such selectivity inevitably discards some pieces of practice as irrelevant. But on the other hand, it eventually upholds the Vienna rules' distinction between practice and agreement. Such selectivity does not discriminate against individual States, their practice, and thus eventually their understanding of the treaty. Instead, it simply acknowledges that individual pieces of practice may be more or less helpful to reliably establish the parties' agreement.

In most cases, however, domestic courts cannot explain their selectivity. Where only few parties generated active conduct, courts should, in particular, address the other parties' omission to act. A lack of express disagreement is not synonymous with agreement. For this reason, the desire to interpret treaties in a uniform fashion may explain why domestic courts take into account how a treaty has been interpreted elsewhere. Yet, it cannot exempt interpreters from complying with the requirements of articles 31–33 VCLT. Unless potentially relevant practice is capable of establishing the parties' agreement, uniformity may be more apparent than real, depend on the interpreter's perspective, and even be self-serving. Selective references to foreign practice may be better than no references at all; nonetheless, references to practice establishing the parties' agreement remain even more desirable.

No one denies that it is challenging to identify active conduct by all parties to a multilateral treaty. Many interpreters presumably lack the resources that are necessary to comprehensively examine how a treaty has been applied. This lack of resources not only relates to those of a technical or financial nature. It also encompasses, for example, a lack of language skills.[160] This may explain why the practice of certain States predominates the jurisprudence of domestic courts. Practice (and especially judicial practice) generated by English-speaking countries seems to represent a high percentage of all practice that is being relied on. Practice in English is readily accessible to most domestic courts, whereas non-English-speaking countries only rarely translate their practice into a format that is understood worldwide. In the end, those States whose practice is more often relied on thus exercise a stronger influence on the interpretation of their treaties than those States whose conduct is not taken into account.

Selected practice may well be representative of practice that was not mentioned. For this reason, the necessary agreement of the parties—albeit difficult to ascertain—may nevertheless exist. However, practice that remained unmentioned may also support an interpretation very different from the one that was finally adopted. Once interpreters refrain from ascertaining the parties' agreement, there is an increased risk that they rely on practice which does *not correspond* to the agreement of all (or at least most) parties. What is more, there is an increased risk that they rely on practice which even *conflicts* with the parties' agreement. This risk is even higher where domestic courts rely on regional practice only or where they impose self-defined criteria relating, for example, to a State's form of government. By pretending that selected practice meets the requirements of article 31(3)(b) VCLT, domestic courts create the impression that their construction rests on the parties' agreement although no one actually knows whether it does.

Thus, domestic courts vest their constructions with an undeserved interpretative legitimacy. In addition, they grant individual parties or even individual State actors,

[160] Not only the process of treaty interpretation but also scientific research in international law is inevitably challenged by a lack of language skills. For this reason, this study does not claim to be representative of all legal traditions, geographical regions, or cultures either. Instead, it leaves room for further research on subsequent agreements and subsequent practice in domestic jurisprudence, see 1.3.2.2.

such as a particular court, a stronger influence on the interpretation of the treaty than other parties. This imbalance eventually undermines the very idea of an agreement of the parties.

8.3 Conclusion

Chapter 8 focused more closely on the normative heart of article 31(3)(b) VCLT, namely the notion of agreement. At any rate, practice in the application of a treaty can be taken into account as a supplementary means of interpretation under article 32 VCLT. But to acquire the status of a primary means of interpretation, potentially relevant practice must be capable of establishing the agreement of all parties regarding the treaty's interpretation.

On its face, subsequent agreements and subsequent practice under article 31(3) VCLT do not fit to the other elements of the general rule because they are extrinsic means of interpretation. Thus, they are detached from the text of the treaty, which offers the best evidence of what the parties jointly agreed on. But if the notion of 'agreement' is understood as requiring the agreement of all parties, subsequent practice can be regarded as recognising the continuing interpretative authority of the parties as a whole. If the notion of agreement was not understood as requiring the agreement of all parties, it would become meaningless. Whose 'agreement' should otherwise justify the status of a primary means of interpretation: The agreement of most parties? The agreement of some parties? Or the agreement of only two parties?

These considerations do not seek to deprive 'other' subsequent conduct of its interpretative relevance. Such 'other' conduct may still be taken into account as a supplementary means of interpretation under article 32 VCLT. But when relying on practice as a primary means of interpretation, interpreters should recall that they assign to that practice the same interpretative value as possesses, for example, the ordinary meaning. By claiming that their interpretation corresponds to the parties' agreement, interpreters vest their interpretation with a particular force of persuasion vis-à-vis other interpreters and the parties themselves. Their interpretation may be followed by other interpreters and thus even turn into potentially relevant practice in the end. If the claim to reflect the parties' agreement is untrue, interpreters will ultimately distort the correct meaning of the treaty and disregard the authority of the parties as a whole, as the ultimate masters of the treaty.

Domestic jurisprudence shows that this risk is particularly high in two situations: Firstly, when interpreters have to deal with silence by one or more parties, and secondly in case of selectivity. Silence seldom amounts to acquiescence. Nevertheless, domestic courts quite readily rely on active and inactive conduct alike to establish the parties' agreement. This approach seems to be justified in cooperative or institutionalised contexts where the parties anticipated their consent. If silence is generally equated with consent, it will be more problematic. This equation imposes upon States obligations to object to any practice that does not conform to their own understanding of the treaty. In addition, States must ensure that they are capable of disagreeing in the first place. As regards bilateral treaties, these burdens are difficult to manage. But as regards multilateral treaties, they are illusory. States that are incapable of disagreeing gradually lose their influence on the treaty's development. This development will then be influenced by those States that have the resources to generate more practice or that, in basic terms, 'shout loudest'.

Interpreters may, for whatever reasons, take it for granted that silence is tantamount to acquiescence. Thus, they may mistakenly 'identify' an agreement that does not exist. An agreement that does not exist may also be asserted if interpreters select the practice upon which they rely. In most cases, domestic courts did not address the parties' agreement. In other words, any practice upon which they relied under article 31(3)(b) VCLT was simply treated as establishing the parties' agreement. Against this background, selective reliance on practice reduces the chances for arriving at interpretations that truly rest on the parties' agreement. In some cases, domestic courts did not just select the practice upon which they relied in terms of quantity but even presented regional selections or selections in terms of quality. These tendencies are even more disconcerting. They transform the shared interpretative authority of the parties as a whole into an interpretative authority of few parties; they favour particular States or groups of States (eg State parties from Europe) over others; or they introduce idiosyncratic value judgments, held by the interpreter himself (eg in favour of Western democratic forms of government), that find no basis in the treaty.

Surely, it may appear unrealistic to require interpreters to search for relevant practice of all parties. The research that would be necessary to do so would, especially in the case of multilateral treaties, be time-consuming and costly. Moreover, it would often be doomed to fail due to practical impediments such as a lack of language skills. Still, there is a difference between seriously attempting to discover all relevant practice to reliably establish the parties' agreement on the one hand, and deliberately selective reliance on the practice generated by 'the usual suspects' on the other. Article 31 VCLT does not oblige interpreters to present an agreement that does not exist. Where a given body of practice is insufficient to establish the parties' agreement, the interpreter may still have recourse to it as a supplementary means of interpretation. In other words, article 31 VCLT requires that all relevant means of interpretation shall be taken into account. It does not postulate that all means are always relevant.

In this respect, it is perhaps deplorable that the Vienna Convnetion does not expressly state—as originally envisaged—that practice falling short of the requirements of the general rule would still be admissible under article 32 VCLT. This clarification would not have entailed any legal difference. However, it would have unequivocally distinguished the different types of practice-based arguments. Thus, it might have helped to preserve the notion of 'agreement' and the interpretative authority of the parties as a whole.

Chapter 9
Conclusion and Outlook

This study opened with a misleading comparison in that it drew up the image of treaties as messages in a bottle. Domestic courts, like other interpreters, are called on to decipher these messages without positively knowing what their senders wished to communicate. By determining the meaning of the terms of a treaty, they wield an enormous power that cannot be underestimated. In theory, they ought to correctly determine a treaty's meaning by ascertaining the objectivised intention of the parties. But in practice, the Vienna rules undeniably grant interpreters much autonomy and independence in exercising this task.

Article 31(3)(a) and (b) VCLT explicitly reintroduces into the interpretative process, so to speak through the frontdoor, the parties' residual command on the meaning of the terms of the treaty.[1] Under this provision, interpreters shall take into account, together with the context, any subsequent agreement between the parties regarding the interpretation of the treaty or the application of its provisions (a), and any subsequent practice in the application of the treaty which establishes the agreement of the parties regarding its interpretation (b). Article 31(3)(a) and (b) VCLT thus not only stipulates another technical rule of interpretation but contains a principled decision about how interpretative powers shall be distributed.

With this provision in mind, one may envision a more appropriate (albeit still not flawless) comparison than treaties as messages in a bottle. Concluding a treaty is like starting a 'treasure hunt' or 'paper chase' (also known as 'hare and hounds'). The contracting parties are the 'hare', the correct meaning of the terms of the treaty is the 'treasure', and the interpreters seeking to discover this meaning are

[1] In addition, art 32 VCLT implicitly authorises interpreters to have recourse to 'other' subsequent conduct in the application of the treaty which does not establish the parties' agreement. Reliance on such 'other' subsequent conduct—whose interpretative relevance cannot be derived from the agreement of all parties—is subject to additional conditions.

K. Berner, *Subsequent Agreements and Subsequent Practice in Domestic Courts*, Beiträge zum ausländischen öffentlichen Recht und Völkerrecht,
https://doi.org/10.1007/978-3-662-54937-7_9

the 'hounds'. It is unsure whether—and on which route—the 'hounds' will find the 'treasure'. The 'hare', however, can lay a trail to facilitate the chase and the rules of the game prescribe that the 'hounds' had better follow this trail.

In that sense, interpreters ought to act as 'trustees' of the treaty by faithfully determining its meaning while the parties as a whole can, through their subsequent agreements and subsequent practice, continuously influence the treaty's meaning. In a certain way, article 31(3)(a) and (b) VCLT therefore restrains the interpreter's autonomy and independence. Not the interpreter but the parties as a whole ought to be the masters of the treaty. But how do domestic courts, which are both interpreters and organs of a particular State, respond to this distribution of interpretative power? A question like this is presumably ill-suited to receive one straightforward and absolute answer. Yet, it can reveal stronger or weaker tendencies and thus nevertheless permit some generalised conclusions and a cautious outlook.

9.1 Ancient Origins but Undiminished Validity

Article 31(3)(a) and (b) VCLT unambiguously affirms the status of subsequent agreements and subsequent practice ('subsequent conduct') as primary means of treaty interpretation. The significance of this provision does not exhaust itself in that it commits all contracting parties to take relevant subsequent agreements and subsequent practice into account. In addition, it has also come to be considered as reflecting customary law rules of treaty interpretation. Thus, it indirectly possesses a much wider scope of application.

The very idea that subsequent agreements and subsequent practice should influence the interpretative process is far from novel. Instead, its foundations can be traced back to Roman legal principles that gradually diffused into public international law in the mid-nineteenth century. Under Roman law, or, to be more precise, under the *Codex Iustinianus,* the lawmaker inherently possessed the power to determine the meaning of the law. This inherent power has found its expression in the maxim *eius est interpretari legem cuius condere*. According to this traditional understanding, interpretations by the lawmaker were typically endowed with binding force and of a formalised nature.

When public international law recognised the relevance of subsequent conduct, ie subsequent agreements and subsequent practice, as a means of treaty interpretation, it originally justified reliance on it by invoking these historic foundations. Very soon, however, reliance on subsequent conduct was detached from these foundations. Instead, it was linked to more general, consensus-based principles of party autonomy and the idea of the parties as the true masters of the treaty. With this adapted rationale, the relevance of subsequent conduct was recognised in international legal scholarship, international, and (to a lesser extent) domestic jurisprudence. In addition, it was integrated into the first State-sponsored and private efforts to codify the law of treaties.

Altogether, the various precursors to subsequent agreements and subsequent practice under article 31(3)(a) and (b) VCLT were only rudimentarily developed and defined. Nonetheless, they reveal some common ideas about subsequent agreements and subsequent practice as means of treaty interpretation. All of these ideas eventually originate in one basic assumption. This basic assumption was that the respective interpretative value of subsequent conduct depended on how much it rested on an agreement of the parties as a whole. Accordingly, three categories of subsequent conduct were commonly distinguished.

The first category comprised manifest subsequent agreements between all contracting parties. Such agreements were described as authentic and legally binding interpretations. These agreements possessed the utmost interpretative value and were superior to the other categories of subsequent conduct. Despite their legal importance, international and domestic courts only sporadically discussed and even more rarely relied on subsequent agreements. In quantitative terms, subsequent agreements therefore seemed to play an only marginal role in the interpretative practice of international and domestic courts alike.

The second category covered informal subsequent conduct ('subsequent practice' or 'quasi-authentic interpretation') that evidenced a non-manifest agreement of all parties. Incapable of proving this agreement with absolute certainty, such conduct was not legally binding and relied on as a supplementary means of interpretation only. Nevertheless, international and domestic courts more often invoked such informal conduct than authentic interpretations in the strict sense. The third category that was sometimes mentioned comprised informal subsequent conduct that failed to evidence the agreement of all parties. Such conduct was non-binding and a supplementary means of interpretation only. Moreover, it was inferior to informal subsequent conduct that did evidence the agreement of all parties.

The relative importance and perception of subsequent agreements and subsequent practice changed markedly with the adoption of the Vienna Convention. Manifest subsequent agreements are now governed by article 31(3)(a) VCLT and hence form part of the general rule of interpretation. Thus, they are effectively deprived of their binding nature and downgraded to the same status as other primary means of interpretation. Subsequent practice establishing the agreement of all parties, in contrast, is now governed by article 31(3)(b) VCLT. In consequence, it is upgraded from a traditionally supplementary to a primary means of interpretation. In addition, interpreters can still have recourse to conduct that does not rest on the agreements of all parties as a supplementary means of interpretation under article 32 VCLT.

Since the Convention's adoption, the marginal quantitative relevance of subsequent agreements in domestic jurisprudence has not increased significantly. In fact, some courts even seemed positively disinclined to rely on subsequent agreements. This disinclination was largely owed to the difficult and constitutionally problematic distinction between interpretative and modifying agreements. Subsequent practice, in contrast, has much more frequently been relied on by domestic courts than before the Convention's adoption. In this respect, it is noteworthy that domestic courts regarded subsequent practice as evidence of the parties' original intention as it was originally perceived. Besides, they recognised the potential of subsequent practice to evidence the parties' evolved understanding of their treaty.

When domestic courts discussed the various types of subsequent conduct, they typically offered three different justifications for doing so. The most natural, positivistic justification has been to cite article 31(3)(a) or (b) or article 32 VCLT or to point out that subsequent agreements and subsequent practice could be taken into account under customary international law. Occasionally, domestic courts also invoked a more general rationale for considering subsequent conduct. In the one alternative, domestic courts emphasised that reliance on subsequent conduct could contribute to ensuring uniform interpretation of the law.[2] And in the other alternative, they contended that reliance on subsequent conduct was justified because it evidenced the understanding of those who created the treaty.[3]

Taking everything into account, one may be easily tempted to dismiss subsequent agreements and subsequent practice as anachronistic. By incorporating them into the Vienna rules of interpretation, Sir Humphrey Waldock and the ILC did not introduce a novelty but ultimately drew on ancient Roman legal principles. But the underlying rationale of subsequent agreements and subsequent practice, ie that the parties' agreement should be relevant to the interpretative process, is still recognised by domestic courts today and as valid as ever. While subsequent agreements were never particularly important in quantitative terms, the practical relevance of subsequent practice even increased. Despite their ancient origins, the validity of subsequent agreements and subsequent practice therefore remains undiminished.

9.2 Neutral Ingredients for the Crucible

A distinctive feature of the general rule of interpretation pursuant to article 31 VCLT is that all primary means of interpretation are to be taken into account in a 'single combined operation'.[4] In the words of Sir Humphrey Waldock, this means that '[a]ll the various elements, so far as they were present in any given case, would be thrown into the crucible and their interaction would then give the legally relevant interpretation'.[5] Two ingredients for the interpretative crucible are subsequent agreements and subsequent practice that fall under article 31(3)(a) and (b) VCLT. In addition, subsequent conduct that does not satisfy the requirements of the general rule may be taken into account as a supplementary means of interpretation under article 32 VCLT.[6]

[2] See 8.2.3.

[3] See eg 5.1.1.2 and 6.3.1.3.

[4] See 3.3.3.

[5] Sir Humphrey Waldock, 'Sixth Report on the Law of Treaties' [1966-II] YBILC 51, 95 [4].

[6] See 4.4.

As primary means of interpretation, recourse to relevant subsequent agreements and subsequent practice is mandatory. But the 'crucible approach' does not mean that relevant conduct automatically trumped any other means of interpretation. Instead, the various primary means of interpretation are to be balanced and weighed against each other in order to determine the single correct ordinary meaning or scope of meanings. In determining the meaning of the terms of the treaty, subsequent agreements and subsequent practice are, on their face, neutral ingredients for the crucible. This is because they are not designed to exclusively support particular types of results such as static, dynamic, restrictive, or extensive constructions.

At least in one important respect, domestic jurisprudence confirms the image of subsequent agreements and subsequent practice as neutral ingredients for the crucible. Although subsequent agreements and subsequent practice under article 31(3)(a) and (b) VCLT are commonly referred to as 'authentic means of interpretation', domestic courts generally refused to unconditionally recognise that their authentic nature automatically enhanced their legal status.[7] In particular, domestic jurisprudence does not confirm the proposition that subsequent agreements or subsequent practice under article 31(3)(a) and (b) VCLT were necessarily legally binding.

Going into the other extreme, domestic jurisprudence rather indicates that the relative importance of subsequent agreements and subsequent practice as components of the general rule must not be overemphasised.[8] In particular, several decisions conveyed the impression that interpretative agreements and practice are more readily taken into account as supplementary than as primary means of interpretation. This impression is not only owed to the fact that the general rule presupposes an agreement between or of the parties and thus imposes requirements that are difficult to fulfil. Contrary to article 31 VCLT, some courts even insinuated that subsequent conduct could only be taken into account under the conditions that apply to supplementary means of interpretation irrespective of whether the requirements of article 31 VCLT were actually met.

A crucial consideration in this regard has been whether subsequent conduct merely interpreted or de facto amended the terms of the treaty. Yet, domestic courts did not per se deny that subsequent conduct was capable of informally amending a treaty. Instead, they simply refused to take such modifying conduct into account unless it satisfied additional (eg constitutional) requirements.[9] Their concern about unduly exceeding the terms of the treaty illustrates that domestic courts are interpreters that fall between two stools. Interpreting international legal instruments by applying international rules of treaty interpretation, they are still anxious to comply with—and eventually tend to give precedence to—the requirements of their domestic legal system.

In terms of result, the jurisprudence of domestic courts also only partially confirms the image of subsequent agreements and subsequent practice as neutral ingredients for the crucible. On balance, domestic courts used these means of interpretation to

[7] See 5.1.1.

[8] See 5.1.2.

[9] See 6.3.

support static, dynamic, restrictive, and extensive interpretations alike. Nevertheless, they only reluctantly adopted extensive interpretations based on subsequent conduct unless the probative value of this conduct was overwhelmingly high.[10] Furthermore, domestic jurisprudence corroborates the special potential of subsequent conduct to adapt treaties to changed conditions.[11] In this respect, it was interesting to see that subsequent conduct was occasionally utilised to consciously create the impression of continuity and stability. To this end, domestic courts drew on its traditional perception as evidence of the parties' original intentions and thus eventually blurred the difference between static and dynamic interpretations.

To summarise, one may stress two points. Firstly, domestic courts tend to rely more readily on agreements and practice as supplementary than as primary means of interpretation. And secondly, domestic courts do not equate subsequent agreements and subsequent practice with certain types of results. However, they displayed some preference for certain types of results. In conclusion, one can therefore say that the jurisprudence of domestic courts does not falsify but to some extent tarnishes the image of subsequent agreements and subsequent practice as neutral ingredients for the crucible.

9.3 The True Masters of the Treaty

In basic terms, article 31(3)(a) and (b) VCLT sets two strategic directions for distributing interpretative power. While opening the interpretative process for a broad range of potentially relevant material, it nevertheless preserves the ultimate interpretative authority of the parties as a whole. Metaphorically speaking, this provision commits interpreters to utilise two different types of filter mechanisms. In the first step, interpreters ought to employ a rough filter so that active, inactive, isolated, and repeated practice as well as practice of contracting parties and non-party entities can pass alike.[12] This rough filtering serves to ensure that no potentially relevant conduct is categorically excluded at the outset. In the second step, it requires interpreters to employ a much finer filter so as to discard any material that neither forms part of a manifest agreement between nor establishes the agreement of all contracting parties.[13]

The requirement of an agreement between or of all parties does not follow from a literal interpretation of the general rule. All the same, it is indispensable to read this requirement into article 31(3)(a) and (b) VCLT. This follows not only from a sensible construction of the general rule but also from more fundamental considerations.

[10] See 5.2.1. Without meaning to speculate, one may, however, wonder whether State parties themselves generally tend to interpret and apply their treaties more restrictively than extensively.

[11] See 5.2.2.

[12] See 4.3.1.

[13] See 4.2.2 and 4.3.2.

Treaties between States are the solemn expression of a common and concordant will of sovereign equals. Articles 31–33 VCLT are devised to implement this common and concordant will and not individual interests.[14] This is why the Vienna rules treat the text as the 'authentic expression of the intentions of the parties'[15] and mistrust the interpretative value of the *travaux préparatoires*. And this is why subsequent agreements and subsequent practice form part of the general rule of interpretation although they are extrinsic to the text of the treaty.

That subsequent agreements and subsequent practice constitute primary means of interpretation is justified because—and can only be justified if—subsequent agreements and subsequent practice require an agreement of *all* parties, which reliably helps to elucidate the original or evolved concordant will that formed the basis of their agreement. To underline the force of this argument, one may conversely ask whose agreement should otherwise suffice to justify the status of primary means of interpretation—the agreement of most parties, of some, or even only few? Besides, article 31(3)(a) and (b) VCLT ultimately requires an agreement of the parties to the treaty.[16] Other actors may generate potentially relevant conduct. But even if they possess expert knowledge, are endowed with an official nature, or claim a high moral power of persuasion, their understanding does not replace the parties' agreement under article 31(3)(a) and (b) VCLT.

Domestic courts, however, have only selectively endorsed the distribution of interpretative power as envisaged by article 31(3)(a) and (b) and article 32 VCLT. This can be seen, for example, from their approach to non-party practice.[17] Many courts acknowledged that certain types of non-party practice may help to cast a light on the meaning of the terms of the treaty. Still, they regularly indicated that such conduct could, in itself, only be taken into account as a supplementary means of interpretation under article 32 VCLT. More precisely, it was noted that non-party conduct may well reflect or catalyse relevant conduct for the purpose of article 31(3)(a) or (b) VCLT. At the same time, several courts emphasised that such conduct not necessarily coincided with the parties' agreement. Although domestic courts thus reaffirmed the ultimate interpretative authority of the parties, they sometimes deviated from it in practice by approaching non-party conduct in a more lenient fashion without verifying the existence of the parties' agreement.

Equally ambivalent is the way in which domestic courts recognised the interpretative competencies of different branches of State power. On the one hand, most courts readily had recourse to conduct generated by other judicial bodies.[18] But on the other hand, they were rather critical towards executive conduct and in particular subsequent executive agreements.[19] Apparently concerned about the erosion

---

[14] See 1.3.1.2 and 3.3.3.

[15] ILC, 'Draft Articles on the Law of Treaties with Commentaries' [1966-II] YBILC 187, 220 [11].

[16] See 4.2.2.1 and 4.3.2.1.

[17] See 7.

[18] See 6.4 and 8.2.

[19] See 6.3.

of democratic legitimacy by circumventing parliamentary participation, domestic courts neglected that subsequent conduct is no more prone to transgressing the terms of the treaty than other means of interpretation. By refusing to rely on subsequent conduct because it does not interpret but allegedly modifies the terms of the treaty, domestic courts do not act as 'neutral third parties'. Instead, they effectively increase their own interpretative power vis-à-vis those actors whose subsequent conduct they refused to rely on.

A final cause for concern relates to the normative heart of subsequent conduct under article 31(3)(a) and (b) VCLT. In principle, numerous courts accepted that the status of subsequent agreements and subsequent practice as primary means of interpretation was contingent on an agreement of all parties. But in practice, many courts did not even attempt to identify relevant practice of all parties, equated silence with inaction, 'cherry-picked' the conduct upon which they relied, and abstained from carefully establishing the necessary agreement. In doing so, they readily enhanced persuasiveness and apparent legitimacy of their reasoning by creating the impression that their preferred interpretation rested on the parties' agreement—although it was uncertain whether the asserted agreement really existed, whether the parties were divided on the interpretative question, or whether their preferred interpretation actually defied the parties' true agreement.

From a macro perspective, domestic jurisprudence thus reaffirms that it is the parties who are the true masters of a treaty. In particular, domestic courts tended to superordinate the parties' understanding of the treaty to constructions advocated by non-party entities. But at closer inspection, this conclusion needs to be qualified. This is because the jurisprudence of domestic courts reveals two striking discriminatory tendencies. Firstly, domestic courts seemed to prefer judicial over executive conduct. And secondly, domestic courts often failed to establish the agreement of the parties as a whole and thus effectively favoured the understanding of few specific parties.

9.4 Towards Uniform Interpretation?

The last conclusion inspires a cautious outlook on the future impact of subsequent agreements and subsequent practice in the jurisprudence of domestic courts. Optimistically, one might contend that subsequent conduct is not only inherently open-minded to adapting treaties to changing conditions. In addition, it may also foster uniform interpretation of treaty law throughout various legal systems.

In that sense, article 31(3)(a) and (b) and article 32 VCLT could gradually exert a 'normative pull towards convergence'.[20] Yet, the objective of uniform interpretation does not possess a value in itself under the Vienna rules.[21] Moreover, one may

[20] cf André Nollkaemper, *National Courts and the International Rule of Law* (OUP 2011) 226.

[21] See 8.2.3.

wonder whether the kind of uniformity that would be achieved through subsequent conduct as it is presently used is truly desirable. This study exposed a major deficiency in the application of subsequent conduct, ie a high degree of selectivity that is coupled with the failure to faithfully establish the agreement of all parties. This approach may well achieve uniformity if constructions that are erroneously based on article 31(3)(a) and (b) VCLT[22] are taken into account and followed by other interpreters. The same applies to constructions that are based on 'other' subsequent conduct under article 32 VCLT in a rather self-serving manner.

But in following such erroneous or ill-founded constructions, interpreters effectively perpetuate a congenital defect. In doing so, they consolidate interpretations that once merely pretended to reflect the parties' agreement or that concealed material disagreement. Thus, the interpretative power of those parties whose interpretation was given precedence effectively increases at the expense of others. In some cases, such selectivity may be based on good intentions. But in other cases, it may be self-serving and unduly biased. To some people, this shift of interpretative power to a particular group of States may actually be welcome.[23] However, it conflicts with the idea of States as sovereign equals. Besides, uniformity that is achieved at this price is likely to be less sustainable. On the long run, those parties whose conduct did not contribute to this uniform interpretation may presumably be less inclined to comply with it.

How can one avoid this scenario and encourage domestic courts to use both article 31(3)(a) and (b) and article 32 VCLT in a less discriminatory fashion? First of all, courts should appreciate that and why article 31(3)(a) and (b) VCLT requires the parties' agreement. Subsequent conduct under the general rule, ie as an authentic means of interpretation, should be perceived as a valuable but exceptional interpretative tool. At the same time, domestic courts can consider 'other' relevant subsequent conduct under article 32 VCLT. Yet, they should do so openly, cautiously, and without overestimating its interpretative weight.

In addition, State parties should appreciate their own opportunities for influencing the interpretation of their treaties and actively take advantage of them. This presupposes that they enable interpreters to take note of useful material by compiling, translating, and promulgating it in a way that renders it easily accessible and digestible.[24] It is certainly tempting to point the finger at interpreters that disregard the requirements of article 31(3)(a) and (b) VCLT or use 'other' subsequent conduct under article 32 VCLT in a self-serving way. All the same, State parties had better make their own contributions in order to remain the true masters of their treaty.

---

22 In this respect, it is important to recall that domestic judicial decisions may again be taken into account as potentially relevant conduct under arts 31(3)(b) and 32 VCLT.

23 cf Anne-Marie Slaughter, 'International Law in a World of Liberal States' (1995) 6 EJIL 503, 524 f.

24 cf Reem Bahdi, 'Globalization of Judgment: Transjudicialism and the Five Faces of International Law in Domestic Courts' (2002) 34 Geo Wash Int'l L Rev 555, 600.

Bibliography

Alvarez, José, 'The New Treaty-Makers' (2002) 25 BC Int'l & Comp L Rev 213–34

American Law Institute, *Third Restatement of the Law—The Foreign Relations Law of the United States* (American Law Inst Pub 1987)

Ando, Nisuke, 'Permanent Court of Arbitration (PCA)' in Rüdiger Wolfrum (ed), *The Max Planck Encyclopedia of Public International Law* (OUP 2012)

Arato, Julian, 'Subsequent Practice and Evolutive Interpretation: Techniques of Treaty Interpretation over Time and Their Diverse Consequences' (2010) 9 Law & Prac Int'l Cts & Tribunals 443–94

Aust, Anthony, *Modern Treaty Law and Practice* (3rd edn, CUP 2013)

Aust, Helmut and Nolte, Georg (eds), *The Interpretation of International Law by Domestic Courts—Uniformity, Diversity, Convergence* (OUP 2016)

Avery Jones, John, 'Tax Treaty Interpretation in the United Kingdom' in Michael Lang (ed), *Tax Treaty Interpretation* (Kluwer 2001) 357–68

Avi-Yonah, Reuven, 'International Tax as International Law' (2004) 57 Tax L Rev 483–502

Axer, Peter, Isensee, Josef, and Kirchhof, Paul (eds), *Aufgaben des Staates* (3rd edn, CF Müller 2006)

Bahdi, Reem, 'Globalization of Judgment: Transjudicialism and the Five Faces of International Law in Domestic Courts' (2002) 34 Geo Wash Int'l L Rev 555–604

——, 'Truth and Method in the Domestic Application of International Law' (2002) 15 CJLJ 255–79

Bederman, David, 'Revivalist Canons and Treaty Interpretation' (1993) 41 UCLA L Rev 953–1034

——, 'Deference or Deception: Treaty Rights as Political Questions' (1999) 70 U Colo L Rev 1439–89

——, *Classical Canons—Rhetoric, Classicism and Treaty Interpretation* (Ashgate 2001)

Benetar, Marco, 'From Probative Value to Authentic Interpretation: The Legal Effect of Interpretative Declarations' (2011) 44 RBDI 170–96

Benvenisti, Eyal, 'Judicial Misgivings regarding the Application of International Law: An Analysis of Attitudes of National Courts' (1993) 4 EJIL 159–83

——, 'Reclaiming Democracy: The Strategic Uses of Foreign and International Law by National Courts' (2008) 102 AJIL 241–74

——, 'Comments on the Systemic Vision of National Courts as Part of an International Rule of Law' (2012) 4 JRLS 42–49

K. Berner, *Subsequent Agreements and Subsequent Practice in Domestic Courts*, Beiträge zum ausländischen öffentlichen Recht und Völkerrecht, https://doi.org/10.1007/978-3-662-54937-7

—— and Downs, George, 'National Courts, Domestic Democracy, and the Evolution of International Law' (2009) 20 EJIL 59–72

Bernárdez, Santiago, 'Interpretation of Treaties by the International Court of Justice Following the Adoption of the 1969 Vienna Convention on the Law of Treaties' in Gerhard Hafner (ed), *Liber Amicorum: Professor Ignaz Seidl-Hohenveldern in Honour of his 80th Birthday* (Kluwer 1998) 721–48

Berner, Katharina, '"Sovereignty of Parliament" under the Grundgesetz—How the German Constitutional Court Discovers Parliamentary Participation as a Means of Controlling European Integration' (2013) 19 EPL 249–62

——, 'Judicial Dialogue and Treaty Interpretation—Revisiting the "Cocktail Party" of International Law' (2016) 54 AVR 67–90

——, 'Authentic Interpretation in Public International Law' (2016) 76 ZaöRV 845–78

Bernhardt, Rudolf, *Die Auslegung völkerrechtlicher Verträge insbesondere in der neueren Rechtsprechung internationaler Gerichte* (Heymann 1963)

——, 'Interpretation and Implied (Tacit) Modification of Treaties' (1967) 27 ZaöRV 491–506

—— (ed), *Völkerrecht als Rechtsordnung, internationale Gerichtsbarkeit, Menschenrechte—Festschrift für Hermann Mosler* (Springer 1983)

——, 'Evolutive Treaty Interpretation, Especially of the European Convention on Human Rights' (1999) 42 GJIL 11–25

Biermann, Frank, 'The Rising Tide of Green Unilateralism in World Trade Law: Options for Resolving the Emerging North-South Conflict' (2001) 35 JWT 421–48

Bjorge, Eirik, *The Evolutionary Interpretation of Treaties* (OUP 2014)

Bond, Martyn, *The Council of Europe and Human Rights—An Introduction to the European Convention on Human Rights* (Council of Europe Publ 2010)

Bonucci, Nicola and Kothari, Gita, 'Organization for Economic Cooperation and Development (OECD)' in Rüdiger Wolfrum (ed), *The Max Planck Encyclopedia of Public International Law* (OUP 2012)

Bos, Maarten, 'Theory and Practice of Treaty Interpretation' (1980) 27 NILR 135–70

Breuer, Marten (ed), *Der Staat im Recht—Festschrift für Eckart Klein zum 70. Geburtstag* (Duncker & Humblot 2013)

Brierly, James, *The Law of Nations—An Introduction to the International Law of Peace* (5th edn, OUP 1955)

Brower, Charles, 'Investor-State Disputes under NAFTA: The Empire Strikes Back' (2001) 40 Colum J Transnat'l L 43–88

——, 'Why the FTC Notes of Interpretation Constitute a Partial Amendment of NAFTA Article 1105' (2006) 46 Va J Int'l L 347–63

——, 'Arbitration' in Rüdiger Wolfrum (ed), *The Max Planck Encyclopedia of Public International Law* (OUP 2012)

Brunnée, Jutta, 'Consent' in Rüdiger Wolfrum (ed), *The Max Planck Encyclopedia of Public International Law* (OUP 2012)

Bull, Hedley, Kingsbury, Benedict, and Roberts, Adam (eds), *Hugo Grotius and International Relations* (Clarendon 1990)

Butler, William, 'Periodization and International Law' in Alexander Orakhelashvili (ed), *Research Handbook on the Theory and History of International Law* (Edward Elgar 2011) 379–93

Calderón, Jose, 'The OECD Transfer Pricing Guidelines as a Source of Tax Law: Is Globalization Reaching the Tax Law?' (2007) 35 Intertax 4–29

Calliess, Christian, 'Auswärtige Gewalt, § 83' in Peter Axer, Josef Isensee, and Paul Kirchhof (eds), *Aufgaben des Staates* (3rd edn, CF Müller 2006) 964–91

Caron, David, 'The ILC Articles on State Responsiblity: The Paradoxical Relationship between Form and Authority' (2002) 96 AJIL 857–73

Cedeño, Víctor and Torres Cazorla, Maria, 'Unilateral Acts of States in International Law' in Rüdiger Wolfrum (ed), *The Max Planck Encyclopedia of Public International Law* (OUP 2012)

Chanaki, Anthina, *L'adaptation des traités dans le temps* (Bruylant 2013)

Cheng, Bin, 'United Nations Resolutions on Outer Space—"Instant" International Customary Law?' (1965) 5 IJIL 23–48

Corten, Olivier and Klein, Pierre (eds), *The Vienna Conventions on the Law of Treaties—A Commentary* (OUP 2011)

Cottier, Thomas and Müller, Jörg, 'Estoppel' in Rüdiger Wolfrum (ed), *The Max Planck Encyclopedia of Public International Law* (OUP 2012)

Crawford, James, 'Prospects for the Codification and Development of International Law by the United Nations: The Work of the International Law Commission' (1998) 9 FYBIL 9–15

——, *Brownlie's Principles of Public International Law* (8th edn, OUP 2012)

——, 'State' in Rüdiger Wolfrum (ed), *The Max Planck Encyclopedia of Public International Law* (OUP 2012)

——, 'A Consensualist Interpretation of Article 31(3)of the Vienna Convention on the Law of Treaties' in Georg Nolte (ed), *Treaties and Subsequent Practice* (OUP 2013) 29–33

——, *State Responsibility—The General Part* (CUP 2013)

Crema, Luigi, 'Subsequent Agreements and Practice within and outside the Vienna Convention' in Georg Nolte (ed), *Treaties and Subsequent Practice* (OUP 2013) 13–28

Criddle, Evan, 'The Vienna Convention on the Law of Treaties in US Treaty Interpretation' (2003) 44 Va J Int'l L 431–500

Daillier, Patrick, Forteau, Mathias, and Pellet, Alain, *Droit international public—Formation du droit, sujets, relations diplomatiques et consulaires, responsabilité, règlement des différends, maintien de la paix, espaces internationaux, relations économiques, environnement* (8th edn, LGDJ 2009)

d'Amato, Anthony, 'Consent, Estoppel and Reasonableness: Three Challenges to Universal International Law' (1969) 10 Va J Int'l L 1–31

de Quadros, Fausto and Dingfelder Stone, John, 'Act of State Doctrine' in Rüdiger Wolfrum (ed), *The Max Planck Encyclopedia of Public International Law* (OUP 2012)

de Vattel, Emer, *The Law of Nations or the Principles of Natural Law* (Charles Fenwick tr, repr, Hein 1995)

Dicey, Albert, *Introduction to the Study of the Law of the Constitution* (8th edn, Macmillan 1915)

Diederiks-Verschoor, Isabella and de Leon, Pablo Mendes, *An Introduction to* Air *Law* (9th edn, Kluwer 2012)

Dinstein, Yoram, 'The Interaction between Customary International Law and Treaties' (2007) 322 RCADI 243–428

Distefano, Giovanni, 'La pratique subséquente des états parties à un traité' (1994) 40 AFDI 41–71

——, 'L'interprétation evolutive de la norme internationale' (2011) 115 RGDIP 373–96

Djeffal, Christian, *Static and Evolutive Treaty Interpretation—A Functional Reconstruction* (CUP 2016)

Dörr, Oliver, 'Article 31—General Rule of Interpretation' in id and Kirsten Schmalenbach (eds), *Vienna Convention on the Law of Treaties—A Commentary* (Springer 2012) 521–70

—— and Schmalenbach, Kirsten (eds), *Vienna Convention on the Law of Treaties—A Commentary* (Springer 2012)

Dorsen, Normen, 'The Relevance of Foreign Legal Materials in US Constitutional Cases: A Conversation between Justice Antonin Scalia and Justice Stephen Breyer' (2005) 3 ICON 519–42

Durchhardt, Heinz, 'From the Peace of Westphalia to the Congress of Vienna' in Bardo Fassbender and others (eds), *The Oxford Handbook of the History of International Law* (OUP 2012) 628–53

Ehlermann, Claus-Dieter and Ehring, Lothar, 'The Authoritative Interpretation under Article IX:2 of the Agreement Establishing the World Trade Organization: Current Law, Practice and Possible Improvements' (2005) 8 JIEL 803–24

Ehrlich, Ludwik, 'L'interprétation des traités' (1928) 24 RCADI 5–145

Elias, Taslim, 'The Doctrine of Intertemporal Law' (1980) 74 AJIL 285–307

Engelen, Franciscus, *Interpretation of Tax Treaties under International Law—A Study of Articles 31, 32 and 33 of the Vienna Convention on the Law of Treaties and Their Application to Tax Treaties* (IBFD 2004)

Evans, Malcolm (ed), *International Law* (OUP 2003)
Fassbender, Bardo and others (eds), *The Oxford Handbook of the History of International Law* (OUP 2012)
Fatima, Shaheed, 'Using International Law in Domestic Courts—Part I: Domesticated Treaties' (2003) 8 JR 81–89
Fauchald, Ole, 'The Legal Reasoning of ICSID Tribunals—An Empirical Analysis' (2008) 19 EJIL 301–64
Favre, Antoine, 'L'interprétation objectiviste des traités internationaux' (1960) 17 ASDI 75–98
Feldman, Alexander, 'Evolving Treaty Obligations: A Proposal for Analyzing Subsequent Practice Derived from WTO Dispute Settlement' (2009) 41 JILP 655–706
Feller, Erika and Klug, Anja, 'Refugees, United Nations High Commissioner (UNHCR)' in Rüdiger Wolfrum (ed), *The Max Planck Encyclopedia of Public International Law* (OUP 2012)
Fitzmaurice, Sir Gerald, 'The Law and Procedure of the International Court of Justice: Treaty Interpretation and Certain Other Treaty Points' (1951) 28 BYIL 1–28
——, 'The Law and Procedure of the International Court of Justice 1951–4: Treaty Interpretation and Certain Other Treaty Points' (1957) 33 BYIL 203–93
Fitzmaurice, Malgosia, 'Consent to Be Bound—Anything New under the Sun?' (2005) 74 NJIL 483–508
——, 'Dynamic (Evolutive) Interpretation of Treaties—Part I' (2008) 21 Hague YB Int'l L 101–53
——, Elias, Olufemi, and Merkouris, Panos (eds), *Treaty Interpretation and the Vienna Convention on the Law of Treaties—30 Years on* (Martinus Nijhoff 2010)
Fox, Hazel, 'Article 31(3)(a) and (b) of the Vienna Convention and the *Kasikili/Sedudu Island* Case' in Malgosia Fitzmaurice, Olufemi Elias, and Panos Merkouris (eds), *Treaty Interpretation and the Vienna Convention on the Law of Treaties—30 Years on* (Martinus Nijhoff 2010) 59–74
Francioni, Francesco, 'International Law as a Common Language for National Courts' (2001) 36 Tex Int'l LJ 587–98
Franck, Thomas and Fox, Gregory (eds), *International Law Decisions in National Courts* (Transnational Pub 1996)
French, Duncan, 'Treaty Interpretation and the Incorporation of Extraneous Legal Rules' (2006) 55 ICLQ 281–314
Frowein, Jochen and Peukert, Wolfgang, *Europäische Menschenrechtskonvention—EMRK-Kommentar* (3rd edn, Engel 2009)
Fürst, Walther, Herzog, Roman, and Umbach, Dieter (eds), *Festschrift für Wolfgang Zeidler* (de Gruyter 1987)
Gaillard, Emmanuel and Bachand, Frédéric (eds), *Fifteen Years of NAFTA Chapter 11 Arbitration* (Juris 2011)
Gardiner, Richard, 'Treaty Interpretation in the English Courts Since *Fothergill v Monarch Airlines* (1980)' (1995) 44 ICLQ 920–28
——, *Treaty Interpretation* (2nd edn, OUP 2015)
Gautier, Philippe, 'Article 2—1969 Vienna Convention' in Olivier Corten and Pierre Klein (eds), *The Vienna Conventions on the Law of Treaties—A Commentary* (OUP 2011) 33–56
Gebauer, Martin, 'Uniform Law, General Principles and Autonomous Interpretation' (2000) 5 ULR 683–705
Geiger, Rudolf and Fiedler, Wilfried (eds), *Völkerrechtlicher Vertrag und staatliches Recht vor dem Hintergrund zunehmender Verdichtung der internationalen Beziehungen—Symposion vom 28. bis 30. Januar* 1999 *in Leipzig* (Nomos 2000)
Gentili, Alberico, *De iure belli libri tres* (John Rolfe tr, Clarendon Press 1933)
Glensy, Rex, 'Which Countries Count?: *Lawrence v Texas* and the Selection of Foreign Persuasive Authority' (2005) 45 Va J Int'l L 357–449
Grewe, Wilhelm, *The Epochs of International Law* (de Gruyter 2000)
Grotius, Hugo, *De jure belli* ac *pacis libri tres* (Francis Kelsey tr, reprod, Hein 1995)
Hafner, Gerhard (ed), *Liber Amicorum: Professor Ignaz Seidl-Hohenveldern in Honour of his 80th Birthday* (Kluwer 1998)

Haggenmacher, Peter, 'Grotius and Gentili: A Reassessment of Thomas E Holland's Inaugural Lecture 1' in Hedley Bull, Benedict Kingsbury, and Adam Roberts (eds), *Hugo Grotius and International Relations* (Clarendon Press 1990) 133–76

——, 'Hugo Grotius (1583–1645)' in Bardo Fassbender and others (eds), *The Oxford Handbook of the History of International Law* (OUP 2012) 1098–1101

Hall, Christopher, 'The Duty of States Parties to the Convention against Torture to Provide Procedures Permitting Victims to Recover Reparations for Torture Committed Abroad' (2007) 18 EJIL 921–37

Handeyside, Hugh, 'The *Lotus* Principle in ICJ Jurisprudence: Was the Ship ever Afloat?' (2007) 29 Mich J Int'l L 71–94

Haraszti, György, *Some Fundamental Problems of the Law of Treaties* (Akademiai Kiado 1973)

Hart, Herbert, *The Concept of Law* (3rd edn, OUP 2012)

Hathaway, James, *The Rights of Refugees under International Law* (reprint, CUP 2011)

Helmersen, Sondre, 'Evolutive Treaty Interpretation: Legality, Semantics and Distinctions' (2013) 6 EJLS 127–48

Henkin, Louis, 'Is There a "Political Question" Doctrine?' (1976) 85 Yale LJ 597–625

Heppenheimer, Tom, *Turbulent Skies—The History of Commercial Aviation* (Wiley & Sons 1995)

Herdegen, Matthias, 'Interpretation in International Law' in Rüdiger Wolfrum (ed), *The Max Planck Encyclopedia of Public International Law* (OUP 2012)

——, *Völkerrecht* (15th edn, Beck 2016)

Hestermeyer, Holger (ed), *Coexistence, Cooperation and Solidarity—Liber Amicorum Rüdiger Wolfrum* (Martinus Nijhoff 2012)

Higgins, Rosalyn, 'United Kingdom' in Francis Jacobs and Shelley Roberts (eds), *The Effect of Treaties in Domestic Law* (Sweet & Maxwell 1987) 123–39

——, 'Time and the Law: International Perspectives on an Old Problem' (1997) 46 ICLQ 501–20

Hillgruber, Christian, 'Die Fortentwicklung völkerrechtlicher Verträge als staatsrechtliches Problem: Wie weit trägt der Rechtsanwendungsbefehl des Zustimmungsgesetzes nach Art 59 Abs 2 Satz 1 GG?' in Josef Isensee and Helmut Lecheler (eds), *Freiheit und Eigentum—Festschrift für Walter Leisner zum 70. Geburtstag* (Duncker & Humblot 1999) 53–74

Hobbes, Thomas, *Leviathan, sive De materia, forma, & potestate civitatis ecclesiasticæ et civilis* (2nd edn, Typis Joannis Thomsonii 1678)

Hofbauer, Ines, 'Tax Treaty Interpretation in Austria' in Michael Lang (ed), *Tax Treaty Interpretation* (Kluwer 2001) 13–39

Hollis, Duncan, 'Why State Consent Still Matters—Non-State Actors, Treaties, and the Changing Sources of International Law' (2005) 23 Berkeley J Int'l L 137–74

—— (ed), *The Oxford Guide to Treaties* (OUP 2012)

Hyde, Charles, 'Concerning the Interpretation of Treaties' (1909) 3 AJIL 46–61

——, *International Law—Chiefly as Interpreted and Applied by the United States* (Little, Brown & Co 1922)

Isensee, Josef and Lecheler, Helmut (eds), *Freiheit und Eigentum—Festschrift für Walter Leisner zum 70. Geburtstag* (Duncker & Humblot 1999)

Jacobs, Francis, 'Varieties of Approach to Treaty Interpretation: With Special Reference to the Draft Convention on the Law of Treaties before the Vienna Diplomatic Conference' (1969) 18 ICLQ 318–46

—— and Roberts, Shelley (eds), *The Effect of Treaties in Domestic Law* (Sweet & Maxwell 1987)

Janis, Mark and Evans, Carolyn (eds), *Religion and International Law* (Martinus Nijhoff 1999)

Karl, Wolfram, *Vertrag und spätere Praxis im Völkerrecht—Zum Einfluss der Praxis auf Inhalt und Bestand völkerrechtlicher Verträge* (repr, Springer 2012)

Kaufmann-Kohler, Gabriele, 'Interpretive Powers of the Free Trade Commission and the Rule of Law' in Emmanuel Gaillard and Frédéric Bachand (eds), *Fifteen Years of NAFTA Chapter 11 Arbitration* (Juris 2011) 175–94

Keith, Kenneth, 'Treaties and Legislation—Based on *Corocraft Ltd v Pan American Airways Inc*' [1970] ICLQ 127–34

Keller, Helen and Ulfstein, Geir (eds), *UN Human Rights Treaty Bodies—Law and Legitimacy* (CUP 2012)

Kenny, James, 'Manley O Hudson and the Harvard Research in International Law 1927–1940' (1977) 11 Int'l L 319–29

Kirkman, Courtney, 'Fair and Equitable Treatment: *Methanex v United States* and the Narrowing Scope of NAFTA Article 1105' (2002) 34 Law & Pol'y Int'l Bus 343–92

Klabbers, Jan, 'Informal Agreements in International Law: Towards a Theoretical Framework' (1994) 5 FYBIL 267–387

——, *The Concept of Treaty in International Law* (Kluwer 1996)

——, 'Some Problems regarding the Object and Purpose of Treaties' (1997) 8 FYBIL 138–60

——, 'Virtuous Interpretation' in Malgosia Fitzmaurice, Olufemi Elias, and Panos Merkouris (eds), *Treaty Interpretation and the Vienna Convention on the Law of Treaties—30 Years on* (Martinus Nijhoff 2010) 17–37

Knop, Karen, 'Here and There: International Law in Domestic Courts' (2000) 32 JILP 501–35

Köck, Heribert, *Vertragsinterpretation und Vertragsrechtskonvention—Zur Bedeutung der Artikel 31 und 32 der Wiener Vertragsrechtskonvention 1969* (Duncker & Humblot 1976)

Koh, Harold, 'The Ninth Annual John W Hager Lecture, the 2004 Term: The Supreme Court Meets International Law' (2004) 12 Tulsa J Comp & Int'l L 1–22

Kohen, Marcelo, 'Keeping Subsequent Agreements and Practice in Their Right Limits' in Georg Nolte (ed), *Treaties and Subsequent Practice* (OUP 2013) 34–45

Kolb, Robert, *Interprétation et création du droit international—Esquisses d'une herméneutique juridique moderne pour le droit international public* (Bruylant 2006)

——, *The International Court of Justice* (Hart 2013)

Kontou, Nancy, *The Termination and Revision of Treaties in the Light of New Customary International Law* (Clarendon Press 1994)

Krisch, Nico, 'The Decay of Consent: International Law in an Age of Global Public Goods' (2014) 108 AJIL 1–40

Lai, David, 'Interpretation of Double Taxation Agreements in Hong Kong' (2007) 37 HKLJ 137–60

Lampert, Steffen, 'Germany' in Michael Lang (ed), *The Impact of the* OECD *and UN Model Conventions on Bilateral Tax Treaties* (CUP 2012) 466–500

Lang, Michael, 'Later Commentaries of the OECD Committee on Fiscal Affairs, Not to Affect the Interpretation of Previously Concluded Tax Treaties' (1997) 25 Intertax 7–9

—— (ed), *Tax Treaty Interpretation* (Kluwer 2001)

—— (ed), *The Impact of the* OECD *and UN Model Conventions on Bilateral Tax Treaties* (CUP 2012)

—— and Jirousek, Heinz (eds), *Praxis des Internationalen Steuerrechts—Festschrift für Helmut Loukota zum 65. Geburtstag* (Linde 2005)

—— and Brugger, Florian, 'The Role of the OECD Commentary in Tax Treaty Interpretation' (2008) 23 ATF 95–108

Lauterpacht, Sir Hersch, Private *Law Sources and Analogies of International Law: With Special Reference to International Arbitration* (Longman 1927)

——, 'Some Observations on Preparatory Work in the Interpretation of Treaties' (1935) 48 HLR 549–91

——, 'Restrictive Interpretation and the Principle of Effectiveness in the Interpretation of Treaties' (1949) 26 BYIL 48–85

Lesaffer, Randall, 'The Classical Law of Nations (1500–1800)' in Alexander Orakhelashvili (ed), *Research Handbook on the Theory and History of International Law* (Edward Elgar 2011) 408–40

Lewalter, Ernst, 'Die geistesgeschichtliche Stellung des Hugo Grotius' [1933] DVjs 262–93

Lewis, Corinne, 'UNHCR's Contribution to the Development of International Refugee Law—Its Foundations and Evolution' (2006) 17 IJRL 67–90

——, UNHCR *and International Refugee Law—From Treaties to Innovation* (Routledge 2012)

Linderfalk, Ulf, 'On the Meaning of the "Object and Purpose" Criterion, in the Context of the Vienna Convention on the Law of Treaties, Article 19' (2003) 72 NJIL 429–48
——, 'Is the Hierarchical Structure of Articles 31 and 32 of the Vienna Convention Real or Not?—Interpreting the Rules of Interpretation' (2007) 54 NILR 133–54
——, *On the Interpretation of Treaties—The Modern International Law as Expressed in the* 1969 *Vienna Convention on the Law of Treaties* (Springer 2007)
——, 'Doing the Right Thing for the Right Reason—Why Dynamic or Static Approaches Should Be Taken in the Interpretation of Treaties' (2008) 10 Int CL Rev 109–41
——, 'Who are "the Parties"?—Article 31, Paragraph 3(c) of the 1969 Vienna Convention and the "Principle of Systemic Integration" Revisited' (2008) 55 NILR 343–64
——, 'The Application of International Legal Norms over Time: The Second Branch of Intertemporal Law' (2011) 58 NILR 147–72
Lissitzyn, Oliver, 'Efforts to Codify or Restate the Law of Treaties' (1962) 62 Col LR 1166–1205
Llewellyn, Huw, 'United Nations, Sixth Committee' in Rüdiger Wolfrum (ed), *The Max Planck Encyclopedia of Public International Law* (OUP 2012)
Macalister-Smith, Peter, 'Institut de Droit International' in Rüdiger Wolfrum (ed), *The Max Planck Encyclopedia of Public International Law* (OUP 2012)
MacGibbon, Ian, 'The Scope of Acquiescence in International Law' (1954) 31 BYIL 143–86
Mann, Francis, 'The Interpretation of Uniform Statutes' (1946) 62 LQR 278–91
——, 'The Enforcement of Treaties by English Courts' (1958) 44 Transactions of the Grotius Society 29–62
Maresceau, Marc, 'Belgium' in Francis Jacobs and Shelley Roberts (eds), *The Effect of Treaties in Domestic Law* (Sweet & Maxwell 1987) 1–28
Margalioth, Yoram, 'Double Taxation' in Rüdiger Wolfrum (ed), *The Max Planck Encyclopedia of Public International Law* (OUP 2012)
——, 'International Taxation' in Rüdiger Wolfrum (ed), *The Max Planck Encyclopedia of Public International Law* (OUP 2012)
Martinez, Jenny, 'Towards an International Judicial System' (2003) 56 Stan L Rev 429–529
Matz-Lück, Nele, 'The Benefits of Positivism: The ILC's Contribution to the Peaceful Sharing of Transboundary Water' in Georg Nolte (ed), *Peace through International Law—The Role of the International Law Commission: A Colloquium at the Occasion of its Sixtieth Anniversary* (Springer 2009) 125–51
McAdam, Jane, *Complementary Protection in International Refugee Law* (OUP 2007)
——, 'Interpretation of the 1951 Convention' in Andreas Zimmermann (ed), *The 1951 Convention relating to the Status of Refugees and its 1967 Protocol—A Commentary* (OUP 2011) 75–115
McCaffrey, Stephen, 'Is Codification in Decline?' (1997) 20 Hastings Int'l & Comp L Rev 639–60
McDougal, Myres, 'The International Law Commission's Draft Articles upon Interpretation—Textuality Redivivus' (1967) 61 AJIL 992–1000
McGinley, Gerald, 'Practice as a Guide to Treaty Interpretation' (1995) 9 Fletcher F World Aff 211–30
McLachlan, Campbell, 'The Principle of Systemic Integration and Article 31(3)(c) of the Vienna Convention' (2005) 54 ICLQ 279–319
McNair, Arnold, *The Law of Treaties* (repr, Clarendon Press 2003)
McRae, Peter, 'The Search for Meaning: Continuing Problems with the Interpretation of Treaties' (2002) 33 Victoria U Wellington L Rev 209–60
Mechlem, Kerstin, 'Treaty Bodies and the Interpretation of Human Rights' (2009) 42 Vand J Transnat'l L 905–47
Meyring, Bernd, *Die Entwicklung zustimmungsbedürftiger völkerrechtlicher Verträge nach ihrem Abschluss und ihre Auswirkungen in der deutschen Rechtsordnung* (Berliner Wissenschafts-Verlag 2001)
Millett, Piers, 'The Biological Weapons Convention—Securing Biology in the Twenty-First Century' (2010) 15 J Conflict & Sec L 24–43
Moloo, Rahim, 'Changing Times, Changing Obligations? The Interpretation of Treaties over Time' (2012) 106 ASIL PROC 261–64

——, 'When Actions Speak Louder Than Words: The Relevance of Subsequent Party Conduct to Treaty Interpretation' (2013) 31 Berkeley J Int'l L 39–88
Morton, Jeffrey, *The International Law Commission of the United Nations* (University of South Carolina Press 2000)
Mowbray, Alastair, 'The Creativity of the European Court of Human Rights' (2005) 5 Hum Rts L Rev 57–79
Munday, Roderick, 'The Uniform Interpretation of International Conventions' (1978) 27 ICLQ 450–59
Murphy, Sean, 'The Relevance of Subsequent Agreements and Subsequent Practice for the Interpretation of Treaties' in Georg Nolte (ed), *Treaties and Subsequent Practice* (OUP 2013) 82–94
Murswiek, Dietrich, 'Die Fortentwicklung völkerrechtlicher Verträge: Verfassungsrechtliche Grenzen und Kontrolle im Organstreit' [2007] NVwZ 1130–35
Musil, Andreas, 'Steuergerechtigkeit im Verfassungsstaat—Über die Bedeutung der Grundrechte im Steuerrecht' in Marten Breuer (ed), *Der Staat im Recht—Festschrift für Eckart Klein zum 70. Geburtstag* (Duncker & Humblot 2013) 237–48
Myers, Denys, 'The Names and Scope of Treaties' (1957) 51 AJIL 574–605
Neff, Stephen, 'A Short History of International Law' in Malcolm Evans (ed), *International Law* (OUP 2003) 31–58
Nollkaemper, André, *National Courts and the International Rule of Law* (OUP 2011)
Nolte, Georg, 'Die "neuen Aufgaben" von NATO und WEU—Völker- und verfassungsrechtliche Fragen' (1994) 54 ZaöRV 95–123
——, 'Bundeswehreinsätze im kollektiven Sicherheitssystem—Zum Urteil des Bundesverfassungsgerichts vom 12. Juli 1994' (1994) 54 ZaöRV 652–755
—— (ed), *Peace through International Law—The Role of the International Law Commission: A Colloquium at the Occasion of its Sixtieth Anniversary* (Springer 2009)
—— (ed), *Treaties and Subsequent Practice* (OUP 2013)
——, 'Report 1—Jurisprudence of the International Court of Justice and Arbitral Tribunals of Ad Hoc Jurisdiction relating to Subsequent Agreements and Subsequent Practice' in id (ed), *Treaties and Subsequent Practice* (OUP 2013) 169–209
——, 'Report 2—Jurisprudence under Special Regimes relating to Subsequent Agreements and Subsequent Practice' in id (ed), *Treaties and Subsequent Practice* (OUP 2013) 210–306
——, 'Report 3—Subsequent Agreements and Subsequent Practice of States outside of Judicial or Quasi-Judicial Proceedings' in id (ed), *Treaties and Subsequent Practice* (OUP 2013) 307–86
Noyes, John, 'Christianity and Theories of International Law in Nineteenth-Century Britain' in Mark Janis and Carolyn Evans (eds), *Religion and International Law* (Martinus Nijhoff 1999) 235–58
Nuno Sérgio, Marques Antunes, 'Acquiescence' in Rüdiger Wolfrum (ed), *The Max Planck Encyclopedia of Public International Law* (OUP 2012)
O'Flaherty, Michael, 'The Concluding Observations of United Nations Human Rights Treaty Bodies' (2006) 6 Hum Rts L Rev 27–52
OECD, *Draft Double Taxation Convention on Income and Capital* (OECD Pub 1963)
——, *Double Taxation of Income and Capital: Revised Texts of Certain Articles of the 1963* OECD *Draft Convention and of the Commentary Thereon* (OECD Pub 1977)
——, *The Application of the* OECD *Model Tax Convention to Partnerships* (OECD Pub 1999)
——, *Transfer Pricing Guidelines for Multinational Enterprises and Tax Administrations* (OECD Pub 2010)
——, *Model Tax Convention on Income and on Capital 2010* (OECD Pub 2012)
Oesterhelt, Stefan, 'Bedeutung des OECD-Kommentars für die Auslegung von Doppelbesteuerungsabkommen' (2011/2012) 80 ASA 373–96
Oetheimer, Mario and Palomares, Guillem, 'European Court of Human Rights (ECtHR)' in Rüdiger Wolfrum (ed), *The Max Planck Encyclopedia of Public International Law* (OUP 2012)
Oppenheim, Lassa, *International Law—A Treatise* (2nd edn, Longman 1912)
——, Jennings, Robert, and Watts, Arthur, *Oppenheim's International Law* (9th edn, Longman 1992)

Orakhelashvili, Alexander (ed), *Research Handbook on the Theory and History of International Law* (Edward Elgar 2011)
——, 'The 19th-Century Life of International Law' in id (ed), *Research Handbook on the Theory and History of International Law* (Edward Elgar 2011) 441–55
Pauwelyn, Joost, *Conflict of Norms in Public International Law—How WTO Law Relates to other Rules of International Law* (CUP 2003)
Pedone, Joanne and Kloster, Andrew, 'New Proposals for Human Rights Treaty Body Reform' (2013) 22 J Transnat'l L & Pol'y 29–84
Pellet, Alain, 'The Normative Dilemma: Will and Consent in International Law-Making' (1988) 12 AYBIL 22–53
——, 'Between Codification and Progressive Development of the Law—Some Reflections from the ILC' (2004) 6 Int'l LF D Int'l 15–23
Peters, Christopher, 'Subsequent Practice and Established Practice of International Organizations—Two Sides of the Same Coin?' (2011) 3 GOJIL 617–42
——, *Praxis Internationaler Organisationen—Vertragswandel und völkerrechtlicher Ordnungsrahmen* (Springer 2016)
Petersen, Niels, 'Customary Law without Custom?—Rules, Principles, and the Role of State Practice in International Norm Creation' (2007) 23 Am U Int'l L Rev 275–310
Phillimore, Robert, *Commentaries upon International Law* (T & J W Johnson, Law Booksellers 1855)
Pisillo-Mazzeschi, Riccardo, 'Treaty and Custom: Reflections on the Codification of International Law' (1997) 23 Commw L Bull 549–65
Pufendorf, Samuel, *De jure naturae et gentium libri octo* (William Oldfather tr, repr, Hein 1995)
Regelsberger, Elfriede and Kugelmann, Dieter, 'Artikel 15—Gemeinsame Standpunkte' in Rudolf Streinz (ed), *EUV/EGV—Vertrag über die Europäische Union und Vertrag zur Gründung der Europäischen Gemeinschaft* (CH Beck 2003) 76–77
Reimer, Ekkehart, 'Tax Treaty Interpretation in Germany' in Michael Lang (ed), *Tax Treaty Interpretation* (Kluwer 2001) 119–52
Reinisch, August, *International Organizations before National Courts* (CUP 2000)
Ress, Georg, 'Verfassungsrechtliche Auswirkungen der Fortentwicklung völkerrechtlicher Verträge—Überlegungen zum Verhältnis des Grundgesetzes zur Europäischen Wirtschaftsgemeinschaft und zur Europäischen Menschenrechtskonvention' in Walther Fürst, Roman Herzog, and Dieter Umbach (eds), *Festschrift für Wolfgang Zeidler* (de Gruyter 1987) 1775–97
—— and Schreuer, Christoph (eds), *Wechselwirkungen zwischen Völkerrecht und Verfassung bei der Auslegung völkerrechtlicher Verträge* (CF Müller 1982)
Reuter, Paul, *Droit international public* (6th edn, Presses universitaires de France 1983)
Roberts, Anthea, 'Power and Persuasion in Investment Treaty Interpretation: The Dual Role of States' (2010) 104 AJIL 179–225
——, 'Comparative International Law? The Role of National Courts in Creating and Enforcing International Law' (2011) 60 ICLQ 57–92
Rojahn, Ondolf, 'Die Auslegung völkerrechtlicher Verträge in der Entscheidungspraxis des Bundesverwaltungsgerichts' in Rudolf Geiger and Wilfried Fiedler (eds), *Völkerrechtlicher Vertrag und staatliches Recht vor dem Hintergrund zunehmender Verdichtung der internationalen Beziehungen—Symposion vom 28. bis 30. Januar* 1999 *in Leipzig* (Nomos 2000) 123–40
——, 'Artikel 59' in Ingo von Münch and others (eds), *Grundgesetz—Kommentar* (6th edn, CH Beck 2012) 2644–717
Rosenne, Shabtai, 'The Temporal Application of the Vienna Convention on the Law of Treaties' (1970) 4 Cornell Int'l LJ 1–24
——, 'International Court of Justice (ICJ)' in Rüdiger Wolfrum (ed), *The Max Planck Encyclopedia of Public International Law* (OUP 2012)
——, 'Permanent Court of International Justice (PCIJ)' in Rüdiger Wolfrum (ed), *The Max Planck Encyclopedia of Public International Law* (OUP 2012)
Rux, Johannes, 'Das neue "NATO-Konzept"—Anmerkung zum Urteil des BVerfG vom 22.11.2001—2 BvE 6/99' [2002] JA 461–64

Sabharwal, Dipen, 'Treaties are Treaties and Custom is Custom and Never the Twain Shall Meet—Examining the Interplay of Treaties and Custom in International Law' (2000) 12 Student Advoc 113–36
Sachs, Michael and others (eds), *Grundgesetz—Kommentar* (7th edn, CH Beck 2014)
Scalia, Antonin, 'Keynote Address: Foreign Legal Authority in the Federal Courts' (2004) 98 ASIL PROC 305–10
Scelle, Georges, 'Le phénomène du dédoublement fonctionnel' in Walter Schätzel (ed), *Rechtsfragen der internationalen Organisation—Festschrift für Hans Wehberg zu seinem 70. Geburtstag* (Klostermann 1956) 324–42
Schätzel, Walter (ed), *Rechtsfragen der internationalen Organisation—Festschrift für Hans Wehberg zu seinem 70. Geburtstag* (Klostermann 1956)
Scheinin, Martin, 'Human Rights Treaties and the Vienna Convention on the Law of Treaties—Conflicts or Harmony' in Venice Commission (ed), *The Status of International Treaties on Human Rights* (Council of Europe Publ 2006) 43–54
Schmalenbach, Kirsten, 'Article 3—International Agreements Not Within the Scope of the Present Convention' in Oliver Dörr and id (eds), *Vienna Convention on the Law of Treaties—A Commentary* (Springer 2012) 49–79
——, 'Article 4—Non-Retroactivity of the Present Convention' in Oliver Dörr and id (eds), *Vienna Convention on the Law of Treaties—A Commentary* (Springer 2012) 81–88
Schmoeckel, Mathias, 'Lassa Oppenheim (1858–1919)' in Bardo Fassbender and others (eds), *The Oxford Handbook of the History of International Law* (OUP 2012) 1152–55
Schneider, Hans, 'Zur authentischen Interpretation von Gesetzen' in Rudolf Bernhardt (ed), *Völkerrecht als Rechtsordnung, internationale Gerichtsbarkeit, Menschenrechte—Festschrift für Hermann Mosler* (Springer 1983) 849–56
Schreuer, Christoph, 'The Interpretation of Treaties by Domestic Courts' (1971) 45 BYIL 255–301
——, 'Wechselwirkungen zwischen Völkerrecht und Verfassung bei der Auslegung völkerrechtlicher Verträge' in Georg Ress and id (eds), *Wechselwirkungen zwischen Völkerrecht und Verfassung bei der Auslegung völkerrechtlicher Verträge* (CF Müller 1982) 61–92
Schwarzenberger, Georg, *International Law as Applied by International Courts and Tribunals* (3rd edn, Stevens 1957)
——, 'Myths and Realities of Treaty Interpretation—Articles 27–29 of the Vienna Convention on the Law of Treaties' (1968) 9 Va J Int'l L 1–19
Scupin, Hans-Ulrich, 'History of International Law, 1815 to World War I' in Rüdiger Wolfrum (ed), *The Max Planck Encyclopedia of Public International Law* (OUP 2012)
Seidl-Hohenveldern, Ignaz, 'Relation of International Law to Internal Law in Austria ' (1955) 49 AJIL 451–76
Shelton, Dinah, 'The Legal Status of Normative Pronouncements of Human Rights Treaty Bodies' in Holger Hestermeyer (ed), *Coexistence, Cooperation and Solidarity—Liber Amicorum Rüdiger Wolfrum* (Martinus Nijhoff 2012) 553–75
Sinclair, Ian, 'The Principles of Treaty Interpretation and their Application by the English Courts' (1963) 12 ICLQ 508–51
——, 'The Vienna Conference on the Law of Treaties' (1970) 19 ICLQ 47–69
——, *The Vienna Convention on the Law of Treaties* (2nd edn, MUP 1984)
——, *The International Law Commission* (Grotius Publ 1987)
—— and Dickson, Susan, 'Chapter 6—National Treaty Law and Practice: United Kingdom' (1995) 27 Stud Transnat'l Legal Pol'y 223–60
Skubiszewski, Krzysztof, 'Remarks on the Interpretation of the United Nations Charter' in Rudolf Bernhardt (ed), *Völkerrecht als Rechtsordnung, internationale Gerichtsbarkeit, Menschenrechte—Festschrift für Hermann Mosler* (Springer 1983) 891–902
Slaughter, Anne-Marie, 'International Law in a World of Liberal States' (1995) 6 EJIL 503–38
——, 'A Global Community of Courts' (2003) 44 Harv Int'l LJ 191–219
Sloss, David (ed), *The Role of Domestic Courts in Treaty Enforcement—A Comparative Study* (CUP 2009)

——, 'Treaty Enforcement in Domestic Courts—A Comparative Analysis' in id (ed), *The Role of Domestic Courts in Treaty Enforcement—A Comparative Study* (CUP 2009) 1–60
Sorel, Jean-Marc and Boré Eveno, Valérie, 'Article 31—1969 Vienna Convention' in Olivier Corten and Pierre Klein (eds), *The Vienna Conventions on the Law of Treaties—A Commentary* (OUP 2011) 804–37
Stoll, Peter-Tobias, 'Human Rights, Treaty Bodies' in Rüdiger Wolfrum (ed), *The Max Planck Encyclopedia of Public International Law* (OUP 2012)
——, 'World Trade Organization, Dispute Settlement' in Rüdiger Wolfrum (ed), *The Max Planck Encyclopedia of Public International Law* (OUP 2012)
Streinz, Rudolf (ed), *EUV/EGV—Vertrag über die Europäische Union und Vertrag zur Gründung der Europäischen Gemeinschaft* (CH Beck 2003)
——, 'Artikel 59' in Michael Sachs and others (eds), *Grundgesetz—Kommentar* (7th edn, CH Beck 2014) 1363–87
Sur, Serge, *L'interprétation en droit international public* (Pichon & Durand-Auzias 1974)
Tammelo, Ilmar, *Treaty Interpretation and Practical Reason—Towards a General Theory of Legal Interpretation* (Law Book Co 1967)
Tanaka, Yoshifumi, 'Reflections on Time Elements in the International Law of the Environment' (2013) 73 ZaöRV 139–75
Thakore, Kuljit, 'Chapter 3—National Treaty Law and Practice: India' (1995) 27 Stud Transnat'l Legal Pol'y 79–116
Thirlway, Hugh, *The Sources of International Law* (OUP 2014)
Thomas, Christopher, 'A Reply to Professor Brower' (2002) 40 Col J Transnat'l L 433–63
Tomuschat, Christian, 'National Implementation of International Standards on Human Rights' [1984] CHRYB 31–61
——, 'Obligations Arising for States without or against Their Will' (1993) 241 RdC 195–374
——, *Human Rights—Between Idealism and Realism* (3rd edn, OUP 2014)
——, 'International Courts and Tribunals' in Rüdiger Wolfrum (ed), *The Max Planck Encyclopedia of Public International Law* (OUP 2012)
Treves, Tullio, 'Customary International Law' in Rüdiger Wolfrum (ed), *The Max Planck Encyclopedia of Public International Law* (OUP 2012)
Treviranus, Hans and Beemelmans, Hubert, 'Chapter 2—National Treaty Law and Practice: Federal Republic of Germany' (1995) 27 Stud Transnat'l Legal Pol'y 43–77
Türk, Volker, 'UNHCR's Supervisory Responsibility' (2001) 14 RQDI 135–58
Tzanakopoulos, Antonios, 'Domestic Courts as the "Natural Judge" of International Law: A Change in Physiognomy' (2012) 3 Select Proceedings of the European Society of International Law 155–68
Ulfstein, Geir, 'Treaty Bodies and Regimes' in Duncan Hollis (ed), *The Oxford Guide to Treaties* (OUP 2012) 428–47
van Alebeek, Rosanne and Nollkaemper, André, 'The Legal Status of Decisions by Human Rights Treaty Bodies in National Law' in Helen Keller and Geir Ulfstein (eds), *UN Human Rights Treaty Bodies—Law and Legitimacy* (CUP 2012) 356–443
van den Bossche, Peter and Zdouc, Werner, *The Law and Policy of the World Trade Organization—Text, Cases and Materials* (3rd edn, CUP 2013)
van der Bruggen, Edwin, 'The Power of Persuasion: Notes on the Sources of International Law and the OECD Commentary' (2003) 31 Intertax 259–70
van Ert, Gibran, 'Dubious Dualism: The Reception of International Law in Canada' (2010) 44 Val UL Rev 927–34
van Raad, Kees, 'Interpretatie van belastingverdragen' (1978) 47 MBB 49–56
Venice Commission (ed), *The Status of International Treaties on Human Rights* (Council of Europe Publ 2006)
Vierdag, Egbert, 'The Time of the "Conclusion" of a Multilateral Treaty: Article 30 of the Vienna Convention on the Law of Treaties and Related Provisions' (1989) 59 BYIL 75–111
Villiger, Mark, *Customary International Law and Treaties—A Manual on the Theory and Practice of the Interrelation of Sources* (2nd edn, Kluwer 1997)

——, *Commentary on the* 1969 *Vienna Convention on the Law of Treaties* (Martinus Nijhoff 2009)
——, 'The 1969 Vienna Convention on the Law of Treaties—40 Years After' (2009) 344 RCADI 9–192
Vogel, Klaus, 'Double Tax Treaties and Their Interpretation' (1986) 4 Int'l Tax & Bus Law 1–85
Voïcu, Ioan, *De l'interprétation authentique des traités internationaux* (Pédone 1968)
von Münch, Ingo and others (eds), *Grundgesetz—Kommentar* (6th edn, CH Beck 2012)
von Wolff, Christian, *Jus naturae—Methodo scientifica pertractatum* (Rengersche Buchhandlung 1746)
Vranes, Erich, 'Lex Superior, Lex Specialis, Lex Posterior—Zur Rechtsnatur der "Konfliktlösungsregeln"' (2005) 65 ZaöRV 391–405
Vukas, Budislav, 'Treaties, Third-Party Effect' in Rüdiger Wolfrum (ed), *The Max Planck Encyclopedia of Public International Law* (OUP 2012)
Waite, Maurice (ed), *Oxford Thesaurus of English* (3rd edn, OUP 2009)
Ward, David, *The Interpretation of Income Tax Treaties with Particular Reference to the Commentaries on the* OECD *Model* (IFA 2005)
Waters, Melissa, 'Justice Scalia on the Use of Foreign Law in Constitutional Interpretation: Unidirectional Monologue or Co-Constitutive Dialogue?' (2004) 12 Tulsa J Comp & Int'l L 149–61
——, 'Treaty Dialogue in *Sanchez-Llamas*: Is Chief Justice Roberts a Transnationalist, after All?' (2007) 11 LCLR 89–98
Waters, Mike, 'The Relevance of OECD Commentaries in the Interpretation of Tax Treaties' in Michael Lang and Heinz Jirousek (eds), *Praxis des Internationalen Steuerrechts—Festschrift für Helmut Loukota zum 65. Geburtstag* (Linde 2005) 671–89
Watts, Arthur, 'Codification and Progressive Development of International Law' in Rüdiger Wolfrum (ed), *The Max Planck Encyclopedia of Public International Law* (OUP 2012)
Weil, Prosper, 'Towards Relative Normativity in International Law?' (1993) 77 AJIL 413–42
Weiler, Todd, 'NAFTA Investment Arbitration and the Growth of International Economic Law' [2002] Bus L Int'l 158–89
——, 'NAFTA Investment Law in 2001: As the Legal Order Starts to Settle, the Bureaucrats Strike Back' (2002) 36 Int'l L 345–53
Wildhaber, Luzius, 'Parliamentary Participation in Treaty-Making, Report on Swiss Law' (1991) 67 Chi-Kent L Rev 437–58
Wittendorff, Jens, *Transfer Pricing and the Arm's Length Principle in International Tax Law* (Kluwer 2010)
Wolfrum, Rüdiger (ed), *The Max Planck Encyclopedia of Public International Law* (OUP 2012)
——, 'Sources of International Law' in id (ed), *The Max Planck Encyclopedia of Public International Law* (OUP 2012)
Wood, Michael, 'State Practice' in Rüdiger Wolfrum (ed), *The Max Planck Encyclopedia of Public International Law* (OUP 2012)
Woodward, Richard, *The Organisation for Economic Cooperation and Development* (Routledge 2009)
Wuerth, Ingrid, 'Treaty Interpretation, Subsequent Agreements and Practice, and Domestic Constitutions' in Georg Nolte (ed), *Treaties and Subsequent Practice* (OUP 2013) 154–59
Yasseen, Mustafa, 'L'interprétation des traités d'après la Convention de Vienne sur le Droit des Traités' (1976) 151 RCADI 1–114
Zimmermann, Andreas (ed), *The 1951 Convention relating to the Status of Refugees and its 1967 Protocol—A Commentary* (OUP 2011)
——, 'State Succession in Treaties' in Rüdiger Wolfrum (ed), *The Max Planck Encyclopedia of Public International Law* (OUP 2012)
Zoller, Elisabeth, *La bonne foi en droit international public* (Pédone 1977)

Max-Planck-Institut für ausländisches öffentliches Recht und Völkerrecht

Beiträge zum ausländischen öffentlichen Recht und Völkerrecht

Hrsg.: A. von Bogdandy, A. Peters

Bde. 27–59 erschienen im Carl Heymanns Verlag KG Köln, Berlin (Bestellung an: Max-Planck-Institut für Völkerrecht, Im Neuenheimer Feld 535, 69120 Heidelberg); ab Band 60 im Springer-Verlag GmbH

---

268 Katharina *Berner*: **Subsequent Agreements and Subsequent Practice in Domestic Courts.** 2018. XLV, 298 Seiten. Geb. € 114,99 zzgl. landesüblicher MwSt.

267 Josephine *Asche*: **Die Margin of Appreciation.** 2018. XII, 255 Seiten. Geb. € 84,99

266 Nele *Yang*: **Die Leitentscheidung.** 2018. XI, 362 Seiten. Geb. € 84,99

265 Roya *Sangi*: **Die auswärtige Gewalt des Europäischen Parlaments.** 2018. XV, 179 Seiten. Geb. € 69,99

264 Anna Krueger: **Die Bindung der Dritten Welt an das postkoloniale Völkerrecht.** 2018. XII, 434 Seiten. Geb. € 89,99

263 Björnstjern *Baade*: **Der Europäische Gerichtshof für Menschenrechte als Diskurswächter.** 2017. XVIII, 543 Seiten. Geb. € 99,99

262 Felix *Lange*: **Praxisorientierung und Gemeinschaftskonzeption.** 2017. XIV, 403 Seiten. Geb. € 94,99

261 Johanna Elisabeth *Dickschen*: **Empfehlungen und Leitlinien als Handlungsform der Europäischen Finanzaufsichtsbehörden.** 2017. XIX, 277 Seiten. Geb. € 84,99

260 Mohamed *Assakkali*: **Europäische Union und Internationaler Währungsfonds.** 2017. XV, 516 Seiten. Geb. € 99,99

259 Franziska *Paefgen*: **Der von Art. 8 EMRK gewährleistete Schutz vor staatlichen Eingriffen in die Persönlichkeitsrechte im Internet.** 2017. XV, 220 Seiten. Geb. € 69,99

258 Tim René *Salomon*: **Die internationale Strafverfolgungsstrategie gegenüber somalischen Piraten.** 2017. XXXII, 743 Seiten. Geb. € 129,99

257 Jelena *Bäumler*: **Das Schädigungsverbot im Völkerrecht.** 2017. XIX, 379 Seiten. Geb. € 89,99

256 Christopher *Peters*: **Praxis Internationaler Organisationen - Vertragswandel und völkerrechtlicher Ordnungsrahmen.** 2016. XXVIII, 498 Seiten. Geb. € 99,99

255 Nicole *Appel*: **Das internationale Kooperationsrecht der Europäischen Union.** 2016. XVIII, 608 Seiten. Geb. € 109,99

254 Christian *Wohlfahrt*: **Die Vermutung unmittelbarer Wirkung des Unionsrechts.** 2016. XIX, 300 Seiten. Geb. € 84,99

253 Katja *Göcke*: **Indigene Landrechte im internationalen Vergleich.** 2016. XVII, 818 Seiten. Geb. € 139,99

252 Julia *Heesen*: **Interne Abkommen.** 2015. XXI, 473 Seiten. Geb. € 94,99

251 Matthias *Goldmann*: **Internationale öffentliche Gewalt.** 2015. XXIX, 636 Seiten. Geb. € 109,99

250 Isabelle *Ley*: **Opposition im Völkerrecht.** 2014. XXIII, 452 Seiten. Geb. € 94,99

249 Matthias *Kottmann*: **Introvertierte Rechtsgemeinschaft.** 2014. XII, 352 Seiten. Geb. € 84,99

248 Jelena *von Achenbach*: **Demokratische Gesetzgebung in der Europäischen Union.** 2014. XVI, 522 Seiten. Geb. € 94,99

247 Jürgen *Friedrich*: **International Environmental "soft law".** 2014. XXI, 503 Seiten. Geb. € 94,99 zzgl. landesüblicher MwSt.

246 Anuscheh *Farahat*: **Progressive Inklusion.** 2014. XXIV, 429 Seiten. Geb. € 94,99

245 Christina *Binder*: **Die Grenzen der Vertragstreue im Völkerrecht.** 2013. XL, 770 Seiten. Geb. € 119,99

244 Cornelia *Hagedorn*: **Legitime Strategien der Dissensbewältigung in demokratischen Staaten.** 2013. XX, 551 Seiten. Geb. € 99,99

243 Marianne *Klumpp*: **Schiedsgerichtsbarkeit und Ständiges Revisionsgericht des Mercosur.** 2013. XX, 512 Seiten. Geb. € 94,99

242 Karen *Kaiser* (Hrsg.): **Der Vertrag von Lissabon vor dem Bundesverfassungsgericht.** 2013. XX, 1635 Seiten. Geb. € 199,99

241 Dominik *Steiger*: **Das völkerrechtliche Folterverbot und der "Krieg gegen den Terror".** 2013. XXX, 821 Seiten. Geb. € 139,99

240 Silja *Vöneky*, Britta *Beylage-Haarmann*, Anja *Höfelmeier*, Anna-Katharina *Hübler* (Hrsg.): **Ethik und Recht - Die Ethisierung des Rechts/Ethics and Law - The Ethicalization of Law.** 2013. XVIII, 456 Seiten. Geb. € 94,99

239 Rüdiger *Wolfrum*, Ina *Gätzschmann* (eds.): **International Dispute Settlement: Room for Innovations?** 2013. XIV, 445 Seiten. Geb. € 94,95 zzgl. landesüblicher MwSt.

238 Isabel *Röcker*: **Die Pflicht zur rahmenbeschlusskonformen Auslegung nationalen Rechts.** 2013. XXIII, 410 Seiten. Geb. € 89,95

237 Maike *Kuhn*: **Die Europäische Sicherheits- und Verteidigungspolitik im Mehrebenensystem.** 2012. XIII, 325 Seiten. Geb. € 79,95

236 Armin *von Bogdandy*, Ingo *Venzke* (eds.): **International Judicial Lawmaking.** 2012. XVII, 509 Seiten. Geb. € 94,95 zzgl. landesüblicher MwSt.

235 Susanne *Wasum-Rainer*, Ingo *Winkelmann*, Katrin *Tiroch* (eds.): **Arctic Science, International Law and Climate Change.** 2012. XIX, 374 Seiten. Geb. € 84,95 zzgl. landesüblicher MwSt.

234 Mirja A. *Trilsch*: **Die Justiziabilität wirtschaftlicher, sozialer und kultureller Rechte im innerstaatlichen Recht.** 2012. XIX, 559 Seiten. Geb. € 99,95

233 Anja *Seibert-Fohr* (ed.): **Judicial Independence in Transition.** 2012. XIII, 1378 Seiten. Geb. € 169,95 zzgl. landesüblicher MwSt.

232 Sandra *Stahl*: **Schutzpflichten im Völkerrecht - Ansatz einer Dogmatik.** 2012. XXX, 505 Seiten. Geb. € 94,95

231 Thomas *Kleinlein*: **Konstitutionalisierung im Völkerrecht.** 2012. XLII, 940 Seiten. Geb. € 149,95

230 Roland *Otto*: **Targeted Killings and International Law.** 2012. XVIII, 661 Seiten. Geb. € 109,95 zzgl. landesüblicher MwSt.

229 Nele *Matz-Lück*, Mathias *Hong* (Hrsg.): **Grundrechte und Grundfreiheiten im Mehrebenensystem - Konkurrenzen und Interferenzen.** 2012. VIII, 394 Seiten. Geb. € 89,95

228 Matthias *Ruffert*, Sebastian *Steinecke*: **The Global Administrative Law of Science,** 2011. IX, 140 Seiten. Geb. € 59,95 zzgl. landesüblicher MwSt.

227 Sebastian *Pritzkow*: **Das völkerrechtliche Verhältnis zwischen der EU und Russland im Energiesektor.** 2011. XXIV, 304 Seiten. Geb. € 79,95

226 Sarah *Wolf*: **Unterseeische Rohrleitungen und Meeresumweltschutz.** 2011. XXIII, 442 Seiten. Geb. € 94,95

225 Clemens *Feinäugle*: **Hoheitsgewalt im Völkerrecht.** 2011. XXVI, 418 Seiten. Geb. € 89,95

224 David *Barthel*: **Die neue Sicherheits- und Verteidigungsarchitektur der Afrikanischen Union.** 2011. XXV, 443 Seiten. Geb. € 94,95

223 Tilmann *Altwicker*: **Menschenrechtlicher Gleichheitsschutz.** 2011. XXX, 549 Seiten. Geb. € 99,95

222 Stephan *Bitter*: **Die Sanktion im Recht der Europäischen Union.** 2011. XV, 351 Seiten. Geb. € 84,95

221 Holger *Hestermeyer*, Nele *Matz-Lück*, Anja *Seibert-Fohr*, Silja *Vöneky* (eds.): **Law of the Sea in Dialogue.** 2011. XII, 189 Seiten. Geb. € 69,95 zzgl. landesüblicher MwSt.

220 Jan *Scheffler*: **Die Europäische Union als rechtlich-institutioneller Akteur im System der Vereinten Nationen.** 2011. XXXV, 918 Seiten. Geb. € 149,95

219 Mehrdad *Payandeh*: **Internationales Gemeinschaftsrecht.** 2010. XXXV, 629 Seiten. Geb. € 99,95

218 Jakob *Pichon*: **Internationaler Strafgerichtshof und Sicherheitsrat der Vereinten Nationen.** 2011. XXVI, 399 Seiten. Geb. € 89,95

217 Michael *Duchstein*: **Das internationale Benchmarkingverfahren und seine Bedeutung für den gewerblichen Rechtsschutz.** 2010. XXVI, 528 Seiten. Geb. € 99,95

216 Tobias *Darge*: **Kriegsverbrechen im nationalen und internationalen Recht.** 2010. XXXV, 499 Seiten. Geb. € 94,95

215 Markus *Benzing*: **Das Beweisrecht vor internationalen Gerichten und Schiedsgerichten in zwischenstaatlichen Streitigkeiten.** 2010. L, 846 Seiten. Geb. € 139,95

214 Urs *Saxer*: **Die internationale Steuerung der Selbstbestimmung und der Staatsentstehung.** 2010. XLII, 1140 Seiten. Geb. € 169,95

213 Rüdiger *Wolfrum*, Chie *Kojima* (eds.): **Solidarity: A Structural Principle of International Law.** 2010. XIII, 238 Seiten. Geb. € 69,95 zzgl. landesüblicher MwSt.

212 Ramin S. *Moschtaghi*: **Die menschenrechtliche Situation sunnitischer Kurden in der Islamischen Republik Iran.** 2010. XXIII, 451 Seiten. Geb. € 94,95

211 Georg *Nolte* (ed.): **Peace through International Law. The Role of the International Law Commission.** 2009. IX, 195 Seiten. Geb. € 64,95 zzgl. landesüblicher MwSt.

210 Armin *von Bogdandy*, Rüdiger *Wolfrum*, Jochen *von Bernstorff*, Philipp *Dann*, Matthias *Goldmann* (eds.): **The Exercise of Public Authority by International Institutions.** 2010. XIII, 1005 Seiten. Geb. € 149,95 zzgl. landesüblicher MwSt.

209 Norman *Weiß*: **Kompetenzlehre internationaler Organisationen.** 2009. XVIII, 540 Seiten. Geb. € 99,95

MIX
Papier aus verantwortungsvollen Quellen
Paper from responsible sources
FSC® C105338

If you have any concerns about our products,
you can contact us on
ProductSafety@springernature.com

In case Publisher is established outside the EU,
the EU authorized representative is:
Springer Nature Customer Service Center GmbH
Europaplatz 3, 69115 Heidelberg, Germany

Printed by Libri Plureos GmbH
in Hamburg, Germany